The Law and Society Canon

The International Library of Essays in Law and Society
Series Editor: Austin Sarat

Titles in the Series:

Law and Religion
Gad Barzilai

Police and Policing Law
Jeannine Bell

Law and Society Approaches to Cyberspace
Paul Schiff Berman

Law and Families
Susan B. Boyd and Helen Rhoades

Rhetoric of Law
Marianne Constable and Felipe Gutterriez

Law in Social Theory
Roger Cotterrell

Ethnography and Law
Eve Darian-Smith

International Law and Society
Laura Dickinson

Legal Lives of Private Organizations
Lauren Edelman and Mark C. Suchman

Courts and Judges
Lee Epstein

Consciousness and Ideology
Patricia Ewick

Prosecutors and Prosecution
Lisa Frohmann

Intellectual Property
William T. Gallagher

Human Rights, Law and Society
Lisa Hajjar

Race, Law and Society
Ian Haney López

The Jury System
Valerie P. Hans

Regulation and Regulatory Processes
Robert Kagan and Cary Coglianese

Crime and Criminal Justice
William T. Lyons, Jr.

Law and Social Movements
Michael McCann

Colonial and Post-Colonial Law
Sally Merry

Social Science in Law
Elizabeth Mertz

Sexuality and Identity
Leslie J. Moran

Law and Poverty
Frank Munger

Rights
Laura Beth Nielsen

Governing Risks
Pat O'Malley

Lawyers and the Legal Profession, Volumes I and II
Tanina Rostain

Capital Punishment, Volumes I and II
Austin Sarat

Legality and Democracy
Stuart A. Scheingold

The Law and Society Canon
Carroll Seron

Popular Culture and Law
Richard K. Sherwin

Law and Science
Susan Silbey

Immigration
Susan Sterett

Gender and Feminist Theory in Law and Society
Madhavi Sunder

Procedural Justice, Volumes I and II
Tom R. Tyler

Trials
Martha Merrill Umphrey

The Law and Society Canon

Edited by

Carroll Seron

University of California, Irvine, USA

Routledge
Taylor & Francis Group
LONDON AND NEW YORK

First published 2006 by Ashgate Publishing

Reissued 2018 by Routledge
2 Park Square, Milton Park, Abingdon, Oxon, OX14 4RN
711 Third Avenue, New York, NY 10017, USA

Routledge is an imprint of the Taylor & Francis Group, an informa business

A Library of Congress record exists under LC control number: 2005051424

ISBN 13: 978-0-815-39792-2 (hbk)
ISBN 13: 978-1-351-12667-0 (ebk)

Contents

PART IV LAWYERS

PART V POLICING

PART VI ADMINISTRATIVE LAW AND REGULATION

Acknowledgements

The editor and publishers wish to thank the following for permission to use copyright material.

American Sociological Association for the essays: Stewart Macaulay (1963), 'Non-Contractual Relations in Business: A Preliminary Study', *American Sociological Review*, **28**, pp. 55–67; Egon Bittner (1967), 'The Police on Skid-Row: A Study of Peace Keeping', *American Sociological Review*, **32**, pp. 699–715.

Blackwell Publishers for the essays: Alan Hunt (1985), 'The Ideology of Law: Advances and Problems in Recent Applications of the Concept of Ideology to the Analysis of Law', *Law and Society Review*, **19**, pp. 11–37. Copyright © 1985 Law and Society Association; Gunther Teubner (1983), 'Substantive and Reflexive Elements in Modern Law', *Law and Society Review*, **17**, pp. 239–85. Copyright © 1983 Law and Society Association; Abraham S. Blumberg (1967), 'The Practice of Law as Confidence Game: Organizational Cooptation of a Profession', *Law and Society Review*, **1**, pp. 15–39. Copyright © 1967 Law and Society Association.

Copyright Clearance Center for the essays: Laura Nader (1965), 'Choices in Legal Procedure: Shia Moslem and Mexican Zapotec', *American Anthropologist*, **67**, pp. 394–99; Michael K. Young (1984), 'Judicial Review of Administrative Guidance: Governmentally Encouraged Consensual Dispute Resolution in Japan', *Columbia Law Review*, **84**, pp. 923–83. Copyright © 1984 Columbia Law Review.

Journal of Japanese Studies for the essay: John Owen Haley (1978), 'The Myth of the Reluctant Litigant', *Journal of Japanese Studies*, **4**, pp. 359–90.

Korean Journal of International and Comparative Law for the essay: Dai-Kwon Choi (1980), 'Western Law in a Traditional Society Korea', *Korean Journal of Comparative Law*, **8**, pp. 177–202.

Notre Dame Law School and Philip Selznick for the essay: Philip Selznick (1961), 'Sociology and Natural Law', *Natural Law Forum*, **6**, pp. 84–108.

Springer for the essay: Paul G. Chevigny (1990), 'Police Deadly Force as Social Control: Jamaica, Argentina, and Brazil', *Criminal Law Forum*, **1**, pp. 389–425. Copyright © 1990 Paul G. Chevigny.

State University of New York Press for the essay: Setsuo Miyazawa (1992), 'Irony of Effective Supervision and an *Enabling* Legal Environment', in *Policing in Japan: A Study on Making*

Crime, Albany, New York: SUNY Press, pp. 233–44, 244a, 244b. Copyright © 1992 State University of New York.

University of Chicago Press for the essays: Richard L. Abel (1985), 'Comparative Sociology of Legal Professions: An Exploratory Essay', *American Bar Foundation Research Journal*, **1**, pp. 5–79; Edward O. Laumann and John P. Heinz (1977), 'Specialization and Prestige in the Legal Profession: The Structure of Deference', *American Bar Foundation Research Journal*, **1**, pp. 155–216. Copyright © 1997 American Bar Foundation.

Yale Law Journal Company and William S. Hein for the essay: Donald J. Black (1972), 'The Boundaries of Legal Sociology', *Yale Law Journal*, **81**, pp. 1086–100.

Every effort has been made to trace all the copyright holders, but if any have been inadvertently overlooked the publishers will be pleased to make the necessary arrangement at the first opportunity.

Series Preface

The International Library of Essays in Law and Society is designed to provide a broad overview of this important field of interdisciplinary inquiry. Titles in the series will provide access to the best existing scholarship on a wide variety of subjects integral to the understanding of how legal institutions work in and through social arrangements. They collect and synthesize research published in the leading journals of the law and society field. Taken together, these volumes show the richness and complexity of inquiry into law's social life.

Each volume is edited by a recognized expert who has selected a range of scholarship designed to illustrate the most important questions, theoretical approaches, and methods in her/his area of expertise. Each has written an introductory essay which both outlines those questions, approaches, and methods and provides a distinctive analysis of the scholarship presented in the book. Each was asked to identify approximately 20 pieces of work for inclusion in their volume. This has necessitated hard choices since law and society inquiry is vibrant and flourishing.

The International Library of Essays in Law and Society brings together scholars representing different disciplinary traditions and working in different cultural contexts. Since law and society is itself an international field of inquiry it is appropriate that the editors of the volumes in this series come from many different nations and academic contexts. The work of the editors both charts a tradition and opens up new questions. It is my hope that this work will provide a valuable resource for longtime practitioners of law and society scholarship and newcomers to the field.

AUSTIN SARAT
William Nelson Cromwell Professor of Jurisprudence and Political Science
Amherst College

Introduction

Law and Society Canon offers a brief tour through the research essays that shape the discipline of law and society. Today, law and society is a taken-for-granted discipline in universities and colleges in the United States and around the globe. Historically, law and society is, however, a relatively recent arrival on the academic scene and, in fact, one where there is lively and continuous debate around methods and substantive foci. The goal of this volume is to provide a historical perspective on the discipline by bringing together a sampling of the seminal pieces that mark its intellectual canon.

Every discipline, to the extent it is a discipline, develops a canon – a set of standard texts, approaches, problems, examples and stories that its members repeatedly employ or invoke. A canon is what one reads as a rite of passage into an intellectual and professional community of scholars, and what one shares as part of the experience of membership. If the study of law and society 'is a discipline, it too must have its canons and its own sense of the canonical' (Balkin and Levinson, 1996; see also Sarat, 1998). In this sense, a canon of texts is both the objectification of a social process and a discursive engagement that 'mutates continuously' in the frictional spaces of institutional reproduction (Guillory, 1987, p. 498). As the moment's residue of unceasing enterprise, a canon provides, therefore, a foundation for connection and contestation across generations and across sub-fields, promoting new questions and new research (Sarat, 1998). Any particular work is canonical or classical to the extent that it is part of the ongoing, historically sedimented yet immanently unstable referential process.

Canon presents a group of seminal essays that continues to shape the contemporary discipline of law and society, including socio-legal theory, disputing, courts, lawyers, policing and administrative enforcement and regulation. For these purposes, the focus is on those essays of the post-Second World War period that coincided with the founding of the modern Law and Society Association (LSA) in 1964 (Garth and Sterling, 1998; Tomlins, 2000). Although, in its earliest form, LSA was a decidedly American professional association, scholars from other countries did participate in the development of the discipline, often as graduate students and post-doctoral fellows at one of the Law and Society Centers in the United States. Thus, examples of scholarship from various countries are included here. Today, as the Association moves in a decidedly international direction it is especially appropriate to bring together the work that laid the foundation to expand the boundaries of the discipline.

Before turning to a consideration of these essays, however, it is appropriate, first, to offer a working definition, a jumping-off point, of this field. What, then, is the discipline of law and society? Law and society was seeded by a group of scholars – sociologists, political scientists, anthropologists, psychologists, and legal scholars – committed to understanding the role of law in everyday life. In shorthand, it was claimed that traditional law scholars study 'law in the books' (or the formal relationship between, and the evolution of, cases, statutes or constitutions) whereas law and society scholars study the terrain of 'law in action' (or the informal role of law and legality in everyday life). By working outside the boundaries of legal scholars' official territory, law and society scholarship identified for itself a capacious ground. Students of law and society have historically pursued the study of law-in-action in courts, lawyers' offices, juries, regulatory agencies, police stations and on the street. Of late, those sites of study have expanded to include hospitals (Heimer and Staffen, 1998), corporations (Edelman, 1990; Morrill, 1995) or scientific laboratories (Silbey, 2003).

Law and society builds from diverse intellectual roots beginning with classical social theory, including Marx, Weber and Durkheim, and the American school of Legal Realism. In Part I we examine four authors' works – those of Donald Black, Alan Hunt, Philip Selznick and Gunther Teubner who capture contemporary starting points for a theory of law and society. In Part II, we turn to studies of disputing with essays by John Haley on Japan, Stewart Macaulay on the United States and Laura Nader on the Middle East and Mexico. Part III presents seminal studies of courts; the essay by Abraham Blumberg introduces the intellectual legacy of the Legal Realists of the early twentieth century who asked, 'How does law work "in action"?' (also see Schlegel, 1995). The essay by Dai-Kwon Choi on the borrowing of American procedure in a modernizing Korea presents a thoughtful and two-sided looking-glass of law in action. Part IV turns to research on lawyers, key actors in the legal system, who perform central roles in the transformation of disputes from normative conflicts to legal cases that may, or may not, go to court. Richard Abel's synthesis of a comparative study of the legal profession incorporates a neo-Marxist strand of law and society scholarship whereas the essay by Edward Laumann and John Heinz on specialization and prestige in the legal profession illustrates the discipline's close intellectual links to sociology of stratification. Law on the street has also been rich terrain where scholars have made major contributions to our understanding of the role of police as agents of social control. Part V includes Egon Bittner's study of the police on skid-row that also raised questions for the study of policing beyond American shores, including work, also included here, by Paul Chevigny on Latin America and by Setsuo Miyazawa on Japan. Finally, in Part VI we consider essays on administrative law and regulation by Kitty Calavita, Keith Hawkins and Michael Young that have shaped an important agenda both within nation-states and, more recently, across nation-states as international regulatory tribunals play an emergent role to balance due process and social control in a globalizing framework.

Socio-legal Theory

From different analytical points of departure, Marx (1847), Weber (1954) and Durkheim (1947) set out to explain the processes of modernization or the transition from traditional to industrial society. Each pursued the analysis of social phenomena at the broadest level, seeing law as part of the transformation of social, political and economic institutions. Emile Durkheim, for example, argued that law had become an embodiment of the 'collective conscience' in societies with advanced divisions of labour, where interdependence and reciprocity prevailed. For Durkheim, 'law is the example par excellence of the social fact. It is a visible symbol of all that is essentially social' (cited in Hunt, 1978, p. 65). Donald Black (1976) begins, as the article in this volume demonstrates, with the Durkheimian premise that 'it is possible to formulate propositions that explain the quantity and style of law in every setting' (Black, 1976, p. 6). Conceptualizing social control as the 'normative aspect of social life', may take the form of law or, possibly, other variables of social life, such as 'etiquette, custom, ethics, bureaucracy and the treatment of mental illness' (1976, p. 105). Further, Black argues, 'social control is a quantifiable variable' (1976, p. 105). If social control has multiple indicators and is quantifiable then, it follows, '*law varies inversely with other social control*' (1976, p. 107). Black's work represents an important attempt to develop a theory of law that has been tested empirically by many of his students (for example, Morrill, 1995; Baumgartner, 1988).

In marked contrast to Durkheim's call and Black's formulation of a positive, value-neutral science of law in society, Philip Selznick argues that normative considerations, or substantive law, must be central to rigorous investigation of social phenomena, including law. The article by Selznick in this volume focuses on the institution of law that demonstrates a lens and a bridge between ideals and values (Kagan, Kryger and Winston, 2002): a focus on institution encompasses a place for theoretical frame, methodological direction, *and* normative reflection. Law and legality is a particularly apt institution because it embodies a 'mainstay of cultural identity' as well as 'the bridge between justice and community' (Selznick, 1992, p. 435). For the student of law or legality, the task, then, is to 'explore the meaning of legality itself . . . the quality of legality and the gradations within it' in all its many obvious, hidden and emerging sites (Selznick, 1959, p. 124).

For Weber (1947, 1954), the forms of social organization that are characteristically modern are premised upon formal legal rationality and bureaucratic administration. These particularly legal features of modern society generate pronounced, and seemingly insoluble, tensions with which most modern societies struggle: contradictions between demands for predictability and equally valued demands for substantive justice. Gunther Teubner's essay in this volume (Chapter 4) presents a framework for understanding the substantive direction of law in contemporary society as one framed by a 'reflexive' law. Teubner argues that 'reflexive' law incorporates elements of both substantive and 'responsive' (Nonet and Selznick, 1978) law, but supersedes both; or, as he states, 'To put this thesis into Selznick's conceptual framework: it is reflexive rather than substantive rationality that represents the "conceptual readiness" of responsive law to take advantage of the "opportunity structures" emerging in post-modern society' (pp. 90–91).

Marx deals with law somewhat less explicitly than Weber or Durkheim, and more critically. In contributing the concept of ideology and its relationship to both material conditions of production and state power, Marx makes a major contribution to the study of modernization. In this context, both the law as it is written and the law as it is lived or experienced may be examined as a 'hybrid phenomenon of politics and ideology, or a politico-ideological artifact' (Sumner, 1979, p. 266). Whilst law is only one among many ideological 'weapons', it contributes to the concealment or distortion in the formation and transformation of class relations. Thus, the study of law, it may be inferred, provides a lens for understanding how exploitative, unequal class relations are disguised and mystified. As Marx's work enjoyed an intellectual renaissance in the United States beginning in the 1970s, scholars struggled to understand the ideological role of law in society as a 'difficult, slippery, and ambiguous concept' (Hunt, Chapter 2, this volume, p. 39); Hunt argues that the concept of ideology must be central to a theoretically informed sociology of law and, at the same time, avoid the mechanistic, instrumental pitfalls along the way.

Disputing

The body of work that gave distinctive shape and substance to the field of law and society began by looking outside of courts, or any other formal institution of law. In a truly groundbreaking study, *The Cheyenne Way*, Hoebel and Llewellyn (1941) claimed that the place to begin research is the 'trouble case', where the taken-for-granted modes of social interaction break down. The 'trouble case' presents a way of viewing law that fundamentally challenged a claim for the pre-eminence of courts as the central site for legal production and organization. Also, in articulating this 'discovery' of law in society, the discipline of law *and* society began to develop parallel sites for research that were not limited to the Legal Realist's agenda.

Laura Nader, trained in anthropology and one of the group who organized the Law and Society Association and journal, built on the work of Llewellyn and Hoebel as well as post-Second World War anthropologists such as Gulliver (1963), Evans-Pritchard (1940, 1971), Gibbs (1967, 1969), Radcliffe-Brown (1948) and Bohannan (1967) to champion the concept of dispute as the building-block for a socio-cultural study of law; through the lens of the dispute process it is possible, she argued, to develop a social theory that explains the relationship between social control and social change. Equally, Nader argued, as the essay here as Chapter 7 demonstrates, for contextualized ethnographies of courts, if appropriate, but where disputing remained the organizing construct. This body of work begins, then, with the premise that disputes are windows on society, openings in the social fabric, or moments of exploration in which the collectivity is challenged, transformed or repaired.

Anthropologists were not, however, alone in noticing that much law-like activity took place outside of the formal institutions of law, or in noting the virtue of studying trouble and dispute. Stewart Macaulay's (Chapter 6) seminal study of the 'non-contractual' relations among automobile manufacturers and their franchises places disputing squarely in the American context. Although the relationships between manufacturers and dealers are entirely legalized, Macaulay observed that disagreements and disputes between them were handled through informal discussion and negotiation, rather than by invoking the provisions and remedies of the contracts that obligated the parties. He also discovered that binding business agreements were frequently made without knowledge of the relevant rules of contract law and that, in many cases, the contracts might be invalid according to those rules, were they to be challenged in court. However, they were rarely challenged because businessmen routinely sought to avoid the law, lawyers and the courts in conducting their affairs.

Folklore suggests that Japan holds promise for better ways to resolve disputes; Japanese cultural values tend to shun public disagreements and, hence, courts play a relatively insignificant role in society. John Haley's essay (Chapter 5) challenges these claims. He finds that the rate of civil dispute in Japan suggests that private suits do occur at rates that in fact exceed those of Denmark or Australia. Haley argues that post-war legislation was designed to discourage litigation in courts of law in keeping with elitist notions of Japanese values, but that mediation has played a central role and, in addition, complements cultural values and social organization.

Courts and the Discovery of Local Legal Culture

Legal scholars tend to study judges' appellate decisions to identify the legal rules in force at any particular moment; political scientists, working in a behaviourist tradition, studied 'the behavior of individuals or groups of individuals as the primary unit of analysis' (Ulmer, 1961, p. 1; see also Peltason, 1955; Pritchett, 1954, 1966; Schubert, 1965; Schmidhauser, 1960). Law and society scholars focus on courts at the front line. Abraham Blumberg's (1967) study of criminal case decision-making in a local court (Chapter 8) is emblematic of a movement out of appellate courts to examinations of litigation in trial courts. In turning to the local level, Blumberg shows that the overwhelming majority of criminal cases are plea-bargained, rather than tried; further, the work of the local court is more about efficiency and speed than fairness and due process of law (also see Packer, 1968). In mapping his argument, Blumberg describes the organizational structure of the local court and the way in which this system in fact encompasses the work of the judge as well as that of the local prosecutor, the clerk's office, probation and defendant's counsel to form a bureaucratic 'sieve' for the expeditious disposition of cases through negotiated pleas. He concludes that the day-to-day work of local courts is more akin to a rational, efficient bureaucratic system than it is to a procedurally fair, if slow, model of deliberative (judicial-like) decision-making guided by doctrinal rules and procedural constraints. To study only the lofty reaches of appellate decision-making, Blumberg implicitly claims, is to miss the main event in local criminal courts where most of the work of law takes place (see also Feeley, 1977 for a follow-up study).

Choi's article in this volume, 'Western Law in a Traditional Society Korea', explores whether classical sociological theories of modernization that give primacy to the role of legal rationality obtains in Korea. He asks, 'are the kinds of particularism, personal approaches, and substantive rationality that exist in Korea incompatible with a modern society when they are incorporated into a formal legal system?' (p. 201 of article; p. 227 of volume). Interestingly, Choi points out, for example, that Korea's tradition of 'collective responsibility' may be an important value for the development of a Korean welfare state – albeit, a foundation that is quite different from that of Western, industrial societies. In this regard, Choi's comparative look at the role of law in society demonstrates a central theme of law and society, that is, that law must be explained in the context of time and place.

Lawyers

Early law and society scholars borrowed concepts from a long-standing sociological tradition to explain the factors that distinguish a profession such as law from other occupations. Talcott Parsons (1939, 1952) had posited that the growth of the professions is one of the most important characteristics of the twentieth century and, further, that a profession may be distinguished from other occupations by its commitment to serve the public interest, by its organization into small, collegial communities and by its commitment to the self-regulation of entry, education and retention of members. Two early classics pursued these Parsonian questions by looking at how the profession of law is practised in solo settings (Carlin, 1962) and in large firms (Smigel, 1969).

In their study, *Chicago Lawyers* and the essay from that study in this volume (Chapter 11), Edward Laumann and John Heinz take the findings from these in-depth ethnographies of various domains of practice to build an integrated model that seeks to explain the stratification and networks within the profession at large. Based on a survey to a random sample of Chicago lawyers, they conclude that the legal profession may be best understood as two 'hemispheres' organized around client bases of one-shot individuals or repeat player organizations (see Galanter, 1974). If one knows whether an attorney serves individuals or organizational clients, Laumann and Heinz argue, one may predict the social background of the incumbent's father, where the incumbent went to law school, the incumbent's social network for getting more clients, and the social status of the incumbent in the eyes of his peers. In many respects, Laumann's and Heinz's larger, more systematic, and quantitative study of the profession lends support to Carlin's picture of the precarious solo practitioner (Carlin, 1962) and Smigel's portrait of the comforts enjoyed by the elite men of the profession (Smigel, 1969). *Chicago Lawyers* pays less attention to the gender stratification of the profession and, in this regard, underscores the value of Epstein's (1998) study of the 'deviant' and pioneering women who paved the way into elite firms only to find themselves marginalized in relatively low-status niches.

Despite the law and society scholar's ambition to challenge the normative claims of the legal scholar, there was a more fundamental tendency to leave the institutional pillars of the profession unexamined. As the social sciences in the United States took a more critical, neo-Marxist turn in the late 1970s, the sociology of professions developed new conceptual models to explain the relationship between social class and the 'professional project' (Larson, 1977) as well as the deprofessionalization or proletarianization of professional labour (Haug, 1973, 1975; Oppenheimer, 1973). This sociological work, particularly that of Larson (1977), paved the way for a large-scale, comparative study of the legal profession (Abel and Lewis, 1989) that, in many respects, returns the study of lawyers to the intellectual roots of the social sciences, or the role of law and lawyers in modernization. As Richard Abel's essay in this volume argues, the comparative study of lawyers documents the ways in which the profession is laced with structural inequalities, the ways in which the legal scholar's claim to what would be idiosyncratic is found to be normal practice, and the ways in which a professional's background (gender, geographical location, father's occupation) shapes opportunities and outcomes for mobility.

Policing

In contrast to the practice of law, the occupation of policing did not participate in a core project of professionalization (Bittner, 1990, pp. 311–13). Police were studied as part of general sociological and criminological inquiry about deviance, crime and social control. Social movements of the 1960s, particularly the Civil Rights Movement, also contributed to an interest in research on policing. The Civil Rights Movement exposed middle-class college students to something they had never experienced: the surveillance practices of the police. Equally, the Civil Rights Movement gave people '"from the wrong side of the track"' a voice to demand examination of surveillance by police that had long been a part of their daily routines.

Skolnick (1966), Reiss (1971; Black and Reiss, 1967), and Bittner (1970, 1990) conducted seminal studies of policing. Policing, these scholars demonstrate, operates in a context of enormous social and cultural ambiguity. For example, in his classic study of the police on skid-row, Egon Bittner (Chapter 12) demonstrates the ways in which officers' jobs to 'keep the peace' are a response to the 'demand conditions' of their work on the street, rather than the 'legal mandates' written in the 'books'. Working on skid-row, Bittner finds that policing rests on three dimensions: officers use their 'concrete knowledge about people', make judgements about when to arrest based 'mainly on the basis of perceived risk', and focus energies on 'reducing the aggregate total of troubles' rather than 'evaluating individual cases according to merit' (p. 381). This is a familiar law and society theme: law 'in action', or 'on the street', is as much social and cultural as it is legal; indeed, in the case of policing, Bittner suggests, it may be more social and cultural than legal.

Paul Chevigny has made an enormous contribution to law and society in his studies of policing in Latin America. His essay (Chapter 13) presents a framework for weighing the role of police in countries with less firm commitments to democratic governance and a rule of law. His work shows that, on the street, police engage in highly abusive techniques of social control; although there are ways to bring claims against officers, it is the exception rather than the rule. Chevigny argues that police reform should not just be viewed as an aspiration to improve the 'human rights' of Latin American citizens; rather, as a 'practical matter, changing the police by subjecting them to the rule of law is in the interest of all groups, elite as well as poor in a democratic society' (p. 52). These practical steps toward reform can be identified in various cities across Latin America, including the introduction of an ombudsman, legislative steps to increase police accountability, better pay to reduce the probability of corruption, and more training of police. Such reforms have, of course, been tried in the United States as well; and, countries on both sides of the North–South axis can report mixed results to ensure equal treatment by police toward all racial and ethnic groups.

Setsuo Miyazawa's study of the occupation of detective work in Japan demonstrates the subtle ways in which culture and society become part and parcel of policing. The concluding chapter from his book, *Policing in Japan* (1992) that is reprinted as Chapter 14 in this volume, demonstrates the ways in which the occupation of policing shares features specific to Japanese culture and values as well as features that are found in other countries, such as the United States or Canada. Policing in Japan is anchored by the perception of 'aggressive actions and stressful work conditions', creating a culture that is accepted as 'morally right and cognitively natural' (p. 457). In Japan, frontline officers experience a fairly high level of direct supervision, but this internal control may be 'double-edged'; depending on circumstances and external demands, supervisors may push toward 'procedural restraint' or 'aggressive investigation' (ibid.). Thus, while the level or degree of aggressive policing in Japan may not be as great as one finds in the United States, there are structural constraints in the Japanese context that do give legitimacy to assertive practices. Further, Miyazawa concludes, there are few, if any, external pressures coming from the legislature, executive, or public interest law community to exercise a countervailing pressure toward reform of policing practices. This is, then, a cautionary story, like many others about Japan (see Haley, Chapter 5): once we scratch beneath the surface, Japanese legal practice may not offer the panacea that more superficial glances at the East suggest.

For many citizens, their most typical encounter with the law is through the police (Skogan, 1994). Policing takes place 'on the street' where it is seen by the public but is yet largely unobserved or unsupervised by other legal actors. They do the dirty work of the legal system, cleaning up social messes, deploying the situated force and dispensing the violence inherent in all law. Perhaps because of the overwhelming situatedness of policing, as well as the very marked features of the subculture of policing (see, for example, Skolnick, 1966), research on the police has produced some of the most enduring insights about the importance of contingency and context for legal culture.

Administrative Law and Regulation

Echoing findings from policing, discretion is the centre of administrative law enforcement and regulation as well as the shape of the modern (welfare) state. A good part of the early law and society scholarship in the United States focused directly on the work of the various administrative agencies that emerged at the end of the nineteenth and beginning of the twentieth centuries. Taking the moral aspirations of the rule of law quite seriously as an effort to limit official power by a system of rules (Dicey, 1915), a desire to reduce the arbitrariness of power (Selznick, Chapter 3, this volume), and accountability for the use of force (Davis, 1972), observers often found that the regulation of business for the common good fell short of expectations (Bernstein, 1955; Edelman, 1964; Shapiro, 1968; Kolko, 1965; Orren, 1974). The explanations of these failures ranged from a focus on the symbolic nature of the legislative process that produces inconsistent mandates (Edelman, 1964), to analyses of the segmented structure of a system that encourages a division of the commonweal among interested parties to the exclusion of the unorganized public (Lowi, 1969).

Analyses of the symbolism of administrative law have been a rich vein of research in law and society. Administrative law is, after all, a '"mix" of symbolic effect and rational reflection of interests in resources' (Edelman, 1964, p. 703). The essay by Kitty Calavita on immigration law reform (Chapter 15) illustrates this theme nicely. Reviewing the Immigration Reform and Control Act of 1986 (IRCA), Calavita shows how debates over immigration reform capture contradictory impulses in American society between economic demands to encourage labour flows and political concerns to restrict immigration in response to xenophobic spikes among the citizenry. Drawn from a close reading of the legislation, she shows how the IRCA is the 'product of a conflict embedded in the political economy, between the ideology of immigration restrictionism and the economic pressure to provide employers with immigrant labor' (p. 467). Moves, then, toward restrictions are a 'symbolic act' in response to demands to '"regain control of the border"' leavened by economic realities to ensure continued and relatively inexpensive labour (ibid.). Work on immigration has been an important focus among law and society scholars that today takes place on a global stage (see, for example, Calavita, 2005).

Scholars of administrative law also took a closer look inside the agencies to understand how discretion works in practice. Although statutes set theoretical limits to official action, they cannot determine how things are done within those limits (Davis, 1972; Kadish and Kadish, 1973; Lipsky, 1980). How, then, does enforcement unfold in practice? Keith Hawkins' study of the enforcement of water pollution standards in England (Chapter 16) is illustrative of research into this question. Hawkins finds that administrators' quite wide-ranging discretionary authority is balanced by a need to maintain ongoing relations with the regulated. Picking up on Macaulay's insights from his study of contracts, he demonstrates that ensuring compliance with regulatory guidelines is embedded in a social process. Enforcement is an 'elastic concept in practice' (p. 481) where assessments about how to proceed are based on the 'demeanor' of the regulated – that is, whether and to what extent the regulated demonstrates a willingness to cooperate and then the timeliness of that cooperation. Once assessments are made, enforcers often bargain and negotiate with the regulated, sometimes 'bluffing' about the law's reach to secure compliance, but then again recognizing that companies do not want to be seen as 'trouble makers' (p. 497) because it may compromise their reputation among their peers. As Hawkins argues, '[e]nforcement . . . is a social process, founded on reciprocity, which is serial in character: a patterned sequence of demands is placed upon the rule-breaker in return for forbearance' (p. 506). Understood in this manner, Hawkins argues, there is evidence to challenge earlier claims that administrative regulation is a 'failure' or 'ineffective'.

Of course, in a global community, the borrowing of legal forms can take many forms and occur in multiple directions. While Choi's essay in this volume (Chapter 9) considers attempts to incorporate American law into Korea's modernization project, Michael Young's essay on Japan's regulation of disputes over land use planning and automobiles (Chapter 17) offers 'Western legal systems a promising model for regulation and the resolutions of certain kinds of disputes in a postindustrial era' (p. 983). Young shows that Japan's administrative schema rests on a concept of 'guidance' to the regulated party that builds from a process that is negotiated with the party and relies on 'informal pressure' to modify problematic behaviour. After a period of a hands-off approach to administrative guidance, Japanese courts did develop a process of judicial review that 'focus[es] primarily on the agencies' attempt to restructure the bargaining situation. Courts accomplish this task', Young argues, 'by rearticulating the agencies' mandate and refusing to determine the priority of competing claims of right' (p. 983). To be sure, administrative guidance, including court sanction of the practice, is illustrative of Japanese cultural tradition of reaching consensus through negotiation. In returning to the American case, researchers from diverse perspectives have also found that organizational culture is a key variable influencing the dynamics of compliance and the probability of sustainable improvement in administrative regulation. Terms such as 'regulatory culture', 'regulatory style', 'governing style' or 'regulatory context' are currently employed to examine processes of regulation across jurisdictions, agencies, and even across nations (Epp, 2001; Vogel, 1986).

Conclusion

Reading the canon of law and society research, several common themes may be noted. First, the practices and resources of law are unequally distributed and highly stratified. Studies show that social background and organizational capacity matter for access to law and the quality of legal services delivered and received. Second, what may seem aberrant malfeasance, extra-legal and idiosyncratic from the standpoint of law on the books is, in practice, 'normal' (Sudnow, 1965). Third, legal activities are situated and contingent upon the particularities of specific times and places; for example, lawyers, much research shows, are not of one profession, one 'brotherhood' (Goode, 1957); rather, lawyers' work and identities depend on who their clients are (Heinz and Laumann, 1982; Mather *et al.*, 2001; Kritzer, 2004), where they went to school (Landinsky, 1963), and whether they work in the city, the country (Handler, 1967; Landon, 1990) or the suburbs (Seron, 1996). Fourth, as both institutionalized and discursive practice, law consists of historically and culturally developed activities regulating and legitimating the use of force in social groups. It is simultaneously word and deed. Its legitimacy is inseparable from its activity, including the possibility of material violence (what Habermas refers to as its facticity).

Interestingly, and importantly, the sum of these themes is more than their individual parts. In the late twentieth century, across the mainstream social science disciplines there was an important intellectual turn towards a more modest set of claims about the degree to which empirical findings may contribute to a general theory and set of concepts to guide understanding of modern society. It is now commonplace to couch theory and concept in time and place and to recognize the degree to which social patterns are contingent, local, culturally embedded and emerge from negotiating the boundaries of professional and non-professional transactions (see, for example, Lamont and Fournier, 1992). Ironically, given its intimate contract with the legal academy and profession, the discipline of law and society stands poised to make a major contribution to this larger turn in social science theory precisely because the discipline has been discovering this point – the contingency of cultural locations and practices – for generations across multiple sites of legal encounter. What may have begun as a professional weakness or sidestepping of the role of theory qua theory (as discussed in Seron and Silbey, 2002) for the discipline of law and society in the mid-twentieth century may prove to be its most important contribution to the social sciences more generally at the beginning of the twenty-first century.

Acknowledgements

Much of this discussion is drawn from my essay with Susan Silbey (Seron and Silbey, 2004).

When asked to ensure representation of research from scholars working outside the United States, I turned to the international network of the law and society discipline and received thoughtful and prompt responses. In some instances, colleagues forwarded my requests to others in their country so that I might receive additional suggestions. My experience in selecting the essays for this volume demonstrates that, at the beginning of the twenty-first century, law and society is a discipline that transcends national borders in every sense of the term. I would like to thank particularly Eric Feldman, Thomas Ginsburg, Robert Kidder, Rogelio Perez Perdomo, Setsuo Miyazawa, Ji Weidong and Kun Yang. Unfortunately, I am only able to provide an appetizer of their suggestions, but one that invites further sampling.

Anne Dalgish provided exemplary research assistance in preparing this volume, and I remain in her debt for all of her hard work.

References

Abel, Richard and Philip Lewis (eds) (1989), *Lawyers in Society*, Berkeley, CA: University of California Press.

Balkin, Jack M. and Levinson, Sanford (1996), 'How to Win Cites and Influence People', *Chicago Kent Law Review*, **71**, p. 843.
Baumgartner, M.P. (1988), *The Moral Order of a Suburb*, New York: Oxford University Press.
Bernstein, Marver (1955), *Regulating Business by Independent Commission*, Princeton, NJ: Princeton University Press.
Bittner, Egon (1970), *The Functions of the Police in Modern Society*, Washington, DC: Government Printing Office.
Bittner, Egon (1990), *Aspects of Police Work*, Boston, MA: Northeastern University Press.
Black, Donald (1976), *The Behavior of Law*, New Haven, CT: Yale University Press.
Black, Donald and Reiss, Albert Jr (1967), *Patterns of Behavior in Police and Citizen Transactions*, report prepared for The President's Commission on Law Enforcement and Administration of Justice.
Bohannan, Paul (ed.) (1967), *Law and Warfare: Studies in the Anthropology of Conflict*, Garden City, NY: The Natural History Press.
Calavita, Kitty (2005), *Immigrants at the Margins: Law, Race, and Exclusion in Southern Europe*, Cambridge: Cambridge University Press.
Carlin, Jerome E. (1962), *Lawyers on their Own: A Study of Individual Practitioners in Chicago*, New Brunswick: Rutgers University Press.
Davis, Kenneth Culp (1972), *Discretionary Justice*, Baton Rouge: Louisiana State University Press.
Dicey, A.V. (1915), *The Law of the Constitution*, London: Macmillan Co.
Durkheim, Emile (1947), *The Division of Labor in Society*, New York: The Free Press.
Edelman, Lauren (1990), 'Legal Environments and Organizational Governance: The Expansion of Due Process in the American Workplace', *American Journal of Sociology*, **95**, pp. 1401–440.
Edelman, Murray (1964), *The Symbolic Uses of Politics*, Urbana, IL: University of Illinois Press.
Epp, Astrid (2001), 'Contested Cultures of Regulation: The Conflict over GM Food in Germany and in the United States', paper presented at the Law and Society Association meeting in Budapest, Hungary.
Epstein, Cynthia Fuchs (1998), *Women in Law* (2nd ed), Urbana and Chicago, IL: University of Illinois Press.
Evans-Pritchard, Evan E. (1940), *The Nuer: A Description of the Modes of Livelihood and Political Institutions of a Niloltic People*, New York: Oxford University Press.
Evans-Pritchard, Evan E. (1971), *The Azande: History and Political Institutions*, Oxford: Oxford University Press.
Feeley, Malcolm (1977), *The Process is the Punishment*, New York: Russell Sage Foundation.
Galanter, Marc (1974), 'Why the "Haves" Come Out Ahead: Speculations on the Limits of Legal Change', *Law & Society Review*, **9**(1), pp. 95–160.
Garth, Bryant and Sterling, Joyce (1998), 'From Legal Realism to Law & Society: Reshaping Law for the Last Stages of the Activist State', *Law & Society Review*, **32**(2), pp. 409–72.
Gibbs, James L. Jr (1969), 'Law and Personality: Signposts for a New Direction', in Laura Nader (ed.), *Law in Culture and Society*, Berkeley, CA: University of California Press, pp. 176–207.
Gibbs, James L. Jr (1967), 'The Kpelle Moot', in Paul Bohannan (ed.), *Law and Warfare: Studies in the Anthropology of Conflict*, Garden City, NY: The Natural History Press.
Goode, William (1957), 'A Community within a Community: The Professions', *American Sociological Review*, **22**, pp. 194–200.
Guillory. J. (1987), 'Canonical and Non-Canonical Literatary Canon: A Critique of the Current Debate', *English Literary History*, **54**(3), pp. 483–527.
Gulliver, P.H. (1963), *Social Control in an African Society: A Study of the Arusha: Agricultural Masai of Northern Tanganyika*, London: Routledge.
Handler, Joel (1967), *The Lawyer and His Community: The Practicing Bar in a Middle-Sized City*, Madison, WI: University of Wisconsin Press.
Haug, Marie (1973), 'Deprofessionalization: An Alternative Hypothesis for the Future', *Sociological Review Monograph*, **20**, pp. 195–211.
Haug, Marie (1975), 'The Deprofessionalization of Everyone?', *Sociological Focus*, August, pp. 197–213.
Heimer, Carol A. and Staffen, Lisa R. (1998), *For the Sake of the Children: The Social Organization of Responsibility in the Hospital and the Home*, Chicago, IL: University of Chicago Press.

Heinz, John P. and Lauman, Edward (1982), *Chicago Lawyers: The Social Structure of the Bar*, New York: Russell Sage Foundation; Chicago, IL: American Bar Foundation.
Hoebel, E. Adamson and Llewellyn, Karl (1941), *The Cheyenne Way*, Norman, OK: University of Oklahoma Press.
Hunt, Alan (1978), *The Sociological Movement in Law*, London: Macmillan Press.
Kadish, Mortimer H. and Kadish, Sanford (1973), *Discretion to Disobey*, Palo Alto, CA: Stanford University Press.
Kagan, Robert A., Kryger, Martin and Winston, Kenneth (2002), *Legality and Community: Essays in Honor of Philip Selznick*, Berkeley, CA: University of California Press.
Kolko, Gabriel (1965), *Railroads and Regulation*, Princeton, NJ: Princeton University Press.
Kritzer, Herbert (2004), *Risks, Reputation and Rewards: Contingency Fee Legal Practice in the United States*, Stanford, CA: Stanford University Press.
Lamont, Michele and Fournier, Marcel (1992), *Cultivating Differences: Symbolic Boundaries and the Making of Inequality*, Chicago, IL: University of Chicago Press.
Landinsky, Jack (1963), 'Careers of Lawyers: Law Practice and Legal Institutions', *American Sociological Review*, **28**, pp. 47–54.
Landon, Donald D. (1990), *Country Lawyers: The Impact of Context on Professional Practice*, New York: Praeger.
Larson, Magali Safarti (1977), *The Rise of Professionalism: A Sociological Analysis*, Berkeley, CA: University of California Press.
Lipsky, Michael (1980), *Street-level Bureaucracy*, New York: Russell Sage Foundation.
Lowi, Theodore (1969), *The End of Liberalism*, New York: W.W. Norton & Co.
Marx, Karl (1847), 'Wage Labour and Capital', in Karl Marx (1976), *Wage-Labour and Capital & Value, Price, and Profit*, New York: International Publishers.
Mather, Lynn, McEwen, Craig and Maiman, Richard (2001), *Divorce Lawyers*, New York: Oxford University Press.
Morrill, Calvin (1995), *The Executive Way*, Chicago, IL: University of Chicago Press.
Nonet, P. and Selznick, Philip (1978), *Law and Society in Transition: Toward Responsive Law*, New York: Harper & Row.
Oppenheimer, Martin (1973), 'The Proletarianization of the Professional', *Sociological Review Monograph*, **20**, pp. 213–27.
Orren, Karen (1974), *Corporate Power and Social Change*, Baltimore, MD: Johns Hopkins Press.
Packer, Herbert (1968), *The Limits of the Criminal Sanction*, Stanford, CA: Stanford University Press.
Parsons, Talcott (1939), 'The Professions and Social Structure', in Talcott Parsons (ed.) (1954), *Essays in Sociological Theory*, New York: Free Press.
Parsons, Talcott (1952), 'A Sociologist Looks at the Legal Profession', in Talcott Parsons (ed.) (1954), *Essays in Sociological Theory*, New York: Free Press.
Peltason, Jack (1955), *Federal Courts in the Political Process*, Garden City, NY: Doubleday Books.
Pritchett, C. Herman (1954, 1966), *Civil Liberties and the Vinson Court*, Chicago, IL: University of Chicago Press.
Radcliffe-Brown, A.R. (1948), *The Andaman Islanders: A Study in Social Anthropology* (2nd ed), Glencoe, IL: Free Press,
Radcliffe-Brown, A.R. (1931), *The Social Organization of Australian Tribes*, Melbourne: Macmillan & Co.
Reiss, Albert J. (1971), *The Police and the Public*, New Haven, CT: Yale University Press.
Sarat, Austin (1998), 'President's Column', *Law & Society Association Newsletter*, October.
Schlegel, John Henry (1995), *American Legal Realism and Empirical Social Science*, Chapel Hill, NC: University of North Carolina Press.
Schmidhauser, John R. (1960), *The Supreme Court: Its Politics, Personalities and Procedures*, New York: Holt, Rinehard and Winston.
Schubert, Glendon (1965), *Judicial Policy-making: Political Role of Courts*, Chicago, IL: Scott Foresman.
Selznick, Philip (1959), 'The Sociology of Law', in Robert K. Merton, Leonard Broom and Leonard S. Çottrell, Jr (eds), *Sociology Today*, New York: Basic Books, pp. 115–27.

Selznick, Philip (1992), *The Moral Commonwealth: Social Theory and the Promise of Community*, Berkeley and Los Angeles, CA: University of California Press.
Seron, Carroll (1996), *The Business of Practicing Law: The Work Lives of Solo and Small-Firm Attorneys*, Philadelphia, PA: Temple University Press.
Seron, Carroll and Silbey, Susan (2004), 'Profession, Science, and Culture: An Emergent Canon of Law and Society Research', in Austin Sarat (ed.), *The Blackwell Companion to Law and Society*, Malden, MA: Blackwell Publishing, pp. 30–61.
Shapiro, Martin (1968), *The Supreme Court and Administrative Agencies*, New York: Free Press.
Silbey, Susan S. (2003), 'Governing Green Laboratories: Differential Responses to Legal Regulation', San Francisco, CA: American Sociological Association.
Skogan, W.G. (1994), *Contacts Between Police and Public: Findings from the 1992 British Crime Survey*, London: HMSO Books.
Skolnick, Jerome E. (1966), *Justice Without Trial*, New York: John Wiley & Sons.
Smigel, E.O. (1969), *The Wall Street Lawyer: Professional Organization Man*, Bloomington, IN: Indiana University Press.
Sudnow, David (1965), 'Normal Crimes: Sociological Features of the Penal Code in a Public Defender's Office', *Social Problems*, **12**(3), pp. 253–76.
Sumner, Colin (1979), *Reading Ideologies: An Investigation into the Marxist Theory of Ideology and Law*, London: Academic Press.
Tomlins, Christopher (2000), 'Framing the Field of Law's Disciplinary Encounters: A Historical Narrative', *Law & Society Review*, **34**(4), pp. 911–72.
Ulmer, Sidney (1961), *Introductory Readings in Political Behavior*, Chicago, IL: Rand McNally & Company.
Vogel, David (1986), *National Styles of Regulation: Environmental Policy in Great Britain and the United States*, Ithaca, NY: Cornell University Press.
Weber, Max (1947), *The Theory of Social and Economic Organization*, trans. A.M. Henderson and Talcott Parsons, New York: Free Press.
Weber, Max (1954), *Max Weber on Law in Economy and Society*, eds. Max Rheinstein and Edward Shills, New York: Simon and Schuster.

Part I
Socio-legal Theory

[1]

The Boundaries of Legal Sociology*

Donald J. Black†

I

Contemporary sociology of law is characterized by a confusion of science and policy. Its analysis proceeds in the disembodied tongue of science, in the language of "system," "structure," "pattern," and "organization," or in the vocabulary of technique, of "needs," "functions," and "viability." Rarely does the language impart emotion, indignation, or even personal involvement on the part of the investigator. But while legal sociology is presented in this scientific language and scientific tone, normative considerations—the "ought" and the "just"—become subtly implicated.

Although legal sociologists[1] typically criticize one another according to the usual scientific standards of methodological precision and theoretical validity, they frequently become preoccupied with the "policy implications" of their research. Occasionally, in assessing one another, they shed the mantle of science and become unabashedly political. Recently, for instance, a sociologist characterized the literature of legal sociology as bourgeois, liberal, pluralist, and meliorist.[2] He went on to argue that a more radical sociology is required, one that is "more critical in its premises and farther-reaching in its proposals."[3]

* This paper has benefited from the reactions of several readers: Leon Lipson, Maureen Mileski, David Trubek, and Stanton Wheeler. In March, 1972, an early draft occasioned an informal seminar at the Center for the Study of Law and Society of the University of California at Berkeley. I thank the following participants in that seminar for helping me to sharpen my ideas: David Matza, Sheldon Messinger, Philippe Nonet, Jerome Skolnick, and Philip Selznick. Finally, I want to express appreciation to Henry M. Fields, a law student who first suggested that I write this paper and then went on to contribute his considerable scholarly and editorial abilities to its preparation.

† Assistant Professor of Sociology and Lecturer in Law, Yale University.

1. In what follows I shall use the term "sociologists" as a matter of convention, though I intend to refer not only to Ph.D.'s in sociology but also to lawyers and political scientists and anyone else claiming to contribute to the scientific study of law as a social phenomenon. Most of my examples, however, derive from the scholarly literature explicitly labeled "sociology of law" and authored by academic sociologists.

2. Currie, *Book Review*, 81 YALE L.J. 134 (1971), *reviewing* LAW AND THE BEHAVIORAL SCIENCES (L. Friedman & S. Macaulay eds. 1969) *and* SOCIETY AND THE LEGAL ORDER (R. Schwartz & J. Skolnick eds. 1970). These two collections of the legal sociology literature not only collect representative materials but also attempt to explain the relevance of the materials, thereby providing excellent examples of the style of discourse now dominating the field.

3. *Id.* at 145. A striking feature of Currie's review is that he pays little attention to the scientific adequacy of the work he criticizes. Instead, he focuses more upon the reform

The Boundaries of Legal Sociology

Whether liberal or radical, however, legal sociologists tend to share a style of discourse that deserves attention and comment.

It is my contention that a purely sociological approach to law should involve not an assessment of legal policy, but rather, a scientific analysis of legal life *as a system of behavior*. The ultimate contribution of this enterprise would be a general theory of law, a theory that would predict and explain every instance of legal behavior. While such a general theory may never be attained, efforts to achieve it should be central to the sociology of law. By contrast, the core problems of legal policymaking are problems of value. Such value considerations are as irrelevant to a sociology of law as they are to any other scientific theory of the empirical world.

Invoking the language of science and relying upon its aura of respectability, sociologists move, in a special and almost imperceptible way, beyond science and deal with questions of legal evaluation. Because they confuse scientific questions with policy questions, they severely retard the development of their field. At best, they offer an applied sociology of law—at worst, sheer ideology.

After examining the type of discourse that passes for a sociology of law and noting its apparent shortcomings, I shall discuss more directly the nature and aims of a pure sociology of law.

II

With one phrase, *legal effectiveness,* we capture the major thematic concern of contemporary sociology of law. The wide range of work that revolves around the legal-effectiveness theme displays a common strategy of problem formulation, namely a comparison of legal reality to a legal ideal of some kind. Typically a gap is shown between law-in-action and law-in-theory. Often the sociologist then goes on to suggest how the reality might be brought closer to the ideal. Law is regarded as ineffective and in need of reform owing to the disparity between the legal reality and the ideal.[4]

Legal-effectiveness studies differ from one another, however, in the kinds of legal ideals against which their findings are measured. At one

implications of the existing work and condemns it on political rather than methodological or theoretical grounds. Thus, while he suggests that the work could greatly benefit from the perspectives of Marxian scholars, he fails to show that the Marxian approach to law has a superior explanatory power.

4. Because research in legal sociology consistently shows these disparities, the field has become identified with debunkery and the unmasking of law. In legal scholarship this debunking spirit goes back to the legal realism movement which has haunted American law schools since it emerged around the turn of the century. Much legal sociology, then, is a new legal realism, appearing in the prudent garb of social science, armed with sophisticated research methods, new language, and abstract theoretical constructs.

extreme are "impact studies" that compare reality to legal ideals with a very plain and specific operational meaning. Here the legal measuring rod is likely to be a statute whose purpose is rather clearly discernible or a judicial decision unambiguously declarative of a specific policy. The *Miranda* decision, for example, requiring the police to apprise suspects of their legal rights before conducting an in-custody interrogation, has a core meaning about which consensus is quite high.[5] Soon after *Miranda* was handed down by the Supreme Court, research was initiated to evaluate the degree of police compliance with the decision.[6] When the core meaning of a decision thus is clear, this type of research can be expected to show whether or not a decision has, in fact, been implemented.

Sociologists, however, may launch these implementation studies where legislation or judicial opinion is considerably more ambiguous than in *Miranda.* In such instances, the "impact" may be difficult to measure. What must be done, for example, to implement *In re Gault*?[7] Though it is generally recognized that *Gault* guarantees to juvenile suspects constitutional rights previously accorded only to adults, the extent of these juvenile rights is not at all clear.[8] Hence it becomes difficult, perhaps impossible, to identify the degree to which *Gault* has been implemented.[9]

5. Miranda v. Arizona, 384 U.S. 436 (1966). Although there may be some disagreement as to the peripheral meanings of "custody" and "interrogation" (*see, e.g.,* Mathis v. United States, 391 U.S. 1 (1968); Orozco v. Texas, 394 U.S. 324 (1969)), there is little doubt that a suspect under arrest in a police station who is probingly questioned about his involvement in a crime is both in custody and under interrogation as these concepts are used by the Court. Moreover, no question remains as to the required *content* of an apprising of rights. 384 U.S. at 478-79. Yet, there may even be disagreement as to what constitutes an "adequate" and "effective" apprising of rights. *Id.* at 467. *Compare* United States v. Fox, 403 F.2d 97 (2d Cir. 1968), *with* State v. Renfrew, 280 Minn. 276, 159 N.W.2d 111 (1968). For example, would a police procedure of giving the suspect a preprinted card listing his rights meet the requirement of an adequate and effective apprisal? Would that procedure meet the *Miranda* test if the suspect were illiterate?

6. *See, e.g.,* Project, *Interrogations in New Haven: The Impact of Miranda,* 76 YALE L.J. 1519 (1967).

7. 387 U.S. 1 (1967).

8. *See generally* Foster, *Notice and "Fair Procedure": Revolution or Simple Revision?,* in GAULT, WHAT NOW FOR THE JUVENILE COURT? 51 (V. Nordin ed. 1968). For examples of judicial conflict in the applicability of specific rights, *compare*: (1) Stanley v. Peyton, 292 F. Supp. 213 (W.D. Va. 1968), *cert. denied,* 400 U.S. 828 (1970) (dictum) *and* State v. Acuna, 78 N.M. 119, 428 P.2d 658 (1967), *with* Steinhauer v. State, 206 So.2d 25 (Fla. Dist. Ct. App. 1967), *quashed and remanded on other grounds,* 216 So.2d 214 (1968), *cert. denied,* 398 U.S. 914 (1970) (Douglas, J., dissenting on denial of *cert.*) (right to counsel at waiver of juvenile court jurisdiction hearing); (2) *In re* Fletcher, 251 Md. 520, 248 A.2d 364 (1968), *cert. denied,* 396 U.S. 852 (1969), *with In re* D., 30 App. Div. 2d 183, 290 N.Y.S.2d 935 (1968) (necessity of giving *Miranda* warnings to *both* juvenile and parents at pre-trial custodial interrogation); (3) *In re* Wylie, 231 A.2d 81 (D.C. Ct. App. 1967), *with In re* Urbasek, 38 Ill.2d 535, 232 N.E.2d 716 (1967) (right to standard of proof beyond a reasonable doubt).

9. *See, e.g.,* Lefstein, Stapleton, & Teitelbaum, *In Search of Juvenile Justice*: Gault *and its Implementation* 3 L. & SOC. REV. 491 (1969), in which these problems of operationalization are evident.

The Boundaries of Legal Sociology

Finally, the sociologist may attempt to compare legal reality to an ideal grounded in neither statutory nor case law. Here the investigator assesses his empirical materials against standards of justice such as "the rule of law," "arbitrariness," "legality," or a concept of "due process" not explicitly anchored in the due process clause of the Constitution. Jerome Skolnick, for instance, asserts that the police employ the informer system in narcotics enforcement "irrespective of the constraints embodied in principles of due process."[10] But there is no indication of where Skolnick locates these principles. Presumably he realizes that no court in the United States has declared the practice illegal, and there is no reason to think such a decision is likely in the near future.[11] In another study, Skolnick investigates plea-bargaining in the courtroom, concluding that the cooperation underlying this practice "deviates" from some unarticulated adversarial ideal.[12] Similarly, Leon Mayhew, in arguing that the Massachusetts Commission Against Discrimination failed to define discrimination adequately and thereby ignored much illegal conduct, provides neither a legal argument nor an empirical referent for his interpretation of the Commission's proper mission.[13] In short, then, some studies in legal sociology seem to move beyond the law when they measure legal reality against an ideal.

At its most useful, legal-effectiveness research may be valuable to people in a position to reform the legal order. In this sense it consists of studies in *applied* sociology of law. This would appear to be particularly true of those investigations that relate empirical findings to legal ideals which are clearly expressed in the written law. Such research might provide legal reformers with a kind of leverage for change, though the mere evidence of a gap between law-in-action and law-in-theory would not in itself overwhelm all resistance to change.

10. J. Skolnick, Justice Without Trial 138 (1966).

11. Much less than viewing the use of informers as a violation of constitutional safeguards, the Supreme Court has refused even to require that an informer's identity be revealed. Specifically, police reliance upon anonymous informants to provide the requisite information for probable cause to sustain an arrest or search warrant has been held not to violate either the Fourth Amendment or due process clause. *See* McCray v. Illinois, 386 U.S. 300 (1967); Draper v. United States, 358 U.S. 307 (1959). Information supplied by an unnamed informer of apparent reliability under certain circumstances may provide sufficient cause for a search without a warrant. Adams v. Williams, 40 U.S.L.W. 4724 (U.S. June 12, 1972). But if the police utilize an informant as a participant in an illegal narcotics transaction, even where there is no question of entrapment the government will be required to disclose the identity of the informant at trial when such disclosure may be "relevant and helpful to the accused's defense." The failure to disclose in this context would violate due process. Roviaro v. United States, 353 U.S. 53 (1957).

12. Skolnick, *Social Control in the Adversary System,* 11 J. Conflict Resolution 52 (1967).

13. L. Mayhew, Law and Equal Opportunity (1969), *reviewed,* Black, *Book Review,* 40 Soc. Inquiry 179 (1970). *See* Mayhew, *Teleology and Values in the Social System: Reply to Donald J. Black,* 40 Soc. Inquiry 182 (1970).

Who can imagine a study, after all, that would not discover such a gap? Little is more predictable about the law than that these gaps exist.

However, legal-effectiveness research sometimes moves beyond applied sociology. When legal reality is compared to an ideal with no identifiable empirical referent, such as "the rule of law" or "due process," the investigator may inadvertently implant his personal ideals as the society's legal ideals. At this point social science ceases and advocacy begins. The value of legal-effectiveness research of this kind is bound to be precarious, for it involves, perhaps unwittingly, moral judgment at the very point where it promises scientific analysis.

III

As I have described it, the sociology of law significantly resembles a broader style of thought that has come to be known as *technocratic* thought,[14] or, to use an earlier term, scientism. In the technocratic world-view, every problem—factual, moral, political, or legal—reduces to a question of technique. A good technique is one that works, and what works can be learned through science. Any problem that cannot be solved in this way is no problem at all, hardly worthy of our attention. In theory, moreover, every problem can be solved if only the appropriate expertise is applied to it. Among the key words in the technocratic vocabulary are efficiency and, one I noted earlier, effectiveness. It is a style of thought in some respects akin to pragmatism, but it is a pragmatism with unstated goals, a search for the most rational way to go somewhere that is never clearly specified. Rather, we must infer what these goals are, and that is how some technocratic approaches come to be known as liberal and bourgeois, others as radical and critical. Technocrats do not make political arguments in the usual sense; they do not moralize. They simply want to get the job done.

The technocratic style dominates much discussion of social controversy at the higher reaches of American life. We are given to understand that scientific research will reveal whether marijuana should be legalized, that the Vietnam War was a miscalculation, and that economic analysis will determine the most "rational" tax program. The new nations of Africa and Asia are studied to determine what their modernization "requires." Riots, violence, and pornography give rise to government study commissions and research grants for the universities. Moral problems of every sort are translated into problems of

14. For a recent discussion of technocratic thought, see T. Roszak, The Making of a Counter Culture 5-22 (1969).

knowledge and science, of know-how. To discuss the criminal in the moral terms of right and wrong comes to be seen as primitive and unschooled; medical terminology is introduced into the discussion of the treatment of criminal offenders. In the name of science and progress, what was once seen as evil is studied and treated, not condemned.

The logic of this technocratic mentality has helped to catapult sociology to a position of some prominence in these times of rapid social change and conflict. Sociology, it is thought, will point the way to solutions to the many problems before us. The sociologists themselves have shown little reluctance to accept this responsibility. The typical sociologist knows almost nothing about moral or social philosophy, but if public policy is no more than a matter of scientific technique, why should he? In a technocratic era, moral philosophy is an oddity in the real world of action, a quaint remnant of the nineteenth century, something for the undergraduates.

IV

Law can be seen as a thing like any other in the empirical world. It is crucial to be clear that from a sociological standpoint, law consists in observable acts, not in rules as the concept of rule or norm is employed in both the literature of jurisprudence and in every-day legal language.[15] From a sociological point of view, law is not what lawyers regard as binding or obligatory precepts, but rather, for example, the observable dispositions of judges, policemen, prosecutors, or administrative officials.[16] Law is like any other thing in the sense that it is as amenable to the scientific method as any other aspect of reality. No intellectual apparatus peculiar to the study of law is required. At the same time, a social science of law true to positivism, the conventional theory of science, cannot escape the limitations inherent in scientific thought itself.[17] Perhaps a word should be said about these limitations.

15. Hence this sociological concept of law is very different from and not logically incompatible with the legal positivism of Hans Kelsen and his "pure theory of law." *See, e.g.*, H. KELSEN, GENERAL THEORY OF LAW AND STATE (1945). Similarly, to take another well-known example, a sociological approach does not conflict with the rule-oriented jurisprudence of H.L.A. Hart in THE CONCEPT OF LAW (1961).

At the level of social life in its narrow sense, law is behavior and nothing more. If the concept of rule or norm is used in a sociological analysis, it should always refer to a behavioral pattern of some kind. *See, e.g.*, E. DURKHEIM, *The Determination of Moral Facts*, in SOCIOLOGY AND PHILOSOPHY 35-62 (D.F. Pocock transl. 1953).

16. At a later point, I shall propose a sociological definition of law. *See* p. 1096 *infra*.

17. A good introduction to positivism is L. KOLAKOWSKI, THE ALIENATION OF REASON: A HISTORY OF POSITIVIST THOUGHT (N. Guterman transl. 1968).

The Yale Law Journal Vol. 81: 1086, 1972

Within the tradition of positivist philosophy, three basic principles of scientific knowledge can be noted. First, science can know only phenomena and never essences.[18] The quest for the one correct concept of law or for anything else "distinctively legal" is therefore inherently unscientific.[19] The essence of law is a problem for jurisprudence, not science. Second, every scientific idea requires a concrete empirical referent of some kind.[20] A science can only order experience, and has no way of gaining access to non-empirical domains of knowledge. Accordingly, insofar as such ideals as justice, the rule of law, and due process are without a grounding in experience, they have no place in the sociology of law. Third, value judgments cannot be discovered in the empirical world and for that reason are without cognitive meaning in science.[21]

It is for this last reason that science knows nothing and can know nothing about the effectiveness of law. Science is incapable of an evaluation of the reality it confronts. To measure the effectiveness of law or of anything else for that matter, we must import standards of value that are foreign to science.[22] What is disturbing about the contemporary literature on legal effectiveness then is not that it evaluates law,[23] but rather, that its evaluations and proposals are presented as

18. This has been called the principle of phenomenalism. *See id.* at 3-4.

19. Philip Selznick, one of the most ambitious and influential students of legal effectiveness, considers the "cardinal weakness" of the sociological approach to law to be its "failure to offer a theory of the distinctively legal." Selznick, *The Sociology of Law*, 9 INTERNATIONAL ENCYCLOPEDIA OF THE SOCIAL SCIENCES 51 (D.L. Sills ed. 1968).

20. This is the principle of nominalism. *See* KOLAKOWSKI, *supra* note 17, at 5-7.

21. *Id.* at 7-8. Some legal sociologists are willing to tolerate an obfuscation of factual and normative discourse. Selznick, for instance, while conceding that the separation of fact and value has some merit, nevertheless suggests that this distinction is meant for "unsophisticated minds." We must, he continues, unlearn this "easy and reassuring" formula from our "intellectual youth." Selznick finds a natural-law approach more appropriate for the mature thinker. Selznick, *Sociology and Natural Law*, 6 NATURAL L.F. 86 (1961).

22. This does not say that scientific studies of legal effectiveness are impossible. As long as a social goal is introduced into the analysis and is adequately defined for purposes of the investigation, the study of effectiveness is perfectly feasible. Such applied science can be as rigorously conducted as any other research. *Cf.* pp. 1089-90 *supra*.

23. As a rule I do not personally find the policy criticisms and proposals of legal sociologists to be particularly objectionable, the exception being those proposals that increase the power of the government to intervene in citizens' lives. Thus, for instance, I find the therapeutic approach to criminal offenders a frightening advance of an already too powerful criminal justice system. In fact, I align myself more broadly and precisely in the philosophical tradition of anarchism. For me, the validity of law is at all times contingent upon my own assessment of its moral validity, and thus I recognize no a priori legitimacy in the rule of law. For a brief introduction to this political ethic, see R. WOLFF, IN DEFENCE OF ANARCHISM (1970).

I would add that the students of legal effectiveness I am discussing are, politically speaking, the elite of our society, however critical of the legal process they may seem. Indeed, the government often finances their research on its own effectiveness. It is my view that the confusion of fact and value operates as a form of mystification that helps to keep the established order intact. Nevertheless, I do not wish to use my status as a scientist to promote my political philosophy. *See* M. WEBER, FROM MAX WEBER: ESSAYS IN SOCIOLOGY 129-56 (H.H. Gerth & C.W. Mills transl. and eds. 1958).

scientific findings. Far from denying this confusion, Philip Selznick[24] has gone so far in the opposite direction as to claim that "nothing we know today precludes an effort to define 'ends proper to man's nature' and to discover objective standards of moral judgment."[25]

Legal sociologists involved in the study of effectiveness have thus come to advance a conception of scientific criticism of law. This is illogical; it is a contradiction in terms.

It is apparent by now that my critique of contemporary legal sociology is premised on the notion that sociology is a scientific enterprise and, as such, can be distinguished from moral philosophy, jurisprudence, or any other normatively oriented study—in other words, that the study of fact can be distinguished from the study of value. This is not to say that I am unaware of the criticisms that have been levied against a purely value-free social science. But while accepting these criticisms, I cannot understand the conclusion that the effort to develop an objective science of man should be abandoned.

It is important to understand precisely how values become involved in social science. One widely recognized intrusion of values occurs at the first stage of scientific inquiry: the choice of the problem for study. The values of the investigator may determine, for example, whether he selects a problem with great relevance for public policy or one of wholly academic interest. This intrusion of values was long ago noted by Max Weber, perhaps the most illustrious proponent of value-free sociology. Weber contended that the role of values in the choice of a problem is unavoidable and should be faced squarely, but he insisted that the problem, once selected, could and should be pursued "non-evaluatively."[26]

But I would go further than Weber and grant that these value orientations may bias the analysis of the problem as well as its selection. Though various methodological techniques have been developed to minimize the effects of these biases, good social science still requires a disciplined disengagement on the part of the investigator—so disciplined, in fact, that it may rarely be achieved. Various arguments can be made to the effect that bias is built into social science at its very foundations. For example, the claim has been made that every social science study necessarily implicates the investigator in the perspective of an actual hierarchical position, seeing social life from

24. *See* note 19 *supra*.
25. Selznick, *supra* note 21, at 93-94.
26. *See* M. WEBER, THE METHODOLOGY OF THE SOCIAL SCIENCES 21-22 (E.A. Shils & H.A. Finch transls. 1949). For a direct attack on Weber's approach to these questions, see Gouldner, *Anti-Minotaur: The Myth of a Value-Free Sociology*, 9 SOC. PROBLEMS 199 (1962).

either the social top or the bottom, and is therefore inherently biased.[27] For purposes of discussion I grant even this. Similarly it is arguable that all social science is, beyond science, a form of ideology, if only because it is by its nature an instance of social behavior subject to the scrutiny of the very discipline of which it is a part. Sociology, that is, can be analyzed sociologically. Sociology does not occur in a vacuum and is undoubtedly influenced by social forces. Accordingly, sociology may be viewed as ideology supporting either the defenders of the status quo or their opponents.[28]

Finally, because much social science can be interpreted in an ideological framework, its theories and findings can be used as weapons in the arena of public policymaking. The polemical impact of social science may be particularly great at this historical moment, given the enormous prestige of science in modern society. Not only do these theories and findings feed into existing policy debates, but they also can stimulate controversy and change by drawing attention to empirical situations that might otherwise be unknown or ignored by policymakers and social critics. Thus social science performs—willingly or not—an intelligence function in the political process.[29] Because of such political ramifications, the argument has been put forward that the sociologist remains responsible for the consequences of his work. Only by making an explicit moral commitment can the social scientist hope to protect himself and others from the unintended consequences of his work.[30] It is apparent that social science resonates into the realm of ideology, thereby raising serious questions about the scholar's responsibilities to his fellow man.

In several senses, then, values enter into the activity of social science. While values may play a similar role in science of all kinds, it can at least be admitted that their role is especially visible and dramatic when man is studying himself. Values may be all the more prominent in the

27. Becker, *Whose Side Are We On?,* 14 SOC. PROBLEMS 239 (1967).

28. This is a major theme of a recent critique of sociological theory. *See* A. GOULDNER, THE COMING CRISIS OF WESTERN SOCIOLOGY (1970).

29. It should be clear that the policy impact of science is never direct but is always mediated by normative analysis, whether explicit or implicit. Policy cannot be deduced from scientific propositions alone. All of this is dramatically illustrated by the relation between the Marxian theory and public policy. Surely no theory of social science has had more impact upon the world. It has been an important weapon in ideological debate, and it has alerted policymakers and the public to the situation of the working class and the role of class conflict in social change. Yet as a scientific theory the Marxian analysis of society and history has no logical implications for political action. Without passing judgment upon the exploitation and growing misery of the proletariat, one could just as well sit back passively and watch history unfold as join the revolution. Both responses are logically independent of the theory.

30. R. DAHRENDORF, *Values and Social Science: The Value Dispute in Perspective,* in ESSAYS IN THE THEORY OF SOCIETY 17 (1968).

study of man's moral life, of which legal sociology is one branch. The major arguments against the possibility of a pure science of man, in short, seem to have some merit.[31] But the crucial question is what all of this implies for the traditional distinction between fact and value. I say it implies nothing. In fact, much of the criticism of value-free sociology itself rests upon observable patterns of value impact upon social science and for that reason relies upon the fact-value distinction for its own validity.

We have seen that a social scientist may be affected by values in the choice of his problem and may be biased in his approach to it. Critics of a value-free social science assert that these psychological effects, along with the ideological character of social science when viewed as the object of analysis itself, undermine the validity of social science. But this is to confuse the origins and uses of a scientific statement with its validity.[32] *The fact that scientific statements are influenced by values does not make them value statements.* The psychological and social influence of values on scientific inquiry has no logical implications for the validity of a scientific proposition. Its validity is determined only by empirical verification. A value statement, by contrast, is not subject to such a test.[33] How, for example, is the following statement to be empirically verified: "Democratic process is an ultimate good"? The fact that we can distinguish between scientific propositions and such value statements is all we need to assert the possibility

31. Of course in this brief discussion I cannot begin to review the sizable literature on the subject. Perhaps I should note, however, one criticism of the value-neutral strategy that bears directly on the study of law—one, moreover, that seems to me to be wholly without merit. This criticism asserts that the study of normative life, because it is normative, requires a partially normative approach on the part of the investigator if he is to comprehend its empirical character. The investigator must take the normative view of the participants if he is to understand their normative behavior. Selznick, for instance, suggests that the sociologist should make an "assessment" of the degree to which a normative system reaches an ideal "from the standpoint of the normative system being studied" though "the student of a normative system need not have any personal commitment to the desirability of that system." Selznick, *supra* note 21, at 88. In the study of law, therefore, it seems we must include an assessment of legal reality in terms of the ideals of the legal system we study.

In my view this argument incorrectly assumes that such normative ideals can be identified at a wholly empirical level. I do not believe, for example, that the degree of conformity of law with, let us say, a constitutional ideal, is a wholly empirical question. The nature of the ideal is itself a normative question, a question of normative interpretation. In the study of law such interpretation is the heart of legal scholarship, and from a positivist standpoint that activity is, at its core, normative rather than scientific. It advances an "ought" as the proper measure of reality, and it does not matter whether or not the interpreter himself subscribes to the "ought." It remains an unavoidably normative judgment. In effect, then, Selznick's view is that in order to understand normative life we must *be* normative. This view, I believe, is a non sequitur.

32. *See* Dahrendorf, *supra* note 30, at 9-10.

33. Although not subject to empirical verification, a value statement may be subject to other criteria such as its logical status in relation to a more general axiological principle.

of social science. In short, values may affect social science profoundly, but that is no reason to abandon the enterprise.[34]

V

The proper concern of legal sociology should be the development of a general theory of law. A general theory involves several key elements that may not at first be obvious. To say that a theory of law is general means that it seeks to order law wherever it is found. It seeks to discover the principles and mechanisms that predict empirical patterns of law, whether these patterns occur in this day or the past, regardless of the substantive area of law involved and regardless of the society. By contrast, the contemporary study of law is ideographic, very concrete and historical. Legal scholars tend to rebel at the suggestion of a general theory of their subject matter. Nevertheless, unless we seek generality in our study of law, we abandon hope for a serious sociology of law.

If the sweep of legal sociology is to be this broad, a correspondingly broad concept of law is required. I like to define law simply as *governmental social control.*[35] This is one possibility among many consistent with a positivist strategy. It is a concept easily employed in cross-societal analysis, encompassing any act by a political body that concerns the definition of social order or its defense. At the same time it excludes such forms of social control as popular morality and bureaucratic rules in private organizations. It is more inclusive than an American lawyer might deem proper, but more selective than anthro-

34. My critique of contemporary legal sociology arises from a very conventional conception of scientific method, a conception associated with the broader tradition of positivist thought. I have not made and do not intend to make a philosophical defense of this tradition. I wish only to advocate a sociology of law true to basic positivist principles as they have come to be understood in the history of the philosophy of science.

35. I mention this only as a means of delineating the subject matter of legal sociology. A definition of the subject matter is a prerequisite to any scientific inquiry. Just as a physicist must first define motion before he can describe its characteristics, a sociologist of religion, for example, must first define the pattern of social behavior that constitutes religion before he can proceed with his research. This does not mean that there is only one proper definition. Law itself has been defined non-normatively in a variety of ways. *See, e.g.,* M. Weber, The Theory of Social and Economic Organization 127 (T. Parsons ed. & transl. 1964):

> An order will be called *law* when conformity with it is upheld by the probability that deviant action will be met by physical or psychic sanctions aimed to compel conformity or to punish disobedience, and applied by a group of men especially empowered to carry out this function.

I have chosen "governmental social control" as a definition of law for the reasons that follow in the text. I should add, however, that for me the choice of a particular sociological concept of law is not at all critical to my larger aim, since my ultimate interest goes beyond law per se to all forms of social control. For me, the study of law is preliminary and subordinate to the more general study of social control systems of all kinds. Therefore, if my concept of law is too narrow or too broad it does not matter *theoretically,* since it will in any case be relevant to a sociology of social control.

pological concepts which treat law as synonymous with normative life and dispute settlement of every description, governmental or otherwise. If we are to have a manageable subject matter, our concept must construe law as one among a larger array of social control systems. And if we are to have a strategically detached approach, our concept must be value neutral. We need a theoretical structure applicable to the law of the Nazis as well as American law, to revolutionary law and colonial law as well as the cumbersome law of traditional China. What do these systems share, and how can we explain the differences among them?

Ultimately a theory is known and judged by its statements about the world. These statements both guide and follow empirical research. They propose uniformities in the relation between one part of reality and another. Thus a general theory of law is addressed to the relation between law and other aspects of social life, including, for instance, other forms of social control, social stratification, the division of labor, social integration, group size, and the structure and substance of social networks. At the moment we have only a small inventory of theoretical statements, or propositions, of this kind. The relevant literature is sparse, and many of our leads must come from the classic works of Maine,[36] Durkheim,[37] Weber,[38] Ehrlich,[39] Pound,[40] and the like. Marx, too, should not be forgotten, though he gave law only passing attention.[41] Apart from classical sociology and comparative jurisprudence, anthropological literature, notably the work of such scholars as Malinowski,[42] Hoebel,[43] Gluckman,[44] Bohannan,[45] and Nader,[46]

36. *See, e.g.*, ANCIENT LAW (1861); VILLAGE-COMMUNITIES IN THE EAST AND WEST (1871).

37. THE DIVISION OF LABOR IN SOCIETY (G. Simpson transl. 1933); PROFESSIONAL ETHICS AND CIVIC MORALS (C. Brookfield transl. 1957); *Two Laws of Penal Evolution* (M. Mileski transl. 1971) (available in my files).

38. MAX WEBER ON LAW IN ECONOMY AND SOCIETY (M. Rheinstein ed., E. Shils & M. Rheinstein transls. 1954).

39. FUNDAMENTAL PRINCIPLES OF THE SOCIOLOGY OF LAW (W. Moll transl. 1936).

40. *E.g.*, SOCIAL CONTROL THROUGH LAW (1942); *The Limits of Effective Legal Action*, 27 INT'L J. ETHICS 150 (1917); *A Survey of Social Interests*, 57 HARV. L. REV. 1 (1943).

41. Marx did, however, inspire some interesting sociological work on law. *See, e.g.*, K. RENNER, THE INSTITUTIONS OF PRIVATE LAW AND THEIR SOCIAL FUNCTIONS (O. Kahn-Freund ed., A. Schwartzchild transl. 1949); Pashukanis, *The General Theory of Law and Marxism*, in SOVIET LEGAL PHILOSOPHY 111 (H. Babb transl. 1951).

42. The standard work is CRIME AND CUSTOM IN SAVAGE SOCIETY (1926). This study is considered the first ethnography of law.

43. THE LAW OF PRIMITIVE MAN (1954); K. LLEWELLYN & E. HOEBEL, THE CHEYENNE WAY: CONFLICT AND CASE LAW IN PRIMITIVE JURISPRUDENCE (1941).

44. *See, e.g.*, THE JUDICIAL PROCESS AMONG THE BAROTSE OF NORTHERN RHODESIA (1955). Gluckman provides a useful overview of legal anthropology in POLITICS, LAW AND RITUAL IN TRIBAL SOCIETY (1965).

45. JUSTICE AND JUDGMENT AMONG THE TIV (1957); *The Differing Realms of the Law*, in THE ETHNOGRAPHY OF LAW 33 (1965) (supplement to 67 AM. ANTHROPOLOGIST 33 (1965)).

46. *E.g.*, *An Analysis of Zapotec Law Cases*, 3 ETHNOLOGY 404 (1964); *Choices in Legal Procedure: Shia Moslem and Mexican Zapotec*, 67 AM. ANTHROPOLOGIST 394 (1965).

has contributed more than sociology to a general theory of law. Contemporary sociologists tend to limit their attention to the American legal system, and even there, disproportionate emphasis is given the criminal justice system. Rarely do they compare American law to governmental social control in other societies; yet if legal sociology is not comparative, its conclusions will inevitably be time-bound and ethnocentric.

This is not to suggest that American criminal justice is unworthy of study. But one must address problems at a higher level of generality, thereby contributing to and benefiting from scholarship in other realms of law. If we investigate the police, for example, our fundamental interest as sociologists must be in what police work can teach us about law, generically understood, and we must bring to a study of the police whatever we know about other forms of legal life. From my standpoint, in other words, the major shortcoming of most sociological literature on the police is that it concerns the police alone, instead of treating police behavior as an instance of law. Often sociologists occupy themselves with the unique world of the policeman, his attitudes, hopes and fears, his relations with his fellow officers, his social isolation in the wider community—in brief, with the "human" dimensions of police work.[47] Insofar as such studies rise above descriptive journalism or ethnography, then, they tend to focus upon the psychology of the policeman on his day-to-day round. Yet from a purely sociological point of view it is not important to know that policemen are, after all, "human" or to know how their minds work. A pure sociology of law does not study humans in the usual sense. It studies law as a system of behavior.[48] Taken in this sense, law feels nothing. It has no joy or sorrow or wonderment. Scientifically conceived as a social reality in its own right, law is no more human than a molecular structure. It has no nationality, no mind, and no ends proper to its nature.

I do not mean to criticize categorically the rather impressive body of police research that has accumulated in recent years, but only to suggest that its contribution to the sociology of law is limited. We must give up the notion that the sociology of law embraces any and all forms of empirical research relating to the legal system. A scientific discipline is defined by its theoretical mission, by what it tries to ex-

47. *E.g.*, SKOLNICK, *supra* note 10; W. WESTLEY, VIOLENCE AND THE POLICE: A SOCIOLOGICAL STUDY OF LAW, CUSTOM, AND MORALITY (1970); Bittner, *The Police on Skid-Row: A Study of Peace-Keeping*, 32 AM. SOC. REV. 699 (1967); Werthman and Piliavin, *Gang Members and the Police*, in THE POLICE: SIX SOCIOLOGICAL ESSAYS 56 (D. Bordua ed. 1967).
48. *See* p. 1091 *supra*.

plain, not by its sources of data. Thus, research on the human body may contribute to any of a variety of disciplines—biochemistry, genetics, endocrinology, physiological psychology, or whatever. The same is true of research on law or the police. Accordingly, a study of the police contributes to legal sociology only if it provides insights into legal behavior, its empirical profile, the social conditions under which it occurs, and its social implications. I am not saying that every sociologist must be a theorist, but only that any sociologist who does research on a legal topic without knowing, roughly, its theoretical relevance does so at his peril.

Police research should tell us something about the social control function of the police: What legal matters do they handle? How do they come to deal with those matters? What are the principles according to which they process their cases? Ideally a study would also tell us how police behavior resembles other known patterns of legal behavior and how it differs. We know, for example, that the police make arrests relatively infrequently when some other form of social control is available in the situation. Thus, they rarely make an arrest when one family member criminally offends another, a situation where other means of social pressure typically are at hand, whereas the same offense committed by one stranger against another is very apt to result in arrest.[49] This pattern of legal behavior is known to have analogues in a wide variety of legal settings, in civil as well as criminal cases, in the invocation of law as well as its application, in many countries and historical periods, and even in the evolution of law itself.[50] We may state the pattern as a theoretical proposition: Law tends to become implicated in social life to the degree that other forms of social control are weak or unavailable.[51] Hence, what we discover in the behavior of policemen turns out to be simply an instance of a much more general pattern in the conditions under which the law acts upon social life. We thereby add systematically to existing knowledge of this pattern, and, what is more, we can *explain* the behavior of the police, since it can be predicted and deduced from a more general proposition about law.[52] If the likelihood of legal control is greater where other forms of social control are absent, it follows that the police are more likely to arrest a stranger who, let us say, assaults a stranger than a son who assaults his father. To be able to explain something so mundane

49. Black, *The Social Organization of Arrest,* 23 STAN. L. REV. 1087, 1107 (1971).
50. *Id.* at 1107-08 nn.30-34.
51. *Id.* at 1108.
52. For a discussion of this type of explanation, see R. BRAITHWAITE, SCIENTIFIC EXPLANATION: A STUDY OF THE FUNCTION OF THEORY, PROBABILITY AND LAW IN SCIENCE (1953).

The Yale Law Journal Vol. 81: 1086, 1972

and microscopic as behavior in a police encounter with the same proposition that we use to explain the historical emergence of law itself is exciting and encouraging. It provides a glimpse of general theory in action. This kind of theoretical structure is built up and elaborated over time through a process of give-and-take between data and tentative propositions stated at a high level of abstraction. It is the classical pattern of scientific advance, and I cannot see why the sociology of law should be any less ambitious or any less rigorous.

VI

We should be clear about the relation between sociological and legal scholarship. There is, properly speaking, no conflict of professional jurisdiction between the two. A legal problem is a problem of value and is forever beyond the reach of sociology. Jurisdictional conflict arises only when the sociologist makes policy recommendations in the name of science: In matters of legal policy, the lawyer must rely on his own wits.

But a more significant matter than jurisdictional clarity is the relation between pure and applied sociology of law. My view, hardly novel, is that the quality of applied science depends upon the quality of pure science. Just as major advances in mechanical and chemical engineering have been made possible by theoretical formulations in pure physics and chemistry, so legal engineering ultimately requires a general theory of how legal systems behave as natural phenomena. The case for a pure sociology of law does not rest solely on its social usefulness, but if utility is at issue, then in the long run the type of work I advocate is crucial. At present, applied sociology of law has little to apply. What more serious claim could be brought against it?

[2]

THE IDEOLOGY OF LAW: ADVANCES AND PROBLEMS IN RECENT APPLICATIONS OF THE CONCEPT OF IDEOLOGY TO THE ANALYSIS OF LAW

ALAN HUNT*

In this paper I note the growth of analyses of law that focus upon its ideological character and content, and I identify problems and difficulties manifest in the ideological analysis in recent critical and Marxist texts. The paper argues that work focusing upon the ideological character of law realizes significant advances over that produced by the more orthodox approaches within the sociology of law and jurisprudence employing normative analysis. It is possible to make ideological analysis more rigorous. The paper outlines the elements of a theory of and methodology for the ideological analysis of law.

I. INTRODUCTION

The application of the concept "ideology" to the analysis of law has been one of the distinctive features of the strand of critical legal studies that draws upon the Marxist tradition. My objectives in this paper are:

i) to situate the "ideological analysis of law" within contemporary Marxism,

ii) to locate its relevance to the current concerns of the sociology of law and of critical legal studies,[1]

iii) to explore the substantive contribution of work written under the imprint of "the ideological analysis of law" and to identify its major variants,

iv) to show that theoretical and methodological clarification of both the components and scope of the ideological analysis of law is needed, and

v) to outline some elements of a theory of ideological analysis.

---

* This paper was originally delivered as the George Lurcy lecture at Amherst College, Amherst, Massachusetts, in September 1983. I would like to thank Piers Beirne, Maureen Cain, Jeremy Cooper, Steve Redhead, David Sugarman, and Ronnie Warrington for valuable comment and criticism.

1 For my present purpose I distinguish "critical legal studies" as a trend of analysis that, while drawing significantly on the Marxist tradition, is primarily identified by the political project of intervening in the scholarship and practice of legal education.

There is an extensive literature that refers variously to "the ideology of law," the "ideological dimension of law," or "legal ideology." Behind the apparent homogeneity of this writing lie diverse conceptions of ideology and even greater diversity in the way these conceptions are used. Its effects are regularly taken for granted when they should be treated as problematic, and its heuristic potential for the analysis of law is often thwarted by the vagueness and imprecision that one encounters in probing apparently sophisticated conceptualizations. "Ideology," like "dialectics," is all too often invoked as an evasion rather than a solution. If the concept of ideology is poorly used by many of those who write in the Marxist tradition, it is hardly used at all by those who approach the study of law from other perspectives. In the major texts on the sociology of law, both old and new, the concept "ideology" is noticeable by its absence. While no single concept provides a magic key to the mysteries of law, the idea of ideology is important in understanding legal life. There is no concept within the sociology of law that plays the role that is given to ideology within the Marxist tradition. Thus, the ideological analysis of law is not only significant in its own right, but it provides an instructive point of differentiation between Marxist analyses of law and mainstream sociology of law.

Perhaps the closest alternatives to "ideology" within mainstream sociology of law are the concepts "symbolic,"[2] as used by Gusfield (1963) and later by Carson (1974), and "legitimation," as used within the Weberian tradition (Weber, 1966). Neither of these alternatives has, however, either the breadth or the specificity provided by the concept "ideology." If we aspire, as I do, to break what Trubek has aptly characterized as "the stifling debate between instrumental Marxism and liberal legalism" (Trubek, 1977: 553), we must explore the potential utility of the Marxist concept "ideology," not to show the superiority of one tradition over another but to advance the explanatory power of social theory in its application to the analysis of law.

---

2 This paper does not discuss the concept of "symbolism" further. It is, however, important to note the existence of important strands of work which, drawing on the symbolic-instrumental dichotomy, have brought the focus on the symbolic dimensions of law into increasingly close proximity with the concerns of ideology analysis. Such an exploration would require an extended discussion of such diverse authors as Foucault (1977), Ignatieff (1978), and Habermas (1976).

II. MARXISM AND IDEOLOGY

We must, at the outset, recognize that a "correct definition" of ideology cannot be discovered from a search of Marx's texts. Marx used the concept in a variety of ways. Sometimes ideology refers to all ideas, sometimes it refers only to those ideas that are deemed unscientific ("false consciousness"), and sometimes it refers to those ideas that serve the interests of dominant classes, "class beliefs" (cf. Williams, 1977: 66). Not only is the concept open in its texture, but it is also multidimensional. Nevertheless, there are a number of uses of the concept that must be eliminated because they make a definitional assumption about the relationship between "ideology" and "class."

My objective is to use the concept to explore the connection between ideas, attitudes, and beliefs, on the one hand, and economic and political interests, on the other. We can thus ignore ideology as "Ideology," which refers only to a systematic and totalized world view (*Weltanschauung*). Consistent world views may exist, but they must be treated as special or exceptional cases. Second, the idea that ideology necessarily entails some sort of "false consciousness" should also be discarded because it removes the empirically important issue of the association between ideas and interests. For similar reasons we should reject the view that ideology necessarily has a class designation or derivation. For example, the idea that "nationalism" is necessarily traceable to the interests of the "petty bourgeoisie" is empirically problematic and should be replaced by an approach that sees such connections as raising empirical rather than conceptual issues.

While the concept of ideology has often been misused in the ways we describe above, there have been important advances toward a theory of ideology in recent Marxist writing. Our next step is to identify these advances and to relate them to the analysis of law as ideology.[3]

The concept of "ideology" has played a key role for Marxist theorists who make up the "Western Marxist" tradition that

---

[3] To undertake this task systematically would require a thorough study of the historical development of the Marxist theory of ideology. Much of this work has already been undertaken with a greater or lesser degree of success; of particular interest is the work of the Birmingham group (Centre for Contemporary Cultural Studies, 1977), Ernesto Laclau (1977), and Larrain's wide-ranging history of ideology (1979). The decisive intervention of Althusser is to be found in his major texts (Althusser, 1969; 1971) and has been the subject of critical analysis by Hirst (1979) and McLennan (McLennan *et al.*, 1977). The impact of semiology on the theory of ideology is investigated by Coward and Ellis (1977) and Sumner (1979).

has sought to liberate Marxism from the ossification of orthodox "Marxism-Leninism." Central to this project has been the need to reformulate Marxist theory in a way that avoids the related deficiencies of "economism" and "reductionism." If social institutions and ideas are not a simple reflex of economic or class interests and yet are linked to such interests, a sophisticated concept of ideology is needed to explore such linkages in a thorough, empirically grounded manner.

It is thus no accident that the more recent development of a Marxist theory of law, a subject that had previously received little attention, should follow close on the heels of developments in Marxist theories of ideology. Law is interesting and important because it is both close to yet distinct from the state and is, at the same time, the bearer of important ideological values. Albrow characterizes the development within Marxist theory as a movement "from a Gramscian interest in politics to an Althusserian interest in ideology and finding in law a bridge between the two" (Albrow, 1981: 127).

The main thrust of the renewed concern with ideology has been directed towards elaborating a conception of ideology that plays more than the epiphenomenal or marginal role attributed to it within Marxism-Leninism. This goal reflects a political agenda that sees the need to grapple with the persistence of capitalism, while, at the same time, elaborating non-insurrectionary political strategies for socialist transformation within the advanced capitalist democracies. Theorists have realized that to do this ideology needs to be understood in its role of preserving and reproducing capitalist social and economic relations. While much of the debate has often taken an abstract and theoretical form, these real and pressing political concerns are very much present.

As an example of the recent developments in the theory of ideology, consider the use made of the concept of "relative autonomy." The term "relative autonomy" refers to the partial independence of different social elements, such as the legal, political, and ideological, both from each other and, more importantly, from the general interests of a dominant class. This concept serves the interests of the new Marxism because it acknowledges the fundamental importance of the economic base (albeit "in the last instance") while allowing the ideological realm to be treated as an arena of struggle that is not simply the reflex of economic class conflict. This places a heavy theoretical and political burden on the fragile shoulders of the concept, and despite the attractiveness of the idea of "relative autonomy" difficult theoretical problems remain. The primary problem is to achieve what Althusser (1969) described as the necessity of holding on to "both ends of the chain" at the same time; that is, to encompass both the relative autonomy of ideology (or law or state) and the determination of ideology (or law or state), in the last instance by economic relations. There are those within the Marxist tradition who argue that the concept "relative autonomy" cannot overcome such theoretical hurdles and that "there is no middle way" (Cutler *et al.*, 1977: I, 172).

Nevertheless, some real and important advances have been made during the course of the debate on ideology. These achievements can best be illustrated if we look separately at three major issues that Marxist scholars have explored with the aid of the concept of ideology.

A. *Ideology and Human Subjectivity*

A major but insufficiently recognized thrust of the Althusserian tradition was to develop a theory that could at once accommodate the traditional socio-economic concerns of Marxism and a concern for human subjectivity. While this results in some of the most difficult and opaque discussion in Marxist theory, one element is especially important for the analysis of law. The human being according to the Althusserian tradition has three "instances": as a biological being, as a "subject," and as a participant in social relations. For Althusser the "subject" is created by and through a range of different discourses. For example, political discourse produces the individual as "citizen," with its consequent images of atomized but equal citizens existing in a common relationship to the state. Legal discourse transforms both human beings and social entities; for example, corporations become "legal subjects." Legal subjects as the bearers of rights and duties are the primary constituents of the "form of law," which will figure large in my subsequent discussion. The creation of legal subjects involves the recognition of "the law" as the active "subject" that calls them into being. It is by transforming the human subject into a legal subject that law influences the way in which participants experience and perceive their relations with others. Thus, legal ideology provides a constituent of what Althusser called the "lived relation" of human actors (Althusser, 1969: 233). One important implication is that we are encouraged to view law not merely as an external mechanism of regulation but as a constituent of the way in which social relations are lived and experienced. This approach radically changes the role accorded ideology in social life. Ideology is perceived not as a form of consciousness, which is the conventional view, but as a constituent of the unconscious in which social relations are lived. Once this possibility is appreciated, we have in ideology a new and powerful tool for exploring the relationship between "the Law," legal subjects, and social relations.

B. The Determination of the Content of Ideology

Theorists have been concerned both with the generation of specific elements of ideology and with the patterning or structuring of these elements into more or less coherent and integrated systems that make it possible to employ the concept of "bourgeois legal ideology." Here my earlier rejection of the view that every ideological element has a necessary class designation is important. The class dimension of ideology is not an intrinsic property of words or concepts, but instead arises from the way in which ideological elements are combined and interrelated. Ideologies are not to be treated "as if they were political number plates worn by social classes on their backs" (Poulantzas, 1975: 202). Therborn expresses this particularly well:

> [i]deologies actually operate in a state of *disorder*. . . . ideologies operate, constantly being communicated, competing, clashing, affecting, drowning, and silencing one another in social processes of communication (Therborn, 1980: 77, 103).

Thus, an ideology is not a unitary entity. It draws its power from its ability to connect and combine diverse mental elements (concepts, ideas, etc.) into combinations that influence and structure the perception and cognition of social agents. Colin Sumner (1979) expresses something of this approach with his suggestion that ideologies act as grids which select, sort, order, and reorder the elements of thought. This view of ideology is particularly salutary in the field of legal analysis since it counsels us not to assume the coherence and consistency of legal discourse but to search out the resonances of the social, economic, and political struggles that reside behind the smooth surface of legal reasoning and judicial utterance.

The general thrust of the concern with the determination of ideology is the insistence that ideology is a social process that is realized in and through social relations. At the same time ideologies have their own distinctive characteristics, the most important of which are an internal discourse such that the elements of an ideology are not reducible to a mere reflection of economic or social relations. It is this internal dimension of an ideology that semiotics seeks to grasp through the concept of "sign" and its derivatives.

C. *Functions of Ideology*

The third important issue within the theory of ideology concerns the *functions of ideology*; attention is directed towards the role of ideology as an essential element in the process of legitimation and hence in the reproduction of the prevailing social relations. This concern is particularly pronounced in Poulantzas, who, building on Gramsci's metaphor of ideology as the "cement" of society, proposes the general thesis that: "Ideology, which slides into every level of the social structure, has the particular function of *cohesion*" (1975: 207). Poulantzas is of special significance with regard to the ideology of law because his analysis leads him to the view that juridico-political ideology is the "dominant region" within the dominant ideology within capitalist modes of production. From this he concludes that in capitalist societies law fulfills "the key function of every dominant ideology: namely, that of cementing together the social formation under the aegis of the dominant class" (1978: 88). I do not subscribe to the view that to speak of "function" is to lapse into functionalism; rather we must distinguish between function and functionalism and reject the latter. Functionalism assumes that there are necessary functions that must be fulfilled and then proceeds to search for the agency that realizes or fulfills each function. The deficiency of functionalism is that functions are reified. Their existence is assumed and all social practices and institutions must be classified in terms of them. Poulantzas' cement metaphor and his designation of the state as fulfilling "the particular function of constituting the factor of cohesion between the levels of a social formation" (1975: 44) come perilously close to functionalism. This danger can be avoided if we treat the metaphor as an hypothesis about the *effectivity* of ideology. The concept *effectivity* seeks to draw attention to the effects or results of ideology while at the same time leaving open the issue of whether or the degree to which a possible function of ideology is fulfilled. Thus, with respect to law, we should abandon any *a priori* views about its integrative or legitimating functions and treat them as open questions relating to the specific effects or consequences of legal regulation and legal ideology.

Distinguishing among these three different issues within the theory of ideology allows us to identify the significant advances that have been achieved in the recent debate. But these advances have extracted their own price. The most important price has been that in order to establish the "specificity" (distinctive characteristics not reducible to the economic base) of ideology, the Althusserian tradition posited the existence of conceptually distinct "instances" of economic, political, and ideological practices. So pervasive has this tendency been that in many texts these conceptual distinctions are assumed to represent real separations. But there is no location inhabited by ideology; there is no realm of the ideological (Jones, 1982). Nor are all social, political, and economic institutions necessarily associated with specific ideological practices. Much more helpful is Althusser's (1971) suggestion of a distinction between "sites" that "produce" ideology and those that "transmit" ideology. Certain institutions such as the media and the university are identified with the ideological realm because they both "produce" and "transmit" ideology, whereas schools, the family, sports, and the like are primarily transmitters of ideology. Applying this distinction to legal systems, we can immediately identify both the creation and dissemination of ideology and proceed to investigate the extent to which these two activities are separated.

A second deficiency within the theory of ideology is the persistence of the *reflection* metaphor, by which I mean the persistent assumption that there exists an objective social world that is "reflected" in thought and in the process is to a greater or lesser extent distorted. This metaphor is ubiquitous as a means of asserting the determination of ideology by material relations and of expressing the divergence between a "real concrete"—that is, some objective ideology-free reality—and its representation in ideology. This imports a dubious epistemology derived from naive materialism. More significantly, the metaphor has its own logic which leads to notions of ideological "distortion" or, more seriously, "inversion" of the real world. Thus, ideologies are discussed in terms of their truth or falsity, which implies that there is a social reality independent of consciousness and that thought simply corresponds to a greater or lesser extent to this given reality. The dubious nature of the implication is never confronted. While the idea of "reflection" raises the question of how ideology is determined, it does not provide any assistance in pursuing this line of inquiry. As Stuart Hall and his colleagues comment:

> As is often the case in those areas where Marxism is not yet fully developed, the simple formulae are often too simple, too reductive for our purposes. The idea for example, that, broadly speaking, legal norms and rules in a bourgeois society will reflect and support bourgeois economic relations, . . . may provide the first, basic step in such a theory, but it remains, too general, too abstract, too reductive, too sketchy (Hall *et al.*, 1978: 196).

The most important figure in the development of the theory of ideology has been Antonio Gramsci. He has profoundly influenced not only the questions asked but also the general direction of contemporary Marxist discussions. In particular, Gramsci's concern with "hegemony," the processes through which the dominance of capitalist power is secured within civil society, provides both the theoretical and political framework for the ongoing Marxist debate. The issues raised by the idea of "hegemony" go to the very heart of the problems facing the Marxist analysis of law in that this concept poses as a central issue the dialectic of coercion and consent.

The earliest Marxist writings on law, which I have characterized as the "oppositional stage," sought to combat conventional notions of the consensual character of law and strove to demonstrate its repressive or coercive character (Hunt, 1981a). In contrast, most contemporary Marxist writings on law have sought to demonstrate and explore the real significance and deep consequences of the dual character of law as coercion and as consent. Not only is this attempt to grasp and to integrate the elements of coercion and consent a central *leitmotif* of Marxist legal theory but, as I have argued elsewhere, its theorization presents major problems. Moreover, if my argument is correct, the same difficulties are encountered by the non-Marxist sociology of law (Hunt, 1981a).

III. THE IDEOLOGICAL DIMENSIONS OF LAW

A concern with the ideology of law is at the heart of all recent Marxist treatments of law. In this section, I shall examine some of this recent theoretical work in the light of the preceding discussion. I hope to show how some of the ideas advanced above have been fruitfully employed, and I shall point to a number of unproductive features that remain. There has, however, been such an explosion of Marxist, neo-Marxist, and critical theory of law over the past few years that I am forced to be selective. I will concentrate my attention primarily on four recent texts.

These are *The Politics of Law* (Kairys, 1982a), which is especially significant as the first collective presentation of the Critical Legal Studies movement; *Marxism and Law* (Beirne and Quinney, 1982), a collection that brings together some of the more important of the previously published contributions to Marxist debate on law; *Reading Ideologies* (Sumner, 1979), which is the most closely related to my concerns because it focuses on the applicability of the Marxist theory of ideology to the analysis of law; and *Marxism and Law* (Collins, 1982), which sets out to examine the total theoretical field and gives the relationship between law and ideology a crucial role in the attempt to set forth a general Marxist theory of law. As we shall see, a number of the problems that arise are common to all the texts, which in itself suggests the importance of the issues under consideration.

A. *Mystification, Distortion, and All That*

The most general feature of ideological analysis is that it starts from the proposition that there is no direct or necessary correspondence between the realm of "knowledge" and that of "the real." As I have already noted, the most pervasive embodiment of the theory of ideology in Marxism is to be found in the metaphor of "reflection." The merit of the metaphor is that it succeeds in combining two central propositions: (a) the known and the real are not identical, and (b) the real is the "object" that produces or determines the "image." The metaphor of reflection captures the most basic feature of Marx's materialist dictum: "It is not the consciousness of men that determines their being, but on the contrary their social being that determines their consciousness" (Marx, "1859 Preface"). It is thus not surprising that the metaphor of "reflection" and its derivatives are frequently invoked.

In all four of the texts under discussion a reflection theory of ideology is a dominant motif. The linguistic variants are many, but the most frequently employed are: "mirrors," "distorts," "illusion," "fantasy," "facade," "mystifies," and "reifies." The problem that I wish to highlight is that these terms are used in such a way as to imply a theory about the relationship between knowledge and its object, a taken-for-granted "social reality." Propositions such as "law distorts" and "law reflects" are used as if there were some pre-given relationship between the real and its ideological representation. The alternative I propose is that the nature of the relationship between reality and its ideological representation should be seen as "the problem," or object of analysis, without prejudgment as to the way in which the relationship can be captured or portrayed.

For an example of the limitations of reflection theory, consider the essay in Kairys' collection by Nadine Taub and Elizabeth Schneider (1982) on the role of law in the subordination of women. Taub and Schneider argue that the legal distinction between public and private reflects, in a distorted fashion, an actual distinction between the nondomestic and domestic social realms. In so doing the legal distinction functions ideologically and "camouflages the fundamental injustice of existing sexual relations" (1982: 124). This readiness to attribute causality to the legal distinction between public-private leads Taub and Schneider to ignore the question of whether this distortion results from legal ideology or from some other mechanism. For example, no consideration is given to the role of other discourses concerning the family—thus precluding, without discussion, the possibility that the law is largely passive and merely gives effect to an ideological separation between public-private that is produced elsewhere.[4] Now I do not hold any strong view about whether this is the case, but I do wish to suggest that the metaphor of reflection distracts attention from such issues and for that reason should not be invoked as if it were a conclusion.

In contrast, the essay by Peter Gabel on reification in Beirne and Quinney examines the process of legal reasoning in great detail and concludes that "reification" is a result determined by the process rather than a pre-given necessity (Gabel, 1982).[5] In the course of this analysis Gabel makes the important point that we need to distinguish between (a) the processes that create the ideological characteristics embedded

---

[4] For a stimulating discussion of the public-private dichotomy as it relates to family law, see the article by Frances Olsen (1983), which has the great merit, in contrast to "reflection" approaches, of isolating the complex and shifting boundary between the public and the private and, consequently, its tortuous history in legislation.

[5] In the case of reprinted papers, which occur primarily in the Beirne and Quinney collection, I cite the reprint rather than its original publication.

in the law and (b) those consequences flowing from law that have a particular ideological content. With this in mind, we can see a hitherto unrevealed distinction in the usages "mirrors," "distorts," etc., which are often used interchangeably. Some terms (e.g., mirrors, reflects, reifies) have as their primary referrent the process by which the "real" is transformed into an ideological form (see, e.g., Gabel and Feinman, 1982) while others (e.g., mystifies, illusion) focus on the results or consequences of the ideological form (see, e.g., Kennedy, 1982). Ideological analysis should separate, as distinct methodological and expository stages, the analysis of the production of legal ideology from the analysis of the effectivity of legal ideology.[6]

B. *The Form of Law*

It is generally agreed that the ideological character of law can be identified at a number of different levels. I shall specify, at least provisionally, three different levels for analysis since this allows me to explore the interrelationship among them. They are:

(a) the ideological content of concrete legal norms;
(b) the ideological content of what are conventionally referred to, most explicitly by Dworkin (1978), as "principles";
(c) the ideological content of the "form of law."

At the core of any attempt to understand ideology is the question of its material determination. Distinguishing these levels allows us to address the important question of whether legal ideology is primarily the resultant of one of them. There is an unexplored and perhaps unconscious polarization in the texts under consideration. It is possible to identify two broadly distinguishable positions.

The first I call *Concrete Determination*. This position argues that the ideological content of law is largely manifest in the content of specific laws, whether judicial rules or specific legislative enactments. This position emphasizes the role of "struggle" in the formation of legal ideology.

---

6 Note that the reflection theory of ideology is not the only one available within the Marxist tradition. Another version is that derived from Marx's application in *Capital* of the essence/appearance distinction. We should be cautious about assuming a simple continuity between reflection theory and essence/appearance theory. Frequently, these two approaches are conflated in the texts under consideration. The further exploration of the ideological dimension of law requires attention to the issue of Marxist epistemology and the need to challenge the simple empiricist model of both reflection and essence/appearance that characterizes much of the recent discussion of the ideology of law (Hindess, 1977; Cutler *et al.*, 1977).

The second I call *Form Determination*. This perspective sees in the form of law the key to law's ideological role. The concrete level gives effect to the necessary and inescapably general ideological content inscribed in the form of law.

Frequently, the position taken by an author arises naturally from the object of analysis: where the object of analysis is concrete, as with a specific statute or series of cases, the discussion tends to focus on concrete determination (Kairys, 1982b; Horwitz, 1982; Tushnet, 1982; Klare, 1982a; Freeman, 1982). Where the interest is at a more general theoretical level, form determination comes to the fore (Gabel and Feinman, 1982; Picciotto, 1982; Poulantzas, 1978; Rifkin, 1982). But this is not a simple empirical versus theoretical divide; some of the most powerful work operates at all three levels (Klare, 1982b; Hay, 1982).

The distinction among the three levels of analysis not only involves important theoretical questions, but it is also related to political differences and debates. Marxists perennially argue over the extent to which law can be harnessed and mobilized to the advantage of subordinate classes or groups, a question that Collins appropriately calls "the radical predicament" (Collins, 1982: Ch. 6). Those who give priority to form analysis typically deny that the bourgeois form of law can contribute much, apart from defense, to struggles against the capitalist order. As Mark Tushnet puts it, the form of law "serves as an additional barrier to the organisation of the under-dog to upset existing social arrangements" (Tushnet, 1977: 102). On the other hand, those who focus their attention on concrete determination tend to see particular legal outcomes as the results of struggles that depend on the balance of forces involved. This issue is at the heart of the important current controversies concerning the "politics of law." There is significant disagreement among "progressives" about the extent to which struggles over the creation and enforcement of legal rights are politically significant and potentially worthwhile. These questions are currently being raised in the internal debates within the Conference on Critical Legal Studies (Hutchinson and Monahan, 1984; Munger and Seron, 1983; Sparer, 1984; Trubek, 1984), and they continue to be debated in Britain under the insistent prodding of E.P. Thompson (1975; 1980; see also Adlam, 1981; Hunt, 1981b).

Leaving aside these broader political questions, I want to focus attention on questions concerning the form of law. An emphasis on the form of law is attractive in that it provides an escape route from the difficulties of instrumentalist versions of

Marxist theory, which focus on the law as an instrument of the will of the dominant class. The form of law is seen not as a manifestation of the will of a dominant class but as a necessary and inevitable consequence of the very nature of capitalist economic relations. Hugh Collins (1982) suggests that there exist economistic and class instrumentalist versions of the theory. In my view both the "economistic" and "instrumentalist" trends are inherent within classical Marxism, and they come to the fore with the ossification of orthodox Marxism. The common problem of both variants is that of "reductionism"; the difference is that class instrumentalism merely adds another step in the reductive logic since class relations are treated as directly derivable from and so reducible to economic relations.

The discussion of the form of law in recent Marxist literature is heavily influenced by the renewed interest in the writing of the early Soviet jurist Evgeny Pashukanis (Beirne and Sharlet, 1980). Pashukanis' influence has focused discussion on the question of whether a *single* form of law is characteristic of capitalist society (cf. Balbus, 1977; Redhead, 1978; Hirst, 1979; Cotterell, 1980; 1981; Warrington, 1981; Picciotto, 1982). This discussion has typically proceeded at a high level of abstraction, concerning itself with the general and abstract capitalist mode of production rather than with the situation in actual capitalist societies. Analysis at this level views capitalism as a simple totality of exchange relations and leads to the identification of a single form of law, the bourgeois legal form.

If, however, the level of analysis is changed and we focus our attention on concrete social formations (that is, historically given societies), we need to identify more than a single form of law. Capitalism has undergone massive changes and development. It exists within widely different political and state structures, and its internationalization has profoundly affected the relations among nation states. While mainstream sociology of law has for some time been concerned with the phenomenon of legal pluralism (Galanter, 1981), Marxist writers have only more recently paid serious attention to this question (Fitzpatrick, 1983). As David Sugarman argues, studies of the contribution of law to the development of capitalism, from Weber (1966) through E.P. Thompson (1975), Atiyah (1979), Horwitz (1977), and others, can only lead to the conclusion that

> there was no single "capitalist" form of law—whether we call it contractual, commodity form or absolute private property. It is more accurate to view each as one of several *forms* of capitalist law which co-existed over long periods, complementing and conflicting with one another (Sugarman, 1983: 256).

What remains to be done is to identify systematically the various forms of law and to study the general conditions affecting their interaction.

However, the general trend in the texts we are treating as representative of recent critical and Marxist scholarship is either to assume a simple, single form of law or to slip between the singular and plural. The apparently sophisticated concept "the form of law" tends to be invoked as a rhetorical device that points to some underlying uniformity of legal phenomena that remains unexplored. When the form of law is identified, it is by reference to general values or what Balbus calls "abstract universals" (Balbus, 1977: 580). But in listing abstract universals, the distinction between form and content becomes blurred. If the concept of "legal form" or "forms of law" is to advance our understanding of the relationship between law and economy, there is an urgent need for conceptual clarification.

My proposals in this regard are modest. I suggest that when we restrict the concept "form of law" at a high level of abstraction to denote the logically necessary characteristics of a legal order within a specified economic or political order, this makes it possible and, indeed, necessary to address the co-existence of forms of law when analyzing specific societies. With regard to law in capitalist societies, the form of law is characterized by (i) "reification" (separation of the juridico-political realms from the economic), (ii) legal subjectivity (separation of legal status from political or economic status), and (iii) the legal subject (a human or organizational entity vested with legal rights) (Hirst, 1979).

I also believe that the form of law has no *necessary* ideological characteristic or content. Instead, certain ideological values have, to borrow Weber's idea, an elective affinity or homologous relationship to the legal form. Hence, values such as individualism, equality, and private property become universal and preponderant values under capitalism and come to function as if they were the form of law itself. The close association between the concept of law and these values means that these values come to legitimate the existing forms of social relationships. Thus, the legitimating potential of law is shared or taken over by values the law only contingently embraces.

I have not included in my definition of "the form of law" the much emphasized element of "formalism." I am uncertain whether formalism inheres in the form of law or is an ideological value preponderantly associated with law in capitalist society. This uncertainty derives from my reflections on Horwitz's work. What Horwitz brings out most powerfully is the essentially contested character of formalism, a contest between impersonal Weberian legal rationality and the class facilitative character of the transformation of American law (Horwitz, 1975; 1977).

Treating legal formalism as a problematic feature of the legal form has the virtues of not universalizing the ideological values most characteristic of law in capitalist society and of directing attention to struggles that surround all ideological elements. This approach reminds us that the most pervasive values that may be subsumed under the label "ideological forms of law" (universality, certainty, etc.) are subject to contradiction and interact in complex ways in the course of legal disputes. My approach alsc reflects reservations I have about following the realist methodology of starting with legal values and subsequently comparing them to "reality." The viability of this position depends on the questionable assumption that legal values have an existence independent of the concrete legal rules in which they are embedded.

The foregoing analysis of the form of law throws into relief an important problem which I wish to mention but do not have the space here to pursue. The "discovery" of the ideological dimension of law by the Marxist and critical traditions tends towards a conceptualization of law itself as an *ideological phenomenon*. The danger is obvious: the materiality of the law—that is to say, law's real impact on real people and real relations—tends to be ignored. In seeking to establish the extent to which all social practices are suffused by ideology, we must not lose sight, to paraphrase Marx, of "the dull compulsion" of legal regulation, particularly in the spheres where law operates relatively unproblematically to give effect to the existing forms of social, economic, and political relations. If we are to grapple with real world problems, we must not retreat into idealistic theories of ideological determination.

C. *The Function and Effectivity of Legal Ideology*

One of the most distinctive features of the contemporary Marxist and critical trends is the powerful historical scholarship which has been its most notable achievement to date. In Britain there has been the major impact of the project that produced *Whigs and Hunters* and *Albion's Fatal Tree* (Thompson, 1975; Hay *et al.*, 1975) and *Policing the Crisis*, a "contemporary history" study of the "mugging crisis" of 1972-73 (Hall *et al.*, 1978). The latter work is of particular interest because of its self-conscious attempt to integrate theoretical and historical analysis. And in the United States there has been a similar interest in revisionist legal history, spearheaded by Morton Horwitz. These critical legal histories share a common concern with the effectivity of legal ideology as it operates in conjunction with the material and coercive instrumentality of law. Douglas Hay's powerful analysis of the combined impact of "justice," "terror," and "mercy" is a good example of work that focuses on this conjunction (Hay, 1982).

The two most important strands present in this tradition are best characterized by the distinction between "function" and "effectivity." Attention to "function" yields formulations of a general theoretical character about the role of legal ideology at the level of either the abstract modes of production (e.g., Althusser's "ideology secures the reproduction of the social relations of production," 1971: 141) or, more concretely, with respect to historical epochs (e.g., Poulantzas' "juridical ideology written into law becomes the dominant area of ideology in a mode of production in which ideology no longer plays the dominant role," 1978: 88). A concern for "effectivity," on the other hand, leads to a focus on the causal role of legal ideology in specific historical circumstances; e.g., Klare's (1982a) study of the influence of judicial ideology on the formation of labor relations in the U.S.A. before World War II.

The distinction between "function" and "effectivity" rarely appears in pure form. Instead, we frequently find either an oscillation between these foci of inquiry or a conflation of the two levels. This is unfortunate. In the analysis of legal ideology one must keep firmly in mind the different *levels of abstraction* of these related but distinguishable perspectives. Thus, it is perfectly proper to treat a possible function of legal ideology as an hypothesis to be evaluated through concrete historical investigation and discarded, amended, or qualified in the movement from one level of abstraction to another. It is a mistake, however, to treat a possible function of law as given or proven and to use history to "reveal" the operation of this essential or assumed function. It is equally unacceptable to arrive through concrete historical analysis at a conclusion concerning the effectivity of legal ideology and then to pronounce this a "function" fulfilled by law during a particular historical epoch.

As an illustration of the second of these questionable procedures, consider E.P. Thompson's thesis that "the rule of law itself, the imposing of effective inhibitions upon power and the defence of the citizen from power's all-intrusive claims, seems to me to be an unqualified human good" (Thompson, 1975: 266). Thompson arrives at this conclusion from his compelling study of "The Black Act" of 1723. The Act itself and its enforcement are interpreted as a conflict between the "new" landowning Whig gentry and the customary rights of farmers and forest-dwellers. Thompson demonstrates that in the period after the 1688 constitutional "revolution," when the structures and supports for the legal order were still weak, the rule of law had a significant impact on the manner in which this draconian legislation was enforced. But Thompson moves, without further argument, from his historically specific study to a generalization about the function of legal ideology in modern capitalist society.[7] I have considerable sympathy with Thompson's insistence on the contemporary significance of the rule of law, but not with the means by which he arrives at it, for Thompson ignores important differences in levels of analysis.

Having clarified the different levels of analysis involved in the distinction between "function" and "effectivity," we need to consider the risks inherent in functionalist modes of analysis. One such danger is the temptation to lapse into a naive instrumentalism which posits a single dominating function expressed, for example, in theses such as "law reproduces the social relations of capitalist society" or "law legitimates capitalist social relations." Such single function theses are themselves attributable to the ideological reification of law. In such theories law is presented as "the Law" and is discussed as if it were a totally coherent and integrated process. A valuable corrective against tendencies to see law in this way is found in modern Marxist and critical legal theory: the idea of "contradiction." This concept focuses attention on the limits of

[7] The historical studies in the two collections of texts are peppered with less serious and less controversial examples. Genovese in his otherwise very convincing account of the role of law in the slave states asserts, as a given, the hegemonic function of law (Genovese, 1982). In so doing he comes perilously close to the functionalist circle of specifying a necessary function and then showing it revealed in practice. Janet Rifkin (1982), in advancing an abstract, necessary connection between law as hegemonic ideology and the ideology of patriarchy, similarly builds an unnecessarily functionalist account of the rule of law in perpetuating male dominance.

doctrinal coherence and on the variable operation of different legal procedures and institutions.

One of the most important contributions of radical legal historiography has been to breathe life and substance into the abstract category of "contradiction." At the outset this enterprise involves distinguishing between *internal* and *external* contradictions. The shift to a more empirical level of analysis, one of the hallmarks of the Critical Legal Studies movement, has allowed scholars to highlight the contradictory character of legal development; and it has helped them to avoid the pitfalls of instrumentalism. There is, however, a tendency within critical legal studies to focus one-sidedly on either internal or external contradictions. Thus, some work that examines doctrinal development stresses its internal incoherence while another strand emphasizes contradictions arising from the interplay of classes, class fractions, and other social and political forces as they struggle over the creation and practice of law. Both strands of research could be improved if they worked with a more systematic model of internal and external contradictions.

This is not the place to develop such a model, but I want to mention three considerations. First, with respect to both internal and external contradictions different "levels" need to be distinguished. Looking at internal contradictions, for example, we can distinguish among: (a) juridical reasoning and its ideological forms, (b) the ideologies embodied in the policy aspects of legal doctrine, (c) different legal institutions (e.g., types of courts), and (d) the professional ideologies of different kinds of legal actors. Such distinctions involve no profound theoretical insights, but they do provide a checklist of the sources and forces involved in the ideological determination of law. Second, the internal and external dimensions of legal ideology are not watertight compartments, and the interface between the two is a significant location of contradiction. Models of internal and external contradictions must take this into account and allow for some permeability. Finally, I would stress the practical significance for intervention in the politics of law of a careful analysis of contradictions since these pinpoint areas in which the subordinate classes have their greatest potential for effecting change. This speaks to the political importance of the model-building enterprise rather than to how it should be done.

Thinking about contradictions highlights problems with two widespread features of contemporary Marxist writings.

The first is a tendency to overemphasize the independence or autonomy of the internal ideology of law. A clear example is found in Karl Klare's conclusion from his study of the Wagner Act that law-making because of the impersonal, antiparticipatory, suprahistorical forms of thought and procedures involved "is governed by the process of alienation" (1982a: 168). This analysis does not give due weight to the pressures and contradictions that constantly press upon the judicial process and disrupt the calm of formal judicial logic in ways that Klare's substantive analysis demonstrates. I also question the conclusions that Klare draws from this line of argument. His preferred alternative requires "a quest for justice in each concrete historical setting" and the abolition of the rule of law (1982a: 168). In my view the call for individualized justice is not self-evidently a progressive demand. I remain convinced that the most important lesson for legal politics that may be drawn from our experience of "actual socialism" in the Soviet Union and other states is the necessity of retaining formalized and entrenched rights, the core of the rule of law, to protect citizens and social institutions against political usurpation by the state and the bureaucracy.

The second feature of the recent critical literature that my analysis calls into question is what I see as an overemphasis on the autonomy of the general ideological function of law, variously expressed by the legitimating or hegemonic function. Let me take as my example Colin Sumner. His analysis is in many respects parallel to the position I have advanced, but I believe he overstates the general function of legal ideology. "The Law," he argues,

> lies hidden beneath a heavy shroud of discourse, ritual and magic which proclaim the Wisdom and Justice of the Law. . . . Once this shroud is torn into tatters that hegemonic bloc of classes and class fractions which sustain the rule of capital is in trouble because inequality and domination can *only* be justified mystically and that is precisely the ideological function of law (Sumner, 1979: 277; emphasis added).

Now if the ideology of "The Law" is as effective as Sumner suggests, it is difficult to imagine how this shroud could ever be "torn into tatters"; this is a case of pure verbal militancy. More important is the contention that legal ideology provides the *primary* justification for inequality and domination. This is, in my view, quite simply wrong. Capitalist systems employ a wide range of ideological justifications which are used (a) differentially over time and (b) in different combinations.

These include such important legitimating ideas as "economic efficiency," "freedom," "democracy," and "national interest." The significance of legal ideology lies in its articulation along with other nonlegal ideological bases of legitimation. This point is made by Sumner but then seemingly forgotten.

> . . .The effectiveness of law as an ideological force, as a means toward ruling class hegemony, depends upon its ideological encapsulation of a consensus *constructed outside itself* in other economic, political and cultural practices (Sumner 1979: 264; emphasis added).

This point is nicely illustrated in *Policing the Crisis* (Hall *et al.*, 1978). The authors show that it was the combination of legal ideology with other elements, including appeals to moral consensus, the nation, and ethnicity, that made the shift to a more authoritarian mode of governance possible. While it is appropriate to stress the importance of legal ideology in contemporary capitalism, we must avoid any tendency to think that law is the only structure other than naked violence that props up the capitalist social order. It follows that our analysis of legal ideology, and its relationship to the production and reproduction of hegemony, must pay close attention to the way legal ideology is articulated in conjunction with economic, political, and cultural ideologies.

IV. CONCLUSION

Martin Albrow in a perceptive but critical review of recent Marxist texts on law expressed doubt as to whether "a general critique of law as ideology can lead into the scientific study of social relations underpinning and generating law, i.e., the sociology of law" (Albrow, 1981: 127). I hope that the above discussion has gone some way to demonstrate that Albrow is both right and wrong. He is right in castigating a "*general* critique of law as ideology"; but he is wrong in suggesting that the investigation of legal ideology cannot contribute substantially to the sociology of law.

Ideology is and will remain a difficult, slippery, and ambiguous concept, and there is little to be gained by searching for a "better" definition. Problems cannot be avoided, for ideology involves issues that go to the heart of the puzzling interrelationship between human subjectivity and social action. Yet, handled with care, the concept "ideology" provides an indispensable and irreplaceable tool of analysis.

If the potential utility of the concept is to be realized, it is necessary that we attend closely to two separate but related sets of distinctions. The first is between the concrete particular and the concrete totality. The transition from one to the other is not a movement from micro to macro levels. This can be illustrated by taking, for example, the methodology involved in the study of a piece of legislation. The concrete particular focuses attention on the immediate or proximate influences, for example, doctrinal developments in that area of law, the particular "problem" addressed by the legislators, or the internal dynamics of the commission or inquiry proposing legislative action. The concrete totality retains the focus upon the legislation itself but seeks to situate that process in the context of wider economic, social, or political determinants. Understanding the relationship between the particular and the totality requires attention to the existence of distinct levels within the legal framework. We need to distinguish, for example, between the ideological elements present in the substance of the legislation, the legal form in which legislation is cast, and the way in which the form and substance of the law relate to the dominant ideological features of the legal system. These levels within the legal system are in turn related to the different levels of social relations, which means that the next step is to investigate the connections between "legal relations," on one hand, and "social relations," on the other. This involves turning our attention from the specific sets of social relations affected by the projected legislation to broader social forces rooted in economic, political, and other practices and to institutions that affect the creation and application of the legislation.

The second set of distinctions that must be maintained is between more abstract and more concrete conceptualizations. The need to distinguish between levels of abstraction is a theme found both in Marx's own methodological writings (Carver, 1975) and in the recent methodological debate (Echeverra, 1978; Sayer, 1979). What follows from this distinction is that concepts must be appropriate to different levels of abstraction. This implies that the unitary conceptions of the "form of law" derived from an abstract conception of the commodity relation are poorly suited to the analysis of the "forms of law" within historically specific legal systems. More generally, when the object of investigation is a specific legal system, more concrete concepts are needed than those that can be derived from an examination of the relationship among economic, political, and ideological practices at the abstract level of "the capitalist mode of production."

The implications of these two sets of distinctions underline one general theme of this paper: namely, that the ideological analysis of law must be understood as operating at a number of different levels, and that these different levels are both conceptual and empirical.

Colin Sumner suggests a distinction between "ideology" as basic or simple elements and "ideological formations" as complex systematizations of ideologies (Sumner, 1979: 20). I suggest that we can improve upon this scheme if we define "ideological elements" as the constituents of any text or speech act (for example, a legal norm or judicial pronouncement) but depart from Sumner by insisting that these elements are far from "basic" or "simple." Despite their apparent protean quality they involve already complex determinations. Ideology has no primary units or building blocks, for concepts do not themselves have any necessary ideological content; this is only acquired as they are employed in specific discourses. From this it follows that no word, however sensitive and emotive its connotations, has any necessary class content or implication; "equality," "fairness," "democracy," and the other key verbal labels only acquire ideological characteristics in their use.

I would retain Sumner's term "ideological formation" for those phenomena that link different ideological elements. This use allows for inconsistencies and tensions within legal discourse but does not assume any necessary systematization. In a legal system the degree of systematization is an issue for empirical inquiry. Additionally, I suggest the term "ideological form of law" to designate configurations of ideological elements where there has been conscious systematization.

The distinctions that the three concepts defined above allow have a significance with regard to legal phenomena which we can illustrate by contrasting a simple conversation with the judgment of an appellate court. While the former will consist of "elements of ideology," the appellate judgment may either involve an "ideological formation" linking discrete elements or may achieve a more rigorous systematization as "an ideological form of law." This makes the "reading" of legal ideology more complex. In my view it restricts the applicability of semiotic analysis, with its emphasis on discourses reducible to primary units of "signs," because in judicial discourse there is already present a more complex structure derived from the modes of legal reasoning.

The second implication of my classification of legal ideology is that we must be wary of assuming a single function derived from an analysis of the form of law at a high level of abstraction. This means that we should not uncritically accept as proven conceptions of the legal order that seek to identify it in essence as a locus of such phenomena as "mystification," "legitimation," or "alienation." Rather, it is likely that research will disclose a considerable degree of variation in the function and effectivity of different types of legal practice.

The advance of Marxist and critical analyses of law which has been characterized by a special interest in ideological analysis has had a dual impetus. On the one hand, there has been a growing dissatisfaction with the methods and results of traditional legal scholarship and education. On the other hand, there has been a growing consciousness of the need to overcome the limitations and weaknesses of instrumentalist versions of Marxist theory. But the invocation of the concept "ideology" has in its turn necessitated a deepening awareness of both the pitfalls and potential of ideological analysis. This essay has been directed to an exploration of some problems posed by the use of this concept and to advancing some suggestions for the further development of ideological analysis. In it I have tried to stress the need for a greater theoretical self-consciousness in employing the concept of ideology and at the same time to underline the general shift in critical and Marxist studies towards a more concrete historical and empirical analysis of law.

Finally, to avoid any possible misunderstanding of the nature of my current project, I should acknowledge the importance of issues that I have not discussed. I have had nothing to say about the important questions associated with the investigation of the material or social determination of law and legal relations. Nor have I concerned myself with the other side of the same problem: the extent to which law and legal regulation are themselves constitutive of social and economic relations. The omission of these questions should not be read as denying their importance in the analysis of law. The issues involved in the harnessing of the concept "ideology" to the analysis of law are themselves of sufficient importance to merit the specific focus of this essay.

REFERENCES

ADLAM, Diana (ed.) (1981) *Law, Politics and Justice: Politics and Power*, 4. London: Routledge & Kegan Paul.

ALBROW, Martin (1981) ". . . law, ideology, law, ideology, law, ideology . . . sociology?" 32 *British Journal of Sociology* 127.

ALTHUSSER, Louis (1969) *For Marx*. Harmondsworth: Penguin.

——— (1971) "Ideology and the Ideological State Apparatuses," in *Lenin and Philosophy*. London: New Left Books.

ATIYAH, Patrick (1979) *The Rise and Fall of Freedom of Contract*. Oxford: Clarendon Press.

BALBUS, Isaac (1977) "Commodity Form and Legal Form: An Essay on the 'Relative Autonomy' of the Law," 11 *Law & Society Review* 571.

BEIRNE, Piers and Richard QUINNEY (eds.) (1982) *Marxism and Law*. New York: John Wiley & Sons.

BEIRNE, Piers and Robert SHARLET (eds.) (1980) *Pashukanis: Selected Writings on Marxism and Law*. London: Academic Press.

CARSON, W.G. (1974) "Symbolic and Instrumental Dimensions of Early Factory Legislation," in R. Hood (ed.), *Crime, Criminology and Public Policy*. London: Heinemann.

CARVER, Terrell (1975) *Karl Marx: Texts on Method*. Oxford: Blackwell.

CENTRE FOR CONTEMPORARY CULTURAL STUDIES (1977) *On Ideology*. Birmingham: CCCS.

COLLINS, Hugh (1982) *Marxism and Law*. Oxford: Clarendon Press.

COTTERELL, Roger (1980) "Review of Beirne and Sharlet 'Pashukanis: Selected Writings on Marxism and Law'," 7 *British Journal of Law & Society* 317.

——— (1981) "Conceptualizing Law: Problems and Prospects of Contemporary Legal Theory," 10 *Economy & Society* 348.

COWARD, Rosalind and John ELLIS (1977) *Language and Materialism: Developments in Semiology and the Theory of the Subject*. London: Routledge & Kegan Paul.

CUTLER, Antony, Barry HINDESS, Paul HIRST and Attar HUSSAIN (1977) *Marx's 'Capital' and Capitalism Today*. London: Routledge & Kegan Paul.

DWORKIN, Ronald (1978) *Taking Rights Seriously*. London: Duckworth.

ECHEVERRA, Rafael (1978) "Critique of Marx's *1857 Introduction*," 7 *Economy & Society* 333.

FITZPATRICK, Peter (1983) "Marxism and Legal Pluralism," 1 *Australian Journal of Law & Society* 45.

FOUCAULT, Michel (1977) *Discipline & Punish: The Birth of the Prison*. London: Allen Lane.

FREEMAN, Alan (1982) "Legitimizing Racial Discrimination Through Antidiscrimination Law," in P. Beirne and R. Quinney (eds.), *Marxism and Law*. New York: John Wiley & Sons.

GABEL, Peter (1982) "Reification in Legal Reasoning," in P. Beirne and R. Quinney (eds.), *Marxism and Law*. New York: John Wiley & Sons.

GABEL, Peter and Jay FEINMAN (1982) "Contract Law as Ideology," in D. Kairys (ed.), *The Politics of Law: A Progressive Critique*. New York: Pantheon.

GALANTER, Marc (1981) "Justice in Many Rooms: Private Ordering and Indigenous Law," 19 *Journal of Legal Pluralism* 1.

GENOVESE, Eugene (1982) "The Hegemonic Function of Law," in P. Beirne and R. Quinney (eds.), *Marxism and Law*. New York: John Wiley & Sons.

GUSFIELD, Joseph (1963) *Symbolic Crusade: Status Politics and the American Temperance Movement*. Urbana: University of Illinois Press.

HABERMAS, Jürgen (1976) *Legitimation Crisis*. London: Heinemann.

HALL, Stuart, Chas CRITCHER, Tony JEFFERSON, John CLARKE and Brian ROBERTS (1978) *Policing the Crisis: Mugging, the State and Law and Order*. London: Macmillan.

HAY, Douglas (1982) "Property, Authority and the Criminal Law," in P. Beirne and R. Quinney (eds.), *Marxism and Law*. New York: John Wiley & Sons.

HAY, Douglas, Peter LINEBAUGH, John RULE, Edward THOMPSON and Cal WINSLOW (1975) *Albion's Fatal Tree: Crime & Society in Eighteenth-Century England*. Harmondsworth: Penguin.

HINDESS, Barry (1977) *Philosophy and Methodology in the Social Sciences.* Brighton: Harvester.

HIRST, Paul (1979) *On Law and Ideology*. London: Macmillan.

HORWITZ, Morton (1975) "The Rise of Legal Formalism," 19 *American Journal of Legal History* 251.

——— (1977) *The Transformation of American Law 1780-1860.* Cambridge, MA: Harvard University Press.

——— (1982) "The Doctrine of Objective Causation," in D. Kairys (ed.), *The Politics of Law: A Progressive Critique.* New York: Pantheon.

HUNT, Alan (1981a) "Dichotomy and Contradiction in the Sociology of Law," 8 *British Journal of Law and Society* 47; and P. Beirne and R. Quinney (eds.), *Marxism and Law.* New York: John Wiley & Sons.

——— (1981b) "The Politics of Law & Justice," in D. Adlam (ed.), *Law, Politics and Justice: Politics and Power*, 4. London: Routledge & Kegan Paul.

——— (1983) "Marxist Legal Theory and Legal Positivism," 46 *Modern Law Review* 236.

HUTCHINSON, Alan and Patrick MONAHAN (1984) "Law, Politics and the Critical Legal Scholars: The Unfolding Drama of American Legal Thought," 36 *Stanford Law Review* 199.

IGNATIEFF, Michael (1978) *A Just Measure of Pain: The Penitentiary in the Industrial Revolution, 1750-1850.* New York: Pantheon.

JONES, Kelvin (1982) *Law and Economy: The Legal Regulation of Corporate Capital.* London and New York: Academic Press.

KAIRYS, David (ed.) (1982a) *The Politics of Law: A Progressive Critique.* New York: Pantheon.

——— (1982b) "Freedom of Speech," in D. Kairys (ed.), *The Politics of Law: A Progressive Critique.* New York: Pantheon.

KENNEDY, Duncan (1982) "Legal Education as Training for Hierarchy," in D. Kairys (ed.), *The Politics of Law: A Progressive Critique.* New York: Pantheon.

KLARE, Karl (1982a) "Judicial Deradicalization of the Wagner Act and the Origins of Modern Legal Consciousness 1937-1941," in P. Beirne and R. Quinney (eds.), *Marxism and Law.* New York: John Wiley & Sons.

——— (1982b) "Critical Theory and Labor Relations Law," in D. Kairys (ed.), *The Politics of Law: A Progressive Critique.* New York: Pantheon.

LACLAU, Ernesto (1977) *Politics and Ideology in Marxist Theory.* London: New Left Books.

LARRAIN, Jorge (1979) *The Concept of Ideology.* London: Hutchinson.

McLENNAN, Gregor, Victor MOLINA and Roy PETERS (1977) "Althusser's Theory of Ideology," in Centre for Contemporary Cultural Studies, *On Ideology.* Birmingham: CCCS.

MUNGER, Frank and Carol SERON (1983) "Critical Legal Studies versus Critical Legal Theory." Mimeo.

OLSEN, Frances (1983) "The Family and the Market," 96 *Harvard Law Review* 1497.

PICCIOTTO, Sol (1982) "The Theory of the State, Class Struggle and the Rule of Law," in P. Beirne and R. Quinney (eds.), *Marxism and Law.* New York: John Wiley & Sons.

POULANTZAS, Nicos (1975) *Political Power and Social Classes.* London: New Left Books.

——— (1978) *State, Power, Socialism.* London: New Left Books.

REDHEAD, Steve (1978) "The Discrete Charm of Bourgeois Law," 9 *Critique* 113.

RIFKIN, Janet (1982) "Toward a Theory of Law and Patriarchy," in P. Beirne and R. Quinney (eds.), *Marxism and Law.* New York: John Wiley & Sons.

SAYER, Derek (1979) *Marx's Method: Science, Ideology and Critique in 'Capital'.* Brighton: Harvester.

SPARER, Ed (1984) "Fundamental Human Rights, Legal Entitlements and the Social Struggle: A Friendly Critique of the Critical Legal Studies Movement," 36 *Stanford Law Review* 509.

SUGARMAN, David (ed.) (1983) *Legality, Ideology and the State.* London and New York: Academic Press.

SUMNER, Colin (1979) *Reading Ideologies: An Investigation into the Marxist Theory of Ideology and Law*. London: Academic Press.

TAUB, Nadine and Elizabeth SCHNEIDER (1982) "Perspectives on Women's Subordination and the Rule of Law," in D. Kairys (ed.), *The Politics of Law: A Progressive Critique*. New York: Pantheon.

THERBORN, Göran (1980) *The Ideology of Power and the Power of Ideology*. London: New Left Books.

THOMPSON, Edward P. (1975) *Whigs and Hunters: The Origin of the Black Act*. London: Penguin and New York: Pantheon.

——— (1980) *Writing by Candlelight*. London: Merlin.

TRUBEK, David (1977) "Complexity and Contradiction in the Legal Order: Balbus and the Challenge of Critical Social Thought about Law," 11 *Law & Society Review* 529.

——— (1984) "Where the Action Is: Critical Legal Studies and Empiricism," 36 *Stanford Law Review* 575.

TUSHNET, Mark (1977) "Perspectives on the Development of American Law: A Critical Review of Friedman's *A History of American Law*," 1977 *Wisconsin Law Review* 81.

——— (1982) "Corporations and Free Speech," in D. Kairys (ed.), *The Politics of Law: A Progressive Critique*. New York: Pantheon.

WARRINGTON, Ronnie (1981) "Pashukanis and the Commodity Form Theory," 9 *International Journal of Sociology of Law* 1.

WEBER, Max (1966) *Max Weber on Law in Economy and Society*, ed. Max Rheinstein. Cambridge, MA: Harvard University Press.

WILLIAMS, Raymond (1977) *Marxism and Literature*. Oxford: Oxford University Press.

[3]

SOCIOLOGY AND NATURAL LAW*

Philip Selznick

AMONG MODERN SOCIOLOGISTS, the reputation of natural law is not high. The phrase conjures up a world of absolutisms, of theological fiat, of fuzzy, unoperational, "mystical" ideas, of thinking uninformed by history and by the variety of human situations. This is sad, because sociology should have a ready affinity for the philosophy of natural law. Both are anti-formalist in spirit. Each looks beyond what is given and immediate to what is latent and inchoate; each is committed to the study of "nature" as yielding something more permanent and more universal than the transitory judgments of the hour or the epoch.

One of the chief writers on the sociology of law, Eugen Ehrlich,[1] made a cardinal point of his quest for law, not in formal institutions alone, but in the "inner order" of human associations, in the natural settings and adaptive outcomes of group life. "At the present as well as at any other time," Ehrlich wrote, "the center of gravity of legal development lies not in legislation, nor in juristic science, nor in judicial decision, but in society itself."[2] This is not in itself a natural law viewpoint. It does, however, reflect the general emphasis in sociology that education, politics, religion, and other social activities, are found outside of the specialized institutions established to deal with them. Sociology has located these phenomena "in society," that is, in more informal and spontaneous groupings and processes. A corollary view, not usually made explicit, is that sociologists, in looking beyond formal arrangements, are identifying something closer to a "natural" order.

Most sociologists today, addressing themselves to the legal order, would still agree with Ehrlich that "the center of gravity of legal development" lies in altered ways of life and in the changing organization of society. They would argue, however, that it is bootless and sterile to call every kind of order "law" and that the study of legal development, including probable future changes in law, entails no commitment to a theory of justice. There would be a fairly ready acceptance of the distinction between law as com-

* I should like to record my thanks to the Center for Advanced Study in the Behavioral Sciences, where this paper was written. For intellectual assistance and encouragement I am especially indebted to Gertrude J. Selznick, Yosal A. Rogat, and to Robert M. Hutchins and his colleagues at the Center for the Study of Democratic Institutions.

1. FUNDAMENTAL PRINCIPLES OF THE SOCIOLOGY OF LAW, trans. by Walter L. Moll (Cambridge: Harvard U. Press, 1936).
2. *Id.* at xiv. In his Foreword, Ehrlich offers this as a one-sentence summary of his book.

monly understood and the *sources* of law as the whole range of influences on legal development and stability. In this way, they would hope to avoid seemingly endless terminological discussions and vexing philosophical issues.

There is much that is appealing and wholesome in this way of thinking. It does indeed apply to broad areas in the study of law and society. But in some very important respects it is a superficial and profoundly mistaken view. In this essay I shall attempt to state why I think this is so and why I believe that a modern version of natural law philosophy is needed for a proper understanding of the law as well as for the fulfillment of sociology's promise. I speak here of natural law as a legal philosophy and not as a general system of ethics.

In approaching this task, I accept two basic commitments. First is a commitment to naturalism. My approach purports to be in all respects consistent with the spirit and logic of scientific inquiry. I offer only the caveat that it is John Dewey's philosophical pragmatism, and not a narrower positivism, which frames my view of naturalism. A second commitment is to a demanding concept of natural law. We are speaking of something more than a name for the sources of law, or for the moral foundations of law. Natural law is more than "the law that ought to be." If it is to mean anything significant, natural law must be itself legally efficacious, in some sense legally authoritative.

First I shall consider two obstacles to natural law thinking in sociology — the separation of fact and value and the doctrine of moral relativism. Then I shall analyze the meaning of legality and of positive law, finally turning to some attributes of natural law as they bear on sociological inquiry.

I. Master Ideals in Sociology

The main drift of contemporary sociology has been toward positivism, especially toward an ever-greater emphasis on empirical observation and techniques of measurement. A striving for objectivity, for clarity of thought, and for scientific respectability has produced a strong feeling against speculative inquiry and especially against moral philosophy. At least, these ancient preoccupations are thought to have no place in modern sociology, whatever other value they might have as literature. This movement of thought has much to commend it. At the same time, just because it is a "movement," it harbors many illusions and often serves to close minds rather than to open them. It is a procedural canon of inquiry that the study of fact must be assiduously protected from contamination by the value preferences of the observer. From this methodological requirement has been derived a quasi-metaphysical dogma, namely, that fact and value belong to alien spheres.

It is easy to understand why this separation of fact and value should arise. Surely one of the first necessities of education is to impress upon unsophisticated minds the necessity of distinguishing what the world is really like from what they would like it to be. As educators, we certainly have the obligation to lead the student toward realistic understandings. This very often requires that harsh truths be faced and that old habits of thought, so largely influenced by private needs and wishes, be set aside. Furthermore, the advance of science seems to require that we respect the autonomy of nature and recognize that there are structures in being and forces at work whose existence depends not at all on human awareness or contrivance. For these and similar reasons it makes good sense to segregate preference from observation and to stress the logical distinction between normative statements and fact statements.

But the needs of the unsophisticated cannot forever dominate the minds of scholars and teachers. Education also means unlearning, if need be, the easy and reassuring formulae of our intellectual youth. So it must be with the separation of fact and value. It is not that this principle lacks all merit but that too much is claimed for it. We must limit those claims if social science is to deal effectively with some of the most important dimensions of social life.

The entire issue of fact and value is too large to be set forth here, but I shall try to contribute to the discussion, and at the same time advance the argument of this paper, by analyzing briefly one area in which a significant intersection of fact and value occurs. I have in mind those phenomena in the social world whose very nature encompasses the realization of values.

Social scientists are not troubled by the idea of a "norm" or standard of behavior. A great deal of anthropological and sociological writing is devoted to the description and analysis of norms and systems of norms. That a cultural prescription exists, that it changes, that it is related to other prescriptions in determinate ways — these matters of fact can be handled by the social scientist quite blandly, without an uneasy conscience. From the standpoint of the observer, norms are factual data and that is that.

But suppose we are interested in the following: friendship, scholarship, statesmanship, love, fatherhood, citizenship, consensus, reason, public opinion, culture (in its common-sense and value-laden meaning), democracy. These and a great many other similar phenomena are "normative systems," in a special and "strong" sense of that term. I have in mind more than a set of related norms. A democracy is a normative system in that much complex behavior, as well as many specific norms, is governed by a master ideal. Behavior, feeling, thought, and organization are all bound together by a commitment to the realization of democratic values. It is impossible to understand any of these phenomena without also understanding what ideal states are to be approximated. In addition we must understand what forces are produced within the system, and what pressures exerted on it which inhibit or facilitate fulfilling the ideal.[3]

In a normative system, the relation between the master ideal and discrete norms may be quite complex. For example, it might be concluded that under certain circumstances maximizing the number of people who vote, irrespective of competence or interest, would undermine rather than further the democratic ideal. This is one reason for stressing the difference between a normative system and a set of related norms. A normative system is a living reality, a cluster of problem-solving individuals and groups, and its elements are subject to change as new circumstances and new opportunities alter the relation between the system and its master ideal. Put another way, the norms applicable to friendship or democracy are derived, not directly from the master ideal, but also from knowledge of what men and institutions are like. Only thus can we know what specific norms are required to fulfill the ideal.

The study of friendship cannot long avoid an evaluation of the extent to which particular social bonds approximate the ideal. Nor can it properly escape specifying the elements of friendship — what modes of response and obligation are called for by the ideal. None of this is inconsistent with detachment on the part of the observer. The observer need not have any personal commitment to the value in question, at least at the time and in the circumstances at hand. He may assess, quite objectively and impersonally, such connections and discrepancies as may exist between the ideal and its fulfillment.

Though this may be true, there is an odd reluctance on the part of social scientists to deal with normative systems. The disposition is to reduce such phenomena to arrangements that can be studied without assessment by the investigator, even when that assessment would entail nothing more than applying a culturally defined standard as to how far an implicit ideal has been realized. Thus, in the name of objectivity and rigor, the idea of friendship is left largely unanalyzed, and sociometric studies of reciprocal choice or differential association become the major line of inquiry. These measures, of course, say little about the quality of the relationship, not so much because they are incapable of doing so as because the studies do not begin

3. Compare the criticism of Max Weber in LEO STRAUSS, NATURAL RIGHT AND HISTORY 49ff. (Chicago: U. of Chicago Press, 1953).

with the normative perspective that would be appropriate. Similarly, the study of public opinion, where it is not mere polling, looks for stable patterns of response and for underlying attitudes and values, without much concern for public opinion as a normative idea. Again, social scientists have been much happier with the word "culture" since they have been able to strip it of normative significance and to bar the view that the idea of culture has something to do with excellence.

There is another side to this story, however. In theory, as opposed to the main trend of empirical research, some recognition of normative systems does exist. There is not much of a theory of friendship, or of love, in social science, but we do have the concept of the "primary relation," of which love and friendship are characteristic illustrations. What is a primary relation? It is a social bond marked by the free and spontaneous interaction of whole persons, as distinguished from the constrained and guarded arms-length contact of individuals who commit only a part of themselves to the social situation. In the primary relation, there is deep and extensive communication; individuals enter this experience as a way of directly attaining personal security and well-being, not as a means to other ends. This rough and elliptical statement is very close to what most sociologists would accept. Yet clearly it states an ideal only incompletely realized in the actual experience of living persons.

This illustration permits us to clarify the role of assessment in the observation and analysis of normative systems. The normative concept or model tells us what are the attributes of a primary relation. Only with this in mind can we properly classify our observations or identify the significant forces at work. To formulate the ideal primary relation is part of what theory is about in social psychology. This formulation, to be sure, will avoid the language of morality. It will specify social and psychological states, such as the quality of communication. Still, the intellectual function of the model is to provide a framework for diagnosis, including standards against which to assess the experience being studied. The small nuclear family is largely based on primary relations, but where communication between generations is weakened, and where authority requires impersonal judgment and discipline, the fulfillment of the primary-relations ideal is limited.

Whatever the assessment, it is always *from the standpoint of the normative system being studied.* The student of a normative system need not have any personal commitment to the desirability of that system. We may all agree that primary relations are a good thing, and the values they realize "genuine" values, but it is precisely the role of the social scientists to avoid the moralistic fallacy that primary relations are always a good thing. Where impersonality and objectivity are needed, the intimacy and commitment associated with primary relations may well be inappropriate. A different ideal, that of "official" behavior, may be called for. This ideal, too, is a demanding one and it is likely to be fulfilled in practice only partially. The investigator, in making his assessments from the standpoint of some purportedly operating normative system, can be quite detached about whether that system's ideals should be striven for in the circumstances. Indeed, the social scientist should be able to say whether the context is appropriate for the institution and support of a particular normative system. It might well be concluded that in the circumstances the attempt to create a friendship, to sustain a university, or to establish a democracy could only result in a distortion of the ideals these phenomena embody.

These remarks about detachment are made without prejudice to the view that certain ideals may be elements of an objective moral order. Whatever we may think of the appropriateness of friendship or love in a *given* context, we may still conclude that the values inherent in primary relations are of vital importance to man's well-being, and sometimes to his survival. This is only to say that he must find them somewhere, not that they are always appropriate. It may also be argued that no normative system is possible, or at least viable, unless it contains some ideals that all men can recognize as having a general moral validity. This position has much merit, but it is not necessary to the argument I am developing here.

Another illustration of support in sociological theory for the relevance of normative systems is the concept of "public opinion." Again, the trend of empirical research is to neutralize the term, to reduce it to the mere distribution of attitudes in a population. But conceptually a "public" is usually distinguished from a "crowd" or "mass" in that the behavior of a public, including the formation of public opinion, has a greater rational component and a greater self-consciousness. The member of a public acts rationally usually in his own immediate self-interest, but also potentially in the light of a larger sense of public interest. The formation of public opinion involves rational debate and is not merely the result of suggestibility or emotional rapport.

Clearly this view of public opinion presumes a normatively oriented system of organization and interaction. Given such a concept, which specifies standards, we can critically analyze opinion-making, not out of our own subjective preferences, but on the basis of a theory stating the conditions under which public opinion as a distinctive phenomenon is created. It follows that the state of opinion we actually observe will only approximate the theoretical ideal.

Concepts that specify ideal states are familiar enough in social science, and elsewhere as well. Any typology must designate, at least implicitly, a "pure" or "ideal" state with which purported instances of the type may be compared. The term "model" suggests a similar logic. However, not all types or models are normative; they do not necessarily have to do with the realization of values. When the realization of values is involved, social scientists seem to lose their zest for model-building. This probably has much to do with anxieties provoked by the epistemological dogma that values are "subjective."

The study of normative systems is one way of bridging the gap between fact and value. At the same time, the objectivity and detachment of the investigator can remain unsullied. The great gain is that we can more readily perceive latent values in the world of fact. This we do when we recognize, for example, that fatherhood, sexuality, leadership, and many other phenomena have a natural potential for "envaluation." Biological parenthood is readily transferred into a relationship guided by ideals. This occurs, not because of arbitrary social convention, but because the satisfactions associated with parenthood — satisfactions which are biologically functional — are not fully realized unless a guiding ideal emerges. The same holds true for the dialectic of sex and satisfaction. On a different plane, but according to the same logic, if leadership is to be effective and satisfying, it must go beyond simple domination to encompass a sense of responsibility.

This perception of latent values in behavior and organization is no mere sop to the moralizer. It enriches the thought and refines the observations of the student of society. Taken seriously, it may also serve to clear up some difficulties in contemporary sociological theory. Thus much attention is devoted these days to "functionalism." This is the view that items of behavior and of social structure should be examined for the work they do in sustaining or undermining some going concern or system. What is apparently or manifestly propaganda may be interpreted as latently a way of contributing to group cohesion by keeping members busy; a mode of punishment sustains the common conscience; selective recruitment of administrative personnel undermines an established policy or bolsters a shaky elite. Functional analysis is most familiar in the study of personality where a great many items of perception and behavior become meaningful only when their contribution to the maintenance of personal adjustment, including neurotic adjustment, is understood.

In all such interpretations, a system must be posited, whether it be at the level of personality or of group structure. The system is known insofar as a theory can be elaborated stating what the system "needs" to sustain itself. These needs are sometimes called "functional requisites." But here a persistent difficulty arises. There is a strong and understandable tendency to identify what is required for the maintenance of a system with what is required for the *bare survival* of a group or individual. The very term "survival" suggests that what is at stake is the biological extinction of the individual or the complete dissolution of the group. In fact, however, systems may decay despite the continuity of individual or group life. If a man extricates himself from neurotic dependence on another person, then a system has changed. If an organization maintains its personnel and budget, and even its formal identity, but transforms its effective goals, capabilities, commitments, and role in the community, then too a system has changed. To be sure, *some* systems are indispensable if life is to exist at all; but other systems are required if a certain *kind* of life is to survive. And it is fair to say that in social science the most important analyses have to do not with the bare continuity of life but with certain kinds and levels of organization.

A great many such systems are normative in the sense that their organization and development are governed by certain master ideals. A familiar and widespread illustration is the governing ideal of rationality in economic and administrative systems. In normative systems, it should be noted, terms like "maintenance" and "survival" are relevant but not adequate. They do not prepare us for observing, when it occurs, the evolutionary development of the system toward increased realization of its implicit ideals.

Sociology has studied normative systems, and even the self-realization of systems, for a long time (as witness the monumental work of Max Weber on the unfolding of rationality in modern institutions), but we have not thought through the implications of this intellectual concern. When we do, it will be a matter of course to recognize that a system may be known precisely by its distinctive competence or excellence, as well as by its special inner strains and vulnerabilities.

I have offered these remarks with malice prepense. They are meant to suggest that sociological inquiry has ample warrant for the study of law as a normative order. And this is the first, indispensable step toward a rapprochement between sociology and natural law.

II. Relativism and Human Nature

A second barrier to the acceptance of natural law among social scientists is the widespread commitment to moral relativism. But whatever else it may or may not be, the natural law philosophy is not relativist. At least, it is committed to the view that universal characteristics of man, and concomitant principles of justice, are discoverable. It does not necessarily hold that such generalizations are *known,* only that they are *knowable.*

What should a reading of modern sociology, and related subjects, tell us on this issue? Here we must remember the polemical context within which sociology developed. We must also keep in mind the moral impulses, and the high-minded educational aspirations, that have guided writing and teaching in this field. Sociology was nurtured by the revolt against an atomist, individualist image of man and the corollary view of society as the product of human will, albeit an imperfect will. Society was the dependent variable, created by beings endowed *ab initio* with mind and self. Sociological theory countered by stressing the *creative* role of society, especially in making possible just those attributes of self-awareness, reason, and symbolic imagination that are distinctively human. This approach proved seminal indeed, and a great deal of very valuable work, in many special areas, has resulted from it. At the same time, it lent powerful support to the notion that there really is no such thing as "human nature," that, in familiar accents, man may have a history, but not a nature.

The moral and educational aims of sociologists, social psychologists, and anthropologists helped relativism considerably. These social scientists accepted a liberalizing mission, and many pursued this mission with admirable zeal. They sought more tolerance, more sympathetic understanding, a deeper sense of human community. This breadth of vision and generosity of spirit was to be gained by stressing the fateful dependency of man on his social environment. If we realize that what men can achieve and what they strive for, what they respect and what they fear, are deeply and decisively affected by the conditions under which they grow up, then surely sympathetic understanding will be encouraged. If we recognize the great diversity of cultures, with what variety and ingenuity communities have solved the problems of survival and designed valued ways of life, then our parochial views will be modified and the richness of human experience appreciated. Above all, the easy tendency to treat our own ways as natural and to see them as stemming from "human nature" will be rejected. This understanding would contribute to freedom and enlightenment. It would yield benign doctrines encouraging the transformation of social conditions in order to correct moral ills, shifting the locus of responsibility from the individual to organized society.

A critical scrutiny of this intellectual movement suggests, however, that radical conclusions regarding human nature and moral relativism are neither well grounded in theory nor truly supported by the empirical evidence. In particular, the argument from cultural diversity is at best inconclusive. To be sure, the diversity of cultures is impressive. It is especially impressive to undergraduates, and is a very valuable antidote for any tendency to guffaw at strange practices and call other people "gooks." No doubt, many older efforts to identify essential traits of human nature, for example that men are naturally acquisitive or pugnacious, have been discredited. But if older generalizations have been wrong, new and more sophisticated ones may yet be valid.

That there is unity in this diversity — what some anthropologists have called the "psychic unity of mankind" — is often acknowledged. This acknowledgment comes easily if we are speaking of drives, such as hunger or sex, and potentialities, such as the capacity to learn and use language. But there are other features of man's psychic unity (not much studied, to be sure) more directly relevant to what is universal in social organization and pervasive in human values. I have in mind such motivating forces as the search for respect, including self-respect, for affection, and for surcease of anxiety; such potentialities as the union of sex and love, the enlargement of social insight and understanding, reason, and esthetic creativity. That man has morally relevant needs, weaknesses, and potentialities is supported, not contradicted, by the anthropological evidence. Moreover, if there are many different ways in which self-respect can be won, it does not follow that a study of those ways would not reveal certain common attributes. Human dignity, and the conditions for sustaining it, would be a proper subject for sustained inquiry. But there has been little interest in it.

There is an odd paradox in the teachings of cultural relativism. The very impulse which moves these teachings presumes that there is a morally relevant common humanity. *The whole point of the doctrine has been to encourage respect for others as human.* The underlying assumption is that all men need and deserve respect despite their diverse ways of life. What is this if not a theory of human nature? Moreover, the doctrine assumes that there are general principles for showing respect effectively, despite the fact that for each culture there may be variations in detail. The paradox is that a moral impulse, a bid for humility and sympathetic understanding, has become an obstacle to moral judgment. But that need not be so. A more careful consideration of the conclusions regarding man's nature implicit in the doctrine of cultural relativism, and derivable from comparative studies, can remove the paradox and free inquiry from some formidable roadblocks.

I conclude that the findings of modern social science do not refute the view that generalizations about human nature are possible, despite the effects of social environment and the diversity of cultures. Nothing we know today precludes an effort to define "ends proper to man's nature" and to discover objective standards of moral judgment. This does not mean that proper ends and objective standards are knowable apart from scientific inquiry. It does mean that psychic health and well-being are, in principle, amenable to definition; and that the conditions weakening or supporting psychic health can be discovered scientifically. It also means that all such conclusions are subject to revision as our work proceeds.

Whether we are able now to say what human nature consists of, is not important. We are not completely at a loss, but any current formulations would still be very crude. The essential point is that *we must avoid any dogma that blocks inquiry*. Relativism is pernicious when it insists, on woefully inadequate theoretical and empirical grounds, that the study of human nature is a chimera, a foolish fancy. To say we "know" there is no such thing, and that there is no use looking for it, is to abandon the self-corrective method of science. It is also to ignore much evidence regarding the psychic unity of mankind.

III. Positive Law and the Legal Order

Most definitions of law — and they are not really so various as is sometimes suggested — remind us that we are dealing with a normative system and a master ideal, in the sense discussed above. Aquinas is perhaps most explicit, calling law "an ordinance of reason for the common good, made and promulgated by him who has care of the community." But even the efforts of Gray and Holmes to avoid a normative definition surely falter when they emphasize "the rules which the courts, that is, the judicial organs of that body, lay down for the determination of legal rights and duties" or, in the Holmesian formula, "the prophecies of what the courts will do in fact, and nothing more pretentious, are what I mean by the law." For the meaning of "court" or "judicial organ" is plentifully supplied with normative connotations, such as the idea of being duly constituted, independent rather than servile, and offering grounded decisions.

In framing a general concept of law it is indeed difficult to avoid terms that suggest normative standards. This is so because the phenomenon itself is defined by — it does not exist apart from — values to be realized. The name for these values is "legality." Sometimes this is spoken of as "the rule of law" or, simply, "the legal order." Legality is a complex ideal embracing standards for assessing and criticizing decisions that purport to be legal, whether made by a legislature or a court, whether elaborating a rule or applying it to specific cases.

The essential element in legality, or the rule of law, is the governance of official power by rational principles of civic order. Official action, even at the highest levels of authority, is enmeshed in and restrained by a web of accepted general rules. Where this ideal exists, no power is immune from criticism nor completely free to follow its own bent, however well-intentioned it may be. Legality imposes an objective environment of constraint, of tests to be met, of standards to be observed, and, not less important, of ideals to be fulfilled.

This concept of legality is broad enough, but it is not so broad as the idea of justice. Justice extends beyond the legal order as such. It may have to do with the distribution of wealth, the allocation of responsibility for private harms, the definition of crimes or parental rights. Such issues may be decided politically, and law may be used to implement whatever decision is made. But the decision is not a peculiarly legal one, and many alternative arrangements are possible within the framework of the rule of law. How far government should intervene to direct social and economic life is a question of political prudence, in the light of justice, but how the government behaves if it does exercise broader controls or enter new spheres of life quickly raises questions of legality.

The ideal of legality has to do with the way rules are made and with how they are applied, but for the most part it does not prescribe the content of legal rules and doctrines. The vast majority of rules, including judge-made rules, spell out policy choices, choices not uniquely determined by the requirements of legality. Whether contracts must be supported by consideration; whether a defendant in an accident case should be spared liability because of plaintiff's contributory negligence; whether minors should be relieved of legal consequences that might otherwise apply to their actions — these and a host of other issues treated in the common law are basically matters of general public policy. For practical purposes, and especially because they arise in the course of controversies to be adjudicated, a great many of these policy matters are decided by the courts in the absence of, or as a supplement to, legislative determination. In making these decisions, and in devising substantive rules, the courts are concerned with dimensions of justice that go beyond the ideal of legality. Legality is a part of justice, but only a part. It is indeed the special province of jurists, but it is not their only concern. On the other hand, when they act outside the province where the ideal of legality is at issue, the courts share with other agencies of government the responsibility for doing justice. It is not legality alone which determines what the rule should be or how the case should be decided. That depends also on the nature of the subject matter and on the claims and interests at stake. Whether the outcome is just or unjust depends on more than legality.

However, there are times when the ideal of legality does determine the content of a legal rule or doctrine. This occurs when the purpose of the rules is precisely to implement that ideal, the most obvious illustration being the elaboration of procedural rules of pleading and evidence. In addition, principles of statutory interpretation, including much of constitutional law, directly serve the aim of creating and sustaining the "legal state." Some of these rules are "merely" procedural in the sense that they are arbitrary conveniences, chosen because some device was necessary, for which some other procedure might readily be substituted. Others are vital to just those substantial rights which the ideal of legality is meant to protect. These include all that we term civil rights, the rights of members of a polity to act as full citizens and to be free of oppressive and arbitrary official power. Again, it is not the aim of this ideal to protect the individual against all power, but only against the misuse of power by those whose actions have the color of authority. Of course, in our society we may have to extend our notions of who it is that acts "officially."

Perhaps the most difficult area governed by the ideal of legality is the process of judicial reasoning itself. Fundamentally, of course, this is part of the law of procedure, but it has a special obscurity as well as a special significance. The crucial problem here is to justify *as legal* the exercise of judicial creativity. That there is and must be creativity, whatever the name we give to it, is no longer seriously disputed. The question remains, however, whether there is something beyond the bare authority of the court, or reliance on a vague "sense of justice," to support the idea that judge-made policy has the stamp of legality.

One approach to this problem gives special weight to the legal tradition, to the received body of concepts, principles, doctrines, and rules. By working with these pre-existent legal materials, the law is in some weak sense "discovered," at the same time that creativity is permitted. Using familiar concepts establishes a link with the past and tends to create (though it does not guarantee) a smooth, gradual transition from one accepted policy to another. In this way legal craftsmanship, defined by its familiarity with the limits and potentialities of a certain body of materials and certain modes of decision, can ease social change by extending the mantle of legitimacy. A new policy, if it can be blanketed into contract doctrine or fitted into the law of torts, can have a peculiarly "legal" quality simply because of the ideas with which it is associated. It seems fair to say that this peculiar function of the law is weakening because it has become less attractive to the legal profession. This is so in part because of the modern interest in avoiding arcane language, in making policy objectives explicit, and in criticizing conventional legal categories. One may wonder, however, whether enough attention has been given to the role of legal concepts in defining an implicit delegation of power to the courts. This might be thought of as a working arrangement by which society allows the courts to make policy within areas marked out by the received body of legal ideas. It is assumed that these ideas are bounded, not limitless; that legal reasoning and judicial behavior contain some built-in restraints; and there is no contrary action by a legislature.

Another approach is to emphasize, not the "artificial reason" of the law, but the role of natural reason in the ideal of legality. Among the attributes of legality is a commitment to the search for truth, to consistency of thought, and to logical analysis of evidence as relevant, of classifications as inclusive, of analogies as persuasive. In this sense, there is no special legal reasoning; there is only the universal logic of rational assessment and scientific inquiry. The ideals of science and of legality are not the same, but they do overlap. Judicial conclusions gain in *legal* authority as they are based on good reasoning, including sound knowledge of human personality, human groups, human institutions.

The *meaning* of law includes the ideal of legality. That ideal, even though not yet completely clarified or specified, is the source of critical judgment concerning constituent parts of the legal order, especially particular rules and decisions. When a part of the law fails to meet the standards set by that ideal, it is to that extent wanting in legality. It does not necessarily cease to be law, however. It may be inferior law and yet properly command the respect and obligation of all who are committed to the legal order as a whole. At the same time, a mature legal system will develop ways of spreading the ideals of legality and of expunging offending elements.

The subtlety and scope of legal ideas, and the variety of legal materials, should give pause to any effort to define law within some simple formula. The attempt to find such a formula often leads to a disregard for more elusive parts of the law and excessive attention to specific rules. But even a cursory look at the law will remind us that a great deal more is included than rules. Legal ideas, variously and unclearly labeled "concepts," "doctrines," and "principles," have a vital place in authoritative decision. "Detrimental reliance," "attractive nuisance," "reasonable doubt," "exhaustion of remedies," "agency," and "interstate commerce" are among the many familiar concepts which purport to grasp some truth and provide a foundation for the elaboration of specific rules. In addition, of course, there are even more general ideas or principles stating, e.g., the necessary conditions of "ordered liberty" or that guilt is individual rather than collective. It would be pointless to speak of these as merely a "source" of law; they are too closely woven into the fabric of legal thought and have too direct a role in decision-making.

Variety in law is manifest in other ways, too. We may speak, for example, of variety in function: Law is called upon to organize public enterprises; to establish enforceable moral standards; to mediate differences while maintaining going concerns; to arrange contractual or marital divorces; to make public grants; to investigate; to regulate some private associations, to destroy others. These and other functions have yet to be adequately classified or systematically studied. It seems obvious that such study is a precondition for formulating a valid theory of law.

There are also well-known qualitative differences in the authority of legal pronouncements. If opinions are divided; if there is manifest confusion of concepts, monitored by legal scholarship; if rules or concepts are based on received tradition alone; if a particular rule is inconsistent with the general principles of a particular branch of law — then the authority of opinion or judgment is weakened. If all laws are authoritative, some are more authoritative than others.

These considerations support Lon Fuller's view that the legal order has an implicit or internal morality,[4] a morality defined by distinctive ideals and purposes. To say this, of course, is not to end inquiry but virtually to begin it. We must learn to distinguish more sharply between "bad law" that is merely bad public policy and law that is bad because it violates or incompletely realizes the ideals of legality. And we must attain a better understanding of how public purpose affects legal principle, as when we recognize that society binds itself especially tightly in the administration of criminal justice, generally requiring evidence of intent and barring retroactive legislation.

If the legal order includes a set of standards, an internal basis for criticism and reconstruction, then an essential foundation is laid for a viable theory of justice. In his sympathetic treatment of the natural law position,[5] Morris Cohen was almost right in arguing that we must be able to appeal from the law that is to the law that ought to be, from positive law to principles of justice. But he did not quite see that at least some principles of justice

4. Lon L. Fuller, *Positivism and Fidelity to Law — A Reply to Professor Hart*, 71 HARVARD LAW REVIEW 645 (1958).
5. MORRIS R. COHEN, REASON AND NATURE 408 (Glencoe, Ill.: The Free Press, 1953).

are ingredients of the ideal of legality and are therefore part of "the law that is." In many cases, we appeal from specific rules or concepts in the law to other concepts and to more general principles that are also part of the law. This is sometimes put as an appeal from "laws" to "the law,"[6] and there is merit in that approach. But it has the disadvantage of suggesting that "the law" is something disembodied and unspecifiable, when in fact all we mean is that general principles of legality are counterposed to more specific legal materials. Both belong to a normative system whose "existence" embraces principles of criticism and potentialities for evolution.

With this approach in mind, we can give to positive law its proper place and meaning. "Positive law" refers to those public obligations *that have been defined* by duly constituted authorities. This is not the whole of law, and it may be bad law. Law is "positive" when a particular conclusion has been reached by some authorized body — a conclusion expressed as an unambiguous rule or as a judgment duly rendered. This definition differs from the suggestion made by Holmes that law is what the courts *will* do, assuming that he meant to define positive law. I am emphasizing what the courts *have done,* because what they will do may depend on the whole body of legal materials.

Positive law is the product of legal problem solving. The legal order has the job of producing positive law as society's best effort to regulate conduct and settle disputes. What is done may be only imperfectly guided by legal principles, perhaps because those principles themselves are inadequate, but it remains law for the time being. As such, it has a claim on obedience. Positive law invokes a suspension of personal preference and judgment with regard to the *specific issue*. To suspend judgment, of course, is not necessarily to fail to have a judgment, but someone else's judgment is taken as an authoritative guide to behavior. Suspension in this sense is rightfully invoked because obedience to positive law is essential to the survival and integrity of the system as a whole. For the system to function, it is necessary that only specially appointed individuals may disregard a positive law, by changing or reinterpreting it, or by modifying its effect in a particular case when other rules can be brought to bear.

Obedience to positive law, irrespective of private judgment, is not an abandonment of reason. On the contrary, as has been well understood for a long time, it is a natural outcome of reasoned assent to the system as a

6. See Roscoe Pound, 2 Jurisprudence 106 (St. Paul: West Publishing Co., 1959). Note also his comment at 107: "Law in the sense we are considering is made up of precepts, technique, and ideals: A body of *authoritative* precepts, developed and applied by an *authoritative* technique in the light or on the background of *authoritative* traditional ideals." (Emphasis supplied)

whole. It in no way precludes criticism or testing of positive law, including the assertion that it is void and without effect. But criticism, testing, and change proceed within the broader framework of the legal order, appealing to its own ideals and purposes when they are relevant. Of special importance is the duty of legal officers, including private counsel, to respond critically to the positive law.

Plainly, positive law includes an arbitrary element. For him who must obey it, it is to some extent brute fact and brute command. But this arbitrary element, while necessary and inevitable, is repugnant to the ideal of legality. Therefore the proper aim of the legal order, and the special contribution of legal scholarship, is *progressively to reduce the degree of arbitrariness in the positive law.* This rule is comparable to that in science where the aim is to reduce the degree of empiricism, that is, the number of theoretically ungrounded factual generalizations within the corpus of scientific knowledge.

If reducing the degree of arbitrariness is accepted as the central task of jurisprudence, a long step is taken toward natural law philosophy. For whatever its variations, or its special errors, the concept of natural law has survived, and flourished periodically, precisely because of the need to minimize the role of arbitrary will in the legal order. The basic aim of this philosophy is to ground law in reason. The question then is, What shall we understand as the meaning of "reason"? I shall take it to mean what John Dewey meant by "intelligence" and, following his basic teachings, suggest that scientific inquiry, including inquiry about proper ends and values, is the road to a science of justice or natural law.

IV. Natural Law

As a doctrine or perspective, the chief tenet of natural law is that arbitrary will is not legally final. It holds that an appeal to principles of legality and justice is always available. This appeal assumes that every legal order, to the extent that it is one, has an implicit constitution. Thus understood, natural law is more than a "method." It is that surely, because it offers a rule, a guide to inquiry. But it also has content in that it looks to the ultimate formulation of principles stating the conditions of just governance. Science also combines method and content. Even when we emphasize method, there are conclusions to be drawn about the requirements of science as an intellectual enterprise. Similarly, liberalism and conservatism are methods of political thought and action, but they presume some general truths about man and society.

Method and content come together when the conclusions of natural law inquiry become *principles of criticism* to be applied to existing positive law. These conclusions are not more sacrosanct or eternal than any scientific generalization. On the other hand, a conclusion subject to correction is not necessarily precarious. It may be firmly grounded in theory and effectively supported by evidence. Therefore it does not lack the authority of reason as a guide to human action.

By its very name, "natural law" connotes a concern for drawing conclusions about nature. In other words, natural law *presumes inquiry*. And this entails a commitment to the ideals and canons of responsible thought. This does not mean, of course, that legal rules or doctrines are the same as scientific generalizations. The latter are "laws" in a quite different sense. Legal norms or principles are "natural law" to the extent that they are *based upon* scientific generalizations, *grounded in* warranted assertions about men, about groups, about the effects of law itself.

To put the matter this way may seem all too innocent. Among those who seek to improve legal doctrine and the administration of justice, few would question the importance of having more knowledge about how people behave in legal settings. Studies of deterrence and criminal law, of jury behavior, of arbitration, and of legally relevant changes in industrial organization, would all be welcome. Such studies are safe enough when they do not address themselves to the basic ideals of legality and therefore to the constitution of the legal order. In principle, however, there is no reason why the most general concepts of law — equality, reasonableness, fairness, and the like — should not be as subject to criticism, on the basis of scientific investigation, as are narrower legal concerns. When that occurs all innocence is lost and the quest for law is uneasily resumed.

Whatever the scope of our concern, natural law inquiry *presumes a set of ideals or values*. Most broadly, this is the welfare of man in society; law is examined for its potential contribution to that welfare. A more specific objective of natural law inquiry is to study the structure of the legal order as a normative system and to discover how the system can be brought closer to its own inherent ideals. Thus law is tested in two ways: first, against conclusions regarding the needs of man, including his need for a functioning society; second, against tested generalizations as to the requirements of a legal order. To some extent, the latter really includes the former, because among the requirements of a legal order is the capacity to serve human well-being by protecting and facilitating at least some vital aspects of social life.

On one vital point it seems wise to limit our intellectual commitments. It is not necessary for natural law supporters to prove or maintain that man *qua* man has any inherent duties, including the duty to live at all or to choose the good and avoid evil. This may be so on other grounds, but it is not essential to the natural law perspective. To be sure, the duties of man as father or as citizen are subject to social and legal definition, but that is a more limited assertion. Moreover, I should like to shift the emphasis. From the standpoint of natural law, ***the duty lies in the legal order***. If there is to be a legal order, it must serve the proper ends of man. It must not debase him or corrupt him. It must not deprive him of what is essential to the dignity and status of a human being. Whether or not any particular human being accepts a commitment to life, or to the good life, the law has no such freedom. It exists, on any theory, precisely to insure that at least the minimum conditions for the protection of life are established. The master ideals of justice and legality broaden that commitment considerably. But broad or narrow, it is the ***system*** that has the commitment.

As I have suggested earlier, there is nothing strange about this viewpoint to the sociologist acquainted with "functional" analysis. Functionalism, in stating "the requirements of a going concern," must identify what is essential to the system it is studying and then work out what is needed to sustain it at some specified level of activity or achievement. The level specified is not necessarily an arbitrary preference; it is at least partly set by the theory of what "is" a nuclear family or a trade union or an industrial society. To study a type of society is to learn what its distinctive structure is, and what it is capable of, as well as what forces are generated within it tending to break it down or transform it. At no point in that analysis is it necessary to show that all participants desire the system or have a duty to uphold it. But if the system is to be maintained, then certain requirements, taking account of natural processes, must be met.

Thus far I have argued:

a) Natural law presumes scientific inquiry;

b) Natural law presumes an end-in-view, a master ideal which guides inquiry;

c) Natural law searches for and incorporates enduring truths regarding the morally relevant nature of man, e.g., his need for self-respect;

d) Natural law searches for and incorporates enduring truths regarding the morally relevant nature of society, e.g., the distribution and use of social power;

e) Natural law searches for and incorporates enduring truths regarding the nature and requirements of a legal order.

It is obvious that the authority of natural law, and its development, must depend on progress in the social sciences. Where social knowledge is weak, as in the formulation of theoretically well-grounded and empirically tested generalizations about universal psychic or political phenomena, natural law must also be limited in its authority. Just because this is so, the natural law school has the right and the obligation to criticize social science and help make it more fruitful and more sophisticated.

One response to the difficulty of discovering general truths about man and society is to emphasize the "flexibility" or "variable content" of natural law. (This may also be a defensive reaction to the criticism of natural law philosophy as absolutist and dogmatic.) There is an important insight here, but it must be placed in proper perspective. It is true that natural law *presumes changing legal norms,* but this does not require abandoning the quest for universals or the assertion of them when they are warranted. A grasp of this point is essential if the relation between sociology and natural law is to be rightly understood.

Why does natural law presume changing norms? The reason is that its basic commitment is to a governing ideal, not to a specific set of injunctions. This ideal is to be realized in history and not outside of it. But history makes its own demands. Even when we know the meaning of legality we must still work out the relation between general principles and the changing structure of society. New circumstances do not necessarily alter principles, but they may and do require that new rules of law be formulated and old ones changed.

In a system governed by a master ideal, many specific norms, for a time part of that system, may be expendable. The test is whether they contribute to the realization of the ideal. Many norms evolve or are devised to take account of quite specific circumstances; and when those circumstances change, the norm may lose its value for the system. Thus the governing ideal of the system may be administrative rationality, but specific norms will vary depending on the purpose of the enterprise and upon its stage of development. For example, the norm of decentralization does not always serve the end of administrative rationality. Yet that end continues to have a vital influence on the selection of appropriate norms.

There are two valid interpretations of the idea that natural law has a changing content. (1) As inquiry proceeds, it is always possible that basic premises about legality, including underlying assumptions regarding human nature and social life, will be revised. (2) As society changes, new rules and doctrines are needed in order to give effect to natural law principles by adapting them to new demands, new circumstances, new opportunities. These perspectives demand that we detach natural law from illusions of eternal stability. They also require us to reject the notion that natural law must be a directly applicable code or it is nothing. A set of principles is not a code, any more than the principle of the conservation of energy is a specific physical theory. Natural law provides the authoritative materials for devising codes and for criticizing them, in precisely the same way as constitutional principles affect legislation and judge-made rules.

It may be helpful to illustrate briefly the dialectic of continuity and change in natural law. At the same time, we can see something of the relevance of sociological inquiry. Let us consider the idea of "fiduciary responsibility." This is a legal concept containing the implicit principle that where power is exercised under the color of benefit to another, then the one who holds power must comport himself in ways consistent with the fiduciary basis of his authority.[7] A fiduciary cannot treat his beneficiary as if he were merely his obligee in a contractual arrangement. He owes duties of loyalty and good faith appropriate to the status assumed. Different fiduciary relations call for different duties, but they have some attributes in common.

After much more analysis and testing, the general principle stated here may emerge as part of the corpus of natural law. It is based both on ideals of justice and on empirical theories regarding the temptations that beset men under certain conditions. These conclusions are subject to inquiry and to correction as may be necessary. But even as the principle remains, there is still the problem of giving it effect by embodying it in specific rules and doctrines.

Traditionally, the principle of fiduciary responsibility has been applied primarily in the law of property. In effect, a "trustee" is a kind of fiduciary who holds title to property and has a legal obligation to keep or use that property for someone else's benefit. There are fairly elaborate rules, and associated concepts and doctrines, stating how various kinds of trusts may be created and specifying the powers and responsibilities of trustees. This application of the broader principle reflects, of course, the needs of economic and social life in a particular historical epoch, as for pooling of investment funds, for the protection of family interests, of the interests of minors, and of those for the benefit of whom a public trust may be created. Social needs have joined with concepts of fairness to determine what specific rights will be protected, what norms embodied in positive law, and what legal ideas accepted to guide and justify the formulation of new rules. At the same time, legal development is constrained by a more or less conscious awareness of the limitations of positive law as an instrument of social control.

7. This statement does not necessarily include all the obligations, or embrace all the relations, that may be included in the legal concept of fiduciary duty.

There are good reasons why at any given time the general principle of fiduciary responsibility is not universally or automatically applied wherever fiduciary authority exists. The situations to which it could be applied might not be sufficiently important to justify the social cost of exercising formal control; such control might be ineffective because the resources and techniques of the law are inadequate; there might be other values, such as the autonomy of group life, which overweigh the need for justice based upon this principle. Yet the principle remains latent in the law and can be applied when needed as part of authoritative legal materials.

New historical developments, especially the rise of large bureaucratic enterprises, may well give the principle of fiduciary responsibility a fuller role in the law. The principle has already been applied for some time in regulating the conduct of corporation directors. The director is not technically a trustee, but that he is in some sense a fiduciary is not seriously questioned. Difficulties arise as to whether the fiduciary relation extends from the director to the corporation as an institution, to the stockholders, or perhaps to other classes of beneficiaries, including creditors, employees, customers, and the general public. Some voices are heard to say that all of these interests partake of the *beneficium,* though it is hard to formulate workable norms of responsibility to so heterogeneous a constituency. The important point is, however, that the principle of fiduciary responsibility is no longer clearly tied to a definite *res* or property interest, as that is understood in the law of trusts. The responsibility of the corporate director is more diffuse, both as to subject matter and as to beneficiary.

Some steps have been taken to apply the principle of fiduciary responsibility to trade union leaders.[8] It is becoming increasingly clear that at least the trade union "international" has been evolving in a bureaucratic direction, with self-perpetuating leaders and with an essentially passive membership which "buys" a service with its dues. This is not the whole truth, of course, but it is sufficiently true to justify the development of new legal safeguards against overreaching and potentially tyrannical union directorates. The sociological truth is that the modern large trade union, like the modern large corporation, cannot be adequately controlled by internal democratic processes. This is so because of a fundamental change in social organization and not because leaders are venal or members morally debilitated. The nature of membership has been profoundly altered. The trade union member does not see the need for effective participation beyond the payment of dues to support the power of the organization and the professional services

8. See Archibald Cox, *Internal Affairs of Labor Unions under the Labor Reform Act of 1959,* 58 Michigan Law Review 827-29 (1960).

of the union staff. To be sure, this change is probably not as radical as the shift in the meaning of shareholding, but the direction is the same.

The outcome is that members or owners of large enterprises, abdicating effective control, are in need of outside support for the protection of their interests. Such support can come by invoking the principle of fiduciary responsibility. This will not necessarily be effective in the courts, or in legislation, depending on whether the application of it in these circumstances can meet other demands, including consistency with related legal rules and with the effective administration of justice. But the natural law principle can be a starting point for legal craftsmanship.

The application of such a principle often depends on what may be called "institutional assessment." I have in mind the study of a complex enterprise, or type of enterprise, such as a school, church, political party, business firm, or government agency. The aim of institutional assessment is to determine what goals or objectives can be attributed to the enterprise, the capabilities it has, the strategies it lives by, its characteristic weaknesses, the distinctive significance it has for the life of the member, and what its probable line of evolution may be. Institutional assessment is one of the great practical and theoretical aims of social science, to which the sociology of large-scale organizations can make very important contributions. The development of this line of inquiry is still very primitive, but the needs of the legal order may require us to do the best we can with the intellectual tools now available. This is just what is being done in current discussions of the responsibilities of corporation directors and trade union leaders.

As a legal approach to the creation of responsible leadership, the fiduciary principle may have a "competitor." This is the concept of private government. In the assessment of modern industrial institutions, one conclusion taking shape today is that large, stable business enterprises and trade unions are performing significant governmental functions.[9] If this is more than a vaguely suggestive idea, the question is raised whether general principles of just governance should be applied to the exercise of authority in industry. Should the concepts and norms of "due process" be carried over? This would not necessarily depend on a doctrine of implied delegation of powers from the "official" government to the "private" government. It might mean simply that wherever the functions of governance are exercised there should be corresponding restraints on the exercise of authority. If such a view is ultimately clarified and adopted, the principle of fiduciary responsi-

9. See RICHARD EELS, THE MEANING OF MODERN BUSINESS ch. III (New York: Columbia, 1960); also the writings of A. A. Berle and Peter Drucker. For a critical view, see SHELDON S. WOLIN, POLITICS AND VISION ch. X (Boston: Little, Brown, 1960).

bility may drop out as a direct source of guidance. It is arguable, however, that the fiduciary principle underlies the responsibility of governors and therefore would still make its contribution to the legal result.

A general theory of responsibility and authority would be part of natural law. The theory rests on both logic and experience, on the clarification of meanings as well as on propositions about anxiety, aspiration, and group structure. Insofar as its elements withstand the test of inquiry, the theory remains a permanent part of the legal order. But how and where principles of responsible authority are applied depends on social needs and opportunities, as well as on circumstances that determine whether a particular rule will have the desired effect.

The significance of historical opportunity may merit a special word. When we consider the problems of large organization, it is tempting to take the view that the growth of private power has created vast new possibilities of oppression, and to make this the ground for seeking the extension of legal protection. I doubt that this accords with reality, and I think it reflects a mistaken view of legal development. Our problem is not so much the resistance of oppression as it is the fulfillment of opportunities. This is not to say that oppression is absent, or that new forms of it have not developed. But far more important is the fact that we now have opportunities not available before to build the ethic of legality into large segments of the economic order. Extending the ideals of due process to private associations might at any time have been a worthy objective. But the development of an inner order within bureaucratic enterprises brings that objective into close accord with a naturally evolving social reality. Legal ideals cannot always be completely realized, principles of justice cannot always be effectively applied, but they remain as living potentialities, awaiting the appearance of historical developments that will permit their application.

A legal principle, including a principle of natural law, belongs to an intricate, interdependent whole. It is not applied mechanically, in isolation from other legal materials. For this reason, among others, *natural law is applied with caution*. This is not an unfamiliar idea, as students of judicial review well know. Natural law, like constitutional interpretation, presumes a conservative posture. Excesses of logical extrapolation, overconfidence in the power and authority of an abstract idea, will thereby be minimized. This means also that the effects of a change in rule or doctrine on the legal system as a whole, or on some especially integrated parts of it, will be weighed.

The principle of caution recognizes a rebuttable presumption in favor of positive law. This is so for two reasons. First, it helps sustain the authority of the machinery for making positive law, and this is necessary to the integrity and effectiveness of the entire legal order. Second, the presumption recognizes that the funded experience of the political community has a special merit, although not absolute merit. Positive law is always partly a reflection of arbitrary will and naked power politics, but it also registers the problem-solving experience of the community. Above all, it can be a vehicle for the emergence of rational consensus. Therefore positive law makes its own vital contribution to the development of natural law. As a road to natural law, the evolution of positive law has a special claim to respect, because it is a kind of funded experience and because it can bring with it an added dimension of legal authority. This is a corollary of the statement made earlier about "reducing the degree of arbitrariness" in positive law. As that is done, the competence of positive law to aid the development of general legal principles will be enhanced.

In this essay I have outlined some of the foundations for a fruitful collaboration between sociology and natural law philosophy. This has required a critical discussion of both the sociological and the natural law perspectives. I have argued that sociological analysis is quite compatible with the study of social systems, such as the legal order, that are governed by master ideals; and that the relativity of moral judgment is not essential to the sociological view of man and society. I have also offered an interpretation of positive law and of natural law that is consistent with the premises of scientific inquiry. Yet I suggest that this interpretation captures the essential truth in the natural law approach.

I have no doubt that the sociology of law can gain immensely valuable guidance from the study of problems posed by the quest for natural law. I also believe that natural law philosophy would benefit from a greater effort to increase the scientific component of its discourse. A vigorous research program, devoted to the formulation and testing of natural law principles, might do much to advance both the cause of justice and sociological truth.

[4]

SUBSTANTIVE AND REFLEXIVE ELEMENTS IN MODERN LAW

GUNTHER TEUBNER*

The most comprehensive efforts to develop a new evolutionary approach to law are found in the work of Nonet and Selznick in the United States and Habermas and Luhmann in Germany. While these theorists are concerned with a common problem—the crisis of formal rationality of law—they differ drastically in their accounts of the problem and their vision of the future. This paper tries to resolve these differences by first decomposing and then restructuring the diverse neo-evolutionary models. Using a more comprehensive model of socio-legal covariation, the author identifies an emerging kind of legal structure which he calls "reflexive law." Reflexive law is characterized by a new kind of legal self-restraint. Instead of taking over regulatory responsibility for the outcome of social processes, reflexive law restricts itself to the installation, correction, and redefinition of democratic self-regulatory mechanisms. The author identifies areas of private law in which reflexive solutions are arguably emerging, and he spells out the consequences which a concern for reflexivity has for a renewed sociological jurisprudence.

I. NEO-EVOLUTIONARY THEORIES ABOUT LAW

We live in a time of increasing disenchantment with the goals, structures, and performance of the regulatory state. The political debate over "deregulation" (e.g., Breyer, 1982; Mitnick, 1980; Wilson, 1980) is just one manifestation of a much broader reappraisal of the systems of law and public organization.

* This article has changed from a one-man business into almost a transatlantic enterprise. It started at the Center for the Study of Law and Society at Berkeley, where I gave a seminar on comparative legal theory. In this challenging atmosphere, especially due to the presence of Philippe Nonet and Philip Selznick, I wrote the first draft, which then underwent critical examination by many colleagues, among them Richard Buxbaum, Johannes Feest, Wolfgang Fikentscher, Wolf von Heydebrand, James Nickel, and Rainer Walz. I have to thank the Deutsche Forschungsgemeinschaft for financial support.

On the other side of the Atlantic the paper met considerable criticism. My colleagues at Bremen especially and also elsewhere helped me with critical suggestions. I want to mention Gert Brüggemeier, Peter Derleder, Dieter Hart, Christian Joerges, Karl-Heinz Ladeur, Eike Schmidt, Klaus Sieveking, Helmut Willke, and Gerd Winter. Then the paper was exposed to the pleasant surroundings of Florence. I am grateful to the participants of the seminar on "New concepts of jurisprudence," particularly Werner Maihofer and Joseph Weiler, and I also received valuable suggestions from Marc Galanter and Niklas Luhmann. Presenting the paper to an American audience created the urgent need to "de-teutonize" it. David Trubek and Richard Lempert made extremely valuable suggestions regarding the final version. In fact, their cooperation was so intensive and their contributions went so far beyond usual editing activities that one can no longer speak of an individual article but of a collective

Recent debates in legal sociology mirror the more general concern with the effects of welfare-regulatory intervention. Thus, scholars have explored the causes and effects of the "legalization" of various spheres of social life (Voigt, 1980) as well as the sources and implications of movements for delegalization (Galanter, 1980) and informal justice (Abel, 1980; 1982). Attention has also been drawn to systems that might replace formal adjudication with various types of mediation and conciliation (Blankenburg *et al.*, 1980).

At this moment, society seems to be reassessing its commitment to purposive law and to the bureaucratic and legal structures that are associated with it. The classical models of law and the state which we inherited from the nineteenth century stressed what Max Weber called "formal rationality" (Rheinstein, 1954: 61,39). A formal rational legal system creates and applies a body of universal rules, and formal rational law relies on a body of legal professionals who employ peculiarly legal reasoning to resolve specific conflicts. With the coming of the welfare and regulatory state, greater stress has been placed on substantively rational law, i.e., on law used as an instrument for purposive, goal-oriented intervention (Rheinstein, 1954: 63,303). Since substantively rational law is designed to achieve specific goals in concrete situations, it tends to be more general and open-ended, yet at the same time more particularistic, than classical formal law.

European scholars have called this trend away from formality the "rematerialization" of the law. They see it both as an inherent part of the program of the welfare-regulatory state and as a development that leads to the dissolution of formal rationality. Some see the new "materialization" of the law as a threat to important social values (Voigt, 1980). The trend may also threaten individuality by weakening the protections which formal law (at least in theory) provides against arbitrary state action while, at the same time, removing barriers to bureaucratic intervention in what have heretofore been largely localized or private domains of human interaction (family, neighborhood, school).

Legal sociology in Europe and the United States has provided some useful phenomenological accounts of the conflicting and contradictory tendencies in the current

---

enterprise. To be sure, this does not mean collective responsibility; here we should stick to more old-fashioned notions of individual liability.

situation. But while we have become aware that there are movements towards and away from legalization, and shifts from formal to substantive modes of legal thought and practice, we do not know why this is occurring, nor do we know enough to predict the likely outcome of the current trends. Critics, who tell us that legalization cannot deal with the complexity and particularity of modern conflicts, argue for "alternatives" to law (see Blankenburg *et al.*, 1980). But this criticism is met by those who note that delegalization and informalism can, under current social conditions, reinforce rather than erode asymmetric power relations (Abel, 1980). Observers of the "rematerialization of law" note the pernicious effects of this process but are unable to answer critics like Kennedy (1976) who stress the impossibility of realizing the program of formal law.

Many see the current situation as a "crisis." But what is bringing it about? Are the debate over legalization and delegalization and the perceived tension between form and substance evidence of cyclical oscillations between arbitrary, yet antagonistic, principles of legal and social organization? Or is the current crisis the reflection of more basic, underlying forces whose operation can be grasped and whose direction can be anticipated? Because most current analyses of the situation lack either a macro-social or a developmental grounding, they cannot provide answers to these questions.

The purpose of this article is to outline an approach to change in law and society that will allow us to see the current situation as a "crisis" of legal and social evolution, and thus to situate the phenomenological accounts of legalization/delegalization and form/substance in a more comprehensive social theory. The theory shall be in the evolutionary tradition, for "neo-evolutionary" concepts provide a way of seeing the current situation in context. The evolutionary tradition is an old one in the sociology of law. It flourished in the early years of the discipline and then it fell into disrepute (Friedman, 1975). Now there is renewed interest in evolutionary approaches to explaining changes in law and society, both in the United States and in Europe (Brüggemeier, 1980; Buss, 1982; Eder, 1978; Eder *et al.*, 1978; Habermas, 1976c; Luhmann, 1970a; Nonet and Selznick, 1978; Schluchter, 1981; Tugendhat, 1980; Turner, 1974; Unger, 1976; Wiethölter, 1982; Willke, 1981; Zielke, 1980).

The method I shall follow is to analyze the two leading German neo-evolutionary theories of law in society and to contrast these to the most recent American essay in neo-evolutionary legal thought. From this juxtaposition of different but overlapping approaches, I develop a new perspective on the process of legal and social change that permits me to point to a new "evolutionary" stage of law, which I call "reflexive law." This stage, in which law becomes a system for the coordination of action within and between semi-autonomous social subsystems, can be seen as an emerging but as yet unrealized possibility, and the process of transition to a truly "reflexive" law can be analyzed.

This analysis is a preliminary and tentative one. My goals are to show how one can create a theory which avoids the shortcomings of prior evolutionary models and to demonstrate the utility of such an account for a preliminary appraisal of our current situation. But the social theory I build on is itself incomplete, and my efforts to apply it to the current legal scene are at best partial and tentative.

The most comprehensive efforts to develop a new evolutionary approach to law are found in the work of Philippe Nonet and Philip Selznick (1978) in the United States, and Jürgen Habermas (1981) and Niklas Luhmann (1970a) in Germany. These three neo-evolutionary accounts seek to identify different "types" of law, show the progression from one type to another, and explain the processes of transition. While there are substantial differences among them, these theories are concerned with a common problem: the crisis of formal rationality. They treat formal rationality as the dominant feature of modern law (at least until recent times), assert that phenomena like the "rematerialization of law" are a manifestation of the crisis, and seek to explain the situation.

To one degree or another each of these approaches harks back to Max Weber's formulation of the issues. Writing more than half a century ago, Weber both described the system of formal rationality and suggested the possibilities of a "rematerialization of law." Weber set forth a typology which included both formal and substantive rationality (Rheinstein, 1954: 61, 301; Schluchter, 1981: 87; Trubek, 1972: 720). He traced the sociological determinants of the shift from primarily material attributes of legal action (ethically determined, eudaemonistic, or utilitarian) to primarily formal attributes (conceptually abstract, precisely defined, and procedural). In his account, formal rationality is sustained by a set of methodological rules (legal syllogism, rules of legal interpretation) that guarantee uniformity and continuity in the legal system.[1]

Max Weber also pointed to some antiformal tendencies in modern legal development (Rheinstein, 1954: 303). In contract law, for instance, these tendencies manifested themselves in an "increasing particularization" of the law and growing legislative and judicial control of the material content of agreements. Weber interpreted this as a renewed infusion into law of "ethical imperatives, utilitarian and other expediential rules, and political maxims" (Rheinstein, 1954: 63), which in his view would endanger the formal rationality of law. "In any case, the juristic precision of judicial opinions will be seriously impaired if sociological, economic, or ethical argument were to take the place of legal concepts" (Rheinstein, 1954: 320).

Weber thought that these trends were marginal when compared to the overriding process of formal rationalization, but contemporary evolutionary theories seem to attribute high significance to the "materialization of formal law" (see, e.g., Assmann *et al.*, 1980; Eder, 1978; Trubek, 1972; Unger, 1976; Wieacker, 1967; Wiethölter, 1982). The theories I shall focus on search for process models that explain the dissolution of formal rationality in terms of transformation, directionality, and evolutionary potential, and each theory posits a new type of rationality toward which post-modern law may be moving.

While the theories of Habermas, Luhmann, and Nonet and Selznick have a common problematic and, to some degree, a common starting point, the approaches they take and the basis for their theories are very diverse. Nonet and Selznick (1978) present a developmental model with three evolutionary stages—repressive, autonomous, and responsive law. Responsive law, in this account, is the result of a crisis of legal formalism, out of which a new form of law emerges which combines purposiveness and participation (1978: 78, 95). In explaining the transition to responsive law, Nonet and Selznick stress internal developments within autonomous law which erode the law's formal tendencies.

Luhmann and Habermas, on the other hand, ground their analyses in theories that treat the evolution of societal structures and processes of legal and social covariation. Luhmann, who follows the Parsonian-Durkheimian tradition

---

[1] For an interesting reformulation of formal rationality in the context of a modern argumentation theory, see Eder *et al.* (1978: 11).

and is the leading German exponent of "systems theory," employs a three-stage evolutionary scheme which distinguishes among (a) segmented, (b) stratified, and (c) functionally differentiated societies (1982). For each type of social organization he posits a corresponding type of legal order (1970a: 3; 1972a: 132; 1981a: 45). Following this analysis, Luhmann argues that the current crisis in law is generated by the transition from a stratified to a functionally differentiated society. This transition "demands" a parallel transition in the legal order. From this point of view, the current crisis in law results from the inadequacies of the received system of positive law, given the complexities of a functionally differentiated society. For Luhmann, what is needed is not the increased purposiveness and participation suggested by Nonet and Selznick but higher abstraction, functionalist thought, and "self reflection" of the legal system (1972b: 325; 1974: 49; 1979: 176).

Jürgen Habermas approaches the same issue from a different vantage point (1975). The leading spokesman of "critical theory," Habermas has attempted a "reconstruction of historical materialism" along neo-evolutionary lines (1976). Like Luhmann, Habermas identifies evolutionary stages in society and analyzes the relationship between these stages and moral-legal developments. Habermas' model develops stages of "social organizational principles" which arise out of the interaction of structures of social labor and communicative interaction.[2] In his model, law is presented as the institutional embodiment of an historical sequence of "rationality structures": preconventional, conventional, and post-conventional.[3] Formal law in Habermas' scheme embodies a conventional rationality structure: the present situation involves a transition to a very different form of social and legal rationality.

Given the conflicting nature of these models, can one derive plausible features of an emerging post-modern legal rationality? Rather than attempting to choose among the competing models on grounds of theoretical "rightness," I will seek to identify implicit agreements and tacit convergences.

---

[2] Habermas seeks a "view to structural possibilities that are not yet (and perhaps never will be) institutionalized." This seems to be the ultimate goal of all these evolutionist models. They look at modern law from a problem-solving rather than a purely analytical perspective: they aim to help diagnose and cure the troubles that arise from the crisis of formal rationality; cf. Habermas (1976a).

[3] Conventional is a morality which is justified by tradition; postconventional refers to a justification by the interests of all participants; see Habermas (1976c: 260; 1979a: 95).

The goal is to transcend controversies between functionalism and critical theory and transform seemingly irreconcilable standpoints into complementary perspectives. I will attempt to construct an integrated model of legal evolution by decomposing the existing models into their elements and restructuring them in a different way. From this perspective, the three models do not really conflict but instead speak to different aspects of the same problem.

Nonet and Selznick, in order to explain legal change, rely strongly on variables "internal" to the legal system, while Habermas, as well as Luhmann, tends to stress "external" interrelations between legal and social structures. Our strategy shall be to combine "internal" and "external" variables in a model of their covariation. We shall be concerned with both the inherent developmental potentialities of the present legal system (Nonet and Selznick) and with the constraints and necessities of an emerging post-modern society (Habermas and Luhmann). In particular, we wish to explain how the internal dynamics of legal development described by Nonet and Selznick is likely to play itself out in the environment of societal transformation, which forms the basis of the theories developed by Habermas and Luhmann. We can do this with the aid of a concept of law which is similar to Nonet and Selznick's responsive law but differs from it in important respects. I call this concept, which identifies an emerging kind of legal structure, "reflexive law."

The argument proceeds as follows. In Section II, we look more closely at what Nonet and Selznick call "responsive law." Responsive law, as we shall see, involves two separate and potentially contradictory dimensions. Nonet and Selznick see the growth of "responsive law" as a unidimensional movement toward a more participatory *and* purposive system, but their analysis confounds two related but distinct trends in post-modern law, namely, the move towards greater substantive rationality and the emergence of reflexive rationality. Since responsive law includes substantive and reflexive elements, it turns out to be, on closer analysis, an amalgam of two different types of legal rationality. This discovery leads to the question of whether the legal structure Nonet and Selznick call "responsive law" is a stable or plausible "stage" of legal evolution or merely a moment in a transitional situation.

This question is central to this paper. But it cannot be answered within the framework of the evolutionary theory which Nonet and Selznick use since the only dynamic element in their evolutionary model is *internal* change in law. To deal with it, one must develop more complex models of legal and social evolution, in which changes in the legal system are explained in terms that encompass both the internal dynamics of the legal order and the impact of changing social structure. I turn to this task in Section III, where I use insights from Habermas and Luhmann to develop basic principles of socio-legal evolutionary covariation. This preliminary analysis suggests the importance of two concepts: "socially adequate complexity" and "organizational principles of society." Organizational principles, according to Habermas, emerge from the interplay of evolutionary processes in the moral and the social sphere of society. Fundamental legal norms incorporate those organizational principles of society and thus define the learning *niveau* (level) of a given society. The principle of socially adequate complexity, derived from Luhmann, states that the legal order in post-modern societies must have mechanisms that allow it to operate in a complex environment of functionally differentiated, semi-autonomous subsystems. Applied to the problem of post-modern society, both principles lead to the conclusion that a post-modern legal order must be oriented toward self-reflective processes within different social subsystems.

In Section IV, I use these principles to address the question of whether the amalgam of substantive and reflexive rationality contained in Nonet and Selznick's theory of responsive law is a stable or merely transitory stage. This analysis leads me to conclude that the two strands of the amalgam have different probabilities of realization in the conditions of post-modern society. It can be shown that the reflexive dimension of responsive law is more likely to meet the requirements of the principles of socially adequate complexity and congruence than are the purposive or substantive aspects of responsive law. Therefore, even if responsive law accurately describes the current situation in law, the amalgam it describes is unlikely to hold together. Indeed, reflexive law, now just an element in a complicated mixture of legal orientations, may emerge as the dominant form of post-modern law.

II. "TOWARD RESPONSIVE LAW": INTERNAL DYNAMICS OF LEGAL CHANGE

For Nonet and Selznick, responsive law, which combines a purposive orientation with an emphasis on participation in lawmaking processes, is an evolutionary advance over "autonomous law," the stage which Weber referred to as formal rationality. In identifying this new type of law, and explaining its emergence, Nonet and Selznick make an important contribution to the reconstruction of the theory of legal evolution. To understand the nature—and the limits—of this contribution, we must see how they analyze the process of legal evolution. The key lies in what Nonet and Selznick call their "social science" strategy, and the way this approach differs from traditional jurisprudential and sociological approaches to law.

A. Autonomy of Legal Development

Nonet and Selznick consider a whole range of jurisprudential issues from the standpoint of modern social science (1978: 8; Selznick, 1969: 3; 1968: 50). Their approach to law is empirical rather than analytical; they define law as multidimensional rather than unidimensional; they treat the social, political, and institutional dimensions of law as variables that depend on social context; and they conceive of these dimensions as aspects of a system of interrelated elements which can take on only a limited number of evolutionary configurations. The resulting theory of responsive law goes beyond traditional jurisprudence. Legal development is not identified exclusively with the unfolding of norms, principles, and basic concepts of law. Rather, it is determined by the dynamic interplay of social forces, institutional constraints, organizational structures, and—last but not least—conceptual potentials.

This type of social science strategy avoids the fallacies of sociological reductionism (see Luhmann, 1972a; Schelsky, 1980: 77). Law for Nonet and Selznick is neither an epiphenomenon disguising more basic economic contradictions (see, e.g., Wagner, 1976), nor, as in some positivist approaches, is it reducible to a set of decisions determined by power relations, organizational structures, professional roles, and the like. Instead, law is an autonomous social institution, whose development depends on its own internal dynamics. In short, Nonet and Selznick offer us a theory of institutional constraints and response within the legal system whose "main point is that a determinate disposition to change is traced such that systematic forces set in motion at one stage are said to produce characteristic outcomes at another" (Nonet and Selznick, 1978: 20). For example, the first of their three stages, repressive law, serves to legitimate power, but this very function generates pressures within a repressive legal system that undermine its specific structures and lead to the emergence of a new type, autonomous law. Similarly, autonomous law develops internal modes of reasoning and concepts of participation which break the boundaries of formal thought and generate pressures for the transformation toward a more responsive type of law (1978: 51, 71).

This concept of an "institutional logic" of the legal order, central to Nonet and Selznick's neo-evolutionary approach, is strongly supported by their European counterparts. Habermas transforms "economistic" versions of the base/superstructure thesis into more abstract relations between "labor" and social "interaction" and provides for an autonomous "developmental logic" of normative structures. In Habermas' theory, the evolution of moral and legal consciousness follows its own autonomous pattern and cannot be reduced to a mere reflection of "developmental dynamics" in the basic social and economic structures (1979: 130). It is one of Habermas' major theses that the rationalization of the "life-world," in which moral and legal development take place, is not reducible to those processes that tend toward increasing complexity in the economic and political "systems."

Luhmann accounts for the autonomy of legal evolution by defining it as an interaction between different evolutionary mechanisms inside the legal system. Law's normative structures provide for variation; its procedural institutions fulfill the selection function; its conceptual abstractions represent stabilization mechanisms (1970a). Thus, despite substantial differences in the models offered by Nonet and Selznick, Habermas, and Luhmann, one finds a striking convergence in their view of the autonomy of legal evolution.

What does it mean to formulate a theory of legal change in terms of autonomous evolution? Is the development of the idea of an "institutional logic" within the legal system, which forms a central part of the three approaches we are analyzing, a step forward in theory? One might argue that to stress the autonomy of the law is to abandon a key insight of legal sociology, namely, the dependence of law on social factors, and to recreate the traditional division between jurisprudence and social science. But these dangers exist only if the legal system is conceptualized as a "closed" system, self-sufficient and independent from changes in the broader social environment. In the work we are drawing on it is not. For the neo-evolutionists, legal autonomy means that law changes in reaction only to its own impulses, for the legal order—norms, doctrines, institutions, organizations—reproduces itself.[4] But in so doing, the legal system is not insulated from its environment. The key idea, central to the neo-evolutionary theories, is the "self-reference of legal structures." Legal structures so conceived reinterpret themselves, but in the light of external needs and demands. This means that external changes are neither ignored nor directly reflected according to a "stimulus-response scheme." Rather, they are selectively filtered into legal structures and adapted in accordance with a logic of normative development. Even the strongest social pressures influence legal development only insofar as they first shape "legal constructions of social reality." Thus, broader social developments serve to "modulate" legal change as it obeys its own developmental logic.

The concept of the self-reference of the legal system is a vital aspect of neo-evolutionary thought. It presents the legal system as, at the same time, both a "closed" and an "open" system. In this way, neo-evolutionary thought avoids the fallacies of theories which see legal change as either purely internal and independent or exclusively the result of external events. Legal and social changes are, for the neo-evolutionist, related yet distinct processes. Legal change reflects an internal dynamic, which, nevertheless, is affected by external stimuli and, in turn, influences the external environment.

The concept of self-referential legal structures enables us to take account of the "distinctively legal" character of specific normative phenomena, without at the same time losing a broader social science perspective (Trubek, 1977: 540). Sociologically, we can recognize and analyze the differences between legal doctrines and scientific theories, between legal constructions of reality and social science constructs, between doctrinal legal research and sociological empirical research, and between a specific juridical type of rationality and the rationality of other social subsystems.

Most importantly, the concept of self-referential legal development provides the basis for a perspective on social and legal co-evolution that allows us to understand more fully the current crisis. By focusing on this dimension, we can gain new insights into the issues raised by the debate over the "rematerialization of the law" and see how a new form of

[4] The concept of self-reference is employed in biology as well as in the social sciences, in order to identify a system that produces and reproduces by itself the elements of which it consists; see Hejl (1982: 189).

rationality may be emerging. But to do this, we must go beyond the analysis that Nonet and Selznick offer. We must first see that their concept of "responsive law" actually incorporates *two* different types of legal rationality. Then, we must transcend their purely internal account of the dynamics of legal evolution.

B. *Two Dimensions of Responsive Law: Substantive Versus Reflexive Rationality*

Nonet and Selznick's description of the emergence of responsive law is in many respects similar to European ideas about the "rematerialization of formal law." However, they have developed a more coherent and systematic model of autonomous legal change to show the consequences of this transition. Nonet and Selznick assert that legal formalism undergoes a crisis, from which a new substantive orientation—sovereignty of purpose—emerges. The rise of purposiveness transforms fundamentally rigid normative structures into "open-textured" standards and "result-oriented" rules. The new purposive orientation influences basic doctrinal concepts ("obligation and civility"), as well as legal constructions of social reality ("political paradigm") (1978: 78, 84, 87, 93). In this development, classical methods of legal inquiry need to transform themselves into methods of "social policy analysis" that parallel changes in the modes of legal participation ("legal pluralism") (1978: 84, 96, 106). Moreover, materialization of law corresponds to totally new institutional and organizational structures: it demands "regulation, not adjudication" carried out by non-hierarchical "post-bureaucratic organizations." Outside of the legal system, its boundaries need to be redefined with respect to the political and social environment. Substantive rationality requires an "integration of legal and moral judgment and of legal and political participation" (1978: 104, 108, 110).

Much of what Nonet and Selznick say about the transition from autonomous to responsive law is based on their view—shared by many Europeans—that the legal order has shifted from formal to substantive (purposive) modes of rationality. But there is a crucial difference between Nonet and Selznick and others who have discussed the "materialization" of the law. For Nonet and Selznick's idea of responsive law not only includes elements of substantive rationality; they also include in the category elements which seem to be based on very different principles. At least two elements of responsive law—

"institutional design" and "politicization of law"—obey a different form of rationality than other aspects of the concept. Although the authors subsume these elements under the principle of "substantive justice"—as opposed to those of "procedural fairness," which governs autonomous law, and "raison d'état," which dominates repressive law (1978: 16)—we can upon close analysis perceive a significantly different orientation. Indeed, the place that institutional design and politicization occupy in the theory of responsive law suggests the germ of a new type of legal rationality.

Consider first "institutional design and institutional diagnosis" (1978: 111). Here, legal attention focuses on creating, shaping, correcting, and redesigning social institutions that function as self-regulating systems. Legal norms should produce a "harmonious fit" between institutional structures and social structures rather than influence the social structures themselves. Instead of giving substantive guidance to behavior, these norms are directed toward organization, procedure, and competence. Instead of taking over responsibility for concrete social results, the law is restricted to structuring mechanisms for self-regulation such as negotiation, decentralization, planning, and organized conflict. Where substantive rationality requires comprehensive regulation, "institutional design" aims at "enablement and facilitation" (1978: 111).

The same can be said about other features of responsive law. The politicization of law, for instance, as suggested by new modes of political participation (social advocacy, class actions, representation of group interests, etc.) (1978: 95), imports a different set of social conflicts and integrates different interests into the legal process. Yet it does so without commanding the specific results a substantive rationality would require.

What this suggests is that Nonet and Selznick's description of the transformation of autonomous law (legal formalism) incorporates a move from formal rationality to two different types of legal rationality: the "substantive" rationality of results, and the "reflexive" rationality of the process-oriented structuring of institutions and organizing of participation. But what does it mean to speak of these three "types" of legal rationality (formal, substantive, reflexive)?

C. *A Neo-Evolutionary Model of Legal Rationality*

Legal rationality is a compact concept. In order to define the specific rationalities of formal, substantive, and reflexive law, we have to break the concept of rationality up into different dimensions. This can be done by using the dimensions Habermas (1976: 262) uses to analyze modern formal law and then applying them to substantive law and reflexive law. Habermas' categories expand on the original Weberian concepts, which equated legal rationality with internal features, i.e., the construction of general conceptual categories and the systematization of doctrine. For Habermas these features mark only one dimension of legal rationality. Internal rationality is dependent on two other dimensions: system rationality and norm rationality. System rationality refers to the external social functions of law. It designates the capacity of the legal order to respond to the control problems of society at large. Norm rationality, in contrast, refers to fundamental principles which justify the specific way that legal norms should govern human actions. For the moment, we shall ignore the systematic connections between these dimensions and consider only how this scheme may be used to describe the different types of modern and post-modern law. Applying this formal model to our analysis yields the following three dimensions:

(1) justification of law ("norm rationality");
(2) external functions of law ("system rationality");
(3) internal structure of law ("internal rationality").

The *formal rationality* of modern law is defined by a historically specific configuration of these dimensions:

(1) The justification of formal law lies in its contributions to individualism and autonomy and so rests on the continued validity of these values (Kennedy, 1976). The contribution occurs because formal law restricts itself to the definition of abstract spheres of action for the autonomous pursuit of private interests. In doing so, it guarantees a framework within which substantive value judgments are made by private actors. Thus, "formalities" facilitate private ordering. They are "premised on the lawmaker's indifference as to which of a number of alternative relationships the parties decide to enter" (Kennedy, 1976: 1685; cf. Heller, 1979: 187). The corollary elements of formal law are: conventionality, legalism, and universalism (Habermas, 1976: 264; cf. Unger, 1976: 204).

(2) With this orientation, formal law fulfills specific external social functions. Formal law develops its own system rationality insofar as it establishes spheres for autonomous

activity and fixed boundaries for the action of private actors. Thus, it contributes to the mobilization and allocation of natural resources, which is a necessary concomitant of a developed market economy (Habermas, 1976: 264; 1981: 352).[5] Put another way, the "semantics of decentralization" which arises out of the systematization of subjective rights is the adequate legal form for the functional differentiation of an autonomous economic system (Luhmann, 1981a: 80). At the same time formal law fulfills legitimizing functions: "A logically formal legal order appears to be a neutral and autonomous source of normative guidance, and this very neutrality and autonomy of law forms one basis for the claims of political systems in capitalist societies to legitimate authority" (Trubek, 1977: 540).

(3) It is by the interplay of both these elements that we can explain the internal structure of formal law. Internally, law is formally rational to the extent that it is structured according to standards of analytical conceptuality, deductive stringency, and rule-oriented reasoning (Habermas, 1976: 263; 1981: 348). A highly developed rule-orientation results in norms whose legal consequences depend on precise definitions of factual situations. Professionalization is an additional element: legal experts are masters of a body of esoteric knowledge which they are trained to apply in a universalistic way (Friedman, 1973: 14; Trubek, 1972).

The trichotomy of norm, external function, and internal structure may be applied to substantive and reflexive rationality as well. *Substantive rationality* emerges in the processes of increasing state regulation. It is commonly associated with the growth of the welfare state and state intervention in market structures (Assmann *et al.*, 1980; Eder, 1978; Heydebrand, 1982; Voigt, 1980). In these developments, law loses its formal characteristics on all three dimensions.

(1) In its "norm rationality," substantive law shifts the focus from autonomy to regulation. The justification of substantive law is to be found in the perceived need for the collective regulation of economic and social activities to compensate for inadequacies of the market. Instead of delimiting spheres for autonomous private action, the law directly regulates social behavior by defining substantive

5 This is the core of Max Weber's concept of formal rationality; cf. Rheinstein (1954: 61).

prescriptions. In doing so, law becomes increasingly oriented to social roles and statuses (Rehbinder, 1967).

(2) The change in norm rationality is accompanied by a change in the functions that law fulfills. Substantive law demonstrates its "system rationality" by the contributions it offers to political intervention by the welfare-regulatory state. As the political system takes over responsibilities for defining goals, selecting normative means, prescribing concrete actions, and implementing programs, substantive law assumes increasing importance. It is the main instrument by which the state modifies market-determined patterns and structures of behavior.

(3) Insofar as substantive law takes over this new function and develops a regulatory justification, its internal structures change so that the dominant rule-orientation of formal law is supplemented by an increasingly purposive orientation. Substantive law is realized through purposive programs and implemented through regulations, standards, and principles. This trend toward purposive law has grave consequences for the conceptual construction of doctrinal legal systems. There is today considerable dispute about the degree to which legal thinking and legal practice can cope with the cognitive consequences of consequentialism.[6]

Reflexive rationality has emerged only recently in the crisis of the welfare state. It is as yet an undeveloped and not fully defined alternative to the regressive tendencies of the reformalization of substantive law. It shares with substantive law the notion that focused intervention in social processes is within the domain of law, but it retreats from taking full responsibility for substantive outcomes.

(1) The justification for reflexive law is to be found neither in the perfection of autonomy nor in the collective regulation of behavior. Rather, it is justified by the desirability of coordinating recursively determined forms of social cooperation. In this "norm rationality," reflexive law resembles liberal and neo-liberal concepts of the role of law. To the extent it supports social autonomy, it relies on invisible hand mechanisms. But reflexive law does not merely adapt to or support "natural social orders." Quite to the contrary, it searches for "regulated autonomy." It seeks to design self-regulating social systems through norms of organization and

[6] For a profound analysis of the implications of "consequentialism" in purposive law, see Luhmann (1974: 31).

procedure. Reflexive law, unlike formal law, does not accept "natural" subjective rights. Rather, it attempts to guide human action by redefining and redistributing property rights.

(2) The external social functions of reflexive law are different from those of substantive law. The role of reflexive law is to structure and restructure semi-autonomous social systems (Galanter, 1980: 21), by shaping both their procedures of internal discourse and their methods of coordination with other social systems. Thus, reflexive law shows elements of "system rationality" insofar as it facilitates integrative processes within a functionally differentiated society (Willke, 1981). What is important is that to facilitate integrative processes does not, for reflexive law, mean to prescribe authoritatively ways and means of social integration. It means to create the structural premises for a decentralized integration of society by supporting integrative mechanisms within autonomous social subsystems.

(3) The "internal rationality" of reflexive law is represented neither by a system of precisely defined formal rules nor by the infusion of purpose-orientation through substantive standards. Instead, reflexive law tends to rely on procedural norms that regulate processes, organization, and the distribution of rights and competencies. The new procedural orientation characteristics of reflexive law can be observed in different legal fields as an emerging alternative to formal as well as substantive rationality.[7] Under a regime of reflexive law, the legal control of social action is indirect and abstract, for the legal system only determines the organizational and procedural premises of future action (Luhmann, 1970a: 92, 72).

Table 1 summarizes the basic characteristics of formal, substantive, and reflexive law that I have outlined above. To better appreciate what these characteristics mean, consider a concrete example. Take contract law, for instance. If a contractual obligation is disputed, formal law looks only to see if certain formal, general, and objective conditions are met—e.g., whether there was a "meeting of the minds." It is indifferent to the social effects which the formal law allows contracting parties to create. Substantive law, on the other

[7] For German corporation law and labor law, see the analysis of Wiethölter (1982), in which he distinguishes three phases of modern legal change: formalization, materialization, proceduralization; cf. as well Brüggemeier (1980: 60); Ladeur (1982: 74); Winter (1982: 9). For examples of parallel processes in contract law, cf. Schmidt (1980: 153, 155) and in consumer law, Joerges (1981). For a similar interpretation of American constitutional law, cf. Ely (1980).

hand, is concerned with outcomes and is characterized by the direct intervention of legislatures and courts in setting and altering contract terms. Reflexive law approaches the contract relation very differently. It seeks to structure bargaining relations so as to equalize bargaining power, and it attempts to subject contracting parties to mechanisms of "public responsibility" that are designed to ensure that bargaining processes will take account of various externalities. However, within the limits of the arena that has been so structured, the parties are free to strike whatever bargains they will. Reflexive law affects the quality of outcomes without determining the agreements that will be reached. Unlike formal law, it does not take prior distributions as given. Unlike substantive law, it does not hold that certain contractual outcomes are desirable.[8]

As I have already noted, Nonet and Selznick's concept of responsive law includes elements of reflexive as well as substantive rationality. It does not, however, sufficiently distinguish between them. Distinguishing between the two elements is important because reflexive legal rationality requires institutional legal structures, cognitive models of reality, and normative characteristics quite different from its substantive counterpart. Furthermore, only by distinguishing between the two elements can we assess the extent to which the potential of responsive law can be realized. This is because Nonet and Selznick's focus on autonomous internal legal evolution, which is the major theoretical advance of their particular social science strategy, may draw attention away from the systematic interplay between legal and social evolutionary processes. Yet, social developments outside the legal system drastically limit the potential of substantive law while they systematically favor the reflexive type of legal rationality. To put this thesis into Selznick's conceptual framework: It is reflexive rather than substantive rationality that represents the "conceptual readiness" of responsive law to

[8] Another example of a reflexive law "solution" to the inadequacies of both substantive and formal law is the idea of "external decentralization," which is emerging in the European literature as an alternative to the neo-conservative "solutions" of deregulation, reformalization, and privatization (Gotthold, 1982; Lehner, 1979: 178). External decentralization induces the delegation of "public tasks" to semi-public or private institutions under certain constraints designed to ensure that political responsibility prevails. The law, for example, in authorizing a local task-oriented association may mandate certain rights of participation or procedures of decision making. The state also monitors the behavior of such organizations and is ready to step in and further alter institutional arrangements, should the desired degree of social accountability not be achieved.

take advantage of the "opportunity structures" emerging in post-modern society (Selznick, 1968: 50, 55, 57; 1969: 243).

Table 1. Types and Dimensions of Modern Legal Rationality

Dimensions	Types: Formal	Types: Substantive	Types: Reflexive
Justification of Law	the perfection of individualism and autonomy: establishment of spheres of activity for private actors.	the collective regulation of economic and social activity and compensation for market inadequacies	controlling self-regulation: the coordination of recursively determined forms of social cooperation
External Functions of Law	structural premises for the mobilization and allocation of resources in a developed market society and for the legitimation of the political system.	the instrumental modification of market-determined patterns and structures of behavior	structuring and restructuring systems for internal discourse and external coordination
Internal Structures of Law	rule-orientation: conceptually constructed rules applied through deductive logic	purpose-orientation: purposive programs of action implemented through regulations, standards, and principles	procedure-orientation: relationally oriented institutional structures and decision processes

III. "ORGANIZATIONAL PRINCIPLES" AND "SOCIALLY ADEQUATE COMPLEXITY": COVARIATION OF LEGAL AND SOCIAL STRUCTURES

A. *Law Without Society?*

We turn now to the relationship between legal and social structures in the evolutionary process. Our goal is to understand the relationship between changes in law and changes in society. An "evolutionary" or developmental theory cannot merely assert that certain types of law covary with features of social, economic, and political organization. It must also account for the relations between legal and social structures and help us understand how transformations come to occur.

Let us start with the model developed by Nonet and Selznick. Their analysis of the process of legal change assigns a central role to the "internal dynamics" of the legal system. Changes which occur *within* law set in motion forces that, themselves, alter the characteristic configurations of the law (1978: 20). For example, universalism in legal thought—a major feature of autonomous law—leads ineluctably to purposive modes of reasoning. This development, in turn, brings about changes in the nature of legal obligation and modes of legal advocacy (1978: 78).

The Nonet and Selznick model does not, however, overlook entirely the role of external social forces. It explicitly recognizes that such factors play a role in legal development (1978: 21, 23, 16), but the place their developmental theory assigns to them is marginal. The external environment is seen not as *bringing about* changes in law, but as serving principally to block or facilitate the realization of those developmental potentials generated by the internal dynamics of law. Broader social structures encourage or impede the "actualization" of legal potential, determining the stability of an evolutionary stage and the probability of progress and regression (1978: 18, 23, 116). But it is from its internal dynamics that the legal system gains its developmental potential, and this potential defines exclusively the system's pattern of growth and decay. In this respect we seem to have a law without society.

The limited role that Nonet and Selznick assign to external social factors is, in my view, inadequate. To combine their notion of legal autonomy with a satisfactory account of the interrelationship between autonomous legal evolution and broader social developments requires a model in which law and society are treated as separate yet interdependent aspects of an overall system. We must, in other words, model legal and social covariation.

In addition, an adequate model must contain a theory of the developmental "crisis" since notions of "crises of development" are central to evolutionist thinking. Here again, Nonet and Selznick provide a promising beginning, but their model requires further elaboration. In noting the existence of specific internal crises in repressive as well as in autonomous law, they seem to be advancing two rather different ideas. On the one hand, there is the idea that crises in law derive from the inability of law to respond to the need for "*system* integration" in the sense that the legal structure does not provide the conceptual and action resources needed for the maintenance of the overall social system (Habermas, 1975: 1). The authors' stress on "greater capacities for problem solving," on "the economy of power," and on the "precariousness of responsive law" (Nonet and Selznick, 1978: 24, 33, 115), fits nicely into such a functionalist systems approach. On the other hand, there is the idea that the problems of both repressive and responsive law may be diagnosed as legitimation crises. The problems here involve "*social* integration," *social* identity, and the dissolution of *social* norms (Habermas, 1975). Perhaps Nonet and Selznick are deliberately refusing to be forced into making a clear-cut distinction between social and system integration. Their concept of crisis contains elements compatible with both. But, since we cannot equate social integration with system integration, we need to clarify the relationship between *rationality crises*, which concern the social-engineering capacities of the law, and *legitimation crises*, which relate to social identity and social norms.

Let us reconsider the crisis of formal legal rationality. Does it stem from a deficiency of abstract, general, and formal control mechanisms or from the inability of legal formalism to take into account questions of substantive justice (Habermas, 1979: 184)? How one answers this question has important consequences for the concept of responsive law. The challenges to which responsive law responds can be analyzed in terms of an "internal" legitimation crisis, an "external" rationality crisis of autonomous law, or some combination of the two.

I have tried thus far both to emphasize the promise of Nonet and Selznick's approach and to show specific areas where their model is lacking. My basic point is that by shifting the focus of the argument from a theory of internal legal growth to one of socio-legal covariation (e.g., Tugendhat, 1980), it may be possible to pursue the classical goals of a comprehensive socio-legal analysis without sacrificing the insights into the "internal dynamics" of legal evolution that Nonet and Selznick have given us.

A good place to begin our discussion of the covariation of legal and social structures is with the work of Habermas and Luhmann. Both Habermas and Luhmann acknowledge the autonomous nature of the development of norms within the legal system and examine systematically the relationship between law and its social context.

B. *Habermas: "Organizational Principles" of Society*

Habermas argues that post-Darwinian theories of social evolution which rely on the interplay of evolutionary mechanisms (variation, selection, stabilization) cannot account for the characteristics of societal stages of evolution or for the potential to learn from historical experience. These can only be analyzed in terms of "social consciousness" (Habermas, 1976a: 226). In order to identify the autonomous "developmental logic" of normative structures (moral and legal consciousness), Habermas borrows from models of individual moral development in the Piaget-Kohlberg tradition. The resulting "social organizational principles" form logical sequences of "structured wholes" characterized by the common features of irreversibility, structured hierarchy, and directionality (Habermas, 1979: 98).

In Habermas' evolutionary theory, these highly abstract social organizational principles—which include legal institutions (Habermas, 1976c: 266)—designate the "learning level" (*niveau*) of a given society (Habermas, 1971: 270; 1979: 17; 1976a: 200; 1976b: 92; 1976c: 260; 1976d: 129; 1979a: 95; 1979d: 130). The learning level imposes limits on the variation that is possible with respect to types of social integration (social identity, consensus on values) and with respect to system integration (the capacity for control of a society) as well.

Organizational principles emerge as the result of a double learning process that can be explained—according to Habermas—by combining two models. These principles are forms of social patterning that allow a society to deal with its characteristic problems. As such, their capacity to cope with system problems is ordinarily open to functional analysis. But in crisis situations, another mode of analysis, which Habermas calls "rational reconstruction," is needed. Crises occur, according to Habermas, when developments in the social sphere render the governing organizational principles inadequate to meet systemic needs. In such situations, new forms of social learning emerge in the cultural sphere through internal processes that do *not* obey a functional logic. These developments lead to a *normative* evolution which obeys a specific "developmental logic" analogous to the logic of moral evolution that Piaget and Kohlberg identify. This developmental logic can only be interpreted through "rational reconstruction" (Habermas, 1979a: 98):

> These structural patterns depict a *developmental logic* inherent in cultural traditions and institutional change.

> This logic says nothing about the *mechanisms* of development; it says something only about the range of variations within which cultural values, moral representations, norms and the like—at a given level of social organization—can be changed and can find different historical expression. In its developmental *dynamics*, the change of normative structures remains dependent on evolutionary challenges posed by unresolved, economically conditioned system problems and on learning processes that are a response to them.

The interplay between the logic and the dynamics of the development of norms can be seen in the following sequence of explanation:

(1) *Initial State*: The organizational principle of a given historical period has the necessary capacity to solve the problems of social and system integration. Example: the political class structures of medieval feudal society were generally well-suited to agrarian production and urban artisanship.

(2) *Evolutionary Challenge*: Changes in social structure create system problems which surpass the adaptive and learning capacities of the society so long as it is confined by the existing organizational principle. Example: economic problems (international trade and monetary economy) arose that could not be dealt with within the framework of the organizational principle around which medieval politics was structured.

(3) *Experimentation*: Cognitive potentialities which have developed autonomously in the cultural sphere according to an internal logic are used for social organization in an experimental manner. In this way, normative concepts are institutionalized as models for strategic action. Example: the ideas of the market and rational bureaucratic organization emerge and are tried out.

(4) *Stabilization*: If successful, the new organizational principle is institutionalized throughout society and is incorporated in fundamental legal structures. Example: a relationship among the economy, the taxing power of the state, and modern administration emerges, and complementary systems of contract, property, tax, and administrative law are created.

What makes this concept of the "organizational principle" useful for our purposes is its focus on the relationship between the legal and social structures. Fundamental legal structures—seen as incorporating organizational principles at an institutional level—are analyzed in terms of an interplay between normative structures and broader social structures. This model is consistent with Nonet and Selznick's notion of autonomous legal development, since it assumes that normative structures develop according to an autonomous evolutionary logic that can be analyzed by rational reconstruction. It adds to their theory the idea of a system/environment model that can show the influence of the dynamics of social evolution. The result is a more comprehensive model of socio-legal covariation which tells us "that in social evolution higher levels of integration can only be established insofar as legal institutions have emerged in which a moral consciousness of the . . . [higher stages] is embodied" (Habermas, 1981: 261). In this respect Habermas has found a solution to the problem which we considered to be unresolved in Nonet and Selznick's theory. The combination of two different analytical models enables him to analyze legal development in terms of both legal autonomy and social dependency.

It is from this combination that one gains the three-dimensional concept of legal rationality that we used in our preliminary definition of reflexive law (see Section II). Now we are able to more fully understand the bases of the distinction among the normative, social, and cognitive dimensions of legal rationality that we set forth there. Habermas' idea of "rational reconstruction" leads to a concept of "norm rationality" which determines the possible norms and values within a given moral and legal order. His functional or "system/environment model" supplements this internal view with a concept of "system rationality" which determines the capacity of the legal order to respond to problems of social control. Finally, norm rationality and system rationality together determine the constraints on the internal conceptual, procedural, and organizational structures of the legal system, thus defining the "internal rationality" of legal concepts.

C. *Luhmann: "Socially Adequate Complexity"*

The question of how societal organizational principles are "translated" into legal structures is left more or less open in Habermas' theory. Habermas tells us to expect to find co-variation between social and legal organizational principles, but he doesn't tell us how this congruence comes about. Luhmann's concept of the "socially adequate complexity" of legal systems is of some aid here.

By rejecting the key concepts of classical evolutionism—and in particular those of unilinearity, necessity, and progress—Luhmann (1970a; 1972a: 1, 132; 1975a: 150; 1980; 1982) develops a minimalist version of an evolutionary model. His model makes three basic assumptions regarding the dynamics, mechanisms, and directionality of systemic evolution. The dynamics of evolution derive primarily from a fundamental difference in complexity between system and environment (Luhmann, 1972a: 136):

> Evolution presupposes . . . an overproduction of possibilities in regard to which systems can be selectively maintained by structures and, on these premises, it renders probable otherwise improbable systems of order. The impulse and regulation of evolution is the complexity difference between system and environment.

This difference in complexity between a social system and its environment produces changes in the social system. Adaptation for a social system requires the development of specific evolutionary mechanisms for variation, selection, and stabilization (Luhmann, 1975a: 150). In the case of the legal system (Luhmann, 1972a: 140):

> The main source of overproduction of possibilities is the normative, i.e., the temporal dimension. The mechanism of institutionalization serves as a selection factor which chooses among new expectations those for which consensus of third parties can be presumed. Stabilization is reached by linguistic definition of a transferable meaning which can be worked into and preserved in the conceptual structure of law.

Socio-legal evolution, in Luhmann's account, is characterized by the interplay between the legal system's "endogenous" evolutionary mechanisms and the "exogenous" evolution of the society at large (Luhmann, 1972a: 132; 1970a: 7). Law, in following its internal evolutionary logic, has to adapt to specific levels of social differentiation.

Luhmann identifies three organizational principles which have dominated society at different times: segmentation, stratification, and functional differentiation. Each creates particular configurations of the legal system, and each can lead to specific "bottlenecks" of legal evolution (Luhmann, 1970a: 16).

In segmented societies, which are characterized by a "poverty of alternatives," "archaic law" faces the problem of providing for an adequate variety of normative structures. Stratified societies, organized on a hierarchical basis, have solved this problem by producing a greater variety of norms, the resulting law of pre-modern high culture. But the procedures by which decisions are made remain problematic. Finally, in functionally differentiated societies there is a massive overproduction of norms, and the corresponding "positive law" is characterized by sophisticated selection mechanisms (of which legislation is preeminent), but the law's stabilization mechanisms are still bound to traditional doctrinal concepts. Because the status of legal doctrine remains undeveloped in functionally differentiated societies, a crisis of positive law emerges (Luhmann, 1973: 130, 142; 1974: 49). The rigid normative character of modern positive law hinders the emergence of a socially adequate "learning" law. What is missing, according to Luhmann, is a "conceptual system oriented towards social policy which would permit one to compare the consequences of different solutions to problems, to accumulate critical experience, to compare experiences from different fields, in short: to learn" (Luhmann, 1970a: 19).

D. Reinterpretation of Stages of Legal Evolution

Now, having briefly described what Habermas means by the "congruence of organizational principles" and what Luhmann means by "socially adequate complexity," we shall integrate these concepts into Nonet and Selznick's concept of the "internal dynamics" of legal systems and spell out the consequences for each evolutionary stage of law. Because our particular concern is with modern legal rationality, we shall treat "repressive" and "autonomous" law only briefly.

In Nonet and Selznick's theory, the initial stage of legal development is "repressive law"—a legal order whose main function is to provide legitimation for an emerging political order (1978: 29). For Habermas as well as Luhmann, "repressive law" would represent a rather modern type of legal order, reflecting the social organizational principles of an advanced "political society" (Habermas, 1979d: 161; Luhmann, 1972a: 166). This suggests that Nonet and Selznick's typology needs to be expanded by the introduction of a pre-modern type of legal order—"archaic law"—(Luhmann, 1972a: 145), the characteristics of which cannot be subsumed under repressive, autonomous, or responsive law. Archaic law, unlike repressive law, reflects the organizational principle of segmented societies. Such societies are characterized by the predominance of kinship relations and have no state structures as such (Luhmann, 1972a: 145; cf. Habermas, 1976b: 97). Retribution and reciprocity are the main principles of archaic law, which, principally through forms of sacred law, develops concrete and rigid norms, employs ritualistic forms of procedure, and stresses expressive rather than instrumental functions (Luhmann, 1972a: 154). Archaic law will be transformed into "repressive law" only if system problems emerge which surpass the control capacity of the kinship organizational principle and lead to the development of a distinct political organization or state (Habermas, 1979d: 162).

With the emergence of a new social organizational principle (Luhmann: "stratification," 1982: 229; Habermas: "political class domination," 1979d) comes the need for the legal structure to change its character. Nonet and Selznick analyze in detail the intimate connections between the construction of systems of political power and the emergence of "repressive law" (1978: 29). Their account corresponds to Luhmann's account of "high cultural law," the structure of which reflects the supremacy of the political order in stratified societies and the corresponding hierarchical form of domination (1972a: 166). In this transition, adequate legal complexity, in Luhmann's analysis, is achieved by the institutionalization of court procedures which can cope with the much higher degree of social conflict that occurs in stratified societies (1972a: 171). Habermas' analysis of the organizational principle in stratified societies focuses on the specific type of social integration which becomes possible under "political class domination." Through the institutionalization of court procedures, a conventional morality based on the idea that behavior ought to be in accordance with preexisting rules can replace its preconventional predecessor (1979d: 161):

> This was the case when the judge, instead of being bound as a mere referee to the contingent constellations of power of the involved parties, could judge according to intersubjectively recognized legal norms sanctified by tradition, when he took the intention of the agent into account as well as the concrete consequences of action, and when he was no longer guided by the ideas of reprisal for damages caused and restoration of a status quo ante, but punished the guilty party's violation of a rule.

The law that emerges in stratified societies, Nonet and Selznick's repressive law, will, as law and society change, experience both an internal "legitimation crisis" (Nonet and Selznick, 1978: 51) and an external "system crisis" (Habermas,

1976a: 242; Luhmann, 1972a: 190), each of which contributes to the development of a more "autonomous" type of law.

"Autonomous law," as Nonet and Selznick define it, meets the Weberian requisites of formal legal rationality: the separation of law and politics, legal professionalization, strict rule-orientation, universality and precision, "artificial reasoning," and procedural justice (1978: 53; Rheinstein, 1954: 61, 301; Schluchter, 1981: 89). Autonomous law also appears to obey a specific "system rationality" as well as a specific "norm rationality" (Habermas, 1976a: 262). Its conventionality, legalism, and formality allow it to contribute to the mobilization and allocation of natural resources, a normative imperative in a developed market society. At the same time, in its universalist elements, law begins to institutionalize a postconventional norm rationality. Norms must be justified by reasoning via universal principles.[9] To explain the crisis of this modern type of law, its internal dynamics which result in pressure for increased responsiveness (Nonet and Selznick, 1978: 70) needs to be related to inadequacies of legal complexity (Luhmann, 1972a: 190) as well as to an emergent crisis of the dominant organizational principle (Habermas, 1976a: 242).

This tentative reformulation of "repressive" and "autonomous" law suggests the explanatory value of our proposed synthesis. To combine the "congruence of organizational principles" and "adequate social complexity" with the theory of "law and society in transition" requires considerable modification of the latter model. In addition to adding "archaic law," we have had to reassess "repressive" and "autonomous" law in terms of their external functions and internal structures as well as in terms of their inherent crisis tendencies. The increased richness of the resulting model should be obvious, but we must still show how this synthesis improves our understanding of "responsive law."

IV. "REFLEXIVE LAW": A NEW PROCEDURALISM

In order to show how this synthesis improves our understanding of responsive law, we must first confront the problem of how normative integration can occur in modern

[9] From Luhmann's perspective, it appears that "autonomous law" develops adequate complexity with respect to the principle of functional differentiation largely due to the phenomenon of "positivity" and the separation of judicial and legislative procedures (Luhmann, 1970b: 176; 1972a: 190).

society, given the ubiquitousness of disruptive conflicts between the different rationalities of highly specialized social subsystems (cf. Habermas, 1975; Luhmann, 1982). The efforts of Habermas and Luhmann to deal with this problem in the context of legal evolution can be interpreted so as to complement each other. On the one hand, Habermas' account of the tendency towards crisis in organized capitalism fits into the general framework of a systems theory that describes the inherent conflicts between the different rationalities of the political, economic, and cultural subsystems. On the other hand, the integrative mechanisms that Luhmann proposes for highly differentiated societies can be seen to play a role in Habermas' theory: they represent mechanisms of system integration which, in Habermas' account, need to be supplemented by mechanisms of social integration (Habermas, 1975: 113). Thus, an appreciation of Habermas and Luhmann suggests that ideas drawn from both critical theory and neo-functionalism can be used to assess the chances for the realization of responsive law.

A. Substantive Legal Rationality and the Crisis of the Interventionist State

Habermas (1975) has developed a theory of legitimation problems within organized capitalism, which can be systematically linked to the concept of responsive law. The theory argues that organized capitalism is characterized by a series of successive crises shifting between different social subsystems. Those which are economic in origin are partially resolved by state intervention, but this leads to a crisis within the political system. The emerging political legitimation problems lead, in turn, to a politicization of the cultural system with consequent cultural crises that can be resolved only by fundamental changes in normative structures (Habermas, 1975: 33). Within this framework, the crisis of formal legal rationality is closely connected to an external phenomenon: the emergence of modern state interventionism. The system rationality of Nonet and Selznick's "autonomous law," a result of the interplay among a market economy, a formal private law system, state taxation, and bureaucratic administration, is undermined as the political system increasingly takes over the responsibilities for correcting market deficiencies, for global economic policy, and for compensatory social policies (Habermas, 1975: 33). The "rematerialization" of formal law is the corollary development within the legal sphere. Law develops a substantive rationality characterized by particularism, result-orientation, an instrumentalist social policy approach, and the increasing legalization of formerly autonomous social processes (Brüggemeier, 1980: 32, 71; Eder, 1978; Unger, 1976: 192; Voigt, 1980).

Habermas' analysis of the changing role of the state in capitalism helps us understand the forces that bring about the "rematerialization of law" and contribute to the rise of substantive rationality in law. However, the trend toward substantive law is not necessarily a stable one, nor is the program of substantive legal rationality certain to be fully realized. For, according to Habermas, the trend toward substantive law encounters significant limits that make it unlikely that law can ever become fully purposive. These limits arise out of three interrelated crises which drastically limit the potential of political-legal substantive rationality (1975: 50).

First, the program of state intervention encounters what Habermas calls a "rationality crisis." This occurs because of the complexity of socio-economic processes, the contradictory imperatives of economic crisis management, and the cognitive limits of our mechanisms of political-legal control. Social processes and economic arrangements are simply too dense, complex, and potentially contradictory to be adequately accounted for in the kinds of interventionist control mechanisms that have been created. Legal and bureaucratic structures cannot incorporate models of social reality that are sufficiently rich to allow them to cope effectively with crises of economic management and similar challenges. This "rationality" crisis, which ultimately poses a threat to system integration and could endanger social integration, limits the possibilities for substantive rationalization in law and politics.[10]

Related to this is the emergence of a "legitimation" crisis in organized capitalism. Because of the growth of monopoly power and the increased role of the state in managing the economy, the market mechanism loses its power as a device which legitimates what once were portrayed as "naturally" justified distributive outcomes. To the extent that state intervention takes over the political responsibility for market substitution and market compensation, the political system becomes increasingly dependent on mass loyalty for its

[10] It is important to note that in Habermas' account, rationality and legitimation only identify crisis tendencies while the third type of crisis, the motivation crisis, reveals a necessary conflict between the political and the cultural system.

politico-economic decisions. However, the political production of legitimizing ideologies is limited, according to Habermas, by the resistance of normative structures (1975: 68). The inherent "developmental logic" of the cultural system thus necessarily creates a third problem, a "motivation crisis," which sets effective limits to the substantive rationality of the welfare state (Habermas, 1975: 75).

In Habermas' view, only a "discursive" rationality emerging from autonomous evolutionary processes in the normative sphere could finally resolve the legitimation problems of the modern state (1975: 95). This view is based on a theory of political legitimation which asserts that irreversible developments in the normative sphere mean that modern principles of legitimation must be procedural (Habermas, 1976b: 184):

> Since ultimate grounds can no longer be made plausible, the *formal conditions of justification themselves obtain legitimating force*. The procedures and presuppositions of rational agreement themselves become principles.

The subsequent question of institutionalization, i.e., the question of which organizational structures and which discussion and decision mechanisms can produce procedurally legitimate outcomes, depends on "concrete social and political conditions, on scopes of disposition, on information and so forth" (Habermas, 1979b: 186). Habermas' own proposals to institutionalize procedural legitimation include the notion of "organizational democracy" in labor unions, public associations, and functional elites, participatory mechanisms in various social subsystems, mainly in the educational and cultural sector, and a "pragmatistic dialogue model" for an institutionalized cooperation among science, politics, and the public (Habermas, 1962: 228, 269; 1969: 202; 1970: 62; 1973: 9).

This program for the "democratization of social subsystems" has substantial affinities with Nonet and Selznick's concept of responsive law. Responsive law, they tell us, requires broad political participation and institutional redesigns that ensure the adequate representation of various interests in the core organizations of society (Nonet and Selznick, 1978: 95; Selznick, 1969: Ch. 7). However, the affinities between Habermas and Nonet and Selznick exist only with respect to those elements in responsive law that involve what we have called reflexive rationality. If we accept Habermas' analysis, the capacity of responsive law to deal with legitimation problems in post-modern society varies according to the circumstances.

To the extent that responsive law is based on the expansion of substantive rationality, it must encounter the limits set by the crises of rationality, legitimacy, and motivation. These render it unlikely that the substantive or purposive dimension of the responsive law amalgam will ever be realized.

The reflexive rationality component is the strong point of responsive law. As we have noted, reflexive rationality in law obeys a logic of procedural legitimation. This orientation, Habermas suggests, reflects the emerging organizational principle of post-modern society. In a recent publication Habermas (1981) makes an important distinction between law as "medium" and law as "institution." As a medium, law, in a sense, is an independent socio-technological decisional process which replaces the communicative structures that exist within the "life-world" of social subsystems, and so allocates goods according to its own criteria. As an "institution," law functions merely as an "external constitution" for the spheres of socialization, social integration, and cultural reproduction. When it serves as an "institution," law facilitates rather than endangers the self-regulatory processes of communication and learning. Since this facilitative role is congruent with emergent forms of discursive rationality, reflexive law, with its procedural orientation, seems well-suited to the legitimation problems of post-modern society.

B. *Reflexive Legal Rationality in Functionally Differentiated Societies*

So far, we have examined the concept of responsive law in the context of "critical theory." If we translate our problem into the language of the neo-functionalist system theory that Luhmann has developed in the Durkheim-Parsons tradition, we find that the same set of problems appears—although in even more abstract and comprehensive perspective. "Crisis tendencies in organized capitalism" are now interpreted as particular cases of a more general phenomenon. The functional differentiation of society, so Luhmann tells us (1972a: 190; 1982), induces highly specialized subsystems to develop their own specific rationality to such a degree that radical system conflicts are inevitable. "Motivation crisis"—in Habermas' terms the contemporary *Grundwiderspruch* (basic contradiction) between the logic of state-interventionism and the logic of cultural development—now appears as marginal among a variety of equally basic or even more fundamental conflicts. These clashes include those between universal social structures (economy, science) and territorially-bound political and legal structures, between scientific planning and economic production control, and between the temporal requirements of social interdependencies and the slow-developing processes of education and institutionalization (Luhmann, 1971: 374). Finally, the quest for responsive law, emerging from a crisis of formal legal rationality, is now seen in the context of one overriding problem: How does the legal system participate in and react to the secular processes of functional differentiation (Luhmann, 1970a; 1972a: 190)?

In this perspective, Max Weber's description of modern law as "formally rational" seems misleading since the concepts of form and substance are almost interchangeable in the comparison between traditional and modern law (Luhmann, 1972a: 17). Rather, the notion of "autonomous law," in Nonet and Selznick's sense, points to the crucial changes of functional differentiation: the increasing autonomy of the legal system, its separation from moral and scientific structures, and its relative independence from political processes (Trubek, 1977: 540). It is in these developments that the features of legal formalism emerge: strict rule-orientation, professional (artificial) reasoning, and the prominence of procedure (Buss, 1982: 114; Luhmann, 1972b: 207). The "crisis" of autonomous law exists because law, particularly in its conceptual structures, has not yet adapted to the exigencies of a highly differentiated society. Legal doctrine is still bound to the classical model of law as a body of rules enforceable through adjudication. The legal order lacks a conceptual apparatus adequate for the planning and social policy requirements that arise in the interrelations among specialized social subsystems (Luhmann, 1972b: 325).

"Substantive legal rationality," in Max Weber's sense of the term, is supposed to solve the crisis by a remoralization and repoliticization of law, but it appears from this perspective as a clearly regressive tendency. A renewed fusion of the law with the scientific, moral, and political sphere would destroy the specific juridical rationality without replacing it with a new one (Luhmann, 1974: 31). In Luhmann's account as in Habermas', a thoroughgoing "rematerialization" of law would inevitably lead to a rationality crisis of the political-legal system since the various social subsystems in a functionally differentiated society have developed such a high degree of internal complexity that none of them—whether politics, science, economy, morals, or law, either alone or in combination—could evolve the necessary control capacity. Thus, if the substantive dimension of responsive law were to become the dominant feature of the modern legal order, the result would be a regressive dedifferentiation of society, rather than its reintegration.

To achieve integration under conditions of extreme functional differentiation, the different subsystems must, according to Luhmann, be mutually supportive. "[T]hey have not only to fulfill adequately their function, but to stand in a meaningful relation of compatibility to the functions and structural achievements of other systems for which they form an environment" (Luhmann, 1974: 88). Functional differentiation requires a displacement of integrative mechanisms from the level of the society to the level of the subsystems (Luhmann, 1982: 229). Centralized social integration is effectively ruled out today and cannot be achieved by legal, economic, moral, or scientific mechanisms. A decentralized mode of integration is inevitable because to maximize the rationality of one subsystem is to create insoluble problems in other functional systems. To avoid this, "*corresponding restrictions must be built into the reflexion structure of every functional subsystem, insofar as they do not result directly from ongoing relations with its environment*" (Luhmann, 1977: 245). Thus, "reflexion" structures are the key to determining how responsive law can play a role in functionally differentiated societies. The matter needs some clarification.

In Luhmann's theory, each subsystem has open to it three different orientations: (1) towards the entire social system in terms of its *function*; (2) towards other societal subsystems in terms of input and output *performances*; and (3) towards itself in terms of *reflexion* (Luhmann, 1982: 229). It is the incompatibility of these orientations which is crucial. They cannot, Luhmann tells us, be subsumed under a common purpose. In the political system, for instance, there is an inherent tension between social function (the formulation and execution of binding decisions) and performance (the guarding of power resources and the promotion of legitimation) that can be reconciled only internally by processes of political reflexion (focusing on what politics is all about and so imposing limits on what may be done in the name of rendering decisions and preserving power) (Luhmann, 1982: 229).

It is the task of reflexion structures in any social subsystem to resolve conflicts between function and performance by imposing internal restrictions on given subsystems so that they are suitable as components of the environment of other subsystems (Luhmann, 1977: 245): "Reflexion must mediate between performance and function, since for the subsystem, society represents the encompassing system as well as the social environment" (Luhmann, 1979: 176). By reconciling tensions between function and performance, reflexion structures within social subsystems become the main integration mechanisms in functionally differentiated societies. From this theoretical perspective, responsive law needs to develop "reflexive dimensions" if it is to work as an integrative mechanism (Assmann, 1980: 122).

C. *The Point of Convergence: Internal Reflexion and Discursive Democracy in Social Subsystems*

The theoretical approaches that have concerned us thus far converge on the "reflexive" dimension of responsive law. Our translation of responsive law into the languages of neo-functionalism and critical theory has led us to assess skeptically the viability of substantive legal rationality under modern conditions. At the same time, our interpretation of Nonet and Selznick's theory allowed us to identify an important connection between Habermas' procedural concept of legitimation and Luhmann's theory of internal system reflexion. Putting the various elements we have discussed together, our theses are: (1) Reflexion within social subsystems is possible only insofar as processes of democratization create discursive structures within these subsystems. (2) The primary function of the democratization of subsystems lies neither in increasing individual participation nor in neutralizing power structures but in the internal reflexion of social identity.

Before dealing with the role that reflexive law has to play vis-à-vis other subsystems, let us consider the role of reflexion and the limits it imposes within the legal system. This can be most easily seen by considering how the threefold typology, function, performance, and reflexion, applies to the legal system. The function of law can be defined as its capacity to provide congruent generalizations of expectations for the whole of society (Luhmann, 1972a: 94). Its performance is to resolve conflicts which are produced in other social subsystems and which cannot be resolved there (Bohannon, 1967). These orientations both overlap and conflict. The production of congruent normative generalizations may not suffice to provide rules that are well-suited to resolve concrete conflicts, and the legal system, by the processes of conflict resolution, may produce norms which cannot be congruently generalized. It is the role of legal reflexion to reconcile the inherent tensions between function and performance by imposing internal restrictions on the capacities of the legal system.

It is our thesis that law can best do this by imposing restrictions on the legal performance dimension. Instead of the comprehensive regulation of substantive legal rationality, reflexive law restricts legal performance to more indirect, more abstract forms of social control.

What is crucial is the structural correspondence between legal norms and the opportunity structure within social subsystems. Substantive legal rationality does not take sufficient account of this necessary correspondence. It attempts to regulate social structures by legal norms, even though these structures do not always or easily bend to legal regulation.

Aspects of modern educational and welfare systems provide striking examples (Voigt, 1980). In these fields, the current critique of legalization has shown again and again that substantive legal programs obey a functional logic and follow criteria of rationality and patterns of organization which are poorly suited to the internal social structure of the regulated spheres of life. In consequence, law as a medium of the welfare state either turns out to be ineffective or it works effectively but at the price of destroying traditional patterns of social life (Habermas, 1981: 542).

A reflexive orientation does not ask whether there are social problems to which the law must be responsive. Instead it seeks to identify opportunity structures that allow legal regulation to cope with social problems without, at the same time, irreversibly destroying valued patterns of social life.

This brings us to the question of how autonomous reflexion imposes limits on the scope of legality and defines the role of law vis-à-vis other social subsystems. One possibility in vogue today is the policy of the deregulation or reformalization of substantive law. Another one is the policy of proceduralization under which the legal system concerns itself with providing the structural premises for self-regulation within other social subsystems (cf. Moore, 1973: 720; Galanter, 1980: 21). What is involved here is not only the guarantee of autonomy for other social subsystems, but also Habermas' concept of the "democratization of social subsystems," which—with its stress on procedural legitimation—shows the direction in which reflexive law can develop.

Recall Habermas' distinction between law as "medium" and law as an "institution." Although law as a "medium" of societal guidance endangers the communicative structures of the legalized spheres of social life, law as an "institution" rooted in the core morality of a given society may facilitate communicative processes by guaranteeing the "external constitution" of the communicatively structured social sphere. Law as an "external constitution" can promote "discursive decision processes and consensus-oriented procedures of negotiation and decision" (Habermas, 1981: 544). It does so by providing norms of procedure, organization, and competences that aid other social systems in achieving the democratic self-organization and self-regulation which, according to Habermas, are at the heart of procedural legitimacy. Reflexive law, in other words, will neither authoritatively determine the social functions of other subsystems nor regulate their input and output performances, but will foster mechanisms that systematically *further the development of reflexion structures within other social subsystems*.

However, in the light of functional differentiation, one can no longer hope for universal legitimation structures, for a generally applicable morality of discourse, or for a common procedure of reflexion. The legal prerequisites for reflexion processes in, for example, the economy or in politics differ greatly from what will be required by the educational system. Thus, law must act at the subsystem-specific level to install, correct, and redefine democratic self-regulatory mechanisms. Law's role is to decide about decisions, regulate regulations, and establish structural premises for future decisions in terms of organization, procedure, and competencies. Specific outcomes in other subsystems will be influenced by law's role in setting the parameters for decision making, but they will not be legal mandates, for law would not have determined them. This vision of the legal order may be summed up in a sentence: *Law realizes its own reflexive orientation insofar as it provides the structural premises for reflexive processes in other social subsystems*. This is the integrative function of contemporary responsive law.

D. *A New Legal Self-Restraint: Developmental Chances in Modern Private Law*

To be sure, the "result" we have reached is merely hypothetical in nature. That responsive law develops potentialities for a substantive and a reflexive rationality and that this potential is differentially actualized under the differing conditions of post-modern societies is nothing more than a hypothesis derived from theories of socio-legal development. Borrowing "internal" variables from the theory of responsive law and "external" variables from concepts of post-modern society in critical theory and neo-functionalism, we have sketched a model of socio-legal interrelation and have arrived at the proposition that responsive law can respond to the challenges of post-modern society if it succeeds in developing a "reflexive" legal rationality. This hypothesis rests on a number of highly speculative (and debatable) theoretical assumptions. It must withstand strong empirical testing before it might claim any "validity." However, we can lend some empirical support to our thesis by pointing to recent legal trends in which we can recognize the outlines of "reflexive" legal structures, although we have to acknowledge that the "fallacy of misplaced concreteness" is almost inevitable.

Consider again the development of contract law. A trend towards substantive legal rationality is obvious in legislative definitions of minimal conditions and judicial concern with the substance of agreements (Friedman, 1959). Yet, if this trend is to involve more than marginal correction of the formal approach, it will encounter conditions that impose limits on the capacity of the legal system, some of which are already visible today.[11] Labor law, in contrast, is, with respect to collective bargaining, characterized to some degree by a more abstract control technique in which we can recognize a "reflexive" potential. The legal regulation of collective bargaining operates principally by shaping the organization of collective bargaining, defining procedural norms, and limiting or expanding the competencies of the collective actors. Law attempts to balance bargaining power, but this only indirectly controls specific results.

Corresponding efforts at constructing systems of countervailing powers in other spheres, particularly in consumer protection law, have not fared so well (Hart and

[11] This is recognized even by authors who have argued emphatically for a deformalization of modern contract law; cf. Wiethölter (1982: 5).

Joerges, 1980: 83). However, functional parallels might be found in the "artificial" creation of autonomous semi-public institutions (e.g., in Germany the "Stiftung-Warentest" or "Verbraucherzentrale") which provide consumer information and political-legal representation for unorganized social interests (Hart and Joerges, 1980). The role of state law is, again, not substantive regulation but the procedural and organizational structuring of "autonomous" social processes. Organizations are fostered to give consumers a voice. To paraphrase Joerges (1981: 23): the law does not authoritatively decide what constitutes the consumer's interest; it restricts itself to defining competences for the articulation of consumer interests and to securing their representation. The task of the legal system is neither to develop its own purposive program nor to decide goal conflicts between competing policies. It is to guarantee coordination processes and to compel agreement. To these observations one may add the fact that the law can help resolve inter-system conflicts by arbitrating claims across sectors and settling boundary problems.

Perhaps consumer law provides a shaky example of reflexive law at work because it is an example of the limits of the strategy we have called "external decentralization." This strategy necessarily fails if social asymmetries of power and information can resist institutional attempts at equalization. One solution is for law to develop in itself "reflexive" structures which can compensate for inequality of power and information, thus supplementing the operation of decentralized systems through modes of compensatory legal logic. It is possible to interpret the developments of certain "general clauses" or standards as evidence of a reflexive logic within doctrine. For example, even though standards like "good faith" or "public policy" are usually regarded as instruments of substantive judicial interventionism, they might be seen as a means of "socialization of contract" quite different from what is traditionally thought of as state intervention (Teubner, 1981). Using standards like good faith and public policy to compensate for irreducible inequities at, for example, the level of concrete interaction between contractual partners or the level of market and organization, as well as at the societal level, where there is an interplay among politics, economics, culture, and law, is "reflexive" insofar as the legal system itself "simulates" processes of social self-regulation. This means that, in the case of "interaction deficiencies" between contracting parties, objective purposes and duties are defined authoritatively by virtue of law; in the case of "market deficiencies," commercial customs are replaced by the judicial definition of market behavior rules; and in the case of "political deficiencies," the judicial process defines standards of public policy. Common to these examples is a logic of internal simulation. An actual deficiency in subsystem mechanisms of self-regulation is presumed, and the general clause of "good faith" or "public policy" is interpreted as a command to simulate within the legal system self-regulatory processes—as they might exist—internal to non-legal subsystems. Obviously, such a simulation has it own deficiencies. It can be perverted easily into a sheer moralistic appeal, and its cognitive and procedural adequacy is unclear.

The law of private organizations provides a further example. Here again we find tendencies to "substantialize" the formal classical-liberal law, which was restricted to providing politically neutral forms for private organizations. Today, judicial control and state regulation of associational behavior seem to reach the limits of their control capacity. Our approach suggests a quite different strategy to deal with the deficiencies of the current system, namely, the creation of legal structures which systematically strengthen "reflexion mechanisms" within the organization. "Constitutionalization" of the association might make the "organizational conscience" work if it effectively forces the organization to "internalize" outside conflicts in its own decision structure (see Stone, 1975). In this context, the traditional meaning of the "democratization of social institutions" is transformed. The main goal is neither power-equalization nor an increase of individual participation in the emphatic sense of "participatory democracy." Rather, it is the design of organizational structures which makes the institutions—corporations, semi-public associations, mass media, educational institutions—sensitive to the outside effects of their attempts to maximize internal rationality. Its main function is to substitute for outside interventionist control an effective internal control structure (Teubner, 1978b).

E. Some Implications for "Sociological Jurisprudence": Legal Constructions of Social Reality

These examples are intended to illustrate what it means for the law to orient its structure toward a reflexive rationality. Further questions arise concerning the "cognitive competence" of a reflexive legal system, an issue of importance in the theory of "responsive law" (Nonet and Selznick, 1978: 78, 104, 112).

This is a field where future research is needed. Here it is only possible to sketch lines of argumentation that need to be developed in depth. If it is true that legal reflexive processes contribute to social integration insofar as they mediate between performance and function within the legal system, the structural conditions of this legal self-reflexion, particularly in their cognitive aspects, are of crucial importance. Among these conditions, "internal models of reality" play a central role. The relevance of such models—containing descriptive as well as normative elements—for guiding decision processes has been increasingly acknowledged in decision theory as well as in legal theory (Assmann, 1980; Collins, 1976; Galanter, 1980: 12; Reale, 1970; Stachowiak, 1973; Teubner, 1978a). Dworkin, for instance, has developed the thesis that, in the interaction of norms and principles, the judge utilizes—implicitly or explicitly—"political theories" in order to justify the decision of "hard cases" (Dworkin, 1977: 81, 90). More generally, one can reconstruct "theories" of social reality out of legal norms, court opinions, and doctrinal considerations, which in turn serve as a kind of background information, or, to use the hermeneutical phrase, a "preunderstanding" ("Vorverständnis"). For example, legal concepts of contract, of association, or of state-society relations are rooted in peculiarly legal perceptions of social reality. These perceptions differ significantly from our day-to-day understanding of these phenomena as well as from sociological or economic theories. The legal system develops certain specific "social constructions of reality" (Berger and Luckmann, 1966) in order to decide social conflicts under the guidance of legal norms. In creating its own reality from the perspective imposed by the exigencies of conflict resolution, the legal system abstracts highly selective models of the world, thereby neglecting many politically, economically, and socially "relevant" elements.

Obviously, these models change their character in the course of legal development, and there will be covariation between legal model construction and types of legal rationality. Thus, there remains the question of how "rematerialization" has forced formal law to change its perceptions of social reality, and we must also identify the kind of legal model-building required by reflexive legal rationality.

"Sociological Jurisprudence" and related movements in legal theory (Freirechtschule, Interessenjurisprudenz) should be interpreted as methodological corollaries of the rematerialization of formal law (e.g., Heck, 1968; Pound, 1910/11:

591; 1911/12: 140, 489; 1943/44: 1). They attack legal formalism not merely for its conceptualism, as a reading of their criticisms of "mechanical jurisprudence" might suggest, but for its very construction of social reality. Formal legal rationality and sociological jurisprudence were *fundamentally* incompatible because the former conceived of legal actors as abstracted from the world, thus allowing the assertion that taking account of social, economic, and political aspects is not a task for the "lawyer as such" (Windscheid, 1904: 101).

Substantive legal rationality has required a "rescientification" of legal perceptions of reality precisely in the sense which formed the main methodological concern of sociological jurisprudence. This type of sociological jurisprudence, however, is bound to the crisis of substantive legal rationality that we have analyzed in the framework of neo-functionalism and critical theory. If taken seriously, such a sociological jurisprudence requires encompassing models of reality which have to integrate social science theories to a degree that enables the law to take over responsibility for comprehensive planning processes. Legal analysis then tends to be transformed into a full-fledged social policy analysis, which requires an adequate description of the real situation, the perception of problems, the definition of goals, the selection of legal norms, and the implementation of norms in social reality (cf. Lindblom and Cohen, 1979: 30). Obviously, the complexity of the underlying models that would be required for the law to achieve these ends will rapidly surpass the cognitive competence of any existing legal system, even one based on a profound interdisciplinary analysis (Luhmann, 1974: 31).

It seems that sociological jurisprudence—like decision theory—needs to develop a concept of "bounded rationality" in order to construct workable models of reality that are of practical use for legal decision processes (March and Simon, 1966; Simon, 1976). Perhaps an additional role of reflexive processes in the legal system is to define legal self-restraint in the context of building models of social reality.

Reflexive legal rationality requires the legal system to view itself as a system-in-an-environment (Assmann, 1980: 333; Luhmann, 1979: 161) and to take account of the limits of its own capacity as it attempts to regulate the functions and performances of other social subsystems. Thus, its relation to social science knowledge is characterized neither by "reception" nor by "separation." Instead, the relationship involves the "translation" of social knowledge from one social context to the other according to certain translation rules, i.e., specific legal criteria of selectivity (cf. Teubner, 1978a: 27; Walz, 1980). If it is true that law fulfills its integrative function by furthering reflexive processes in other social subsystems, the social knowledge required by the legal system is very specific and the need for model construction is much more limited than it would be in a comprehensive "planning" law. Reflexive law needs to utilize and develop only that knowledge necessary to the control of self-regulatory processes in different contexts. Thus, encompassing social policy models may be replaced by models of how to combine the insights of socio-legal analysis and the dynamics of interaction processes for social problem solving. If the analysis of this paper is correct, the generation of such models is an important next step in the evolutionary development of law.

REFERENCES

ABEL, Richard L. (1980) "Delegalization: A Critical Review of Its Ideology, Manifestations and Social Consequences," in E. Blankenburg, E. Klausa and H. Rottleuthner (eds.), *Alternative Rechtsformen und Alternativen zum Recht*. Opladen: Westdeutscher Verlag.

——— (1982) *The Politics of Informal Justice*. New York: Academic Press.

ASSMANN, Heinz-Dieter (1980) *Wirtschaftsrecht in der Mixed Economy. Auf der Suche nach einem Sozialmodell für das Wirtschaftsrecht*. Frankfurt: Athenäum.

ASSMANN, Heinz-Dieter, Gert BRÜGGEMEIER, Dieter HART and Christian JOERGES (1980) *Wirtschaftsrecht als Kritik des Privatrechts*. Königstein: Athenäum.

BERGER, Peter and Thomas LUCKMANN (1966) *The Social Construction of Reality*. Garden City: Doubleday.

BLANKENBURG, Erhard, Ekkehard KLAUSA and Hubert ROTTLEUTHNER (eds.) (1980) *Alternative Rechtsformen und Alternativen zum Recht*. Opladen: Westdeutscher Verlag.

BOHANNON, Paul (1967) "The Differing Realms of Law," in P. Bohannon (ed.), *Law and Warfare*. Garden City: The Natural History Press.

BREYER, Stephen (1982) *Regulation and its Reform*. Cambridge, MA: Harvard University Press.

BRÜGGEMEIER, Gert (1980) "Probleme einer Theorie des Wirtschaftsrechts," in H.-D. Assmann, G. Brüggemeier, D. Hart and C. Joerges, *Wirtschaftsrecht als Kritik des Privatrechts*. Königstein: Athenäum.

——— (1982) "Drei Modelle der Verflechtung von Staat und Wirtschaft," in V. Gessner and G. Winter (eds.), *Rechtsformen der Verflechtung von Staat und Wirtschaft*. Opladen: Westdeutscher Verlag 60.

BUSS, Eugen (1982) "Das Rechtssystem in komplexen Gesellschaften," 13 *Rechtstheorie* 114.

CAIN, Maureen (1980) "The Limits of Idealism: Max Weber and the Sociology of Law," 3 *Research in Law and Sociology* 53.

COLLINS, Lyndhurst (ed.) (1976) *The Use of Models in Social Sciences*. Boulder: Westview Press.

DURKHEIM, Emile (1933) *The Division of Labor in Society*. New York: Free Press.

DWORKIN, Ronald (1977) *Taking Rights Seriously*. Cambridge, MA: Harvard University Press.

EDER, Klaus (1978) "Zur Rationalisierungsproblematik des modernen Rechts," 29 *Soziale Welt* 247.

EDER, Klaus, Günther FRANKENBERG, Ulrich RÖDEL and Ernst TUGENDHAT (1978) *Die Entwicklung von Gerechtigkeitsvorstellungen im modernen Recht als soziologisches Problem*. Starnberg: Typoscript.

ELY, John Hart (1980) *Democracy and Distrust*. Cambridge: Harvard University Press.

ERD, Rainer (1978) *Verrechtlichung industrieller Konflikte. Normative Rahmenbedingungen des dualen Systems der Interessenvertretung*. Frankfurt: Campus.

ESSER, Josef (1970) *Vorverständnis und Methodenwahl*. Frankfurt: Athenäum.

FRIEDMAN, Lawrence (1973) *A History of American Law*. New York: Simon and Schuster.

——— (1975) *The Legal System: A Social Science Perspective*. New York: Simon and Schuster.

FRIEDMAN, Wolfgang (1959) *Law in a Changing Society*. Berkeley: University of California Press.

GALANTER, Marc (1980) "Legality and Its Discontents: A Preliminary Assessment of Current Theories of Legalization and Delegalization," in E. Blankenburg, E. Klausa and H. Rottleuthner (eds.), *Alternative Rechtsformen und Alternativen zum Recht*. Opladen: Westdeutscher Verlag.

GOTTHOLD, Jürgen (1982) "Privatisierung oder Entbürokratisierung kommunaler Sozialpolitik," in R. Voigt, *Entrechtlichung*. Königstein: Athenäum.

GROSER, Manfred (1979) "Stabilität und Wandel im System der Arbeitsbeziehungen," 20 *Politische Vierteljahresschrift* 258.

HABERMAS, Jürgen (1962) *Strukturwandel der Öffentlichkeit*. Neuwied: Luchterhand.

——— (1969) "Für ein neues Konzept der Hochschulverfassung," in J. Habermas, *Protestbewegung und Hochschulreform*. Frankfurt: Suhrkamp.

——— (1970) "The Scientization of Politics and Public Opinion," in J. Habermas, *Toward a Rational Society*. Boston: Beacon.

——— (1971) "Luhmanns Beitrag zu einer Theorie der gesellschaftlichen Evolution," in J. Habermas and N. Luhmann, *Theorie der Gesellschaft oder Sozialtechnologie*. Frankfurt: Suhrkamp.

——— (1973) "Zum Begriff der politischen Beteiligung" (1958), in J. Habermas, *Kultur und Kritik*. Frankfurt: Suhrkamp.

——— (1975) *Legitimation Crisis*. Boston: Beacon.

——— (1976a) "Geschichte und Evolution," in J. Habermas, *Zur Rekonstruktion des Historischen Materialismus*. Frankfurt: Suhrkamp.

——— (1976b) "Können komplexe Gesellschaften eine vernünftige Identität ausbilden?" in J. Habermas, *Zur Rekonstruktion des Historischen Materialismus*. Frankfurt: Suhrkamp.

——— (1976c) "Überlegungen zum evolutionären Stellenwert des modernen Rechts," in J. Habermas, *Zur Rekonstruktion des Historischen Materialismus*. Frankfurt: Suhrkamp.

——— (1976d) "Zum Theorienvergleich in der Soziologie: am Beispiel der Theorie der sozialen Evolutionstheorie," in J. Habermas, *Zur Rekonstruktion des Historischen Materialismus*. Frankfurt: Suhrkamp.

——— (1976e) "Zur Rekonstruktion des Historischen Materialismus," in J. Habermas, *Zur Rekonstruktion des Historischen Materialismus*. Frankfurt: Suhrkamp.

——— (1979a) "Historical Materialism and the Development of Normative Structures," in J. Habermas, *Communication and the Evolution of Society*. Boston: Beacon.

——— (1979b) "Legitimation Problems in the Modern State," in J. Habermas, *Communication and the Evolution of Society*. Boston: Beacon.

——— (1979c) "Moral Development and Ego Identity," in J. Habermas, *Communication and the Evolution of Society*. Boston: Beacon.

——— (1979d) "Toward a Reconstruction of Historical Materialism," in J. Habermas, *Communication and the Evolution of Society*. Boston: Beacon.

——— (1981) *Theorie des kommunikativen Handelns*. Frankfurt: Suhrkamp.

HABERMAS, Jürgen and Niklas LUHMANN (1971) *Theorie der Gesellschaft oder Sozialtechnologie—Was leistet die Systemforschung?* Frankfurt: Suhrkamp.

HART, Dieter and Christian JOERGES (1980) "Verbraucherrecht und Marktökonomik: Eine Kritik ordnungstheoretischer Eingrenzung der Verbraucherpolitik," in H.-D. Assmann, G. Brüggemeier, D. Hart and C.

Joerges, *Wirtschaftsrecht als Kritik des Privatrechts*. Königstein: Athenäum.
HECK, Philipp (1968) *Das Problem der Rechtsgewinnung. Gesetzesauslegung und Interessenjurisprudenz. Begriffsbildung und Interessenjurisprudenz*. Bad Homburg: Gehlen.
HEJL, Peter M. (1982) *Sozialwissenschaft als Theorie Selbstreferentieller Systeme*. Frankfurt: Campus.
HELLER, Thomas (1979) "Is the Charitable Exemption from Property Taxation an Easy Case? General Concerns About Legal Economics and Jurisprudence," in D. Rubinfeld (ed.), *Essays on the Law and Economics of Local Governments*. Washington D.C.: Urban Institute.
HEYDEBRAND, Wolf von (1982) "Die Technokratisierung des Rechts und der Justizverwaltung," in V. Gessner and G. Winter (eds.), *Rechtsformen der Verflechtung von Staot und Wirtschaft*. Opladen: Westdeutscher Verlag 93.
JOERGES, Christian (1981) *Verbraucherschutz als Rechtsproblem*. Heidelberg: Recht und Wirtschaft.
KALBERG, Stephen (1980) "Max Weber's Types of Rationality: Cornerstones for the Analysis of Rationalization Processes in History," 85 *American Journal of Sociology* 1145.
KENNEDY, Duncan (1973) "Legal Formality," 2 *Journal of Legal Studies* 351.
——— (1976) "Form and Substance in Private Law Adjudication," 89 *Harvard Law Review* 1685.
LADEUR, Karl-Heinz (1982) "Verrechtlichung der Ökonomie—Ökonomisierung des Rechts?" in V. Gessner and G. Winter (eds.), *Rechtsformen der Verflechtung von Staat und Wirtschaft*. Opladen: Westdeutscher Verlag 74.
LEHNER, Franz (1979) *Grenzen des Regierens*. Königstein: Athenäum.
LINDBLOM, Charles E. and David K. COHEN (1979) *Usable Knowledge: Social Science and Social Problem Solving*. New Haven: Yale.
LUHMANN, Niklas (1970a) "Evolution des Rechts," 3 *Rechtstheorie* 1.
——— (1970b) "Positivität des Rechts als Voraussetzung einer modernen Gesellschaft," 1 *Jahrbuch für Rechtssoziologie und Rechtstheorie* 176.
——— (1970c) "Reflexive Mechanismen," in N. Luhmann, *Soziologische Aufklärung 1*. Opladen: Westdeutscher Verlag.
——— (1971) "Systemtheoretische Argumentationen. Eine Entgegnung auf Jürgen Habermas," in J. Habermas and N. Luhmann, *Theorie der Gesellschaft oder Sozialtechnologie*. Frankfurt: Suhrkamp.
——— (1972a) *Rechtssoziologie 1*. Reinbek: Rowohlt.
——— (1972b) *Rechtssoziologie 2*. Reinbek: Rowohlt.
——— (1973) "Gerechtigkeit in den Rechtssystemen der modernen Gesellschaft," 4 *Rechtstheorie* 130.
——— (1974) *Rechtssystem und Rechtsdogmatik*. Stuttgart: Kohlhammer.
——— (1975a) "Evolution und Geschichte," in N. Luhmann, *Soziologische Aufklärung 2*. Opladen: Westdeutscher Verlag.
——— (1975b) "Die Weltgesellschaft," in N. Luhmann, *Soziologische Aufklärung 2*. Opladen: Westdeutscher Verlag.
——— (1977) *Funktion der Religion*. Frankfurt: Suhrkamp.
——— (1979) "Selbstreflexion des Rechtssystems," 10 *Rechtstheorie* 176.
——— (1980) *Gesellschaftsstruktur und Semantik*, Vol. 1. Frankfurt: Suhrkamp.
——— (1981a) *Gesellschaftsstruktur und Semantik*, Vol. 2. Frankfurt: Suhrkamp.
——— (1981b) *Politische Theorie im Wohlfahrtsstaat*. München: Olzog.
——— (1982) *The Differentiation of Society*. New York: Columbia University Press.
MARCH, James G. and Herbert SIMON (1966) *Organizations*. New York: Wiley.
MAYNTZ, Renate (1979) "Regulative Politik in der Krise," in Joachim Matthes (ed.), *Sozialer Wandel in Westeuropa*. Frankfurt: Campus.
MITNICK, Barry (1980) *The Political Economy of Regulation*. New York: Columbia University Press.
MOORE, Sally F. (1973) "Law and Social Change: The Semi-Autonomous Social Field as an Appropriate Object of Study," 7 *Law & Society Review* 719.
NEUMANN, Franz (1967) "Der Funktionswandel des Gesetzes im Recht der bürgerlichen Gesellschaft," in F. Neumann, *Demokratischer und autoritärer Staat*. Frankfurt: Europäische Verlagsanstalt.

NONET, Philippe and Philip SELZNICK (1978) *Law and Society in Transition: Toward Responsive Law*. New York: Harper.

PATEMAN, Carol (1970) *Participation and Democratic Theory*. Cambridge: Cambridge University Press.

POUND, Roscoe (1910/11) "The Scope and Purpose of Sociological Jurisprudence," 24 *Harvard Law Review* 591.

——— (1911/12) "The Scope and Purpose of Sociological Jurisprudence," 25 *Harvard Law Review* 140, 489.

——— (1943/44) "A Survey of Social Interests," 57 *Harvard Law Review* 1.

RADBRUCH, Gustav (1965) *Vorschule der Rechtsphilosophie*. Göttingen: Vandenhoeck.

REALE, Miguel (1970) "Pour une théorie des modèles juridiques," 5 *Acts of IV International Congress for Philosophy* 144.

REHBINDER, Manfred (1967) "Status—Kontrakt—Rolle," in *Festschrift für Ernst E. Hirsch*. Berlin: Duncker.

RHEINSTEIN, Max (1954) *Max Weber on Law in Economy and Society*. Cambridge: Harvard University Press.

ROTTLEUTHNER, Hubert (1973) *Rechtswissenschaft als Sozialwissenschaft*. Frankfurt: Fischer.

SELZNICK, Philip (1968) "Law: The Sociology of Law," 9 *International Encyclopedia of the Social Sciences* 50.

——— (1969) *Law, Society and Industrial Justice*. New York: Russell Sage.

SCHELSKY, Helmut (1980) "Die Soziologen und das Recht," in H. Schelsky, *Die Soziologen und das Recht*. Opladen: Westdeutscher Verlag.

SCHLUCHTER, Wolfgang (1981) *The Rise of Western Rationalism: Max Weber's Developmental History*. Berkeley: University of California Press.

SCHMIDT, Eike (1980) "Von der Privat—zur Sozialautonomie," 35 *Juristenzeitung* 153.

SIMON, Herbert (1976) *Administrative Behavior*. New Haven: Yale.

STACHOWIAK, Herbert (1973) *Allgemeine Modelltheorie*. New York: Springer.

STONE, Christopher (1975) *Where the Law Ends: The Social Control of Corporate Behavior*. New York: Harper.

STREECK, Wolfgang (1979) "Gewerkschaftsorganisation und industrielle Beziehungen," in J. Matthes (ed.), *Sozialer Wandel in Westeuropa*. Frankfurt: Campus.

STREECK, Wolfgang, P. SEGLOW and P. BAYLEY (1978) *Railway Unions in Britain and West Germany: Structural Sources of Crossnational Differences and Similarities*. Berlin: Wissenschaftszentrum.

TEUBNER, Gunther (1978a) "Generalklauseln als sozio-normative Modelle," in Lüderssen (ed.), *Generalklauseln als Gegenstand der Sozialwissenschaften*. Baden-Baden: Nomos.

——— (1978b) *Organisationsdemokratie und Verbandsverfassung. Rechtsmodelle für politisch relevante Verbände*. Tübingen: Mohr.

——— (1981) "Die Generalklausel von Treu und Glauben," *Alternativkommentar zum Bürgerlichen Gesetzbuch*, Vol. 2. Neuwied: Luchterhand.

TRUBEK, David M. (1972) "Max Weber on Law and the Rise of Capitalism," [1972] *Wisconsin Law Review* 720.

——— (1977) "Complexity and Contradiction in the Legal Order: Balbus and the Challenge of Critical Social Thought About Law," 11 *Law & Society Review* 529.

TUGENDHAT, Ernst (1980) "Zur Entwicklung von moralischen Begründungsstrukturen im Recht," 14 *Archiv für Rechts—und Sozialphilosophie*. Beiheft. Wiesbaden: Steiner.

TURNER, Jonathan H. (1974) "A Cybernetic Model of Legal Development," 5 *Western Sociological Review* 3.

UNGER, Roberto M. (1976) *Law in Modern Society*. New York: Free Press.

VOIGT, Rüdiger (1980) *Verrechtlichung. Analysen zu Funktion und Wirkung von Parlamentarisierung, Bürokratisierung und Justizialisierung sozialer, politischer und ökonomischer Prozesse*. Königstein: Athenäum.

WAELDE, Thomas (1979) *Juristische Folgenorientierung*. Königstein: Athenäum.

WAGNER, Heinz (1976) *Recht als Widerspiegelung und Handlungsinstrument*. Köln: Paul-Rugenstein.

WALZ, Rainer (1980) *Steuergerechtigkeit und Rechtsanwendung*. Hamburg: Decker.

WIEACKER, Franz (1967) *Privatrechtsgeschichte der Neuzeit*. Göttingen: Vandenhoeck & Ruprecht.
WIETHÖLTER, Rudolf (1982) "Entwicklung des Rechtsbegriffs," in V. Gessner and G. Winter (eds.), *Rechtsformen der Verflechtung von Staat und Wirtschaft*. Opladen: Westdeutscher Verlag 38.
WILLKE, Helmut (1978) "Zum Problem der Integration komplexer Sozialsysteme," 30 *Kölner Zeitschrift für Soziologie und Sozialpsychologie* 228.
——— (1981) *Zur Steuerungsfunktion des Staates in hochkomplexen Gesellschaften*. Köln: Typoscript.
WILSON, James Q. (ed.) (1980) *The Politics of Regulation*. New York: Basic Books.
WINDSCHEID, Bernhard (1904) "Die Aufgaben der Rechtswissenschaft," in B. Windscheid, *Gesammelte Reden und Abhandlungen*. Leipzig: Duncker.
WINTER, Gerd (1982) "Literaturbericht zum Thema," in V. Gessner and G. Winter (eds.), *Rechtsformen der Verflechtung zwischen Staat und Wirtschaft*. Opladen: Westdeutscher Verlag 9.
ZIELKE, Andreas (1980) "Zur Rationalität des modernen Rechts," 11 *Rechtstheorie* 85.

Part II
Disputing

[5]

The Myth of the Reluctant Litigant

JOHN OWEN HALEY

And if any man will sue thee at the law, and take away thy coat, let him have thy cloak also. (Matthew 5:40.)

Now therefore there is utterly a fault among you, because ye go to law one with another—Why do ye not rather take wrong? Why do ye not rather suffer yourselves to be defrauded? (I Corinthians 6:7.)

Introduction

The belief that the Japanese are an exceptionally nonlitigious people is remarkably pervasive. Commentators, both within and without Japan, are almost unanimous in attributing to the Japanese an unusual and deeply rooted cultural preference for informal, mediated settlement of private disputes and a corollary aversion to the formal mechanisms of judicial adjudication. As a result, they say, Japanese do not take advantage of the available mechanisms for formal dispute resolution. These attitudes, they commonly add, are bolstered by a peculiar Japanese penchant for compromise, distrust of clearcut "all or none" solutions and distaste for both public quarrels and their public resolution.[1] As explained by Kawashima

The initial version of this article was presented as a paper entitled "The Litigious Japanese?" to the Southern California Japan Seminar (USC-UCLA Joint Center in East Asian Studies) on December 10, 1976.

1. This idea is repeated so frequently that a sampling of sources must suffice. The most ubiquitous are the works of Kawashima Takeyoshi. Particularly influential are his popular book *Nihonjin no hō ishiki* (Tokyo: Iwanami, 1967), especially pp. 125–203, in the title of which he coined the phrase "Japanese legal consciousness," and his article, "Dispute Resolution in Contemporary Japan," in Arthur T. von Mehren (ed.), *Law in Japan: The Legal Order in a Changing Society* (Cambridge: Harvard University Press, 1963), pp. 41–72, probably the most widely cited English language article on Japanese law. Dan F. Henderson, *Conciliation and Japanese Law: To-*

Takeyoshi, one of Japan's leading legal sociologists and most articulate exponents of this belief, the endurance of a traditional concern for preserving cooperative personal relationships makes unwanted any definitive delineation of rights and duties through litigation. Bringing a lawsuit has meant issuing a "public challenge and provoking a quarrel."[2]

The importance of this notion is difficult to exaggerate. Most critical, upon it rests the conventional evaluation of the role of the judiciary within Japan's political and social order. The standard introductory works in English on Japanese government, for instance, uniformly dismiss the courts as politically insignificant on the basis of this perceived unwillingness of the Japanese to litigate.[3] Without

kugawa and Modern (2 vols., University of Washington Press, 1965), especially chapter VIII in vol. 2, pp. 191–200, is a frequently footnoted source for this idea, as a result of his reference to "an unusually pronounced tendency [on the part of Japanese] to avoid litigation." Most fail, however, to note the extent to which Henderson qualifies this in his analysis of "didactic" conciliation (discussed below). For other references in English, see Hideo Tanaka, *The Japanese Legal System: Introductory Cases and Materials* (Tokyo: University of Tokyo Press, 1976), pp. 254–263, 286–310; Yosiyuki Noda, *Introduction to Japanese Law* (English trans. from French; Tokyo: University of Tokyo Press, 1976), pp. 181–182; Kahei Rokumoto, "Problems and Methodology of the Study of Civil Disputes, Part I," *Law in Japan*, vol. 5 (1973), pp. 102–110; D. J. Danielski, "The Supreme Court of Japan: An Exploratory Study" in Glendon Schubert and David J. Danielski (eds.), *Comparative Judicial Behavior* (New York and London: Oxford University Press, 1969), pp. 121–156; Charles R. Stevens, "Modern Japanese Law as an Instrument of Comparison," *American Journal of Comprehensive Law*, vol. 19 (1971), pp. 673–681; Charles R. Stevens, "Japanese Law and the Japanese Legal System: Perspectives for the American Business Lawyer," *Business Lawyer*, vol. 27 (1972), pp. 1271–1273 also in Richard C. Allison (ed.), *Current Legal Aspects of Doing Business in the Far East* (Chicago: American Bar Association, 1972), pp. 13–14. Others are cited elsewhere in this paper.

A few have ventured qualifications, see, e.g., Tomoyuki Ohta and Tadao Hozumi, "Compromise in the Course of Litigation," in *Law in Japan*, vol. 6 (1973), pp. 97–110; and at least two scholars, outright rejection, Kazuaki Sono and Warren L. Shattuck, "Personal Property as Collateral in Japan and the United States," *Washington Law Review*, vol. 39 (1964), p. 571 fn. 6.

These observations have had significant influence on general comparative legal studies, particularly concern with what is fashionably referred to as "legal culture." See, e.g., Henry W. Ehrmann, *Comparative Legal Cultures* (Englewood Hills: Prentice Hall, 1976), pp. 82–86; Roberto Mangabeira Unger, *Law in Modern Society* (New York: Free Press, 1976), pp. 124–131; Lawrence M. Friedman, "Legal Cultures and Social Development," *Law and Society Review*, vol. 4 (1969), pp. 19–46.

2. Kawashima, *Nihonjin no hō ishiki*, p. 140.

3. See, e.g., Ardath W. Burks, *The Government of Japan* (New York: Crowell, 1961), pp. 149–172; Nobutaka Ike, *Japanese Politics: Patron-Client Democracy*

cases the courts cannot act. Unlike other arms of the state, the courts do not apply or enforce laws on their own initiative. They must wait passively for controversies to be brought before them for decision. This notion of the nonlitigious Japanese raises obvious doubts as to the efficacy of the postwar legal reforms, which were premised on an active, American-styled judiciary. Yet even as optimistic an observer as Alfred C. Oppler, who was among those who contributed most to the Occupation's efforts to realize a judiciary capable of implementing the ideals of the postwar constitution, accepts it without question.[4]

The dilemma posed by the institutional ideal of an active judiciary in a nonlitigious society is surmounted at least in part by those, such as Kawashima, who view Japanese aversion to litigation as a gradually fading, "traditional" response.[5] Indeed, the literature is replete with observations on rising litigation rates in postwar Japan,[6] which some take as a convenient index to measure Japan's progress toward a "modern" society.[7]

Despite the ubiquity of these ideas few have bothered to appraise their accuracy or, more important, to analyze with care their implications, particularly as to the role of law and the courts. Even the most basic question has not been fully answered. Are the Japanese, in fact, unusually loath to resort to court? The common retort is to pose another question: If not, then how does one explain the apparent lack of litigation in Japan relative to the United States and the failure of the judiciary to exert a more positive influence on the political process?

This article represents an attempt to respond to these questions and, in so doing, to suggest areas for profitable future research that,

(New York: Alfred A. Knopf, 2d ed. 1972), pp. 30–32; Robert E. Ward, *Japan's Political System* (Englewood Hills: Prentice-Hall, 1967), p. 102.

4. Alfred C. Oppler, *Legal Reform in Occupied Japan: A Participant Looks Back* (Princeton: Princeton University Press, 1976), p. 107.

5. See, e.g., Takeyoshi Kawashima, "The Status of the Individual in the Notion of Law, Right and Social Order in Japan," in Charles A. Moore (ed.), *The Japanese Mind* (Honolulu: East-West Center Press, 1967), pp. 271–275. This is Kawashima's main theme in this work as well as the others cited above.

6. See, e.g., Tanaka, p. 262; Charles R. Stevens, Remarks on Panel on "Developing a Pacific Community," in *Proceedings of the 71st Annual Meeting of the American Society of International Law* (1977), p. 70.

7. See, e.g., Takeyoshi Kawashima and Kurt Steiner, "Modernization and Divorce Rate Trends in Japan," *Economic Development & Social Change* (1960), pp. 213–239.

I believe, are obscured by the orthodox emphasis on Japanese aversion to litigation.

A Paradigm

The threshold problem is to define "litigiousness" in some meaningful fashion. There is little question that the Japanese generally use their courts less frequently than do Americans (although the contrast may not actually be as great as some have suggested). As indicated in Table 1, relative to the number of registered motor vehicles and motor vehicle accidents resulting in deaths, Californians filed twice as many suits as the Japanese in Tokyo and Osaka, jurisdictions with a combined population roughly equivalent to that of California (20 million).

This relative lack of litigation is not, however, a uniquely Japanese phenomenon. In Austin Sarat's and Joel B. Grossman's study of litigation rates in a selection of ten countries (Table 2), resort to court in civil cases in Japan appears to be modestly frequent.[8]

In California in 1972-73, it might be noted, 4,838 civil cases (including probate, guardianship, personal injury, death, property damage, eminent domain and small claims actions) were filed in superior and municipal courts per 100,000 persons.[9] This rate is slightly below Denmark's on the Sarat and Grossman index. As Sarat and Grossman recognize, however, the data are too crude for an accurate index of "litigiousness" or other analytical purpose.[10] They do not indicate what is meant by "civil cases" in each instance. In the Japanese case, for example, statistics on civil cases filed typically include all forms of summary proceedings as well as cases docketed for formal trial proceedings (see Figure 1). Moreover, such statistics do not take into account differences among these jurisdictions as to matters where judicial intervention is legally required, such as probate and divorce; the availability of extrajudicial institutions for adjudication of particular types of disputes, such as labor relations boards; or welfare and insurance schemes, such as workman's com-

8. Austin Sarat and Joel B. Grossman, "Courts and Conflict Resolution: Problems in the Mobilization of Adjudication," *American Political Science Review*, vol. 69 (1975), pp. 1200–1217, 1208.

9. Judicial Council of California, *Annual Report* (Sacramento, 1974), pp. 107, 136.

10. Sarat and Grossman, p. 1208.

FIGURE 1

* New Civil Cases, Including Formal Trial (*soshō*), Compromise (*wakai*), Conciliation (*chōtei*), Summary (*tokusoku*), Provisional Attachment (*kari-sashiosae*), and Provisional Disposition (*kari-shobun*) proceedings filed in Courts of First Instance from 1890 through 1972.

** Cases Docketed for Formal Trial Proceedings.

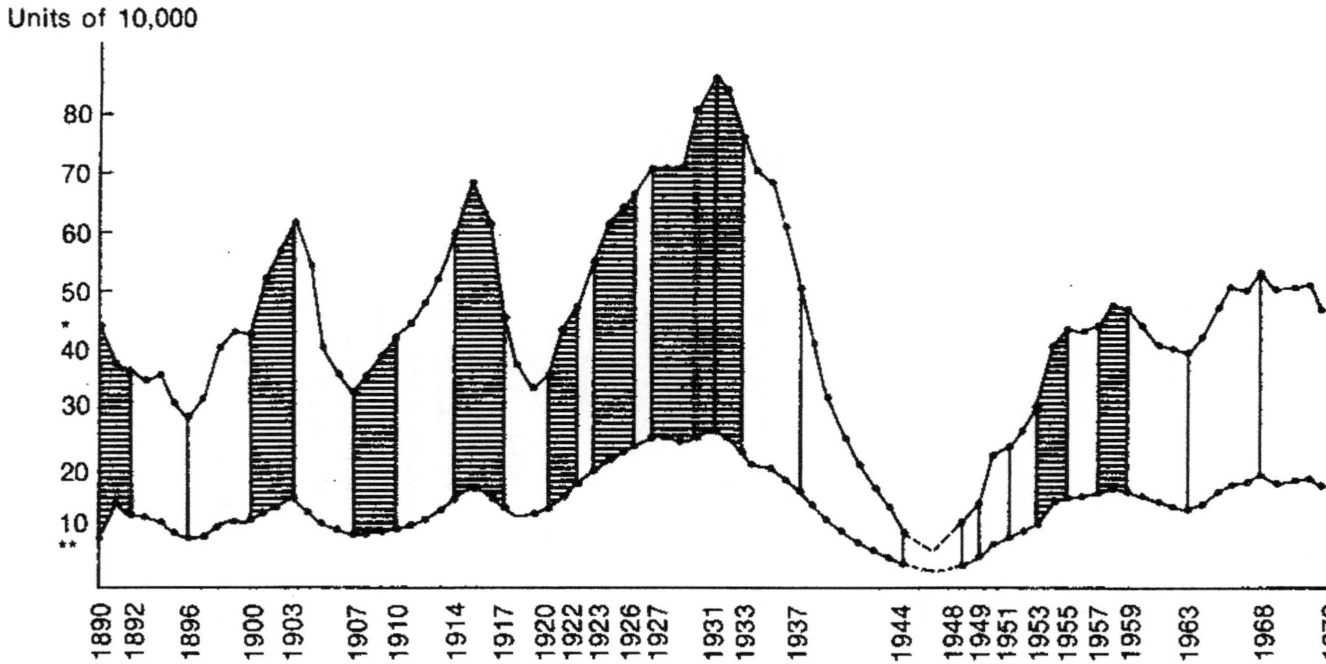

Source: Nihon Bengoshi Rengōkai (Japan Federation of Bar Associations), *Shihō Hakusho* (White paper on the legal system) (Tokyo, 1974) p. 19.

TABLE 1
COMPARISON OF PERSONAL INJURY ACTIONS INVOLVING MOTOR VEHICLE ACCIDENTS FILED IN SUPERIOR COURTS IN CALIFORNIA AND DISTRICT COURTS IN OSAKA AND TOKYO.

	Registered Motor Vehicles	Motor Vehicle Accident Deaths	Actions Filed
California, 1972–73:	11,901,000	5,114	43,521
Tokyo and Osaka, 1969:	3,533,460	1,672	6,090
Ratio:	3.4:1	3:1	7:1

Sources: Judicial Council of California, *Annual Report* (Sacramento, 1974), p. 106; Saikō Saibansho (Supreme Court), *Shihō tōkei, Shōwa 44* (Annual report of judicial statistics for 1969) (Tokyo, 1970), pp. 122, 123; *Japan Statistical Yearbook* (Tokyo, 1971), p. 628; *Statistical Abstracts of the United States* (Washington, D.C.: Department of Commerce, 1974), p. 562.

TABLE 2

Country	Civil Cases per 100,000 Population
Australia	5,277 (1969)
Denmark	4,844 (1969)
New Zealand	4,423 (1969)
Great Britain	3,605 (1969)
West Germany	2,085 (1969)
Japan	1,257 (1970)
Sweden	683 (1970)
Finland	493 (1970)
Norway	307 (1970)
South Korea	172 (1963)

pensation; any of which may reduce or preclude resort to courts.[11] Nor do they attempt to analyze the effect of jury systems with their uncertainties of result, compulsory conciliation schemes (as in Norway), or the relationship between the number of lawyers and litigation. Nonetheless, to the extent their data permit a rough, impressionistic comparison, then if by "litigious" is meant simply the number of suits filed or disposed of per capita, Japan is quite litigious relative to some societies and notably nonlitigious compared to others.

11. For instance, use of registries in Japan for marriage, adoption, divorce, inheritance and real property transfers reduces significantly the use of courts and lawyers. See Dan F. Henderson and John O. Haley, *Law and the Legal Process in Japan*. (Mimeographed materials, University of Washington Law Library, 1977), pp. 439-468.

The orthodox view of Japanese "litigiousness," however, relates to a reluctance to litigate, not simply the amount of litigation. Even assuming such a reluctance to exist, to be meaningful in terms of evaluating the role of the judiciary it must involve more than simply a desire to avoid lawsuits. While we might conceive of an individual or community as a whole that delights in engaging the complex litany of trial procedures or activating the public intervention of a magistrate, if such exist, they are rare. For most persons a lawsuit is a last resort. Litigation, is, after all, almost always a costly and cumbersome process for resolving disputes, and ordinarily an aggrieved party to a dispute will attempt to reach informal private settlement. The overwhelming majority of disputes in most societies are in fact resolved informally.[12] As the quotes prefacing this article indicate, traditional moral censure of litigation is arguably as Christian as it is Confucian.

The paradigm process of dispute resolution for most societies, including Japan, is two or three-tiered. A dispute will typically move through several steps before reaching the courts—private negotiation between the immediate parties, perhaps mediation with the aid of a third party—but ultimately to the litigated solution only where there has been a failure to reach a settlement at each preceding stage. (These steps can be, and most often are, conducted concurrently with negotiation, mediation, and possibly both, taking place throughout trial proceedings, in some instances even after a judgment but before all appeals have been exhausted.)[13]

The critical issue is whether the parties will settle only when neither believes he has more to gain by judicial intervention. If this is

12. This is common knowledge, but of possible interest are a number of studies on how disparate types of legal disputes are resolved in the United States. See, e.g., H. Lawrence Ross, *Settled Out of Court: The Social Process of Insurance Claims Adjustment* (Chicago: Aldine Publishing Co., 1970); Alfred F. Conrad, *Automobile Accidents Costs and Payments* (Ann Arbor: University of Michigan Press, 1964) ch. 6, pp. 181–182. Curtis J. Buger and Patrick J. Rohan, "The Nassau County Study: An Empirical Look Into Practices of Condemnation," *Columbia Law Review*, vol. 67 (1967), pp. 430, 440–441. Conard's University of Michigan study is particularly interesting when contrasted with the study by Professor Zensuke Ishimura and Yuriko Kaminaga, "Attorneys and Automobile Accident Cases," *Law in Japan*, vol. 9 (1976), pp. 83–116.

13. By definition this is a highly generalized model meant to be used as a tool for analysis and not necessarily as a description of a universally applicable process for all societies or all types of disputes. As I discuss later (*infra* note 57), the bulk of cases settled privately in the United States between lawyers do not involve mediation at all. See also Sarat and Grossman.

the case, a decision to settle necessarily involves an assessment of the outcome of the potential lawsuit, and the private settlement should reflect that outcome discounted by the costs (including time) and uncertainties of litigation. In this process, the judicial model operates in a manner similar to economic markets. And if the paradigm functions effectively, the legal norms that courts apply in these isolated cases become the standards used, albeit discounted, in resolving similar subsequent disputes.

Consequently, whether the Japanese are nonlitigious is in itself significant for our purposes here only if by "nonlitigious" we mean that Japanese involved in a dispute tend to reach negotiated or mediated settlements that do not reflect the litigated outcomes and one of the parties accepts a less favorable result because of an aversion to litigation in general. The frequency of litigation alone is not meaningful since the availability and successful utilization of alternative mechanisms for settlement may reduce litigation without impairing the efficacy of judicially-imposed norms. Also, a number of institutional factors can preclude litigation as a realistic option and thereby diminish substantially the influence of the courts. Indeed, resort to court would be rare to the extent that access is assured, the costs are minimal, judicial relief is effective, and the outcome is certain.

Litigation in particular types of disputes—for example, suits by children against their parents—should be distinguished. Inasmuch as in most instances litigation commonly involves a rupturing of relations as a result of public acknowledgement of the parties' inability to reach an amicable settlement between themselves in private, litigation is less likely where the parties wish to continue their relationship or where rupturing the relationship offends widely held social norms. Also, in many of these areas as a matter of public policy the courts may be given very limited jurisdiction to intervene (e.g. in disputes between husbands and wives). While we might want to isolate and investigate such specific areas where the judicial model may not be as effective, none involves the question of a general and peculiarly Japanese desire to avoid available mechanisms for formal resolution of disputes.

The Myth Reconsidered

Is there, then, any evidence of an unusual Japanese aversion toward lawsuits that leads a party to accept a settlement less beneficial than one he anticipates he would gain by suing? The answer, I believe, is negative. What little evidence there is suggests the opposite—that most Japanese are willing to go to court in such circumstances. The recent pollution cases[14] and the thalidomide case[15] are illustrative.

A recently published inquiry into the decisions to litigate in the pollution cases documents a variety of cultural factors causing the litigants to hesitate to sue.[16] These included a sense of "shame" for physical and mental deformity, constraints on individual initiative and "selfish" behavior imposed by the demands of community unity and group consciousness, and hostility against an association with what was perceived to be—correctly, I believe—a leftist, antigovernment cause reflected in the politics of the lawyers who dominated the conduct of these trials. This experience was paralleled in part in the thalidomide case, where the apparent reason for reluctance to sue was a fear of public exposure of the children's deformities. "In a society strongly prejudiced against deformity," one of the plaintiffs' lawyers wrote, "it took considerable courage to sue."[17] In each of these cases the plaintiffs filed suit only reluctantly and as a last resort. The reluctance, however, was based on a variety of factors related to the particular circumstances and nature of the disputes, not an unwillingness to sue in general.[18]

The one arguable exception was the attitude that bringing an action for damages reflected socially unacceptable "selfishness." At first blush this would appear to be a cultural barrier to litigation in

14. Komatsu v. Mitsui Kinzoku Kōgyō, *Hanrei Jihō* (No. 635) 17 (Toyama Dt. Ct., June 30, 1971); aff'd *Hanrei Jihō* (No. 674) 25 (Nagoya High Ct., Kanazawa Br., Aug. 9, 1972); Ōno v. Shōwa Denkō K.K., *Hanrei Jihō* (No. 642) 96 (Niigata Dt. Ct. Sept. 29, 1971); Watanabe v. Chisso K.K. *Hanrei Jihō* (No. 696) 15 (Kumamoto Dt. Ct., Mar. 20, 1973); Shiono v. Shōwa Yokkaichi Sekiyu K.K., *Hanrei Jihō* (No. 672) 30 (Tsu Dt. Ct., Yokkaichi Br., July 24, 1972). For a brief discussion of these cases in English, see Tomohei Taniguchi, "A Commentary on the Legal Theory of the Four Major Pollution Cases," *Law in Japan*, vol. 9 (1976), pp. 35–62.

15. These series of cases were settled before decided by the courts; hence there is no official report. For an account of the progress of the suits, see "Diary of the Plaintiff's Attorney's Team in the Thalidomide Litigation," *Law in Japan*, vol. 8 (1975), pp. 136–187 [hereafter referred to as "Diary"].

16. Frank K. Upham, "Litigation and Moral Consciousness in Japan: An Interpretative Analysis of Four Japanese Pollution Suits," *Law and Society Review*, vol. 10 (1976), pp. 579–619.

17. Statement by Koichi Nishida in "Diary," p. 141.

18. Inasmuch as the plaintiffs did litigate eventually, of course, they could be regarded as exceptional and this an unreliable basis for generalization. But this line of reasoning leaves us with little to work with. The details of settlements reached privately in unlitigated disputes are seldom disclosed fully and thus are shielded from public scrutiny.

general. It was overcome in these instances, however, by justifying the lawsuit as a means of bringing wrongdoers to justice, coupling compensation with a desire to prevent others from inflicting similar harm.[19] But such justifications are among the principal policies behind damage awards and private tort actions, and few plaintiffs would find similar rationalization of their motives difficult. Moreover, the success of the initial suits in these cases has produced others as well as a significant change in the standards being applied in private settlements of similar disputes.[20]

The few direct surveys of Japanese attitudes that have been made provide further support for rejecting the orthodox view. For example, in the survey by Sasaki Yoshio cited by both Dan F. Henderson and Kawashima,[21] when asked, "What would you do if a civil dispute arose and despite discussions with the opposite party you could not settle it?" 64% of the 2,098 respondents replied that they would willingly go to court.

Even more persuasive, however, is the pattern of litigation in Japan from 1890 to the present. As indicated in Figure 1 and Table 3, litigation has been *less* frequent in absolute numbers in the postwar years than the period from 1890 to the outbreak of the Sino-Japanese War in 1937. Relative to population, the contrast is even more startling. In 1934, for example, 302 new civil cases involving formal trial proceedings were initiated in courts of first instance per 100,000 persons, while in 1974 there were 135 such cases per 100,000 persons—2.2 times as many per capita in 1934 than there were in 1974.

By and large this pattern holds true for all categories of cases. While there is a slight variation in the frequencies of certain types of suits in some years, overall, over longer periods, there is a parallel rise or fall in the rate of litigation in each category. Nor do statistics reveal any aberration resulting from the prevalence of a particular type of suit during the prewar period, such as rural tenancy cases.

There was a greater frequency of litigation in absolute numbers in the prewar years in almost every category. (In the postwar period the increase in use of automobiles has led to a significant increase in personal injury actions.) Table 4, for example, shows the actual

19. Upham, p. 588.

20. These cases have produced additional litigation and at least in one instance (the Morinaga Milk poisoning case) a renegotiation of a previously settled dispute. See, e.g., Tanaka, pp. 417–443.

21. Henderson, vol. 2, p. 192; Kawashima, "The Status of the Individual in the Notion of Law, Right and Social Order in Japan," p. 272.

TABLE 3.
New Cases for Formal Trial Proceedings (soshō)
Filed 1891–1943, 1949–1974

1891	136,589		1917	132,531		1949	45,435	
1892	118,474	(293)	1918	120,641	(220)	1950	68,488	(82)
1893	111,246		1919	118,825		1951	87,817	
1894	107,442	(261)	1920	129,152	(233)	1952	87,480	(104)
1895	90,241		1921	148,850		1953	100,643	
1896	79,546	(189)	1922	169,239	(298)	1954	133,595	(157)
1897	83,927		1923	188,164		1955	144,036	
1898	98,564	(230)	1924	208,774	(358)	1956	145,935	(169)
1899	105,736		1925	225,429		1957	151,274	
1900	104,739	(239)	1926	237,244	(394)	1958	162,786	(184)
1901	121,346		1927	248,999		1959	157,252	
1902	131,758	(293)	1928	248,406	(400)	1960	147,673	(161)
1903	144,084		1929	242,757		1961	135,656	
1904	127,004	(275)	1930	249,030	(390)	1962	132,191	(140)
1905	100,681		1931	261,760		1963	128,654	
1906	90,956	(193)	1932	255,187	(387)	1964	135,849	(141)
1907	85,489		1933	228,224		1965	159,324	
1908	90,570	(189)	1934	204,731	(302)	1966	169,979	(173)
1909	94,386		1935	196,777		1967	173,383	(174)
1910	99,900	(203)	1936	180,501	(274)	1968	185,021	(184)
1911	106,499		1937	158,874		1969	172,020	(170)
1912	117,049	(231)	1938	132,069	(188)	1970	175,164	(170)
1913	130,598		1939	106,294		1971	179,256	(172)
1914	148,177	(285)	1940	88,160	(123)	1972	168,753	(160)
1915	162,545		1941	74,854		1973	150,662	(140)
1916	159,351	(298)	1943	39,905	(50)	1974	149,688	(135)

Sources: The statistics for 1891–1941 are from Nihon Teikoku Shihōshō (Ministry of Justice of the Empire of Japan) *Dai 67 Minji Tōkei Nenpō* (67th Annual report on civil case statistics) (Tokyo, 1943), pp. 103–104, Those for 1950–1974 are from Saikō Saibansho (Supreme Court) *Shōwa 49 Shihō Tōkei* Annual report of judicial statistics for 1974) (Tokyo, 1975), p. xx.

Note: These statistics represent actions involving ordinary trial procedures in civil cases. They do not include actions involving summary or special procedures (such as suits on bills and notes for provisional relief) or formal conciliation. The statistics for the postwar period include administrative suits, precluded for the prewar courts by jurisdictional limitations. Thus, as noted in the graph in Figure 1, these actions constitute only one part of the total caseload of the courts. The figures in parentheses indicate the number of new cases filed per 100,000 persons in Japan. See Table 5.

number of new filings for civil trials in courts of first instance for selected categories of cases in 1926 and 1969. The categories selected represent, with the exception of divorce actions, the standard bread and butter fare of litigation and the most numerous types of actions filed in both years. Again, in absolute numbers in 1926, several years prior to the prewar peak in 1934, there was far more

TABLE 4
COMPARISON OF CASES DOCKETED FOR FORMAL TRIAL PROCEEDINGS (*soshō*) IN COURTS OF FIRST INSTANCE, 1926–1969.

Subject of Action	1926*	1969**
a. Divorce	1383 (Dt. Cts. only)	2935 (Dt. Cts. only)
b. Actions relating to land	6894 Dt. Ct.—2890 Ward Ct.—4004	15,151 Dt. Ct.—10,193 Summ. Ct.—4958
c. Eviction & Delivery of Buildings Actions	10,315 Dt. Ct. 757 Ward Ct. 9558	7073 Dt. Ct. 4063 Summ. Ct. 3010
d. Actions for Contract Price	41,231 Dt. Ct.—2634 Ward Ct.—38,597	30,639 Dt. Ct.—11,362 Summ. Ct.—19,277
e. Actions for Money Lent	64,796 Dt. Ct.—4852 Ward Ct.—59,944	20,960 Dt. Ct.—12,215 Summ. Ct.—8754
f. Actions for Damages	5991 Dt. Ct.—2215 Ward Ct.—3776	20,071 Dt. Ct.—18,006 Summ. Ct.—2065 (Traffic Accidents = 10,968)

Sources: (*) Nihon Teikoku Shihōshō (Ministry of Justice of the Empire of Japan), *Dai-gōjuni Minji Tōkei Nenpō Taishō 15* (52nd annual report on civil case statistics: 1926) (Tokyo, 1928), pp. 30–32, 162–64.
(**) Saikō Saibansho (Supreme Court), *Shihō Tōkei Nenpō Shōwa 44* (Annual report of judicial statistics for 1969) (Tokyo, 1970), pp. 88–89, 122–23.

litigation than in 1969. Since Japan's population increased by 40% during the interval, on a per capita basis there was only a slight increase in divorce actions and suits relating to land in 1969 and, if we discount traffic accidents as peculiar to the postwar environment, no significant increase in damage actions.

Moreover, the conclusion reached after a trend analysis of the series of trial actions filed from 1891 through 1941 and from 1949 through 1974 is that there is no discernible trend *upwards* or *downwards* during either of these periods (see Table 5). This is evident graphically in Figure 2.

It is apparent that these patterns are inconsistent with conventional ideas about the reluctance of Japanese to litigate; moreover, they contradict the widely held belief that there has been a greater willingness to sue in the postwar period. In short, most of what is said or written about Japanese attitudes toward the legal process is

TABLE 5

Period	Equation Best Predicting Percentage of Change of Litigation	R^2
1891–1941:	$v_t = -.006 + .996v_{t-1} - .347v_{t-2} + u_t$	$R^2 = .582$
1949–1974:	$v_t = .054 + u_t - .711u_{t-1}$	$R^2 = .371$

v_t = percentage change in new civil trial actions (cases docketed for formal trial proceedings) filed in year t.

u_t = normally distributed random variables with mean o and variance of 1.

Note: The estimated constants in both equations were found to be statistically insignificant from 0 and as such constitute a rejection of the hypothesis that there is trend in the numbers new civil trial actions filed.

myth. But as with many myths, it contains an important element of truth.

Although, at least since the middle of the Meiji Period and perhaps even earlier, the Japanese in general may not have been unusually reluctant to litigate, the evidence points to the conclusion that to do so was offensive to some—that is, those who wished to maintain a paternalistic order based on a hierarchical submission to authority. As Henderson has detailed in his often cited (but apparently seldom read) study of conciliation in Japanese law, Tokugawa officialdom had constructed a formidable system of procedural barriers to obtaining final judgment in the Shogunate's courts. The litigant was forced each step of the way to exhaust all possibilities of conciliation and compromise and to proceed only at the sufferance of his superiors. We can only marvel at the endurance and perseverance of those who eventually prevailed. Conciliation was coerced—to use Henderson's phrase "didactic"—not voluntary.[22] Yet, as Henderson tells us, litigation increased.[23]

The modern analogues to Tokugawa conciliation are equally revealing. Formal conciliation proceedings (*chōtei*) were not instituted until enactment of the Land Lease and House Lease Conciliation Law in 1922.[24] This measure was followed in succession by the Farm Tenancy Conciliation Law of 1924,[25] the Commercial Affairs Conciliation Law of 1926,[26] the Labor Disputes Conciliation Law of 1926,[27] the Monetary Claims Temporary Conciliation Law of 1932,[28]

22. Henderson, vol. 1, p. 4.
23. Henderson, vol. 1, p. 107.
24. *Shakuchi shakuya chōtei hō* (Law No. 41, 1922).
25. *Kosaku chōtei hō* (Law No. 18, 1924).
26. *Shōji chōtei hō* (Law No. 42, 1926).
27. *Rōdō sōgi chōtei hō* (Law No. 57, 1926).
28. *Kinsen saimu rinji chōtei hō* (Law No. 26, 1932).

FIGURE 2

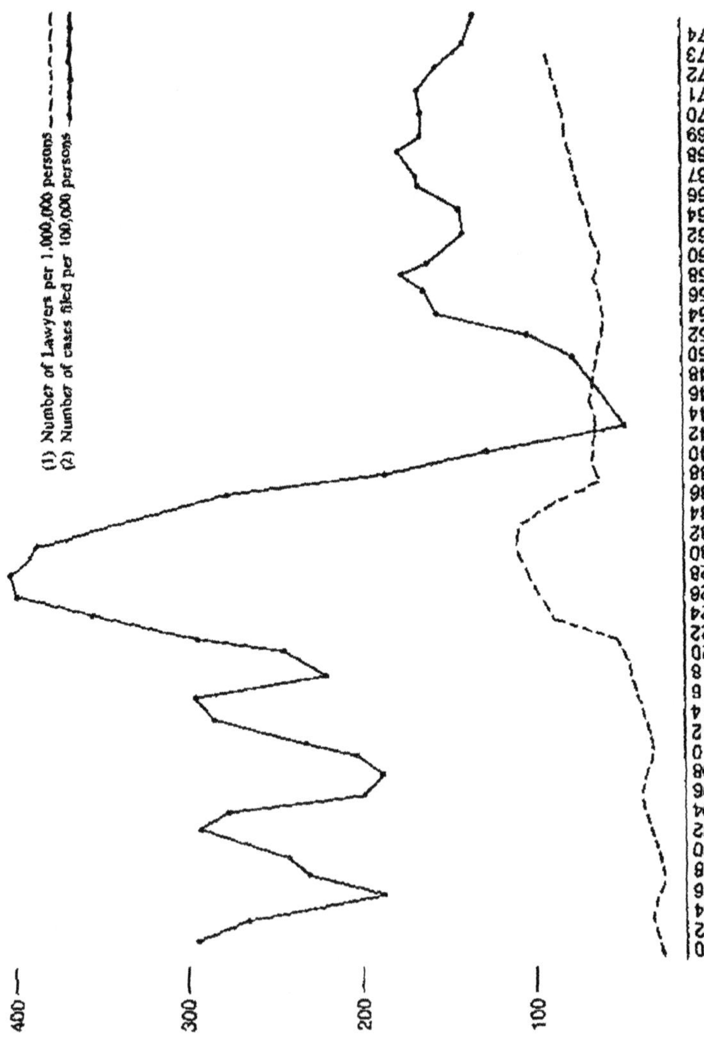
(1) Number of Lawyers per 1,000,000 persons
(2) Number of cases filed per 100,000 persons
400
300
200
100
1890
1892
1894
1896
1898
1900
1902
1904
1906
1908
1910
1912
1914
1916
1918
1920
1922
1924
1926
1928
1930
1932
1934
1936
1938
1940
1942
1944
1946
1948
1950
1952
1954
1956
1958
1960
1962
1964
1966
1967
1968
1969
1970
1971
1972
1973
1974

the conciliation provisions added to the Mining Law[29] in a 1939 amendment and to the Placer Mines Law[30] in a 1940 amendment,[31] the Agricultural Land Adjustment Law of 1938,[32] the Personal Status Conciliation Law of 1939,[33] and finally the conciliation provisions of the Special Wartime Civil Affairs Law of 1942.[34]

Kawashima relies heavily on the enactment of these statutes in arguing that the Japanese have been loath to litigate.[35] Yet there is nothing to suggest that they were the product of popular demand for an alternative to litigation more in keeping with Japanese sensitivities. Rather it seems more accurate to conclude that they reflected a conservative reaction to the rising tide of lawsuits in the 1920s and early 1930s and a concern on the part of the governing elite that litigation was destructive to a hierarchial social order based upon personal relationships. Thus Kawashima's views are perhaps accurate so long as limited to description of the attitudes of those who came into power in the late 1920s and 1930s rather than the Japanese people as a whole, the residual effect of which may explain (at least in part) the persuasiveness today of the idea that the Japanese are not litigious.[36]

Indicative of the rationale for modern conciliation was the recommendation of the 1919 Special Investigation Commission on Legal Institutions (*Rinji Hōsei Shingikai*) to establish conciliation proceedings for family disputes (translated by Henderson):

> It was recognized that to cleave to the type of lawsuit such as is used in the present system for family disputes would not preserve the

29. *Kōgyō hō* (Law No. 45, 1905) as amended by the Mining Law Partial Amendment Law (*Kōgyō hō chū kaisei hōritsu*), Law No. 23, 1939.

30. *Sakō hō* (Law No. 13, 1909).

31. The Placer Mines Law Partial Amendment Law (*Sakō hō chū kaisei hōritsu*), Law No. 103, 1940.

32. *Nōchi chōsei hō* (Law No. 67, 1938).

33. *Jinji chōtei hō* (Law No. 11, 1939).

34. *Senji minji tokubetsu hō* (Law No. 63, 1942).

35. Tables with comprehensive statistics on conciliation are included in Kawashima; "Dispute Resolution in Contemporary Japan," pp. 60–72; see also, Kawashima, "The Status of the Individual in the Notion of Law, Right and Social Order in Japan," p. 273.

36. This, of course, is not at all what Kawashima and others have in mind when they refer to the prevalence of traditional attitudes. Theirs is a linear model of transition from tradition to modernity. What is suggested here is more complex. The contemporary Japanese belief that they are a traditionally unlitigious people may reflect a very successful transmission of values and perceptions by those in power in the immediate prewar years.

> virtuous ways and beautiful tradition from the past, but rather it was recognized as extremely important to establish a special system to solve them amicably with compassion and based on morality.[37]

Although unsuccessful in 1919, such arguments became increasingly persuasive as litigation increased and the influence of "revisionists" in the civil and military bureaucracies grew (the Personal Affairs Conciliation Law, which provided for conciliation of such disputes, was not enacted until 1940).[38] The initial statutes for conciliation of urban and rural landlord-tenant disputes were confined to providing an optional alternative to lawsuits. But by the end of the 1930s almost all civil disputes were subject to conciliation procedures, and judges or special commissioners were empowered to require the parties to conciliate.[39] The Special Wartime Civil Affairs Law of 1942 capped the progression toward a modern version of "didactic" conciliation by providing for conciliation in all civil disputes and authorizing judges to enter a judgment without a trial where in the course of conciliation the parties failed to reach voluntary settlement.[40] During the immediate postwar period, as Justice Mano Tsuyoshi remarked in his dissent to the decision in *Suzuki v.*

37. Henderson, vol. 2, p. 216.

38. See, e.g., Robert M. Spaulding Jr., "Bureaucracy as a Political Force, 1920–45," in James W. Morley (ed.), *Dilemmas of Growth in Prewar Japan* (Princeton: Princeton University Press, 1971), pp. 33–80. The attitudes of the "revisionist bureaucrats" (to use Spaulding's term) have been aptly described under the rubric of a "collectivist ethic" in R. P. Dore and Tsutomo Ōuchi, "Rural Origins of Japanese Fascism," in *ibid.*, pp. 201–211. See also, Kenneth B. Pyle, "Advantages of Followership: German Economics and Japanese Bureaucrats 1890–1925," *Journal of Japanese Studies*, vol. 1, (No. 1 Autumn, 1974), p. 164.

39. The Land Lease and House Lease Conciliation Law of 1922 provided that trial proceedings would be suspended upon the court's receipt of a petition for conciliation by one of the parties (art. 5). The statute was amended in 1924 (Law No. 17, 1926) to provide that the trial judge could require conciliation *ex officio* (article 4–2). Similar authority was given to official rural tenancy conciliators (*kosakukan*) and judges for rural tenancy disputes under the 1938 Agricultural Law Adjustment Law (arts. 10(1), 10(2)). Comparable provisions for coercive conciliation were included in the Commercial Affairs Conciliation Law, the Monetary Claims Temporary Conciliation Law and the statutes providing for conciliation in mining cases. For detailed discussion, see Etō Yoshihiro, "*Chōtei seido no kinō to yakuwari*" (The function and role of the conciliation system), in Toshitani Nobuyoshi (ed.), *Hō to saiban* (Law and adjudication) (Tokyo: Gakuyō shobō, 1972), pp. 178–182.

40. Special Wartime Civil Affairs Law arts. 14, 16, 17, 18. Article 19(2) incorporated the "judgment in lieu of conciliation" provision of article 7(1) of the Monetary Claims Temporary Conciliation Law of 1932.

Ishigaki,[41] (upholding under the postwar constitution the Special Wartime Civil Affairs Law provision for judgment in lieu of conciliation), "there developed a tendency to regard lawsuits as a kind of vice."[42]

These measures, it should be emphasized, did not reflect objections to what the courts were doing in these cases. The period from about 1905 through the early 1920s was one of the most creative eras in Japanese jurisprudence. The judiciary was extraordinarily innovative in adapting the new European-based codes to the Japanese environment, rationalizing traditional norms within the framework of Western law. In a series of cases, the courts recognized the right of the citizen to sue the government for damages in the ordinary courts,[43] expanded the liability of private industry for pollution,[44] restricted the arbitrary power of the househead,[45] limited the exercise of private property rights where it would cause undue economic harm to the community,[46] recognized traditional security devices[47] and redefined the law on leases to insure fair treatment of tenants.[48] Although in some of those instances the courts' decisions were contrary to what we today might consider a "conservative" position, in

41. 10 Minshū 1355 (Sup. Ct., G.B., Oct. 31, 1956), translated in J. O. Haley, *The Public Law System of Japan* (Mimeographed materials, University of Washington School of Law Library, 1976). Susuki Ishigaki was effectively overruled in Nomura v. Yamaki, 14 Minshū 1657 (Sup. Ct., G.B. July 6, 1960).

42. 10 Minshū at 1361.

43. City of Tokushima v. Ose, 22 Minroku 1088 (Gr. Ct. Cass., June 1, 1916).

44. Osaka Alkali K.K. v. Tonomura, *Shinbun* (No. 1659) 11 (Osaka Ct. App., Dec. 27, 1919), on remand from 22 Minroku 2474 (Gr. Ct. Cass., Dec. 29, 1916).

45. Sonoda v. Sonoda, 7 Minroku 47 (Gr. Ct. Cass., June 20, 1901); Ikeda v. Ikeda, *Shinbun* (No. 493) 17 (Osaka Ct. App., Mar. 26, 1908); Saitō v. Saitō *Shinbun* (No. 2550) 11 (Yamagata Dt. Ct., Mar. 18, 1926); Iwabuchi v. Iwabuchi, *Shinbun* (No. 2865) 10 (Tokyo Ct. App., April 9, 1928); Nozaki v. Nozaki, *Shinbun* (No. 3111) 7 (Nagasaki Ct. App., Mar. 28, 1929). These cases are cited and discussed in Aoyama Michio, "Wagakuni ni okeru kenri ran'yo riron no hatten" (Development of Abuse of Rights Theory in Japan), in *Kenri no ran'yo* (Abuse of Rights) (Yūhikaku, 1965), p. 9, translated in Henderson and Haley, pp. 406–422.

46. See, e.g., Shinagawa v. Kurobe Rwy K.K., 14 Minshū 1965 (Gr. Ct. Cass., Oct. 5, 1935), translated in Tanaka, p. 118. See also, Kazuaki Sono and Yasuhito Fujioka, "The Role of the Abuse of Right Doctrine in Japan," *Louisiana Law Review*, vol. 35 (1975), p. 1037.

47. See discussion of the *jōto tampo* cases in J. O. Haley, *The Non-Code Security Interests: A Study of Japanese Case Law* (Unpublished LL.M. paper, University of Washington Law Library, 1971), pp. 8–52.

48. See landlord-tenant cases discussed in Tadao Hozumi, "The Structure and Function of the 'Interpretation' of Juristic Acts, Part II," *Law in Japan*, vol. 5 (1972), p. 132.

fact, often despite the thrust of the new Japanese codes, the courts adhered to a traditional scheme of values that gave priority to community welfare over individual interests and placed emphasis on social obligations and duties rather than legal rights. The results reached in such cases conformed in many cases to provisions enacted in subsequent statutes, for example the House Lease Law[49] and the Land Lease Law[50] enacted a year before the Land Lease and House Lease Conciliation Law.[51]

Another example is the Farm Tenancy Conciliation Law of 1924, enacted in response to the rural tenancy disputes of the 1920s. One recent study attributes these disputes to an increase in absentee landlords and their abandoning traditional obligations toward tenants and the local community.[52] Similarly, it appears that the rupture of the patron-client relation evidenced in suits by landlords against tenants as well as tenants against landlords, rather than the merits of their claims, was a critical concern for those who pressed for enactment of the Farm Tenancy Conciliation Law.[53] The courts had already proven their capacity to reinforce traditional relationships and concepts of responsibility despite provisions in the codes. But conciliation insured that extralegal instruction could be given the parties to remind them of their proper roles and that the traditional village hierarchy, not just the parties and the judges, would be involved.[54]

Those such as Kawashima who argue that the modern conciliation statutes evidence a generally-held desire for an alternative to lawsuits have ignored these considerations. Equally telling, however, are the statistics on the frequency of conciliation versus lawsuits during the 1920s and 1930s. As seen in Figure 3, despite enactment of the conciliation statutes, lawsuits continued to increase until the mid-1930s. At that point the number of both new trials and conciliation proceedings began to fall precipitously. The availability of conciliation as an alternative to a formal trial—even when subject to a discretionary judicial order despite the parties' wishes—did not

49. *Shakuya hō* (Law No. 50, 1921).

50. *Shakuchi hō* (Law No. 49, 1921).

51. Hozumi, pp. 54–61.

52. Ann Waswo, "The Origins of Tenant Unrest," in Bernard S. Silberman and H. D. Harootunian (eds.), *Japan in Crisis* (Princeton: Princeton University Press, 1974), pp. 386–397.

53. Adachi Mikio, "*Kosaku chōtei hō*" (Farm Tenancy Conciliation Law), in Ukai, Kawashima, Fukushima & Tsuji (eds.), *Nihon kindaihō hattatsu shi* (History of the development of modern Japanese law) (Heisō shobō, 1959), p. 57.

54. *Ibid.*, vol. 7, pp. 66–68.

FIGURE 3

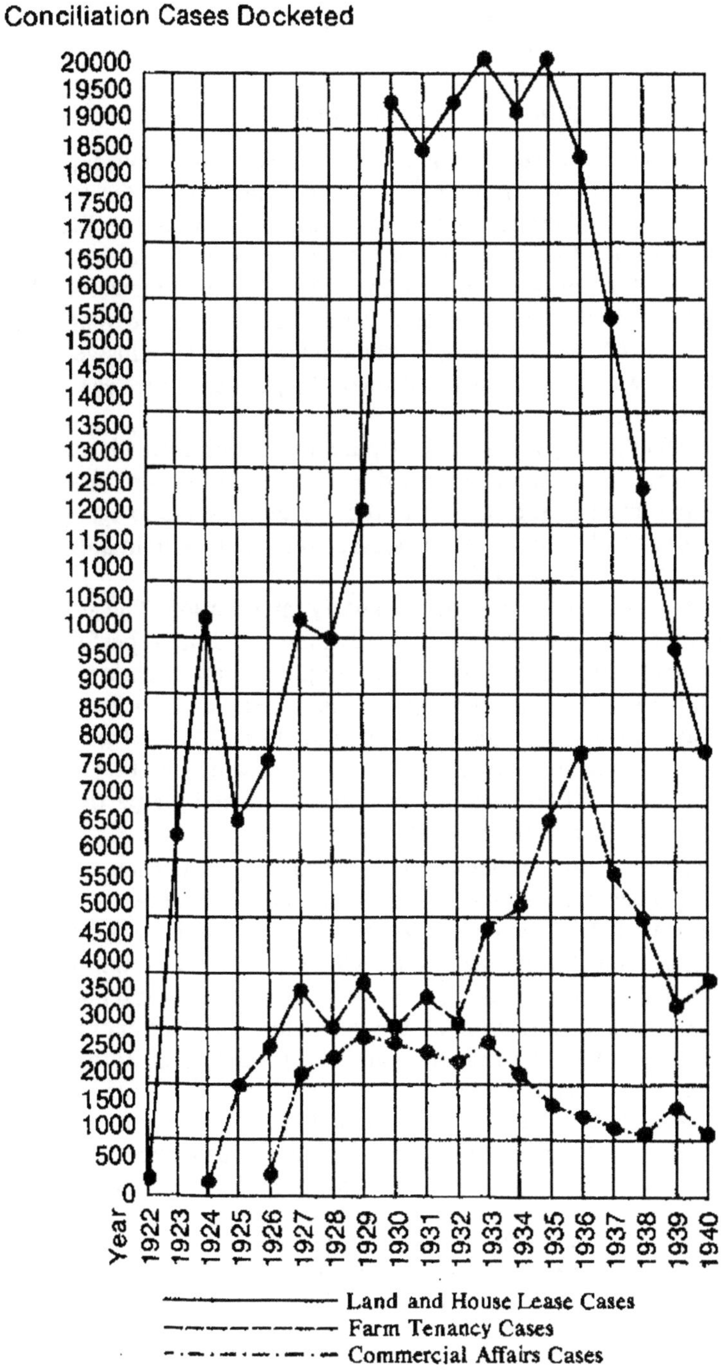
Conciliation Cases Docketed
20000
19500
19000
18500
18000
17500
17000
16500
16000
15500
15000
14500
14000
13500
13000
12500
12000
11500
11000
10500
10000
9500
9000
8500
8000
7500
7000
6500
6000
5500
5000
4500
4000
3500
3000
2500
2000
1500
1000
500
0
Year
1922
1923
1924
1925
1926
1927
1928
1929
1930
1931
1932
1933
1934
1935
1936
1937
1938
1939
1940
Land and House Lease Cases
Farm Tenancy Cases
Commercial Affairs Cases

lead to a decrease in litigation. Instead the creation of an additional process for formal dispute resolution led to an even greater increase of cases channelled into the formal process.

The Reality of Institutional Incapacity

If the Japanese are not particularly averse to litigation, how then can we explain why they appear to use their courts far less frequently than do Americans and perhaps others? Why has litigation decreased since the war (and continues to do so)? Also, what accounts for the pervasive acceptance by Japanese themselves that they are unusually "nonlitigious"? And how do such explanations relate to the efficacy of the judicial model in Japan? To answer these questions, we should first reconsider the paradigm process of dispute resolution.

Typically, the parties to a dispute will move through stages—from direct negotiation, to third party mediation and finally to litigation—as a result of failure in the preceding stage to agree to an acceptable resolution. In this process, a relative lack of litigation can be explained by several factors.

One is the effectiveness of third party intervention. The availability of suitable third parties who are willing and able to perform this role reduces the need to invoke formal judicial intervention. At the outset, mediation requires the presence of persons who, because of position or personal relationships, command respect and are able to exercise some measure of authority. In other words, to be effective, the mediator must be someone who can command the parties' trust and their obedience to the settlement.

One would thus anticipate that suitable third parties are more readily available in a stable, closely-integrated and hierarchical society like Japan, than in a more geographically mobile, less cohesive society like the United States in which individual autonomy and social equality are emphasized. Societal expectations and habits are equally relevant. The role of the mediator becomes increasingly legitimate for both the mediator and the parties to disputes where there is repeated reliance on third parties to settle disputes. A contrast in police attitudes in Japan and the United States pointed out by David H. Bayley[55] is especially interesting in this respect. Japanese commonly rely on the police for assistance in settling disputes.[56] But

55. David H. Bayley, *Forces of Order: Police Behavior in Japan and the United States* (Berkeley: University of California Press, 1976), p. 87.

56. Henderson, vol. 2, p. 191.

despite similar popular demand in the United States, "what is different," says Bayley, "is that American police organizations have not adapted willingly to perform this function."[57] Another Japanese example is the mediating service some companies provide for employees involved in traffic accidents.[58] In short, the Japanese may be more successful in avoiding litigation because of social organization and values more conducive to informal dispute resolution through mediation.

The tendency of the Japanese to mediate does not necessarily impair the effectiveness of the judiciary, however. As we have seen, the judicial model does not depend on the actual frequency of litigation, but rather the influence of the perceived outcome of the litigation on the mediated settlement.

Resort to court is, however, reduced by another set of factors that do inhibit or enhance the utility of the judicial model as a vehicle for social control and development.[59]

First, for courts to have an impact through decisions in individual cases beyond those persons immediately affected in those cases, information about the courts and these decisions must be disseminated in order that parties to similar disputes are sufficiently aware of the legal norm for it to influence informal resolution of their dis-

57. Bayley, p. 87. Some police departments in the United States have moved toward the Japanese practice. In Seattle, for instance, a recently established Community Service Officer Section now provides counseling services, especially in landlord-tenant disputes and potentially violent family quarrels.

The lawyer in the United States is often said to perform a mediative function. See, e.g., Sarat and Grossman, p. 1204. This is not true for most cases, however. Because of the adversarial nature of a lawyer's work and the strictures of the lawyer-client relation, few lawyers are in a position to "mediate" as a neutral third party, and once one party brings a lawyer into the dispute usually the other side does likewise. Thus it is probably more accurate to view a lawyer's intervention as a form of direct negotiation. Since if the dispute is not settled litigation is the obvious next step once lawyers are involved, the mediation state of the paradigm would be skipped in these cases.

58. Ishimura and Kaminaga, p. 96.

59. Excluded from consideration is the effect of the outcome of litigation on the frequency of lawsuits. There will be less litigation where, for instance, those who are more likely to sue (e.g., those with greater financial means) perceive that they are likely to lose or that the judges are not sympathetic and the courts or the law being applied is not responsive to commercial or other needs. This may explain the relative lack of suits in Japan among businesses. Compare, e.g., J. Toshio Sawada, *Subsequent Conduct and Supervening Events; A Study of Two Selected Problems in Contract Jurisprudence* (Ann Arbor: University of Michigan Press, 1968) with Morton J. Horowitz, *The Transformation of American Law 1780–1860* (Cambridge: Harvard University Press, 1977), pp. 140–159.

putes. This does not mean the judicial model cannot work unless people are fully aware of what the courts will do. But people must be generally cognizant that the courts do provide an available option, and they must have the means to become informed about what the probable outcome will be in the specific case. Thus in societies where illiteracy rates are high or little is communicated about the courts, the judicial model will be less successful. A lack of law trained persons and the absence of published reports of court decisions, for example, are serious barriers to the effectiveness of the judiciary.

There must also be meaningful access to the courts. Access can be denied directly by jurisdictional barriers that prevent the courts from adjudicating certain types of disputes altogether.[60] Bond-posting requirements that may place an intolerable burden on the parties seeking relief[61] illustrate another form of conscious policy designed to prevent resort to courts. Limited institutional capacity also inhibits access. There must be a sufficient number of courts, of judges and lawyers, to insure that the costs and delays of litigation do not preclude lawsuits as a realistic option.

A third factor is the capacity of the courts to provide adequate relief. Courts must have available a range of remedial measures and forms of relief to suit the variety of controversies that arise. An award of monetary damages or declarations of the rights and duties of the parties will not always help the aggrieved party. In addition, especially in cases where the legal norm and thus the outcome is reasonably certain, filing suit may evidence a recalcitrant party against whom coercive measures have become necessary. Indeed, many of the cases courts handle each day do not involve any real controversy of fact or law, but simply a last resort to force the other party to perform an acknowledged legal duty. For relief to be adequate the courts must be able to provide a remedy that fits the case and have the capacity to enforce its judgments.

60. A Japanese example of this is article 61 of the Meiji Constitution, which, following continental practice, deprived judicial courts of jurisdiction over cases brought against illegal administrative actions. These cases were adjudicated exclusively by a special administrative court. (Unlike in France and Germany, in Japan there was only one.) For an exhaustive account of the establishment and role of the Japanese Administrative Court, see Hideo Wada, "The Administrative Court under the Meiji Constitution," *Law in Japan*, vol. 10 (1977), p. 1ff. Wada emphasizes the antipathy of the civil bureaucracy to judicial intervention.

61. See articles 107–117 of the Japanese Code of Civil Procedure (*Minji soshō hō*), Law No. 29, 1890.

Assessing the effectiveness of Japanese courts in terms of these criteria, one finds first that lack of information in Japan is not a particular problem. Law is among the most popular fields of undergraduate study. The newspapers and other media cover the courts and regularly report judicial decisions. There is also in Japan an amazing abundance of legal journals and books on the law, including a plethora of layman's *Handobukku* for particular legal problems to advise the average person.[62] But evidence of other institutional barriers to litigation is ample.

The courts in Japan are even more strained to capacity than in the United States. Superior courts in California in 1971–72, for example, disposed of 964 cases per judge. In 1974, United States District Courts had a caseload of only 325 cases per judge.[63] These caseloads are considered to be excessively high.[64] Yet District Courts in Tokyo and Osaka disposed of 1,525 cases per judge in 1969 and the total Japanese caseload in 1974 was 1,708 cases per judge.[65] This results from a lack of judges. As indicated in Table 6, the number of judges in Japan has grown but little for the entire period from 1890 to the present. Thus as the population has grown the ratio of judges to the population has declined from one judge to 21,926 persons in 1890 to one judge to 52,800 persons in 1926 and one judge to 56,391 persons in 1969.

As a result of overcrowded courts, aggravated by the form of trials in Japan that (as in other civil law jurisdictions) involve recurring hearings typically spaced at one month intervals, delay is acute. The simplest trial can take over a year at the district court level, and the average is two years (Table 7). If there are appeals, the case will take about five years, but proceedings that continue for eight to ten years are not uncommon.

The relationship of delay and a lack of lawyers to frequency of litigation is revealed rather starkly in analysis of litigation in prewar Japan. As seen in Table 5 for the period between 1891–1941, the

62. See, e.g., Richard W. Rabinowitz, "Law and the Social Process in Japan," *Transactions of the Asiatic Society of Japan*, vol. 10 (3d Series, Tokyo, 1968), pp. 41–43.

63. Director of the Administrative Office of the U.S. Courts, 1974 *Annual Report* (Washington D.C., 1974), p. 196.

64. See, e.g., "Chief Justice Burger's 1977 Report to the American Bar Association," *American Bar Association Journal*, vol. 63 (April, 1977), p. 504, in which the Chief Justice called for the creation of 132 new federal judgeships.

65. Nihon Bengoshi Rengōkai (Japan Federation of Bar Associations), *Shihō hakusho* (White paper on the judiciary) (Tokyo, 1974), pp. 326–327.

TABLE 6
THE LEGAL PROFESSION IN JAPAN 1890–1973

Year	Judges	Public Procurators	Private Attorneys	Private Attorneys per 1 million persons
1890	1,531	481	1,345	33.7
1892	1,532	482	1,423	35.1
1894	1,221	383	1,562	38.0
1896	1,221	383	1,578	37.6
1898	1,244	473	1,464	34.1
1900	1,244	473	1,590	36.3
1902	1,208	363	1,727	38.4
1904	1,197	374	1,908	41.4
1906	1,179	379	2,027	43.1
1908	1,234	401	2,006	42.7
1910	1,125	390	2,008	40.8
1912	1,129	390	2,036	40.3
1914	898	386	2,256	43.4
1916	903	359	2,665	49.8
1918	1,004	478	2,947	53.8
1920	1,134	570	3,082	55.6
1922	1,150	578	3,914	68.9
1924	1,155	574	5,485	94.0
1926	1,121	564	5,936	98.6
1928	1,245	656	6,304	101.5
1930	1,249	657	6,599	103.3
1932	1,345	628	7,055	107.1
1934	1,370	648	7,082	104.6
1936	1,391	648	5,776	87.6
1938	1,470	686	4,866	69.2
1940	1,541	734	5,498	70.7
1942	1,581	625	5,231	70.3
1944	1,188	610	5,174	70.1
1946	1,232	668	5,737	75.7
1948	1,842*	1,387*	5,992	74.8
1950	2,261	1,673	5,862	70.5
1952	2,323	1,717	5,872	69.9
1954	2,327	1,717	5,942	69.7
1956	2,327	1,717	6,040	69.9
1958	2,347	1,717	6,235	70.4
1960	2,367	1,761	6,439	70.2
1962	2,450	1,796	6,740	71.3
1964	2,475	1,829	7,108	73.9
1966	2,518	1,844	7,687	78.2
1968	2,525	1,871	8,016	80.4
1969	2,580	1,946	8,580	84.6
1970	2,605	1,983	8,868	86.2
1971	2,619	2,019	9,167	88.2
1972	2,681	2,071	9,483	90.2
1973	2,688	2,076	9,921	92.0

* The figures after 1948 include the number of summary court judges and assistant procurators.

Source: Nihon Bengoshi Rengōkai (Japan Federation of Bar Associations) *Shihō Hakusho* (White Paper on the Legal System) (Tokyo, 1974), pp. 102–03.

TABLE 7
COURTS AND PROCEDURE

Average Time Required for Disposition of Civil Cases
(not including administrative cases)

A. Cases First Brought In Summary Courts
The Period from Filing in the Court of First Instance to Decision

Year	Summary Courts	District Courts (kōso)	High Courts (jōkoku)
1960	4.9 months	22.4 months	42.8 months
1965	5.7	31.6	50.7
1970	4.8	36.2	53.9

B. Cases First Brought In District Courts
The Period from Filing in Court of First Instance to Decision

Year	District Courts	High Courts (kōso)	Supreme Court (jōkoku)
1960	12.6 months	38.2 months	67.5 months
1965	12.1	40.4	67.7
1970	12.8	40.0	66.0

Source: Hideo Tanaka, *The Japanese Legal System: Introductory Cases and Materials* (Tokyo: University of Tokyo Press, 1976), p. 476.

percentage change in new civil actions filed in any given year was best predicted by a model in which a rise in actions filed in one year tended to predict a rise in the next year, but a fall in the third year. Such a trend can be explained in terms of legal institutions that are very responsive to "market" forces. As the availability of judicial relief becomes known, more lawsuits are filed. As the number of lawsuits increase so the number of lawyers also increases, resulting in even greater information about and access to the courts. If, however, the number of judges is not expanded to meet such increases, there will be greater delay as caseloads per judge become heavier. Such delay contributes in turn to a decrease in litigation.

However unlikely such an appraisal of the Japanese legal process may appear, it is consistent with subsequent analysis of the data. When the hypothesis that potential litigants respond positively to the number of lawyers per capita and delay (using the ratios of first instance civil trials completed in three months to the total number of first instance civil trials and first instance civil trials completed after one year to total first instance civil trials), the results (Table 8) show that there is a significant correlation between the number of trial actions filed in a given year with the number of lawyers per capita in that year and delay in the previous year.

TABLE 8
REGRESSIONS
(t Values in Parentheses)

Regression Equations	Dependent Variable	Constant	Independent Variables				R^2	d.f.	D.W.
(1)	NCTA	= −3566.2	+ 10400.7 AGEMP/POP	+ 2116.2 LAG 3 MON/TO	− 21894 7 LAG YEAR/TO	+ 47.833 LAWYER	.838	27	1.186
		(−.5151)	(1 3209)	(.1873)	(−.6123)	(11.4056)			
(2)	NCTA IDIFF	= −4103.0	+ 3817.6 AGEMP/POP	+ 5769.3 3 MON/TO	+ 7212.0 YEAR/TO	+ 5.767 LAWYER	.401	27	.841
		(−1.0435)	(.7978)	(.8924)	(3544)	(2.3677)			
(3)	NCTA IDIFF	= −10642.7	+ 11903.6 AGEMP/POP	+ 13411 3 LAG 3 MON/TO	+ 45077.5 LAG YEAR/TO	+ 6.279 LAWYER	.481	27	1.126
		(−2.8291)	(2.7821)	(2.1846)	(2.3199)	(2.7758)			
(4)	NCTA IDIFF	= −7440.4	+ 11295.9 AGEMP/POP	+ 8930.3 LAG 3 MON/TO	+ 41563.1 LAG YEAR/TO	− 27.451 JUDGES	.349	27	.790
		(−1.8642)	(2.0766)	(1.3453)	(1.8113)	(−1 8038)			

NCTA = New Civil Trial Actions (cases docketed for formal trial proceedings) Filed.
AGEMP/POP = Ratio of Agricultural Employment to Total Population (from: Kazushi Ohkawa and Henry Rosovsky, *Japanese Economic Growth—Trend Acceleration in the Twentieth Century*. [Palo Alto: Stanford University Press], pp. 310–311).
LAWYERS = Per Capita Number of Lawyers.
NCTA IDIFF = Change in NCTA.
3 MON/TO = Ratio of First Instance Trial Actions Disposed of Within 3 Months to Total First Instance Trial Actions Concurrent with REAL NCTA.
YEAR/TO = Ratio of First Instance Trial Actions Disposed of Within One Year to Total First Instance Trial Actions Concurrent with REAL NCTA.
JUDGES = Per Capita Number of Judges.
LAG 3 MON/TO = Ratio of First Instance Trial Actions Disposed of Within 3 Months to Total First Instance Trial Actions Lagged One Year Behind REAL NCTA.
LAG YEAR/TO = Ratio of First Instance Trial Actions Disposed of Within One Year to Total First Instance Trial Action Lagged One Year Behind REAL NCTA.

Moreover, when the ratio of agricultural employment to the total population is included, the results show a *positive* correlation. That is, *lower* rates of agricultural employment coincide with *decreases* (or smaller increases) in the number of new civil actions. This of course does not mean that decreasing agricultural employment necessarily causes or even contributes to decreasing litigation, other factors may explain parallel declines. This result is, however, inconsistent with the notion that litigation in Japan is an index to modernization, or at least industrialization.

The postwar data is more troubling. The analysis of postwar litigation noted above (Table 5) produces a very different result from the prewar pattern. The estimate is that a positive change in one or more random variables will contribute to an increase in the number of civil suits filed in that year and to a decrease in the year thereafter (perhaps explained by delay as above), but there is no indication that these random variables operate in any cyclical fashion and as random variables they may be positive or negative in any given year. (Since the data base for the postwar period is relatively weak—25 as opposed to 50 years—no attempt was made to analyze further the postwar data.)

The failure of Japan to provide more judges and lawyers has been clearly a matter of governmental policy. As to lawyers, since the mid-1930s, entry has been limited by a strictly enforced examination system. (This would explain why the number of lawyers would have levelled off after 1935, but not the extraordinary decrease in lawyers between 1934 and 1938. [See Table 6.] For reasons that are not at all clear, nearly a third of all Japanese attorneys withdrew from their bar associations during this period.) In the postwar system with few exceptions, all members of the legal profession have had to complete an apprenticeship under the Legal Training and Research Institute (*Shihō Kenshū Sho*). To enter, a person must pass the national judicial examination (*shihō shiken*). As can be seen from the data in Table 9, the number of applicants has increased tenfold, while the number of those who pass has been limited to about 500. The most common reason given is budgetary constraint—those who attend the Institute receive government stipends. For purposes of comparison—and to put to rest any doubts about contemporary Japanese attitudes toward the legal profession[66]—the number per capita of

66. Often repeated comments on the lack of interest on the part of Japanese to become attorneys and low status of the bar are manifestly in error. See particularly Danielski, pp. 124–125; remarks by Charles R. Stevens, "Developing a Pacific Community," p. 79; Oppler, p. 107.

TABLE 9
THE JAPANESE NATIONAL LAW EXAMINATION

Year	Applicants	Persons passing final examinations (and entering the LTRI)	Percentage of successful Applicants
1949	2514	265	10.5%
1950	2755	269	9.8%
1951	3648	272	7.5%
1952	4765	253	5.3%
1953	5141	224	4.4%
1954	5172	250	4.8%
1955	6306	264	4.2%
1956	6714	297	4.4%
1957	6920	286	4.1%
1958	7074	346	4.9%
1959	7819	319	4.1%
1960	8302	345	4.2%
1961	10921	380	3.5%
1962	10802	459	4.2%
1963	11725	456	3.9%
1964	12728	508	4.0%
1965	13681	528	3.9%
1966	14867	554	3.7%
1967	16460	537	3.3%
1968	17727	525	3.0%
1969	18453	501	2.7%
1970	20160	507	2.5%
1971	22336	533	2.6%
1972	23425	537	2.3%
1973	25259	537	2.1%
1974	26708	491	1.8%
1975	27791	472	1.7%

Source: Tanaka, p. 577.

Japanese taking the judicial examination in 1975 was slightly higher than that of Americans taking a bar examination.[67] Since in the United States 74% passed compared to 1.7% in Japan, the desire to become a lawyer on the part of Japanese may be significantly higher than Americans if self-selection is considered. Moreover, the attraction of the legal profession has grown in both Japan and the United States by almost an identical degree.[68]

67. In 1975 in Japan, 27,791, persons took the judicial exam (Table 9). While in the United States 46,414 persons (36,873 first timers) took a state (or D.C.) bar examination *The Bar Examiner*, vol. 45 (1976), p. 95.

68. In 1963 there were 11,725 applicants for the Japanese judicial examination (Table 9) and 15,761 persons (11,397 first timers) who took a U.S. bar examination. *Bar Examiner*, vol. 33 (1963), p. 87.

The limited range of remedies available to Japanese courts and the lack of contempt power to enforce their decisions are equally serious. Japanese courts in the postwar period have continued to rely on continental notions of judicial power that restrict available remedies to those provided by statute. In the area of civil law this has meant that the courts can order specific performance, award damages, or enter declaratory judgments affirming the legal relations of parties in the suit. In most instances, these remedies are effective because of voluntary compliance. But lacking the power of contempt, a court has no way to enforce its decrees on its own motion. Instead, it must rely on procurators to initiate criminal proceedings.[69]

The problem of adequate relief is even more critical in the area of actions by private citizens against the government. The options open to a court in these cases are very limited. They include, for example, declaratory relief of affirming the legality or invalidity of administrative actions or decisions of the failure of officials to act and revocation of administrative acts, and decisions.[70] The law provides the power to suspend administrative actions but includes a provision permitting the Prime Minister to object, thereby requiring the court to retract its order.[71] There is no clear provision empowering the courts to order an administrative agency to take affirmative action, although there is considerable argument on this issue among scholars, there is as yet no authoritative court decision.[72]

The limitations of the courts' capacity to respond in such instances is illustrated in the decision in *Kurokawa v. Chiba Prefecture Election Commission*,[73] holding unconstitutional the 1972 electoral system. The Japanese Supreme Court in that case was faced

69 See Japanese Penal Code (*Keihō*), Law No. 45, 1907, art. 96-2.

70. For a brief discussion in English, see Ichirō Ogawa, "Judicial Review of Administrative Actions in Japan," *Washington Law Review*, vol. 43 (1968), p. 1075.

71. The former Administrative Case Special Regulations Law (*Gyōsei jiken soshō tokurei hō*), Law No. 81, 1948), art. 10; the current Administrative Case Litigation Law (*Gyōsei jiken soshō hō*), Law No. 139, 1962, art. 27.

72. See, e.g., Naohiko Harada, "Preventive Suits and Duty-Imposing Suits in Administrative Litigation," *Law in Japan*, vol. 9 (1976), pp. 63–82. Harada cites only one case of a preventive declaratory action—Kinoshita v. Chief of the Fuchū Criminal Affairs Office, 14 *Gyōsai reishū* 1316 (Tokyo Dt. Ct., July 29, 1963) in which a prisoner sought to have the court prohibit compulsory haircuts. *Id*. at fn. 30. But see the more recent Supreme Court decision in *Higaki v. Nagano Prefecture*, 26 Minshū (No. 9) 1746 (Sup. Ct., 1st P.B., Nov. 30, 1972), recognizing declaratory preventive suits.

73. 30 Minshū (No. 3) 223 (Sup. Ct., Gt. B., April 14. 1976).

with three alternatives aside from upholding the system on the merits as it had done in its 1964 Grand Bench decision in *Koshiyama v. Tokyo Prefecture Election Commission*.[74] It could have avoided the decision through a variety of devices denying justiciability.[75] Or it could have declared the 1972 election null and void, hence raising doubts as to the validity of the Diet elected thereunder and thus all subsequent legislative actions. The third alternative, and the one it chose to follow, was to declare the system unconstitutional but to refrain from invalidating the election. As a result the government has all but ignored the decision, and the Supreme Court and the judiciary, as one-third of the justices predicted, has appeared naked and powerless as a political organ. The contrast to American reapportionment cases[76] is revealing. American courts had the power to retain jurisdiction and to force state legislatures to redistrict, setting precise guidelines for what was constitutional in these cases; while some debate the courts' wisdom in acting,[77] few question their ability to do so.

The executive in Japan is equally limited in enforcing law. In the United States regulatory law is enforced principally through the civil process with the courts acting in partnership with administrative agencies. Orders issued by agencies are ultimately backed up by court order and the threat of contempt for disobedience. Criminal sanctions are cumbersome and seldom invoked.[78] In Japan, how-

74. 18 Minshū 270 (Sup. Ct., G.B., Feb. 5, 1964).

75. Justice Amano, the sole dissenter on the merits of the election case, argued that the case should have been dismissed on the technical ground that the Chiba Prefectural Election Commission was not the proper party defendant.

76. See Baker v. Carr, 369 U.S. 186 (1962); Scholle v. Hare 369 U.S. 429 (1962); Wesberry v. Sanders, 376 U.S. 1 (1963), especially discussion on the ability of lower courts to fashion an appropriate remedy.

77. See, e.g., Alexander M. Bickel, *The Least Dangerous Branch: The Supreme Court at the Bar of Politics* (Indianapolis: Bobbs Merrill 1962).

78. See, e.g., Kenneth G. Elzinga and William Breit, *The Antitrust Penalties* (New Haven: Yale University Press, 1976), pp. 30–43, one of the few studies to evaluate the effectiveness of various types of sanctions. The authors conclude that, "until judges and juries are convinced beyond a reasonable doubt that the well-dressed, wealthy, articulate pillar of the community facing them is in actuality the real instigator and director of a conspiracy to cut back production, rig prices, and rob consumers and taxpayers just as effectively as a common mugger or bank robber, it is unlikely that prison sentences often will be imposed for violations of the antitrust laws. The sentence of this penalty in the antitrust arsenal is not a realistic deterrent to corporate criminality." *Ibid.*, p. 43. Similar considerations plus a marked reticence to apply criminal sanctions in most instances would appear to make resort to criminal sanctions even less effective in Japan than in the United States. On this last point,

ever, the government must rely exclusively on a criminal process that for cultural and other reasons seems to be even less available.

From this perspective the prevalence of conciliation of private disputes and "administrative guidance" (*gyōsei shidō*) by administrative authorities can be explained as basically similar responses to the absence of effective law-enforcing mechanisms in Japan.[79] If we ignore the obfuscating gloss that these are endemically Japanese phenomena, we are left with processes and a necessary reliance on consensus present in any legal order lacking effective sanctions. Both conciliation and administrative guidance invoke negotiated agreement and voluntary compliance. To the extent that sanctions exist, they tend to be indirect, informal and extralegal.

Conclusion

Few misconceptions about Japan have been more widespread or as pernicious as the myth of the special reluctance of the Japanese to litigate. In emphasizing this peculiar Japanese response, most commentators ignore the distaste for litigation and preference for informal dispute resolution common to most societies. As noted at the outset of this article, censure of litigation is arguably as much a part of the traditional Christian heritage as it is a legacy of Confucianism. What distinguishes Japan is the successful implementation of this interdiction through institutional arrangements. When we disregard the shared nature of these attitudes, we also fail to note applicable lessons from the Japanese experience. By increasing the number of judges to reduce our court delays, for instance, we may simply spur more litigation and greater social disintegration.

see, e.g., Bayley, pp. 134–159; Shigemitsu Dando, "System of Discretionary Prosecution in Japan," *American Journal of Comparative Law*, vol. 18 (1970), pp. 518–531. Dando cites statistics showing that prosecution was suspended in 87.1% of all cases involving abuse of authority by public officials as compared to 6.3% of robbery cases. *Ibid.*, p. 524 (Table 2).

79. For evidence that conciliation is used in lieu of litigation at least in part because of the inability of the legal system to provide adequate relief, see Nibu Yoshitaka, *Kaji jiken no rikō kakuho seido* (System for enforcing performance in family affairs cases) (6 *Shihō kenkyū hokokusho* (No. 8, 1954), pp. 2–7 in which it is reported that failure to comply with court judgments in family cases for distribution of property, child support and "mental suffering" awards ranged from 30 to 90 per cent by prefecture. However, compliance was significantly higher where there was conciliation. Also, it has been noted that landlords resorted to conciliation in the prewar rural tenancy cases because of difficulty in enforcing favorable court judgments. Adachi, p. 53.

The myth also directs attention away from factors that may help us to understand better some of the dynamics of Japanese life and hides from view relationships that we might otherwise profitably explore. Does the failure of the courts to provide adequate relief explain, at least in part, such apparent social abnormalities such as gangsterism and recurrent bouts of violence in Japan's otherwise remarkably crime-free society? On the other hand, does limited access to the courts also have the effect of promoting beneficial forms of mediation and other mechanisms for disputes resolution? What is the relationship between the number of lawyers and litigation in other societies?

Finally, attributing a relative lack of litigation in Japan to pervasive cultural—and thus more immutable—causes, provides justification for continuing intended and unintended barriers to a more effective judiciary. It hinders inquiry into what the proper balance should be between the need to assure adequate judicial relief and the need to maintain social harmony. "Why should we have more judges" a Minister of Finance preparing the budget might ask, "since we are not a very litigious people."

UNIVERSITY OF WASHINGTON

[6]

NON-CONTRACTUAL RELATIONS IN BUSINESS: A PRELIMINARY STUDY *

STEWART MACAULAY

Law School, University of Wisconsin

Preliminary findings indicate that businessmen often fail to plan exchange relationships completely, and seldom use legal sanctions to adjust these relationships or to settle disputes. Planning and legal sanctions are often unnecessary and may have undesirable consequences. Transactions are planned and legal sanctions are used when the gains are thought to outweigh the costs. The power to decide whether the gains from using contract outweigh the costs will be held by individuals having different occupational roles. The occupational role influences the decision that is made.

WHAT good is contract law? who uses it? when and how? Complete answers would require an investigation of almost every type of transaction between individuals and oganizations. In this report, research has been confined to exchanges between businesses, and primarily to manufacturers.[1] Futhermore, this report will be limited to a presentation of the findings concerning when contract is and is not used and to a tentative explanation of these findings.[2]

This research is only the first phase in a scientific study.[3] The primary research technique involved interviewing 68 businessmen and lawyers representing 43 companies and six law firms. The interviews ranged from a 30-minute brush-off where not all questions could be asked of a busy and uninterested sales manager to a six-hour discussion with the general counsel of a large corporation. Detailed notes of the interviews were taken and a complete report of each interview was dictated, usually no later than the evening after the interview. All but two of the companies had plants in Wisconsin; 17 were manufacturers of machinery but

---

* Revision of a paper read at the annual meeting of the Americal Sociological Association, August, 1962. An earlier version of the paper was read at the annual meeting of the Midwest Sociological Society, April, 1962. The research has been supported by a Law and Policy Research Grant to the University of Wisconsin Law School from the Ford Foundation. I am grateful for the help generously given by a number of sociologists including Robert K. Merton, Harry V. Ball, Jerome Carlin and William Evan.

[1] The reasons for this limitation are that (a) these transactions are important from an economic standpoint, (b) they are frequently said in theoretical discussions to represent a high degree of rational planning, and (c) manufacturing personnel are sufficiently public-relations-minded to cooperate with a law professor who wants to ask a seemingly endless number of questions. Future research will deal with the building construction industry and other areas.

[2] For the present purposes, the what-difference-does-it-make issue is important primarily as it makes a case for an empirical study by a law teacher of the use and nonuse of contract by businessmen. First, law teachers have a professional concern with what the law ought to be. This involves evaluation of the consequences of the existing situation and of the possible alternatives. Thus, it is most relevant to examine business practices concerning contract if one is interested in what commercial law ought to be. Second, law teachers are supposed to teach law students something relevant to becoming lawyers. These business practices are facts that are relevant to the skills which law students will need when, as lawyers, they are called upon to create exchange relationships and to solve problems arising out of these relationships.

[3] The following things have been done. The literature in law, business, economics, psychology, and sociology has been surveyed. The formal systems related to exchange transactions have been examined. Standard form contracts and the standard terms and conditions that are found on such business documents as catalogues, quotation forms, purchase orders, and acknowledgment-of-order forms from 850 firms that are based in or do business in Wisconsin have been collected. The citations of all reported court cases during a period of 15 years involving the largest 500 manufacturing corporations in the United States have been obtained and are being analyzed to determine why the use of contract legal sanctions was thought necessary and whether or not any patterns of "problem situations" can be delineated. In addition, the informal systems related to exchange transactions have been examined. Letters of inquiry concerning practices in certain situations have been answered by approximately 125 businessmen. Interviews, as described in the text, have been conducted. Moreover, six of my students have interviewed 21 other businessmen, bankers and lawyers. Their findings are consistent with those reported in the text.

none made such items as food products, scientific instruments, textiles or petroleum products. Thus the likelihood of error because of sampling bias may be considerable.[4] However, to a great extent, existing knowledge has been inadequate to permit more rigorous procedures—as yet one cannot formulate many precise questions to be asked a systematically selected sample of "right people." Much time has been spent fishing for relevant questions or answers, or both.

Reciprocity, exchange or contract has long been of interest to sociologists, economists and lawyers. Yet each discipline has an incomplete view of this kind of conduct. This study represents the effort of a law teacher to draw on sociological ideas and empirical investigation. It stresses, among other things, the functions and dysfunctions of using contract to solve exchange problems and the influence of occupational roles on how one assesses whether the benefits of using contract outweigh the costs.

To discuss when contract is and is not used, the term "contract" must be specified. This term will be used here to refer to devices for conducting exchanges. Contract is not treated as synonymous with an exchange itself, which may or may not be characterized as contractual. Nor is contract used to refer to a writing recording an agreement. Contract, as I use the term here, involves two distinct elements: (a) Rational planning of the transaction with careful provision for as many future contingencies as can be foreseen, and (b) the existence or use of actual or potential legal sanctions to induce performance of the exchange or to compensate for non-performance.

These devices for conducting exchanges may be used or may exist in greater or lesser degree, so that transactions can be described relatively as involving a more contractual or a less contractual manner (a) of creating an exchange relationship or (b) of solving problems arising during the course of such a relationship. For example, General Motors might agree to buy all of the Buick Division's requirements of aluminum for ten years from Reynolds Aluminum. Here the two large corporations probably would plan their relationship carefully. The plan probably would include a complex pricing formula designed to meet market fluctuations, an agreement on what would happen if either party suffered a strike or a fire, a definition of Reynolds' responsibility for quality control and for losses caused by defective quality, and many other provisions. As the term contract is used here, this is a more contractual method of creating an exchange relationship than is a home-owner's casual agreement with a real estate broker giving the broker the exclusive right to sell the owner's house which fails to include provisions for the consequences of many easily foreseeable (and perhaps even highly probable) contingencies. In both instances, legally enforceable contracts may or may not have been created, but it must be recognized that the existence of a legal sanction has no necessary relationship to the degree of rational planning by the parties, beyond certain minimal legal requirements of certainty of obligation. General Motors and Reynolds might never sue or even refer to the written record of their agreement to answer questions which come up during their ten-year relationship, while the real estate broker might sue, or at least threaten to sue, the owner of the house. The broker's method of *dispute settlement* then would be more contractual than that of General Motors and Reynolds, thus reversing the relationship that existed in regard to the "contractualness" of the *creation* of the exchange relationships.

TENTATIVE FINDINGS

It is difficult to generalize about the use and nonuse of contract by manufacturing industry. However, a number of observations can be made with reasonable accuracy at this time. The use and nonuse of contract in creating exchange relations and in dispute settling will be taken up in turn.

The creation of exchange relationships. In creating exchange relationships, businessmen may plan to a greater or lesser degree in relation to several types of issues. Before reporting the findings as to practices in cre-

[4] However, the cases have not been selected because they *did* use contract. There is as much interest in, and effort to obtain, cases of nonuse as of use of contract. Thus, one variety of bias has been minimized.

ating such relationships, it is necessary to describe what one can plan about in a bargain and the degrees of planning which are possible.

People negotiating a contract can make plans concerning several types of issues: (1) They can plan what each is to do or refrain from doing; e.g., S might agree to deliver ten 1963 Studebaker four-door sedan automobiles to B on a certain date in exchange for a specified amount of money. (2) They can plan what effect certain contingencies are to have on their duties; e.g., what is to happen to S and B's obligations if S cannot deliver the cars because of a strike at the Studebaker factory? (3) They can plan what is to happen if either of them fails to perform; e.g., what is to happen if S delivers nine of the cars two weeks late? (4) They can plan their agreement so that it is a legally enforceable contract—that is, so that a legal sanction would be available to provide compensation for injury suffered by B as a result of S's failure to deliver the cars on time.

As to each of these issues, there may be a different degree of planning by the parties. (1) They may carefully and explicitly plan; e.g., S may agree to deliver ten 1963 Studebaker four-door sedans which have six cylinder engines, automatic transmissions and other specified items of optional equipment and which will perform to a specified standard for a certain time. (2) They may have a mutual but tacit understanding about an issue; e.g., although the subject was never mentioned in their negotiations, both S and B may assume that B may cancel his order for the cars before they are delivered if B's taxi-cab business is so curtailed that B can no longer use ten additional cabs. (3) They may have two inconsistent unexpressed assumptions about an issue; e.g., S may assume that if any of the cabs fails to perform to the specified standard for a certain time, all S must do is repair or replace it. B may assume S must also compensate B for the profits B would have made if the cab had been in operation. (4) They may never have thought of the issue; e.g., neither S nor B planned their agreement so that it would be a legally enforceable contract. Of course, the first and fourth degrees of planning listed are the extreme cases and the second and third are intermediate points. Clearly other intermediate points are possible; e.g., S and B neglect to specify whether the cabs should have automatic or conventional transmissions. Their planning is not as careful and explicit as that in the example previously given.

The following diagram represents the dimensions of creating an exchange relationship just discussed with "X's" representing the example of S and B's contract for ten taxi-cabs.

	Definition of Performances	Effect of Contingencies	Effect of Defective Performances	Legal Sanctions
Explicit and careful	X			
Tacit agreement		X		
Unilateral assumptions			X	
Unawareness of the issue				X

Most larger companies, and many smaller ones, attempt to plan carefully and completely. Important transactions not in the ordinary course of business are handled by a detailed contract. For example, recently the Empire State Building was sold for $65 million. More than 100 attorneys, representing 34 parties, produced a 400 page contract. Another example is found in the agreement of a major rubber company in the United States to give technical assistance to a Japanese firm. Several million dollars were involved and the contract consisted of 88 provisions on 17 pages. The 12 house counsel—lawyers who work for one corporation rather than many clients—interviewed said that all but the smallest businesses carefully planned most transactions of any significance. Corporations have procedures so that particular types of exchanges will be reviewed by their legal and financial departments.

More routine transactions commonly are handled by what can be called standardized planning. A firm will have a set of terms and conditions for purchases, sales, or both printed on the business documents used in these exchanges. Thus the things to be sold and the price may be planned particularly for each transaction, but standard provisions will further elaborate the performances and cover the other subjects of planning. Typically, these terms and conditions are lengthy and printed in small type on the back of the forms. For example, 24 paragraphs in eight point type are printed on the back of the purchase order form used by the Allis Chalmers Manufacturing Company. The provisions: (1) describe, in part, the performance required, e.g., "DO NOT WELD CASTINGS WITHOUT OUR CONSENT"; (2) plan for the effect of contingencies, e.g., ". . . in the event the Seller suffers delay in performance due to an act of God, war, act of the Government, priorities or allocations, act of the Buyer, fire, flood, strike, sabotage, or other causes beyond Seller's control, the time of completion shall be extended a period of time equal to the period of such delay if the Seller gives the Buyer notice in writing of the cause of any such delay within a reasonable time after the beginning thereof"; (3) plan for the effect of defective performances, e.g., "The buyer, without waiving any other legal rights, reserves the right to cancel without charge or to postpone deliveries of any of the articles covered by this order which are not shipped in time reasonably to meet said agreed dates"; (4) plan for a legal sanction, e.g., the clause "without waiving any other legal rights," in the example just given.

In larger firms such "boiler plate" provisions are drafted by the house counsel or the firm's outside lawyer. In smaller firms such provisions may be drafted by the industry trade association, may be copied from a competitor, or may be found on forms purchased from a printer. In any event, salesmen and purchasing agents, the operating personnel, typically are unaware of what is said in the fine print on the back of the forms they use. Yet often the normal business patterns will give effect to this standardized planning. For example, purchasing agents may have to use a purchase order form so that all transactions receive a number under the firm's accounting system. Thus, the required accounting record will carry the necessary planning of the exchange relationship printed on its reverse side. If the seller does not object to this planning and accepts the order, the buyer's "fine print" will control. If the seller does object, differences can be settled by negotiation.

This type of standardized planning is very common. Requests for copies of the business documents used in buying and selling were sent to approximately 6,000 manufacturing firms which do business in Wisconsin. Approximately 1,200 replies were received and 850 companies used some type of standardized planning. With only a few exceptions, the firms that did not reply and the 350 that indicated they did not use standardized planning were very small manufacturers such as local bakeries, soft drink bottlers and sausage makers.

While businessmen can and often do carefully and completely plan, it is clear that not all exchanges are neatly rationalized. Although most businessmen think that a clear description of both the seller's and buyer's performances is obvious common sense, they do not always live up to this ideal. The house counsel and the purchasing agent of a medium size manufacturer of automobile parts reported that several times their engineers had committed the company to buy expensive machines without adequate specifications. The engineers had drawn careful specifications as to the type of machine and how it was to be made but had neglected to require that the machine produce specified results. An attorney and an auditor both stated that most contract disputes arise because of ambiguity in the specifications.

Businessmen often prefer to rely on "a man's word" in a brief letter, a handshake, or "common honesty and decency"—even when the transaction involves exposure to serious risks. Seven lawyers from law firms with business practices were interviewed. Five thought that businessmen often entered contracts with only a minimal degree of advance planning. They complained that businessmen desire to "keep it simple and avoid red tape" even where large amounts of money and significant risks are involved. One stated that he was "sick of being told, 'We can trust old Max,' when the problem is not one of honesty but one of reaching an agreement that both sides understand." Another said that businessmen when bargaining often talk only in pleasant generalities, think they have a contract, but fail to reach agreement on any of the hard, unpleasant questions until forced to do so by a lawyer. Two outside lawyers had different views. One thought that large firms usually planned important exchanges, although he conceded that occasionally matters might be left in a fairly vague state. The other dissenter represents a large utility that commonly buys heavy equipment and buildings. The supplier's employees come on the utility's property to install the equipment or construct the buildings, and they may be injured while there. The utility has been sued by such employees so often that it carefully plans purchases with the assistance of a lawyer so that suppliers take this burden.

Moreover, standardized planning can break down. In the example of such planning previously given, it was assumed that the purchasing agent would use his company's form with its 24 paragraphs printed on the back and that the seller would accept this or object to any provisions he did not like. However, the seller may fail to read the buyer's 24 paragraphs of fine print and may accept the buyer's order on the seller's own acknowledgment-of-order form. Typically this form will have ten to 50 paragraphs favoring the seller, and these provisions are likely to be different from or inconsistent with the buyer's provisions. The seller's acknowledgment form may be received by the buyer and checked by a clerk. She will read the *face* of the acknowledgment but not the fine print on the back of it because she has neither the time nor ability to analyze the small print on the 100 to 500 forms she must review each day. The face of the acknowledgment—where the goods and the price are specified—is likely to correspond with the face of the purchase order. If it does, the two forms are filed away. At this point, both buyer and seller are likely to assume they have planned an exchange and made a contract. Yet they have done neither, as they are in disagreement about all that appears on the back of their forms. This practice is common enough to have a name. Law teachers call it "the battle of the forms."

Ten of the 12 purchasing agents interviewed said that frequently the provisions on the back of their purchase order and those on the back of a supplier's acknowledgment would differ or be inconsistent. Yet they would assume that the purchase was complete without further action unless one of the supplier's provisions was really objectionable. Moreover, only occasionally would they bother to read the fine print on the back of suppliers' forms. On the other hand, one purchasing agent insists that agreement be reached on the fine print provisions, but he represents the utility whose lawyer reported that it exercises great care in planning. The other purchasing agent who said that his company did not face a battle of the forms problem, works for a division of one of the largest manufacturing corporations in the United States. Yet the company may have such a problem without recognizing it. The purchasing agent regularly sends a supplier both a purchase order and another form which the supplier is asked to sign and return. The second form states that the supplier accepts the buyer's terms and conditions. The company has sufficient bargaining power to force suppliers to sign and return the form, and the purchasing agent must show one of his firm's auditors such a signed form for every purchase order issued. Yet suppliers frequently return this buyer's form *plus* their own acknowledgment form which has conflicting provisions. The purchasing agent throws away the supplier's form and files his own. Of course, in such a case the supplier has not acquiesced to the buyer's provisions. There is no agreement and no contract.

Sixteen sales managers were asked about the battle of the forms. Nine said that frequently no agreement was reached on which set of fine print was to govern, while seven said that there was no problem. Four of the seven worked for companies whose major customers are the large automobile companies or the large manufacturers of paper products. These customers demand that their terms and conditions govern any purchase, are careful generally to see that suppliers acquiesce, and have the bargaining power to have their way. The other three of the seven sales managers who have no battle of the forms problem, work for manufacturers of special industrial machines. Their firms are careful to reach complete agreement with their customers. Two of these men stressed that they could take no chances because such a large part of their firm's capital is tied up in making any one machine. The other sales manager had been influenced by a law suit against one of his competitors for over a half million dollars. The suit was brought by a customer when the competitor had been unable to deliver a machine and put it in operation on time. The sales manager interviewed said his firm could not guarantee that its machines would work perfectly by a specified time because they are designed to fit the customer's requirements, which may present difficult engineering problems. As a result, contracts are carefully negotiated.

A large manufacturer of packaging materials audited its records to determine how often it had failed to agree on terms and conditions with its customers or had failed to create legally binding contracts. Such failures cause a risk of loss to this firm since the packaging is printed with the customer's design and cannot be salvaged once this is done. The orders for five days in four different years were reviewed. The percentages of orders where no agreement on terms and conditions was reached or no contract was formed were as follows:

1953	75.0%
1954	69.4%
1955	71.5%
1956	59.5%

It is likely that businessmen pay more attention to describing the performances in an exchange than to planning for contingencies or defective performances or to obtaining legal enforceability of their contracts. Even when a purchase order and acknowledgment have conflicting provisions printed on the back, almost always the buyer and seller will be in agreement on what is to be sold and how much is to be paid for it. The lawyers who said businessmen often commit their firms to significant exchanges too casually, stated that the performances would be defined in the brief letter or telephone call; the lawyers objected that nothing else would be covered. Moreover, it is likely that businessmen are least concerned about planning their transactions so that they are legally enforceable contracts.[5] For example, in Wisconsin requirements contracts—contracts to supply a firm's requirements of an item rather than a definite quantity—probably are not legally enforceable. Seven people interviewed reported that their firms regularly used requirements contracts in dealings in Wisconsin. None thought that the lack of legal sanction made any difference. Three of these people were house counsel who knew the Wisconsin law before being interviewed. Another example of a lack of desire for legal sanctions is found in the relationship between automobile manufacturers and their suppliers of parts. The manufacturers draft a carefully planned agreement, but one which is so designed that the supplier will have only minimal, if any, legal rights against the manufacturers. The standard contract used by manufacturers of paper to sell to magazine publishers has a pricing clause which is probably sufficiently vague to make the contract legally unenforceable. The house counsel of one of the largest paper producers said that everyone in the industry is aware of this because of a leading New York case concerning the contract, but that no one cares. Finally, it seems likely that planning for contingencies and defective performances are in-between cases—more likely to occur than planning for a legal sanction, but less likely than a description of performance.

Thus one can conclude that (1) many business exchanges reflect a high degree of planning about the four categories—description, contingencies, defective performances and legal sanction—but (2) many, if not most, exchanges reflect no planning, or only a minimal amount of it, especially concerning legal sanctions and the effect of defective performances. As a result, the opportunity for good faith disputes during the life of the exchange relationship often is present.

The adjustment of exchange relationships and the settling of disputes. While a

[5] Compare the findings of an empirical study of Connecticut business practices in Comment, "The Statute of Frauds and the Business Community: A Re-Appraisal in Light of Prevailing Practices," *Yale Law Journal*, 66 (1957), pp. 1038–1071.

significant amount of creating business exchanges is done on a fairly noncontractual basis, the creation of exchanges usually is far more contractual than the adjustment of such relationships and the settlement of disputes. Exchanges are adjusted when the obligations of one or both parties are modified by agreement during the life of the relationship. For example, the buyer may be allowed to cancel all or part of the goods he has ordered because he no longer needs them; the seller may be paid more than the contract price by the buyer because of unusual changed circumstances. Dispute settlement involves determining whether or not a party has performed as agreed and, if he has not, doing something about it. For example, a court may have to interpret the meaning of a contract, determine what the alleged defaulting party has done and determine what, if any, remedy the aggrieved party is entitled to. Or one party may assert that the other is in default, refuse to proceed with performing the contract and refuse to deal ever again with the alleged defaulter. If the alleged defaulter, who in fact may not be in default, takes no action, the dispute is then "settled."

Business exchanges in non-speculative areas are usually adjusted without dispute. Under the law of contracts, if B orders 1,000 widgets from S at $1.00 each, B must take all 1,000 widgets or be in breach of contract and liable to pay S his expenses up to the time of the breach plus his lost anticipated profit. Yet all ten of the purchasing agents asked about cancellation of orders once placed indicated that they expected to be able to cancel orders freely subject to only an obligation to pay for the seller's major expenses such as scrapped steel.[6] All 17 sales personnel asked reported that they often had to accept cancellation. One said, "You can't ask a man to eat paper [the firm's product] when he has no use for it." A lawyer with many large industrial clients said,

> Often businessmen do not feel they have "a contract"—rather they have "an order." They speak of "cancelling the order" rather than "breaching our contract." When I began practice I referred to order cancellations as breaches of contract, but my clients objected since they do not think of cancellation as wrong. Most clients, in heavy industry at least, believe that there is a right to cancel as part of the buyer-seller relationship. There is a widespread attitude that one can back out of any deal within some very vague limits. Lawyers are often surprised by this attitude.

Disputes are frequently settled without reference to the contract or potential or actual legal sanctions. There is a hesitancy to speak of legal rights or to threaten to sue in these negotiations. Even where the parties have a detailed and carefully planned agreement which indicates what is to happen if, say, the seller fails to deliver on time, often they will never refer to the agreement but will negotiate a solution when the problem arises apparently as if there had never been any original contract. One purchasing agent expressed a common business attitude when he said,

> if something comes up, you get the other man on the telephone and deal with the problem. You don't read legalistic contract clauses at each other if you ever want to do business again. One doesn't run to lawyers if he wants to stay in business because one must behave decently.

Or as one businessman put it, "You can settle any dispute if you keep the lawyers and accountants out of it. They just do not understand the give-and-take needed in business." All of the house counsel interviewed indicated that they are called into the dispute settlement process only after the businessmen have failed to settle matters in their own way. Two indicated that after being called in house counsel at first will only advise the purchasing agent, sales manager or other official involved; not even the house counsel's letterhead is used on communications with the other side until all hope for a peaceful resolution is gone.

Law suits for breach of contract appear to be rare. Only five of the 12 purchasing agents had ever been involved in even a negotiation concerning a contract dispute where both sides were represented by lawyers; only two of ten sales managers had ever gone this far. None had been involved in a case that went through trial. A law firm with more than 40 lawyers and a large commercial practice handles in a year only

---

6 See the case studies on cancellation of contracts in *Harvard Business Review*, 2 (1923–24), pages 238–40, 367–70, 496–502.

about six trials concerned with contract problems. Less than 10 per cent of the time of this office is devoted to any type of work related to contracts disputes. Corporations big enough to do business in more than one state tend to sue and be sued in the federal courts. Yet only 2,779 out of 58,293 civil actions filed in the United States District Courts in fiscal year 1961 involved private contracts.[7] During the same period only 3,447 of the 61,138 civil cases filed in the principal trial courts of New York State involved private contracts.[8] The same picture emerges from a review of appellate cases.[9] Mentschikoff has suggested that commercial cases are not brought to the courts either in periods of business prosperity (because buyers unjustifiably reject goods only when prices drop and they can get similar goods elsewhere at less than the contract price) or in periods of deep depression (because people are unable to come to court or have insufficient assets to satisfy any judgment that might be obtained). Apparently, she adds, it is necessary to have "a kind of middle-sized depression" to bring large numbers of commercial cases to the courts. However, there is little evidence that in even "a kind of middle-sized depression" today's businessmen would use the courts to settle disputes.[10]

At times relatively contractual methods are used to make adjustments in ongoing transactions and to settle disputes. Demands of one side which are deemed unreasonable by the other occasionally are blocked by reference to the terms of the agreement between the parties. The legal position of the parties can influence negotiations even though legal rights or litigation are never mentioned in their discussions; it makes a difference if one is demanding what both concede to be a right or begging for a favor. Now and then a firm may threaten to turn matters over to its attorneys, threaten to sue, commence a suit or even litigate and carry an appeal to the highest court which will hear the matter. Thus, legal sanctions, while not an everyday affair, are not unknown in business.

One can conclude that while detailed planning and legal sanctions play a significant role in some exchanges between businesses, in many business exchanges their role is small.

TENTATIVE EXPLANATIONS

Two questions need to be answered: (A) How can business successfully operate exchange relationships with relatively so little attention to detailed planning or to legal sanctions, and (B) Why does business ever use contract in light of its success without it?

Why are relatively non-contractual practices so common? In most situations contract is not needed.[11] Often its functions are served by other devices. Most problems are avoided without resort to detailed planning or legal sanctions because usually there is little room for honest misunderstandings or good faith differences of opinion about the nature and quality of a seller's performance. Although the parties fail to cover all foreseeable contingencies, they will exercise care to see that both understand the primary obligation on each side. Either products are standardized with an accepted description or specifications are written calling for production to certain tolerances or results. Those who write and read specifications are experienced professionals who will know the customs of their industry and those of the industries with

[7] *Annual Report of the Director of the Administrative Office of the United States Courts*, 1961, p. 238.

[8] State of New York, The Judicial Conference, Sixth Annual Report, 1961, pp. 209–11.

[9] My colleague Lawrence M. Friedman has studied the work of the Supreme Court of Wisconsin in contracts cases. He has found that contracts cases reaching that court tend to involve economically-marginal-business and family-economic disputes rather than important commercial transactions. This has been the situation since about the turn of the century. Only during the Civil War period did the court deal with significant numbers of important contracts cases, but this happened against the background of a much simpler and different economic system.

[10] New York Law Revision Commission, *Hearings on the Uniform Code Commercial Code*, 2 (1954), p. 1391.

[11] The explanation that follows emphasizes a *considered* choice not to plan in detail for all contingencies. However, at times it is clear that businessmen fail to plan because of a lack of sophistication; they simply do not appreciate the risk they are running or they merely follow patterns established in their firm years ago without reexamining these practices in light of current conditions.

which they deal. Consequently, these customs can fill gaps in the express agreements of the parties. Finally, most products can be tested to see if they are what was ordered; typically in manufacturing industry we are not dealing with questions of taste or judgment where people can differ in good faith.

When defaults occur they are not likely to be disastrous because of techniques of risk avoidance or risk spreading. One can deal with firms of good reputation or he may be able to get some form of security to guarantee performance. One can insure against many breaches of contract where the risks justify the costs. Sellers set up reserves for bad debts on their books and can sell some of their accounts receivable. Buyers can place orders with two or more suppliers of the same item so that a default by one will not stop the buyer's assembly lines.

Moreover, contract and contract law are often thought unnecessary because there are many effective non-legal sanctions. Two norms are widely accepted. (1) Commitments are to be honored in almost all situations; one does not welsh on a deal. (2) One ought to produce a good product and stand behind it. Then, too, business units are organized to perform commitments, and internal sanctions will induce performance. For example, sales personnel must face angry customers when there has been a late or defective performance. The salesmen do not enjoy this and will put pressure on the production personnel responsible for the default. If the production personnel default too often, they will be fired. At all levels of the two business units personal relationships across the boundaries of the two organizations exert pressures for conformity to expectations. Salesmen often know purchasing agents well. The same two individuals occupying these roles may have dealt with each other from five to 25 years. Each has something to give the other. Salesmen have gossip about competitors, shortages and price increases to give purchasing agents who treat them well. Salesmen take purchasing agents to dinner, and they give purchasing agents Christmas gifts hoping to improve the chances of making sale. The buyer's engineering staff may work with the seller's engineering staff to solve problems jointly. The seller's engineers may render great assistance, and the buyer's engineers may desire to return the favor by drafting specifications which only the seller can meet. The top executives of the two firms may know each other. They may sit together on government or trade committees. They may know each other socially and even belong to the same country club. The interrelationships may be more formal. Sellers may hold stock in corporations which are important customers; buyers may hold stock in important suppliers. Both buyer and seller may share common directors on their boards. They may share a common financial institution which has financed both units.

The final type of non-legal sanction is the most obvious. Both business units involved in the exchange desire to continue successfully in business and will avoid conduct which might interfere with attaining this goal. One is concerned with both the reaction of the other party in the particular exchange and with his own general business reputation. Obviously, the buyer gains sanctions insofar as the seller wants the particular exchange to be completed. Buyers can withhold part or all of their payments until sellers have performed to their satisfaction. If a seller has a great deal of money tied up in his performance which he must recover quickly, he will go a long way to please the buyer in order to be paid. Moreover, buyers who are dissatisfied may cancel and cause sellers to lose the cost of what they have done up to cancellation. Furthermore, sellers hope for repeat for orders, and one gets few of these from unhappy customers. Some industrial buyers go so far as to formalize this sanction by issuing "report cards" rating the performance of each supplier. The supplier rating goes to the top management of the seller organization, and these men can apply internal sanctions to salesmen, production supervisors or product designers if there are too many "D's" or "F's" on the report card.

While it is generally assumed that the customer is always right, the seller may have some counterbalancing sanctions against the buyer. The seller may have obtained a large downpayment from the buyer which he will want to protect. The seller may have an exclusive process which the buyer needs. The seller may be one of the few firms which has the skill to make the item to the tolerances set by the buyer's engineers and within the time available. There are costs and delays involved in turning from a supplier one has dealt with in the past to a new supplier. Then, too, market conditions can change so that a buyer is faced with shortages of critical items. The most extreme example is the post World War II gray market conditions when sellers were rationing goods rather than selling them. Buyers must build up some reserve of good will with suppliers if they face the risk of such shortage and desire good treatment when they occur. Finally, there is reciprocity in buying and selling. A buyer cannot push a supplier too far if that supplier also buys significant quantities of the product made by the buyer.

Not only do the particular business units in a given exchange want to deal with each other again, they also want to deal with other business units in the future. And the way one behaves in a particular transaction, or a series of transactions, will color his general business reputation. Blacklisting can be formal or informal. Buyers who fail to pay their bills on time risk a bad report in credit rating services such as Dun and Bradstreet. Sellers who do not satisfy their customers become the subject of discussion in the gossip exchanged by purchasing agents and salesmen, at meetings of purchasing agents' associations and trade associations, or even at country clubs or social gatherings where members of top manangement meet. The American male's habit of debating the merits of new cars carries over to industrial items. Obviously, a poor reputation does not help a firm make sales and may force it to offer great price discounts or added services to remain in business. Furthermore, the habits of unusually demanding buyers become known, and they tend to get no more than they can coerce out of suppliers who choose to deal with them. Thus often contract is not needed as there are alternatives.

Not only are contract and contract law not needed in many situations, their use may have, or may be thought to have, undesirable consequences. Detailed negotiated contracts can get in the way of creating good exchange relationships between business units. If one side insists on a detailed plan, there will be delay while letters are exchanged as the parties try to agree on what should happen if a remote and unlikely contingency occurs. In some cases they may not be able to agree at all on such matters and as a result a sale may be lost to the seller and the buyer may have to search elsewhere for an acceptable supplier. Many businessmen would react by thinking that had no one raised the series of remote and unlikely contingencies all this wasted effort could have been avoided.

Even where agreement can be reached at the negotiation stage, carefully planned arrangements may create undesirable exchange relationships between business units. Some businessmen object that in such a carefully worked out relationship one gets performance only to the letter of the contract. Such planning indicates a lack of trust and blunts the demands of friendship, turning a cooperative venture into an antagonistic horse trade. Yet the greater danger perceived by some businessmen is that one would have to perform his side of the bargain to its letter and thus lose what is called "flexibility." Businessmen may welcome a measure of vagueness in the obligations they assume so that they may negotiate matters in light of the actual circumstances.

Adjustment of exchange relationships and dispute settlement by litigation or the threat of it also has many costs. The gain anticipated from using this form of coercion often fails to outweigh these costs, which are both monetary and non-monetary. Threatening to turn matters over to an attorney may cost no more money than postage or a telephone call; yet few are so skilled in making such a threat that it will not cost some deterioration of the relationship between the firms. One businessman said that customers had better not rely on legal rights or threaten to bring a breach of contract law suit against him since he "would not be treated like a criminal" and would fight back with every means available. Clearly actual litigation is even more costly than making threats. Lawyers demand substantial fees from larger business units. A firm's executives often will have to be transported and maintained in another city during the proceedings if, as often is the case, the trial must be held away from the home office. Top management does not travel by Greyhound and stay at the Y.M.C.A. Moreover, there will be the cost of diverting top management, engineers, and others in the organization from their normal activities. The firm may lose many days work from several key people. The non-monetary costs may be large too. A breach of contract law suit may settle a particular dispute, but such an action often results in a "divorce" ending the "marriage" between the two businesses, since a contract action is likely to carry charges with at least overtones of bad faith. Many executives, moreover, dislike the prospect of being cross-examined in public. Some executives may dislike losing control of a situation by turning the decision-making power over to lawyers. Finally, the law of contract damages may not provide an adequate remedy even if the firm wins the suit; one may get vindication but not much money.

Why do relatively contractual practices ever exist? Although contract is not needed and actually may have negative consequences, businessmen do make some carefully planned contracts, negotiate settlements influenced by their legal rights and commence and defend some breach of contract law suits or arbitration proceedings. In view of the findings and explanation presented to this point, one may ask why. Exchanges are carefully planned when it is thought that planning and a potential legal sanction will have more advantages than disadvantages. Such a judgment may be reached when contract planning serves the internal needs of an organization involved in a business exchange. For example, a fairly detailed contract can serve as a communication device within a large corporation. While the corporation's sales manager and house counsel may work out all the provisions with the customer, its production manger will have to make the product. He must be told what to do and how to handle at least the most obvious contingencies. Moreover, the sales manager may want to remove certain issues from future negotiation by his subordinates. If he puts the matter in the written contract, he may be able to keep his salesmen from making concessions to the customer without first consulting the sales manager. Then the sales manager may be aided in his battles with his firm's financial or engineering departments if the contract calls for certain practices which the sales manager advocates but which the other departments resist. Now the corporation is obligated to a customer to do what the sales manager wants to do; how can the financial or engineering departments insist on anything else?

Also one tends to find a judgment that the gains of contract outweigh the costs where there is a likelihood that significant problems will arise.[12] One factor leading to this conclusion is complexity of the agreed performance over a long period. Another factor is whether or not the degree of injury in case of default is thought to be potentially great. This factor cuts two ways. First, a buyer may want to commit a seller to a detailed and legally binding contract, where the consequences of a default by the seller would seriously injure the buyer. For example, the airlines are subject to law suits from the survivors of passengers and to great adverse publicity as a result of crashes. One would expect the airlines to bargain for carefully defined and legally enforceable obligations on the part of the airframe manufacturers when they purchase aircraft. Second, a seller may want to limit his liability for a buyer's damages by a provision in their contract. For example, a manufacturer of air conditioning may deal with motels in the South and Southwest. If this equipment fails in the hot summer months, a motel may lose a great deal of business. The manufacturer may wish to avoid any liability for this type of injury to his customers and may want a contract with a clear disclaimer clause.

Similarly, one uses or threatens to use legal sanctions to settle disputes when other devices will not work and when the gains are thought to outweigh the costs. For example, perhaps the most common type of business contracts case fought all the way through to the appellate courts today is an action for an alleged wrongful termination of a dealer's franchise by a manufacturer. Since the franchise has been terminated, factors such as personal relationships and the desire for future business will have little effect; the cancellation of the franchise indicates they

---

[12] Even where there is little chance that problems will arise, some businessmen insist that their lawyer review or draft an agreement as a delaying tactic. This gives the businessman time to think about making a commitment if he has doubts about the matter or to look elsewhere for a better deal while still keeping the particular negotiations alive.

have already failed to maintain the relationship. Nor will a complaining dealer worry about creating a hostile relationship between himself and the manufacturer. Often the dealer has suffered a great financial loss both as to his investment in building and equipment and as to his anticipated future profits. A cancelled automobile dealer's lease on his showroom and shop will continue to run, and his tools for servicing, say, Plymouths cannot be used to service other makes of cars. Moreover, he will have no more new Plymouths to sell. Today there is some chance of winning a law suit for terminating a franchise in bad faith in many states and in the federal courts. Thus, often the dealer chooses to risk the cost of a lawyer's fee because of the chance that he may recover some compensation for his losses.

An "irrational" factor may exert some influence on the decision to use legal sanctions. The man who controls a firm may feel that he or his organization has been made to appear foolish or has been the victim of fraud or bad faith. The law suit may be seen as a vehicle "to get even" although the potential gains, as viewed by an objective observer, are outweighed by the potential costs.

The decision whether or not to use contract—whether the gain exceeds the costs—will be made by the person within the business unit with the power to make it, and it tends to make a difference who he is. People in a sales department oppose contract. Contractual negotiations are just one more hurdle in the way of a sale. Holding a customer to the letter of a contract is bad for "customer relations." Suing a customer who is not bankrupt and might order again is poor strategy. Purchasing agents and their buyers are less hostile to contracts but regard attention devoted to such matters as a waste of time. In contrast, the financial control department—the treasurer, controller or or auditor—leans toward more contractual dealings. Contract is viewed by these people as an organizing tool to control operations in a large organization. It tends to define precisely and to minimize the risks to which the firm is exposed. Outside lawyers—those with many clients—may share this enthusiasm for a more contractual method of dealing. These lawyers are concerned with preventive law—avoiding any possible legal difficulty. They see many unstable and unsuccessful exchange transactions, and so they are aware of, and perhaps overly concerned with, all of the things which can go wrong. Moreover, their job of settling disputes with legal sanctions is much easier if their client has not been overly casual about transaction planning. The inside lawyer, or house counsel, is harder to classify. He is likely to have some sympathy with a more contractual method of dealing. He shares the outside lawyer's "craft urge" to see exchange transactions neat and tidy from a legal standpoint. Since he is more concerned with avoiding and settling disputes than selling goods, he is likely to be less willing to rely on a man's word as the sole sanction than is a salesman. Yet the house counsel is more a part of the organization and more aware of its goals and subject to its internal sanctions. If the potential risks are not too great, he may hesitate to suggest a more contractual procedure to the sales department. He must sell his services to the operating departments, and he must hoard what power he has, expending it on only what he sees as significant issues.

The power to decide that a more contractual method of creating relationships and settling disputes shall be used will be held by different people at different times in different organizations. In most firms the sales department and the purchasing department have a great deal of power to resist contractual procedures or to ignore them if they are formally adopted and to handle disputes their own way. Yet in larger organizations the treasurer and the controller have increasing power to demand both systems and compliance. Occasionally, the house counsel must arbitrate the conflicting positions of these departments; in giving "legal advice" he may make the business judgment necessary regarding the use of contract. At times he may ask for an opinion from an outside law firm to reinforce his own position with the outside firm's prestige.

Obviously, there are other significant variables which influence the degree that contract is used. One is the relative bargaining power or skill of the two business units. Even if the controller of a small supplier succeeds within the firm and creates a contractual system of dealing, there will be no contract if the firm's large customer prefers not to be bound to anything. Firms that supply General Motors deal as General Motors wants to do business, for the most part. Yet bargaining power is not size or share of the market alone. Even a General Motors may need a particular supplier, at least temporarily. Furthermore, bargaining power may shift as an exchange relationship is first created and then continues. Even a giant firm can find itself bound to a small supplier once production of an essential item begins for there may not be time to turn to another supplier. Also, all of the factors discussed in this paper can be viewed as *components* of bargaining power—for example, the personal relationship between the presidents of the buyer and the seller firms may give a sales manager great power over a purchasing agent who has been instructed to give the seller "every consideration." Another variable relevant to the use of contract is the influence of third parties. The federal government, or a lender of money, may insist that a contract be made in a particular transaction or may influence the decision to assert one's legal rights under a contract.

Contract, then, often plays an important role in business, but other factors are significant. To understand the functions of contract the whole system of conducting exchanges must be explored fully. More types of business communities must be studied, contract litigation must be analyzed to see why the nonlegal sanctions fail to prevent the use of legal sanctions and all of the variables suggested in this paper must be classified more systematically.

* Presented at the annual meetings of the American Sociological Association, August, 1962, in Washington, D.C.

[1] Cf. William M. Evan, "Power, Bargaining, and Law: A Preliminary Analysis of Labor Arbitration Cases," *Social Problems*, 7 (Summer, 1959), pp. 5–16.

[7]

Choices in Legal Procedure: Shia Moslem and Mexican Zapotec[1]

LAURA NADER

Center for Advanced Study in the Behavioral Sciences Stanford, California

INTRODUCTION

IN AN article on "The Use of Typology in Anthropological Theory" Clyde Kluckhohn (1960) called for more exploratory studies into typologies of relations. In the field of kinship much of this kind of investigation has been carried on, but what we have done in comparative law is indeed minimal. Although we do not have abundant data on legal procedure we probably have sufficient information about cultures from different parts of the world so that one could at least construct a descriptive typology illustrating the range of variation in legal procedure. The work of Hoebel (1954), in his book *The Law of Primitive Man*, was in part an attempt to describe this range of variation and to relate complexity in the law to different levels of subsistence.

In this paper I compare the formal conflict-settling procedures in two villages which share the same subsistence level. They are both peasant villages and thereby share certain features. There are also many differences between them, but only three differences are specifically relevant in this discussion: (1) patterns of social grouping; (2) formal political organization; (3) the mechanics of settling conflicts by public means. My general aim is to understand what factors affect the choice of settling disputes by court or by other means. More specifically, I am interested in the relation between legal procedure and types of social grouping.

DESCRIPTION[2]

The first village, Libaya, is a Shia Moslem community of the Metwalli sect with a population size of approximately 1400 people. This town, located in the southern Beqá Valley in Lebanon, is not easily found on a map because villages do not get on maps if they are not connected by road, and this village only had its road a few years ago. It is a town of mud and stone houses interrupted only by the tall whiteness of the village mosque. The people who live here are peasant farmers, some of whom also specialize in carpentry, stone masonry, and other activities. The major crops, wheat and barley, are subsistence crops and a few people grow the cash crop tobacco.

The land is divided for use into individual family plots but much of the land is owned by one landlord who is absentee. At different times in the life cycle the household may be extended with two or more nuclear families, or it may be only nuclear. The villagers recognize ten lineage groups in this community. These lineages are not localized; rather their members are scattered throughout the village.

Excluding the political and economic control which may be exerted by the landlord, there is little of what may be called village government in Libaya. According to Lebanese statute any community of 50 persons or more should elect a ***mukhtar*** and a council. During my stay no mention was made of any council (the members of which are theoretically supposed to function as public decision makers); nor did mention of such a group crop up in the ethnographic material. Libaya does, however, have a mukhtar, a mayor, who is supposedly elected every four years by the village men. The duties of this mukhtar are primarily organizational and administrative. He signs deeds of sale, identity cards, bills of assessment, etc. He is theoretically responsible to the central government for maintenance of peace and for collection of taxes. His position is unpaid and primarily prestigious. There is no village court; there is no village police force. If there is a serious dispute, the local government gendarmerie will be called in by one or both parties.

In Libaya the position of mukhtar has alternated for several generations between the two leading and opposed families of the town—the Akls and the Abrahams. And when one of these two families succeeds in getting into power, it usually holds on to the position for ten to fifteen years. Libaya is a village which for as long as anyone can remember has been split into two opposing factions based on family alliances—one headed by the Akls, and the other by the Abrahams. Each faction (except for the rare marriage by capture) is endogamous. The balance of power between factions shifts from time to time, according to one informant, because one or two of the smaller families, described as being peripheral, may ally themselves one way or the other. All the recreative as well as political activities and family or life cycle activities are patterned along lines of this dual division. No one from the Abraham group attends funerals, weddings, or participates in the men's winter discussion groups with the members of the Akl group or vice-versa. There is almost a touch of humor about this avoidance, especially when informants are reporting on face-to-face "non-interaction."

In order to get at the procedures or processes for settling conflicts I collected a series of conflict stories. For our purposes here, I will differentiate between two classes of conflict—the first involves persons within one or the other half, and the second involves conflict between individuals belonging to the two opposing groups or between an individual and an outsider (i.e., a member of another town). The procedure involving the settlement of conflict within one half of the town is described as friendly and peaceful; often these quarrels are mediated by older members of the families, or by *awadeem*—respected individuals who may be from the same half or from nearby Shia towns. Conflicts that arise between the two sides or between a member of the village and an outsider are by far the more serious and are not settled in this way, although a kind of intermediary is used. This second class of conflict usually ends up in the district's civil court at Jeb Jannine, or, if not settled there, in the Zahle civil court. Remember, there is no court in Libaya. Remember also that the mukhtar, theoretically at least, is a man who is supposed to maintain peace. But he does not in fact function very effectively as a village peacemaker because of the dual division in the village. He may be consulted to settle problems for his own side, but he is never called upon to settle conflicts between the two sides because he is "biased." How then do Libayans settle such conflicts? This can best be illustrated by citing one short case:

> There was a man named Hassan from Libaya. He bought a goat in order to feed his three youngsters from her milk. One day Hassan decided to send the goat out to the prairie with the shepherd for one day. At the end of the day the shepherd returned without the goat. Hassan started to look around the village and to ask this one and that if he had seen the goat, but the goat was nowhere to be found. He went to the mukhtar and told him the story asking him to accompany him in search of neighbors' homes—that is, those houses which the goat would have had to pass on the way home. They went out and began to search in various homes but did not find anything. The owner of the goat then turned to the mukhtar and said, "I would like to look in your house to see if my goat is there."
>
> The mukhtar and the owner of the goat entered the animal shelter and found the goat lying down on the floor with a young man sitting on her in order to prevent her from raising her voice. The mukhtar went over and struck the young man, a cousin of his named Moh. The owner of the goat, one of the worst enemies of the mukhtar and a leading member of the 'other side,' left the mukhtar's house with his goat shouting and screaming, "I found my goat in the house of the mukhtar. . . . "
>
> The police came and took the story from both sides. . . . Weeks later the case had been scheduled at the district court. The judge ordered the mukhtar of Libaya to come as a witness, since he had indeed been one of the two men who had caught the thief. The mukhtar complied once but then refused to return to the court trial because his father and the father of the young thief were first cousins; they had pleaded with him not to go as a witness in the case. When the judge insisted that the mukhtar be present, the mukhtar began to see various doctors in order that he be given sick permission to be absent. This was done with the help of K.N., the Bekka congressman. The judge would not, however, give his final decision until the mukhtar was present.
>
> Now K.N. paid a great deal of attention to this case because the mukhtar and his cousin paid him to untie the knot of the case. They did this because K.N. knows the judge personally, and if there was anyone who could make a *wasta* he could. K.N. went to see the judge in Jeb Jannine and talked with him, principally asking him to set the thief free, which the judge actually did. When the goat owner heard that the thief had been freed, he went to Zahle and began to ask, "Who knows the judge, who has influence with the judge?" He found such a person. His name was S.H., a man who had been a close friend of the judge since they were studying law together. S.H. prepared for a lone meeting with the governor and pleaded rights for Hassan. . . . The judge then set a hearing date. The mukhtar, Hassan, and the two 'lawyers' were there to hear the mukhtar tell the story of the goat thief. The mukhtar could not lie because what he had said previously was still in the hands of the judge. The judge, finding himself in a dilemma between two friends, decided the case according to the law, and did not pay any attention to any of the wastas. He judged that the thief should pay 100 liras to the owner of the goat, that he should spend one month in prison and pay 25 liras to the court. When S.H. heard the decision he refused to accept it, convinced that K.N. had pressured the judge. After this decision in the Jeb Jannine court, S.H. took the case of Zahle, and until this time the case is still with the courts. K.N. is still working by means of the wasta method for his client; as for the goat owner, S.H. and J.S., Zahle's congressman, are making wastas for him.[3]

There are several interesting things to note about all of the cases. First there is almost no mention made of Moslem written law at the village level. Second, wastas—or remedy arrangements—are made by specialists, and for the most part these wasta specialists are Lebanese politicians. Another way to state this is that Lebanese politicians, or aspiring politicians, must by definition be professional wasta makers. It is considered the duty of a Lebanese politican to settle the grievances of his constituents and these grievances may deal with murder or stolen goats. Their interest in the settlement of a case is a political one, and not so much an interest in 'justice.' A single case won in Libaya can mean the votes of half the village. On the other hand, the villager in trouble, if he is to find the right wasta-maker, must have a most detailed knowledge of interpersonal relations among the politico-elite of Lebanon, and it is a rather admirable game they play--both plaintiff and defendant--to see who can get to the best connections fastest. In looking for a wasta, the Shia Moslem villager comes into contact with a whole series of people, and they may be of almost any religious affiliation (except perhaps Sunni Moslem). The arrangements made about a case are usually made outside of any courtroom and always outside of the village itself—often in the homes of politicians. I was visiting in such a Beirut household and awoke at 6:30 one morning to note that along with the first cup of coffee, the head of the household and his wife received, while still in bed, villagers in singles, in groups, even in busloads. The professional wasta-maker, unlike the tribal sheikh, is not to judge a situation but rather to use his personal influence to swing the decision of the judge in favor of his constituent. There is a kind of adversariness involved except that the decision of the judge is usually based on the relative efficacy of personal power rather than on the facts of the case.

The Zapotecan town of Ralu'a is both similar and different. It has a population of 2000 people. These, too, are mountain, peasant farmers, with mud houses surrounding not a mosque but a large Catholic church. The inhabitants grow corn, beans, and sugar cane as subsistence crops, and coffee as their cash crop. This town has also been relatively isolated and was connected by road to the state capital the same year that Libaya acquired its road.

There is no landlordism here as in Lebanon; 90 per cent of all Ralu'ans have their own land. Although some households are extended, the predominant family pattern is nuclear. There are no recognized lineages or large family groups as in Libaya. There is general village endogamy.

In very strong contrast to Libaya, there are many ties which link citizens in Ralu'a: ties of kinship, locale, common work groups; there are musicians' groups—savings and loan groups, religious associations—all kinds of ties which link a number of men together in a group or as individuals, but other ties which divide them by linking some of them with different groups. Whereas in Libaya all of the ties that bind merge within one group to cause a dual, deep rift in town, in Ralu'a the groupings by not coinciding, but by countering each other, cause a complexity in relations serving to unify the village as a whole.

The presence of village government, which is outlined in the Oaxacan state code, is immediately symbolized by a large town hall. And within this town hall there are many officials: the *presidente*, the *sindico*, the *alcalde*, the *policia*, the *regidores*, the *secretario*, the *tesorero*, etc. Apart from this village officialdom, there are frequent town meetings.

Three of these men, elected by the town citizens for one year's service, constitute the town court of justice: the presidente, the sindico, and the alcalde (Nader 1964). The presidente and the sindico have administrative and judicial duties while the duties of the alcalde are only judicial. The following case illustrates how conflicts are publicly settled in Ralu'a:

> Having been detained over night in jail, Francisco Chavez appeared in court today to render his declaration. The plaintiff Manuel Gonsalez, also present, told the following story. The previous night at about 11:00 there were various people in his *cantina* drinking *mezcal*. When Manuel Gonsalez refused to serve Francisco Chavez any more alcohol on credit, the defendant struck Manuel a blow that made him fall over. At this point, the defendant grabbed the machete behind the table and attempted to stab (kill) the plaintiff. It was only because of the other men present that the machete was torn away from him. The plaintiff took advantage of this scuffle to run and call the police. At this point, the presidente asked the defendant to speak. The defendant declared that it was true that he had committed all these acts, but that it was only because he was so drunk. "As everybody knows," he said, "he has never had reason to fight with Manuel Gonsalez." The defendant asked that the court fine him. The presidente decided to fine both parties. The owner of the cantina was fined 25 pesos because he had violated the closing hour rule set by the *municipio*. The defendant had to pay 100 pesos on a charge of battery and threat to kill. (If this case had not been settled by the presidente, it would have been referred to the alcalde.)

DISCUSSION

In summary, then, both towns are peasant farming villages, homogeneous in religion—one being Moslem, the other Catholic. They differ, however, in the following important respects: Libaya is divided into two endogamous groups; it lacks a development of secondary groups not based on kinship or strong alliance to one of the two factions; it lacks a viable organization for village government. Loyalties are unidirectional and directed to the half in which an individual belongs. Conflicts within the half are resolved by the use of go-between intermediaries; conflicts between halves or between a member of one half and an outsider are settled ultimately at appeal courts in larger towns by means of wasta-makers who act as biased intermediaries between villager and judge. At the village level, conflict divides by accentuating the hostility which members of each half have toward each other. At the national level, it may be argued, the mechanics of conflict resolution function as an integrative factor. Villagers involved in serious disputes must rely on the formal and informal processes of a civil court which they can often influence only by manipulation of interpersonal relations. Usually this forces Shia villagers, for example, out of the Shia community, into interaction with members of other religious groups. Winning a case in a civil court means learning how to deal successfully with Lebanese officials.

Ralu'a is a village composed of many groups which serve to cross-link town citizens. Loyalties are multidirectional, certainly none being directly antithetical to the village as a united whole. There is a proliferation of secondary groups not based on kinship factors. Conflicts between individuals and groups are publicly solved by means of a court system which succeeds in terminating most cases without referring them to courts outside of the village.

The data suggest that villages with dual organization are incompatible with village court or council systems of settling conflict.[4] It also suggests the reverse: that wherever village court systems do develop (in contrast to where they are imposed), secondary groupings which cross-link citizens will be found. If, as in Libaya, loyalties within the village are only attached to a large kin group or to the intermarrying half of the village, this situation will compete with any system of adjudication that may pretend to be impartial. Villages which have a proliferation of secondary groupings which cross-link citizens, like Ralu'a or Zuni, for example, provide a good setting for councils or courts of adjudication. Also, societies like Tzintzuntzan in Mexico, where in place of various groupings we have a series of social relations based on the dyadic contract, there is absent a unit which can serve as a basis for feuding (Foster 1961). In Libaya there are two units which may well serve as a basis for feuding and it is more than likely that before Libaya was linked to the Lebanese national scene they probably did settle disputes by means of institutionalized feuding.

Perhaps the reader will object that the contrast presented here ignores the problem of comparable units. This is a question to be considered seriously in any kind of comparison. It is possible, for example, that I should have compared the village court of Ralu'a with conflict settling procedures in one half of the Shia village, in which case I would have been comparing a court system with the proceedings as carried out by go-betweens. Or I could have contrasted the Ralu'an court with the civil court in Jeb Jannine, in which case I would be contrasting a court of elected peers, as among the Zapotec, with a court of politically appointed, professionally trained judges. In this paper, however, I chose to compare the village unit, that is, the largest number of people who share a common settlement, and recognize that it is common regardless of other differences they might have, because my central question evolved about this unit.

NOTES

[1] This paper was presented at the 1962 meetings of the American Anthropological Association in Chicago, Illinois. I wish to thank Michael Moerman for his useful suggestions in the preparation of this manuscript.

[2] The data upon which this paper is based were gathered during two field trips. Between 1957 and 1959 I spent nine months working among the Zapotec of Oaxaca, Mexico. This work was sponsored by the Milton Fund at Harvard University, Radcliffe College, and the Mexican government. Fieldwork in the Shia Moslem community was carried out during the summer of 1961 and supported by a grant from the Institute of International Studies, University of California.

[3] Unfortunately I was unable to witness any court cases during my field trip to Lebanon. Because of a national strike of practicing lawyers, court business was suspended during the summer of 1961.

[4] H. T. Nuñez reports the presence of a dual division and the absence of a village court system for Cajititlán, Galiaco, Mexico.

REFERENCES CITED

Foster, George M.
1961 The dyadic contract: a model for the social structure of a Mexican peasant village. American Anthropologist 63:1173–1192.

Hoebel, E. Adamson
1954 The law of primitive man. Cambridge, Harvard University Press.

Kluckhohn, Clyde
1960 The use of typology in anthropological theory. In Selected Papers of the Fifth International Congress of Anthropological and Ethnological Sciences. Anthony F. C. Wallace, ed.

Nader, Laura
1964 An analysis of Zapotec law cases. Ethnology 3:404 419.

Part III
Courts and the Discovery of Local Legal Culture

[8]

THE PRACTICE OF LAW AS CONFIDENCE GAME

Organizational Cooptation of a Profession

ABRAHAM S. BLUMBERG

State University of New York at Stony Brook

A RECURRING THEME in the growing dialogue between sociology and law has been the great need for a joint effort of the two disciplines to illuminate urgent social and legal issues. Having uttered fervent public pronouncements in this vein, however, the respective practitioners often go their separate ways. Academic spokesmen for the legal profession are somewhat critical of sociologists of law because of what they perceive as the sociologist's preoccupation with the application of theory and methodology to the examination of legal phenomena, without regard to the solution of legal problems. Further, it is felt that "... contemporary writing in the sociology of law ... betrays the existence of painfully unsophisticated notions about the day-to-day operations of courts, legislatures and law offices."[1] Regardless of the merit of such criticism,

EDITOR'S NOTE: *In an essay contest sponsored by the Institute on American Freedoms for graduate students in sociology, this article (submitted under the title of: Covert Contingencies in the Right to the Assistance of Counsel) won first prize, in the amount of $1,000, in February 1967.*
AUTHOR'S NOTE: *The article is a revised version of a paper read at the meetings of the American Sociological Association, Miami Beach, Florida, August 30, 1966.*

1. H. W. Jones, *A View From the Bridge*, Law and Society: Supplement to Summer, 1965 Issue of SOCIAL PROBLEMS 42 (1965). See G. Geis, *Sociology, Criminology, and Criminal Law*, 7 SOCIAL PROBLEMS 40–47 (1959); N. S. Timasheff, *Growth and Scope of Sociology of Law*, in MODERN SOCIOLOGICAL THEORY IN CONTINUITY AND

scant attention—apart from explorations of the legal profession itself—has been given to the sociological examination of legal institutions, or their supporting ideological assumptions. Thus, for example, very little sociological effort is expended to ascertain the validity and viability of important court decisions, which may rest on wholly erroneous assumptions about the contextual realities of social structure. A particular decision may rest upon a legally impeccable rationale; at the same time it may be rendered nugatory or self-defeating by contingencies imposed by aspects of social reality of which the lawmakers are themselves unaware.

Within this context, I wish to question the impact of three recent landmark decisions of the United States Supreme Court; each hailed as destined to effect profound changes in the future of criminal law administration and enforcement in America. The first of these, *Gideon v. Wainwright*, 372 U.S. 335 (1963) required states and localities henceforth to furnish counsel in the case of indigent persons charged with a felony.[2] The Gideon ruling left several major issues unsettled, among them the vital question: What is the precise point in time at which a suspect is entitled to counsel?[3] The answer came relatively quickly

CHANGE 424–49 (H. Becker & A. Boskoff, eds. 1957), for further evaluation of the strained relations between sociology and law.

2. This decision represented the climax of a line of cases which had begun to chip away at the notion that the Sixth Amendment of the Constitution (right to assistance of counsel) applied only to the federal government, and could not be held to run against the states through the Fourteenth Amendment. An exhaustive historical analysis of the Fourteenth Amendment and the Bill of Rights will be found in C. Fairman, *Does the Fourteenth Amendment Incorporate the Bill of Rights? The Original Understanding*, 2 STAN. L. REV. 5–139 (1949). Since the Gideon decision, there is already evidence that its effect will ultimately extend to indigent persons charged with misdemeanors—and perhaps ultimately even traffic cases and other minor offenses. For a popular account of this important development in connection with the right to assistance of counsel, see A. LEWIS, GIDEON'S TRUMPET (1964). For a scholarly historical analysis of the right to counsel see W. M. BEANEY, THE RIGHT TO COUNSEL IN AMERICAN COURTS (1955). For a more recent comprehensive review and discussion of the right to counsel and its development, see Note, *Counsel at Interrogation*, 73 YALE L.J. 1000–57 (1964).

With the passage of the Criminal Justice Act of 1964, indigent accused persons in the federal courts will be defended by federally paid legal counsel. For a general discussion of the nature and extent of public and private legal aid in the United States prior to the Gideon case, see E. A. BROWNELL, LEGAL AID IN THE UNITED STATES (1961); also R. B. VON MEHREN, et al., EQUAL JUSTICE FOR THE ACCUSED (1959).

3. In the case of federal defendants the issue is clear. In Mallory v. United States, 354 U.S. 449 (1957), the Supreme Court unequivocally indicated that a person under federal arrest must be taken "without any unnecessary delay" before a U.S. commissioner

in *Escobedo v. Illinois*, 378 U.S. 478 (1964), which has aroused a storm of controversy. Danny Escobedo confessed to the murder of his brother-in-law after the police had refused to permit retained counsel to see him, although his lawyer was present in the station house and asked to confer with his client. In a 5–4 decision, the court asserted that counsel must be permitted when the process of police investigative effort shifts from merely investigatory to that of accusatory: "when its focus is on the accused and its purpose is to elicit a confession—our adversary system begins to operate, and, under the circumstances here, the accused must be permitted to consult with his lawyer."

As a consequence, Escobedo's confession was rendered inadmissible. The decision triggered a national debate among police, district attorneys, judges, lawyers, and other law enforcement officials, which continues unabated, as to the value and propriety of confessions in criminal cases.[4] On June 13, 1966, the Supreme Court in a 5–4 decision underscored the principle enunciated in *Escobedo* in the case of *Miranda v. Arizona*.[5] Police interrogation of any suspect in custody, without his consent, unless a defense attorney is present, is prohibited by the self-incrimination provision of the Fifth Amendment. Regardless of the relative merit of the various shades of opinion about the role of counsel in criminal cases, the issues generated thereby will be in part resolved as additional

---

where he will receive information as to his rights to remain silent and to assistance of counsel which will be furnished, in the event he is indigent, under the Criminal Justice Act of 1964. For a most interesting and richly documented work in connection with the general area of the Bill of Rights, see C. R. SOWLE, POLICE POWER AND INDIVIDUAL FREEDOM (1962).

4. See N.Y. Times, Nov. 20, 1965, p. 1, for Justice Nathan R. Sobel's statement to the effect that based on his study of 1,000 indictments in Brooklyn, N.Y. from February–April, 1965, fewer than 10% involved confessions. Sobel's detailed analysis will be found in six articles which appeared in the New York Law Journal, beginning November 15, 1965, through November 21, 1965, titled *The Exclusionary Rules in the Law of Confessions: A Legal Perspective—A Practical Perspective.* Most law enforcement officials believe that the majority of convictions in criminal cases are based upon confessions obtained by police. For example, the District Attorney of New York County (a jurisdiction which has the largest volume of cases in the United States), Frank S. Hogan, reports that confessions are crucial and indicates "if a suspect is entitled to have a lawyer during preliminary questioning . . . any lawyer worth his fee will tell him to keep his mouth shut", N.Y. Times, Dec. 2, 1965, p. 1. Concise discussions of the issue are to be found in D. Robinson, Jr., *Massiah, Escobedo and Rationales For the Exclusion of Confessions*, 56 J. CRIM. L. C. & P.S. 412–31 (1965); D. C. Dowling, *Escobedo and Beyond: The Need for a Fourteenth Amendment Code of Criminal Procedure*, 56 J. CRIM. L. C. & P.S. 143–57 (1965).

5. Miranda v. Arizona, 384 U.S. 436 (1966).

cases move toward decision in the Supreme Court in the near future. They are of peripheral interest and not of immediate concern in this paper. However, the *Gideon, Escobedo,* and *Miranda* cases pose interesting general questions. In all three decisions, the Supreme Court reiterates the traditional legal conception of a defense lawyer based on the ideological perception of a criminal case as an *adversary, combative* proceeding, in which counsel for the defense assiduously musters all the admittedly limited resources at his command to *defend* the accused.[6] The fundamental question remains to be answered: Does the Supreme Court's conception of the role of counsel in a criminal case square with social reality?

The task of this paper is to furnish some preliminary evidence toward the illumination of that question. Little empirical understanding of the function of defense counsel exists; only some ideologically oriented generalizations and commitments. This paper is based upon observations made by the writer during many years of legal practice in the criminal courts of a large metropolitan area. No claim is made as to its methodological rigor, although it does reflect a conscious and sustained effort for participant observation.

COURT STRUCTURE DEFINES ROLE OF DEFENSE LAWYER

The overwhelming majority of convictions in criminal cases (usually over 90 per cent) are not the product of a combative, trial-by-jury process at all, but instead merely involve the sentencing of the individual after a negotiated, bargained-for plea of guilty has been entered.[7]

---

6. Even under optimal circumstances a criminal case is a very much one-sided affair, the parties to the "contest" being decidedly unequal in strength and resources. See A. S. Goldstein, *The State and the Accused: Balance of Advantage in Criminal Procedure,* 69 YALE L.J. 1149–99 (1960).

7. F. J. DAVIS et al., SOCIETY AND THE LAW: NEW MEANINGS FOR AN OLD PROFESSION 301 (1962); L. ORFIELD, CRIMINAL PROCEDURE FROM ARREST TO APPEAL 297 (1947).

D. J. Newman, *Pleading Guilty for Considerations: A Study of Bargain Justice,* 46 J. CRIM. L. C. & P.S. 780–90 (1954). Newman's data covered only one year, 1954, in a midwestern community, however, it is in general confirmed by my own data drawn from a far more populous area, and from what is one of the major criminal courts in the country, for a period of fifteen years from 1950 to 1964 inclusive. The English experience tends also to confirm American data, see N. WALKER, CRIME AND PUNISHMENT IN BRITAIN: AN ANALYSIS OF THE PENAL SYSTEM (1965). See also D. J. NEWMAN, CONVICTION: THE DETERMINATION OF GUILT OR INNOCENCE WITHOUT TRIAL (1966),

Although more recently the overzealous role of police and prosecutors in producing pretrial confessions and admissions has achieved a good deal of notoriety, scant attention has been paid to the organizational structure and personnel of the criminal court itself. Indeed, the extremely high conviction rate produced without the features of an adversary trial in our courts would tend to suggest that the "trial" becomes a perfunctory reiteration and validation of the pretrial interrogation and investigation.[8]

The institutional setting of the court defines a role for the defense counsel in a criminal case radically different from the one traditionally depicted.[9] Sociologists and others have focused their attention on the deprivations and social disabilities of such variables as race, ethnicity, and social class as being the source of an accused person's defeat in a criminal court. Largely overlooked is the variable of the court organization itself, which possesses a thrust, purpose, and direction of its own. It is grounded in pragmatic values, bureaucratic priorities, and administrative instruments. These exalt maximum production and the particularistic career designs of organizational incumbents, whose occupational and career commitments tend to generate a set of priorities. These priorities exert a higher claim than the stated ideological goals of "due process of law," and are often inconsistent with them.

Organizational goals and discipline impose a set of demands and conditions of practice on the respective professions in the criminal court, to which they respond by abandoning their ideological and professional commitments to the accused client, in the service of these higher claims of the court organization. All court personnel, including the

---

for a comprehensive legalistic study of the guilty plea sponsored by the American Bar Foundation. The criminal court as a social system, an analysis of "bargaining" and its functions in the criminal court's organizational structure, are examined in my forthcoming book, THE CRIMINAL COURT: A SOCIOLOGICAL PERSPECTIVE, to be published by Quadrangle Books, Chicago.

8. G. FEIFER, JUSTICE IN MOSCOW (1965). The Soviet trial has been termed "an appeal from the pretrial investigation" and Feifer notes that the Soviet "trial" is simply a recapitulation of the data collected by the pretrial investigator. The notions of a trial being a "tabula rasa" and presumptions of innocence are wholly alien to Soviet notions of justice. . . . "the closer the investigation resembles the finished script, the better . . ." *Id.* at 86.

9. For a concise statement of the constitutional and economic aspects of the right to legal assistance, see M. G. PAULSEN, EQUAL JUSTICE FOR THE POOR MAN (1964); for a brief traditional description of the legal profession see P. A. Freund, *The Legal Profession,* Daedalus 689–700 (1963).

accused's own lawyer, tend to be coopted to become agent-mediators[10] who help the accused redefine his situation and restructure his perceptions concomitant with a plea of guilty.

Of all the occupational roles in the court the only private individual who is officially recognized as having a special status and concomitant obligations is the lawyer. His legal status is that of "an officer of the court" and he is held to a standard of ethical performance and duty to his client as well as to the court. This obligation is thought to be far higher than that expected of ordinary individuals occupying the various occupational statuses in the court community. However, lawyers, whether privately retained or of the legal-aid, public defender variety, have close and continuing relations with the prosecuting office and the court itself through discreet relations with the judges via their law secretaries or "confidential" assistants. Indeed, lines of communication, influence and contact with those offices, as well as with the Office of the Clerk of the court, Probation Division, and with the press, are essential to present and prospective requirements of criminal law practice. Similarly, the subtle involvement of the press and other mass media in the court's organizational network is not readily discernible to the casual observer. Accused persons come and go in the court system schema, but the structure and its occupational incumbents remain to carry on their respective career, occupational and organizational enterprises. The individual stridencies, tensions, and conflicts a given accused person's case may present to all the participants are overcome, because the formal and informal relations of all the groups in the court setting require it. The probability of continued future relations and interaction must be preserved at all costs.

This is particularly true of the "lawyer regulars" *i.e.*, those defense lawyers, who by virtue of their continuous appearances in behalf of defendants, tend to represent the bulk of a criminal court's non-indigent case workload, and those lawyers who are not "regulars," who appear almost casually in behalf of an occasional client. Some of the "lawyer regulars" are highly visible as one moves about the major urban centers of the nation, their offices line the back streets of the courthouses, at times sharing space with bondsmen. Their political "visibility" in terms of local club house ties, reaching into the judge's chambers and prose-

10. I use the concept in the general sense that Erving Goffman employed it in his ASYLUMS: ESSAYS ON THE SOCIAL SITUATION OF MENTAL PATIENTS AND OTHER INMATES (1961).

cutor's office, are also deemed essential to successful practitioners. Previous research has indicated that the "lawyer regulars" make no effort to conceal their dependence upon police, bondsmen, jail personnel. Nor do they conceal the necessity for maintaining intimate relations with all levels of personnel in the court setting as a means of obtaining, maintaining, and building their practice. These informal relations are the *sine qua non* not only of retaining a practice, but also in the negotiation of pleas and sentences.[11]

The client, then, is a secondary figure in the court system as in certain other bureaucratic settings.[12] He becomes a means to other ends of the organization's incumbents. He may present doubts, contingencies, and pressures which challenge existing informal arrangements or disrupt them; but these tend to be resolved in favor of the continuance of the organization and its relations as before. There is a greater community of interest among all the principal organizational structures and their incumbents than exists elsewhere in other settings. The accused's lawyer has far greater professional, economic, intellectual and other ties to the various elements of the court system than he does to his own client. In short, the court is a closed community.

This is more than just the case of the usual "secrets" of bureaucracy which are fanatically defended from an outside view. Even all elements of the press are zealously determined to report on that which will not offend the board of judges, the prosecutor, probation, legal-aid, or other officials, in return for privileges and courtesies granted in the past and to be granted in the future. Rather than any view of the matter in terms of some variation of a "conspiracy" hypothesis, the simple explanation is one of an ongoing system handling delicate tensions, managing the trauma produced by law enforcement and administration, and re-

---

11. A. L. Wood, *Informal Relations in the Practice of Criminal Law*, 62 AM. J. SOC. 48–55 (1956); J. E. CARLIN, LAWYERS ON THEIR OWN 105–09 (1962); R. GOLDFARB, RANSOM—A CRITIQUE OF THE AMERICAN BAIL SYSTEM 114–15 (1965). In connection with relatively recent data as to recruitment to the legal profession, and variables involved in the type of practice engaged in, will be found in J. Ladinsky, *Careers of Lawyers, Law Practice, and Legal Institutions*, 28 AM. SOC. REV. 47–54 (1963). See also S. WARKOV & J. ZELAN, LAWYERS IN THE MAKING (1965).

12. There is a real question to be raised as to whether in certain organizational settings, a complete reversal of the bureaucratic-ideal has not occurred. That is, it would seem, in some instances the organization appears to exist to serve the needs of its various occupational incumbents, rather than its clients. A. ETZIONI, MODERN ORGANIZATIONS 94–104 (1964).

quiring almost pathological distrust of "outsiders" bordering on group paranoia.

The hostile attitude toward "outsiders" is in large measure engendered by a defensiveness itself produced by the inherent deficiencies of assembly line justice, so characteristic of our major criminal courts. Intolerably large caseloads of defendants which must be disposed of in an organizational context of limited resources and personnel, potentially subject the participants in the court community to harsh scrutiny from appellate courts, and other public and private sources of condemnation. As a consequence, an almost irreconcilable conflict is posed in terms of intense pressures to process large numbers of cases on the one hand, and the stringent ideological and legal requirements of "due process of law," on the other hand. A rather tenuous resolution of the dilemma has emerged in the shape of a large variety of bureaucratically ordained and controlled "work crimes," short cuts, deviations, and outright rule violations adopted as court practice in order to meet production norms. Fearfully anticipating criticism on ethical as well as legal grounds, all the significant participants in the court's social structure are bound into an organized system of complicity. This consists of a work arrangement in which the patterned, covert, informal breaches, and evasions of "due process" are institutionalized, but are, nevertheless, denied to exist.

These institutionalized evasions will be found to occur to some degree, in all criminal courts. Their nature, scope and complexity are largely determined by the size of the court, and the character of the community in which it is located, *e.g.*, whether it is a large, urban institution, or a relatively small rural county court. In addition, idiosyncratic, local conditions may contribute to a unique flavor in the character and quality of the criminal law's administration in a particular community. However, in most instances a variety of stratagems are employed—some subtle, some crude, in effectively disposing of what are often too large caseloads. A wide variety of coercive devices are employed against an accused-client, couched in a depersonalized, instrumental, bureaucratic version of due process of law, and which are in reality a perfunctory obeisance to the ideology of due process. These include some very explicit pressures which are exerted in some measure by all court personnel, including judges, to plead guilty and avoid trial. In many instances the sanction of a potentially harsh sentence is utilized as the visible alternative to pleading guilty, in the case of recalcitrants. Probation and psychiatric reports are "tailored" to organizational needs, or are at least responsive to the court organization's requirements for the refurbishment of a defendant's social biography, consonant with his new status. A resourceful judge can, through his subtle domination of the proceedings, impose his will on the final outcome of a trial. Stenographers and clerks, in their function as record keepers, are on occasion pressed into service in support of a judicial need to "rewrite" the record of a courtroom event. Bail practices are usually employed for purposes other than simply assuring a defendant's presence on the date of a hearing in connection with his case. Too often, the discretionary power as to bail is part of the arsenal of weapons available to collapse the resistance of an accused person. The foregoing is a most cursory examination of some of the more prominent "short cuts" available to any court organization. There are numerous other procedural strategies constituting due process deviations, which tend to become the work style artifacts of a court's personnel. Thus, only court "regulars" who are "bound in" are really accepted; others are treated routinely and in almost a coldly correct manner.

The defense attorneys, therefore, whether of the legal-aid, public defender variety, or privately retained, although operating in terms of pressures specific to their respective role and organizational obligations, ultimately are concerned with strategies which tend to lead to a plea. It is the rational, impersonal elements involving economies of time, labor, expense and a superior commitment of the defense counsel to these rationalistic values of maximum production[13] of court organization that prevail, in his relationship with a client. The lawyer "regulars" are frequently former staff members of the prosecutor's office and utilize the prestige, know-how and contacts of their former affiliation as part

13. Three relatively recent items reported in the New York Times, tend to underscore this point as it has manifested itself in one of the major criminal courts. In one instance the Bronx County Bar Association condemned "mass assembly-line justice," which "was rushing defendants into pleas of guilty and into convictions, in violation of their legal rights." N.Y. Times, March 10, 1965, p. 51. Another item, appearing somewhat later that year reports a judge criticizing his own court system (the New York Criminal Court), that "pressure to set statistical records in disposing of cases had hurt the administration of justice." N.Y. Times, Nov. 4, 1965, p. 49. A third, and most unusual recent public discussion in the press was a statement by a leading New York appellate judge decrying "instant justice" which is employed to reduce court calendar congestion ". . . converting our courthouses into counting houses . . ., as in most big cities where the volume of business tends to overpower court facilities." N.Y. Times, Feb. 5, 1966, p. 58.

of their stock in trade. Close and continuing relations between the lawyer "regular" and his former colleagues in the prosecutor's office generally overshadow the relationship between the regular and his client. The continuing colleagueship of supposedly adversary counsel rests on real professional and organizational needs of a *quid pro quo,* which goes beyond the limits of an accommodation or *modus vivendi* one might ordinarily expect under the circumstances of an otherwise seemingly adversary relationship. Indeed, the adversary features which are manifest are for the most part muted and exist even in their attenuated form largely for external consumption. The principals, lawyer and assistant district attorney, rely upon one another's cooperation for their continued professional existence, and so the bargaining between them tends usually to be "reasonable" rather than fierce.

FEE COLLECTION AND FIXING

The real key to understanding the role of defense counsel in a criminal case is to be found in the area of the fixing of the fee to be charged and its collection. The problem of fixing and collecting the fee tends to influence to a significant degree the criminal court process itself, and not just the relationship of the lawyer and his client. In essence, a lawyer-client "confidence game" is played. A true confidence game is unlike the case of the emperor's new clothes wherein that monarch's nakedness was a result of inordinate gullibility and credulity. In a genuine confidence game, the perpetrator manipulates the basic dishonesty of his partner, the victim or mark, toward his own (the confidence operator's) ends. Thus, "the victim of a con scheme must have some larceny in his heart." [14]

Legal service lends itself particularly well to confidence games. Usually, a plumber will be able to demonstrate empirically that he has performed a service by clearing up the stuffed drain, repairing the leaky faucet or pipe—and therefore merits his fee. He has rendered, when summoned, a visible, tangible boon for his client in return for the requested fee. A physician, who has not performed some visible surgery or otherwise engaged in some readily discernible procedure in connection with a patient, may be deemed by the patient to have "done nothing" for him. As a consequence, medical practitioners may simply

14. R. L. Gasser, *The Confidence Game,* 27 FED. PROB. 47 (1963).

prescribe or administer by injection a placebo to overcome a patient's potential reluctance or dissatisfaction in paying a requested fee, "for nothing."

In the practice of law there is a special problem in this regard, no matter what the level of the practitioner or his place in the hierarchy of prestige. Much legal work is intangible either because it is simply a few words of advice, some preventive action, a telephone call, negotiation of some kind, a form filled out and filed, a hurried conference with another attorney or an official of a government agency, a letter or opinion written, or a countless variety of seemingly innocuous, and even prosaic procedures and actions. These are the basic activities, apart from any possible court appearance, of almost all lawyers, at all levels of practice. Much of the activity is not in the nature of the exercise of the traditional, precise professional skills of the attorney such as library research and oral argument in connection with appellate briefs, court motions, trial work, drafting of opinions, memoranda, contracts, and other complex documents and agreements. Instead, much legal activity, whether it is at the lowest or highest "white shoe" law firm levels, is of the brokerage, agent, sales representative, lobbyist type of activity, in which the lawyer acts for someone else in pursuing the latter's interests and designs. The service is intangible.[15]

The large scale law firm may not speak as openly of their "contacts," their "fixing" abilities, as does the lower level lawyer. They trade instead upon a facade of thick carpeting, walnut panelling, genteel low pressure, and superficialities of traditional legal professionalism. There are occasions when even the large firm is on the defensive in connection with the fees they charge because the services rendered or results obtained do not appear to merit the fee asked.[16] Therefore, there is a recurrent problem in the legal profession in fixing the amount of fee, and in justifying the basis for the requested fee.

Although the fee at times amounts to what the traffic and the conscience of the lawyer will bear, one further observation must be made with regard to the size of the fee and its collection. The defendant in a criminal case and the material gain he may have acquired during the course of his illicit activities are soon parted. Not infrequently the ill gotten fruits of the various modes of larceny are sequestered by a

15. C. W. MILLS, WHITE COLLAR 121–29 (1951); J. E. Carlin *supra*, note 11.

16. E. O. SMIGEL, THE WALL STREET LAWYER 309 (1964).

defense lawyer in payment of his fee. Inexorably, the amount of the fee is a function of the dollar value of the crime committed, and is frequently set with meticulous precision at a sum which bears an uncanny relationship to that of the net proceeds of the particular offense involved. On occasion, defendants have been known to commit additional offenses while at liberty on bail, in order to secure the requisite funds with which to meet their obligations for payment of legal fees. Defense lawyers condition even the most obtuse clients to recognize that there is a firm interconnection between fee payment and the zealous exercise of professional expertise, secret knowledge, and organizational "connections" in their behalf. Lawyers, therefore, seek to keep their clients in a proper state of tension, and to arouse in them the precise edge of anxiety which is calculated to encourage prompt fee payment. Consequently, the client attitude in the relationship between defense counsel and an accused is in many instances a precarious admixture of hostility, mistrust, dependence, and sycophancy. By keeping his client's anxieties aroused to the proper pitch, and establishing a seemingly causal relationship between a requested fee and the accused's ultimate extrication from his onerous difficulties, the lawyer will have established the necessary preliminary groundwork to assure a minimum of haggling over the fee and its eventual payment.

In varying degrees, as a consequence, all law practice involves a manipulation of the client and a stage management of the lawyer-client relationship so that at least an *appearance* of help and service will be forthcoming. This is accomplished in a variety of ways, often exercised in combination with each other. At the outset, the lawyer-professional employs with suitable variation a measure of sales-puff which may range from an air of unbounding selfconfidence, adequacy, and dominion over events, to that of complete arrogance. This will be supplemented by the affectation of a studied, faultless mode of personal attire. In the larger firms, the furnishings and office trappings will serve as the backdrop to help in impression management and client intimidation. In all firms, solo or large scale, an access to secret knowledge, and to the seats of power and influence is inferred, or presumed to a varying degree as the basic vendible commodity of the practitioners.

The lack of visible end product offers a special complication in the course of the professional life of the criminal court lawyer with respect to his fee and in his relations with his client. The plain fact is that an accused in a criminal case always "loses" even when he has been exonerated by an acquittal, discharge, or dismissal of his case. The hostility of an accused which follows as a consequence of his arrest, incarceration, possible loss of job, expense and other traumas connected with his case is directed, by means of displacement, toward his lawyer. It is in this sense that it may be said that a criminal lawyer never really "wins" a case. The really satisfied client is rare, since in the very nature of the situation even an accused's vindication leaves him with some degree of dissatisfaction and hostility. It is this state of affairs that makes for a lawyer-client relationship in the criminal court which tends to be a somewhat exaggerated version of the usual lawyer-client confidence game.

At the outset, because there are great risks of nonpayment of the fee, due to the impecuniousness of his clients, and the fact that a man who is sentenced to jail may be a singularly unappreciative client, the criminal lawyer collects his fee *in advance*. Often, because the lawyer and the accused both have questionable designs of their own upon each other, the confidence game can be played. The criminal lawyer must serve three major functions, or stated another way, he must solve three problems. First, he must arrange for his fee; second, he must prepare and then, if necessary, "cool out" his client in case of defeat[17] (a highly likely contingency); third, he must satisfy the court organization that he has performed adequately in the process of negotiating the plea, so as to preclude the possibility of any sort of embarrassing incident which may serve to invite "outside" scrutiny.

In assuring the attainment of one of his primary objectives, his fee, the criminal lawyer will very often enter into negotiations with the accused's kin, including collateral relatives. In many instances, the accused himself is unable to pay any sort of fee or anything more than a token fee. It then becomes important to involve as many of the accused's kin as possible in the situation. This is especially so if the attorney hopes to collect a significant part of a proposed substantial fee. It is not uncommon for several relatives to contribute toward the

17. Talcott Parsons indicates that the social role and function of the lawyer can be therapeutic, helping his client psychologically in giving him necessary emotional support at critical times. The lawyer is also said to be acting as an agent of social control in the counseling of his client and in the influencing of his course of conduct. See T. PARSONS, ESSAYS IN SOCIOLOGICAL THEORY 382 et seq. (1954); E. Goffman, *On Cooling the Mark Out: Some Aspects of Adaptation to Failure*, in HUMAN BEHAVIOR AND SOCIAL PROCESSES 482–505 (A. Rose ed., 1962). Goffman's "cooling out" analysis is especially relevant in the lawyer-accused client relationship.

fee. The larger the group, the greater the possibility that the lawyer will collect a sizable fee by getting contributions from each.

A fee for a felony case which ultimately results in a plea, rather than a trial, may ordinarily range anywhere from $500 to $1,500. Should the case go to trial, the fee will be proportionately larger, depending upon the length of the trial. But the larger the fee the lawyer wishes to exact, the more impressive his performance must be, in terms of his stage managed image as a personage of great influence and power in the court organization. Court personnel are keenly aware of the extent to which a lawyer's stock in trade involves the precarious stage management of an image which goes beyond the usual professional flamboyance, and for this reason alone the lawyer is "bound in" to the authority system of the court's organizational discipline. Therefore, to some extent, court personnel will aid the lawyer in the creation and maintenance of that impression. There is a tacit commitment to the lawyer by the court organization, apart from formal etiquette, to aid him in this. Such augmentation of the lawyer's stage managed image as this affords, is the partial basis for the *quid pro quo* which exists between the lawyer and the court organization. It tends to serve as the continuing basis for the higher loyalty of the lawyer to the organization; his relationship with his client, in contrast, is transient, ephemeral and often superficial.

DEFENSE LAWYER AS DOUBLE AGENT

The lawyer has often been accused of stirring up unnecessary litigation, especially in the field of negligence. He is said to acquire a vested interest in a cause of action or claim which was initially his client's. The strong incentive of possible fee motivates the lawyer to promote litigation which would otherwise never have developed. However, the criminal lawyer develops a vested interest of an entirely different nature in his client's case: to limit its scope and duration rather than do battle. Only in this way can a case be "profitable." Thus, he enlists the aid of relatives not only to assure payment of his fee, but he will also rely on these persons to help him in his agent-mediator role of convincing the accused to plead guilty, and ultimately to help in "cooling out" the accused if necessary.

It is at this point that an accused-defendant may experience his first sense of "betrayal." While he had perhaps perceived the police and prosecutor to be adversaries, or possibly even the judge, the accused is wholly unprepared for his counsel's role performance as an agent-mediator. In the same vein, it is even less likely to occur to an accused that members of his own family or other kin may become agents, albeit at the behest and urging of other agents or mediators, acting on the principle that they are in reality helping an accused negotiate the best possible plea arrangement under the circumstances. Usually, it will be the lawyer who will activate next of kin in this role, his ostensible motive being to arrange for his fee. But soon latent and unstated motives will assert themselves, with entreaties by counsel to the accused's next of kin, to appeal to the accused to "help himself" by pleading. *Gemeinschaft* sentiments are to this extent exploited by a defense lawyer (or even at times by a district attorney) to achieve specific secular ends, that is, of concluding a particular matter with all possible dispatch.

The fee is often collected in stages, each installment usually payable prior to a necessary court appearance required during the course of an accused's career journey. At each stage, in his interviews and communications with the accused, or in addition, with members of his family, if they are helping with the fee payment, the lawyer employs an air of professional confidence and "inside-dopesterism" in order to assuage anxieties on all sides. He makes the necessary bland assurances, and in effect manipulates his client, who is usually willing to do and say the things, true or not, which will help his attorney extricate him. Since the dimensions of what he is essentially selling, organizational influence and expertise, are not technically and precisely measurable, the lawyer can make extravagant claims of influence and secret knowledge with impunity. Thus, lawyers frequently claim to have inside knowledge in connection with information in the hands of the D.A., police, probation officials or to have access to these functionaries. Factually, they often do, and need only to exaggerate the nature of their relationships with them to obtain the desired effective impression upon the client. But, as in the genuine confidence game, the victim who has participated is loathe to do anything which will upset the lesser plea which his lawyer has "conned" him into accepting.[18]

18. The question has never been raised as to whether "bargain justice," "copping a plea," or justice by negotiation is a constitutional process. Although it has become the most central aspect of the process of criminal law administration, it has received virtually no close scrutiny by the appellate courts. As a consequence, it is relatively free of legal control and supervision. But, apart from any questions of the legality of bargaining, in terms of the pressures and devices that are employed which tend to violate due process of law, there remain ethical and practical questions. The system

In effect, in his role as double agent, the criminal lawyer performs an extremely vital and delicate mission for the court organization and the accused. Both principals are anxious to terminate the litigation with a minimum of expense and damage to each other. There is no other personage or role incumbent in the total court structure more strategically located, who by training and in terms of his own requirements, is more ideally suited to do so than the lawyer. In recognition of this, judges will cooperate with attorneys in many important ways. For example, they will adjourn the case of an accused in jail awaiting plea or sentence if the attorney requests such action. While explicitly this may be done for some innocuous and seemingly valid reason, the tacit purpose is that pressure is being applied by the attorney for the collection of his fee, which he knows will probably not be forthcoming if the case is concluded. Judges are aware of this tactic on the part of lawyers, who, by requesting an adjournment, keep an accused incarcerated awhile longer as a not too subtle method of dunning a client for payment. However, the judges will go along with this, on the ground that important ends are being served. Often, the only end served is to protect a lawyer's fee.

The judge will help an accused's lawyer in still another way. He will lend the official aura of his office and courtroom so that a lawyer can stage manage an impression of an "all out" performance for the accused in justification of his fee. The judge and other court personnel will serve as a backdrop for a scene charged with dramatic fire, in which the accused's lawyer makes a stirring appeal in his behalf. With a show of restrained passion, the lawyer will intone the virtues of the accused and recite the social deprivations which have reduced him to his present state. The speech varies somewhat, depending on whether the accused has been convicted after trial or has pleaded guilty. In the main, however, the incongruity, superficiality, and ritualistic character of the total performance is underscored by a visibly impassive, almost bored reaction on the part of the judge and other members of the court retinue.

Afterward, there is a hearty exchange of pleasantries between the lawyer and district attorney, wholly out of context in terms of the sup-

of bargain-counter justice is like the proverbial iceberg, much of its danger is concealed in secret negotiations and its least alarming feature, the final plea, being the one presented to public view. See A. S. TREBACH, THE RATIONING OF JUSTICE 74–94 (1964); Note, *Guilty Plea Bargaining: Compromises by Prosecutors to Secure Guilty Pleas,* 112 U. PA. L. REV. 865–95 (1964).

posed adversary nature of the preceding events. The fiery passion in defense of his client is gone, and the lawyers for both sides resume their offstage relations, chatting amiably and perhaps including the judge in their restrained banter. No other aspect of their visible conduct so effectively serves to put even a casual observer on notice, that these individuals have claims upon each other. These seemingly innocuous actions are indicative of continuing organizational and informal relations, which, in their intricacy and depth, range far beyond any priorities or claims a particular defendant may have.[19]

Criminal law practice is a unique form of private law practice since it really only appears to be private practice.[20] Actually it is bureaucratic practice, because of the legal practitioner's enmeshment in the authority, discipline, and perspectives of the court organization. Private practice, supposedly, in a professional sense, involves the maintenance of an organized, disciplined body of knowledge and learning; the individual practitioners are imbued with a spirit of autonomy and service, the earning of a livelihood being incidental. In the sense that the lawyer in the criminal court serves as a double agent, serving higher organizational rather than professional ends, he may be deemed to be engaged in bureaucratic rather than private practice. To some extent the lawyer-client "confidence game," in addition to its other functions, serves to conceal this fact.

---

19. For a conventional summary statement of some of the inevitable conflicting loyalties encountered in the practice of law, see E. E. CHEATHAM, CASES AND MATERIALS ON THE LEGAL PROFESSION 70–79 (2d ed. 1955).

20. Some lawyers at either end of the continuum of law practice appear to have grave doubts as to whether it is indeed a profession at all. J. E. Carlin, *op. cit. supra* note 11, at 192; E. O. Smigel *supra,* note 16, at 304–305. Increasingly, it is perceived as a business with widespread evasion of the Canons of Ethics, duplicity and chicanery being practiced in an effort to get and keep business. The poet, Carl Sandburg, epitomized this notion in the following vignette: "Have you a criminal lawyer in this burg?" "We think so but we haven't been able to prove it on him." C. SANDBURG, THE PEOPLE, YES 154 (1936).

Thus, while there is a considerable amount of dishonesty present in law practice involving fee splitting, thefts from clients, influence peddling, fixing, questionable use of favors and gifts to obtain business or influence others, this sort of activity is most often attributed to the "solo," private practice lawyer. See A. L. Wood, *Professional Ethics Among Criminal Lawyers,* SOCIAL PROBLEMS 70–83 (1959). However, to some degree, large scale "downtown" elite firms also engage in these dubious activities. The difference is that the latter firms enjoy a good deal of immunity from these harsh charges because of their institutional and organizational advantages, in terms of near monopoly over more desirable types of practice, as well as exerting great influence in the political, economic and professional realms of power.

THE CLIENT'S PERCEPTION

The "cop-out" ceremony, in which the court process culminates, is not only invaluable for redefining the accused's perspectives of himself, but also in reiterating publicly in a formally structured ritual the accused person's guilt for the benefit of significant "others" who are observing. The accused not only is made to assert publicly his guilt of a specific crime, but also a complete recital of its details. He is further made to indicate that he is entering his plea of guilt freely, willingly, and voluntarily, and that he is not doing so because of any promises or in consideration of any commitments that may have been made to him by anyone. This last is intended as a blanket statement to shield the participants from any possible charges of "coercion" or undue influence that may have been exerted in violation of due process requirements. Its function is to preclude any later review by an appellate court on these grounds, and also to obviate any second thoughts an accused may develop in connection with his plea.

However, for the accused, the conception of self as a guilty person is in large measure a temporary role adaptation. His career socialization as an accused, if it is successful, eventuates in his acceptance and redefinition of himself as a guilty person.[21] However, the transformation is ephemeral, in that he will, in private, quickly reassert his innocence. Of importance is that he accept his defeat, publicly proclaim it, and find some measure of pacification in it.[22] Almost immediately after his

21. This does not mean that most of those who plead guilty are innocent of any crime. Indeed, in many instances those who have been able to negotiate a lesser plea, have done so willingly and even eagerly. The system of justice-by-negotiation, without trial, probably tends to better serve the interests and requirements of guilty persons, who are thereby presented with formal alternatives of "half a loaf," in terms of, at worst, possibilities of a lesser plea and a concomitant shorter sentence as compensation for their acquiescence and participation. Having observed the prescriptive etiquette in compliance with the defendant role expectancies in this setting, he is rewarded. An innocent person, on the other hand, is confronted with the same set of role prescriptions, structures and legal alternatives, and in any event, for him this mode of justice is often an ineluctable bind.

22. "Any communicative network between persons whereby the public identity of an actor is transformed into something looked on as lower in the local scheme of social types will be called a 'status degradation ceremony.'" H. Garfinkel, *Conditions of Successful Degradation Ceremonies*, 61 AM. J. SOC. 420–24 (1956). But contrary to the conception of the "cop out" as a "status degradation ceremony," is the fact that it is in reality a charade, during the course of which an accused must project an appropriate and acceptable amount of guilt, penitence and remorse. Having adequately

plea, a defendant will generally be interviewed by a representative of the probation division in connection with a presentence report which is to be prepared. The very first question to be asked of him by the probation officer is: "Are you guilty of the crime to which you pleaded?" This is by way of double affirmation of the defendant's guilt. Should the defendant now begin to make bold assertions of his innocence, despite his plea of guilty, he will be asked to withdraw his plea and stand trial on the original charges. Such a threatened possibility is, in most instances, sufficient to cause an accused to let the plea stand and to request the probation officer to overlook his exclamations of innocence. The table that follows is a breakdown of the categorized responses of a random sample of male defendants in Metropolitan Court[23] during 1962, 1963, and 1964 in connection with their statements during presentence probation interviews following their plea of guilty.

It would be well to observe at the outset, that of the 724 defendants who pleaded guilty before trial, only 43 (5.94 per cent) of the total group had confessed prior to their indictment. Thus, the ultimate judicial process was predicated upon evidence independent of any confession of the accused.[24]

As the data indicate, only a relatively small number (95) out of the total number of defendants actually will even admit their guilt, following the "cop-out" ceremony. However, even though they have

---

feigned the role of the "guilty person," his hearers will engage in the fantasy that he is contrite, and thereby merits a lesser plea. It is one of the essential functions of the criminal lawyer that he coach and direct his accused-client in that role performance. Thus, what is actually involved is not a "degradation" process at all, but is instead, a highly structured system of exchange cloaked in the rituals of legalism and public professions of guilt and repentance.

23. The name is of course fictitious. However, the actual court which served as the universe from which the data were drawn, is one of the largest criminal courts in the United States, dealing with felonies only. Female defendants in the years 1950 through 1964 constituted from 7–10% of the totals for each year.

24. My own data in this connection would appear to support Sobel's conclusion (see note 4 *supra*), and appears to be at variance with the prevalent view, which stresses the importance of confessions in law enforcement and prosecution. All the persons in my sample were originally charged with felonies ranging from homicide to forgery; in most instances the original felony charges were reduced to misdemeanors by way of a negotiated lesser plea. The vast range of crime categories which are available, facilitates the patterned court process of plea reduction to a lesser offense, which is also usually a socially less opprobious crime. For an illustration of this feature of the bargaining process in a court utilizing a public defender office, see D. Sudnow, *Normal Crimes: Sociological Features of the Penal Code in a Public Defender Office*, 12 SOCIAL PROBLEMS 255–76 (1964).

TABLE 1

Defendant Responses as to Guilt or Innocence After Pleading Guilty

N = 724 **Years — 1962, 1963, 1964**

NATURE OF RESPONSE		*N OF DEFENDANTS*
INNOCENT (Manipulated)	"The lawyer or judge, police or D.A. 'conned me'"	86
INNOCENT (Pragmatic)	"Wanted to get it over with" "You can't beat the system" "They have you over a barrel when you have a record"	147
INNOCENT (Advice of counsel)	"Followed my lawyer's advice"	92
INNOCENT (Defiant)	"Framed"— Betrayed by "Complainant," "Police," "Squealers," "Lawyer," "Friends," "Wife," "Girlfriend"	33
INNOCENT (Adverse social data)	Blames probation officer or psychiatrist for "Bad Report," in cases where there was pre-pleading investigation	15
GUILTY	"But I should have gotten a better deal" Blames lawyer, D.A., Police, Judge	74
GUILTY	Won't say anything further	21
FATALISTIC (Doesn't press his "Innocence," won't admit "Guilt")	"I did it for convenience" "My lawyer told me it was only thing I could do" "I did it because it was the best way out"	248
NO RESPONSE		8
TOTAL		724

affirmed their guilt, many of these defendants felt that they should have been able to negotiate a more favorable plea. The largest aggregate of defendants (373) were those who reasserted their "innocence" following their public profession of guilt during the "cop-out" ceremony. These defendants employed differential degrees of fervor, solemnity and credibility, ranging from really mild, wavering assertions of innocence which were embroidered with a variety of stock explanations and rationalizations, to those of an adamant, "framed" nature. Thus, the "Innocent" group, for the most part, were largely concerned with underscoring for their probation interviewer their essential "goodness" and "worthiness," despite their formal plea of guilty. Assertion of his innocence at the post plea stage, resurrects a more respectable and acceptable self concept for the accused defendant who has pleaded guilty. A recital of the structural exigencies which precipitated his plea of guilt, serves to embellish a newly proffered claim of innocence, which many defendants mistakenly feel will stand them in good stead at the time of sentence, or ultimately with probation or parole authorities.

Relatively few (33) maintained their innocence in terms of having been "framed" by some person or agent-mediator, although a larger number (86) indicated that they had been manipulated or "conned" by an agent-mediator to plead guilty, but as indicated, their assertions of innocence were relatively mild.

A rather substantial group (147) preferred to stress the pragmatic aspects of their plea of guilty. They would only perfunctorily assert their innocence and would in general refer to some adverse aspect of their situation which they believed tended to negatively affect their bargaining leverage, including in some instances a prior criminal record.

One group of defendants (92), while maintaining their innocence, simply employed some variation of a theme of following "the advice of counsel" as a covering response, to explain their guilty plea in the light of their new affirmation of innocence.

The largest single group of defendants (248) were basically fatalistic. They often verbalized weak suggestions of their innocence in rather halting terms, wholly without conviction. By the same token, they would not admit guilt readily and were generally evasive as to guilt or innocence, preferring to stress aspects of their stoic submission in their decision to plead. This sizable group of defendants appeared to perceive the total court process as being caught up in a monstrous organizational apparatus, in which the defendant role expectancies were not clearly defined. Reluctant to offend anyone in authority, fearful that clear cut statements on their part as to their guilt or innocence would be negatively construed, they adopted a stance of passivity, resignation and acceptance. Interestingly, they would in most instances invoke their lawyer as being the one who crystallized the available alternatives for them, and who was therefore the critical element in their decision-making process.

In order to determine which agent-mediator was most influential in altering the accused's perspectives as to his decision to plead or go to trial (regardless of the proposed basis of the plea), the same sample of defendants were asked to indicate the person who first suggested to them that they plead guilty. They were also asked to indicate which of the persons or officials who made such suggestion, was most influential in affecting their final decision to plead.

The following table indicates the breakdown of the responses to the two questions:

TABLE 2

Role of Agent-Mediators in Defendant's Guilty Plea

PERSON OR OFFICIAL	*FIRST SUGGESTED PLEA OF GUILTY*	*INFLUENCED THE ACCUSED MOST IN HIS FINAL DECISION TO PLEAD*
JUDGE	4	26
DISTRICT ATTORNEY	67	116
DEFENSE COUNSEL	407	411
PROBATION OFFICER	14	3
PSYCHIATRIST	8	1
WIFE	34	120
FRIENDS AND KIN	21	14
POLICE	14	4
FELLOW INMATES	119	14
OTHERS	28	5
NO RESPONSE	8	10
TOTAL	724	724

It is popularly assumed that the police, through forced confessions, and the district attorney, employing still other pressures, are most instrumental in the inducement of an accused to plead guilty.[25] As Table 2 indicates, it is actually the defendant's own counsel who is

25. Failures, shortcomings and oppressive features of our system of criminal justice have been attributed to a variety of sources including "lawless" police, overzealous district attorneys, "hanging" juries, corruption and political connivance, incompetent judges, inadequacy or lack of counsel, and poverty or other social disabilities of the defendant. See A. BARTH, LAW ENFORCEMENT VERSUS THE LAW (1963), for a journalist's account embodying this point of view; J. H. SKOLNICK, JUSTICE WITHOUT TRIAL: LAW ENFORCEMENT IN DEMOCRATIC SOCIETY (1966), for a sociologist's study of the role of the police in criminal law administration. For a somewhat more detailed, albeit legalistic and somewhat technical discussion of American police procedures, see W. R. LAFAVE, ARREST: THE DECISION TO TAKE A SUSPECT INTO CUSTODY (1965).

most effective in this role. Further, this phenomenon tends to reinforce the extremely rational nature of criminal law administration, for an organization could not rely upon the sort of idiosyncratic measures employed by the police to induce confessions and maintain its efficiency, high production and overall rational-legal character. The defense counsel becomes the ideal agent-mediator since, as "officer of the court" and confidant of the accused and his kin, he lives astride both worlds and can serve the ends of the two as well as his own.[26]

While an accused's wife, for example, may be influential in making him more amenable to a plea, her agent-mediator role has, nevertheless, usually been sparked and initiated by defense counsel. Further, although a number of first suggestions of a plea came from an accused's fellow jail inmates, he tended to rely largely on his counsel as an ultimate source of influence in his final decision. The defense counsel, being a crucial figure in the total organizational scheme in constituting a new set of perspectives for the accused, the same sample of defendants were asked to indicate at which stage of their contact with counsel was the suggestion of a plea made. There are three basic kinds of defense counsel available in Metropolitan Court: Legal-aid, privately retained counsel, and counsel assigned by the court (but may eventually be privately retained by the accused).

TABLE 3

Stage at Which Counsel Suggested Accused to Plead

N = 724

	COUNSEL TYPE							
CONTACT	PRIVATELY RETAINED		LEGAL-AID		ASSIGNED		TOTAL	
	N	%	N	%	N	%	N	%
FIRST	66	35	237	49	28	60	331	46
SECOND	83	44	142	29	8	17	233	32
THIRD	29	15	63	13	4	9	96	13
FOURTH OR MORE	12	6	31	7	5	11	48	7
NO RESPONSE	0	0	14	3	2	4	16	2
TOTAL	190	100	487	101*	47	101*	724	100

* Rounded percentage.

26. Aspects of the lawyer's ambivalences with regard to the expectancies of the various groups who have claims upon him, are discussed in H. J. O'Gorman, *The Ambivalence of Lawyers*, paper presented at the Eastern Sociological Association meetings, April 10, 1965.

The overwhelming majority of accused persons, regardless of type of counsel, related a specific incident which indicated an urging or suggestion, either during the course of the first or second contact, that they plead guilty to a lesser charge if this could be arranged. Of all the agent-mediators, it is the lawyer who is most effective in manipulating an accused's perspectives, notwithstanding pressures that may have been previously applied by police, district attorney, judge or any of the agent-mediators that may have been activated by them. Legal-aid and assigned counsel would apparently be more likely to suggest a possible plea at the point of initial interview as response to pressures of time. In the case of the assigned counsel, the strong possibility that there is no fee involved, may be an added impetus to such a suggestion at the first contact.

In addition, there is some further evidence in Table 3 of the perfunctory, ministerial character of the system in Metropolitan Court and similar criminal courts. There is little real effort to individualize, and the lawyer's role as agent-mediator may be seen as unique in that he is in effect a double agent. Although, as "officer of the court" he mediates between the court organization and the defendant, his roles with respect to each are rent by conflicts of interest. Too often these must be resolved in favor of the organization which provides him with the means for his professional existence. Consequently, in order to reduce the strains and conflicts imposed in what is ultimately an over-demanding role obligation for him, the lawyer engages in the lawyer-client "confidence game" so as to structure more favorably an otherwise onerous role system.[27]

CONCLUSION

Recent decisions of the Supreme Court, in the area of criminal law administration and defendant's rights, fail to take into account three crucial aspects of social structure which may tend to render the more libertarian rules as nugatory. The decisions overlook (1) the nature of courts as formal organization; (2) the relationship that the lawyer-regular *actually* has with the court organization; and (3) the character of the lawyer-client relationship in the criminal court (the routine rela-

27. W. J. Goode, *A Theory of Role Strain*, 25 AM. SOC. REV. 483–96 (1960); J. D. Snoek, *Role Strain in Diversified Role Sets*, 71 AM. J. SOC. 363–72 (1966).

tionships, not those unusual ones that are described in "heroic" terms in novels, movies, and TV).

Courts, like many other modern large-scale organizations possess a monstrous appetite for the cooptation of entire professional groups as well as individuals.[28] Almost all those who come within the ambit of organizational authority, find that their definitions, perceptions and values have been refurbished, largely in terms favorable to the particular organization and its goals. As a result, recent Supreme Court decisions may have a long range effect which is radically different from that intended or anticipated. The more libertarian rules will tend to produce the rather ironic end result of augmenting the *existing* organizational arrangements, enriching court organizations with more personnel and elaborate structure, which in turn will maximize organizational goals of "efficiency" and production. Thus, many defendants will find that courts will possess an even more sophisticated apparatus for processing them toward a guilty plea!

28. Some of the resources which have become an integral part of our courts, *e.g.*, psychiatry, social work and probation, were originally intended as part of an ameliorative, therapeutic effort to individualize offenders. However, there is some evidence that a quite different result obtains, than the one originally intended. The ameliorative instruments have been coopted by the court in order to more "efficiently" deal with a court's caseload, often to the legal disadvantage of an accused person. See F. A. ALLEN, THE BORDERLAND OF CRIMINAL JUSTICE (1964); T. S. SZASZ, LAW, LIBERTY AND PSYCHIATRY (1963) and also Szasz's most recent, PSYCHIATRIC JUSTICE (1965); L. Diana, *The Rights of Juvenile Delinquents: An Appraisal of Juvenile Court Procedures*, 47 J. CRIM. L. C. & P.S. 561–69 (1957).

[9]

WESTERN LAW IN A TRADITIONAL SOCIETY KOREA

by Dai-Kwon Choi*

I. Introduction

Koreans, perhaps more than others, used to say that there is a gap between the law and the reality. For some the gap borders on an outright lawlessness as seen in the high rate of traffic violations on the streets of metropolitan cities, in the number of public officials dismissed or prosecuted on a bribery charge, and in the business practices believed as invariably associated with tax evasions, reckless discharge of pollutants, etc. For others the gap represents an attribute of human nature. An ideal is always not fully realized; in a sense, the harder to realize, the more ideal. In fact, there is no society in which there is no gap between the law and the reality. For still others the gap is symptomatic of social malaise afflicted with by a society in rapid transition such as Korea.

For some others the gap is actually between Western and Oriental cultures. In this shrinking world a tension and conflict between two cultures is only natural according as Korea is extensively exposed to Western influences. The formal Korean law is based on Western concepts, particularly German ones, which were forcefully introduced by the Japanese for their colonial rule at the turn of the century—American influence is also felt in its ideological contents, following the World War II.

Traditional Korean culture was greatly influenced by two thousand years of Confucian teachings. Naturally, Confucian notions of propriety and law became deeply ingrained in Korean attitudes toward law. In the Analects, Confucius says:

> "Lead the people with governmental measures and regulate them by law and punishment, they will avoid wrongdoing but will have no sense of honor and shame. Lead them with virtue and regulate them by the rules of propriety (*li*), and they will have a sense of shame and, moreover, set themselves right."

*Currently Professor of Law (Assistant Professor), Law School, Seoul National University; Associate Director of the Korea Law Research Institute of Seoul National University. LL.B., 1960, Seoul National University; M.C.L., 1967, University of Michigan Law School; LL.M., 1969, University of California School of Law at Berkeley; Ph.D., 1976, University of California at Berkeley.

Even at the level of ordinary persons, the most popular expression toward an upright neighbor or a good colleague today is "a person who can live without law." One's insistence on the formal law tends to make a Korean frown upon him.

Apart from the formal law, there is a remarkable orderliness. This stands out especially when the formal law completely collapses because of a political upheaval or a disaster. The kind of orderliness showed up right after the fall of President Syng Man Rhee's regime and the accompanied collapse of the formal law apparatus that followed the students' revolt of April 19, 1960. The same students that took to streets to revolt had promptly organized themselves to do the job of cleaning streets, controlling traffic, and patrolling neighborhoods. The same orderliness prevailed a few years ago in the town of Iri where there was a giant explosion of the freight train carrying a large amount of explosives at night. The explosion caused heavy damages to humans and properties accompanied by a total blackout like a town devastated by a severe earthquake. Thus one is reminded of the newspaper articles that carried a contrasting picture of New York when the city had a blackout. In Korea, the orderliness resides in the persisting traditional social structure.

What is said above of the gap, the traditional Korean cultural patterns, and the social orderliness, all has truth about law in Korean society. The gap between the law and the reality in Korea is more complex than the simple gap in any normative system; the former gap has three dimensions of conflicts: between the social norms residing in the persisting social structure and their reality; between the formal Western law and its reality; and between the Western values embodied in the formal law and the social norms embodied in the social structure. However, the last dimension is more significant than the other two; it highlights one of the core problems with the gap between the law and the reality in Korea today.

Even with the last dimension of the gap, a thorny issue is how to approach it. Understanding of the entire scope of the dimension is not tried here. In this paper, only an attempt is made to bring a more focused light on five antinomies around which tensions, conflicts, interactions, and interrelationships between Western formal law and the persisting traditional social structure manifestedly evolve. These are: (1) universalism vs. particularism, (2) impersonal vs. personal relationships, (3) competition vs. cooperation, (4) individual vs. collective responsibility, and (5) conflict vs. harmony. Modern Western law incorporates the first variables of these five antinomies as overarching principle and underlying values. The second variables of these five antinomies are embodied in the Korean traditional social structure. No doubt, the five characteristic features of Western law considered here have their historical roots in Western society. Likewise, the five traits of the traditional Korean social structure have their historical roots in Korean society. Even this simple historical consideration makes apparent the presence and pervasiveness of the five antinomies in various social contexts. It obviously precludes the idea that the imposition of a Western, modern, formal legal system on a non-Western—and non-Communist—society such as Korea will alone transform a traditional social structure into one with modern characteristics. At the same time, however, there is a danger of overdichotomizing the five antinomies against which we must guard. A closer examination will reveal a complicated combination of the variables involved in the dichotomies.

II. Universalism vs. Particularism

Since particularism is defined as interchangeable with ascriptive principle or with status, universalism is in our scheme defined as a principle negating particularism. Thus understood, universalism differs from uniformity. Even a particularistic (or ascriptive) rule can be perfectly uniform throughout a society or a state. Uniformity—that is, generality or regularity—is an inseparable feature of law whether it applies to group, nation, or state. Of course, there is room for local variation (localism or federalism) in territorial uniformity to some extent within certain areas of human activity. But in other areas territorial uniformity is the rule. Even the kind of social and/or political-institutional localism that once prevailed in China and feudal Japan never existed in Korea. In law of nationality (naturalization and immigration), a personal principle is the rule in the Continental Europe and in Korea. In the Anglo-American world, a territorial principle is the rule. In a conflict of law situation, the law of nationality (or of domicile) is relied on for certain issues whereas the law of the forum is for other issues, according to the forum's choice of law rule.

Historically, particularism is associated with class, race, and religion. In this connection the evolution from status to contract best describes the present state of universalistic law. In the transformation the French revolution is the symbolic and political turning point in Europe. The introduction of the Western formal legal system in Korea at the turn of the century marks the start of universalistic law in this society at least in formal legal principle. In dynastic Korea, particularism was the rule.

Social and (formal) legal norms were structured along official class lines and order of rank among *yangban* officials.

In dynastic Korea, for example, there were sumptuary laws that differentially regulated one's mode of life with respect to clothing, housing, and rituals in accordance with one's social and legal status.[1] Scholar-officials for the centralized bureaucratic organizations were recruited exclusively from the ruling yangban class on the basis of performance at the royal examinations for civil and military officials. As the philosopher-king producing ruling class, the yangban received differential treatment legally from other classes with respect to both privileges and obligations. For example, members of this class were not subject to compulsory military service and labor—corresponding to the Western corvée. These obligations were borne entirely by the commoners. On the other hand, more exacting behavioral rules and standards, based on Confucian moral norms, were required of yangbans than of non-yangbans. These included rules against extravagance,[2] making a profit, corruption,[3] immoral behavior,[4] superstition including practices in Buddhism,[5] and sexual promiscuity.[6] This latter included prohibitions against taking a wife with-

1. As for clothing, for example, see *Kyongkukdaejon* (The Great Codes of Governance), a modern Korean translation, (Seoul: Bopjaech'o, 1962), I; 216 ff. and II, 166; *Sokdaejon*, a modern Korean translation, (Seoul: Bopjaech'o, 1965), 202; as for housing *Kyongkukdaejon*, II, 210; *Han'guksa* (History of Korea), (Seoul: Kuksa p'yonch'an wiwonhoe, 1974), XI, 393–396; as for rituals, *Kyongkukdaejon*, I, 233 ff., 261, and 266–268.

2. For example, it constituted a crime entailing a flogging of 100 strokes for a yangban lady to have a picnic in a wood or on a beach. *Kyongkukdaejon*, *ibid.*, II, 165. Similar prohibitive rules had existed against various forms of "extravagance."

3. Like a yangban lady who had "befouled her virtue" (see note 6 *infra*), a yangban (official) who had embezzled public funds, taken bribe, or illegally enriched himself was also recorded in the public records which were kept by various ministries and offices. *Kyongkukdaejon*, *ibid.*, II, 167. He was not only punished but also permanently barred from taking another official position and from taking the royal examination. His son and grandson were also barred from taking the royal examination as well as from being appointed to major official positions specified in the Code. *Kyongkukdaejon*, I, 23 and 201.

4. A yangban whose behavior was "against the proper human relations" was also in the official records kept by various ministries and offices. *Kyongkukdaejon*, *ibid.*, II, 167.

5. It also constituted a crime entailing 100 strokes for a Confucian scholar (or a lady) to go to a Buddhist temple. *Kyongkukdaejon*, *ibid.*, II, 165.

6. It was prohibited for a yangban man to marry within three years after his former wife had died, and for a yangban lady to marry for the second time. For the

in three years after a previous wife had died and against a yangban lady marrying for a second time, and the requirement of three years of mourning at the death of a parent,[7] during which period a yangban had to live a monk-like ascetic life by the parent's graveyard. Due to this requirement any official who had an official position had to resign, and any misconduct unworthy of a yangban, especially sexual misconduct, during the mourning period entailed harsh punishment.[8] A yangban in mourning who

former prohibition, see *Kyongkukdaejon, ibid.*, I, 267. Probably the former rule must have been more effective than the latter, even though there was no negative formal legal sanction for the former rule. The social censor against a yangban who violated the former rule, however, must have been extremely strong among the yangban class especially when he was ambitious in the officialdom. For the latter rule, there were official records in which a yangban lady who had "befouled her virtue" by having married for the third time was recorded. These records were kept by the Ministry of Officials (*Ijo*), the Ministry of Armed Forces (*Pyongjo*), and the two censorial offices. *Kyongkukdaejon*, II, 167. Descendants (son or grandson) of a lady who had married for the second time or otherwise "befouled her virtue" were not only allowed to take the royal examination for civil officials (*Kyongkukdaejon*, 1, 201), but also were barred from their being appointed to major official positions specified in the Code of Officials (*Kyongkukdaejon*, I, 23). See also Yi Sang-paek, "Chaeka kumji supsokui yurae-e daehan yon'gu" (A Study of the Origin of the Prohibition against Ladies' Second Marriage), *Han'guk munhwasa yon'guron'go* (Studies on Korean Cultural History), (Seoul: Eulyumunhwasa, 1954), Chapter 3, 205-248.

Having a concubine was socially tolerated. But there was the strong sanction against taking a concubine in the form of permanently disqualifying descendants of a concubine from taking the royal examination for civil officials and thus barring them from becoming officials. *Kyongkukdaejon*, II, 201. See also Yi Sang-paek, "So-ol ch'adaeui yonwon-e daehan ilmunjae" (A Problem of the Origin of Discrimination Against Descendants of a Concubine), *Han'guk munhwasa yon'guron'go*, Chapter 2, 172-204. Descendants of others than common law wives were generally classified among the middlemen class even though their father was a yangban.

An official's going to a prostitute constituted a crime entailing a flogging of 100 strokes. If a son of an official was caught for committing the crime, his name went to an official record for consideration in the future official appointment. *Daemyongnyul jikhae*, a Modern Korean Translation of the Ming Codes in Use during the Yi Dynasty, (Seoul: Bopjaech'o, 1964), 479.

7. *Kyongkukdaejon, ibid.*, I. 233 ff.; *Han'guksa* (History of Korea), (Seoul: Chindan hakhoe, 1962), III, 333 ff.

8. One who married, had a party, or did not wear mourning clothes and wore instead ordinary clothes during the mourning period, among others, was regarded as having committed a crime of being not filial, and a wife who did the same thing at her husband's death was regarded as having committed a crime of being not righteous.

came personally to the court to institute a lawsuit was punished, and his suit would not even be received.[9] These rules were neither required nor expected of commoners. As centuries passed, however, certain yangban practices, notably rituals related to ancestor worship, were diffused among members of other classes to a great extent.

On the other hand, different rules were applied for crimes committed by a yangban. The punishment for identical crimes was more favorable to yangbans than to non-yangbans in kind and degree,[10] different procedural rules were followed for members of this class, and extra care was taken in cases involving yangbans.[11] Furthermore, an outcaste—i.e., a servant or slave—who committed a crime such as battery or adultery

These two crimes are listed in the ten most heinous crimes. *Daemyongnyul jikhae, op. cit.* (note 6), 51–52.

9. *Sason'gyuch'wi* in *Wonsinbo Sukyojiprok-Sason'gyuch'wi*, a modern Korean translation, (Seoul: Bopjaech'o, 1964), 483. If he did not have a servant or other who could proceed on his behalf, he was allowed to institute the suit after the funeral. If the defendant was in mourning, the hearing would be had also after the funeral.

10. For officials, eunuchs, sons of a certain level of the former high-ranking officials, and those who had passed the royal examination for civil officials, punishment by flogging was as a rule substituted by payment of redemption money, unless they had committed one of the ten most heinous crimes such as high and petty treasons, or adultery, stealing, murder, or bribery. *Kyongkukdaejon, op. cit.* (note 1); Suh Il-kyo, *Choson wangjo hyongsajaedo ui yon'gu* (A Study of the Criminal System of the Yi Dynasty), (Seoul: Han'guk bopryong p'yonch'anhoe, 1968), 188. In sentencing, yangbans were generally spared their lives as far as possible. They were instead sent into exile to a remote place for their crime. *Han'guk Il-bo,* Feb. 17, 1974.

11. Those who came under one of the eight specified groups of royal family members, prominent military men who had performed meritorious services in war, great wise men, extra-talented scholars, high-ranking civil and military officials, etc., could be subpoenaed for criminal investigation only upon the king's special instruction; facts investigated and relevant legal rules were required to be reported to the king for instruction of sentencing, and sentence of punishment was to be decided upon the concurrence of a number of high-ranking officials concerned and then upon the king's approval, unless the crime under consideration was treason. *Daemyongnyul jikhae, op. cit.* (note 6), 53–56. Civil and military officials and ascendants, descendants, wife, and other relatives of those who came under one of the eight specified groups of persons were also provided the special treatment of similar nature even though the requirements were less and less vigorous as the rank order of the official under investigation became lower and as the family relationship of the criminal suspect to one of those eight groups of persons became distant. *Daemyongnyul jikhae,* 56–60. See also Suh Il-kyo, *ibid.*, 292–293.

against a commoner incurred a heavier degree of punishment, and, conversely, a commoner was visited by a degree lighter punishment than usual for a crime against an outcaste.[12]

The ruling-class work ethic that existed in Korea was in fact geared to the scholar-officialdom. The whole political and social system was so arranged that once one became a scholar-official, one could have power, wealth, and prestige. These benefits were invariably conferred on both the individual official and his extended family. The division of labor was organized so that the three other classes formed supporting classes for the yangban scholar-officials. Being a scholar-official was the only career choice for a yangban. A member of this class would go jobless rather than become a professional such as a herb doctor, a jurist, an interpreter, an accountant, or a meteorological observer, or engage in a productive activity such as farming, craftmanship, or commerce. Moreover, a yangban would not take a low-ranking official position in the civil or military hierarchy. These professional careers and low-ranking official positions were held exclusively by members of the middle men class, not because yangbans were excluded but because they regarded them demeaning for a yangban. Commoners engaged in farming, craft, and commerce. The outcaste produced sailors, butchers, shamans, actors, and private and official servants who were sold or inherited like slaves.

The major material burden of support for the yangban class and the bureaucratic political organization of the state fell upon the shoulders of the commoners among others. The absolute majority of these commoners were peasants. Peasants were tied strongly to the land. In fact, it was almost impossible for a peasant to leave the land. The stability of the whole system depended upon the ties that held all classes to their respective professions, especially peasants to the land. It was crucial for the system to maintain the ties undisturbed. There were, for example, the *hopaebop* which required everyone to carry his ID card showing, among others, status and vocation, the *hokubop* (a kind of household census law), and the *okajaktongbop* which made five households a unit for mutual cooperation and collective crime prevention. These devices were in the main designed to discourage peasants from leaving their land.[13] Craft industry and commercial activity were also equally under strict governmental control, which was extremely unfavorable for their prosperity.

12. *Daemyongnyul jikhae, ibid.*, 426–427 and 478–479. See also *Kyongkukdaejon, op. cit.* (note 1), I, 164.

13. See *Han'guksa* (History of Korea), *op. cit.* (note 1), X, 635.

Since it was (and it is) racially and linguistically homogeneous, Korea did not have any problems with ethnic minorities. Because of its Confucian bias, however, discrimination did exist against Buddhism.[14] This discrimination existed in the various forms of governmental control. In the early stage of Yi dynasty, Buddhism underwent a drastic reorganization which resulted in its reduction to a less important social force. The matters related to Buddhism that were under the governmental control had once included the nation-wide Buddhist hierarchy organized on the basis of performance at the Buddhist national examination and promotion thereafter, the size of the landed Buddhist property, and building and repair permits of Buddhist temples. For another example, a special license was once required to become a Buddhist monk. In the later stage, however, the license system was abolished, and, officially albeit ineffectively, no one was allowed to become a monk. Confucian alone enjoyed the monopoly of patronization by the ruling yangban class and the government.

Upon introduction of the Western formal legal system, under the aegis of the Japanese, law in Korea became a universalistic one, at least formally. Particularism as a formal legal principle disappeared with the Japanese so far as the former official class distinctions were concerned. When it came to matters between Japanese and Koreans, however, discrimination against Koreans in favor of the Japanese was legal and systematic. This amounted to a reinforced particularism. Socio-economically, Korean society was reorganized into one composed of the ruling Japanese landlord and Korean sharecropper classes. In the reorganization of Korean society into the two socio-economic classes, however, the former yangban officials were politically *de facto* favored over other former classes among Koreans.

Under the Land Reform Act of 1949 following the liberation of Korea and the founding of the democratic republic, even the landlord class as a readily identifiable socio-economic class, disappeared from the Korean social scene. Today, social discrimination based on former class distinctions—especially in favor of the yangban and against the outcaste—does not exist beyond preference being given to a former yangban descendant and conversely low preference being given to a former out-

14. See *Han'guksa, op. cit.* (note 7), III, 707 ff.; *Han'guksa, ibid.;* IX; 144–151; Yi Sang-paek, *Han'guk munhwasa yon'guron'go, op. cit.* (note 6), Chapter I, 1–170; Kim Yong-tae, "Han'guk pulkyosa" (History of Buddhism in Korea), *Han'guk Munhwasa daekye* (Korean Cultural History Series), (Seoul: Korea University Research Institute of Korean Culture, 1970), VI; 269–364.

caste descendant as a marriage partner if one's origin is ever known. Thus in this respect Korean society is perhaps more egalitarian than Japanese.

Traditionally in Korea, government towers far above the rest of society. This situation in dynastic Korea was associated closely with its centralized bureaucratic political organization, the predominance of Confucianism, and the pre-eminence of the yangban ruling class. The prevailing system was so entrenched that no other organization, ideological or learning system, and no other social group or class that the ones that dynastic Korea actually had was able to compete with or to change the overtowering position of government in society into something else: nothing existed in society that could effectively challenge, or overthrow, its political organization, Confucianism, or the yangban class. All the wealth, power, and honor in society centered around the three elements. Moreover, there was only a single channel to any combination of these. Upward mobility was perceived and attained through this channel alone. To reach the top of the societal hierarchy, one had to become a yangban official, which position could be attained through successful performance at the royal examination.

The door to a cherished governmental position was open only to yangbans. A civilian position was especially coveted and monopolized exclusively by yangbans. Among yangbans, moreover, technically only those who could prove that one of their ancesters at least within the last three generations was an appointed official were allowed to take the royal examinations. Only in the royal examination for military officials could persons of lower class origins compete. There was considerable pressure for persons of common origins to become a yangban—or even to become an outcaste—to avoid the enormous burdens and disadvantages of being a commoner.[15] Toward the end of the Yi dynasty, there are indications that the ratio of the yangban of the total population had remarkably increased and the commoners became considerably thinned. A study even shows that the yangban constituted 68.8% of the population of a community—Taegu—in the middle of the 19th century.[16] Of course, there

15. See *Han'guksa, op. cit.* (Kuksa p'yonch'an wiwonhoe, 1974, note 1), XIII, 446–487 and 492 ff.; Kim Yong-mo, *Choson jipaech'ung yon'gu* (A Study on the Ruling Class of Yi Dynasty), (Seoul: Iljokak, 1977), 42 ff.

16. Shikata Hiroshi, "Richojinkoni kansuru mibunkaikyubetsuteki kansatsu" (An Observation of the Population of Yi Dynasty on the Basis of Status-Class Distinction), *Chosenkeizaino kenkyu* (Study of Korean Economy), Keijoteikokudaikaku hogakkai (Seoul Imperial University, Law Society), X, (Tokyo: Iwanami, 1938), 363–482, especially 387–417. See also Kim Yong-mo, *ibid.*; 43–52.

must have been a natural attrition of the commoner population, caused by famine, epidemic disease, and wars. But a vertical mobility is also involved, although its precise picture is difficult to draw. Many apparently took a military career to facilitate their upward mobility. A fabrication of yangban *chokpo* (family geneology record usually associated with yangban families) to support one's claim to yangban status has been a clandestine trend ever since. There is a number of classical novels and folktales about bribing to get or purchasing a yangban title.[17] During wars or famine many took advantage of being granted a yangban title upon performing a meritorious military deed or turning in a required amount of grain. There are also tales of commoners pretending to be or taking refuge among outcastes such as slaves, Buddhist monks, and travelling entertainers. We have here a picture showing that upward mobility was visualized in terms of buying a yangban title or smuggling oneself into the yangban class rather than in terms of becoming a rich farmer, merchants, or successful craftman or manufacturer who was to form the middle class challenging the privileged class or the political power held by the upper class. At the later stages of the Yi dynasty, Korea became a top-heavy class society in a class analysis. Consequently, it became an easy prey to the Japanese. By toppling the top, Japan took over Korea with relative ease. Within the greatly expanded yangban class, a considerable degree of stratification took place. Only a small number of yangban families virtually monopolized the top-ranking governmental positions, landed wealth, and honor.[18]

The centralized bureaucratic political system closely associated with Confucianism and the yangban class was thoroughly permeated with, and supported by, universal variables such as the work ethic, ability, and performance—initially, among yangbans. The overarching position of the political system in society helped make these universalistic variables permeate the society's value system. Today, these values and the work ethic in the cultural system, and the towering importance of the state in the social structure, remain as two elements from the past that are related to the universal-particular variable, even though the former class lines have disappeared and the social base has been broadened with respect to upward mobility. To the extent that persons of yangban origin were alone allowed to take the royal examination, the Yi dynasty's system was

17. For example, *Yangban chon* (The Tale of a Yangban) by Pak Chi-won (1737–1805) in *Upper-Class Culture in Yi-dynasty Korea*, (Seoul: International Cultural Foundation, 1973), 17–25.

18. Kim Yong-mo, *Choson jipaech'ung yon'gu*, 130–159.

particularistic. However, no official title or position was ever inherited. There was no primogeniture institution in Korea. The social structural picture in which the state is large and in which government officials monopolize power, wealth, and honor in society is, however, inherited by contemporary Koreans from their past. In this particular sense, Korean society is structured by a particularistic principle. Among yangban families, there was an internal hierarchical order. Passing the royal examination was necessary for a highly regarded governmental appointment. This was especially the case for a yangban of lower-family status. For those yangbans whose father or grandfather was a meritorious minister or whose family background was otherwise influential, there was even a chance that they might acquire an appointment without passing through the royal examination.[19] But the top posts were beyond the reach of those who were thus appointed without examination. It was absolutely necessary for one to pass the examination to acquire an appointment in the top notch. At the same time, however, the higher one went on the hierarchical ladder of bureaucratic organization, the more decisive one's family ties were for promotion even among those who passed the examination.[20] One's ability and performance both in the examinations and in the bureaucratic hierarchy[21] were critically important for one's initial status and promotion. But one's family ties were critically important for later stages of promotion. Both the universal norms and traditional primary group ties are still decisive for upward mobility in contemporary Korea.

The family was the "holy community" in the Confucian ideological system upon which the yangban scholar-official dominated centralized political system was based. The family was regarded as the basic social unit. Family relations received not only the moral and ideological but also political and legal spotlight. Differential legal treatment in accord-

19. Kim Yong-mo, *ibid.*, 94–97; *Han'guksa*, Chindan hakhoe, *op. cit.* (note 8), III, 203–296. See also note 51 *infra.*

20. Kim Yong-mo, "Yissi wangjosidae ui jipaech'ung ui hyongsong kwa idong e kwanhan yon'gu" (A Study of the Formation and Social Mobility of the Power Elites in the Yi Dynasty), *Chung-ang University Theses Collection.* No. 11, 167–199, and No. 12, 127–178.

21. Merit system was the integral part of the centralized bureaucratic organization. Performance and ability not only in the royal examination but also on the job in the official hierarchy, along with restrictions on the basis of status distinction, were critical for appointment, job assignment, and promotion. For example, there was an elaborate system of job performance evaluation of officials which was made twice a year. *Kyongkukdaejon, op. cit.*, I, 144.

ance with one's status in the family was the rule. Essentially the same treatments and spotlight were extended to the relationships between teacher and his students, and between the officials representing the king as the parent of people and the subjects. The legal codes of the Yi dynasty included criminal provisions of *high treason* and *petty treason* which were met with the most severe forms of punishment.[22] This situation is comparable to that in the ancient English law.[23] Unfilial behavior such as filing a lawsuit, a criminal charge,[24] or making abusive or defamatory statements,[25] against parents or grandparents, having a separate household from one's parents or grandparents while they were alive,[26] failing to support them or to obey their orders,[27] and marrying or indulging in sex during the mourning period after their death, constituted punishable crimes. A husband who killed his wife or concubine for beating and using abusive language against one of his parents or grandparents incurred only floggings.[28] A parent or grandparent who had beaten his son to death for disobeying his order was punished only with floggings or servitude.[29] Entering into a compromise settlement with the killer who killed one's parent or grandparent constituted a punishable criminal conduct.[30] Taking revenge was a morally imposed obligation on the part of the victim's son or grandson sanctioned by the law.[31] Similar

22. *Daemyongnyul jikhae, op. cit.*, 381–382 and 405–496.

23. In the ancient English law, petty treason was malicious homicide which involved a killing of husband by wife, master by servant, or prelate by clergyman. In England, it was abolished in 1828 by statute. Sir James Fitzjames Stephen, *A History of Criminal Law of England*, (London: Macmillan, 1883), III, 34–35; Rollin M. Perkins, *Criminal Law*, 2nd ed., (Mineola, New York: Foundation Press; 1969); 9–10.

24. *Kyongkukdaejon, op. cit.*, II, 164. The punishment was death by hanging which could be contrasted with exile plus floggings in the Ming Codes. A Chinese son or grandson incurred capital punishment only when he filed a false accusation against his parent or grandparent. Cf. *Daemyongnyul jikhae, op. cit.*, 451–453. See also *Sokdaejon, op. cit.*, 286.

25. *Daemyongnyul jikhae, ibid.*, 440.

26. It constituted one of the ten most heinous crimes. *Daemyongnyul jikhae, ibid.*, 51–52 and 202.

27. *Daemyongnyul jikhae, ibid.*, 454–455.

28. *Daemyongnyul jikhae, ibid.*, 411–412.

29. *Daemyongnyul jikhae, ibid.*, 433–434.

30. *Daemyongnyul jikhae, ibid.*, 415–416.

31. *Daemyongnyul jikhae, ibid.*, 437. One who had beaten another who was beating one's parent or grandparent did not incur any punishment, and if one inflicted a serious injury upon another, one's punishment was commuted by three degrees. If

rules existed with regard to relationships between officials and the ruled and between teachers and students. For example, a subject who killed the magistrate under whose jurisdiction he lived, or an inferior official who killed his superior, or a student who killed his former teacher was visited by heavier punishment than one would have been in the absence of such a relationship.[32] A subject who filed a lawsuit or a criminal charge against the magistrate under whose jurisdiction he lived was punished with floggings and servitude, and the suit or charge was dropped.[33]

Petty treason in Korea included acts of beating or killing committed by a wife against her husband, or against her husband's parents. It also included acts of beating or killing committed by a servant against his master. The crime of filing a lawsuit or a criminal charge against one's own parents included a wife filing one against her husband or against her husband's parent. The crime also included a servant's filing a lawsuit or criminal charge against his master. Conversely, a parent, grandparent, husband, or master, who committed the same crimes against son, wife, or servant would, in fact, or by written provisions, be given lighter punishment or no punishment at all.[34] The rules determining

one killed the murderer who killed one's parent or grandparent, one would incur only 60 strokes. If one killed the murderer on the spot, one would go free.

32. *Daemyongnyul jikhae, ibid.*, 405, 422–424, 425, 438–439; etc.; *Kyongkukdaejon, op. cit.*, II, 164.

33. *Kyongkukdaejon, ibid.*, II, 174.

34. For example, a son (grandson or wife) who filed a criminal charge against a parent (grandparent, or husband) before the court had incurred capital punishment, even though the criminal charge was true. See note 24 *supra*. And the criminally charged parent (grandparent or husband) was not to be punished because he was officially treated as if he voluntarily surrendered himself to justice. *Daemyongnyul jikhae, op. cit.*, 452. On the other hand, a parent (grandparent, or husband) who filed a criminal charge against his (or her) son (grandson, wife, or servant) did not incur any punishment, even though it was a false accusation. *Daemyongnyul jikhae*, 454. A similar differential treatment did exist in connection with the crime of using abusive or defamatory language, battery, and killing, depending on the family relationship. Those kinds of crimes committed by a son, grandson, wife, or servant against a parent (grandparent, husband, or master) were regularly met by heavier punishment than ordinary. The same kinds of crimes committed by a parent (grandparent, husband, or master) against a son (grandson, wife, or servant) were met by ordinary, much commuted, or no punishment at all. Punishment of a parent using abusive language against his son and punishment of a husband beating his wife or older brother (or sister) beating his younger brother (or sister) were out of the question unless the beating was followed by serious injury or death (for the latter

degree of punishment on the basis of hierarchical rank in the family were extended to include to some degree the more extended family relations, such as the older-younger brother relationship, the uncle—i.e., father's brother—nephew relationship, and relationships between cousins.[35] The rules were even extended to former family relations in one case, specifically, to an ex-wife who killed her ex-husband's parent or grandparent.[36] A husband who killed his adulterous wife and her paramour on the spot was exempted from all punishment.[37]

Larceny committed by one against his relative or by a servant against his master or fellow servant incurred commuted punishment the degree of which depended upon the determination of whether their family relationship was close or remote and upon that of whether they were members of the same household.[38] Hiding a criminal who was one's relative or master, or helping him escape from arrest by giving the fugitive a tip needed for escaping or in other way entailed likewise commuted punishment for the one who gave the help to the criminal or fugitive.[39]

To a great extent, legal particularism in accordance with one's status in the family has survived Japanese rule and the subsequent political and socio-economic transformation of Korean society. Actually, it was reinforced during Japanese rule by the Japanese version of familial particularism which ran from the worship of the emperor to the institution of patriarchal family headship. Legal particularism finds its most eloquent expression in the criminal and family law. At this point, it will suffice to cite only a few examples which include a differential legal treatment of patricide or infanticide from an ordinary murder in the criminal

crime). *Daemyongnyul jikhae*, 427–434. There is no specific provision for punishment of a parent killing his son (or husband killing his wife). It is hard to believe that a parent (or husband) regularly went unpunished. It seems that he was punished probably lightly. See Suh Il-kyo, *op. cit.* (note 10), 94–98.

35. For example, in case of a crime of using abusive language, *Daemyongnyul jikhae, ibid.*, 439–440; in case of a crime of filing a criminal charge, *Daemyongnyul jikhae*, 453–454; in case of battery, *Daemyongnyul jikhae*, 430–433.

36. *Daemyongnyul jikhae, ibid.*, 407. And ex-servant or ex-employee who beat, use abusive language against, or filed a criminal charge against, his ex-master or ex-employer regularly incurred punishment two degrees heavier than ordinarily the case would be. *Kyongkukdaejon, op. cit.*, II, 164.

37. *Daemyongnyul jikhae, ibid.*, 406. This is contrasted with the ancient Roman criminal law in which not her husband but her father had the right to kill his adulterous daughter and her lover on the spot. Stephen, *op. cit.* (note 23), I, 14–16.

38. *Daemyongnyul jikhae, ibid.*, 393–394.

39. *Daemyongnyul jikhae, ibid.*, 95–97.

law.[40] The same differential rule is extended to other violent crimes committed against one's parents or grandparents.[41] The rule for the exemption of punishment on the ground of familial relation also obtains for stealing, perjury, and hiding or helping fugitives.[42] The proscription against filing a criminal charge against one's parents or close relatives is also retained in criminal procedure law.[43] The family law amendment of 1977 deleted from the Civil Code a number of particularistic legal rules which were related to sexual inequality. But other particularistic rules still remain in the family law. These include the institution of family headship and the broad definition of the exogamous group.

Particularistic social norms in accordance with one's station in the family and other primary social organizations, as we have defined these, are adhered to in society. Rarely are two persons equal in Korean social interactions when they are related to each other by way of either traditional primary social group or a formal organization. It is more likely that they understand their relationship in terms of father-son, superior-subordinate, leader-follower, teacher-student, and senior-junior contrasts. It is apparent that, to some extent, particularism in social norms overlaps personal considerations when they are related to the formal legal rules. Since in legal theory particularist social norms beyond those provided for in the formal law are *de facto* practices, they, as well as personal considerations, are reflected either legitimately or illegitimately in the administration of the formal law. There are formal legal channels through which particularist social norms, as well as personal considerations, are legitimately reflected in the administration of the formal law. These include a number of the "general clauses" such as "good morals"[44]—the public policy—, the public welfare,[45] faith and sincerity,[46] and extenuating, or mitigating, circumstances,[47] involving a good deal of a judge's discretion. There is room for particularism and personal considerations in situations in which a judge, public prosecutor, or other decision-maker exercises his discretionary powers.

40. Criminal Code(1956), Articles 250, Section 2 and 251.

41. Criminal Code, Articles 257, Section 2; 258, Section 2; 259, Section 2; 260, Section 2; 271, Section 2; 273; 276, Section 2; and 283, Section 2.

42. Criminal Code, Articles 151, 155, 328, 344, etc.

43. Code of Criminal Procedure(1954), Article 224.

44. Civil Code(1958), Article 103.

45. Constitution(1972), Article 32, Section 2.

46. Civil Code, Article 2.

47. Criminal Code, Article 53.

III. Impersonal vs. Personal Relationships

It seems that the "impersonal" variable overlaps the "irrational" variable to a great extent, even though these two are not identical. The impersonal-personal contrast is related to subjective states of minds of actors whereas the rational-irrational contrast is related to the objective nature of actions which are, or will be, taken by actors. It is questionable whether absolute rationality exists. Rationality appears to be a relative term. An economically unsound decision can be rational in relation to the actor's aesthetic or moral perceptions, or an official's illegal action can be rational in relation to his felt need for political survival. It seems that rationality is a predominantly Western middle-class, value-laden term. Rationality is largely related to scientific-economic variables and to Weberian legal rational variables. What is scientifically and/or economically sound is rational. What is other than scientifically, economically, or legally rational is irrational, and, moreover, morally wrong. A rational action is morally right to take. Thus defined, rationality dictates that "personal" considerations must not be taken into account in scientific, economic, and legal judgments because it will be irrational. When it does not affect rational judgments, however, personal considerations do not cause problems. But when they do affect rational judgments, personal considerations cause a normative problem of choice between rational actions and irrational but personal approach. Of course, there can be a conflict between scientific rationality and legal rationality. Furthermore, there is a conflict between substantive rationality and formal rationality in law.[48] Naturally, there can arise a problem of choice or preference among conflicting rational actions to take.

The impersonal-personal contrast seems to be related to an actor's orientation in its cognitive, emotional, evaluative, and behavioral aspects. In the West, an impersonal-rational action in which nothing but scientifically or economically rational considerations are taken into account is not only morally but also religiously endorsed as, for example, in the Protestant ethic.[49] A scientifically or economically rational legislation is also judged as morally right. Once legislated, formal legal rationality is stressed, and relatively little room is left for substantive legal rationality.

In Korea, a substantial rationality in relation to the Confucian es-

48. Max Weber, *Economy and Society*, ed. by Guenther Roth and Claus Wittich, (New York: Bedminster Press, 1968), II, 809 ff.

49. Max Weber, *The Protestant Ethic and the Spirit of Capitalism*, trans, by Talcott Parsons, (New York: Charles Schribner's Sons, 1958).

sential truth (tao) of human being, of nature, and of society has traditionally been emphasized. Formal rationality has been devalued. In traditional Korean law, substantive rationality was the rule. The essential truth of human being, nature, and society is inseparably associated with such concepts as propriety (禮), virtue (德), humanity or benevolence (仁), righteousness or justice (義), faithfulness and loyalty (義理), and their contrasts, dignity or "face" (体面), and shame or disgrace (羞恥). Moreover, these concepts are defined not abstractly but in concrete human terms represented by the five relations—of prince and subject, father and son, husband and wife, brothers, and friends. Consequently, personal considerations related to these concepts are required to be seriously taken in relation to actions and judgments. Personal considerations, for example, an action motivated purely by selfish economic interests, that disregard the concepts are completely another matter. They are regarded as other than virtuous, humane, righteous, faithful, loyal, and graceful. They are shameful and disgraceful. It is in this sense that traditional Korean social structure is "personal."

It is particuluarly the ruler's obligation to practice virtue, benevolence, righteousness, and faithfulness, and to avoid disgraceful or shameful acts. It has been sufficiently embedded in the on-going social structure, although, on the level of popular perception, it is not so clearly articulated as in the Confucian intellectual conceptions. In interpersonal transactions such as negotiation, mediation, and conciliation, and in formal official and legal settings, personal considerations such as humaneness, selflessness, faithfulness, loyalty, "face," disgrace, apology, begging humbly, and repentant attitudes are extremely important. To that extent, particularistic ties are as important in official transactions as they are in private ones. They can be determining elements for an action. But they take forms which appear to be inseparably intertwined with those personal considerations.

Not only intellectually—in terms of Confucianism—but also popularly, "the man is more important than a formal institution" has been a consistent theme, negating formal rationality. It is apparent that since there are few formal institutional guidelines and controls substantive rationality demands an extra strong moral achievement or discipline on the part of actors. Otherwise, this type of system with the emphasis on substantive rationality can be an arbitrary one. This is particularly so with respect to the ruler. The legal system of the Yi dynasty was a system which for its success depended critically upon the moral achievement of the ruler. It is no wonder that Confucian teachings were essentially addressed to the rulers. The rulers were supposed to be able to detach themselves sufficiently from mundane concerns, private personal interests, and private ties, and thereby to maintain a serenity and peace of mind "when being alone" (愼獨).[50] Overall social harmony and solidarity were to be achieved through moral exemplary deeds taken personally by the rulers and through their morally well-balanced governmental actions. Otherwise, the judgment of what is virtuous, humane, righteous, faithful, and/or graceful would be difficult to make in concrete situations, and confusion of private interests with virtue, righteousness, and humanity would be inevitable, and a compartmentalization would be likely along the lines of private and factional interests. The king and his yangban scholar-officials were teachers of morals at the same time. Even in contemporary Korea a leader is expected to be morally superior to others, especially his followers. To a great extent, this expectation intertwined with cross-cutting primary social ties is an antidote to the possible moral depredation and social divisiveness. Finally, it must be pointed out that there was no concept of "rationality" as such in the intellectual vocabulary of traditional Korea.

Certain aspects of substantive rationality and certain personal traits were newly experienced—and even further reinforced—under the Japanese rule. Whatever actions that were considered rational for the Japanese colonial rulers of Korea were readily taken without being hindered by moral principles or by the principles of formal rationality that were engrained in Japanese Westernized formal law. Substantive rationality guided by the principle that political need justifies anything and everything was the norm. Particular personal considerations such as submissive attitudes toward the authority, repentant attitudes in criminal processes, shame, and face were the critical factors in transactional relationships between the Japanese rulers and their Korean subjects.

IV. Competition vs. Cooperation

It seems that competition and cooperation are a universal phenomenon. However, their pattern, conceptualization, and relative importance vary from society to society. It is characteristic of modern Europe that unparalleled intellectual and ideological light has been shed exten-

50. Chong Yak-yong, *Kukyok Mokminsimso* (A Modern Korean Translation of *Mokminsimso*), (Seoul: Minjok munhwa ch'ujinhoe, 1969, originally 1818), III, 361; *The Great Learning* in *A Source Book in Chinese Philosophy*, trans. and compiled by Wing-tsit Chan (Princeton University Press, 1963), 89.

sively and intensively on competition both as a pervasive social phenomenon and as a moving force for social progress. As inseparably interwoven with liberal and democratic ideas and practices as an expression of liberty, competition is presupposed by Western democratic political systems and market economies as one of their indispensable elements. The principle of competition is also a basic presupposition of Western judicial ideas, practices, and procedures involving litigation. This is especially the case in the Anglo-American legal system. Competition, however, presupposes an equality of socio-economic and political powers between competitors. It is therefore natural that Western political and economic ideas and practices revolve around matters of attaining substantial socio-economic and political equalities between individuals, social strata, and political groups as much as around competition as such. A few examples of such ideas and practices include those of pluralism, the general franchise, civil rights, progressive taxation, welfare state, equal justice, legal aids and state-appointed counsel or public defender system. Moreover, Western ideas and practices of competition coupled with those of equality presuppose individualism and a closely related individualistic nuclear family social structure. Competition again coalesces with universalism. Competition is not regarded as a goal but only a means to attain a higher goal such as social harmony, equilibrium, or justice. Equality is also not a final goal. Equality is regarded as consisting in equality of opportunity. Intellectually and ideologically, however, both equality and competition are exalted to the point of their being almost the final goal to achieve in society.

In dynastic Korea, the notion of competition did not receive as much intellectual and ideological attention. Competition failed to be conceptualized as an important social, economic, and political idea. Since the royal examinations and the bureaucratic political organization occupies the central place in society, it may be said that competition received indirect conceptual attention as part of the universalistic values and formal legal and social norms that were associated with the examination system and the governmental bureaucracy. Consequently, individual performance and ability rather than competition as such stood out in social and political concepts and ideas. No doubt, there were individual competitions in the royal examinations and in governmental appointments, on the formal political organizational level. But there were no ideological and social bases to conceptualize individual competition. Confucian teachings, as the official ideology, stressed the obligation of the rulers to exercise a parental care for the people. Litigation was visualized not as a competition between individual parties but as a personal appeal of aggrieved parties to the magistrate for his parental care. Social harmony and peace were envisioned as being realized by the moral achievement of individual rulers through their exemplary deeds and wise decisions. Even today, Korean culture is elitist. Intra and inter group harmony and peace are visualized as attainable through the roles of leaders rather than through competition between individuals and groups. On the other side of the same coin, leaders are seen in their leadership role which includes, among others, that of bringing intra and inter group harmony and solidarity.

The pattern of competition is affected by the traditional social structure. Competition in Korea is as much group or organizational competition as it is competition between individual members of society. It is conducted both as an individual and as a group phenomenon along lines of traditional primary social groups and formal organizations.

Whether conceptualized in terms of ability, performance, competition, or all of these, the traditional themes that are closely associated with passing the major examinations, such as great honor and prestige awarded to an individual examination passer and to his family and as a promised future, are deeply engrained in the value system today. These themes are now associated with passing an entrance examination to a prestigious university, the national bar examination or the national higher civil service examination, and governmental positions. These themes were in fact reinforced during the Japanese rule even though only a few Koreans were able to pass the prestigious Japanese universities'—namely, imperial universities'—, bar, and civil service examinations.

V. Individual vs. Collective Responsibility

Because of strong tradition of liberalism and individualism, the principle of individual responsibility has been the rule in the modern West. In relatively recent years, however, particularly following the two world wars, a growing socialism or welfare state, that is, a form of collective responsibility borne by whole society for the well-being of individual members, has been witnessed in the West. It is fair to say that as the fact of human interdependency is recognized more and more the idea of collective responsibility will grow stronger in this quarter of the world.

In Korea, collective responsibility has been the rule because of the strong influence of the traditional social structure and notions of government developed within its patriarchal political organization. With the introduction of the Western formal legal system, however, individual responsibility became the formal legal rule.

The variable of individual-collective responsibility is related to goal achievement, competition, social harmony, social control, legal consequences of actions, individual well-being, and other social phenomena. In the broad spectrum of social phenomena with which this variable is associated, legal responsibility is an important facet. It is characteristic of modern Europe that the notion of individual responsibility has received more attention as an overarching principle governing legal consequences of actions than as one governing also other social phenomena such as goal achievement, individual material well-being, competition, and social control. In traditional Korea, however, collective responsibility stands out as the legal as well as social principle governing the broad range of social phenomena. It is an aspect of the traditional group social structure. Individual well-being is a matter of group responsibility. Social control is also a group oriented phenomenon. In dynastic Korea, those aspects of collective responsibility that were regarded as essential to the functioning of the centralized bureaucratic political organization and to social harmony as envisioned by Confucian scholar-officials were conceptually and practically more attended to.

Examples of such collective responsibility include the following: High ranking officials were privileged and also required each year to recommend three learned and able persons for governmental appointment. If an official committed a crime or other irregularity, however, liability fell upon the one who recommended him for governmental appointment as well as upon himself.[51] A formal legal principle of collective family responsibility by which not only the criminal but also his family

51. In the spring each year, high-ranking military as well as civil officials were privileged and also obligated to recommend up to three able persons for official positions or the magistrate or local garrison commander's position. A high-ranking official who recommended a person for a position was collectively responsible for the crime of corruption (embezzlement of official funds, taking bribery, or illegally enriching himself) or the "crime against the fundamental moral rules" that were committed by the officials thus recommended and appointed. *Kyongkukdaejon, op. cit.* (note 1), 140–141. See also *Daemyongnyul jikhae, op. cit.* (note 6), 90–92; *Kyongkukdaejon*, II, 151. When "crime against the fundamental moral rules" was committed, i.e., when a son, wife, or servant killed his parent, husband, or master, his wife and children were made slaves, his whole property was confiscated, his house was demolished, the title of the town or village in which he lived was downgraded, and the magistrate was to be fired. *Sokdaejon, op. cit.* (note 1), 174.

members were subjected to punishment was practiced rather widely. An extreme example was the rule that one's three families (families on his father's, mother's, and wife's side) as well as he himself were to be perished in case he was convicted of treason. Finding a spouse for one of marriageable age under one's protection was not only social but also legal responsibility of family, especially borne by the one who played the parental role.[52] A son was socially and even legally responsible for debts incurred by his father, and a father was responsible for debts incurred by his son.[53] Certain taxes in kind were levied on villages as collective entities. Default of a family to pay its share of these taxes resulted in an increased share of the total by the rest of the member families of the village.[54]

Some examples of legally relevant collective responsibility today include the case of security clearance for governmental appointment and for issuance of passports. A governmental appointment or issuance of a passport is refused to one whose father was a communist who, for instance, went north. Another example includes a disciplinary demotion or dismissal of a ranking official if a subordinate commits a certain crime or has made a serious mistake in his official duties. Collective responsibility

52. The ministry of rituals was required to report to the king for instruction regarding daughter of a yangban family who was not able to get married because of poverty, and also required to provide her with proper amounts of necessary goods and articles for her marriage. If her family was not that poor and yet did not have her get married by age 30, the household head of her family would be subjected to punishment. *Kyongkukdaejon, ibid.*, I, 286. Matching unmarried bachelors and spinsters into couples was part of the governmental business, and usually the duty to match devolved upon the magistrate. A magistrate within whose jurisdiction there were unmarried bachelors and especially spinsters were officially even reprimanded. In folktales, those who died unmarried became bad spirits haunting the magistrate. The magistrate would usually make efforts to match bachelors and spinsters in his juridiction, sometimes by using coercion (e.g., flogging the household head who had an unmarried son, daughter, nephew, or niece), sometimes by persuation; or some other times by providing for expenses or granting funds if those unmarried were poverty-stricken. See Yi Tae-kyu, *Kaehwa paekkyong* (Hundred Scenes of Modernization), (Seoul: Sint'aeyangsa, 1969), II, 284–285 and 382.

53. *Kyongkukdaejon, ibid.*, I, 188, *Sason'gyuch'wi* in *Wonsinbo Sukyojiprok-Sason'gyuch'wi, op. cit.* (note 9), 498. When public debts of a certain amount or more were in default, the debtor's wife and children all would be even made servants in substitution for the debts. *Sokdaejon, op. cit.* (note 1), 110.

54. *Han'guksa*, Chindan hakhoe, *op. cit.* (note 7), III, 430 ff.; *Han'guksa*, Kuksa p'yonch'an wiwonhoe, *op. cit.* (note 1), X, 502–503.

as a principle of after-the-fact responsibility in discipline or social control (deviation control), especially that practiced in the army as a collective disciplinary measure, have been receiving critical attention in Korea. It is so because it collides with the formal legal principle of individual responsibility governing consequences of actions. In general, however, collective responsibility is widely practiced as an intrinsic element of the social structure. This is particularly so with regard to goal achievements, associated with groups, large organizations, and the nation as a whole. To a great extent, the recent Korean industrialization efforts were an expression of collective responsibility geared to a goal achievement with the nation as the collectivity.

Some aspects of collective responsibility were reinforced by the Japanese because of their wide use. Collective disciplinary measures consisting of corporal punishment practiced in the Japanese army and even in schools were notorious. This is one reason why collective disciplinary measures are discredited, at least ideologically, today in Korea. The Western idea of individual responsibility is also responsible for this development. As for Korean nationalist activities under the Japanese rule, a whole village and family were brutally retaliated. But it was also a collective preventive measure.

VI. Conflict vs. Harmony

Dispute and harmony are also universal social phenomena whose patterns and conceptualization vary from society to society. Disputes, conflicts, struggles, and revolutions are not only recognized but are given positive roles to play in the modern West. They are regarded as important means for social change. Ideologically, moreover, they prevail over harmony, cooperation, and equilibrium to a great extent. Many social theories and social and political institutions are built on the basis of these facets of social life, positively recognized. Western legal system and jurisprudence are also built on the same ideological basis. Dispute, conflict, struggle, and revolution in the West are more or less individualistic in their pattern as affected by individualism. On the other hand, they generally center around individual (convictional), religious, and socio-economic cleavages and divisions.

Because of the strong influence of Confucian ideology, closely associated with the yangban-dominated centralized bureaucratic political organization, dynastic Korea presented an opposite intellectual picture. Intellectually and ideologically, harmony and equilibrium were predominant, and themes of dispute and conflict found no positive place. At the individual level, disputes, conflicts, struggles, and revolutionary changes were unusually negatively depicted. Confucius' saying, "The superior man is conciliatory but does not identify himself with others; the inferior man identifies with others but is not conciliatory"[55] was the motto. In the Oriental world, political changes involving the ruling group or sector was alone recognized in the periphery of intellectual awareness. Even there the legitimacy of political change alone was the major issue, which was debated in accordance with the intellectually articulated theme of "voice of people" equated with "voice of the Heaven." The theme of orthodoxy vs. heresy was also an intellectual tool for dealing with political change. Even such political changes had relatively less relevancy to Korea because of the dynastic stability that had prevailed for many centuries, as compared with, for example, China. Individual, religious, ideological, and socio-economic cleavages and divisions did not loom large in dynastic Korea.

Theory is one thing, and a culture which is engrained in social structure and in individual personalities is another thing. Individual, religious, ideological and socio-economic cleavages and divisions, especially those of the West, are widely known to educated Koreans as knowledge. They—or their appearance—do exist to some extent in Korea. It is characteristic of Korean culture, however, that in emotional and evaluative orientation disputes, conflicts, and revolutions are conceived negatively, and harmony and equilibrium are conceived positively. In Korea, for example, both disputants in a conflict tend to be viewed as morally wrong regardless of the material issues involved. The same observation applies to litigants. Loss of face, or shame, is usually imputed to both participants in dispute or in litigation. Change is also deplored as seen in such a popular slang expression as "changing one's face" (anmyonul bakkunda). A conciliatory and harmonious person is highly regarded as "one who can live without law." Being conciliatory and harmonious does not mean that as a disputeless or conflictless person one is morally unprincipled, but, on the contrary, principled and morally committed. As an element in personality, this political (legal) culture is widely and uniformly distributed. As an element in social structure, however, it is affected by morphological structural considerations. The culture is strong among those who share common traditional social ties. Among those who do not share such ties, the culture is not necessarily a controlling factor. A dispute or conflict may become more furious than otherwise, when two parties share the

55. *The Analects* in *A Source Book in Chinese Philosophy*, *op. cit.* (note 49), 41.

same social group tie. In such a situation, hatred may run high, and a dispute may become more difficult to mediate, harmonize, or settle.

VII. Concluding Remarks

Both universalism and particularism exist in the traditional social structure in Korea. Moreover, particularism in social norms is closely associated with the morphological elements of the social structure, including the state. The primacy of personal approaches which stand out in Korean interpersonal relationship overlaps the traditional emphasis on both substantive rationality and particularism to some extent. The primacy of collective responsibility, social harmony, and cooperation in social norms is imprinted in the traditional social structure of which personal approaches are integral parts.

As to the relationship between morality and law, morality in Korea is associated with the kinds of particularism (interwoven with the kind of universalism), personal approaches, substantive rationality, collective responsibility, cooperation, and social harmony that are prominent in the Korean traditional social structure. On the other hand, law in Korean conception is associated with the denial of the kind of particularism, lack of personal considerations (like merciless individualism, competition, and dispute or litigation oriented attitudes), and lack of the primacy given to cooperation, harmony, and collective responsibility. Consequently, law represents undesirable, necessary but evil, elements in social norms while morality represents desirable, proper elements of the antinomies. In the Korean value system, formal rationality is lowly evaluated. In the West, morality and law reinforce each other, and both are intertwined with universalism, impersonal approaches, and formal rationality, individual responsibility, competitively oriented values, and the positive recognition given to disputes in society.

The critical question is that of whether a modern society capable of coping with contemporary problems such as nation building and industrialization, on the one hand, and the creation of a modern legal system, on the other, are impossible with the kinds of particularism, personal approaches, collective responsibility, and the primacy of cooperation that prevail in the traditional Korean social structure? In particular, are the kinds of particularism, personal approaches, and substantive rationality that exist in Korea incompatible with a modern society when they are incorporated into a formal legal system?

A positive answer without resort to a revolution may be possible.

And the recent industrialization of Korea may indicate what that is. A growing awareness of human interdependency, the need for fraternal love, and primacy of collective responsibility, social harmony, and co-operation are on the horizon in the West in the form of welfare state or socialism. The other end of the continuum—e.g., individualism, competition, impersonal approaches—alone is obviously not the only controlling principle for human relationships. Since collective responsibility is already a part of the social structure, it may be easier to realize the idea of a welfare state in Korea. Danger of compartmentalization along the lines of traditional primary groups is a problem in Korea. A solution to the question of how to overcome the danger of compartmentalization and yet to realize an overall community in which traditional principles prevail seems to hinges on roles of leaders to a greater extent in Korea than in a Western society. Substantive rationality may be ideologically better than formal rationality when (or if) a mechanism can be invented or developed to prevent a substantive-rational system from degenerating into an arbitrary one. As a humane, emotionally and evaluatively responsive system, a legal system into which personal approaches are integrated may be desirable. For we are too much deprived of personal touches in many aspects of our contemporary life. This kind of particularism cannot be eliminated in a stroke by a piece of legislation because they are very much part of society. We have to discover ways to live with this aspect of social life instead of ignoring it. Finally, the main question is what mechanism we can have or we can develop to restrain governmental power? This issue is particularly important in view of the fact that the state component and its related leadership roles in society have been traditionally strong, on the one hand, and substantive rationality has been a traditional formula for law, on the other. We cannot provide a definite answer. But some answers may be found in traditional social structure, too.

No doubt, an understanding of the gap between the law and the reality in Korea will not be complete without an appreciation of its dimension of the conflict between the Western and Oriental cultures. This appreciation must go beyond a condemnation of one set of variables as totally bad or as far better than the other without a discriminating assessment. One difficult problem arising from the conflict, however, is that in Korea there are two sets of social standards for action neither of which is triumphant over the other or diminishing its social relevancy. Naturally, one is easily led to rely on one set of the standards at one time and on another at other time without consistency as situation dictates. Consequently, the final question is how to cope with the inconsistency that borders on arbitrariness which arise from the double standards.

Part IV
Lawyers

[10]

Comparative Sociology of Legal Professions: An Exploratory Essay

Richard L. Abel

The author surveys and compares the legal professions of 15 nations, including both civil law and common law countries. The essay is organized around the ways that legal professionals control their markets—first by controlling "production of producers" or who and how many enter the profession (with formal education or apprenticeship requirements, examinations, access to entry-level positions). Legal professionals also control "production by *producers"—both external competitors and lawyers themselves. This occurs, for example, through definition and defense of the professional monopoly, control of competition between licensed professionals, and creation of demand. The discussion takes place against the background of the legal profession's recent history—assessing changes in its composition (by race, age, gender), in lawyers' practice settings, in the categories of work they perform, and in the income and status associated with these categories and with the profession in general.*

I. Introduction: A Theoretical Framework

This article is a preliminary attempt to elaborate a theoretical framework for understanding legal professions. It draws on two sources: the writings of Eliot Freidson and of Magali Sarfatti Larson on the sociological theory of the

Richard L. Abel is professor of law at the University of California at Los Angeles. B.A. 1962, Harvard University; LL.B. 1965, Columbia University; Ph.D. 1974, University of London.

The present article grows out of the activities of the Working Group for Comparative Study of Legal Professions, a component of the Research Committee on Sociology of Law of the International Sociological Association. Since 1980, several dozen lawyers and social scientists from some 20 countries have been meeting annually to develop a series of comparable national reports on their legal professions. In the summer of 1984 we met for a week to discuss those reports and additional theoretical and comparative essays building on them. We are grateful to the Rockefeller Foundation and the American Bar Foundation for making that meeting possible and particularly to Terence Halliday for his administrative assistance. The present essay, which was presented at that conference, is based exclusively on the national reports on the legal professions of Scotland, England and Wales, Norway, Germany, Belgium, France, Italy, Spain, Yugoslavia, Canada, the United States, Venezuela, Brazil, Japan, and India. For this reason, it includes no references. I am grateful to the members of the Working Group for allowing me to use the data contained in those unpublished papers. I also am grateful for financial support from the National Science Foundation (Grant No. SES 83-10162) and the UCLA Law School Dean's Fund. Finally, I wish to acknowledge the helpful editorial comments of Terence Halliday, Alan Paterson, and two anonymous reviewers.

This essay will be revised to include additional national reports and other published sources and will appear in the third of three volumes containing the papers of the Working Group: Richard L. Abel & Philip Lewis, eds., Lawyers in Society: A Comparative Approach, vol. 3, Comparative and Theoretical Studies (University of California Press, forthcoming).

professions, and descriptions of 15 legal professions—11 from advanced capitalist countries, 1 from a socialist country, and 3 from Third World countries. I have used the theories of Freidson and Larson because I find them the single most powerful tool for comprehending the phenomenon of professionalism and for understanding the changes that contemporary legal professions are undergoing. At the same time, the reports on the 15 national legal professions clearly demonstrate the need to elaborate or amend the theories, which were derived largely from the American and English experience, particularly in medicine, in order to account for the situation in other countries, especially those with civil law systems. This essay is preliminary both in the sense that I am acutely aware of the need to gather more data and reflect more deeply and because it offers neither a coherent theory nor a comprehensive description but rather an uneasy compromise between those objectives.

Like any theoretical framework, the one I advance (which departs significantly from Freidson and Larson) emphasizes some aspects of lawyers in society at the expense of others. My starting point is the uncontroversial observation that all occupations in capitalist economies must seek to control the markets for their goods and services. Professions can be distinguished from occupations in part by the ways in which they pursue this goal and their relative success in attaining it. Changes in the nature of market control illuminate many facets of the recent history of legal professions. Those changes also influence the composition of the profession, the structures within which lawyers practice, their work, income, and status, and the organization and activities of professional associations. I outline these linkages below.

The first way in which legal professions seek to control their markets is by regulating the production of producers. The simplest method, an explicit *numerus clausus,* no longer is ideologically acceptable. Although professions differ historically in the extent to which they emphasize either formal education or apprenticeship, the former everywhere has grown in importance, progressively supplanting or incorporating the latter. As a result, the profession has lost significant control to those who determine how many graduate from university and who does so. The centrality of the university also has tended to reduce the significance of professional examinations, although they remain a major barrier in some countries. The last hurdle, entry into practice, would seem to represent control *of* the profession *by* the market, but obstacles to independent practice combined with the fact that most lawyers begin their careers as employees constitute a new mode of professional supply control.

These changes in the nature of supply control are reflected in the size and growth of the profession. During the nineteenth century, class was the primary barrier to entering the profession in most countries, but recruitment within the small population of those eligible seems to have fluctuated with demand. The success of supply control in the first half of the twentieth century is visible in the failure of the profession to grow in response to the enormous increase in population and economic activity and to make up for the losses suffered during two world wars. In the last two decades, however, virtually every national profession has experienced an unprecedented and constant expansion, although growth seems to have slowed in recent years. An essential ingredient in this expansion was the entry of women into the profession in significant numbers for the first time—in all but two countries they now represent a third to a half of new lawyers. But the fact that the proportion of lawyers who are women appears to have stabilized also may explain why the rate of entry has leveled off. The profession has reasserted control over the market, though at new levels of production.

The nature and degree of control over the production of producers influence the profession in many ways. These aspects of control affect the distribution of lawyers across work settings. In most countries, the growth of the profession has increased the ratio of lawyers to judges, introducing or aggravating problems of case overload and court delay. Divisions among practitioners based on the courts within which they practice and the functions they perform have declined, while the distinction between employed lawyers and independent practitioners has sharpened. In the civil law countries of northern Europe, where employed lawyers dominate the profession, the absence of sufficient jobs to absorb the growing numbers has enlarged the ranks of independent practitioners; in common law countries, where independent practitioners constitute the largest category, an increasing number of new recruits have sought employment.

Control over the production *of* producers is only half the project of market control; it also is necessary to control production *by* qualified producers. Employment is one such mechanism: Bureaucratic organizations, whether public or private, regulate the rate of production. But private practitioners must mobilize other regulatory devices. First, they must define and defend their monopoly against lay competitors and resentful consumers. Second, they must limit competition among lawyers, a task that becomes both more pressing and more difficult as the number of practitioners increases. The decline of control over the production *of* producers has been accompanied by an erosion of control over production *by* producers: Geographic limitations on practice have fallen, lawyers are associating themselves with other professions, they are engaging in advertising, and professional restrictions on price competition are giving way to state control over fees (through legal aid programs). Third, private lawyers have been stimulated by their growing numbers to take an interest in creating demand, both by persuading potential clients that they need legal services and by securing state subsidies to reduce the cost of those services. Yet this new strategy has serious drawbacks: Individuals (and even businesses) consume legal services only reluctantly; the level of state subsidy depends on the party in power and the availability of state revenues; and demand creation, unlike supply control, seems inevitably to foster concentration among producers.

The new modes of supply control, and especially the changing role of the university, affect not only how many lawyers there are but also who becomes a lawyer. Since the 1960s, the university has allowed women to enter the professions and other high-status occupations. But women who obtain a credential once again confront overt and covert sexism; it remains an open question whether they will seek and attain careers equivalent to those of men or be relegated to subordinate positions. Yet if the meritocracy is gender blind, it continues to confer advantages on class. Indeed, because the entry of women has doubled the number of potential applicants from upper-class backgrounds, it seems to have narrowed the class composition of the legal profession still further. In no country with a significant ethnic minority has that group gained a representation within the legal profession equivalent to its proportion of the population. But the mere increase in numbers has changed the age composition dramatically, from an elderly profession to one that is relatively youthful.

I discussed above the impact of increased numbers on the allocation of lawyers to employment or private practice; numbers also affect those within private practice. The growth of the profession appears to accentuate the concentration of lawyers in capitals and other major cities at the expense of the countryside. Although the proportion of sole practitioners has declined everywhere, small firms and loose associations appear to have multiplied. These structures seem likely to survive unless intensified competition forces rationalization and concentration, as exemplified by the legal clinic, which offers standardized services at cut-rate prices to a mass clientele. The large firm, by contrast, is found only in the common law world (and a few Latin American countries); in-house counsel plays a similar role in civil law countries. But where the large firm exists, it enjoys a prominence far greater than its numbers might suggest, both because of its symbolic position at the top of the professional hierarchy and because it offers a first job to many who later pursue other careers. We can expect large firms to expand in both size and numbers in order to capture or retain their constantly growing clientele and to enhance partnership profits by hiring more subordinated employees.

Changes in the market for legal services naturally have affected the work, income, and status of lawyers. The competitive pressures of greater numbers have compelled those legal professions accustomed to offering a narrow range of services to diversify. But whereas the nineteenth-century legal profession emerged by erecting boundaries against external competitors, today the struggle for market control sets one legal specialty against another and all against the remaining generalists. A number of recent developments combine to depress the income of lawyers: the change in age composition (for young lawyers earn much less than old), the shift from independent practice to employment, and growing reliance by private practitioners on public funds. This, in turn, may lower the social standing of the profession.

Finally, the professional association has been an instrument of market control and has been affected by changes in the nature of that control. The association was far more salient in common law countries than in the civil law world, where organizations tended to be local rather than national and official rather than voluntary, and where a large fraction of the profession were employees rather than independent practitioners. But today, even in the common law countries, professional associations are confronting divisions arising out of the increasing heterogeneity of the profession (age, gender, and ethnicity), the growth in numbers of employed lawyers (who have less need for an association), and greater reliance on public funds (which diminishes professional independence). Furthermore, the association's claim to exercise effective control over misconduct or incompetence is increasingly problematic, which undermines the legitimacy of self-regulation.

The following pages trace the changes in the nature of the market for legal services and their impact on a wide variety of legal professions.

II. Market Control: Production of Producers

Control of the market for its services is one of the elements that define a profession. Nevertheless, national legal professions differ greatly in the methods they use to control supply and in the success of that endeavor. Both can be explained in terms of historical accident, educational institutions, and the structure of the state, among other factors. In turn, the method and success of supply control deeply influence the structure and activities of the legal profession.

A. Quotas and Exclusions

The most obvious way of controlling supply, and the most easily enforced, is a *numerus clausus* imposed by the state or by a professional body with state support. Such a mechanism is feasible when lawyers are either state officials or members of a feudal guild. There was a *numerus clausus* for Rechtsanwalte in some German states at the end of the nineteenth century. Even today the numbers of notaries in Belgium, Germany, and Spain remain limited, as do the numbers of avocats at the Conseil D'Etat and the Cour de Cassation in France and of Rechtsanwalte at the Supreme Court in the Federal Republic of Germany. When the Lord Chancellor of England keeps the number of Queen's Counsel at about 10% of the practicing Bar, he maintains a modified *numerus clausus*. But explicit state control is inconsistent with the independence of a liberal profession, and guild control violates the free market ideology of capitalism. Therefore an explicit *numerus clausus* no longer is an acceptable means of controlling supply. Calls for numerical limitations, which reappear whenever supply outruns demand (as occurred during the Depression and is happening again today), have been rebuffed in the United States, Canada, and the United Kingdom; recently, a plea by lawyers for a limitation on the number of stagiaires was rejected in Belgium. Furthermore, a *numerus clausus* does not specify *who* can become a lawyer.

One way of answering that latter question (and simultaneously limiting numbers) is to use ascribed characteristics. Thus, as we will see below, most legal professions excluded women by law until well into the present century and by social practice until the 1970s. Nazi Germany excluded Jews. Noncitizens were excluded by the United States until 1973, by the solicitor's branch in England and Wales until 1974, and still are excluded by Canada, Japan, Belgium, Germany, and Spain. American jurisdictions require a vague test of character that allows discrimination and sometimes has been used to discriminate, not just against those with ascribed characteristics but also against those with dissenting politics. These disqualifications not only give a competitive advantage to those admitted but also enhance professional prestige by excluding those in low-status categories. However, explicit discrimination on grounds of gender, religion, or race no longer is acceptable. Even preferences for citizens may not withstand the pressures of international trade, as expressed in the European Community. Nevertheless, class background still may influence entry into and distribution within the legal profession, especially when it is mediated by meritocratic tests, as we will see below.

B. Formal Education

The four principal mechanisms presently limiting the supply of lawyers are university education, apprenticeship, professional examinations, and the difficulty of obtaining employment or business during the early years of practice. Most continental European and Latin American countries imposed the requirement of a university law degree during the nineteenth century: Norway as early as 1736, Belgium in 1835, Brazil in 1827 (though *any* university degree was acceptable until 1934), Italy by the 1880s. By contrast, the common law world did not require a law degree until much later: the interwar decades in the United States; only after World War II in Canada; a law degree still is not required in England and Wales or in Scotland. Japan, though otherwise strongly influenced by continental legal systems through its nineteenth-century adoption of the German codes, also does not require a university law degree. However, Japanese legal professionals virtually always obtain such degrees (as they do in Great Britain).

But the mere requirement of a degree says little about its efficacy in controlling supply. There are enormous variations in the ease of access to university (entry barriers of financial means, geography, class, and prior education), in the length and cost of education, in the availability of financial support and part-time employment, and in the rate of attrition. To oversimplify, the civil law world imposed the requirement of a law degree at an early date; although these jurisdictions allowed easy access to university, they provided no financial support and offered an unstructured education whose quality and relationship to professional practice were problematic, with the result that there was a high rate of attrition (often class biased), sometimes followed and reinforced by a difficult state examination. By contrast, the common law world, which imposed the requirement only recently, tends to have highly competitive entrance standards but to provide substantial financial and pedagogic support so that most entrants complete the course and pass any further examinations without difficulty. In the first category, students receive a general liberal education, at least in their early years (e.g., Brazil, Japan); in the second, the education is narrowly technical and its content dictated largely by the profession, which thereby preserves its influence even though the university has overshadowed the apprenticeship (85% of the courses taken by U.S. law students teach matter tested on the bar examination; in England and Wales and in Scotland, two-thirds of the courses are taken in order to obtain exemptions from the professional examinations).

Some civil law countries grant entrance to university as of right to all who complete secondary school: Italy began doing so in 1969, and similar rules apply in Spain, France, and Germany. Belgium recently eased entrance requirements and expanded the number of secondary schools that qualified graduates for university. In many of these countries, law is a favored subject of study because it is less demanding than medicine or engineering (which, unlike law, have entry quotas) and yet appears to guarantee middle-class status. Thus 24% of all Brazilian university matriculants in 1961 were studying law (though this fell to 9% in 1980); in Italy, the proportion was 14% in 1977; in Yugoslavia, 18%; by contrast, only about 3% of Canadian and 5% of U.S. graduate students and a similar proportion of British undergraduates were studying law in 1978. In some civil law countries (such as Venezuela and Brazil), lectures are given by full-time practitioners who are poorly paid for teaching and devote minimal effort to that activity (which they perform because it enhances their practice). Student bodies are enormous: Southern Italian law faculties have 10,000–15,000 students; northern Italian faculties have 3,000–5,000; the Universidad Complutense of Madrid had 14,476 in 1978/79; the Universidad Central of Barcelona had 11,559. Few students in these countries attend classes regularly because the teacher merely reads from notes that can be purchased; students are expected to memorize these notes and regurgitate them on their examinations. In Norway, where the student/teacher ratio today is 80:1, private "crammers" prepare students for the final examination.

By contrast, admission to law school in the common law world tends to be highly competitive. Four times as many applicants take the Law School Aptitude Test in the United States as are admitted to law school; elite schools have 10 times as many applicants as places (though the highly stratified system of legal education offers *some* place to almost every applicant). In England and Wales, university law departments have up to 17 applicants per place (though many students apply to several schools); there are more than twice as many male applicants as places and more than 4 times as many female applicants. In Scotland, only one-fifth of all applicants are admitted. Canadian law schools have 5 to 10 times as many qualified applicants as they can accept. In all these countries, however, the constriction of supply through university admission is a fairly recent phenomenon. Only a small minority of lawyers in Britain and Canada studied law at university until well after World War II. Almost anyone could gain admission to some American law school in the 1920s and 1930s and pay the bills by working while attending part time; today there are hardly any part-time students. Schools in these countries also have seen a shift from part-time to full-time law teachers, as well as an enormous expansion in numbers of academic lawyers. In the United Kingdom, one-quarter of all university law teachers were practitioners in 1963/64; by 1981 the proportion had shrunk to one-tenth; furthermore, the number of law teachers grew from 130 in 1933/34 to 1,282 in 1980/81. In the United States, the proportion of part-time teachers dropped from 43 to 33% of the professoriate between 1947 and 1980, while the overall number grew from 1,727 to 6,755. The number of full-time law teachers in Canada increased from 40 in 1950 to 650 in 1980.

Another measure of the role of university entrance requirements in controlling supply is the ratio between the sizes of the law student body and the legal profession. In India in 1971 there were more than twice as many law students as lawyers; in Italy in 1978 the ratio was almost three to one; in Spain the ratio presently is between two and three to one; in Brazil it is one and a half to one; and in Venezuela, about one to one. At the same time, it is important to remember that in some of these countries both higher education and membership in a profession are privileges enjoyed by only a tiny elite. Thus in Brazil today only 4.6% of the population attends university, and in Yugoslavia the proportion also is small, whereas about half of the United States population obtains some post-secondary education. By contrast, there are only about one-fifth as many law students as legal professionals in the United States and Belgium, three-fifths to four-fifths in Norway, one-sixth in Scotland, and one-third in England and Wales.

In those civil law countries where access to university is easy and law student bodies are large, students suffer financial hardship, the course is long, and attrition is high. Most Spanish law students live at home; students in Italy, Brazil, and Venezuela work to support themselves while attending school full time; in India, a fifth of all students attend school part time. In Norway, half the students are part time, and two-thirds of those finance their educations themselves. Partly because of this, the law course takes long to complete: five years in Belgium, four to seven in Brazil, five to seven in Spain, five in Venezuela, and six in Norway. By contrast, a law degree takes only three years in England and Wales and in Scotland, and almost all those studying for a first degree receive means-tested grants. A law degree in the United States also takes three years to acquire, but it follows a four-year undergraduate degree; furthermore, tuition at private universities is high, and there is little support for living expenses. These differences are reflected in attrition rates. In countries whose law student populations are large compared with their legal professions, attrition is very high: In India, only 2–5% of entrants become practitioners; in Venezuela about 20% graduate; in Norway, a third to a half do (pass rates have been declining since the early 1960s); in Spain, where a fifth of those enrolled in the five-year program might be expected to enter the profession each year, less than 10% actually do so; in Belgium about half complete the course. By contrast, 88% of U.S. students who began law school in 1972 graduated at the end of their course (even more at the elite schools); and 90–95% of university law students in England and Wales finish their degrees today (though only two-thirds to three-quarters of polytechnic students, and less than a third of those studying part time).

It is difficult to use the requirement of a law degree to limit entry to the profession if there are no controls on the number or size of law schools. In the United States in the first four decades of this century, anyone could open a law school without obtaining state or professional approval and with only the most minimal capital investment. Consequently the number of law school places increased tenfold in 40 years, from 4,486 in 1889 to 44,341 in 1927. By 1928, two-thirds of all law students were studying part time, and two-thirds (though not necessarily the same students) were enrolled in schools not approved by the American Bar Association. Only strenuous efforts by the ABA and state bar associations succeeded in cutting unapproved schools to 3% of the total (in 1971) and part-time students to 15% of the total (in 1979). In Brazil today, two-thirds of the 130 law schools are proprietary, even profit making, and these enroll three-quarters of the country's 135,000 students. The same is true in India, which had 105 law schools in 1978. But even where most universities are state institutions or where the profession acts as an accrediting body, it is difficult to control supply by limiting the number of university places. For one thing, the interests of the state and the profession diverge. The state is extremely sensitive to the demands of middle-class voters, who look to education to ensure that their children reproduce their own class position. Indeed, much of the increase in the number of law students in the last two decades does not represent a shift from other subjects —law as a proportion of total enrollments rose only from 2.2% of Canadian undergraduates in 1962/63 to 2.9% in 1976/77—but rather reflects the expansion of tertiary education. Furthermore, the universities also seek to expand, and creating a law department is a cheap and prestigious way of doing so.

The result, virtually everywhere, has been a dramatic increase in the number of universities, law faculties, and law students in the last two decades. In some instances this has meant the founding of new institutions or law departments: In England and Wales, only the universities of Oxford, Cambridge, and London produced significant numbers of law graduates before the war; today there are more than 50 university and polytechnic law departments. In Spain, the number of law students at public universities doubled in the four years between 1971/72 and 1975/76 and tripled by 1978/79. In Norway, the opening of what was only the second law faculty in the country (in Bergen in 1970) heralded a major expansion. Even in the United States, 37 new schools gained ABA accreditation between 1966 and 1981 (an increase of 27% in the number of accredited schools), and those already accredited also expanded, with the result that the number of law students in accredited schools more than tripled between 1961 and 1980. The growth in the number of entrants in England and Wales, Scotland, Canada, the United States, France, Italy, Spain, Belgium, Brazil, and India is shown in appendix table 1.

C. Apprenticeship

The second major barrier constricting supply is apprenticeship, which today usually is required after university training. There appears to be an inverse (if loose) relationship between the prominence of formal education and apprenticeship, with the former gradually displacing the latter. Thus English solicitors traditionally underwent long and arduous apprenticeships. Until the 1960s, nonlaw graduates had to complete five years of articles, for which they paid a substantial premium (up to £500) as well as a stamp tax, and for which they received no salary. But less than half of new entrants were university graduates as late as 1970. Barristers, by contrast, underwent only 12 months of pupillage (optional until 1959), during which they could accept briefs (though, after 1965, only in the second six months). Four-fifths of all new barristers were university graduates by the mid-1960s. In 1963, articles for aspiring solicitors were reduced to three years for nonlaw graduates and to two years for law graduates (now 90% of entrants); premiums began to disappear in the 1950s; and today an articled clerk receives a salary, if barely enough to live on. A similar evolution occurred in Scotland. In the United States, formal schooling rapidly replaced apprenticeship about the turn of the century; yet something like the latter seems to have revived recently, as an ever higher proportion of law graduates are taking first jobs they view as only temporary: as associates in law firms, clerks to judges, or in legal aid or government. At the other extreme, Spain has no apprenticeship at all—law graduates are fully qualified to practice (though most become employees of experienced lawyers); and Germany's lengthy requirement (two and a half years) is ameliorated by the ample salary the apprentice earns as a civil servant (the same is true for the two-year apprenticeship in Norway). Canadian law graduates are assured of articles, at least in their own province. It seems reasonable, therefore, to see the length, cost, and difficulty of obtaining an apprenticeship as complementing the length, cost, and difficulty of entering and graduating from university, one diminishing as the other increases.

The formal requirements of apprenticeship limit the number of entrants; decisions by individual lawyers to accept or reject applicants for apprenticeship also influence the composition of the profession and do so much more particularistically than university admission policies. Thus women are accepted by English universities and polytechnics on the basis of the same credentials as men, but they have much greater difficulty obtaining articles and especially pupillages; so do ethnic minorities. And personal contacts strongly influence who obtains which apprenticeship in France and Belgium (where, at least in the smaller cities, the local bar exercises considerable control), and also in Italy. Similarly, ascribed characteristics weigh heavily in the selection of associates by large law firms in the United States and Canada.

Both characteristics just described help to explain the declining significance of apprenticeship. First, the greater centrality of formal education renders apprenticeship less relevant as a means of supply control (it is hard to justify denying an apprenticeship to someone who has completed a university degree). Second, apprenticeship is under attack by disadvantaged groups, which fear that its private, less visible selection procedures tolerate more discrimination. But there are other reasons for its decline. In a period of rapid professional expansion, too few qualified attorneys are willing to supervise the hordes of apprentices. English law graduates have had difficulty finding places, especially as articled clerks; Belgian graduates also are encountering a shortage of positions as stagiaires; even U.S. law graduates bemoan the scarcity of associate jobs. Furthermore, whereas apprentices used to be an important source of cheap labor for supervising attorneys, the flood of recent graduates who have completed their apprenticeships but cannot or will not practice on their own amply fills this need. Under these circumstances, criticism of the educational value of apprenticeship—a constant undercurrent for many years—now meets less resistance from the profession. Not only does apprenticeship compare unfavorably with university education in terms of quality, but it prepares the apprentice for only a narrow subset of the growing range of opportunities open to lawyers—for commercially oriented private practice in a larger firm but not for employment in government or industry or for a legal aid practice. It is significant, therefore, that a number of countries have introduced formal, postgraduate practical training (the popularity of clinical education in the United States may be analogous). Law graduates in England and Wales must complete a year of vocational training before beginning their apprenticeships, and most do so at schools (whose quality has improved considerably) organized by the professional associations. Scotland recently instituted a mandatory one-year postgraduate vocational course conducted by the university law faculties. France established a similar program in 1971. Canada has one as well. Although all four jurisdictions still require apprenticeship after these courses, formal training may further displace apprenticeship in the future. It is important to note, however, that formal postgraduate training also serves to control numbers: less financial support is available for the vocational year than for university education, and Scotland actually has imposed a *numerus clausus* on enrollment in its postgraduate course (as has the Inns of Court School of Law, although other alternatives are available to English Bar students).

D. Professional Examination

A third entry barrier is a state or professional examination, usually administered at the end of a university course or an apprenticeship. Logically, one might expect this to be the principal hurdle: It appears meritocratic in the sense that it both is universalistic and demonstrates the examinee's mastery of the relevant technical skills; yet it also allows examiners to control the number of successful candidates by adjusting the passing grade. Nevertheless, examinations actually have been less important than either university degrees (except where they constitute the final examination for that degree) or apprenticeships. They were imposed fairly late: The first written statewide examination in the United States was held in 1876, and bar exams did not become widespread until well into the twentieth century (a few states still grant university law graduates a "diploma privilege"). The English Bar first required an examination in 1872, though barristers were recognized as professionals hundreds of years earlier. Brazil did not require an examination until the 1930s, and this did not become a significant barrier until 1963. France required one for lawyers only in 1941 (although magistrates have had to pass an examination since the beginning of the century). Scotland still exempts most university law graduates from any further examination. Spain and Venezuela have no postdegree examinations at all.

Some countries do seem to have used examinations to control supply, especially where university education was not a requirement (as in England and Wales until recently) or attrition during the university course was low (as in the United States). Thus in England and Wales, the pass rates for the Law Society examinations show a steady secular decline from the date of their first administration in the early or mid-nineteenth century until the 1950s, broken by rises during and following the two world wars and during the Depression, when supply was reduced by external forces. Yet even the Law Society examinations had pass rates close to 100% when they first were instituted. So did the English Bar examinations, which consistently have admitted more than 80% of applicants. And in 1982, the pass rate on the French C.A.P.A. examination (Certificat d'aptitude à la profession d'avocat) was 97%. Of course, use of an examination to control entry depends on who sets and marks the papers.

One reason for the high pass rates, even in jurisdictions where the profession sought to depress them, was the emergence of unregulated private "crammers," who used previous examinations to prepare candidates—as was the case in England from the mid-nineteenth to the mid-twentieth century (when the Law Society absorbed the main crammer, Gibson & Welden) and still is in the United States, Norway, and Germany. (This is a useful reminder that controls over supply are difficult to achieve and always transitory.) Furthermore, just as universities have displaced apprenticeships, so they have undermined the barrier of professional examinations. In England and Wales and in Scotland, a law degree exempts graduates from part or all of the final examination. And everywhere, academic legal education seems to lower the hurdle of professional examinations. Thus in the United States, pass rates increased about 15 percentage points from the late 1940s to the early 1970s, as a growing proportion of examinees attended accredited law schools. And in England and Wales the pass rate on the Law Society final exam rose from 48% in the early 1950s (when less than half of all articled clerks had law degrees) to 74% in 1977 (when most clerks had them). Not only do law students acquire knowledge and skills in taking exams; they also obtain a formal credential, which makes it hard to justify denying them the right to practice. Even if the examination may be easy for most, it frequently remains an obstacle for a distinct few—those whose general educational backgrounds are inadequate or irrelevant. Students from the new Commonwealth (the U.K.'s former colonies) who sought admission to their own jurisdictions through Call to the English Bar had considerable difficulty passing the examination (though two-thirds of those who persisted ultimately succeeded). Ethnic minorities in the United States also have a much lower pass rate on the bar examination. Thus what appears superficially to be the most universalistic mechanism for controlling supply turns out to correlate strongly with ascribed characteristics.

Examinations are a major barrier in only two of the countries considered. In Italy, though entrance to a law faculty is guaranteed for all secondary-school graduates, attrition at university seems to be low, and apprenticeship lasts only a year, the professional examination requires three or four years of additional preparation, and pass rates vary between 13 and 70%, depending on the examination center. But the extreme case is Japan: The professional examination for entry to the Institute of Legal Training and Research (the only route to becoming a judge, prosecutor, or private practitioner with a right of audience in court) requires three to five years of cramming, sometimes full time, after a four-year university law degree; and less than 2% pass each year (500 out of 29,000), although many retake the examination numerous times. But this hurdle is somewhat misrepresented as a mechanism of supply control because even those who fail can and do offer legal advice and representation outside of court, primarily as corporate employees.

E. Starting Practice

The last step in entering the profession is finding an initial position. At first sight, this barrier appears to represent control of the profession *by* the market rather than professional control *of* the market. Yet here, too, the profession has imposed rules that hinder the free play of market forces. The English Bar is the most extreme example, perhaps because it required a university degree (*not* a law degree) only recently, demands only a brief one-year apprenticeship, and sets an easy professional examination. The aspiring barrister first must obtain a tenancy in an existing set of chambers—a process in which women, ethnic minorities, and those without social connections encounter great difficulties. Then the barristers must wait passively for briefs from solicitors, hoping that the clerk of the chambers will recommend them when a solicitor expresses no preference for a particular barrister or when a more senior member of chambers is overcommitted. In some years during the early 1970s, there were almost twice as many pupils seeking to start practice as there were tenancies available, and even now there are almost half as many "floaters" (qualified practitioners without permanent tenancies) as there are barristers starting practice each year. It is not surprising, therefore, that even at this late stage of the entry process, attrition is high; 40–80 young barristers have left practice annually since 1975, or 15–20% of the 270–382 who started each year.

Even in countries without such restrictive formal rules it may be difficult or impossible to start practice except as an employee. In the United States, 90% of those entering the private sector for the first time in 1978 began as employees (and so, of course, did all those entering the public sector). In Spain, which offers easy access to university and requires neither an examination nor an apprenticeship, obtaining a first position is the most difficult hurdle. In Venezuela, only a third of those who qualify as abogados enter private practice. In Brazil, the proportion of bachareis who became legal professionals fell from 61% in 1950 to 44% in 1980 as the number of bachareis expanded rapidly. And in India, only 2–5% of those who begin law courses ultimately enter practice. The hurdle of finding a first position is likely to increase in importance as the universities turn out more graduates who pass the professional examinations with ease and as apprenticeship is displaced by a combination of formal training and employment. Furthermore, as the units within which legal services are produced grow in size (see below) and require greater capital investment (in computers and word processing equipment and perhaps in advertising) and higher labor costs (for nonprofessional workers), employment will become the only mode of entry. This is troubling because the decision to hire, even more than the decision to take on an apprentice, allows scope for employer prejudice: Although the profession may feel an obligation to ensure that every law graduate obtains an apprenticeship (since it is the profession that requires such an experience), there is no comparable obligation to ensure a first job or a start in practice. Thus it may be significant that a smaller proportion of Brazilian women than men law graduates began practice and a smaller proportion of male English Bar pupils than female. I will return to this issue in the discussion of women lawyers below.

F. Reprise

This brief overview of mechanisms of supply control in some dozen countries allows me to offer some tentative generalizations. First, in every country the profession exercises some degree of control, either autonomously or through its influence over the state. We are very far from the nineteenth century, when anyone with some religious education could practice as a vakil in India, innkeepers advised litigants in Japan, and any white male could practice law in some American states. Second, there are significant differences in the means of control. Some countries stress ostensibly meritocratic devices: competitive entry into law school in the United States and the United Kingdom, university examinations in Norway, and state examinations in Germany, Italy, and Japan. Other countries allow ascribed characteristics a more explicit role; thus family support may influence who attends and completes law school in the United States, Italy, Spain, and Latin America; and class, gender, and race may influence who obtains apprenticeships and first positions in England and Wales. Third, although the profession justifies its restrictions on supply in terms of quality control, there is *no* evidence that the particular requirements—university education, apprenticeship, or passage of an examination—correlate with professional competence. Indeed, the enormous variety of measures used in different countries, and in the same country at different times, strongly suggests that at least some of them are irrelevant to performance. Fourth, although the stringency of one mechanism often compensates for the laxity of others, still there are overall differences between countries. Japan certainly seems to be the most exclusive. Other global comparisons perhaps are most meaningful between similar countries. It appears to be more difficult to qualify as a barrister in England and Wales than as an advocate in Scotland, as a lawyer in Canada than in the United

States, as an avocat in France than as an avvocato in Italy, as an avvocato in Italy than as an abogado in Spain. It would be interesting to compare these differences with variations in anticompetitive practices within the profession, in income and status, and in the coherence of professional associations.

Finally, some trends are common to many countries. Everywhere the university has become the dominant institution: on the Continent and in Latin America in the nineteenth century; in the United States in the early twentieth; and in Canada, Australia, and England and Wales since World War II. Although formal education initially may have seemed an effective means of controlling supply, in the long run the profession thereby relinquished control to the universities and to the state that supports them in most countries. With the worldwide expansion of university education in the last two decades there has been an explosion in the production of lawyers, which the profession could not stem. The university has overshadowed and marginalized apprenticeship, incorporating some of its functions (through clinical programs) and appending others (in postgraduate vocational courses). There has been a convergence between university and state examinations, so that the former have either displaced the latter or prepared students to pass them. But if the university has gained power at the expense of the profession, new forces are emerging to influence who and how many become what kind of legal professional: These are the large employers of the public sector (government, the judiciary) and the private (corporations, large law firms), which can have an impact very different from that of the atomistic employers of the past.

III. Fluctuations in the Numbers of Lawyers

A. Periodization

The effects of changes in the nature and degree of supply control are visible in the fluctuations in the number of lawyers and in the size of entering cohorts over the last century and a half (see appendix tables 1 and 2). Although data for the nineteenth century (the first period considered here) are available for only a few countries, and even then are incomplete and unreliable, they reveal erratic alternations between rapid growth and stasis or even decline, which is consistent with the view that lawyers were subject to, rather than in control of, market forces. Thus the ratio of population to lawyers fluctuated irregularly in the United States between 1850 and 1920, perhaps in response to the business cycle of booms and busts. Solicitors and barristers in England and Wales, solicitors and advocates in Scotland, and lawyers in Belgium displayed similar patterns. Although entry barriers—typically class and gender—excluded the vast bulk of the population, they did not regulate precisely the number who qualified, which waxed and waned with demand.

The first six decades of the present century (the second period) present a very different picture. Perhaps the strongest way of stating the difference is to note that the profession failed to grow at certain critical periods when demand for lawyers' services arguably exceeded supply, either because supply had been curtailed by external disasters (the two world wars) or because demand was rising rapidly (the economic expansions following those world wars, especially the second). As a result, many very different countries ended the half century with roughly the same number of lawyers they had at the beginning, despite the fact that population grew dramatically (creating a pool seeking entry to the middle class, for which law was a favored portal) and demand skyrocketed (because an expanding economy coincided with massive state intervention). The impact of the world wars on any country depended on whether that country mobilized an army. Thus Belgium, which rapidly was conquered in both wars, actually saw an increase in recruitment to the legal profession during the first world war and a constant rate of lawyer recruitment during the second. In England and Wales, by contrast, enrollment of new solicitors fell from 485 in 1913 to 81 in 1918 (a decline of 83%) and from 952 in 1938 to 117 in 1944 (87%). And in the United States it dropped from 7,706 in 1941 to 1,853 in 1944 (76%). In both countries, the catch-up after the war did not begin to compensate for this reduced rate of lawyer recruitment or for the deaths and disabilities of lawyers who had served in the armed forces. In the United States, the number admitted during the five-year peak of lawyer recruitment following World War II (1948–52: 63,325) exceeded the number admitted during the five years preceding the war (1937–41: 41,910) by only 51%. In England, the number of solicitors admitted during the five years after World War I (1920–24: 2,334) actually was 8% lower than the number admitted during the five years preceding it (1909–13: 2,530); and the number of solicitors admitted during the five years after World War II (1947–51: 4,319) was only 14% higher than the number admitted during the five years before it (1934–38: 3,799).

The static size of the profession during these six decades (which contrasts sharply with earlier and later periods, as we shall see) is recorded in the number of admissions and of practitioners and the ratio of population to practitioners. Belgium granted 200 law degrees in 1890; 58 years later the number was only 273; after a brief postwar surge (to a high of 550 in 1950), it fluctuated between 300 and 400 until 1968. France also experienced a low level of recruitment in the 1930s and again in the 1950s and 1960s. There were 756 stagiaires in the Paris bar in 1924, and 45 years later there were only 750. Japan had 5,976 private practitioners in 1936 and 20 years later had 6,040—virtually no growth at all. Similarly, the province of Ontario, Canada, had 2,792 lawyers in 1951 and 3,388 in 1971—an average annual growth of only 1%; in the rural mining town of Sudbury, in northern Ontario, the ratio of population to lawyers actually *rose* from 2,847:1 in 1921 to 4,762:1 in 1951. In Norway, a fairly constant 150 lawyers a year were admitted between 1930 and 1970. But perhaps the most striking figures are found in the United States and the United Kingdom. In the former, the ratio of population to lawyers was 696:1 in 1900 and exactly the same in 1951; 10,685 lawyers were admitted to the profession in 1928 and 10,788 in 1963. In England and Wales, 16,265 solicitors held practicing certificates in 1902 and 16,318 in 1949; 633 solicitors were admitted in 1899 and 663 in 1964; the number of barristers recorded by the census actually fell from 4,733 in 1901 to 3,084 in 1951. And in Scotland the number of solicitors also remained relatively constant—3,621 in 1901 and 3,780 in 1961—while the number of advocates declined from 349 in 1901 to 285 in 1967.

The third period, from the 1960s to the present, differs from either of the previous two in displaying steady growth at rates higher than any attained in the past. This growth is closely connected to the postwar baby boom, university expansion, and the entry of significant numbers of women for the first time. Now that we are seeing the effects of a falling birth rate, declining educational budgets, and a stabilization in numbers of women law students at less than their proportion of the population (in part because of strong residual discrimination), the rate of expansion appears to be slowing. We can see this most clearly by looking again at the countries with legal professions that grew little or not at all during the first half of this century. In Belgium, a profession that had grown an average of only 1.8% a year between 1961 and 1970 grew 5.5% a year between 1970 and 1982; the number of law degrees conferred annually increased 2.4 times between 1969 and 1976 (from 496 to 1,188), after which it leveled off. In Norway, admissions doubled from 150 to 300 a year. The number of stagiaires at the Paris bar, which had been constant for decades, more than tripled in the seven years following 1964 (from 340 to 1,059). The number of avocats increased at an average annual rate of 10.3% between 1971 and 1981, whereas there was no growth in categories of the profession that retained supply control, such as avoués and notaires. The number of Dutch lawyers grew 1.4% a year between 1947 and 1970, but 8.6% a year between 1970 and 1980. In Canada, law student enrollments more than tripled between 1962/63 and 1976/77. In Ontario, the number of law degrees conferred grew almost fourfold between 1958 and 1972 (from 231 to 873); as a result, the legal profession grew at an average annual rate of 3.8% between 1951 and 1967, 5.1% between 1967 and 1971, and 10.1% between 1971 and 1981. The ratio of population to lawyers was halved (from 1,142:1 to 574:1) between 1960 and 1981. In the United States the number of students enrolled at ABA-accredited law schools increased more than threefold between 1960 and 1980 (from 40,381 to 125,397), and the number of law graduates rose even more (from 9,638 in 1963 to 35,059 in 1980). Bar admissions increased even more rapidly (from 10,788 in 1965 to 46,108 in 1979)—at an annual growth rate of 9.4% between 1965 and 1970, 24.1% between 1970 and 1973, 4.5% between 1973 and 1977, and 13.2% between 1977 and 1979. The profession grew at an annual average rate of 3.1% between 1951 and 1967, falling to 2.7% during the next five years, but then doubling to 6.4% between 1972 and 1980 before declining to 4.9% between 1980 and 1984.

Again, the United Kingdom displays even more extreme variation. In England and Wales the number of law degrees conferred annually almost tripled between 1965 and 1980 (from 1,290 to 3,706). But the number of solicitors admitted annually increased more than fivefold during that period (from 663 in 1964 to 3,538 in 1980), with the result that the number of solicitors holding practice certificates grew at an average annual rate of 2.9% between 1962 and 1970 and 5.9% between 1970 and 1982. The number of barristers starting practice annually also increased almost fivefold (from 80 in 1964 to 382 in 1976), with the result that the Bar grew at an average annual rate of 3.5% from 1962 to 1969, 8.5% from 1969 to 1977, and 3.9% from 1977 to 1982. In Scotland, the number of solicitors admitted annually grew more than threefold in the 1970s (from 116 in 1970 to 397 in 1980); the number of practicing solicitors actually declined an average of 0.3% a year in the decade 1954–64, increased at the same insignificant rate until 1971, but then climbed 3.1% a year in the first half of the seventies (1971–75) and 6.5% a year thereafter (1975–82). Although the number of practicing advocates grew only 0.2% a year in the decade 1951–62, the number of practicing advocates grew an average of 3.6% a year in the next two decades and an average of 7.9% in each of the last three years. The number of private practitioners in Japan, a category that had displayed no growth from 1936 to 1956, grew an average of 3.9% a year during the next two decades. In Germany, the annual average rate of growth in the number of private practitioners increased from 2.9% between 1961 and 1974 to 6.6% between 1974 and 1980. Between 1971 and 1978, Spain witnessed a tripling of the number of both law students (from 24,824 to 74,117) and degrees granted (1,678 to 4,650). And in Italy, the law student population increased almost tenfold in less than a decade (from 13,859 in 1969 to 128,604 in 1977). In almost every country, rates of growth began to taper off at the end of the 1970s and beginning of the 1980s.

B. The Entry of Women

Women made a major contribution to the profession's rapid growth during the last two decades, illustrated by the three countries for which detailed historical statistics are available (see appendix table 3). In Belgium, the number of male law students grew at an average annual rate of 6.2% from 1965 to 1969 while the number of female students was growing at a rate of 12.1%; during the next five years male enrollment grew at an annual average of 3.7% while female enrollment grew an average of 22.5% a year (thereafter growth declined in both categories). In the United States, male enrollment in law school actually declined at an average rate of 0.1% a year in the 1970s, whereas female enrollment increased at an average annual rate of 41.4%. Male entry to the profession also declined after 1973, and *all* further increases in the rate of growth are attributable to new women lawyers. In England and Wales, the number of male university law graduates increased at an average annual rate of 5.4% between 1967 and 1978, but the number of female graduates increased at a rate of 31.2%. The number of male full-time polytechnic law students grew 1% a year from 1966 to 1978, but the number of female students increased 30.6% a year. Admissions of male solicitors grew an average of 11.3% a year between 1968 and 1981, but admissions of female solicitors grew 77% a year; the number of male solicitors grew 4.5% a year between 1968 and 1980, but the number of female solicitors grew 41.5% a year. The number of male barristers grew 6.5% a year between 1965 and 1982, but the number of female barristers grew 25.3% a year. And in Scotland, male entry to the solicitors profession was constant during the two decades 1961–82, but female entry increased 4.5 times. Fragmentary data from other countries confirm this picture. In Canada, the number of male law students doubled between 1962/63 and 1980/81 while the number of female students increased 24 times. And in Norway, the proportion of women in the profession doubled between 1970 and 1980. Only in India and Japan have women remained an insignificant fraction of the profession. Yet the growth in the proportion of women in the profession appears to have halted—in most countries at between 30 and 40%, in a few (such as France and Yugoslavia) at close to 50%, but nowhere more than that.

IV. Internal Differentiation: Categories of Producers

I have written of the efforts of lawyers to control their market as though national professions were unitary. But of course there are major internal divisions—in terms of training, entry, function, lateral mobility, status, income, and relative growth rates—within each of which market control has a different meaning. National legal professions may draw these lines differently, but certain major fissures tend to reappear. Perhaps most important is the division between law graduates and others who perform legal functions (at least in those countries where formal education is the sole or principal portal to private practice). This boundary creates categories of sub- or paraprofessionals who actually may outnumber law graduates and who perform essential functions. Thus, in Japan, there are as many judicial scriveners as there are private attorneys, almost four times as many tax accountants, and six times as many administrative scriveners. In Germany, Rechtsbeistande who used to give legal advice have been absorbed by the Rechstanwalte. In England and Wales, the solicitor's managing clerk (now renamed the legal executive) performs many routine functions in conveyancing and litigation. Many countries allow nonlawyers to appear as representatives before lower or specialized tribunals, such as labor, housing, and social security courts. The legal profession exercises no control over the number or qualifications of paraprofessionals; the most it can do is secure laws delimiting the competence of paraprofessionals or requiring paraprofessionals to practice only as employees of lawyers.

A second major boundary divides private practitioners from employed lawyers. Market control obviously has a very different meaning for the latter: Their numbers are determined by their employer (traditionally the state), and they do not compete for business. In some countries—Germany and Japan, for instance—the public profession (judges, prosecutors, and civil servants) historically was preeminent, and private practitioners only gradually gained autonomy and grew in numbers. In Norway, even private practitioners were civil servants from 1809 until 1848. Other countries reverse the emphasis. In England and Wales, barristers long remained independent professionals; well into the nineteenth century the attorney general remained a private practitioner: He was briefed by the Crown but retained his own chambers and also accepted work from private clients. The distinction between independent and employed professionals has acquired expanded significance as an increasing number of lawyers have entered employment in private industry and commerce. The distinction between employed and self-employed lawyers may reflect differences in training as well: The former often have obtained law degrees but need not have completed their apprenticeships or passed further examinations—examples are syndic attorneys in Germany, law graduates in Japan, legal advisers in France, and employed barristers in the United Kingdom. The centrality of employed lawyers in both the public and the private sectors in continental European legal professions may help to explain the relative weakness of other forms of market control (such as entry to university, state examinations, or apprenticeship).

A third kind of division within the profession turns on the functions that particular categories of private practitioners can perform. The notary specializes in the authentication and registration of documents and transactions but does no litigation. In southern Europe and Latin America this is a distinct category; in some German states, Canada (except Québec), and the United States, notarial functions are performed by lawyers. Another boundary separates lawyers who conduct the preliminary stages of litigation (solicitors, avocats, avvocati, abogados) from those who actually appear in court (barristers, avoués, procuratori, procuradores). The latter function may be differentiated still further by the particular court in which the lawyer is entitled to appear (e.g., a special bar for the highest court). All of these distinctions serve to divide the market and suppress competition by outsiders.

Some forms of internal differentiation have diminished over time. With the unification and rationalization of the judiciary, lawyers admitted to (and by) particular courts gained the right to practice in all courts (though not everywhere, as I discuss below under anticompetitive practices). Thus England saw the union of solicitors and attorneys when the distinction between law and equity collapsed and the elimination of proctors and doctors of law with the integration of the ecclesiastical courts. Specialist litigators often did not survive colonial transplants, as in the United States, Canada, some Australian states, New Zealand, and India. Long-standing distinctions recently have been obliterated: the elimination of avoués in Belgium in 1967 and in France in 1971 (except in the Cour d'Appel) and of the Rechtsbeistande in Germany in 1981. On the other hand, the proliferation in government, industry, and commerce, and even in private practice, of employed lawyers who often cannot appear in court by reason of their employed status may be laying the groundwork for new divisions.

Countries differ greatly in the permeability of the boundaries between categories. At one extreme, there are no legal barriers in the United States between judges, civil servants, private practitioners, academics, and employed lawyers, and there is considerable lateral mobility between these careers. Similarly, in Venezuela, three-quarters of a sample of 1936 law graduates had held positions in at least three of the following categories: private practice, judge, civil servant, government official, and research and teaching. And in Norway, the higher judiciary is less the culmination of a separate career and more a reward that can be earned toward the end of many different careers. By contrast, judges, civil servants, and private practitioners are almost distinct professions in many continental European countries, with few transfers between them. Even in England, only barristers can become judges in the higher courts, and employed barristers virtually never enter private practice; there also is very little exchange between the Bar and the solicitors profession. But even when there are no legal barriers, moving between categories is an individual act and relatively rare, except following certain transitory statuses held by novices, such as district judges in Norway or judge's clerks in the United States, assistant solicitors in England and Wales or associates in American law firms.

The size and growth of these categories in different countries are a function of the relative importance of public and private sectors in the national economy and of the varying roles of judges and lawyers in processing contentious matters (see appendix table 4). Germany and Norway represented one extreme until recently, with judges, employed lawyers, and private practitioners each constituting approximately equal thirds of the legal profession. Furthermore, the number of lawyers in the public sector in Norway increased 44% in the 1970s, while the number in the private sector increased only 15%. By contrast, judges in the United States never constituted more than 5% of the profession and, as recently as 20 years ago, three-fourths of all lawyers were private practitioners. In India in 1970 there were 15 times as many lawyers as judges. However, several factors seem to be producing a convergence of these extremes. First, categories that preserved a very high degree of supply control may have kept their numbers constant but only at the cost of marginalizing themselves—notaires in Belgium (whose numbers have remained unchanged for almost 50 years) and notaires, avoués, syndics, huissiers, and greffiers in France. Second, everywhere the number of judges has grown more slowly than that of other categories, presumably because governments have refused to expand the budget of the judiciary. Thus the number of judges in Japan increased by little more than half in the 80 years from 1896 to 1976, whereas the number of prosecutors tripled and the number of private practitioners grew almost sevenfold. The number of judges in Brazil doubled between 1950 and 1980, whereas the number of lawyers increased more than fivefold. The number of judges in Norway doubled between 1830 and 1980, while the number in the legal profession as a whole grew more than tenfold. Thus the increased production of lawyers in the last two decades is likely to swell the ratio of private practitioners to judges in all countries.

Third, all countries have seen the category of employed lawyers grow more rapidly than that of independent professionals. One reason has been the growth of the welfare state in the 1960s and 1970s (a decade earlier in some countries). Thus between 1972 and 1982, the number of solicitors in local government in England and Wales increased almost twice as fast as did the number of principals in private practice; in Scotland, this number increased five times as fast. In the United States between 1954 and 1970, the self-employed lawyer population increased only 19%, whereas the population of lawyers employed in the federal government increased 108%, and the population of lawyers employed in state and local government increased 167%. Between 1947 and 1970, the number of private practitioners in Belgium increased only 16%, whereas the number of lawyers employed in government increased 127%. An additional reason for the relative decline of private practice is the proliferation of large corporations, which prefer to hire their own lawyers, at least for certain functions. Thus in Belgium, the number of lawyers employed in commerce and industry has increased even more rapidly than the number in government—189% in the same period. In Norway between 1970 and 1983, the number of private practitioners increased only 40%, but the number of advocates employed in commerce and industry doubled and the number of licensed agents tripled. In England and Wales, the population of lawyers employed in business grew 244% between 1957 and 1982, more than three times as fast as that of private principals. In Scotland, the former category grew 147% in the seven years 1975–82, while the latter grew only 20%; and in the United States, the former increased almost fivefold between 1951 and 1980, while the latter did not even double. Another category of employed lawyers that has grown rapidly in recent years is law teachers: from 40 to 650 in Canada between 1950 and 1983; from 1,724 to 6,755 in the United States between 1944 and 1980; and from 130 to 1,282 in England and Wales between 1933–34 and 1980–81.

The final category that increased faster than the profession as a whole is that of lawyers employed by private practitioners—associates in the United States, assistant solicitors in England and Wales and in Scotland. This category is limited to the common law world: In many civil law countries, advocates lose their right of audience when they are employed; and law firms in civil law countries never approach the size of their American counterparts—indeed, very few have more than ten lawyers. The growing number of lawyers employed in private practice is partly a function of the greater size of entering cohorts, for many neophytes always have begun their careers as employees. But in the United States a higher proportion of new lawyers are beginning their careers as employees and remaining longer in that condition. Thus the number of associates increased more than fourfold in the United States between 1951 and 1980, while the number of self-employed lawyers did not even double, and the number of assistant solicitors in England and Wales increased 5.6 times, whereas the number of principals barely doubled. The net result of these various trends is a universal decline in the proportion of the profession that is self-employed—the prototype of the independent professional: from 70% to 57% in England and Wales between 1939 and 1982 (excluding judges); from 85% to 59% in the United States between 1948 and 1980; from 86% to 70% in Ontario, Canada, between 1971 and 1982; from 74% to 60% in Scotland between 1954 and 1982; and from 59% to 31% in Belgium between 1937 and 1982. In Norway in 1970, private practitioners made up only 24% of the profession.

It seems plausible that there is a connection between the two major historical trends identified thus far: the erosion of professional control over the production of producers and the growth in numbers of employed lawyers.

On the one hand, the public sector, private corporations, and law firms offered jobs to the rapidly growing number of new recruits, who would have had great difficulty finding work as independent practitioners. Potential employment in these settings thus acted as a pull factor, helping to explain the intensity of the pressure to enter the profession. On the other, employers (whether governments, corporations, or law firm partners) represent a new form of control over numbers, since they unilaterally decide how many they will employ. Of course, this is heteronomous, not professional, control. Furthermore, it extends only to the employed sector; as jobs dry up there we can expect an increase in the number of independent professionals and in competition among practitioners in a market that may be growing only slowly, if at all. I return to this subject below when I discuss control over production *by* producers.

One remaining career line is not easily compared with any of the above: that of lawyer politicians. On the one hand, because only a tiny proportion of law graduates enter politics, those who do so represent a relatively insignificant fraction of the legal profession and perhaps should not be considered a part of it at all if they never have practiced or never will return to practice. On the other, lawyers clearly are overrepresented in the political system in comparison with their numbers in the general population. But the significance of this disproportionality is problematic: Does law offer a privileged route to a political career, so that entry to the legal profession skews access to political power? Or do legal training and practice influence the way politicians exercise their power? The relationship between politics and other legal careers is complex and varied: Participating in party politics (including service in Parliament) is one way English barristers can improve their chances of being elevated to the bench (it also used to ensure appointment as a QC); prominent U.S. politicians often become "rainmakers" in large corporate law firms. In many countries, lawyers constitute the largest occupational category in both the legislative and the executive branches. In India, they made up about a third of each of the first four post-independence Parliaments (1952–71) and still constituted this proportion in 1980. In addition, just under a third of all ministers and almost two-thirds of cabinet ministers were lawyers. Furthermore, before independence they so dominated municipal and provincial administration that it was referred to as the "vakil-raj." Similarly, lawyers consistently have constituted half of the United States Congress, the cabinet, and most state legislatures. Four of the last seven Canadian prime ministers have been lawyers, governing for 30 of the last 50 years; today a quarter of the federal House of Commons and half of the provincial premiers are lawyers. In Brazil, the period 1841–89 is referred to as the "Empire of the Bachareis"; 57% of the ministers were law graduates, as were 71% of the senators from 1831 to 1840; and from 1871 to 1880 these proportions increased to 86% and 72% (on the other hand, only a small fraction of these law graduates ever practiced law). In Venezuela between 1936 and 1982, half the presidents had studied law (and a third had practiced it), and between one-third and two-thirds of the cabinet members were lawyers, as were 25–40% of the National

Congress and a third to a half of the leadership of the political parties. The Liberal party in Norway in the nineteenth century was nicknamed the "Advocates party" because of the professional backgrounds of its members.

Yet lawyer dominance has diminished in many countries. In France, a quarter of the deputies in the Third Republic were lawyers, but this dropped to a sixth in the 1930s, an eighth in the Fourth Republic, and a twentieth in the Fifth Republic (although several recent premiers and prominent cabinet ministers have been lawyers). In Italy the proportion of lawyer members of Parliament (MPs) dropped from 38% in 1949 to 15% in 1969. In Norway, 20% of MPs between 1814 and 1884 were lawyers, but only 10% have been since World War II. In Scotland, 35% of MPs were lawyers in 1901 but only 4% in 1955, although the proportion has risen to 18% today. Several reasons for the decline have been suggested. Legal practice has become more demanding in recent years and thus harder to combine with political activity, especially for lawyers whose practice is far from the capital. The skills required for government have shifted from rhetoric, drafting, and interpersonal abilities to technocratic knowledge (though the law and economics movement in America and elsewhere in the common law world may be a response to this threat of obsolescence). Stated another way, until recently, lawyers represented the *only* "profession" whose technical knowledge, formal education, wealth, and social standing qualified them for public office; today many other professions can make equal or stronger claims. Finally, the labor voters and governments of the postwar period often have been hostile to lawyers, for reasons of both class and ideology.

V. Market Control: Production by Producers

A. Definition and Protection of the Professional Monopoly

Controlling the production *of* producers (i.e., entry into the profession) is only half of market control. Lawyers who sell their services on the market (i.e., private practitioners) also must control production *by* producers—both external competitors and lawyers themselves. Control over production *of* producers necessarily precedes control over production *by* producers: professionals who voluntarily curtailed their production of services at a time when anyone could claim the title of lawyer would be committing economic suicide. The stringency of control over the production of producers appears to be directly related to the stringency of control over production by producers. For the same reason, the present erosion of professional control over the production of lawyers seems to be undermining restrictive practices. Furthermore, just as employment appears to represent an alternative means of controlling the production of producers (especially in northern European countries), so it diminishes the salience of restrictive practices. Concern with the unauthorized practice of law, for instance, seems to be an obsession of legal professions in common law countries.

The first step in controlling production by producers is defining the professional monopoly. The core of the monopoly, everywhere, is practice in the higher courts (though, as we will see below, this often is the exclusive privilege of only a fraction of the profession). In many countries (including Brazil, Germany, Italy, Spain, and Venezuela), the profession is protected not only against other representatives but also against self-representation by the parties themselves (though few parties are eager to risk appearing alone even where this is allowed). In Norway, lay counsel can appear for criminal defendants and can act in individual civil cases (though not in the Supreme Court). The other major category of lawyers' work—noncontentious matters—actually occupies a much larger proportion of their time; but it is less well protected, perhaps because it is less visible and less obviously requires technical expertise. Only in the United States and Canada do lawyers claim an exclusive right to give legal advice (although Belgian lawyers recently extended their monopoly to advice in order to eliminate competition from the law shops operated by students and apprentices, perhaps because the government was offering to pay for legal aid and advice for the first time). In 1913, the Norwegian state limited the right to sell legal advice to lawyers and others licensed by the municipality, and the latter category was eliminated in 1936; it is noteworthy that this was done in the heart of the Depression and for the express purpose of increasing lawyer income. The monopoly was extended to *public* legal assistance in 1980, at a time when the profession was growing rapidly. However, real estate agents and architects, for example, can give legal advice as part of their trade, and company employees can advise fellow workers. Lawyers in other countries have staked out particular transactions as their private domains. Undoubtedly the most important is the transfer of real property—the conveyancing monopoly—which earns English solicitors more than half their total income and successfully withstood attack until just last year. In Venezuela, lawyers must sign all documents; in many continental European countries this is the prerogative of notaries.

The borders of the monopoly constantly are threatened by other occupations. Even the core, representation in contentious matters, has not gone unchallenged in specialized courts and administrative tribunals, which may eschew formal legal procedures. Self-representation is permitted before labor courts in Brazil and Belgium, and social workers represent parties in Spanish labor courts; in France, the occupations of agréé and mandataire assumed the function of representation in the commercial courts and before justices of the peace, respectively, early in this century. Some countries, such as Brazil and Germany, have a specific category of partially qualified lawyers who can practice in the lower courts. In Japan, lawyers have lost patent and copyright matters to nonlegal specialists. More threatening has been the rise in the number of judicial scriveners (one and a half times as numerous as lawyers themselves), who advise unrepresented litigants. In 1978 the legal profession persuaded the government to impose a formal licensing examination almost as difficult as the lawyers' exam itself (only 2.5% passed in 1982). In every country the lawyers' monopoly over noncontentious matters has been far more vulnerable to incursions from accountants, real estate agents, banks and trust companies, and employees of other companies and trade unions. Thus English solicitors long ago lost much of the market for tax advice to accountants and are likely to lose a good deal of the market for residential real estate transactions to licensed conveyancers. And informalism or delegalization constantly threatens to eliminate all advisers and representatives: 89% of all divorces in Japan are uncontested and handled by the parties themselves; nonlawyers can represent parties in mediation; and small claims courts in the United States often prohibit legal representation.

We know little about how these boundaries are defended. In the United States and in England and Wales, professional associations have vigorously condemned individual incursions, successfully seeking criminal prosecutions for unauthorized practice, and have negotiated market divisions with other occupations. In Canada, the recent influx of lawyers has been accompanied by a rise in the number of lawyer complaints about unauthorized practice: from 10–15 a year in Ontario between 1968 and 1973 to 35–90 a year between 1974 and 1981. Yet the ideologies of the market and of central planning both seem hostile to professional monopolies: A recent Canadian decision held that lawyers can exclude other practitioners from performing particular functions only if they can show that such behavior places the public at risk. Elsewhere the issue does not seem to be litigated and, in any case, proceedings are initiated by the public prosecutor, not the profession. But we can expect further confrontations between the legal profession, competing occupations, and the public interest as a result of the enormous inflow of licensed practitioners unable to find sufficient work.

B. Competition Among Licensed Professionals

An effective defense of the professional monopoly does not complete the task of market control, for the problem of internal competition remains. The legal profession has restrained such competition in a wide variety of ways. First, it has divided the market—most clearly in England and Wales, between barristers, who have an exclusive right of audience in the higher courts, and solicitors, who alone can brief barristers for clients and who also have enjoyed the conveyancing monopoly until this year. English barristers are further divided into QCs (or silks or seniors, fixed at 10% of the practicing Bar for at least the last half century) and juniors; the former are briefed only in weightier matters and are precluded from handling the preliminary phases of litigation. In exchange, it was the rule until recently (and still is the prevailing custom) that a junior must be briefed together with a senior and paid two-thirds of the latter's fee. Another, and more widespread, division is the creation of a separate bar for the highest court, protected by a *numerus clausus*, as in France and Germany. Until 1978, practice in the Norwegian Supreme Court was limited to those who graduated *laudabilis* from university (about 30%); today anyone can qualify for such practice, but Supreme Court advocates retain a separate title.

The market also may be divided geographically—in part a historical residue of localized sovereignty and of the fact that lawyers originally were admitted to practice by, and in, specific courts. National boundaries in legal practice are the most enduring form of this division. In France, lawyers can practice only in the court to which they have been admitted (although members of the Paris bar can practice in its suburbs). In Germany, lawyers can practice only in the trial or appellate court to which they have been admitted (unless accompanied by a Rechtsanwalt from that court) and must live in that state. In the United States, Canada, and Australia, lawyers are admitted to practice in particular jurisdictions, but it is possible to gain admission in more than one, though the applicant typically must pass the bar examination and satisfy the residence requirement in each. Similarly, in Spain, lawyers can practice only within the jurisdiction of the local bar association to which they belong (which used to restrict access to the Supreme Court to Madrid lawyers), but they can join as many as they wish. British barristers are restrained by strong traditions. They must practice from chambers staffed by a clerk (whereas Scottish advocates all practice from the Advocates' Library and must share the staff of clerks); QCs must have chambers in London; barristers must join one of six provincial circuits if they wish to practice in any of them, and clients used to have to pay additional fees to brief barristers appearing outside their own circuit. There are no intranational restrictions on practice in Brazil, Japan, India, or Italy (except for procuratori). I would expect many of these restrictions on practice within or even between countries to be relaxed under pressure from the national or multinational clients whom elite lawyers serve and from law firms seeking to capture or retain this business. (The European Community already has taken steps in this direction.)

The other limitations on intraprofessional competition complement those just discussed by making it more difficult for any lawyer to gain a competitive advantage. One such restraint is the prohibition on combining law with another occupation. Lawyers in the United States and Canada can practice other occupations but cannot enter partnerships with nonlawyers. In Belgium, private practitioners cannot sell real estate or insurance. In England and Wales, solicitors cannot even share office space with those in other occupations, nor can they form a limited company with other solicitors. English barristers cannot form partnerships with anyone (even other barristers); historically, those preparing for the Bar could not support themselves by engaging in a variety of "undignified" trades. Germany represents the other extreme: Rechtsanwalte can qualify as accountants and can form partnerships with accountants, patent lawyers, and tax advisers. Among other things, Norwegian lawyers can conduct auctions, speculate in property, manage housing, collect debts. Closely related to these restrictions are those on employed lawyers (who pose a competitive threat to private practitioners). Barristers in England and Wales and lawyers in Belgium, Germany, and France cannot appear in courts if they are employed; in Brazil and Italy they can represent only their employers. In England and Wales, employed solicitors generally cannot act on behalf of fellow employees. In Spain and the United States, however, there are no distinctions between employed and independent practitioners.

Finally, there are stringent restraints on practices that might allow a lawyer or law firm to concentrate business. Law societies in three Canadian provinces currently are suing lawyers who have established cut-rate high-volume legal clinics. Until recently, advertising was forbidden almost everywhere. It still is in most of Canada, France, Brazil, Germany, Spain, Italy, and Belgium. Indeed, the cab rank rule of English barristers (that they *must* take any brief offered to them) appears to go one step further in dispersing business. In practice, of course, barristers' clerks energetically seek business for their principals and find plausible excuses for rejecting unwanted briefs. But the blanket prohibition on advertising is crumbling: It has been permitted in the United States since 1977; in Scotland and some Canadian provinces and Australian states, more recently; and it was authorized by the Law Society of England and Wales just last year (as a result of the impending loss of the conveyancing monopoly and the threat of advertising by lay competitors). Solicitation still is prohibited everywhere (and the professional proscription has been upheld by the U.S. Supreme Court), but the practice is widespread in India and Venezuela. In Italy, connections with a trade union ensure a steady flow of clients from the membership. The legal profession has been slow to institutionalize formal specialization, largely because generalists (still the majority of lawyers) fear they would lose business to certified specialists.

A primary (if unstated) objection to advertising is fear of price competition (and falling profits). Norwegian advocates, although permitted to advertise, cannot indicate prices. But lawyers have addressed this concern more directly through price controls. These range from mandatory fees fixed by the state for all matters in Germany, to mandatory fees set by courts for solicitors in contentious matters in England and Wales, to advisory fee schedules set by the profession in Norway, Canada, Brazil, France, Spain, and Japan. In the United States, most local bar associations used to circulate minimum fee schedules, which they or the courts sometimes enforced through disciplinary proceedings, but the U.S. Supreme Court struck down such practices in 1975 as violations of the antitrust laws. In England and Wales, minimum fee schedules for conveyancing were abolished in 1972 (although fees actually rose as a result); and the rule by which junior barristers were paid two-thirds the fee of their seniors also was abolished in 1977, though it still is followed in practice. But if professional fee regulation is increasingly problematic, the growing role of the state in subsidizing legal services through legal aid has introduced a new form of control over professional charges, which has influenced fees negotiated in the private market.

Just as many of the functional and geographic divisions within the profession have dissolved in recent years, so the anticompetitive practices just discussed are in retreat. Cooperation, if not partnership, with other experts—such as economists, psychiatrists, and scientists—seems inevitable. The increase in the number of employed lawyers relative to independent professionals, traced in the preceding section, should allow the former to expand their competence. But as employment opportunities become scarcer, new lawyers will be forced into private practice, increasing competition among independent professionals. Competition from other occupations will compel lawyers, in turn, to advertise and to compete in price. All of this will lead to greater concentration in the production of legal services (for which there are other pressures, discussed below). At the same time, the growth of legal aid will reduce professional autonomy in setting fees. The model of an uncompetitive market in which individual practitioners enjoy small but equal shares, protected by rules established and enforced by the professional association, clearly is anachronistic.

C. Demand Creation

The professional project of market control ideally seeks a situation in which supply remains constant (or even declines) while demand increases. We have seen above how and to what extent the former goal is achieved. The latter, less subject to professional influence, is a function of economic activity (according to studies in Belgium, France, England, and the United States), which has expanded greatly in most countries, especially since World War II, and of the size and structure of the state. Belgian notaires present a perfect example of market control: Their numbers increased only 11% between 1900 and 1970, whereas the number of notarized documents rose 135% between 1899 and 1968. Most legal professions have been less successful. Not only have they lost considerable control over the production of producers and competition among them (or never attained it), but demand has remained constant, and low, or actually has declined. One problem is that many countries lack the middle class that would use lawyers for entrepreneurial and personal problems. In Brazil, less than a third of the population earns more than three times the minimum wage ($50 a month); in the five years 1979–84, the middle class lost 16% of its numbers and 20% of its income. In Venezuela, one hour of quality legal services costs the equivalent of five days' income of an average worker. Other factors curtail demand still further. In Brazil, the expansion of military jurisdiction together with the inaccessibility of courts led to a decline in the number of proceedings. In Italy, the delay, cost, and cumbersomeness of litigation also discourages potential litigants. In every country the enormous increase in the number of new lawyers coincided with the worldwide recessions of the 1970s and 1980s.

Lawyers sometimes have responded to rising supply and flat or declining demand by seeking to stimulate the latter. But it is important to remember that all legal professions have adopted this strategy very hesitantly, and many have rejected it in whole or in part. Thus French lawyers were opposed to legal aid when it was introduced in 1972 and have accepted it only recently. There still is no legal aid in Italy, little in Spain, and state support in Belgium began only in 1984. On the other hand, wherever legal aid has been considered, the profession has argued vigorously (and generally persuasively) for the provision of legal services by private practitioners rather than by state employees. Thus "judicare" is the dominant mode of delivering legal services in the United Kingdom, Canada, Australia, New Zealand, the Netherlands, France, Sweden, and Germany. Only in the United States did early opposition by solo practitioners and small-firm lawyers to *any* government support for legal aid lead to exclusive reliance on employed lawyers, and even there the federal government now requires that 10% of its funds be spent on representation by private practitioners. Similarly, although the organized profession has resisted individual advertising, professional organizations in the United States and the United Kingdom have spent considerable sums on collective advertisements and on lawyer referral services that distribute paying clients randomly among participating lawyers, although there is no evidence that these methods have created significant demand.

In two countries, state programs have offered significant benefits to limited segments of the profession. In the Netherlands, legal aid accounts for a fourth to a third of all professional income, and a tenth of the profession relies on it almost entirely. In England and Wales, junior barristers earn half their income from legal aid, though QCs earn only a fourth. But it must be remembered that there are ten times as many solicitors as barristers. Legal aid represents only 6% of solicitors' gross fees, although it is very unevenly distributed (e.g., legal aid paid for 80% of contentious work by solo practitioners in 1975–76). In Scotland, junior advocates earn 39% of their fees from legal aid, although seniors earn only 9% (and again, there are 30 times as many solicitors as advocates). But in no other country does legal aid have anything like this impact on the profession. In Canada (outside Québec) and in France, it supports a small specialized legal aid bar. In Norway it provides only 5% of total lawyer income and pays poorly. Furthermore, only 15–20% of the Norwegian population ever has consulted a lawyer. In the United States, most legally aided criminal and civil matters are handled by salaried public defenders or legal services lawyers. Nor has the attempt to stimulate demand without state subsidies been much more successful: Legal insurance plans, though pervasive in Germany, have not caught on in the United States, England and Wales, Canada, or Scotland. Individual advertising has not stimulated new demand, though it may have redistributed existing demand among service providers.

Like efforts to restrict the production of and by lawyers, interest in demand creation seems more pronounced where private practitioners rather than employees dominate the legal profession, in both numbers and centrality. Thus the common law countries have been quicker to ease rules against advertising and have spent more substantial sums on legal aid payments to private practitioners (the Netherlands is an exception). The choice of a strategy reflects national attitudes toward state and market: The growth of legal aid in Britain is one facet of the expansion of its welfare state; individual lawyer advertising and the emergence of legal clinics in the United States reflect our attachment to a market ideology. But the strategy of demand creation is unlikely to compensate for the erosion of other forms of market control. Even when successful, it intensifies intraprofessional competition (whereas supply control dampens it) and encourages concentration (whereas supply control seeks to preserve inefficient production units). Although the project of supply control was simultaneously an assertion of professional autonomy and status, the project of demand creation may be a surrender of autonomy (to the state, which funds legal aid) and a relinquishment of status (by engaging in commercial promotion). But most important, the profession exercises less control over demand than over supply, and the very project of demand creation seems doomed to failure: People remain reluctant to consult lawyers even when their services are free and accessible.

VI. Internal Differentiation: Ascription in Recruitment and Allocation

In analyzing market control, we have seen that legal professions differ significantly in the barriers they erect to entry. It is reasonable to expect that these differences will be reflected in the backgrounds of lawyers. Furthermore, the transformation in entry procedures effected by the growth of universities and the dramatic expansion of all legal professions in recent decades also should have an impact on the composition of the profession. Have new categories of people entered the profession or occupied new roles within it?

A. Class Background

Despite the enormous changes that have occurred within the legal profession in the last two decades, recruitment remains strongly biased toward upper-class families. This should not be surprising. Although the numbers entering the profession have increased, entry has become more selective, if anything, with the almost universal adoption of the requirement of a university degree. In some countries, competition for university places has become more severe in recent years, and success in securing admission (even where determined by "meritocratic" criteria) correlates closely with class background. The entry of women into the profession, which has almost doubled the number of upper-class aspirants, has narrowed class composition still further.

Fragmentary data support these generalizations, although we often lack historical perspective and comparable data on the class composition of the larger society. In Italy, half of all law students are the children of entrepreneurs, and a third have parents who are university graduates. In Norway in 1958, 36% of the fathers of law students were professionals (20% were lawyers), another 19% were civil servants, and 18% were in business (although the proportion of students from working-class backgrounds increased after World War II). By 1983, 46% of the fathers of law students were professionals, though the proportion who were civil servants and businessmen had decreased to 12 and 8% respectively, and the number of working-class fathers had increased from 14 to 24%. In Japan, 14% of law students' fathers were professionals, 13% managers, 19% clerical or technical workers, 28% proprietors, 19% in agriculture, and only 5% laborers. In the United States in 1972, 86% of law students' fathers had white-collar jobs, and 50% had college degrees; only 2.9% had family incomes less than $10,000 a year (compared with 10.5% of the population). By contrast, among Chicago lawyers' fathers in 1975–76, 52% were professionals or managers, 20% lower white-collar employees, and 22% working class (the highly stratified system of legal education and the absence of a requirement of an undergraduate degree until after World War II explain the relatively large proportion of lawyers from lower-class backgrounds). Of the same group of Chicago lawyers, 15% had a lawyer parent, and more than half had a lawyer relative. In England and Wales in 1976, more than half the Bar had attended a private secondary school, and a third had graduated from Oxbridge; 76% had professional or managerial fathers (compared with 21% of the population), whereas only 14% had working-class fathers (compared with 60% of the population). Solicitors in 1975 were only slightly less privileged: 44% had attended private secondary schools, 32% had managerial fathers, 29% had fathers who were professionals (of whom 18% were solicitors or managing clerks), but only 3% had working-class fathers. This situation has changed only slightly: 54% of law students in the 1970s had professional or managerial fathers, and only 16% were from working-class families. In Scotland in 1978–79, 27% of articled clerks had employer or manager fathers (compared with 5% of male household heads in Britain in 1976), but only 4% had fathers in unskilled occupations (compared with 21% of male household heads). About a fifth of all apprentices had lawyer relatives.

The striking exception to this pattern is Yugoslavia, where 80% of all judges (who enjoy the highest status within the legal profession) come from lower-class farming families and only 8% have fathers who were judges, though this is changing; on the other hand, 93% of all judges were members of the Party when they were appointed. There is some evidence that law is becoming more accessible in other countries as well. In Belgium, the increase in the number of places, the entry of women, and discrimination in favor of Flemish speakers after 1965 all helped to make the law student body at the Catholic University of Leuven (east of Brussels) more representative of the larger population, although by 1981 this trend may have begun to reverse. In Brazil (where lawyers can qualify at proprietary as well as at state law schools), less than a third of all law students have parents with university educations, and three-quarters of all students live at home and work part time to pay tuition. This is strongly reminiscent of American legal education in the 1920s and 1930s; if the parallel is accurate, I would expect class recruitment to narrow in the future.

In some countries, a hierarchy of law schools and student rankings within each school allow background to exert continuing influence on the professional success of those who become lawyers. The stratification of law schools is most explicit and most extreme in the United States—where the results of opinion polls are published periodically and the most prestigious employers recruit from only a few of the nearly 200 accredited law schools—and in England and Wales, where Oxbridge still overshadows the newer universities and polytechnics. In Spain, Brazil, and Venezuela, the older public universities have higher status than the newer private schools. On the other hand, there is no hierarchy in Belgium or Germany. Law schools in the United States, the United Kingdom, and Norway rank their students on the basis of examinations, performance on which strongly influences not only the graduate's first job but the entire career. These data, though incomplete, strongly suggest that increasing reliance on "meritocratic" criteria to admit students to law school and to place law graduates actually amplifies the class advantage in stratified societies.

B. Race

There is little information on the racial composition of the profession (or on other social divisions, such as language or religion), but underrepresentation of minorities is a constant. In pre-partition India, Moslems and Sikhs were underrepresented in the legal profession in the Punjab. In the United States, blacks were grossly underrepresented until the 1970s, when the civil rights movement, rising numbers of black undergraduates, and affirmative action programs increased minority enrollment in law schools from 4.3% in 1969/70 to 8.1% in 1976/77. Since then it has leveled off (at about half the proportion of ethnic minorities in the larger population), although the number of Asian-American law students continues to grow. In addition, the bar examination remains a major hurdle for many minority students, as does discrimination by law firms and corporate employers. In 1973, the United States Supreme Court struck down state laws excluding noncitizens from the profession. On the other hand, the Canadian Supreme Court sustained a similar ban in 1984, in the face of a constitutional challenge. In 1973 there were only 3 native-Canadian lawyers; by 1980/81 there still were only 45 native-Canadian law students. Large Canadian law firms continue to discriminate on the basis of ethnicity. Two of the largest had only 19 and 22 members of ethnic or religious minorities among their 100 and 140 members in 1984. Noncitizens were excluded from the solicitors' profession in England until 1974, and blacks still account for less than 1% of that profession today. Although they never have been excluded from the Inns of Court, and were called to the Bar in large numbers in the 1950s and 1960s, most noncitizens returned home to practice. Overseas students (mostly from the new Commonwealth) represented three-quarters of all calls to the Bar in 1963 but only a third in 1971 and a fourth in 1977. Today, blacks make up about 5% of the Bar and tend to be concentrated in all-black chambers as a result of discrimination by barristers in granting pupillages and tenancies and by solicitors in assigning briefs. Given the overlap between class and race in most multiethnic capitalist societies, it is not surprising that meritocracy continues to exclude racial minorities from the legal profession and to assign those admitted to inferior roles in the professional hierarchy.

C. Gender

I discussed above the extent to which the growth of the profession during the last two decades is attributable to the entry of women. It is important to stress just how recent this phenomenon is: For most of the present century women were excluded from the profession either by law or by cultural and social constraints. In Brazil in 1950, 3.3% of law graduates were women, but by 1980, 24.6% were; the change must have occurred by the mid-1960s (earlier than in most other countries) because women as a proportion of lawyers and public defenders increased from 2.2% in 1950 to 21.7% in 1980. Women also began to enter the profession in England and Wales as university and polytechnic legal education expanded in the 1960s. They accounted for 17% of all law students by 1967 and 39% by 1978; 42% of entering university law students between 1979 and 1981 were women, as were 46% of polytechnic law students in 1983. But the impact on the profession has been more gradual. Women were admitted only as a result of a 1919 statute. The number of women barristers rose slowly to 5% by 1951 and 10% by 1965. Today, 20% of those called to the Bar are women, but they encounter discrimination in finding pupillages and tenancies and in getting work from solicitors; they see barristers' clerks as unsympathetic, and few women have succeeded in reconciling the demands of the early years at the Bar with those of raising young children. Compared with men, a smaller proportion of women who are called actually start practice, and a higher proportion of those who start drop out. Women initially encountered even greater difficulty in becoming solicitors, but the change there has been more dramatic. Only 2% of all solicitors were women as late as 1957, but in 1969 they accounted for 7.3% of new solicitors, and are more than a third today. Yet many who qualify fail to practice, and attrition is high. In Scotland the situation is similar, although the increase has been even more pronounced. Women as a proportion of law students rose from less than 20% in 1970 to 35–40% in 1980—and constitute more than half of the student body in Edinburgh. Only 3% of all advocates in 1975 were women, but they accounted for 13% of new advocates between 1975 and 1981 and 7.5% of all advocates in 1982. Only 4% of all solicitors in 1972 were women, but the proportion rose to 11% of new solicitors in 1975 and to 36% in 1982, by which time they accounted for 16% of all solicitors.

The first woman was admitted to practice by a U.S. state in 1869, but many states excluded women for another half century, and some law schools continued to do so as late as 1950. The number of women entering the profession rose sharply during World War II (and their proportion of all entrants rose even higher), but thereafter their representation fell back to about 5% and began to increase only in 1968. Today 34% of new admittees are women. In Norway, women made up 5% of the profession in 1970, and the proportion is estimated to be 10% today. In New Zealand, they made up less than 2% of the profession as late as 1971 but more than half of those admitted to the bar in 1983.

A few countries deviate from this pattern. In Belgium, 10–15% of law graduates were women as early as 1950, though by the 1970s the proportion approximated the same 35–40% found elsewhere. In France, women were admitted in 1900 but constituted a small proportion of the profession until recently; today, however, more than half of new entrants and a third of all avocats are women. (It is interesting that they also make up a higher proportion of law students in French than in English Canada—45 versus 34% in 1980/81.) In Norway, they accounted for 54% of all law students in 1983, although a smaller percentage entered the profession. And in Yugoslavia as early as the 1970s, half of all private practitioners were women, as are more than half of all law graduates today. At the other extreme, women still account for only 1% of Indian lawyers and for 10% of university law students in Japan (and undoubtedly a much smaller proportion of lawyers, prosecutors, and judges).

Formal qualifications are only the first hurdle, and indeed the easiest, for universities and professional examinations are gender blind. Indeed, women law students graduate and obtain honors degrees in England and Wales in the same proportions as men do. But in many countries a smaller proportion of women graduates than men enter the profession: In Belgium, 64% of 1961 women law graduates had law jobs, 71% of 1970 graduates; in Brazil, only 38% of 1980 women law graduates became legal professionals compared with 44% of all graduates. Decisions by lawyers to take on apprentices or hire new entrants are less visible and centralized, allowing greater scope for the expression of prejudice. The fragmentary evidence strongly suggests that women are becoming concentrated in positions that are less prestigious and remunerative, that deal with personal plight, and that can be held part time. In the United States in 1979, 17 to 19% of associates in the 32 largest firms in New York City were women, but only 2% of the partners were (though this is partly a function of the relative youth of women lawyers). A recent decision by the United States Supreme Court that law firms cannot discriminate in partnership decisions may help to redress this inequality. On the other hand, women are overrepresented in American government positions (as were black lawyers before them) and in teaching law. In Canada, there were only 13 and 16 women lawyers in two large Toronto firms with 100 and 140 lawyers respectively. In England and Wales the situation is no better. In 1976, a third of all London chambers had no women barristers, and another third had only one. There were few women heads of sets, QCs, or judges. Women barristers were concentrated in the less remunerative fields of criminal defense, family law, and general civil matters and were notably absent from chancery, tax, and commercial law chambers. Women were underrepresented in the leading City solicitors firms and even less visible among the partners. In Scotland in 1961, there were 5 women among the 1,209 principals in solicitors firms in Edinburgh and Glasgow (0.4%); 20 years later there were 86 out of 1,530 (5.6%) but only 2 out of 148 principals in the six largest firms (1.4%). In France, women are overrepresented in the less prestigious suburban bars and underrepresented in that of Paris; in Norway they are underrepresented in private practice, business, and advocacy and overrepresented in teaching and lower positions in central government. In Belgium they are underrepresented in the judiciary (especially at the higher levels) and overrepresented in nonprofit organizations. In Brazil, almost all judges are men, although 20% of attorneys, prosecutors, and public curators are women. Even in Yugoslavia, where the proportion of women judges has increased from 5 to 30% of all judges since World War II, they are concentrated at the lower levels. In every country, by contrast, women are greatly overrepresented in subprofessional positions: they make up 67–78% of Japanese law clerks, and there are similar proportions in the United States and the United Kingdom.

This distribution of women across the professional hierarchy is reflected in lower earnings (although the data are very incomplete and have to be adjusted for age). In the United States in 1949, women lawyers averaged half the income of men. They earned 88% as much as men in the Chicago Loop (i.e., downtown) in 1979 but only 42% in suburban Chicago and 31% in the rest of the state. English women barristers under 30 made three-fourths as much as men, but those over 50 made only half as much (controlling for type of practice). Overall, women barristers made just over half the income of men. And in Brazil in 1980, 5% of men lawyers made less than 3 times the national minimum wage compared with 15% of women, whereas 21% of men made more than 20 times the national minimum wage compared with 5% of women.

It seems to be true almost universally that once the legal and sociocultural barriers against women lawyers were removed, they entered the profession in numbers approximating those of men. Unlike aspirants from working-class backgrounds or ethnic minorities, women entrants do not suffer from economic, cultural, or educational disadvantages. Indeed, because they must surmount significant residual bias, women lawyers tend to come from more advantaged backgrounds than do men lawyers. Yet once they leave the meritocratic arena of formal education and examinations, they once again encounter prejudice and role conflict. The result is that qualified women lawyers fail to enter practice, leave early, or accept less attractive positions. These forms of inequality will not change until there is a transformation of the sexual division of labor. But even if we can grasp the broad outlines of the impact on women of becoming lawyers, we have much less sense of the impact on law of the presence of a substantial minority of women. Will the pace of work change? Do women exhibit distinctive styles in negotiating, advising, advocating, or judging? The questions call for cross-cultural research.

D. Age

The age composition of the profession is a function of changes in rates of recruitment; because law generally is a lifetime career, departures from the profession, largely through death, are fairly constant, even during wars. In the few nations where the profession has not (or not yet) experienced major expansion, it is dominated numerically by older lawyers. In Italy in 1980, only 6% of lawyers were under 30, only 17% were under 36, and 10.5% were over 65. In Tokyo today, only 5% are under 30 (partly because of the late age of qualification), and another 27.5% are between 30 and 39, whereas 9% are in their 60s, and 10% are 70 or older. In Belgium in 1970, 54% of lawyers were 25–44 and 36% were 45–64. In Norway that same year, 42% were 30–49, and 46% were 50–69.

In the United States, by contrast, half of all lawyers today have practiced less than 10 years and therefore are less than 35 years of age (although an increasing proportion are entering law school later). In New Zealand in 1981, 53% of all lawyers were under 35. In France we can see the extent to which the youthfulness of the profession is a function of the entry of women. A fourth of all women lawyers were under 30 in 1983, more than half under 35, almost three-quarters under 40, and four-fifths under 45. And in the United Kingdom we have data that allow us to trace changes in the age distribution over time. In England and Wales, 53% of solicitors were 40 or older in 1939, and the proportion was the same in 1969; 7 years later, 58% had been in practice 16 years or less (which would make most of them under 40). In 1966, 34% of all barristers were within 10 years of Call (most of whom would be less than 35 years old); a decade later the proportion had risen to 57%; and a staggering 71% of barristers were under 40. In Scotland, the proportion of solicitors under 40 increased from 33.2% in 1962 to 56.9% in 1982; the proportion under 30 rose from 10.5% to 26.9%.

These demographic shifts are of considerable importance. They reveal a profession that still does not reflect the class or ethnic composition of heterogeneous stratified societies. They reveal a substantial minority of women occupying inferior positions. And they reveal a youthful profession still governed almost exclusively by elderly males (as we will see below). These tensions of class, ethnicity, gender, and age pose acute problems for professional associations.

VII. Structure of Private Practice

The demographic changes sketched above, especially the rapid increase in the number of recent entrants, have influenced the distribution of lawyers, both geographically and across the structures in which they practice. At the same time, this distribution has been affected by other forces common to capitalist economies as well as specific to the late twentieth century.

A. Geographic Distribution

Where lawyers practice is an index of their accessibility to business and to individual clients. The geographic distribution also offers insights into the relationship between the profession and the state and affects the nature and efficacy of professional associations. A wide variety of countries display similar patterns. First, lawyers cluster in the capital. Historically, this reflects the close connection between lawyers and courts and between courts and Courts—the executive power of the nation-states that emerged in Europe and were imposed on the Third World. A third of Belgian private practitioners have offices in Brussels; a third of French avocats practice in Paris; a third of Spanish abogados have offices in Madrid; two-thirds of Venezuelan lawyers practice in Caracas (which has a third of the country's population); nearly half of all Japanese lawyers practice in Tokyo. About 60% of all Norwegian lawyers work in the Oslo region—50% of private practitioners; the ratio of population to lawyers in the southeast of Norway (which contains Oslo) is 476:1, but in northern Norway it is 2,000:1. From 1911 to 1976, Edinburgh consistently contained about a quarter of all Scottish solicitors but only a tenth of all Scots. In England and Wales, two-thirds of the Bar is located in London; although two-thirds of those barristers nominally belong to a circuit, only a third to a fifth frequently appear in courts outside London. Even a third of all solicitors are located in the capital. Toronto contains a tenth of the Canadian population but a quarter of its lawyers. And of course these figures omit the concentration in the capital of lawyers who are civil servants and judges. Only the United States, with its federal government and decentralized economy and financial markets, departs from this pattern: In 1970, less than 5% of American lawyers lived in Washington, D.C., and less than 1% of private practitioners (though more undoubtedly lived in the suburbs).

The second generalization, somewhat less pronounced and more qualified, is that outside the capital, lawyers are concentrated in the cities and scarce in the countryside. Sixty percent of Belgian lawyers are found in the 4 largest cities; 54% of French lawyers in the 8 largest; 64% of Japanese lawyers in the 3 largest; half of all Brazilian lawyers in São Paulo and Rio; two-thirds to three-fourths of provincial British barristers in the 6 next largest cities; three-fourths of Scottish solicitors in the 4 main cities (which contain only a third of the Scottish population); 90% of Norwegian lawyers in cities or towns with more than 6,000 people (which together contain only 47% of the population). Ninety percent of Indian lawyers are found in cities, but only 47% of legal assistants (the other 53% thus serve the rural population). Once again the United States is exceptional: Less than 40% of American lawyers lived in the 27 cities with more than 500,000 people in 1970, and almost an equal proportion lived in cities with fewer than 100,000 people. Interestingly, there do not seem to be enormous differences between rural and urban counties in New Zealand. The shift from solo practice to employment, described in the next two sections, may have accelerated this concentration of lawyers in the largest cities, because that is where employers, both private and public, are located. Yet, despite this consistent pattern, cities and regions of similar size differ greatly in the ratio of population to lawyers, although this ratio seems to correlate with indexes of legal business, such as the number of property transactions or the level of production, sales, or services.

B. Solo and Firm Practice

The ideology of common law legal professions is grounded on the independent practitioner. English barristers and Scottish advocates cannot form partnerships or enter employment; New Zealand, whose legal profession is integrated (i.e., not divided into solicitors and barristers), still retains the institution of the barrister sole. Even in France, a civil law country, only the autonomous avocat is considered a member of a liberal profession. Yet reality increasingly departs from this ideal. We have seen above that a growing proportion of lawyers are found outside private practice, as employees of the state, of private industry, or of educational and research institutions. Here I will consider the extent to which the private practitioner has abandoned the ideal of the autonomous professional.

One index of this change is the decline, both absolute and relative, in the number of solo practitioners. In the United States in 1948, 64% of all lawyers practiced by themselves; this had fallen to 37% by 1970 and to 33% by 1980; only 16% of Chicago lawyers were solo practitioners in 1975. Yet it is important to note that the decline has slowed and that half of all private practitioners still practiced alone in 1980. In England and Wales, the proportion of solo practitioners declined from a quarter of those who held practice certificates in 1939 to a mere 8% in 1982, although the proportion may have begun to rise since then. In Scotland, the proportion of solo practitioners declined from 13% of solicitors in 1970 to 10% in 1977. Yet in countries that do not idealize the independent professional, solo practice remains the mode. In Japan, half of all lawyers practice by themselves, and another 9% are solo practitioners who employ a lawyer assistant. In Rio de Janeiro in 1980, 61% of private practitioners worked alone; 51% of those in Milan did so in 1978. More than 80% of French avocats still practice alone. It would be interesting to speculate about why solo practice almost disappeared in England and Scotland and dropped by half in the United States but still dominates private practice in civil law countries.

One reason for the decline of solo practice is the economic advantage of a loose association of two or three lawyers. Such arrangements have spread widely, not as a transitional step toward larger law firms but as a way of retaining autonomy while collectivizing some resources and expenses and perhaps referring clients. These agreements range from mere office sharing (in which only rent is communal) through the pooling of other expenses (library, secretary, and receptionist) and the exchange of client referrals, to true partnerships that divide income and perhaps even adopt the corporate form (as is being discussed seriously in England for the first time). Office sharing with the pooling of some expenses is common in France (about 15% of avocats, compared with only 5% in true partnerships), Japan (14% of lawyers), Brazil, Germany, Italy, and Spain.

These tend to be very small groupings: In Japan, half of all office-sharing arrangements involve only 2 lawyers, and another third involve 3 to 5. Small partnerships also are common in many countries, often between father and son or between brothers. In Japan, 9% of private practitioners are partners in law firms; of these firms, half have only 2 partners and 87% have fewer than 6. In the United States in 1980, 29% of firm practitioners were in partnerships of 2 or 3 lawyers, 44% were associated with fewer than 6 lawyers, and three-quarters with up to 20 lawyers. If solo practitioners are included, two-thirds of American private practitioners are in firms of 4 lawyers or fewer, and three-quarters are in firms with 5 or fewer. In England and Wales, three-quarters of all firms in 1966 had only 1 or 2 solicitors, and these contained half of all solicitors in private practice; 13 years later these proportions had shrunk to a half and a fourth. In Scotland in 1979, almost four-fifths of all firms contained fewer than 5 lawyers. Thus if the pure form of independent professional—the solo practitioner—is being displaced, the successor is the small association of lawyers, which may or may not be a partnership. One reason why the movement is to small rather than large associations of lawyers is that their clients remain individuals and small businesses, and the growth of legal aid is likely to increase demand by the former. There are signs that this development will continue. Whereas 20% of the French avocats practice in some form of association (15% in a loose affiliation), 26% of Paris avocats practice together—6% sharing office space, 5% sharing other expenses, and the remaining 15% (three times the national proportion) in either a partnership or a civil professional corporation. Another step in this direction is an association among small firms. In England and Wales in 1983, a third of all solicitors firms had branch offices in another part of the city, in the suburbs, or in a secondary city. In Scotland, 90 new branches were opened between 1975 and 1980; the number in Edinburgh and Glasgow grew from 7 to more than 40 during the 1970s. In both the United States and the United Kingdom, small firms are sharing advertising expenses. But only in the United States have legal clinics emerged, attracting a mass clientele through extensive advertising and price cutting and growing to hundreds of lawyers in many offices in several states.

C. Large Firms

Thus solo and small-firm lawyers continue to dominate private practice. But large firms nevertheless deserve some attention (if less than they receive), not only because they are growing in number and size, but also because they represent such a different environment for legal practice and influence the entire profession. In the United States, 14% of firm practitioners are located in firms with more than 50 lawyers and a quarter in firms with more than 20. There were 90 American law firms with more than 100 lawyers in 1979; the 50 largest firms had a median of 188 lawyers, and the 20 largest had a median of 234 lawyers. After the United Kingdom removed the ceiling of 20 partners in 1967, solicitors firms grew rapidly; in 1983 in England and Wales, one firm had more than 60 lawyers, five had 50–59, four had 40–49, and four had 30–39. Although barristers cannot pool their incomes, they must practice out of chambers (or sets) in which they pool expenses and in which the senior clerk commonly directs business that one barrister cannot handle to another in the same chambers. Although most barristers practiced alone in the nineteenth century, in 1959 the average set had 7.5 barristers in London and 5.6 in the provinces; by 1982 these figures had doubled to 16.7 and 12.4 per set. In London today, only 3% of sets have fewer than 5 barristers, and 50% have more than 15. In Scotland, the largest solicitors firm has only 32 lawyers, but 6 have more than 20, and 47 have more than 10 (there were only 27 this large in 1977, 7 in 1971, 2 in 1960, and none in 1950). Elsewhere, the phenomenon of the large firm is rare or non-existent. In Brazil in 1980, there were very few firms larger than 50, and a firm with even 20 lawyers was considered quite large; only 8% of firms in Rio de Janeiro contained more than 5 lawyers. In

Venezuela, the largest firm has 30 lawyers, only 10 have more than 10 lawyers, and the total number of lawyers in large firms is about 300. In Japan, only 0.4% of all firms contained more than 20 lawyers and only 1.6% contained more than 10. In Germany, few firms are bigger than 10–15, and in France, Italy, and Spain there are hardly any large firms. In these countries, the large corporations that would retain large firms instead have many lawyer employees, some acting as general executives and others as in-house counsel.

A concomitant, and also a cause, of the growth of firms has been the increase in the number of employed lawyers. In some countries (such as Spain and Italy), solo practitioners and small firms employ recent graduates, who later may be taken into the firm. In Japan, 9% of private practitioners are solo employers, and 18% are their employees. But in the United States and the United Kingdom, a higher proportion of employees are found in larger firms. The ratio of the total number of associates to the total number of partners in American firms rises from 0.25 for firms with 2–5 lawyers to 1.04 for firms with more than 50 lawyers. In the 50 largest U.S. firms, the ratio rose from 1.1 in 1975 to 1.6 in 1979; in the 10 largest New York City firms, the ratio was 2.36. In England and Wales in 1976, there were 0.4 assistant solicitors for each solo practitioner but 0.7 for each principal in a firm with 10 principals or more. These figures are lower than those in the United States because English firms also use articled clerks (whose ratio to principals increased with firm size from 0.3 to 0.5) and legal executives (whose ratio to principals increased from 0.7 to 1.0), so that the ratio of employees whose time is billed to principals who reap the profits ranges from 1.25 for firms with 2 principals to 2.2 for firms with 10 or more. Nevertheless, firms recently have been replacing legal executives with assistant solicitors. The enormous growth of new lawyer cohorts allows partners to increase their profits by charging more per hour for associates and assistant solicitors than their labor costs; it also allows partners to be highly selective in taking associates and assistants into their firms. The use of subordinated personnel to enhance profitability may explain part of the correlation between partner income and law firm size. This relationship, together with the growth in the size of corporate clients and the complexity of their problems, is likely to lead to further expansion of the large-firm sector of the profession: in both the number of such firms and their size. At the same time, these large corporate clients also have the means and the economic and political incentives to develop in-house legal staffs rather than to use large firms. We still lack an explanation for why law firms expand in some countries and corporate legal departments grow in others.

The influx of lawyers during the last 20 years has had a significant impact on the distribution of all lawyers across locations and types of practice. It appears to have contributed to the further concentration of the profession in the capital and other major cities, although some lawyers have moved to the suburbs, following changing residential patterns. Competitive pressures seem to have driven lawyers out of solo practice and into small, loose associations. But the growth of a clientele of individuals as a result of legal aid programs, and the preservation of restrictive practices (in fact, if not always in law) have allowed this sector to survive and even to expand, despite its inefficiencies. Only in the United States have these small associations of lawyers been threatened by legal clinics. The greatest change has been the growth of large-firm practice, both in the number of such units and in their size, though this development is restricted to the common law world and Latin America. The significance of these firms exceeds their numbers, for they represent the environment in which a disproportionate fraction of beginning lawyers enter the profession, and the high status of corporate law firms makes them a model for lawyers in other sectors. Thus in private practice, as in private and public employment, the ideal of the independent professional has been supplanted by that of the salaried worker and the organization.

VIII. Work, Income, and Status

Logically, these three elements should be the starting points for an understanding of the professional phenomenon. Professionals are defined by the work they do (the technical skills displayed) and the rewards they earn (material and intangible). Yet these are the subjects about which we often know least. Social scientists study the organization of professional work, not its content—the latter is esoteric, invisible, and often concealed by the practitioners themselves. And professionals are equally secretive about their incomes, fearing public envy and the tax officials.

A. Work

Nevertheless, we can say something about lawyers' work and how it has changed in response to the changes in the nature and efficacy of market control. First, countries differ considerably in the extent to which legal work is either concentrated on a narrow range of functions and subject matters or broadly diversified. England and Wales exemplify the first alternative. Solicitors obtain half their income from residential conveyancing, two-thirds from conveyancing and probate (in Scotland they obtain a third from conveyancing and half from conveyancing and trusts and estates). Barristers on circuit at all levels of seniority earn more than half their income from government payments for representation in criminal cases, both as prosecutors and as defense lawyers under the legal aid scheme. These forms of monoculture are precarious: English solicitors are about to lose their conveyancing monopoly, and barristers rely on the government's willingness to appropriate funds and to raise their fees to keep pace with inflation. No other legal profession is so tied to one or even a small number of tasks. Just as the growth of the housing market (both the number and value of transactions) and of legal aid allowed the English legal profession to expand so rapidly in the 1970s, so the stagnant economy, the loss of the conveyancing monopoly, and a conservative Government dedicated to cutting welfare programs threaten a sharp decline in demand.

Representation in court is the functional core of all legal professions, at least historically, but they differ greatly between countries in the extent to which they have assumed the functions of counseling, drafting, and negotiating. In Italy, Venezuela, Brazil, and Japan, legal practice seems to be limited largely to litigation. This seriously restricts lawyers' ability to engage in demand creation and can lead to professional impoverishment when supply control is lost, as seems to have happened in Italy, where only 4.9 civil cases were filed per avvocato in 1961 (even fewer in central and southern Italy), a third of which were dismissed. Even in Japan, lawyers have an average of only 30 to 40 cases a year, and many have fewer than 20. By contrast, noncontentious matters long ago became the staple of practice in the United States and Norway and among solicitors in the United Kingdom. But the functions lawyers perform vary widely between countries and over time, and legal professions have very imperfect control over this. Divorce—the staple of legal aid practice in the United Kingdom and the Netherlands—usually is handled without lawyers in Japan. Many small U.S. and Canadian law firms earn significant income from personal injury litigation undertaken for plaintiffs on a contingent-fee basis; but such arrangements are prohibited almost everywhere else, and no-fault compensation schemes handle most injuries in many other countries, particularly in New Zealand. The conveyancing that is so essential to English solicitors is handled by nonlawyers in many U.S. and Australian states—and soon may be in England as well.

Within the range of functions the profession has carved out for itself and defended against competing occupations, there are further differences in the degree to which particular lawyers specialize. Some of this specialization is highly institutionalized, as we have seen above. Thus advocacy in the higher courts is the exclusive province of barristers in the United Kingdom; of avoués in the French Cour d'Appel, and certain avocats in the Cour de Cassation and the Conseil d'Etat; of Rechtsanwalte admitted to the Supreme Court of Germany; of litigantes in Spain and Venezuela; and of Supreme Court advocates in Norway. Much advice, drafting, and negotiation for large corporations is carried out by house counsel in the United States, the United Kingdom, Japan, Brazil, Venezuela, and Spain. In addition, there is a great deal of less formalized specialization. Several United States commentators have documented the division of that legal profession into two hemispheres: large firms serving large corporations and rich individuals; small firms and solo practitioners serving small businesses and middle-class individuals. In Norway, by contrast, only about a fifth of lawyers' work comes from individuals. A similar bifurcation is found in many other countries, although the role of large firms may be performed by smaller partnerships or master lawyers, often on retainer and assisted by lawyer employees (in Japan), by law professors (in Norway, Germany, and Spain), or by retired judges (in Spain). Finally, within each hemisphere lawyers may specialize further by client or subject matter. In Japan and Italy, for instance, some lawyers and law firms are closely associated with particular trade unions and political parties. A significant portion of barristers' sets in London specialize in subjects such as copyright, patent, admiralty, defamation, taxation, and commercial law. A number of American jurisdictions have certified specialists in certain fields and allowed them to advertise that fact, though they have not excluded generalists. Everywhere the degree of specialization is related to location (urban lawyers are more specialized than rural) and firm size (larger firms permit greater internal specialization, though smaller "boutique" firms may be more specialized as a whole).

It seems very likely that the range of functions performed by lawyers will increase in the future (especially as comfortable monopolies on conveyancing, divorce, and personal injury are dissolved), with the result that specialization both *by* firms (and other structures of practice) and *within* them will increase. The only alternative is a steady loss of business to competing occupations. The erosion of supply control should accelerate this: Young lawyers will have to carve new niches for themselves if they are not to compete with each other by cutting prices for the traditional repertoire of routine services. Yet where the earlier struggle for market control constructed the profession, the struggle to reassert control of submarkets threatens to deconstruct it.

B. Income and Status

Lawyers are even more reticent about what they earn than about what they do. The self-reported data, especially when collected for tax purposes, are highly suspect. French lawyers earn about 50% more than they report to the tax authorities. Although the poor economic situation of Italian lawyers is consistent with the relative lack of supply control and the extraordinarily low ratio of cases filed to practicing lawyers, it seems unlikely that 41% of avvocati really earn less than $500 a year (as they declare) and that the average lawyer earns no more than the national average for all occupations, less than manual workers or office clerks. We may place somewhat greater faith in comparisons within professions and occupations, though once again the fact that private practitioners are paid by clients rather than by employers, often in cash, may allow them to conceal a higher proportion of their income. Nevertheless, there are striking differences in the place of lawyers within national income distributions. At one extreme, lawyers are very well off. In a developing country like Brazil, only 7% make less than 3 times the national minimum wage (compared with 71% of all workers), and 17.5% make more than 20 times that minimum (compared with 0.6% of the general population). Law graduates of Recife (in northeastern Brazil) between 1935 and 1970 were in the top 5% of the income distribution and averaged 25 times the national minimum. A striking contrast can be found in an advanced industrialized country like Norway, with a homogeneous population and a highly developed welfare state. Lawyers in 1970 averaged only 2.5 times the median national income; 40% earned less than 2 times that median. Nevertheless, the 60% who earned more than 2 times the national average income must be compared with the 7% of the Norwegian population who enjoyed that level in 1979, and the 9% of lawyers who earned 4 times the national average compared with only 0.7% of the Norwegian population who earned that much.

Thus, even in Norway, lawyers remain at the top of the income spectrum, although the range of incomes is a good deal more compressed. One reason for the difference, of course, is that most Brazilian lawyers are private practitioners, whereas most Norwegian lawyers are employed. Even in Yugoslavia, lawyers are found in the middle of the top income bracket (which contains those employed in the socialized sector).

Another way of locating lawyers within the system of statification is to compare them with professions they see as competitors. Here they do less well and seem to be losing ground. In France, lawyers earn less than notaires (who have retained almost total supply control), surgeons, specialist doctors, dentists, architects, higher civil servants, and even veterinarians. In the United States, they fell behind physicians in the 1930s (again a reflection of the relative stringency of supply control in the two professions) and even behind dentists in the 1950s. In Canada between 1970 and 1980, lawyer income increased 70% but that of other professions grew more rapidly: accountants gained 76%, physicians 79%, and dentists 143%. In the United Kingdom, the income of barristers and solicitors also dropped below that of physicians and dentists before World War II but rose above it again with the creation of the National Health Service, which transformed most health care professionals into state employees. The average income of lawyers everywhere seems to have fallen in the last decade, with the entry of large numbers of newcomers who earn low salaries.

But these generalizations about professional income are very misleading because, as we have seen above, lawyers really encompass a multiplicity of professions, which differ enormously in earnings. Among private practitioners, the range seems to be greatest in Japan, where the highest decile of lawyers earns 5 to 9 times the lowest decile and 2 to 2.5 times the median. Similarly, the highest decile of English barristers earns 2.2 times the median (perhaps because of the explicit differentiation of QCs and the limitation on their numbers). The highest decile of English solicitors, by contrast, earns only 1.6 times the median. All legal professions seem to have not only a few "high fliers" at the top but also a depressed stratum at the bottom who barely manage to live on their professional incomes.

Income within the profession varies with a number of factors. Age is very important: The notion of a career in which the ambitious (or even the dogged) can aspire to greater income and prestige over time is virtually part of the definition of a profession; furthermore, the unsuccessful tend to drop out, thereby inflating the average income of the senior generation. In Japan, lawyers 50 years of age or older earn three times as much as those under 30 (partly because of the late age of entry). There are geographic differences also, with the highest earnings found in the capital (though this really is a surrogate for other variables). On average, private practitioners everywhere do better than salaried lawyers (although the latter typically start higher). Employees in the private sector are paid more than those in the public (except in Yugoslavia). Within private practice there are further distinctions. Specialists earn more than generalists; those specializing in high court litigation usually earn the most. Law firm partners earn more than solo practitioners (and of course more than law firm employees). Sometimes these differences are very large: Principals in English solicitors firms with 20 partners or more earn five times as much as solo practitioners; partners in Canadian firms with more than 40 partners earned more than three times as much as solo practitioners in 1979. On the other hand, there is little correlation between income and firm size in Scotland, perhaps because there are few large firms. Another way of expressing these differences is to note that lawyers who serve corporations earn more than those who handle the problems of individuals. Similarly, there is an inverse relationship between the proportion of income a private practitioner receives from public funds (i.e., legal aid) and the level of earnings. Thus, to the extent that the profession responds to the loss of supply control by creating publicly subsidized demand, it is likely to lose income as well as status and autonomy.

The status of lawyers in the eyes of the public is seriously at odds with their material privileges, for in almost every country their status seems to fall well below that of occupations with lower incomes. The prestige of national professions appears to vary inversely with the prominence of private practitioners within them, for "independent" professionals have the greatest difficulty balancing fidelity to client and loyalty to larger social interests, including the integrity of the judicial process. In France, lawyers rank at the very bottom of the prestige hierarchy, apparently because of public ambivalence about law; tension between lawyers' protestations of high ideals and their obviously selfish economic motives; and the taint of dirty work, clients, and environment. In Italy their prestige is low and declining, especially because they are seen as resisting necessary reforms of the legal system. In Spain, lawyers are thought to be dishonest if not actually corrupt, a suspicion that extends even to procuradores and judges. And in the United States lawyers are believed to be unethical and discourteous and to charge high fees for unnecessary work. Even in Germany they are respected less than doctors and academics. In Yugoslavia, judges and prosecutors are respected because of the security and income of their positions and their visible public service, but this does not extend to private practitioners. Similarly, judges are highly respected in common law countries like the United States, Canada, and the United Kingdom.

The demographic shifts in the composition of legal professions—both the large number of new entrants and their greater heterogeneity in gender and sometimes race—influence the work, income, and status of those professions. More intense competition will lead to a diversification of functions as lawyers seek protected niches, and this will produce a more fragmented profession. At the same time, the income distribution should grow more unequal, and the lower end should expand, depressing average income. The growth in numbers of employed lawyers and increasing reliance by private practitioners on public funds can only intensify those trends. And occupational status will continue to reflect a common contradiction: Individual clients respect their lawyers, but the general public has a very low regard for the profession as a whole.

IX. Self-Regulation

A. Professional Associations

A collegial association that promotes the general welfare is a central element of professional ideology. Although every legal profession described in the national reports possesses at least one such association, they differ greatly in organization, governance, and function. Some are local, others are national. Because lawyers initially were differentiated from other occupations through their relationship to courts, in which they have exclusive rights of audience and by which they are admitted and controlled, the earliest professional association was a local group attached to each court with compulsory membership. In Belgium there are 26 local bars; in France there are 179 barreaux; in Germany there are 19 Anwaltskammer, each connected with a court of appeal; in Italy membership in a local association is mandatory; in Spain an abogado must belong to at least 1 of the 52 provincial colegios de abogados or the 30 traditional local bars but can join any number; membership in 1 of the 21 regional colegios is mandatory in Venezuela.

English lawyers depart from this pattern in significant respects. For many centuries, barristers have been grouped in two mandatory institutions—the Inns of Court, which trained and admitted them, and the circuits, which regulated practice outside London; though each is associated with the higher courts (in London and in the provinces), these institutions were self-regulating and independent of courts or judges (though the latter did sit on their governing bodies). English solicitors, on the other hand, were wholly subordinate to the courts, which admitted them and could discipline and expel them. However, outside London and a very few large provincial cities, solicitors had no professional association until 1826, and the Law Society founded that year was national and voluntary rather than local and compulsory. Similarly, many local law societies in the United States died out in the early nineteenth century as the power to admit and discipline lawyers shifted to the states and their supreme courts; professional associations were largely dormant until the founding of the American Bar Association in 1878. This localism in continental European and Latin American professional associations probably permitted a high degree of informal control over who was admitted and how they behaved as lawyers, but it also hindered concerted action at the national level. And the official status of these institutions restrained them from acting as aggressive advocates of professional self-interest.

It is instructive to contrast the role of national associations in the formation of the English solicitors profession. The Society of Gentlemen Practicers, founded in 1739, was instrumental in negotiating the conveyancing monopoly in 1804, which later became the staple of solicitors' practice (if few recognized its significance at the time); but the society atrophied soon thereafter. The Law Society, founded in 1826, had to compete with rival provincial associations for half a century, yet ultimately, it eclipsed or absorbed them. Throughout the nineteenth century it played a major role in defining and policing the boundaries of the solicitors' monopoly, setting and raising the barriers to entry, and initiating solicitor training. Thus the Society more or less fits the theoretical model of a category of technical specialists who form a voluntary association in order to pursue their collective goal of becoming a profession.

But this was very atypical. National associations did not emerge as significant forces in most countries until well into the twentieth century, long after the professions had assumed their present form (partly because some countries were unified only in the late nineteenth century). And these associations tend to be reactionary forces rather than progressive, dedicated to preserving professional privileges and characteristics that are threatened by recent changes in the market, the educational system, and the state. English barristers, previously divided into four Inns and seven circuits, formed the Bar Council in 1883, and 90% had joined by 1968. Nevertheless, the organization was poor, weak, and relatively ineffective until 1966, when it was reorganized into the Senate, a federal structure that represents the Inns as well as individual members. In Belgium, a weak national association was created only in 1968. In Brazil, the national bar association had to be launched by federal legislation in 1930. In France, a national organization emerged in 1900 as a counterweight to the dominant Paris bar (just as the Metropolitan and Provincial Law Society was the rival of the Incorporated Law Society in nineteenth-century England), but it had little influence. In the United States, the American Bar Association did not become a potent force until the twentieth century; even today less than half of all lawyers are members, and the Association enjoys no legal authority over them, although the state bars that do exercise power pay great heed to the ABA. In Germany, Italy, Spain, and Venezuela, both mandatory and voluntary local bar associations are integrated in national federations, but it is the former that appear to retain most influence. In Scotland, a national association with compulsory membership was created by statute only in 1948. In Norway, lawyers need not belong to *any* professional association, though most join the national organization.

One reason why national professional associations arrive on the scene so late, tend to be fairly passive, and often are ineffective even when they take action is the heterogeneity of the profession they seek to represent: regional differences and variation in the structure of practice, clientele, subject matter, income, and status. The relative success of the Law Society in England and Wales may be attributable partly to the dominant role of conveyancing, which gives most solicitors a common interest (but then how to explain why Scottish solicitors, who rely almost as much on conveyancing, failed to form a strong national association). Therefore, it is not surprising that much professional activity is narrowly devoted to protecting the material interests that unite most lawyers. Another unifying principle is ideological attachment to the rule of law—the ultimate justification for legal representation. Thus professional associations of lawyers were prominent in the Indian independence movement and in the resistance to fascism in Spain and to military rule in Brazil and Ghana; and lawyers tend to support political liberalism in most other countries (even if they also are economic conservatives).

But such unity is exceptional and superficial. The irreducible heterogeneity of legal professions is mirrored more accurately in the failure of the governing bodies of professional associations to represent the multiple, diverse, and often antagonistic constituencies of lawyers. In the United States, Canada, New Zealand, and England and Wales, national associations are dominated by large-firm lawyers at the expense of solo and small-firm practitioners and lawyers employed in government or in industry and commerce, by urban lawyers at the expense of rural, by older lawyers at the expense of younger, and by men at the expense of women. The first woman was elected to the 70-member Council of the Law Society of England and Wales only in 1977/78. In Ontario, there are only 3 women among the 40 benchers of the Law Society.

This problem of reconciling the divergent interests of different categories of lawyers is certain to increase as the profession becomes more heterogeneous in background, structure, and function. Some categories, such as employed lawyers, are explicitly excluded from some kinds of professional associations. Even when admitted, they generally find such associations irrelevant to their concerns and choose, instead, to form their own groupings. Thus organizations of house counsel have emerged in Japan, Belgium, and the United Kingdom. Some ascriptive categories have suffered exclusion or prejudice in the past and continue to experience discrimination today. Although they may fight for a voice within mainstream organizations, they also establish their own: Ethnic minorities have done so in the United States, Canada, Australia, and the United Kingdom; and women have done so in many countries. Younger lawyers often feel alienated from traditional associations, especially when excluded from governance; they have formed their own organizations in France, Italy, the United States, and England. Political ferment has generated estrangement from traditional organizations, which either are politically conservative or refuse to take positions on controversial issues. Thus the Haldane Society was founded in England after World War I and the National Lawyers Guild in the United States during the Depression; associations of left lawyers and magistrates emerged in France and Italy during the 1960s; and the Ontario Law Union and the Australian Legal Workers Group were established more recently. I would expect the same to occur in New Zealand, if it has not happened already, for an extraordinary 24% of a sample of members of the Auckland Law Society in 1982 declared that their political ideology was radical left. On the other side of the political spectrum, those lawyers most threatened by the erosion of supply control and of anticompetitive practices have rejected the traditional organizations as insufficiently devoted to professional self-interest and formed groups that can advocate more vigorously because they are free from public responsibilities—the British Legal Association (which at one time claimed a membership of 10% of solicitors), voluntary associations in American states with unified bars and, more recently, the Ontario Lawyers' Association. Lawyers employed by government, by legal aid offices, and even by private firms specializing in legal aid in the United States and in England and Wales have gone one step further and sought to unionize, often affiliating with national trade unions. And private practitioners in Brazil, France, and Italy also have chosen the syndicalist form. Although French lawyers have created an umbrella organization to coordinate all these different groupings, it seems likely that professional associations will continue to fragment in order to reflect the increasing heterogeneity of law practice and will find themselves antagonists rather than allies on many important issues.

B. Discipline

Self-discipline is both one of the reasons why occupations professionalize and one of the foundations for their claim to continued autonomy. Yet the record of the legal profession in actually exercising discipline is not impressive. Most legal professions either have no code of professional conduct or have enacted one only recently: the United States in 1908, Brazil in 1934, and Canada in 1974 (replacing a very vague 1920 code). Scotland has few written rules, and English barristers have just codified theirs; Italy currently is debating whether to adopt a code. Those codes that do exist typically are written from the perspective of the private practitioner and have little to say about lawyers employed in government or industry or even those employed in private practice. Indeed, to the extent that employed lawyers are not members of the bar or other professional associations, there may be no effective sanctions for misconduct.

Discipline is exercised by a variety of forums. In most countries, the profession seems to have won both complete control over the early stages of the disciplinary process and exemption from any outside scrutiny (although English judges did not relinquish control to solicitors until 1919). This is crucial for, as we will see below, most complaints are resolved at these early stages. Nevertheless, the accused lawyer (not the aggrieved client) typically has the right to appeal to a body that includes judges as well as lawyers or to a court (as in Germany, Italy, the United States, and the United Kingdom). Recently, external criticism of the integrity of the disciplinary process led Canadian lawyers and Scottish and English solicitors to add laypeople to disciplinary bodies or appeal tribunals, though they remain a small minority with no significant impact on outcome or sanctions. The English Law Society also created a position for a "Lay Observer," who hears complaints from clients dissatisfied with the disciplinary process. Nevertheless, professional autonomy survives effectively intact.

The principal failing of professional discipline is its irrelevance to the vast bulk of client grievances. In every country these concern discourtesy, delay, incompetence, and overcharging. In Brazil, clients complain about lawyers who keep their papers too long, fail to inform them of the progress of their cases, and are impolite. In Scotland between 1976 and 1981, 38% of complaints against solicitors concerned delay, 23% lack of communication, and 13% negligence. A fourth of all complaints against English barristers concern inadequate representation, and another fourth allege bad advice, acting without instructions, lack of courtesy, withholding information, refusing to act, and delay. Clients of English solicitors complain about delay, inefficiency, negligence, discourtesy, and cost. These complaints are increasing; in Ontario the number of claims made against the now compulsory liability insurance more than tripled between 1972 and 1980, even when adjusted for the greater number of lawyers.

Yet professional disciplinary bodies typically disclaim jurisdiction over negligence or incompetence (which they relegate to malpractice litigation) and over fee disputes (which they view as contract matters), and they treat discourtesy and delay as too trivial to merit punishment. Instead, they focus on offenses against lawyers rather than against clients—breaches of honor or professional etiquette by other lawyers and unauthorized practice of law by laypersons—and on financial misconduct. Indeed, the latter is the one subject that many professions take very seriously because of the damage it does to professional reputation and because of the lack of ambiguity or excuse. In Ontario, 89% of disbarments between 1945 and 1965 were for financial misconduct. England and Wales, Scotland, and Canada all require solicitors to submit their accounts to periodic inspections, some make spot audits, and all have established funds (through compulsory solicitor contributions) from which *ex gratia* payments are made to clients who have been defrauded.

When clients do complain, the infrequency and mildness of the penalties imposed tend to confirm the popular suspicion that lawyers look after their own. In the United States, some 90% of all complaints are dismissed without a hearing, and only 1% of lawyers accused are subjected to court-imposed penalties (typically disbarment or suspension). In Paris in 1981, only 9 of the 5,542 practicing avocats (0.2%) were punished; of these, 2 were disbarred, 1 was suspended for three years, and 6 received mild sanctions. Three-fourths of all complaints against British barristers are dismissed without a hearing; 85% of complaints against solicitors were dismissed in the 1960s; 70% are dismissed today. Only 17–25% of hearings lead to punishment of a solicitor; as a result, only 0.8% of the complaints received between 1973 and 1979 led to punishment. In Scotland, the solicitors complaint department used to find two-thirds of the 600–1,000 annual complaints justified, but now it investigates only a third; 3% of all complaints are heard; and in the last two years, only 5 solicitors were struck from the rolls and 3 suspended. No advocate has been disbarred for 100 years. Given the mismatch between client grievances and the priorities and lenient penalties of disciplinary tribunals, it is not surprising that only 2% of British clients with grievances against their solicitors even complained to the Law Society.

The professional association has been central to common law legal professions, as both the vehicle for pursuing the professional project and a symbol of the autonomy thereby achieved, especially the power of self-regulation. But it has played a very different, and far less pivotal, role in civil law countries, where organizations frequently were local rather than national (reflecting divisions in the polity) and official rather than voluntary (inhibiting them from actively pursuing self-interest). Furthermore, these organizations were irrelevant to that large and prestigious segment of the civil law professions who were state (and later private) employees. Indeed, in some northern European countries the civil servant, not the private practitioner, was the prototypical lawyer. For the same reason, civil service bureaucracies, not professional associations, were the important agencies of discipline. The changes in both categories of legal profession in the last several decades have had significant implications for self-regulation. Civil law countries have produced lawyers more rapidly than public or private employment could absorb them, expanding the number of private practitioners. The latter are forming national associations that, for the first time, vigorously advocate professional interests and ideologies. Yet because the profession has grown more heterogeneous, the proliferating associations do not speak with a single voice. The common law world, on the other hand, is experiencing a rapid growth in numbers of employed lawyers, who neither look to the national professional association as their representative nor are effectively regulated by it. Even in private practice, the law firm exercises more meaningful control over employed lawyers than does the professional association. And the influence of the state over the profession has increased with the proliferation of administrative agencies and specialized courts that seek to regulate those who practice before them and with the growth of state legal aid programs that control the lawyers who receive public funds. Given these internal divisions and external pressures, it is not clear that the professional association will continue to perform a central role as either spokesperson or disciplinarian.

X. Conclusion

I have had two objectives in this article: to illustrate the insights that comparative analysis offers into the legal profession and to explore the strengths and weaknesses of a theoretical framework grounded on market control. The availability, for the first time, of sociological descriptions of 15 common law and civil law legal professions contributed to both goals. Civil law professions do not readily fit the model of professionalism that Freidson and Larson constructed, largely from their studies of the United States and England. In continental European countries and their former Latin American colonies, the university has played a central role in the production of lawyers for centuries, exerting a strong influence on both their numbers and their characteristics. The majority of these lawyers enter public or private employment, which further regulates numbers and dampens competition among them. Given the importance of these external institutions—university, state, and private employer—it is not surprising that voluntary associations have been relatively insignificant in the history and governance of the profession. Such global comparisons between total legal professions—more difficult but also more rewarding than the item-by-item comparisons that constitute most of this article—show the need to adapt the theory of market control to civil law countries. But they also reveal the existence of functional equivalents in both categories: Whereas apprenticeship, a first job, and more recently, competitive entry to university law departments are the principal modes of supply control in common law countries, completing a law degree and passing the state examinations have performed a similar function in civil law countries. And global comparisons also suggest that the two systems are converging under the influence of similar internal and external forces: Judges are declining as a proportion of civil law professions, while employed lawyers are rising as a proportion of common law professions, and the university legal education systems are growing more similar.

The theory of market control also highlights the ways in which the professional paradigm that emerged during the nineteenth and early twentieth centuries—most clearly in the common law world—appears to be disintegrating. Legal professions that limited numbers through apprenticeship and professional examinations have lost much of their control to the universities, which have produced lawyers at greatly increased rates during the last two decades. These larger numbers have intensified competition within the profession and led to the erosion of restrictive practices. They also have induced the profession, if reluctantly, to turn to strategies of demand creation, which inevitably encourage both concentration and greater reliance on the state. Expanded university entry has made the profession more heterogeneous, complicating efforts at concerted action and intensifying (and delegitimating) professional stratification. The archetype of the independent professional—the sole practitioner—has declined in numbers and been replaced by the lawyer employed by government, business, or a law firm. Notwithstanding the visibility of a few high fliers, the income and status of the profession as a whole have declined. Although professional associations have proliferated, none can claim to speak for the entire profession or engage in meaningful self-regulation.

The cumulative effect of these changes clearly has undermined the professional project. The unanswered question is what configuration the occupations of law will assume next.

APPENDIX TABLE 1 Entry to the Legal Profession

	England and Wales						Scotland				
			Barristers		*Solicitors*				*Solicitors*		*Advocates*
	Full-Time Univ. & Poly. Law Degree Candidates	Law Degrees[a]	Calls[b]	Starts	Admitted	Change in No. of Practice Certificates	Law Students	Law Degrees	Entering Apprenticeship	Admissions	Admissions
1982	....	....	682	282	2,241	1,943	....	....	392	381	....
1981	....	....	657	270	3,223	1,963	....	....	....	396	13
1980	12,603	3,706	624	309	3,538	3,742	1,850	529	253	397	15
1979	12,105	3,556	670	302	2,552	1,226	1,897	545	430	350	17
1978	11,817	3,494	671	285	2,538	56	1,887	503	390	308	15
1977	11,430	3,374	654	326	2,480	1,562	1,864	487	385	307	11
1976	11,136	3,015	628	382	2,184	1,400	....	443	354	283	13
1975	10,273	2,749	663	364	2,203	1,109	1,700	406	328	292	17
1974	9,223	2,615	529	299	1,849	1,362	....	371	314	....	....
1973	8,259	2,428	561	321	1,764	1,052	....	350	315	247	....
1972	7,335	2,341	586	275	1,713	961	....	329	278	....	....
1971	6,574	2,134	556	222	1,682	959	....	352	245	245	....
1970	5,998	2,021	471	241	1,877	833	1,260	312	248	116	....
1969	....	2,015	370	137	1,365	787	....	....	215	....	....
1968	....	1,824	246	139	997	564	....	....	....	....	....
1967	....	1,556	247	206	1,107	551	....	....	....	....	....
1966	....	1,480	236	129	1,123	417	....	....	....	....	....
1965	4,204	1,290	283	138	1,009	572	1,034	....	....	....	....
1964	3,838	....	237	80	663	414	....	....	113	....	....
1963	3,543	....	198	158	805	479					
1962	3,401	....	205	110	766	352					
1961	3,169	....	211	108	685	369					
1960	3,070	963	192	85	711	329					
1959	3,002	....	252	88	784	218					
1958	3,041	....	234	91	673	178					
1957	....	....	241	97	734	179					
1956	....	....	265	111	745	22					
1955	....	....	288	114	695	312					

NOTE: The presence of four dots in a column indicates unavailable data. [a]Includes External London LL.B. [b]British Domiciliaries

	England and Wales						Scotland				
			Barristers		*Solicitors*				*Solicitors*		*Advocates*
	Full-Time Univ. & Poly. Law Degree Candidates	Law Degrees[a]	Calls[b]	Starts	Admitted	Change in No. of Practice Certificates	Law Students	Law Degrees	Entering Appenticeship	Admissions	Admissions
1954	....	....	303	136	603	144	....	....	108	....	....
1953	2,604	....	328	155	649	59	....	....	....	....	....
1952	....	....	350	165	588	232	....	....	....	....	....
1951	....	....	340	174	717	361	....	....	....	....	....
1950	....	....	336	156	926	717	....	....	174	....	....
1949	....	....	317	196	895	751	....	....	....	....	....
1948	....	576	322	177	877	219	....	....	....	....	....
1947	....	....	253	131	904	....	....	....	....	....	....
1946	....	....	....	....	441	....	....	....	....	....	....
1945	....	....	....	....	180	−84	....	....	....	....	....
1944	....	....	....	....	117	−277	....	....	....	....	....
1943	....	....	....	....	122	−495	....	....	....	....	....
1942	....	....	....	....	104	−595	....	....	....	....	....
1941	....	....	....	....	194	−1,454	....	....	....	....	....
1940	....	....	....	....	323	−1,218	....	....	....	....	....
1939	....	....	....	....	567	203	....	....	....	....	....
1938	1,515	....	....	....	932	421	....	....	....	....	....
1937	....	....	....	....	831	179	....	....	....	....	....
1936	....	....	....	....	751	167	....	....	....	....	....
1935	....	....	....	....	630	191	....	....	170	....	....
1934	....	....	....	....	655	158					
1933	1,804	....	....	....	595	167					
1932	....	....	....	....	695	−52					
1931	....	....	....	....	615	220					
1930	....	....	....	....	680	122					
1929	....	....	....	....	610	129					
1928	....	....	....	....	580	25					
1927	....	....	....	....	440	--9					

NOTE: The presence of four dots in a column indicates unavailable data.

[a]Includes External London LL.B.

[b]British Domiciliaries

APPENDIX TABLE 1 Entry to the Legal Profession—*Continued*

	England and Wales					
			Barristers		*Solicitors*	
	Full-Time Univ. & Poly. Law Degree Candidates	Law Degrees[a]	Calls[b]	Starts	Admitted	Change in No. of Practice Certificates
1926	....	....	....	....	455	20
1925	....	....	....	....	455	61
1924	....	....	....	....	455	45
1923	....	....	....	....	444	137
1922	....	....	....	....	446	266
1921	....	....	....	....	383	−114
1920	....	....	....	....	606	387
1919	....	....	....	....	335	1,083
1918	....	....	....	....	81	194
1917	....	....	....	....	95	−516
1916	....	....	....	....	111	−626
1915	....	....	....	....	158	−889
1914	....	....	....	....	351	−852
1913	....	....	....	....	485	−20
1912	....	....	....	....	494	20
1911	....	....	....	....	489	−102
1910	....	....	....	....	501	−4
1909	....	....	....	....	561	120
1908	....	....	....	....	512	−16

NOTE: The presence of four dots in a column indicates unavailable data.

[a]Includes External London LL.B.
[b]British Domiciliaries.

	Belgium		France	Italy	Spain		India
	Law Students	Law Degrees Awarded	Stagiaires Paris Bar	Law Students	Law Students	Law Degrees	Law Students
1981	4,216	1,170	....	....	....	....	....
1980	4,119	1.118	....	....	....	....	....
1979	4,106	1,087	....	....	....	....	....
1978	3,993	1,060	....	....	74,117	4,650	....
1977	4,069	1,117	....	128,604	....	....	....
1976	3,807	1,188	....	....	....	....	....
1975	3,914	1,144	....	....	47,450	2,704	....
1974	3,980	977	....	....	....	....	....
1973	3,907	853	....	....	....	....	....
1972	3,572	909	....	....	....	....	....
1971	3,327	781	1,059	....	24,824	1,678	200,000
1970	3,036	671	842	....	....	....	....
1969	2,866	496	750	13,839	....	....	....
1968	2,321	404	653	....	....	....	....
1967	1,847	360	491	....	....	....	....
1966	1,491	358	503	....	....	....	....
1965	1,341	343	419	....	....	....	....
1964	1,221	327	340	....	....	....	....
1963	1,180	301	323	....	....	....	....
1962	1,132	374	331	....	....	....	....
1961	1,182	368	334	....	....	....	32,519
1960	1,325	415	316	....	....	....	....
1959	1,294	418	354	....	....	....	....
1958	1,395	435	469	....	....	....	....
1957	1,507	474	467	....	....	....	....
1956	1,593	495	492	....	....	....	....
1955	1,685	511	484	....	....	....	....
1954	1,750	494	482	....	....	....	....
1953	1,791	514	511	....	....	....	....
1952	1,788	495	557	....	....	....	....
1951	1,832	535	633	....	....	....	13,649

NOTE: The presence of four dots in a column indicates unavailable data.

APPENDIX TABLE 1 Entry to the Legal Profession—*Continued*

	Belgium		France	Italy	Spain		India
	Law Students	Law Degrees Awarded	Stagiaires Paris Bar	Law Students	Law Students	Law Degrees	Law Students
1950.....	....	550	792	....	....	....	....
1949.....	1,877	417	875	....	....	....	....
1948.....	1,740	273	897	....	....	....	....
1947.....	1,417	340	902	....	....	....	....
1946.....	1,148	335	797	....	....	....	....
1945.....	1,008	284	730	....	....	....	....
1944.....	....	276	589	....	....	....	....
1943.....	....	279	451	....	....	....	....
1942.....	....	270	442	....	....	....	....
1941.....	923	241	484	....	....	....	....
1940.....	832	267	524	....	....	....	....
1939.....	739	246	607	....	....	....	....
1938.....	....	248	643	....	....	....	....
1937.....	876	317	770	....	....	....	....
1936.....	....	322	840	....	....	....	....
1935.....	1,024	350	872	....	....	....	....
1934.....	....	272	857	....	....	....	....
1933.....	....	271	863	....	....	....	....
1932.....	....	222	792	....	....	....	....
1931.....	....	229	644	....	....	....	....
1930.....	....	240	611	....	....	....	....
1929.....	....	229	575	....	....	....	....
1928.....	....	205	711	....	....	....	....
1927.....	....	197	709	....	....	....	....
1926.....	....	196	730	....	....	....	....
1925.....	....	198	734	....	....	....	....
1924.....	....	....	756	....	....	....	....
1920.....	....	184	....	....	....	....	....
1910.....	....	142	....	....	....	....	....

NOTE: The presence of four dots in a column indicates unavailable data.

	Brazil	Canada			United States		
		No. of Law Degrees Awarded			*No. of Law Students*		
	No. of Law Students	Canada Total	Ontario	No. of Law Students	ABA Schools	All Schools	No. of Bar Admissions
1983.....	....	....	....	....	127,195	....	....
1982.....	....	....	....	....	127,828	....	....
1981.....	....	....	....	....	....	....	....
1980.....	135,026	....	....	....	125,397	128,983	....
1979.....	....	....	...	....	122,860	126,915	46,108
1978.....	....	....	....	....	121,606	126,937	41,662
1977.....	....	....	....	....	118,557	126,085	36,463
1976.....	....	....	....	9,351	117,451	125,010	35,741
1975.....	....	....	....	....	116,991	122,542	34,930
1974.....	....	....	....	....	110,713	116,517	33,358
1973.....	....	....	....	....	106,102	114,800	30,879
1972.....	....	2,268	873	....	101,664	105,245	25,086
1971.....	....	2,152	777	....	93,118	95,943	20,510
1970.....	....	1,949	726	....	82,041	86,028	17,922
1969.....	....	1,502	600	....	68,386	72,032	19,123
1968.....	....	1,323	517	....	62,779	68,562	17,764
1967.....	....	1,190	520	....	64,406	70,332	16,007
1966.....	....	1,041	419	....	62,556	68,121	14,637
1965.....	....	932	400	....	59,744	65,057	13,109
1964.....	....	767	315	....	54,625	59,813	12,023
1963.....	....	701	298	....	49,552	54,433	10,788
1962.....	....	588	249	2,896	44,805	48,663	10,784
1961.....	23,519	661	260	....	41,499	45,012	10,729
1960.....	....	697	305	....	40,381	43,695	10,505
1959.....	....	629	244	....	39,144	43,507	10,744
1958.....	....	712	231	....	39,144	42,645	10,465
1957.....	....	....	....	....	38,832	42,271	9,592
1956.....	....	....	....	....	37,949	41,888	9,450

NOTE: The presence of four dots in a column indicates unavailable data.

APPENDIX TABLE 1 Entry to the Legal Profession—*Continued*

	Brazil	Canada			United States		
		No. of Law Degrees Awarded			*No. of Law Students*		
	No. of Law Students	Canada Total	Ontario	No. of Law Students	ABA Schools	All Schools	No. of Bar Admissions
1955.....	....	....	....	....	35,792	40,347	9,587
1954.....	....	....	....	....	35,015	39,565	9,928
1953.....	....	....	....	....	34,423	39,339	10,976
1952.....	....	....	....	....	35,634	41,276	11,900
1951.....	....	....	....	....	39,626	47,610	13,141
1950.....	....	....	....	....	43,685	53,025	13,641
1949.....	....	....	....	....	46,645	57,759	13,344
1948.....	....	....	....	....	46,647	56,914	11,299
1947.....	....	....	....	....	....	51,015	6,782
1946.....	....	....	....	....	....	38,331	4,815
1945.....	....	....	....	....	....	10,752	2,142
1944.....	....	....	....	....	....	7,465	1,853
1943.....	....	....	....	....	4,797	6,428	2,973
1942.....	....	....	....	....	....	9,839	6,591
1941.....	....	....	....	....	....	22,033	7,706
1940.....	....	....	....	....	....	30,830	7,942
1939.....	....	....	....	....	....	33,508	8,531
1938.....	....	....	....	....	23,827	35,755	8,797
1937.....	....	....	....	....	24,029	38,056	8,934
1936.....	....	....	....	....	22,094	40,529	8,591
1935.....	....	....	....	....	20,430	41,418	8,971
1934.....	....	....	....	....	....	37,872	9,099
1933.....	....	....	....	....	....	37,057	9,258
1932.....	....	....	....	....	....	37,259	9,340
1931.....	....	....	....	....	17,483	39,868	9,676
1930.....	....	....	....	....	....	39,013	10,012
1929.....	....	....	....	....	....	43,876	10,397
1928.....	....	....	....	....	....	42,323	10,685

NOTE: The presence of four dots in a column indicates unavailable data.

	Brazil	Canada			United States		
	No. of Law Students	No. of Law Degrees Awarded		No. of Law Students	No. of Law Students		No. of Bar Admissions
		Canada Total	Ontario		ABA Schools	All Schools	
1927.....	....	....	....	....	....	44,341	10,026
1926.....	....	....	....	....	....	42,042	9,576
1925.....	....	....	....	....	....	38,412	8,211
1924.....	....	....	....	....	....	36,639	7,846
1923.....	....	....	....	....	....	36,211	7,106
1922.....	....	....	....	....	....	32,111	7,068
1921.....	....	....	....	....	....	....	5,777
1920.....	....	....	....	....	....	20,992	6,004
1919.....	....	....	....	....	....	24,503	....
1910.....	....	....	....	....	....	19,567	4,125
1909.....	....	....	....	....	....	19,498	....
1900.....	....	....	....	....	....	12,516	2,750
1899.....	....	....	....	....	....	12,408	....
1889.....	....	....	....	....	....	4,486	....

NOTE: The presence of four dots in a column indicates unavailable data.

APPENDIX TABLE 2 Size of Legal Professions

Belgium			Brazil			Canada (Ontario Only)					
	No.	% Average Annual Change		No.	% Average Annual Change		No.	% Average Annual Change		No.	% Average Annual Change
1982	22,100	5.3	1980	98,460	11.4	1981 . . .	15,294	6.5	1967 . . .	6,327	3.1
1970	13,463	1.8	1970	46,036	3.5				1966 . . .	6,136	3.3
1961	11,554	0.2	1960	34,047	7.8	1976 . . .	11,542	9.2	1965 . . .	5,942	1.6
1947	8,143		1951	19,177		1975 . . .	10,572	5.5	1964 . . .	5,850	3.5
						1974 . . .	10,025	8.1	1963 . . .	5,651	2.7
						1973 . . .	9,277	7.0	1962 . . .	5,501	3.5
						1972 . . .	8,668	13.9	1961 . . .	5,316	3.5
						1971 . . .	7,610	−0.7	1951 . . .	3,932	3.6
						1970 . . .	7,666	3.9			
						1969 . . .	7,381	8.3	1936 . . .	2,556	

England and Wales

	Barristers		Solicitors	
	No.	% Average Annual Change	No.	% Average Annual Change
1982	4,864	3.8	41,738	4.9
1981	4,685	2.1	39,795	5.2
1980	4,589	4.0	37,832	11.0
1979	4,412	3.5	34,090	3.7
1978	4,263	4.6	32,864	0.2
1977	4,076	5.0	32,812	5.0
1976	3,881	6.4	31,250	4.7
1975	3,646	8.3	29,850	3.9
1974	3,368	7.4	28,741	5.0
1973	3,137	7.5	27,379	4.0
1972	2,919	7.4	26,327	3.8
1971	2,714	5.0	25,366	3.9
1970	2,584	5.6	24,407	3.5
1969	2,448	2.9	23,574	3.5
1968	2,379	2.0	22,787	2.5
1967	2,333	4.2	22,223	2.5
1966	2,239	3.5	21,672	2.5
1965	2,164	2.2	21,255	2.0
1964	2,118	2.2	20,683	2.8
1963	2,073	5.5	20,269	2.0
1962	1,964	2.4	19,790	2.5
1961	1,918	−0.1	19,438	1.8
1960	1,919	−0.2	19,069	1.9
1959	1,923	−1.2	18,740	1.8
1958	1,947	−1.1	18,522	1.1
1957	1,968	−0.3	18,344	1.0
1956	1,973	−1.7	18,165	1.0
1955	2,008	−0.1	18,143	0.1
1954	2,010	5.4	17,831	1.7
1953	1,907		17,687	0.3
1952			17,628	1.3
1951			17,396	2.1
1950			17,035	4.4
1949			16,318	4.8
1948			15,567	1.4
1947			15,438	9.1
1945			12,979	−0.6
1944			13,063	−2.1
1943			13,340	−3.6
1942			13,385	−4.1
1941			14,430	−9.1
1940			15,884	−7.1
1939			17,102	1.2
1938			16,899	2.6
1937			16,478	1.1
1936			16,299	1.0
1935			16,132	1.2
1934			15,941	1.0

APPENDIX TABLE 2 Size of Legal Professions—*Continued*

Federal Republic of Germany

	No.	% Average Annual Change
1980 ...	36,081	6.6
1974 ...	25,851	2.9
1961 ...	18,720	5.8
1951 ...	11,818	

France

	No.	% Average Annual Change
1982 ...	15,315	−2.3
1981 ...	15,715	3.6
1980 ...	15,170	4.8
1979 ...	14,480	3.7
1978 ...	13,959	12.5
1977 ...	12,408	4.5
1976 ...	11,869	6.3
1975 ...	11,169	7.8
1974 ...	10,365	24.8
1973 ...	8,307	4.6
1972 ...	7,941	2.4
1970 ...	7,756	

Italy

	No.	% Average Annual Change
1980 ...	46,620	1.5
1968 ...	39,415	2.1
1966 ...	37,800	

Japan

	No.	% Average Annual Change
1976 ...	10,792	3.9
1956 ...	6,040	0.0
1936 ...	5,976	6.2
1916 ...	2,665	3.5
1896 ...	1,568	

Netherlands

	No.	% Average Annual Change
1980.....	3,726	9.6
1976.....	2,694	5.8
1970.....	2,000	0.3
1960.....	1,947	2.2
1947.....	1,509	

New Zealand

	No.	% Average Annual Change		No.	% Average Annual Change
1981 ...	4,041	2.9	1911 ...	950	4.2
1976 ...	3,525	6.5	1906 ...	785	0.8
1971 ...	2,660	2.5	1901 ...	636	1.0
1966 ...	2,366	2.1	1896 ...	604	1.2
1961 ...	2,091	1.5	1891 ...	571	2.3
1956 ...	1,945	3.1	1886 ...	511	8.2
1945 ...	1,455	−1.9	1881 ...	362	9.0
1936 ...	1,762	0.8	1878 ...	285	6.0
1926 ...	1,635	6.5	1874 ...	230	0.0
1921 ...	1,234	1.9	1871 ...	229	
1916 ...	1,125	3.7			

Norway

	No.	% Average Annual Change
1979.....	6,572	2.7
1969.....	5,188	−0.2
1959.....	5,206	

Scotland								
	Solicitors				Advocates			
	Enrollments		Practitioners		Enrollments		Practitioners	
	No.	% Average Annual Change	No.	% Average Annual Change	No.	% Average Annual Change	No.	% Average Annual Change
1982.....	....		5,329	6.5	387	2.4	183	7.9
1981.....	5,830	4.3	....	....	....	....	....	....
1979.....	....	....	....	....	361	3.0	148	3.9
1975.....	....	....	3,666	3.1	322	1.6	128	1.5
1971.....	4,083	0.8	3,267	0.3	....	....	....	....
1967.....	....	....	....	....	285	0.2	114	1.5
1964.....	....	....	3,198	−0.3	....	....	....	
1962.....	....	....	....		281	0.2	106	
1961.....	3,780	0.4	....		....	....	....	
1954.....	....	....	3,306		....	....	....	
1951.....	3,629	1.6	....		276	0.7	....	
1938.....	3,128	−0.6	....		....	....	....	
1931.....	3,321	0.0	....		259	−1.1	....	
1921.....	3,349	−1.4	....		292	−1.5	....	
1911.....	3,900	0.8	....		345	−0.1	....	
1901.....	3,621	2.9	....		349	1.8	....	
1891.....	2,815	2.3	....		296	8.7	....	
1881.....	2,284	1.7	....		158	−1.2	....	
1871.....	1,946	0.0	....		179	−1.8	....	
1861.....	1,973		....		219		....	

NOTE: The presence of four dots in a column indicates unavailable data.

APPENDIX TABLE 2 Size of Legal Professions—*Continued*

United States						Venezuela		
	No.	% Average Annual Change		No.	% Average Annual Change		No.	% Average Annual Change
1983	622,000	4.5	1967	316,856	1.8	1982	15,000	1.8
1982	595,107	4.6	1963	296,069	1.2	1978	14,000	10.4
1981	569,000	4.9	1960	285,933	3.0	1971	8,102	9.0
1980	542,205	5.8	1957	262,320	2.9	1961	4,256	9.4
1977	462,000	5.7	1954	241,514	3.0	1950	2,087	13.1
1972	358,920	0.5	1951	212,605	1.8	1941	957	
1970	355,242	4.0	1941	179,567				

APPENDIX TABLE 3 Entry of Women into the Legal Profession (Percent of Total)

Belgium

Year[a]	Law School Enroll-ment	Receiving Law Degree	Holding Law or Notary Degree
1981	36	35	....
1980	35	37	....
1979	36	36	....
1978	35	33	....
1977	33	35	....
1976	34	35	....
1975	34	33	....
1974	33	27	....
1973	31	28	....
1972	29	22	....
1971	25	23	....
1970	23	24	11
1969	22	21	....
1968	22	16	....
1967	21	13	....
1966	17	16	....
1965	16	15	....
1964	16	15	....
1963	16	17	....
1962	15	19	....
1961	16	15	7.9
1960	14	12	....
1959	14	13	....
1958	13	13	....
1957	13	14	....
1956	13	12	....
1955	13	12	....
1954	12	15	....
1953	13	14	....
1952	14	14	....

Year[a]	Law School Enroll-ment	Receiving Law Degree	Holding Law or Notary Degree
1951	14	11	....
1950	....	....	....
1949	12	9	....
1948	11	2	....
1947	8	5	3.5
1946	7	7	....
1945	5	7	....
1944	....	....	....
1941	4	6	....
1940	5	4	....
1939	5	7	....
1938	....	5	....
1937	6	5	1.7
1936	....	8	....
1935	8	7	....
1934	....	5	....
1933	....	4	....
1932	....	5	....
1931	....	4	....
1930	....	6	....
1929	....	7	....
1885	....	0.5	....

Brazil

Year[a]	Holding Law Degree
1980	25
1970	13
1960	7
1950	3.3

Canada

Year[a]	Students	Ontario Lawyers
1980	37	....
1962	5	....
1960	....	3.3
1950s[s]	....	3.3 (1951)
1940s[s]	....	2.6 (1941)
1930s[s]	....	1.1 (1931)

NOTE: The presence of four dots in a column indicates unavailable data.

[a] Academic year beginning in fall.

[s] Average for decade.

APPENDIX TABLE 3 Entry of Women into the Legal Profession (Percent of Total)—*Continued*

	England and Wales								
	University		*Polytechnic*			*Barristers*		*Solicitors*	
Year[a]	Entrants	Degrees	Full-Time Day	Other	Degrees	Calls	Bar	Admissions	Practicing Certificates
1982	....	....	....	....	....	....	11	35	....
1981	....	....	....	...	39	....	10	30	....
1980	....	....	....	....	32	....	10	28	10
1979	....	....	...	....	31	....	9	....	....
1978	39	31	....	30	30	....	9	25	....
1977	37	30	34	28	....	....	9	....	7
1976	34	29	28	26	....	....	8	....	6
1975	31	27	24	20	....	17	7	....	5
1974	30	23	23	16	....	19	8	15	5
1973	28	24	22	17	....	17	8	13	4
1972	27	19	21	15	....	15	7	12	4
1971	23	18	18	15	....	16	6	10	3
1970	23	18	16	13	....	19	6	9	3
1969	20	16	15	10	....	25	5	7	3
1968	19	14	10	10	....	....	6	9	3
1967	17	14	11	11	....	....	5	8	....
1966	....	....	....	....	....	....	5	6	....
1965	....	....	....	....	....	15	5	6	....
1964	....	....	....	....	....	....	5	....	....
1963	....	....	....	....	....	....	5	....	2
1962	....	....	....	....	....	....	5	....	....
1961	....	....	....	....	....	....	5	....	....
1960	....	....	....	....	....	17	....	....	....
1959	....	....	....	....	....	....	....	7	...
1958	....	....	....	....	....	....	4	5	....
1957	....	....	....	....	....	....	4	....	2

NOTE: The presence of four dots in a column indicates unavailable data.

[a]Academic year beginning in fall.

England and Wales

	University		Polytechnic			Barristers		Solicitors	
Year[a]	Entrants	Degrees	Full-Time Day	Other	Degrees	Calls	Bar	Admissions	Practicing Certificates
1956	....	....	....	....	....	....	3	....	....
1955	....	....	....	....	....	....	3	....	....
1954	....	....	....	...	....	...	4	....	....
1951	....	....	....	....	...	...	....	....	3
1950s[s]	....	....	....	....	....	....	....	4	....
1948	....	....	....	....	....	....	....	....	....
1940s[s]	....	....	....	....	...	....	....	3	....
1930s[s]	....	....	....	....	....	....	....	2	0.7
1920s[s]	....	....	....	....	...	....	....	2	....

NOTE: The presence of four dots in a column indicates unavailable data. [a]Academic year beginning in fall. [s]Average for decade.

New Zealand

Year[a]	Lawyers
1981	8.9
1976	4.2
1971	1.8
1966	1.3
1961	1.6

Scotland

	Solicitors		Advocates
Year[a]	Admissions	On Roll	
1982	36	17	8
1981	34	16	....
1980	33	15	....
1979	30	13	5
1978	22	12	....
1977	27	11	....
1976	21	11	....
1975	11	9	3

APPENDIX TABLE 3 Entry of Women into the Legal Profession (Percent of Total)—*Continued*

United States								
Year[a]	Law School Enrollment[b]	Lawyers	Year[a]	Law School Enrollment[b]	Lawyers	Year[a]	Law School Enrollment[b]	Lawyers
1984	....	13	1967	5	....	1953	4	....
1980	34	12	1966	4	3–4	1952	4	....
1979	31	11	1965	4	....	1951	4	....
1978	30	10	1964	4	....	1950	3	....
1977	27	9	1963	4	3	1949	3	....
1976	26	8–9	1962	4	....	1948	3	2
1975	23	7	1961	4	....	1944	22	....
1974	20	6	1960	4	3	1943	25	....
1973	16	5	1959	4	....	1940	....	2
1972	12	5	1958	3	....	1930	....	2
1971	9	5	1957	3	3	1920	....	1
1970	9	5	1956	3	....	1910	....	1
1969	7	....	1955	4	....			
1968	6	....	1954	4	2			
			1953	4	....			

NOTE: The presence of four dots in a column indicates unavailable data. [a]Academic year beginning in fall. [b]ABA-approved schools.

APPENDIX TABLE 4 Professional Divisions: Size and Growth

Belgium

	Private Practitioners		EMPLOYMENT: Government and Education		EMPLOYMENT: Private		EMPLOYMENT: All Employment		Judges		Notaries	
	No.	% Change	No.	% Change	No.	% Change	No.	% Change	No.	% Change	No.	% Change
1982	6,886	80	....		....		12,332	80	1,671	5	1,226	2
1970	3,827	5	2,390	19	4,458	22	6,848	21	1,586	45	1,202	3
1961	3,641	10	2,008	91	3,648	137	5,656	118	1,091	−2	1,166	3
1947	3,309	−9	1,052	47	1,540	47	2,592	47	1,116	37	1,128	−3
1937	3,627		....		....		1,759		813		1,165	

Brazil

	Lawyers & Public Defenders		Attorneys, Prosecutors, & Public Curators		Judges	
	No.	% Change	No.	% Change	No.	% Change
1980	85,716	127	8,130	73	4,624	28
1970	37,719	25	4,693	186	3,624	55
1960	30,066	93	1,640	22	2,341	3
1950	15,566		1,346		2,265	

TABLE 4 Professional Divisions: Size and Growth—*Continued*

England and Wales

	SOLICITORS										BARRISTERS	
	Private Practitioners				**Employed**							
	Principals		*Consultants & Assistants*		*Local Government*		*Central Government*		*Industry/ Commerce*			
	No.	% Change	No.	% Change	No.	% Change	No.	% Change	No.	% Change	No.	% Change
1982	23,083	38	12,633	102	2,899	61	66	38	1,799	111	4,864	67
1972	16,669	20	6,241	99	1,804	17	48	−11	851	63	2,919	49
1962	13,940	6	3,141	23	1,544	10	54	108	523	21	1,964	
1957	13,178	21	2,559	13	1,409		26		430	−16	1,968	
1939	10,923		2,256				1,991[a]		512			

[a]Employment in both local and central government.

France

	Lawyers			*Advocates*		*Syndics & Administrateurs Judiciares*	*Legal Advisers*	*Notaries*	*Marshalls*	*Court Registrars*
	All Lawyers[a]	Apprentices	% Change	Court of Appeal	Cour d'Etat/ Cour de Cassation					
1982	15,315	....	−2.3	291	74	352	4,271	6,897	2,765	240
1981	15,715	4,033	3.6	280	67	350	4,312	6,785	2,763	236
1980	15,170	3,975	4.8	267	64	302	4,142	6,686	2,744	234
1979	14,480	3,631	3.7	270	62	298	4,153	6,585	2,687	264
1978	13,959	3,574	12.5	266	62	298	4,047	6,539	2,671	249
1977	12,408	....	4.5	262	60	285	....	6,448	2,637	234
1976	11,869	....	6.3	257	60	288	....	6,416	2,607	228
1975	11,169	....	7.8	250	60	286	....	6,352	2,501	236
1974	10,365	....	24.8	247	60	295	....	6,348	2,544	224
1973	8,307	....	4.6	245	60	292	....	6,333	....	213
1972	7,941	....	2.4	243	60	292	....	6,365	2,432	208
1971	7,756	....		239	60	286	....	6,339	2,403	206

[a]Includes apprentices.

Germany	Lawyers	Prose-cutors	Judges
1982	38,000	3,600	17,000

India	Lawyers	Judges
1970	90,906	5,943

Japan	Judges			Prosecutors			Private Practitioners			
	No.	% of Total	% Change	No.	% of Total	% Change	No.	% of Total	% Change	*Total*
1976	1,912	13.8	20	1,173	8.5	17	10,792	77.8	79	13,877
1956	1,597	18.5	15	1,000	11.6	54	6,040	69.9	1	8,637
1936	1,391	17.4	54	648	8.1	66	5,976	74.6	124	8,015
1916	903	22.8	−26	389	9.8	2	2,665	67.3	70	3,957
1896	1,221	38.5		383	12.1		1,568	49.4		3,172

APPENDIX TABLE 4 Professional Divisions: Size and Growth—*Continued*

	Norway						
	Percent						
	Private Practice	Government Administration	Police & Prosecution	Private Employment	Bus. & Org. Management	Judicial	Education
1970	24	31	5	6	20	8	3

	Scotland													
	SOLICITORS										ADVOCATES		JUDGES	
	Private Practitioners				**Employed**									
	Principals		*Consultants & Assistants*		*Local Government*		*Central Government*		*Industry/ Commerce*					
	No.	% Change	No.	% Change	No.	% Change	No.	% Change	No.	% Change	No.	% Change	No.	% Change
1982	3,142	20	1,187	253	500	25	411	45	89	147	173	35	*ca.* 100	
1975	2,608	8	336	−24	400	58	283	167	36	−25	128			
1954	2,420		445		253		106		48					

United States

Lawyers in Private Practice or Employed in the Private Sector

	Private Practitioners						Employed					
	Solo & Partners			*Associates*			*Private Sector*			*Education*		
	No.	% of Total	% Change	No.	% of Total	% Change	No.	% of Total	% Change	No.	% of Total	% Change
1980	321,528	59.3	39	47,714	8.8	76	59,017	10.9	47	6,606	1.2	55
1970	231,263	65.1	10	26,998	7.6	18	40,142	11.3	20	4,263	1.1	49
1966	209,759	66.2	4	22,814	7.2	19	33,587	10.6	11	2,852	0.9	20
1963	201,919	68.2	0	19,244	6.5	16	30,199	10.2	15	2,369	0.8	18
1960	201,297	70.4	2	16,584	5.8	29	26,306	9.2	21	2,002	0.7	27
1957	197,265	75.2	1	12,854	4.9	13	21,773	8.3	31	1,574	0.6	9
1954	195,143	80.8	7	11,351	4.7	11	16,664	6.9	32	1,449	0.6	9
1951	182,159	82.2		10,194	4.6		12,631	5.7		1,330		
1948	....	84.8		....	4.4							

United States

Lawyers in the Judiciary and Government

	Judiciary			Government								
				Federal			*State*[a]			*Local*		
	No.	% of Total	% Change	No.	% of Total	% Change	No.	% of Total	% Change	No.	% of Total	% Change
1980	19,160	3.6	69	20,132	3.7	−2	30,358	5.6	61	....	....	....
1970	11,368	3.2	12	20,604	5.8	16	10,302	2.9	25	8,526	2.4	3
1966	10,139	3.4	4	17,744	5.6	7	8,238	2.6	16	8,238	2.6	−4
1963	9,770	3.3	7	16,580	5.6	12	7,106	2.4	46	8,586	2.9	−9
1960	9,150	3.2	6	14,869	5.2	7	4,861	1.7	9	9,436	3.3	9
1957	8,657	3.3	0	13,903	5.3	40	4,459	1.7	15	8,657	3.3	−8
1954	8,695	3.6	9	9,902	4.1	9	3,864	1.6	−3	9,419	3.9	9
1951	7,978	3.6		9,086	4.1		3,989	1.8		8,643	3.9	
1948	....	4.6		....	3.6		....			....	4.7	

NOTE: The presence of four dots in a column indicates unavailable data.

[a]Data for 1980 combined state and local government.

[11]

Specialization and Prestige in the Legal Profession: The Structure of Deference

Edward O. Laumann and John P. Heinz

The process of specialization is now well advanced within the legal profession, and the specialties have acquired clearly varying levels of prestige among the practicing bar. What are the characteristics of the specialties, or of the lawyers who practice in them, that might account for these variations in prestige? In describing the prestige differences and several of the variables that might be thought to account for them, the authors analyze the results of a survey of a large random sample of Chicago lawyers. Among the findings are a strong relationship between prestige within the legal profession and the type of clients that the specialty serves, a substantial correlation between prestige and the degree of intellectual challenge presented by the subject matter of the specialty, and the perhaps surprising result that prestige is not significantly associated with the income earned by lawyers practicing in the specialty. The authors conclude that legal specialties that regularly confront personal suffering lose social standing as a result, that prestige within the profession is directly proportional to the degree to which the specialty facilitates the conduct of corporate enterprise, and that the varying prestige of the specialties is likely to affect the political and professional power of the lawyers who practice in them and to influence the patterns of recruitment of lawyers into law practice.

INTRODUCTION

Seventy percent of a large, random sample of Chicago lawyers say that they consider themselves specialists in one or more of the subfields

---

Edward O. Laumann is Professor of Sociology and Director of the Center for Social Organization Studies, University of Chicago, and Affiliated Scholar, American Bar Foundation. A.B. Oberlin College, 1960; Ph.D. Harvard University, 1964.

John P. Heinz is Professor of Law, Northwestern University, and Visiting Scholar, American Bar Foundation. A.B. Washington University, St. Louis, 1958; LL.B. Yale Law School, 1962.

This study has been conducted under the sponsorship of the American Bar Foundation, with funding provided by the American Bar Endowment and by the Russell Sage Foundation. The researchers have received valuable advice from more than a score of members of the Chicago bar, as well as from their colleagues at the University of Chicago and Northwestern University, most notably Edward Shils, Morris Janowitz, and Spencer Kimball. Especially helpful in the technical aspects of executing the data analysis were our research assistants, Charles Cappell, Peter Marsden, and Scott Marden. The authors wish to acknowledge, with gratitude, their considerable debts to all of these persons and institutions.

of law. Some of their responses may, of course, have been biased by the connotation of expertise and prestige that is carried by the term "specialist." But these connotations are, themselves, of some relevance to the subject of this paper, which is the relationship between prestige within the legal profession and specialization in the various types of legal work.

The article begins with a brief description of some characteristics of the legal profession that are particularly relevant to the phenomenon of specialization. We then comment on the sociological literature concerning the nature of prestige; the concept is rather more elusive than it may seem. After summarizing the design and scope of our research, we turn to the description and analysis of the findings. Most simply, the research addresses two major questions: First, what is the relative prestige standing within the legal profession of the various specialties or types of legal work? Second, what differences among these specialties or among the lawyers who practice in them might account for the variations in professional prestige?

In the final section of the article, we explore some of the possible implications of the findings. The varying prestige of the specialties might, for example, help to account for their differential attractiveness to lawyers making career choices. And because friendships and professional relationships are more likely to occur between persons of equal social status, perceptions of prestige differences may also influence the patterns of communication within the profession, thus tending to restrict the diffusion of information across specialty lines. This limitation of communication might not only affect the transmission of information about the law and the profession but also tend to limit the communication of social value positions or of positions on issues of legal ethics. If so, the pressure that peers might bring to bear on questions of values or ethics would be restricted to that of practitioners within like specialty groups. Thus, the perceptions of prestige differences among the specialties may enhance the fragmentation of the profession into a number of discrete, insular groups, each composed of lawyers with homogeneous social or professional status and, perhaps, a common point of view. The prestige differences might, then, also influence the flow of clients and cases within the profession by segmenting the referral networks. Yet another possible consequence of disparities in professional prestige might be the creation or enhancement of corresponding disparities in power or influence within the profession or the broader community. Only a few of these implications of prestige differences are specifically addressed in this paper. Other papers will be forthcoming from this research project, which aims at a reasonably comprehensive description and analysis of the social structure of the legal profession in a major city.

THE PROFESSION: CONTEXT

Only in the last two or three years have a few states begun to recognize and certify legal specialties in a manner at all analogous to the recognition of specialization that has so long been established in the medical profession. These initial steps in the certification of legal specialties are, moreover, highly tentative, recognizing only a few specialties and being formally labeled as "experimental."[1] The bar examinations require some minimal level of competence in all of the major, traditional fields of law as a condition of entry into the profession, and, with the few exceptions already noted, there is no further examination available to the lawyer who may wish to demonstrate special competence in a particular field. Moreover, some legal institutions buttress the resistance to specialization. Most American courts have "general jurisdiction," and thus the lawyers who become judges should, in theory, be competent to decide the full range of legal issues. And yet, in spite of the continuing vitality of the myth of the omnicompetent lawyer, the inexorable advance of the division of labor within the legal profession has been too obvious to ignore. More than 40 years ago, Karl Llewellyn said of the "modern metropolitan bar":

> Most of its best brains, most of its inevitable leaders, have moved masswise out of court work, out of a general practice akin to that of the family doctor, into highly paid specialization in the service of large corporations.[2]

Llewellyn also noted the social differentiation that specialization had enhanced:

> "The Bar" is in this country an almost meaningless conglomeration. What we have is lawyers, by their tens of thousands–individual lawyers without unity of tradition, character, background, or objective; as single persons, many of them powerful; as a guild, inert beyond easy understanding.[3]

In the four decades since Llewellyn wrote, the degree of differentiation within the profession has increased further as the size of the profession has grown, recruitment has broadened, and specialization has proceeded.

While specialization was reinforcing social differentiation at the individual level, however, a process of integration was occurring in the organizational contexts within which the law is practiced. Industrialization, the rise of large corporations, and the consequent growth of

1. Richard F. Zehnle, Specialization in the Legal Profession: An Analysis of Current Proposals (Chicago: American Bar Foundation, 1975).
2. K. N. Llewellyn, The Bar Specializes–With What Results? 167 Annals 177 (1933).
3. *Id.* at 178.

government regulation of economic enterprise have for at least a century steadily increased the consolidation of law practice into larger and larger firms. Though two-thirds of the lawyers in private practice at the end of World War II were individual entrepreneurs, or solo practitioners, the solos had declined to half of the private practitioners by 1970, and the trend was even more pronounced in large cities.[4] Moreover, the number of private practitioners of all sorts, including lawyers in firms, declined from 89 percent of the bar in 1948 to 73 percent in 1970 as a result of large increases in the numbers of salaried lawyers employed by corporations as "house counsel" or by the various levels of government.[5] There is reason to believe that these trends have continued since 1970.[6]

These developments—specialization, social differentiation, and changes in organizational work setting—have taken place within the context of a rapid increase in the overall size of the profession. In the last 25 years the estimated number of lawyers in the nation has increased steadily; there were about 220,000 in 1951, 285,000 in 1960, 355,000 in 1970, and well in excess of 400,000 in 1975.[7] This has meant a decline in the population per lawyer from 696 persons per lawyer in 1951 to 572 per lawyer in 1970. In 1974 there were just under 14,000 lawyers with offices in the city of Chicago, and interviews with a random sample of those lawyers have provided the primary body of data analyzed in this paper.

FOR THE SOCIOLOGICALLY INCLINED: A COMMENT ON PRESTIGE

This paper will address two major substantive issues: First, what is the nature and extent of the differences among a selected set of legal specialties in a metropolitan bar in terms of their social and educational composition, characteristic work activities and clients served, and levels of extrinsic and intrinsic rewards for the performance of these services? Second, to what extent do these bases of differentiation help to explain the varying prestige or deference standing accorded legal specialties within the profession?

These questions, specifically referring to the legal profession, are

4. Bette H. Sikes, Clara N. Carson, & Patricia Gorai, The 1971 Lawyer Statistical Report (Chicago: American Bar Foundation, 1972); Jack Ladinsky, The Impact of Social Backgrounds of Lawyers on Law Practice and the Law, 16 J. Legal Educ. 127, 139 (1963).

5. Sikes, Carson, & Gorai, *supra* note 4.

6. John P. Heinz, Edward O. Laumann, Charles L. Cappell, Terence C. Halliday, & Michael H. Schaalman, Diversity, Representation, and Leadership in an Urban Bar: A First Report on a Survey of the Chicago Bar, 1976 A.B.F. Res. J. 717.

7. Sikes, Carson, & Gorai, *supra* note 4. 1975 figure is ABA estimate.

only particular instances of two heated controversies raging in the literature on the emerging theory of social differentiation and inequality in social systems.[8] On the one hand, sharply divergent answers have been advanced to the question of how the differences among social positions come to be treated as grounds for according unequal rewards, privileges, and social regard to them. On the other, there have been extended debates over the nature of the consequences of these inequalities for the incumbents of these positions as well as for the system as a whole. In addition, characterizing the nature of social differentiation among social positions–given the plethora of possible bases of differentiation that could be deemed relevant–has proven especially troublesome in empirical work. This problem has been most acutely encountered in the study of modern societies with their multifaceted occupational structures. By focusing on a single occupation, we have circumvented some of these difficulties because it has been possible to gather more detailed data than could realistically be acquired for a society's occupational structure as a whole. Thus, while the main focus of the following analysis is necessarily on the legal profession, we do hope to illuminate more general theoretical issues regarding the process of prestige allocation.

The literature on prestige and deference is rife with conceptual confusion and methodological disagreements on what should be meant by the term "prestige" and, once that issue is somehow resolved, on how best to measure prestige differences and to describe the prestige-generating process. Most theoretical and empirical discussions are oriented almost exclusively to the differential evaluation of positions in the society as a whole, as in the National Opinion Research Center (NORC) studies of occupational or ethnic group prestige[9] of Shils's dis-

8. *Cf.* Kingsley Davis & Wilbert E. Moore, Some Principles of Stratification, 10 Am. Soc. Rev. 242 (1945); Bernard Barber, Social Stratification: A Comparative Analysis of Structure and Process (New York: Harcourt Brace, 1957); Dennis H. Wrong, The Functional Theory of Stratification: Some Neglected Considerations, 24 Am. Soc. Rev. 772 (1959); Ralf Dahrendorf, On the Origin of Inequality Among Men, *in* his Essays in the Theory of Society 151 (Stanford, Cal.: Stanford University Press, 1968); James C. Kimberly, The Emergence and Stabilization of Stratification in Simple and Complex Social Systems: Some Implications of Small Group Research, 40 Soc. Inquiry 73 (1970); Gerhard Lenski, Power and Privilege: A Theory of Social Stratification (New York: McGraw-Hill, 1966); Randall Collins, Conflict Sociology: Toward an Explanatory Science (New York: Academic Press, 1975); Edward O. Laumann & Franz U. Pappi, Networks of Collective Action: A Perspective on Community Influence Systems (New York: Academic Press, 1976); Edward O. Laumann & Richard Senter, Subjective Social Distance, Occupational Stratification, and Forms of Status and Class Consciousness: A Cross-National Replication and Extension, 81 Am. J. Soc. 1304 (1976).

9. *Cf.* Albert J. Reiss, Jr., Occupations and Social Status (New York: Free Press, 1961); Robert W. Hodge, Paul M. Siegel, & Peter H. Rossi, Occupational Prestige in the United States: 1925-1963, *in* Reinhard Bendix & Seymour Martin Lipset, eds., Class, Status, and Power 322 (2d ed. New York: Free Press, 1966); Paul M. Siegel, Prestige and the American Occupational Structure (1971) (unpublished doctoral thesis, University of Chicago).

cussion of deference,[10] to the virtual neglect of prestige differentiation within a given occupational or status community.[11] Thus, hints gleaned from the literature concerning deference entitlements in the society at large, to use Shils's felicitous phrase, must be carefully recast to have any useful implications for our problem of explaining prestige differences within an occupation.

In their excellent discussion of the theoretical and methodological difficulties of current empirical work on occupational prestige, Goldthorpe and Hope note that prestige has classically been defined as "a particular form of social power and advantage that is of a symbolic rather than of an economic or political character, and which gives rise to structured relationships of deference, acceptance and derogation."[12] They stress the importance of recognizing that "advantage and power in the form of prestige remain distinctive in that they *entirely depend upon* the existence of some shared universe of meaning and value among the actors concerned."[13] Further, they provide a number of reasons to suspect that prestige judgments of the sort elicited by NORC-type questions[14] may not tap this classical conception of prestige. On the contrary, these judgments may merely provide a more or less adequate summary of general socioeconomic status or of the general "goodness" or social desirability of given occupations (so far as goodness is related to economic rewards, cleanliness of work, and other extrinsically or intrinsically rewarding features of particular occupations). But not all occupations enjoying social and economic rewards are prestigious in the classical sense of engendering deferent behavior from nonincumbents and of regulating intimate associations between incumbents and nonincumbents. If such were the case, then the concept of prestige, in the opinion of Goldthorpe and Hope, would add nothing to what we already know about occupations by knowing their relative levels of social and economic rewards.[15]

10. Edward Shils, Deference, *in* J. A. Jackson, ed., Social Stratification 104 (Cambridge: Cambridge University Press, 1968).

11. For an important exception see Allan M. Schwartzbaum, John H. McGrath, & Robert A. Rothman, The Perception of Prestige Differences Among Medical Subspecialties, 7 Soc. Sci. & Med. 365 (1973).

12. John H. Goldthorpe & K. Hope, Occupational Grading and Occupation Prestige, *in* Keith Hope, ed., The Analysis of Social Mobility: Methods and Approaches 19, 21 (Oxford: Clarendon Press, 1972).

13. *Id.* at 25.

14. The form of such questions is illustrated by the question we posed to the sample of lawyers (see note (1) to table 1).

15. When we speak of the prestige standing of an occupation or specialty, let us be quite clear about what we mean. A lawyer active in divorce work may enjoy the highest personal esteem and regard of fellow attorneys familiar with his work and the competence, skill, and ethical sensitivity with which he performs his work tasks. This high esteem can exist in spite of

While possessing some merit, the Goldthorpe and Hope argument can be overstated. Good theoretical reasons can certainly be adduced to explain a fairly high correspondence between the hierarchies of wealth and power in a society and the prestige-oriented behavior of deference or derogation.[16] Only in situations where the population's commitment to values and beliefs legitimating the social order is completely out of phase with the processes generating wealth and power differentials in the society, as in times of revolutionary upheaval, would we expect marked disjunctures among the three systems. Now, it is true that NORC-type prestige judgments are not in themselves evidence of the attractiveness or repulsiveness of incumbents of particular occupations for social intercourse—admittedly a key issue in classical discussions of prestige. Some research not noted by Goldthorpe and Hope, however, has shown substantial correlations between the prestige of occupations (as measured, for example, by the Duncan Index of Socioeconomic Status) and people's subjective social distance reactions toward them,[17] as well as a marked patterning of actual choices of partners for friendship and other intimate relations according to the principle of equal status contact.[18]

We do agree with Goldthorpe and Hope, however, when they emphasize the importance of recognizing prestige judgments as being in some sense functionally autonomous from the hierarchies of wealth and power—that is, as being subjective responses to particular social positions that are rooted in generally shared value orientations. Thus, as they observe, while it is meaningful to speak of a person's possessing "naked power" or wealth through which his will may be enforced, it is

---

the fact that lawyers generally tend to hold divorce work in low regard when compared with work in other specialties. Sociological usage restricts the term "prestige" to the evaluation of the standing of a general social position when compared with others (each of which has a number of incumbents). The esteem in which a given individual is held in the legal community is a combination of the prestige of the varied social positions that he simultaneously occupies (including his work specialties, ethnic group membership, seniority, etc.) and the social evaluation of the personal competence and skill with which he occupies them. We, of course, are concerned here only with the general social evaluation of legal specialties and not with the relative esteem or personal reputation of individual lawyers.

16. *Cf.* Shils, *supra* note 10.

17. *Cf.* Frank R. Westie, Social Distance Scales: A Tool for the Study of Stratification, 43 Soc. & Soc. Research 251 (1959); Edward O. Laumann, Prestige and Association in an Urban Community: An Analysis of an Urban Stratification System (Indianapolis: Bobbs-Merrill, 1966); Laumann & Senter, *supra* note 8.

18. *Cf.* Richard F. Curtis, Differential Association and the Stratification of the Urban Community, 42 Soc. Forces 68 (1963); Morton B. King, Jr., Socioeconomic Status and Sociometric Choice, 39 Soc. Forces 199 (1961); Laumann, *supra* note 17; Lois M. Verbrugge, Adult Friendship Contact: Time Constraints and Status-Homogeneity Effects, Detroit and Julich, West Germany (1974) (unpublished doctoral thesis, University of Michigan); Karl-Heinz Reuband, Differentielle Assoziation und Soziale Schichtung (1974) (unpublished doctoral thesis, University of Hamburg).

meaningless to speak of a person's "naked prestige" because giving deference to another ultimately requires the complicity of the lower status person.

The reason we stress here the importance of values in understanding prestige is that we wish to explore Shils's idea that deferent behavior is elicited in response to various "entitlements," most notably including the positional incumbent's role in controlling, mediating, or allocating core values in the society.[19] Following his classic distinction between the society's center and periphery, Shils argues that positions are differentiated with respect to proximity to the core values of the society and the power to allocate them; and, correspondingly, the closer a position is to the putative power centers at the societal level, the higher its prestige. Such an argument is a useful reformulation of Davis and Moore's earlier functional theory of social inequality[20] because it moves away from the more objectionable features of a theory that assumes that a structure, to be functional, must contribute to the "survival" of a society. In this reformulation, we need not assume that a functionally important position is awarded high prestige, among other rewards, but merely that a position believed to serve core values will be highly regarded and its incumbents deferred to. If these values should change, for whatever reason—that is, so as to lower their core legitimacy—then the position should lose prestige to those who serve the newly legitimated core values more closely. The issue of the society's survival is thus avoided.

Broadly speaking, theories of prestige conferral may be distinguished according to whether they have a macrostructural or a microstructural focus. Macrostructural theories of prestige generation attempt to account for the patterning of prestige and deference across and within institutional sectors in terms of some functional model of society in which the society's members are making differing valuations of social activities according to what is usually assumed to be a widely shared value system.[21] Prestige or its obverse, derogation, in this view becomes expressive of the deep-seated feelings about the core symbols or meanings that constitute the very definition of that society's identity and basis of existence. Other macrostructural theorists, following a more

19. Shils, *supra* note 10.

20. Davis & Moore, *supra* note 8.

21. *Cf.* Talcott Parsons, Equality and Inequality in Modern Society, or Social Stratification Revisited, *in* Edward O. Laumann, ed., Social Stratification: Research and Theory for the 1970s, at 13 (Indianapolis: Bobbs-Merrill, 1970); Davis & Moore, *supra* note 8; Shils, *supra* note 10; Piotr Sztompka, System and Function: Toward a Theory of Society (New York: Academic Press, 1974).

conflict-oriented perspective that questions the broad value consensus postulated by the functionalists,[22] tend to regard prestige as a more manipulative or instrumental strategy of those who hold power positions to screen their exploitative activities and to bolster their domination by eliciting the voluntary compliance and respect of the persons who occupy subordinated positions in the system. Prestige here alludes to its original Latin meaning of creating illusion or bedazzlement. Both the functionalist and conflict perspectives, despite their radical differences in the underlying processes postulated, imply almost identical predictions with regard to which positions will enjoy high or low prestige (although, admittedly, prestige in the conflict perspective tends to be a more precarious phenomenon).

Microstructural perspectives on theories of prestige conferral, on the other hand, direct attention to the social-psychological processes by which individuals come to make their subjective evaluations of the relative standings of various social positions according to some specified valuational criteria. Concern here is with identifying the various factors an individual takes into account in making such judgments, how the judgments are affected by detailed information or ignorance about a particular position or by personally held values and social attributes of the judges, such as age, sex, race, or class, and so on.[23] Being based on much more empirical, quantitative work than the macrostructural theories, microstructural approaches tend to be descriptively oriented, to be tied to particular techniques of measurement, and to avoid more qualitative interpretations of why certain individual-level variables are more predictive than others of relative prestige standing.

In the following analysis we shall draw on the diverse suggestions of these several perspectives in developing an account of differential

---

22. *E.g.*, Dahrendorf, *supra* note 8; Alvin W. Gouldner, The Coming Crisis of Western Sociology (New York: Basic Books, 1970); Collins, *supra* note 8.

23. *Cf.* Reiss, *supra* note 9; Goldthorpe & Hope, *supra* note 12; Paul M. Siegel, Occupational Prestige in the Negro Subculture, *in* Edward O. Laumann, ed., Social Stratification: Research and Theory for the 1970s, at 156 (Indianapolis: Bobbs-Merrill, 1970); Siegel, *supra* note 9.

Of course, there is yet another important microstructural tradition growing most recently out of Goffman's work (Erving Goffman, The Presentation of Self in Everyday Life (Garden City, N.Y.: Doubleday, 1959), and his Interaction Ritual: Essays in Face-to-Face Behavior (Garden City, N.Y.: Doubleday, 1967); Collins, *supra* note 8) that sensitively portrays the dynamic interplay between status display and deference-demanding or avoiding behavior in face-to-face interaction. Most useful as a source of rich qualitative description of ongoing status-linked behavior that can be used to gain insight on where to look for such behavior and the conditions under which it is elicited, this approach requires a radically different set of data-gathering and analytic techniques than those employed here. It is very much our impression, however, from our extended informal observations of lawyers with different practice characteristics, that the empirical results generated by the two approaches are broadly compatible and mutually reinforcing.

prestige among the legal specialties. Because these approaches refer to quite disparate levels of analysis and empirical contexts, we obviously cannot hope to devise a theoretically integrated model that resolves all of their intrinsic differences or to test all of the empirical propositions that can be deduced from a close examination of each of them.

After briefly describing the sources of the data, we turn to an extended empirical analysis that falls into three parts. First, we describe in some detail the nature and extent of social differentiation among the legal specialties. Second, we explore the multifaceted manner in which judgments about the relative prestige of the specialties are presumably organized in the subjective perceptions of the practitioner judges. And, finally, we attempt to account for the prestige rank order of the specialties on the basis of several alternative models employing selected features of the specialties. A concluding section discusses the implications of these results in conceptualizing the prestige allocation process within the legal profession and the society more generally.

THE SOCIAL DIFFERENTIATION OF A PROFESSION

The Sources and Nature of the Data

As part of a larger study of the legal profession and the politics of the organized bar,[24] we conducted 777 personal interviews with a representative cross section of lawyers whose offices were located within the city limits of Chicago.[25] The interviews were conducted in the spring and summer of 1975, averaged 66 minutes in length, and were almost always conducted at the respondent's place of work during

---

24. See Heinz et al., *supra* note 6, for a more comprehensive description of the objective of this larger study and some preliminary results.

25. The population universe was defined to include all lawyers who had office addresses within the city limits of Chicago, as listed in either *Sullivan's Law Directory for the State of Illinois, 1974-75* or *Martindale-Hubbell Law Directory, 1974.* We used two directories to insure complete coverage and to avoid any biases of either directory in their listing rules. (Of course, these procedures could not eliminate biases that both directories share.) Our 777 completed interviews represent 82.1 percent of our original target sample. Only 8.4 percent explicitly refused to grant us an interview, while the remaining 9.5 percent were missed due to the subject's illness, time constraints, and the like. An examination of the known characteristics of those lawyers whom we failed to include, for whatever reasons, reveals that we have probably slightly underenumerated nonmembers of the Chicago Bar Association, the principal bar association in the city, and those engaged in solo practice, especially those who maintain only accommodation addresses in the city. This underenumeration, however, is sufficiently small that we can, for most purposes, treat the completed sample as representative of the defined population universe.

regular business hours. The comprehensiveness and quality of the information gathered provide us with a unique opportunity to describe some of the central features of the metropolitan bar. This information includes the nature of the respondents' legal practice and clients, their personal and social characteristics, their attitudes on major social and legal issues, their membership and participation in the various bar associations, and their critical evaluations of the accomplishments or failures of these associations. The three sets of data that constitute the empirical basis of the analysis presented in this paper are described in greater detail below.

Tables 1 and 2 present standardized prestige scores for each of 30 specialties or types of legal work, standard scores on five characteristics of those specialties as judged by a selected group of legal scholars, and several types of information about the lawyers who practice in the specialties.

As we use the term "specialty" in this article, it refers only to an area or field of law practice that has a more or less distinct content or set of tasks. We do not mean to imply any particular degree of specialization in the area—*i.e.*, that lawyers who perform that sort of work tend to do it to the exclusion of any other.[26] Nor do we mean to suggest that the legal profession is now or in the foreseeable future likely to recognize the field as a formal specialty—*i.e.*, that lawyers may hold themselves out as, or be officially certified as, specialists in the field. Unlike the medical profession, where many specialties are formally recognized and certified, the legal profession enshrines the myth of the omnicompetent practitioner. With only minor and recent exceptions,[27] the ethical rules of the profession forbid lawyers to hold themselves out as specialists except in two relatively small and particularly abstruse fields, patents and admiralty (those we refer to below as the "classic specialties").[28] Thus, the differentiation within the legal profession that this article explores takes place against a background of the official endorsement of a holistic conception of the profession.

26. Though concentration in one field may be regarded as "true" specialization, the work type categories that we use vary considerably in the degree to which they possess this attribute (see table 2, column 14).

27. Zehnle, *supra* note 1.

28. See ABA Code of Professional Responsibility (1975) DR 2-105(A)(1), "Limitation of Practice." In addition to the fields mentioned in the text, this rule also permits the relatively small number of lawyers engaged in trademark law to mention that field on their letterheads and office signs.

TABLE 1
Prestige and Imputed Characteristics of Legal Specialties

		Prestige and Imputed Characteristics[a]				
Legal Specialty	Prestige Score (1)	Intellectual Challenge Score (2)	Rapidity of Change Score (3)	*Pro Bono* Score (4)	Ethical Conduct Score (5)	Freedom of Action Score (6)
1. Securities	68	63	62	44	57	39
2. Tax	67	67	66	43	55	46
3. Antitrust (Defendants)	65	64	56	40	53	39
4. Patents	61	56	44	45	62	47
5. Antitrust (Plaintiffs)	60	65	57	46	47	65
6. Banking	59[a]	47	42	42	58	35
7. Public Utilities	59[b]	55	53	48	56	39
8. General Corporate	59[c]	51	48	44	59	41
9. Probate	58	45	32	44	57	46
10. Municipal	56	44	38	45	56	41
11. Admiralty	55	52	34	42	62	48
12. Civil Litigation	54	52	48	51	45	55
13. Labor (Management)	53	52	53	45	46	38
14. Real Estate	51	45	37	43	48	50
15. Commercial	49[a]	52	48	46	55	48
16. Labor (Unions)	49[b]	53	53	51	47	42

TABLE 1—*Continued*

Legal Specialty	Prestige Score (1)	Intellectual Challenge Score (2)	Rapidity of Change Score (3)	*Pro Bono* Score (4)	Ethical Conduct Score (5)	Freedom of Action Score (6)
	Prestige and Imputed Characteristics[a]					
17. Environmental (Defendants)	49[c]	61	65	47	51	43
18. Personal Injury (Defendants)	48	33	42	43	38	46
19. Environmental (Plaintiffs)	47	61	65	72	58	66
20. Civil Rights/Liberties	46	61	65	77	64	70
21. Criminal (Prosecution)	44	48	56	56	47	53
22. General Family (Paying)	42	38	41	52	54	55
23. Criminal (Defense)	41	51	57	57	33	64
24. Consumer (Creditor)	40	50	60	46	43	41
25. Personal Injury (Plaintiffs)	38[a]	35	43	43	25	64
26. Consumer (Debtor)	38[b]	52	59	65	50	62
27. Condemnations	37[a]	35	36	43	39	49
28. Landlord-Tenant	37[b]	43	47	55	41	52
29. Divorce	35	30	45	50	30	54
30. General Family (Poverty)	34	38	51	76	61	64
Total Sample	50	50	50	50	50	50

[a]The following notes (1)-(6) explain each of the column headings.

(1) A random subsample ($N = 224$) of the total sample of Chicago lawyers was asked the following question: "On the following specialty list would you please indicate the general prestige of each specialty within the legal profession at large." The respondents rated each specialty on a five-point scale, from "outstanding" to "poor." We then computed the mean rating for each specialty. To facilitate comparing the prestige ratings, we calculated a standard score for each specialty by determining the grand mean of the 30 specialty means and its standard deviation and then subtracting the grand mean from each specialty mean and dividing by the standard deviation. To eliminate decimal points and negative numbers, we multiplied the standard score by 100 and added 50 to the result. Thus, "50" represents the average mean prestige rating, with 10 points being the standard deviation. To illustrate: "Securities," the most highly regarded specialty, is 1.8 standard deviations above the average mean prestige rating, while "General Family (Poverty)," with its score of 34, is 1.6 standard deviations below the average mean.

(2) An expert sample of 19 persons, composed of Northwestern Law School professors and American Bar Foundation research specialists on the legal profession, answered the following question for the 30 specialties: "The legal doctrines, cases, statutes, and regulations involved in some types of practice are characteristically more difficult, complex, and intellectually challenging than are those in others. Would you say that the degree of intellectual

challenge presented by the *substance* (as opposed to the strategic considerations) of this type work is: very great, higher than average, average, lower than average, or very little." The resulting means were standard scored, following the procedure described in note (1), *supra.* A high score indicates a specialty above average in intellectual challenge.

(3) The expert sample described in note (2), *supra,* was asked the following question: "The substantive law involved in some areas of practice changes more rapidly than it does in others. The practitioner, thus, may find it more difficult to keep up with developments in the former specialties than in the latter. Would you say that the law involved in this type of work: changes very rapidly, changes relatively quickly, changes at a moderate or average pace, changes relatively slowly, or changes very little or seldom." The resulting means were standard scored, following the procedure described in note (1), *supra.* A high score indicates a specialty above average in rapidity of change.

(4) The expert sample described in note (2), *supra,* was asked the following question: "Some types of legal work are more often done *pro bono publico,* or for altruistic or reformist motives, while other sorts of legal work much more clearly involve a profit motive. Would you say of this type of work that it is: highly money- or profit-oriented, substantially profit-oriented, neither or average, substantially *pro bono,* or mostly *pro bono.*" The resulting means were standard scored, following the procedure described in note (1), *supra.* A high score indicates a specialty above average in *pro bono* motivation.

(5) The expert sample described in note (2), *supra,* was asked the following question: "Some types of legal work have a reputation for 'sharp practice' or for a higher incidence of unethical conduct than is common in some other types of legal work. Would you say of this type of work that its reputation for ethical conduct is: very good, above average, average, below average, or poor." The resulting means were standard scored, following the procedure described in note (1), *supra.* A high score indicates a specialty above average in ethical reputation.

(6) The expert sample described in note (2), *supra,* was asked the following question: "In the practice of some types of law, the practitioner is, to a considerable degree, a 'free agent,' free to pursue whatever strategic course of action his own professional judgment may suggest. By contrast, the freedom of action of a practitioner of some other types of law is more highly constrained by knowledgeable clients or by organizational superiors who supervise and guide his decisions. Would you say that the practice of this type of law is characterized by: a high degree of freedom of action, above average freedom of action, average, below average freedom of action, or little freedom of action." The resulting means were standard scored, following the procedure described in note (1), *supra.* A high score indicates a specialty above average in freedom of action.

TABLE 2
Characteristics of Lawyers Devoting 25 Percent or More of Their Time to Selected Kinds of Legal Work

Selected Characteristics[a]

Legal Specialty	Row Case Base (1)	Mean Age (2)	% Metro-politan (3)	% Jewish (4)	% Repub-lican (5)	% Elite School (6)	% Solo (7)	% Large Firm (8)	Mean % Blue Collar Clients (9)	Mean % Major Corporate Clients (10)	% Stable Clients (11)	% Profes-sional Expertise (12)	% Negoti-ating & Advising (13)	% Concen-tration (14)	% Law Incomes $50,000 or More[b] (15)
1. Securities	20	38	65	15	30	50*	0*	75*	0	60*	54	90*	20	75*	33
2. Tax	67	42	69	29	30	20	10*	25	8*	26	60	66*	22*	65*	26
3. Antitrust (Defendants)	20	38*	55*	5*	25	45*	0*	80*	4	72*	47	40	60	45	43
4. Patents	35	46	60*	14	31	17	14	6	22	55*	70*	66	32	77*	32
5. Antitrust (Plaintiffs)	10	37	90	11	10	40	10	30	0	32	34	40	10	50	43
6. Banking	30	44	72	37	27	33	7	30	6*	41	66	55	18*	46	41
7. Public Utilities	20	43	90	30	30	20*	10	5	19	41	86*	45	63	70*	24
8. General Corporate	126	46	72	32	29*	32*	20	19	10*	26	65*	61	38	27*	29
9. Probate	97	50*	73	18*	30	24	30*	11*	16*	16*	66*	48	43	25*	24
10. Municipal	15	39	80	33	7	27	7	7	24	23	50	68	36	33	28
11. Civil Litigation	57	42	81	14*	20	25	10	40*	18	41	54	50	26*	32	24
12. Labor (Management)	19	41	68	37	10	21	5	26	3	59*	51	68	58	58	24
13. Real Estate[c]	169	47*	79	33	22	20	28*	14	26	25*	56	50	43	39	19
14. Commercial	24	38*	74	38	21	29	21	29	17	37	58	54	44	21*	41
15. Labor (Unions)	13	42	77	46	0	15	8	0	38	41	70	54	31	77*	36
16. Personal Injury (Defendants)	34	40	88	6*	21	9	12	26	23	64*	59	42	32	41	36
17. Civil Rights/Liberties	13	41	92	15	8	54*	0	15	38	40	63	69	31	38	41
18. Criminal (Prosecution)	14	39	86	14	7	0	N.A.	N.A.	N.A.	N.A.	N.A.	50	18	50	0

TABLE 2—*Continued*

Selected Characteristics[a]

Legal Specialty	Row Case Base (1)	Mean Age (2)	% Metro-politan (3)	% Jewish (4)	% Repub-lican (5)	% Elite School (6)	% Solo (7)	% Large Firm (8)	Mean % Blue Collar Clients (9)	Mean % Major Corporate Clients (10)	% Stable Clients (11)	% Profes-sional Expertise (12)	% Negoti-ating & Advising (13)	% Concen-tration (14)	% Law Incomes $50,000 or More[b] (15)
19. General Family[d]	22	52*	80	33	14	14	50*	4	49*	6*	58	29*	68*	4*	26
20. Criminal (Defense)	43	42	98*	33	2*	5*	46*	7	40*	13*	26*	43	45	46	22
21. Consumer[e]	12	42	75	42	17	25	8	8	40	25	54	58	50	33	14
22. Personal Injury (Plaintiffs)	54	43	100*	32	9*	6*	37*	2*	47*	23	43*	40	48	32*	27
23. Divorce	56	44	96*	46*	11	9*	61*	0*	39*	7*	41*	37*	56*	24*	23
Total Sample		44	78	28	21	20	21	18	26	34	55	52	39	45	26
No. of Valid Cases	---	(688)	(688)	(686)	(690)	(683)	(692)	(692)	(339)	(421)	(486)	(677)	(671)	(648)	(652)

N.A. = Not applicable.

*Statistically significant at the .05 level, contrasting practitioners in the specialty with all respondents not in the specialty.

[a]The following notes (1)-(15) explain each of the characteristics.

(1) "Row case base" refers to the number of persons who devoted at least 25 percent or more of their time to this legal specialty. All the other entries in the row for the specialty are on this sample base, but are reduced to exclude those very few cases that did not provide the requisite information reported in a given column.

We used the following question to determine the lawyer's distribution of time across legal specialties: "While a lawyer's time is often spread over many different areas of the law, we wish, for comparative purposes, to characterize those areas in which you spent the major part of your time during the last 12 months. [The respondent was handed a card listing 30 specialties.] In which of the listed areas have you spent: more than 50% of your time, between 25% and 50% of your time, between 5% and 25% of your time?"

(2) "Mean age" is the average age of persons active in a given specialty.

(3) "Percent metropolitan" refers to the proportion of persons active in this specialty who were living in a suburb of a large city or in a large city (over 250,000 people) during most of the time they were in high school.

(4) "Percent Jewish" refers to the percentage of persons who answered "Jewish" to the following question: "Do you have a religious preference? That is, are you either Protestant, Roman Catholic, Jewish, or something else?"

(5) "Percent Republican" refers to the percentage of respondents who expressed a Republican party preference in national politics.

(6) "Percent elite school" refers to the percentage of respondents who received their law degrees from one of the elite law schools: University of Chicago, Columbia, Harvard, University of Michigan, Stanford, or Yale.

(7) "Percent solo" refers to the percentage of respondents who selected "solo" to describe their current type of practice from the following list of alternatives: solo, firm, government (federal, state, or municipal/county government; or military legal service), house counsel (corporate, insurance, banking, or railroad), or other.

(8) "Percent large firm" refers to the percentage of respondents who indicated, in response to the question described in note 7, that they worked for a firm employing 30 or more lawyers.

(9) "Mean percent blue collar clients" refers to the average percentage reported by those respondents who had indicated that they had done at least 10 percent or more of their work on personal matters and who were then asked the following question: "Would you now think about the clients for whom you have handled personal matters in the last 12 months. What proportion of your clients fall into the occupational categories listed?" Categories included professional, technical, managerial; sales and clerical; blue collar; unemployed; retired; in school; keeping house.

(10) "Mean percent major corporations" refers to the average percentage reported by those respondents who had indicated that they received 10 percent or more of their income from work on business and who then

answered the following question: "What proportion of your business income would come from the following size business clients?" The categories included major corporations (*e.g.*, Standard Oil, American National Bank, Abbott Laboratories, Playboy Enterprises, Pepper Construction—*i.e.*, those with over $10 million in sales per year), medium-sized firms, or small businesses (*e.g.*, neighborhood stores, local restaurants, local real estate brokers, etc.—*i.e.*, those with less than $250,000 in sales per year).

(11) "Percent stable clients" refers to the average of the estimates of the respondents answering the following question: "What proportion cf all your clients have you represented for three years or more?"

(12) "Percent professional expertise" refers to the proportion of respondents who described their legal practice in the following way: "The type and content of my practice is such that even an educated layman couldn't really understand or prepare the documents." This was in contrast with a description of their practice as follows: "A paraprofessional could be trained to handle many of the procedures and documents in my area of the law."

(13) "Percent negotiating and advising" refers to the proportion of respondents who described their legal practice in the following way: "My specialty and type of practice requires skill in negotiating and advising clients, rather than detailed concern with technical rules." This was in contrast with a description of their practice as follows: "My area demands skill in handling highly technical procedures rather than skill in negotiation and advising clients."

(14) "Percent concentration" refers to the proportion of respondents who described their legal practice in the following way: "The area of law in which I work is so highly specialized that it demands I concentrate in just this one area." This was in contrast with: "The nature of my legal practice is such that I can handle a range of problems covering quite a number of different areas of legal practice."

(15) "Percent law income $50,000 or more (age adjusted)" refers to the proportion of respondents, adjusted for age composition, who reported their annual income from the practice of law as being $50,000 or greater. Respondents reported their earnings in 1 of 13 categories. Since the individual-level correlation between age and income was .22 ($p < .01$), we employed a direct standardization procedure whereby we calculated the age-specific income proportions for respondents in each specialty who earned more than $50,000. These proportions were then weighted by the age distribution for the total sample. The adjusted income proportion reported here is the sum of the weighted age-specific rates within each specialty (*cf.* Joseph L. Fleiss, Statistical Methods for Rates and Proportions (New York: Wiley Press, 1973)). Because these are age standardized income rates, we have not performed tests of the statistical significance of the differences between specialists and nonspecialists on these data.

[b] Age adjusted.

[c] Due to insufficient cases of persons active in the two subspecialties of real estate included in our list (viz., condemnations and landlord-tenant), we combined them with the general category of "real estate."

[d] Due to insufficient cases of persons active in this specialty, we combined lawyers active in "general family (paying)" and "general family (poverty)" into one category, "general family."

[e] Due to insufficient cases of persons active in this specialty, we combined the creditors' and debtors' lawyers into one category, designated "consumer law."

The first item of our survey presented the respondents with a list of 30 specialties composed from the collective judgments of our research group after we had consulted the very limited amount of published work on the subject. One of the sources was Carlin's study of solo practitioners in Chicago,[29] which used a list of 14 specialties. Though a few of our categories are identical to Carlin's, many are considerably more narrowly defined, and we have added some fields that have emerged only recently (*e.g.*, environmental law). We decided to use relatively fine-grained categories with the intention of combining them later if our sample proved to contain insufficient numbers of respondents in any specialty to permit separate analysis of it. Some of the categories, although expected to have few practitioners, were included because they are traditionally recognized as distinct specialties (*e.g.*, admiralty), and others because we were particularly interested in one or more of their characteristics (*e.g.*, condemnations, where a successful practice is reputed to be heavily dependent on good political connections).

Each respondent in the survey was then asked to indicate the percentage of his professional time that he devoted to each of the 30 types of work—less than 5 percent, 5 to 25 percent, 25 to 50 percent, or more than 50 percent. The answers to this question were used to identify the practitioners in each of the various specialties. Since there was, unavoidably, some overlap among the categories, there is certainly some degree of imprecision in the manner in which our respondents classified their work. The defense of a person charged with a crime, for example, might often plausibly be classified as "civil liberties" work as well as "criminal defense." Several other such sources of ambiguity exist; but the most important one, undoubtedly, is the "civil litigation" category, which may include litigation in any of the fields other than criminal. This problem is compounded by the fact that "litigation time" may well include not only the actual time in court but also the time spent preparing for trial or attempting to negotiate a settlement. It seemed advisable to include litigation as a separate specialty, however, because many of the large law firms contain separate litigation departments and because many lawyers think of themselves as "litigators" of a variety of types of cases.

A randomly selected, one-in-four subsample of our survey respondents was also asked to rate the "general prestige within the legal pro-

29. Jerome E. Carlin, Lawyers on Their Own: A Study of Individual Practitioners in Chicago (New Brunswick, N.J.: Rutgers University Press, 1962).

fession at large" of each of the 30 specialties. This was rated on a five-point scale, ranging from "outstanding" to "poor."[30] The resulting prestige scores of each of the specialties, converted to a standard scale,[31] are presented in table 1, where the specialties are listed in the rank order of declining prestige.[32] (In the survey instrument, the specialties were listed in alphabetical order.) Table 2, which also lists the specialties in declining prestige order, presents several types of informa-

30. *Cf.* National Opinion Research Center, Jobs and Occupations: A Popular Evaluation, *in* Reinhard Bendix & S. M. Lipset, eds., Class, Status & Power: A Reader in Social Stratification 411 (New York: Free Press, 1953); Hodge, Siegel, & Rossi, *supra* note 9.

31. See note (1) to table 1.

32. The degree of consistency among the respondent-judges in their prestige evaluations, especially with respect to the impact of their own specializations on their allocations of prestige, is a matter of considerable theoretical import. If lawyers active in the specialties that rank low in the overall prestige standing tend to invert the order of prestige of the specialties, or if the higher prestige specialists tend to inflate the prestige of their own specialties to an exaggerated degree, then a key assumption of the analysis—namely, that deferent behavior requires the voluntary complicity of the subordinate member of the transactional exchange—is cast into serious doubt.

We have examined the data in a number of ways to determine the degree of interjudge agreement on prestige evaluations and the extent to which there are systematic departures in prestige evaluations as functions of the judges' own specialty status and personal values. *E.g.*, lawyers espousing strong civil libertarian and social welfare values might accord higher prestige to specialties serving these values, while lawyers holding strong pro-business values might accord inordinate prestige to specialties serving business interests and lower the standing of more welfare-oriented specialties. In order not to overburden this already lengthy paper with an extended discussion of the details of our analytic procedures and results, we shall only report here the overall conclusions to be drawn from these serveral analyses. In general, there are comfortingly high rank-order correlations between the mean evaluations of judges located, on the basis of their specialties, in one of three broad prestige levels—high, middle, or low—and the overall mean evaluation of the sample of judges as a whole. (These correlations range between .85 and .97.) But there are some statistically significant differences between the judges in high-ranked and in low-ranked specialties with respect to evaluations of particular specialties. Moreover, there is a discernible pattern of these differences, low-ranked judges tending to assign higher prestige to low-ranked specialties and, conversely, high-ranked judges assigning higher prestige scores to high-ranked specialties (*cf.* Laumann, *supra* note 17, at 41-53, for parallel results obtained for subjective social distance judgments of broadly dispersed occupations in the socioeconomic status hierarchy by a general sample of men active in the labor force). While such systematic departures can be detected in the data, their magnitude or importance should not be exaggerated. The overwhelming tendency is for judges at all prestige levels to concur on the general prestige rank order of the specialties—providing strong evidence for the general complicity of the lower status lawyers in according higher prestige to their "betters."

As a more concrete illustration of this general tendency, consider the fact that the six specialties rated highest in prestige by practitioners of the top five specialties in overall prestige were (in order of declining prestige) securities, antitrust defense, tax, general corporate, banking, and antitrust plaintiffs' work; while the top six as rated by practitioners of the five specialties rated *lowest* in overall prestige were securities, tax, probate, civil litigation, antitrust defense, and banking. Similarly, practitioners of the five highest prestige specialties assigned the six lowest places on the prestige scale to consumer (buyer), landlord-tenant, condemnations, family (poverty), personal injury plaintiffs' work, and divorce (again in declining order of prestige); while practitioners in the five lowest prestige specialties chose for those same positions personal injury plaintiffs' work, condemnations, family (poverty), landlord-tenant, consumer (seller), and consumer (buyer). Thus, even raters who practice at the respective extremes of the prestige order display a high degree of similarity in their prestige ratings.

tion about the lawyers who devote 25 percent or more of their working hours to those specialties. Table 2 contains fewer specialties than table 1 because we dropped specialties from the list or combined them if fewer than ten of our respondents reported that they spent as much as 25 percent of their time in the field. In the case of admiralty, for example, only one of our respondents indicated that the field occupied 25 percent or more of his time and only six respondents devoted as much as 5 percent of their time to the specialty. Because of the manner in which these data are constructed, then, it is quite possible that some of the 777 lawyers in our total sample are not included at all in the data presented in table 2, while others are included in more than one specialty category. If, for example, a lawyer devoted 25 percent of his time to real estate work, 25 percent to commercial law, 25 percent to probate, and the remainder to a scattering of other types of work, he would be counted in the "real estate," "commercial," and "probate" categories. While this means that some individuals are "double counted," this does not present problems for the manner in which we have analyzed those data.

The characteristics of the practitioners in each field, reported in table 2, constitute a substantial amount of information on matters that might be thought to be highly relevant to determining the prestige structure of the specialties. The information includes, for example, the patterns of recruitment and education, the work environment, the type of clients served, and the differential reward structure. None of this material obtained from the survey, however, gave us information about the nature of the law of the field or about the tasks or practices characteristically involved in that sort of work. Because such variables are not so amenable to objective measurement, we sought opinions about them from a relatively small group of experts. These experts consisted of 15 Northwestern University professors in various fields of law and four lawyer-researchers on the staff of the American Bar Foundation. We sought experts who were not active in the practice of law in the hope that this would minimize bias or defensive reactions.[33] The

33. An alternative research strategy would have been to have the same practitioner judges who rated prestige also rate these characteristics, thus permitting us to compare their prestige judgments to their ratings of the individual characteristics. To have done so would have greatly extended already crowded interviews, however, and it was thus not practical to pursue this strategy. We do not regard this as a great loss. We are not so much interested in analyzing the interrelationships among various sorts of evaluations by the individual rater—*i.e.*, among the individual's ratings of specialty prestige and his ratings of the specialties on other sorts of evaluative dimensions. Rather, we were concerned to examine whether some "real" objective properties of the types of work might be discovered that would help account for the differences among specialty prestige at the aggregate level. Thus, we used independent experts to judge the presence or absence of these properties.

results of these expert judgments, converted to the same sort of standard scores used for the prestige judgments of the general sample, are presented in columns (2) through (6) of table 1.

All of these imputed characteristics of the specialties, summarized in table 1, were hypothesized to have significance for the prestige structure of the types of legal work. The first of these, "intellectual challenge," might be expected to be highly valued within a community that characterizes itself as a "learned profession." If, as our question put it, "the legal doctrines, cases, statutes, and regulations involved in some types of practice are characteristically more difficult, complex, and intellectually challenging than are those in others," then we would expect the specialties that are regarded as more demanding to command a higher degree of respect and, thus, of prestige. Similarly, the second imputed characteristic, "rapidity of change," was also intended to address a factor that would make the practice of a specialty more difficult and, therefore, more entitled to respect. If the substantive law involved in an area of practice changes only seldom or slowly, the practitioner will not have to work as hard at keeping up with developments in the law, and his practice is likely to become more routine. By contrast, the practitioner in a rapidly developing specialty will have to devote more effort to keeping abreast of the field, he is likely to have more opportunities for creativity in his work, and he may thus be regarded as more deserving of deference. The third imputed characteristic, referred to in table 1 as the "*pro bono* score," was intended to measure the degree to which work in the specialty tends to be done *pro bono publico,* or for altruistic or reformist motives, as opposed to being motivated primarily by a desire for profit. Our hypothesis was, of course, that altruism or dedication to public service might be positively valued and, thus, might enhance the prestige of specialties where such motivations are characteristic. The "ethical conduct" dimension also represents a quite straightforward hypothesis, in some respects similar to the hypothesis concerning altruistic motivation. A reputation for rectitude may be thought to enhance prestige and power,[34] and a specialty that is thought to have a high incidence of unethical conduct or "sharp practice" may, conversely, be derogated. Finally, the "freedom of action" characteristic refers to the degree to which practitioners in the specialty are free to pursue the courses of action suggested by their own professional judgments, as opposed to being constrained by knowledgeable clients or by organizational superiors who supervise and guide their

34. Harold D. Lasswell & Abraham Kaplan, Power and Society: A Framework for Political Inquiry (New Haven, Conn.: Yale University Press, 1950).

decisions. Autonomy has often been proposed as one of the characteristics that distinguishes the "professions" from other occupations.[35] In addition to the value given to independence in society generally and in the other professions, the legal profession might be thought to give special weight to the ideal of the individual advocate fighting lonely, gallant battles, as opposed to the lawyer as bureaucrat, as small cog in a large machine. Thus, we hypothesized that freedom of action might also enhance the prestige of a specialty.

With respect to the characteristics of the practitioners active in each of the legal specialties, presented in table 2, we were confronted with an embarrassment of riches. The literature on deference entitlements suggested at least four broad categories to consider: (1) the social origins of incumbents (*i.e.*, persons of higher social origins are expected to gravitate toward more prestigious work while persons of derogated origins are relegated to the less attractive work tasks)—in an important sense, this is a result of a prestige hierarchy rather than a cause, although obviously one would expect such a differential distribution of personnel according to esteemed and derogated social origins to reinforce and, therefore, to perpetuate perceptions of the prestige differences among positions; (2) work context and task characteristics (*i.e.*, in addition to the features of work activities noted in discussing table 1, such work aspects as the size of the employer organization have implications for predictability and routinization of work flow, for the range and variety of tasks performed, for the dependency of one's goal achievement on the satisfactory performance of others, and so on);[36] (3) the social evaluation of the relative importance (in power or social status) of the organizations and persons for whom services are being rendered (*i.e.*, client characteristics)—this rests on the proposition of honor or derogation by association with or proximity to the high and the mighty or the low and despised; and (4) the characteristic levels of extrinsic and intrinsic rewards associated with performing particular tasks, including direct financial rewards, the quality of working conditions (such as office furnishings and space, or access to secretaries and other work assistants), and the personal job satisfaction arising from the presence or absence of monotony, excitement, risk-taking, or challenge in one's work. Each of these broad categories could manifest itself in an almost indefinite number of ways in different substantive contexts and,

---

35. Ernest Greenwood, Attributes of a Profession, Soc. Work, July 1957, at 45; Richard H. Hall, Occupations and the Social Structure (Englewood Cliffs, N.J.: Prentice-Hall, 1969).

36. *Cf.* Davis & Moore, *supra* note 8; James D. Thompson, Organizations in Action: Social Science Bases of Administrative Theory (New York: McGraw-Hill, 1967).

in addition, these manifestations might vary considerably in their empirical or analytic independence from one another and in their sensitivity to the hypothesized construct underlying a particular basis for deference entitlement.

The Prestige Order

Turning to the data itself, let us initially note some of the most striking general properties of the prestige scores indicated in table 1. First, the top of the prestige ranking is quite clearly dominated by specialties that might be characterized as "big business" law. Of the first eight specialties in the rank order, only tax is a type of work that is likely to be done for "individual" as well as for "business" clients, and the great predominance of tax work that lawyers do is almost certainly done for businesses or well-to-do individuals. The respondents spending 25 percent or more of their time doing tax work indicated that they derived 38 percent of their income from individuals—somewhat less than average—and that, of these individual clients, 70 percent were in the highest status ("professional, technical, or managerial") category. Not until we reach probate work, ranked ninth in prestige, do we come to a type of legal work that is likely to be done for individuals, and it may be significant to note that it is, in its nature, concerned with the transmission of wealth.

At the other end of the prestige ranking, we find the sorts of legal work that are characteristically done for individuals—general family practice, divorce, personal injury, consumer, and criminal law. Some of these types of practice may be derogated, not only because of the lower socioeconomic status of their clients, but because of the "distasteful" or "unsavory" nature of the work. Divorce work involves emotionally charged, embarrassingly personal situations, the clients are often at their worst, and the fate of children frequently hangs in the balance; personal injury work usually deals with grisly facts and with claimants who are badly maimed; and criminal work is concerned with highly antisocial acts and quite frequently requires the lawyer to associate with persons who are not very nice. Thus, the low prestige of these specialties may be seen as analogous to the derogation of refuse collectors, coal miners, and others whose work involves unpleasant tasks.[37]

Toward the middle of the prestige ranking, we find types of work that are done to some degree by large numbers of lawyers (*e.g.*, real estate, civil litigation, and commercial work) and that might, thus, be

37. Shils, *supra* note 10; Goldthorpe & Hope, *supra* note 12.

seen as "mediating" specialties. A type of work done by a great many lawyers, with widely differing characteristics, is unlikely to be regarded as either particularly high or particularly low in prestige. There are also some specialties near the middle of the ranking that might be regarded as problematic; they possess ambivalent characteristics and may thus be inconsistently valued. For example, the practice of labor law (both for unions and for management) involves considerable financial stakes, but it also involves association with blue collar workers or their representatives. Similarly, the lawyers who represent defendants in personal injury cases usually work for high status clients, since those defendants are typically insurance companies, but their work also involves unsavory fact situations.

Let us now examine in some detail each of the characteristics included in tables 1 and 2 and the ways in which those characteristics are related to prestige. In order to focus on the nature of the specialties as well as on the individual characteristics—*i.e.*, on the rows as well as on the columns of the tables—we have selected five specialties for particular attention, though we will not be slavish about following them through all of their characteristics. These five are more or less evenly spaced along the prestige ranking: securities, the highest in prestige; public utilities, which has a moderately high prestige rating; real estate, which ranks near the middle; criminal defense, which has a moderately low rating; and divorce, which is the lowest prestige specialty for which we have a large enough number of respondents to make generalization sensible. These particular types of work have not been chosen because of any special substantive significance but rather because they represent a range of positions in the prestige order. We will also call attention to other specialties that are particularly noteworthy on one or more of the dimensions.

Imputed Characteristics of Legal Specialties

Beginning with the first independent variable of table 1, we find that securities work ranks fourth in degree of "intellectual challenge." Its score is exceeded only by those of tax and of antitrust plaintiffs' and defendants' work. Thus, the four highest intellectual challenge scores are held by specialties that rank among the top five in prestige. The consistency of this tendency throughout the ratings is reflected in the fact that the intellectual challenge and prestige scores are correlated at .65.

Securities work is concerned with the legal requirements and regulations governing the distribution and resale of stocks, bonds, and other securities. The sorts of matters dealt with include the registration of securities being sold by corporations; the disclosure of information by corporations; insider trading; corporate take-over and proxy solicitations; and the regulation of underwriters, broker-dealers, securities exchanges, investment companies, and other entities involved in the securities industry. As such, it deals with a complex set of federal statutes and regulations. It is very interesting to note that all four of the specialties rated highest in intellectual challenge and all of the top six in the prestige ranking deal predominantly with federal rather than state law, and that all of them require their practitioners to deal with federal regulatory boards, commissions, agencies, or departments (as well as, potentially, with the federal courts). Thus, involvement with the federal government would appear to enhance the prestige of a specialty. This observation is strengthened by noting that the correlation between the prestige of a specialty and the frequency of appearances by its practitioners in the state courts is −.68. (The frequency of appearance in state courts is also correlated at −.65 with the intellectual challenge scores of the specialties.) At the other end of the scale, we find that divorce is assigned the lowest intellectual challenge score of all the specialties. Other specialties with notably low scores on this dimension are personal injury work (for both plaintiffs and defendants) and condemnation law (eminent domain), all of which also rank relatively low in the prestige order.

All of the four specialties rated highest in intellectual challenge also have rapidity of change scores that are well above average, with tax again receiving the highest score. Keeping up with developments in a rapidly changing specialty may make that field more demanding than it would otherwise be, or slow change may make it less so. Probably for this reason, the rapidity of change and intellectual challenge scores are correlated at .69. The other high scores on the rapidity of change dimension were assigned to environmental law (plaintiffs and defendants) and to civil liberties work, which have been areas of rapid and substantial change in public policy in recent years. The lowest change scores went to probate and admiralty law, both of which are fields with very long histories and traditions.

On the dimension that dealt with the extent to which work in the specialties is motivated by altruism (work *pro bono publico*) as opposed to a desire for profit (see table 1, column 4), we find that securities work received one of the lowest scores, as did the other high prestige specialties. The only specialties with lower *pro bono* scores were antitrust defense, banking, admiralty, and real estate. Real estate work deals with the transmission of property or with real estate development, both of which pretty clearly involve the profit motive—as do banking law, the defense of companies charged with antitrust violations, and the representation of shipowners or insurers in admiralty cases. Divorce work, by contrast, received one of its higher scores on this dimension—it reached the mean, 50. By comparison, it may be interesting to note that the personal injury lawyers were not given much credit for altruistic motivation—the specialty received a score of 43, tied with real estate—while criminal defense work was scored substantially above average. The highest *pro bono* scores were assigned to civil liberties work, understandably enough, and to general family practice with poverty level clients, the specialty ranked *lowest* in prestige. More generally, the *pro bono* score is negatively correlated with prestige at −.51. If altruistic motivation is highly valued within the legal profession, then, the weight given it does not seem to be sufficient to offset the value attached to other factors that influence prestige judgments.[38]

The ethical conduct score (see table 1, column 5) behaves very differently than the *pro bono* score; and ethical behavior appears, therefore, to be seen as quite separate from altruistic motivation. This would be consistent with the role conception of the lawyer as "hired gun" providing professional representation, within the ethical rules, for anyone who is able to afford his services. Securities work, like most of the high prestige specialties, has an ethical conduct score that is well above average. Though the highest ethical conduct score was assigned to civil liberties work, as was the case on the *pro bono* dimension, and one of the highest scores went to general family work for poverty clients, most of the high ethical conduct scores were assigned to specialties that represent big business clients and, particularly, to the more traditional

38. Note that the question on which the *pro bono* dimension is based did not ask for an assessment of the "social worth" or "contribution to the public good" of each of the specialties. Such a question would be even more difficult to answer than the one that we did, in fact, pose. Rather, our question asked the panel of scholars to judge the extent to which practitioners in each specialty were likely to undertake the work because of the money to be made in it, rather than because of "altruistic" or "reformist" motives. Thus, the distinction is whether the work of the specialty is more often motivated by the practitioner's desire for profit or by ideological motives—*e.g.,* those addressed to "law reform," to more general social or political reforms, or to "service" apart from personal gain. We recognize (and think it safe to assume that our panel of scholars did, as well) that the choices open to any lawyer may well be limited both by opportunity and by personal circumstances. Some lawyers may take relatively low-paying work—criminal prosecution or real estate title searches, for example—because it is the only type of work open to them. Nonetheless, some lawyers no doubt choose to take the types of cases that will earn them only small fees (or a small salary) or no fee at all. And it may well be, to pursue our examples, that decisions to undertake criminal prosecution are more likely to reflect such a choice than are decisions to do real estate title searches. Our panel of scholars thought that such altruistic or reformist motivations were even more common in civil rights work and in poverty law, and this makes sense to us.

of those specialties, such as patents and admiralty. The lowest ethics scores were given to specialties that represent individuals in the sorts of cases that we have already characterized as "unsavory"—personal injury plaintiffs' work, divorce, and criminal defense. That is, the circumstances of the cases are unsavory, by hypothesis, for reasons quite distinct from the unethical conduct of practitioners in the field. There may be a tendency, then, to see work that is "dirty" in one respect as dirty in another, or the labeling process may lead to unethical conduct in work that is already derogated for other reasons.[39] The score of personal injury plaintiffs' work on this dimension, for example, is particularly striking: 25, the lowest score that any of the specialties received on any of the dimensions. The image of the "ambulance chaser" remains, apparently, quite vivid. The ethical conduct score is correlated with prestige at .53.

The freedom of action score (see table 1, column 6) summarizes the scholars' judgments of the extent to which practitioners in the specialty are free to pursue their own course of action, rather than constrained by clients or superiors. Both securities work and public utilities work, for example, have quite low scores on this dimension. These types of work are typically carried out in large organizations, with senior lawyers supervising juniors, and the clients are highly knowledgeable. Forty percent of the lawyers who devote at least 25 percent of their time to public utilities work are corporate house counsel—a far larger percentage than is the case for any other specialty. And 75 percent of the securities lawyers practice in the largest firms, those with more than 30 lawyers (see table 2, column 8). The practice of securities law is, in fact, reputed to be confined largely to a few major urban centers where the securities underwriters are located. The only specialties with lower freedom of action scores than securities and public utilities are banking and the management side of the labor law practice, both of which serve very sophisticated clients who are capable of assessing the situation and guiding the lawyers' actions. Thus, the higher prestige specialties serving business clients tend to have low freedom of action scores; consequently, this dimension is correlated negatively with prestige (−.54).

Criminal defense work has a very high score on this dimension. This may reflect not only the large number of solo practitioners among criminal defense lawyers, functioning as individual entrepreneurs, but also the characteristic lack of sophistication and influence of their

39. Edwin M. Lemert, Human Deviance, Social Problems, and Social Control 40-64 (Englewood Cliffs, N.J.: Prentice-Hall, 1967), on "secondary deviation."

clients, persons charged with crimes. The only specialties with higher freedom of action scores than criminal defense are civil liberties, environmental plaintiffs', and antitrust plaintiffs' work. In the case of civil liberties, the powerlessness of the clients may be one of the factors accounting for the score, but another contributing factor may well be the inherent creativity or lack of legal structure of the field, which permits the civil liberties lawyer great freedom of action in devising the theory and strategy of his case. This explanation may also apply to environmental plaintiffs' work, which is a new and relatively unstructured field.

The other specialty receiving a high score, antitrust plaintiffs' work, is a very interesting deviant case. That specialty ranks fifth in prestige and has a freedom of action score of 65—not until we descend to nineteenth position in the prestige order (environmental plaintiffs' work) do we find another freedom of action score in the 60s. The lawyers who represent the plaintiffs in antitrust cases must have all the same knowledge and abilities as those who represent the large corporations that are the defendants in these cases. In addition, however, the plaintiffs' lawyers have the task of creating novel theories on which to base antitrust treble damage actions—in recent years, some of these have involved class actions on behalf of large numbers of consumers[40]—and the fact that they search out their clients, rather than being presented with a problem by a client, enhances their freedom of action. The antitrust plaintiffs' lawyers tend to be seen by other lawyers as, in a sense, "traitors to their class"—they have all the special skills of the antitrust lawyers, but they misuse those skills by making them available to the "wrong" sort of client (and profit handsomely by doing so, if they are successful). The profession's view of the antitrust plaintiffs' lawyer as a species of pariah may also be reflected by the specialty's score on the ethical conduct dimension, which is substantially lower than would be anticipated from its prestige rank.

Characteristics of Practitioners in the Specialties

Demographic and Recruitment Characteristics

Columns 2 through 5 of table 2 report demographic characteristics of the practitioners who devote 25 percent or more of their time to each of 23 specialties. (Some of the specialty categories used in table 1 have been combined here to increase the number of cases in the spe-

40. *Cf.* Benjamin S. DuVal, Jr., The Class Action as an Antitrust Enforcement Device: The Chicago Experience (I), 1976 A.B.F. Res. J. 1021, 1032.

cialties; the 23 specialties presented in the table are those that include at least ten cases.)[41] We should note at the outset the high degree of differentiation among the legal specialties on most of the variables presented in table 2. This differentiation is all the more noteworthy since the "specialists" in each field were defined by a criterion that permitted the practitioners to spend up to 75 percent of their time on other sorts of legal work, a criterion that results in a conservative (or, in a sense, "contaminated") measure of the characteristics of the lawyers in each field. Because the lawyers may, in fact, be more active in one or two other specialties (where they will also be counted in our data), the degree of differentiation that we observe in table 2 is the more remarkable.

The correlation between the mean age of the practitioners and the prestige of the specialties is not significant, but it may be of interest to note that it is negative (–.23). The average age of securities practitioners, as is the case in four of the top five specialties in prestige rank, is below the overall mean of 43.9. The two lowest mean ages belong to specialties that are in the top five in prestige, the two sides of antitrust work. This tendency for high prestige to be associated with disproportionate numbers of youthful practitioners may be attributable either to the fact that these sorts of work tend to be done by large firms, where many younger lawyers who are "associates" assist the senior partners, or to the fact that the rapidly changing nature of the law in these fields gives an advantage to younger lawyers who have received their instruction in the subject more recently. The specialties with the highest mean ages–real estate, probate, and general family practice–are types of work that are performed by many solo practitioners, who are significantly older than the average age for the profession.[42]

The extent to which the practitioners in a specialty have their origins in a metropolitan community has a strong negative correlation with the prestige of the specialty (–.69). That is, lawyers who resided during their high school years in cities with populations in excess of 250,000, or in suburbs of such cities, make up a larger percentage of the practitioners in the lower prestige specialties than in the types of work enjoying higher prestige (see table 2, column 3). Securities work, for example, has one of the lowest percentages of practitioners of metropolitan origin. The only specialties with lower percentages are two of the other top prestige fields, antitrust defendants' work and patents. By contrast, many of the lowest prestige specialties have very high

41. See notes (c), (d), and (e) to table 2.
42. See Heinz et al., *supra* note 6.

percentages—divorce, criminal defense, and personal injury plaintiffs' work all range between 95 and 100 percent.

We find, then, a process of selection in the recruitment of practitioners to the various specialties that results in a negative correlation between metropolitan origin and the prestige of the specialties. Some of this may well be self-selection. Our sample was drawn only from lawyers with offices in the city of Chicago, and persons of rural or small town origin who have chosen to practice law in such a large city might be expected to be highly motivated for success or "upward mobility." The recruitment of lawyers for the high prestige specialties may also be more wide-ranging, resulting in a greater diversity of origin of the practitioners. The large law firms and corporations that employ disproportionate numbers of the lawyers in the high prestige fields are likely to recruit at the top national law schools (see column 6) and to select students with high academic achievement, regardless of whether they grew up in the firm's locality. In the lower prestige specialties, by contrast, the lawyers tend to be solo practitioners (see column 7) or to be in smaller firms. The sorts of contacts that are facilitated by the kinship and acquaintance networks of locals may be more important to survival in these fields—that is, the flow of legal work to these lawyers is not so likely to be guaranteed by affiliation with a large, ongoing organization.

The percentage of Jewish practitioners in each specialty (see table 2, column 4) and the percentage of Republicans (column 5) appear to be almost mirror images of one another. Securities work has a relatively low percentage of Jews and a relatively high percentage of Republicans, which is the general tendency for the higher prestige specialties—though the Republican percentage is more strongly correlated with prestige (.67) than is the Jewish percentage (– .45).[43] Divorce and consumer work both have relatively high percentages of Jewish practitioners and relatively low percentages of Republicans, as is the case with the other lowest prestige specialties.

The interpretations of these tendencies are rather obvious. Jews are, perhaps, the most derogated of the ethnic groups that are repre-

---

43. All respondents were asked their religious preferences and their ethnic or national origins. Only the percentage of Jewish practitioners in each specialty is reported here because the "percent Jewish" had a stronger negative correlation with prestige than did any of the other religious and ethnic categories, and it is, in our opinion, the most interesting and important of those variables. "Percent Catholic" was also negatively correlated with prestige, though not to a statistically significant degree, and "percent Protestant" had a strong *positive* correlation with specialty prestige (.67, even stronger than the negative correlation of percent Jewish).

sented in the bar in any substantial numbers,[44] and the Republicans tend to be, conversely, high on deference entitlements such as family wealth and social origins.[45] These factors may bias both the actions of the gatekeepers who limit entry into the high prestige specialties and the perceptions of the prestige of the specialties that have high concentrations of the derogated or "privileged" group. Thus, two complementary tendencies may reinforce one another here. Jews have tended to be excluded from the high prestige specialties and Republicans (or persons with the sort of social origins, family wealth, and connections that Republicans tend to possess in disproportion) to be welcomed in them, leaving the Jews with only the less prestigious work available to them if they choose to practice law and leaving the Republicans free of the necessity of doing such work. The presence of Republicans in the higher prestige specialties may then serve further to enhance the prestige of those specialties by association, and the presence of Jews in the lower prestige specialties may serve further to depreciate the prestige of those specialties in the eyes of lawyers who derogate that ethnic group.

A phenomenon that is in some respects similar may be observed in the data on the percentage of practitioners in each of the specialties who attended one of six "elite" American law schools.[46] Fifty percent of the securities lawyers had graduated from these schools, while only 9.4 percent of the divorce practitioners, 5.6 percent of the personal injury plaintiffs' attorneys, 4.8 percent of the criminal defense lawyers, and none of the criminal prosecutors had done so. The two sides of antitrust work both have high percentages of elite school graduates, which is consistent with both their high prestige and intellectual challenge scores. Noteworthy here is the substantial correlation of .65 between the percentage of elite law school graduates practicing in a specialty and the intellectual challenge score assigned to the specialty by our scholar judges.

44. *Cf.* Nathan Glazer & Daniel Patrick Moynihan, Beyond the Melting Pot: The Negroes, Puerto Ricans, Jews, Italians and Irish of New York City (Cambridge, Mass.: MIT Press, 1963); Edward O. Laumann, Bonds of Pluralism: The Form and Substance of Urban Social Networks (New York: John Wiley & Sons, 1973); Heinz et al., *supra* note 6.

45. E. Digby Baltzell, Philadelphia Gentlemen: The Making of a National Upper Class (Glencoe, Ill.: Free Press, 1958).

46. The six "elite" schools are Chicago, Columbia, Harvard, Michigan, Stanford, and Yale. These six were ranked among the "top five" law schools substantially more often than were any other schools by the 104 law school deans responding to the survey conducted by Peter M. Blau & Rebecca Zames Margulies, A Research Replication: The Reputations of American Professional Schools, 6 Change, Winter 1974-75, at 44. Though their survey is unsatisfactory in many respects, it seems adequate for our purposes here. The lowest ranked of these six schools, Stanford, was rated in the top five by 45 of the 104 deans. The next closest school received only 19 such ratings.

One of the most intriguing findings on this dimension is that the highest percentage of elite school graduates is found in the "civil rights/liberties" specialty. (Since this specialty has one of the smallest case bases, however, we should be somewhat cautious regarding this result.) Civil rights/liberties ranks only twentieth in prestige on the original list of 30 specialties, and its prestige is seventeenth among the 23 specialties for which we present the percentage of elite school graduates. Given the high percentage of elite law school graduates practicing civil liberties law, what might account for its relatively low prestige? There is not a great deal that is noteworthy about the other characteristics of the lawyers practicing in the field, except that the percentage of solo practitioners who do civil liberties work is zero in our sample, a fact that would also tend to be associated with high prestige (see column 7). We have already noted, however, that civil liberties was ranked highest on three of the five imputed characteristics—the *pro bono* score, the ethical conduct dimension, and the freedom of action score—and near the top of the ratings on the other two. Of those scores, particularly extreme ratings occurred on the freedom of action and *pro bono* dimensions (where the scores were 70 and 77, respectively) and these two imputed characteristics also happen to be the ones that are negatively correlated with prestige. On the face of these data, then, one interpretation might be that the prestige of civil liberties work suffers because its practitioners enjoy too much autonomy in their work and have an unseemly reputation for altruistic motivation! But perhaps it would be well to be tentative about this conclusion, having a decent regard for the limitations of our data—in particular, the sample size. Another, perhaps more plausible, explanation may lie in the lack of congruence between the dominant social and political values of the legal profession and those of the civil liberties specialty.

Work Context

Moving from data that concern demographic and recruitment characteristics of practitioners in each of the specialties, we turn to characteristics of the work context of the specialties. These include the nature of the organizations within which the specialties are practiced, the type of clients served, and the stability of the attorney-client relationship in each of the fields (see columns 7 through 11). The first four of these characteristics (columns 7-10) constitute two more pairs of items that are to a considerable degree mirror images. The percentage of solo practitioners in a specialty tends to be inversely related to the percentage of the specialists who practice in firms with more than 30 lawyers, and the two are correlated with prestige at −.58 and .63, respectively. (These are, of course, only two among several possible practice settings—the others include positions in smaller firms, as corporate house counsel, or as government lawyers at the federal, state, or local level. All of these other possibilities, however, have smaller correlations with prestige than do the two presented here.) A similar relationship exists between the percentage of "blue collar" clients of the specialists and the percentage of their law practice income that comes from "major corporations" (defined as corporations with more than $10 million in sales per year). These two variables are correlated with prestige at .86 and .54, respectively. (These are, of course, only two among several possible client types, but these categories were chosen for their extremity of type rather than for the degree of their correlations with prestige. The percentage of income derived from major corporate clients has, in fact, the lowest correlation with prestige of the five client-type categories.)[47]

The securities specialty has one of the largest percentages of lawyers who practice in large firms and its percentage of solo practitioners, in our sample, is zero. Its percentage of large firm lawyers is surpassed only by that of the antitrust defendants' lawyers, another of the highest prestige specialties. These two specialties also have the highest percentages of practice income derived from major corporate clients, and among the lowest percentages of clients who are blue collar workers. The low prestige specialties, by contrast, reverse this pattern. Divorce, the lowest prestige specialty, has the highest percentage of solo practitioners, the lowest percentage of large firm lawyers, one of the two lowest percentages of income from major corporations, and a percentage of blue collar clients that is well above the mean. The pattern of the divorce lawyers is repeated, in a degree that is only slightly less extreme, by criminal defense counsel and by the other lowest prestige specialties—in particular, general family practice and personal injury plaintiffs' work. (The direction of these findings would certainly be anticipated, but the clarity of the pattern is impressive when one recalls that the practitioners included as "specialists" in these fields may have devoted up to 75 percent of their time to other types of work.)

Public utilities practitioners are a somewhat deviant case, with relatively small percentages both of solo practitioners and of large firm

47. The other three client-type categories that we analyzed and their correlations with prestige are "mean percentage of law practice income derived from personal (versus 'business') clients" (−.71); "mean percentage of personal clients who have professional, technical, or managerial occupations" (.79); and "mean percentage of income from business clients that is derived from 'small businesses' (*e.g.*, neighborhood stores, local restaurants, local real estate brokers, etc.—less than $250,000 in sales per year)" (−.71).

lawyers and with substantial amounts of business with both blue collar and major corporate clients. Part of the explanation of these results may be found in the very high percentage of corporate house counsel among the public utilities specialists. Forty percent of the public utilities lawyers are house counsel, a considerably higher percentage than is the case for any of the other specialties. (The next highest percentages of house counsel are found among banking and personal injury defense counsel, about 23 percent of each.) Government lawyers and those who practice in the smallest firms (fewer than ten lawyers) also make up substantial percentages of the public utilities lawyers, each accounting for 20 percent of them. It seems probable that the major corporate clients of the public utilities specialists are, for the most part, served by those who are house counsel, while the blue collar clients are represented in the other sorts of work done by those in the small firms or in solo practice. Rather than generalize further, however, it might be well to recall that only a small number of public utilities specialists are included in our sample.

Public utilities work also has by far the highest percentage of "stable clients," clients whom the lawyer has represented for three years or more (see column 11). That is, again, perhaps attributable to its high percentage of house counsel and of government lawyers (both of whom have, by definition, no client turnover). In general, the higher prestige specialties tend to have greater stability of clientele, though the correlation of this variable with prestige just fails statistical significance at the .05 level (.33). Criminal defense has the lowest percentage of clients represented for three years or more, in spite of the well-publicized delay in bringing criminal cases to trial. But it is interesting to note that lawyers engaged in general family practice report that they have, on the average, represented 58 percent of their clients for three years or more. Apparently the clientele of the neighborhood lawyer is fairly stable. As on several of the other variables, we find that the antitrust plaintiffs' lawyers are somewhat out of line here, given what one would expect from their position in the prestige order—they have one of the lowest percentages of stable clients. Some of this tendency may well reflect the relative youth of practitioners in this field, as well as the nature of their specialty.

Work Task Characteristics

All of the respondents in our survey were asked to characterize the nature of the tasks involved in their legal work in terms of dimensions defined by sets of polar opposites. The results on three of these dimensions are summarized in columns 12 through 14 of table 2. The first reports the percentage of the practitioners in each specialty who characterized their work as demanding a high degree of professonal expertise. Ninety percent of the securities specialists responded that it would not be possible to train paraprofessionals to handle many of the tasks involved in their practice. Though this percentage was far higher than that of any of the other specialties, there was a general tendency for the more prestigious specialties to be relatively high on this dimension—it correlates .49 with prestige. The two sides of antitrust work were, however, both somewhat out of line on this dimension. In spite of their high prestige standing, only 40 percent of each of those sorts of practitioners believed that a professional's skills were so uniformly required in antitrust work.

At the other end of the prestige order, only about 30 percent of the general family practitioners believed that professional expertise was indispensable in their work. Divorce, criminal defense, and personal injury plaintiffs' lawyers were slightly more likely to feel that a professional's training was essential to performing the tasks required in their practices—approximately 40 percent of the practitioners in each of those fields responded that paraprofessionals could not be trained to handle much of the work. And civil liberties had, again, a position on this dimension that was inconsistent with its relatively low prestige rank—nearly 70 percent of the civil liberties lawyers believed that their work required professional expertise. This result may be related to the high percentage of civil liberties lawyers who are graduates of the elite law schools or to the high rate of change in the law of the field.

The second of these work task dimensions deals with the extent to which the practice of each of the specialties requires "skill in negotiating and advising clients, rather than detailed concern with technical rules" (see column 13). Though this may sometimes be associated with the relative proportions of corporate and individual clients, that is not always the case. To the extent that the big business lawyer spends his time putting big business deals together, as many lawyers certainly do, he functions as a negotiator and advisor. The overall tendency, however, is for the negotiating and advising tasks to be inversely related to prestige; the correlation is −.42. The largest percentages of practitioners who define their tasks as negotiating and advising are to be found in such specialties as general family practice and divorce. Securities work, by contrast, has one of the lowest percentages on this dimension, the other conspicuously low ones being antitrust plaintiffs' work, banking, and criminal prosecution. (Apparently, the negotiation of plea bargains does not consume much of the prosecutors' time or attention.) Note, however, that the antitrust defense practitioners differ from those on the other side of their cases and from lawyers in the other high prestige specialties in that antitrust defense has one of the highest percentages defining their tasks as negotiating and advising.

The third work task dimension concerns the extent to which practitioners in the specialty find that the nature of their work requires them to concentrate on one field of law (see column 14). This dimension is, then, a measure of the degree of "true specialization" (or, at least, of the lawyers' perceptions of it). Securities has one of the highest percentages of practitioners reporting that their work is concentrated in one field. The only specialties higher on this dimension are patents—a "classic" specialty that traditionally commands the exclusive attention of its practitioners—and labor union work, perhaps the purest of the "new" specialties. Divorce has one of the lowest percentages on this dimension. Other specialties low on this dimension are probate, commercial work, and—especially low—general family practice. The dimension correlates .52 with prestige.

It is interesting to note that, on all three of these dimensions, general family practice is found at one of the extremes. Perhaps this result is attributable to the fact that a general family practice is perceived as the sole remaining refuge of the general practitioner, the small town lawyer in the big city. In fact, the range of problems handled by these lawyers is, no doubt, rather severely limited. They are highly unlikely to handle any antitrust law, or securities, or patents, or municipal bond work, or labor law. Still, it is no doubt true that the general family practice is as close as we come in today's major cities to the practice of law as it existed before the rise of specialization and of the large firm.

Income

Finally, we turn to the extrinsic rewards of law practice—the percentage of practitioners in each of the specialties who have incomes from law practice of $50,000 per year or more (see column 15). (The income figures used in computing the percentages presented in the table were adjusted to take account of the differences in the age distributions of the practitioners in the various specialties.)[48] The financial rewards

48. Because an individual's income tends to increase with age and higher prestige specialties tend to have disproportionately younger lawyers, we were concerned to eliminate the confounding influence of age on income and prestige of specialties. To do so, we projected incomes of persons active in a particular specialty as if all the specialties had the same age distribution. When the income distribution is thus standardized by age, its correlation with specialty prestige (.40) just fails to achieve statistical significance.

of law practice do not quite achieve a significant correlation with the prestige of the specialties and, when the income variable is included with others in a regression equation, it makes no additional contribution whatsoever to the prediction of prestige.[49] The highest incomes are, however, those of specialties near the top of the prestige ranking, and the lowest income specialties are also relatively low in prestige. The two highest percentages of practitioners with incomes of $50,000 or more are found in the two sides of antitrust work, the antitrust plaintiffs' and defendants' lawyers. High income rates are also found in the banking, commercial, and civil liberties specialties. The civil liberties practitioners are probably corporate lawyers doing this work *pro bono publico*. The lowest percentages are found in criminal prosecution (where there is a system constraint on income—all of the practitioners are required to be full-time, salaried public employees, doing this sort of work exclusively), in consumer law, and in real estate. Real estate, thus, has fewer high income practitioners than would be suggested by the more moderate prestige level of the specialty. While securities lawyers do not achieve as extreme a position on this dimension as they do on several of the others, the specialty nonetheless has one of the larger percentages of high income practitioners. The correlation of law practice income with the prestige of the specialties is certainly in the expected direction, then, but it is important to note that the extrinsic reward system seems to affect the prestige judgments less than several of the more intrinsic characteristics of the practice—including, specifically, client type, the nature of the work, and the characteristics of the lawyers engaged in the practice.

The lack of a strong relationship between income and prestige seems to surprise some lawyers. It may not appear so surprising, however, if we consider the possible impact of specialty prestige on the market for legal services. Prestige may tend to increase the supply of lawyers in the high status specialties and to decrease supply in the types of work that have lower prestige. If these hypothesized effects of prestige on supply did occur, their impact on income would, of course, tend to increase remuneration in the lower status specialties and, conversely, tend to decrease income in the high prestige specialties—producing, perhaps, a result like the one we observe. The result gains additional credence from a study of the medical profession that found no significant correlation between income and the professional prestige of the medical specialties.[50]

49. See our Technical Appendix at table 6, *infra*.

50. See Schwartzbaum, McGrath, & Rothman, *supra* note 11, at 370.

THE MULTIFACETED STRUCTURE OF PRESTIGE

Let us now turn to a closer examination of the prestige evaluations of the 30 specialties by the subsample of Chicago lawyers that were used in constructing the standardized prestige scores, the central dependent variable. The reader will recall that these lawyers were asked to evaluate the general prestige of each specialty in terms of a five-point scale, ranging from "outstanding" to "poor." In attempting to discern the operation of any underlying principles that might account for the ways in which the judges allocated prestige among the various specialties, we shall use two structure-revealing techniques, smallest space analysis and hierarchical clustering. Another way of formulating our task is to ask: since the specialties are elements in a reasonably well defined conceptual universe, can we detect systematic patterns in the ways in which they are differentially evaluated? Once we have described these patterns, we can then consider how the extensive differentiation of the specialties discussed in the preceding section helps to account for these prestige judgments.

As the first step in our analysis, we computed the product-moment correlations of the judges' prestige evaluations for every possible pair of specialties.[51] A high positive correlation between the prestige scores given any two specialties tells us that the judges tend to see the two specialties in a similar way from the standpoint of their relative prestige standings—that is, as both having relatively high or relatively low social standing in the profession. A negative correlation, on the other hand, tells us that judges who evaluate one specialty as having a high prestige standing in the profession tend to regard the other as having a lower social standing. A lack of correlation (*i.e.*, a coefficient approximately zero in value) indicates no correspondence in the judges' evaluations of the specialties under consideration.

These correlation coefficients can be treated as estimating the relative proximities of specialties to one another with respect to their prestige standings. That is, specialties similarly evaluated and thus having comparatively high positive coefficients are in some sense closer or more

51. Put most crudely, this coefficient measures the degree to which two variables co-vary in a linear fashion. Another way of putting it is to say that the coefficient tells us how well we can predict the value of one variable from knowing the value of another. That is, the higher the positive coefficient, the more strictly or closely an increase in the value of one variable is associated with an increase in the value of the other. Conversely, the larger the negative correlation, the more closely an increase in the value of one variable is associated with a decrease in the other. The absence of a linear association between the two variables is indicated by a coefficient of zero. More formally, we can say that a product-moment correlation coefficient is the ratio of the covariation of the two variables to the square root of the product of the variation in the first variable and the variation in the second (*cf.* Hubert M. Blalock, Jr., Social Statistics 285-92 (New York: McGraw-Hill Book Co., 1960)). This coefficient can only have numerical values between plus or minus 1.0.

proximate to one another than specialties that are dissimilarly evaluated and that thus have either zero or negative coefficients.[52] These latter specialties would appear to be farther apart in the minds of the judges. Note, however, that in comparing these proximities with one another, we do not expect them to order themselves automatically along a single or unidimensional prestige ranking unless prestige is, in fact, a unidimensional variable—as income, for example, would be. The patterning of the coefficients could also indicate the presence of several divergent dimensions or bases underlying the generation of prestige judgments. In other words, our general conceptual framework and method of analysis permit prestige to be a multifaceted subjective phenomenon that need not map neatly into a single prestige hierarchy.

The structure of the resulting 30-by-30 matrix of correlation coefficients, which contains 435 coefficients, is obviously very difficult to discern by visual inspection of the matrix itself. Happily for us, however, a number of techniques have recently been developed to facilitate the recovery of the underlying structure of such a matrix. Because we were prepared to make only ordinal assumptions about our measures, rather than some of the more restrictive assumptions required to employ factor analytic techniques,[53] we turned to smallest space analysis.[54]

---

52. Peter Rossi has kindly brought to our attention that interpretations of correlation coefficients of this nature are somewhat ambiguous. If, on the one hand, all the judges agreed on their prestige evaluations of the specialties, there could only be small correlations between judgments across specialties. This is so because correlation is based on covariation and, in this case, covariation would be minimal. Such small correlations among the prestige evaluations of a cross section of occupations in the labor force are, in fact, typically observed. On the other hand, when judges are in agreement concerning the attributes on which they evaluate specialties (*e.g.*, type of client) but disagree in the evaluations they make on the basis of these attributes, substantial correlations of the sort observed in our study are the result. Other analyses we have done support this speculation. *E.g.*, in examining the data using analysis of variance techniques, we found that characteristics of the judges themselves, including such things as their type of specialty, law school, and value orientations, were related to systematic differences in their prestige judgments. See Charles Cappell, Differential Evaluations of the Status of Legal Specialties: A Detailed Analysis with Theoretical Implications (1977) (unpublished paper, American Bar Foundation).

53. Because of the relative crudeness with which we have measured prestige differences among the specialties, we certainly do not want to assume that our prestige scale is as precise, valid, and invariant a measuring device as the use of a yardstick would be in measuring physical distances between pairs of points in physical space. While we are prepared to assume that the specialties can generally be reliably arranged in a rank order from high to low prestige standing, we are not prepared to say that the interval separating the top-ranked and second-ranked specialties is equal to the interval between the third- and fourth-ranked or the twenty-ninth- and thirtieth-ranked specialties, or that specialty *X* has twice the prestige that specialty *Y* has. This, among other things, is what is meant when we say that we can treat the prestige scale used to rank specialties as meeting the ordinal or ranking assumption about scale measurement but that it fails to meet the much more restrictive assumptions of ratio (*e.g.*, a yardstick) or interval (*e.g.*, a thermometer) scales. Although frequently violated in practice, factor analysis ideally requires scale measurement at the level of interval scales.

54. *Cf.* Louis Guttman, A General Nonmetric Technique for Finding the Smallest Coordinate Space for a Configuration of Points, 33 Psychometrika 469 (1968); David D. McFarland

This technique was explicitly designed to represent graphically such a matrix in the fewest possible number of dimensions of a Euclidean space. Most readers will be familiar with such graphic representations from their exposure to plane and solid geometry in high school or college.[55] Perhaps an analogy will help clarify the procedure and its purpose. If one were to perform a smallest space analysis of the mileage chart presenting the distances between all the principal cities of the United States, he would obtain the conventional two-dimensional map of the United States on which the locations of the individual points—representing the cities—are so arranged that they accurately reflect, according to a specified scale (say, of one inch equal to 20 miles), the distances between any given city and every other city. Similarly, the original matrix of correlation coefficients among prestige judgments estimates the relative (*i.e.*, rank-ordered) distances between each specialty and all the others in terms of their similarities (or systematic differences) in eliciting prestige judgments.

Figure 1 presents the three-dimensional smallest space solution, with a coefficient of alienation equal to .129, indicating a satisfactory goodness of fit.[56] In considering how this picture can best be interpreted, we should first emphasize that three dimensions were, in fact, required to achieve an adequate representation of the original matrix of correlations. The one-dimensional solution had a very high coefficient of alienation, indicating that a single dimension, presumably arranging the

---

& Daniel J. Brown, Social Distance as a Metric: A Systematic Introduction to Smallest Space Analysis, *in* Edward O. Laumann, Bonds of Pluralism: The Form and Substance of Urban Social Networks 213 (New York: John Wiley & Sons, 1973); James C. Lingoes, The Guttman-Lingoes Nonmetric Program Series (Ann Arbor, Mich.: Mathesis Press, 1973).

55. In principle, one can always represent exactly the interpoint distances among n points in $n - 1$ dimensions in a Euclidean space. Of course, since we cannot physically represent a space having more than three dimensions, we are usually interested in seeing if it is possible to sacrifice some accuracy of representation for a minimum number of dimensions, ideally three or fewer, consistent with an acceptable level of distortion between the "real world" distances and those represented in the smallest space model of the real world. Two-dimensional world maps are examples of representing a three-dimensional object, the earth, in a more convenient and easily comprehended graphic form. Note, however, the distortions necessitated by adopting such an expedient. Similarly, smallest space analysis tells us whether we have found an acceptable goodness of fit between the original matrix of proximity estimates, treated here as providing information only about the rank order of the distances among the points, and the calculated Euclidean distances between the points of a particular smallest space solution (*cf.* Peter V. Marsden & Edward O. Laumann, The Social Structure of Religious Groups: A Replication and Methodological Critique, *to appear in* Samuel Shye, ed., Festschrift (Jerusalem: Hebrew University Press, forthcoming)). When the coefficient of alienation, the measure of goodness of fit, is zero, it indicates a perfect congruence between the real world proximities and the distances portrayed in the smallest space solution. As the coefficient increases in value, it indicates growing distortions or discrepancies between the real world data and the smallest space solution. Experience has shown that a coefficient of alienation $\leqslant .15$ indicates a satisfactory or acceptable smallest space solution.

56. See discussion of SSA-1 in Lingoes, *supra* note 54.

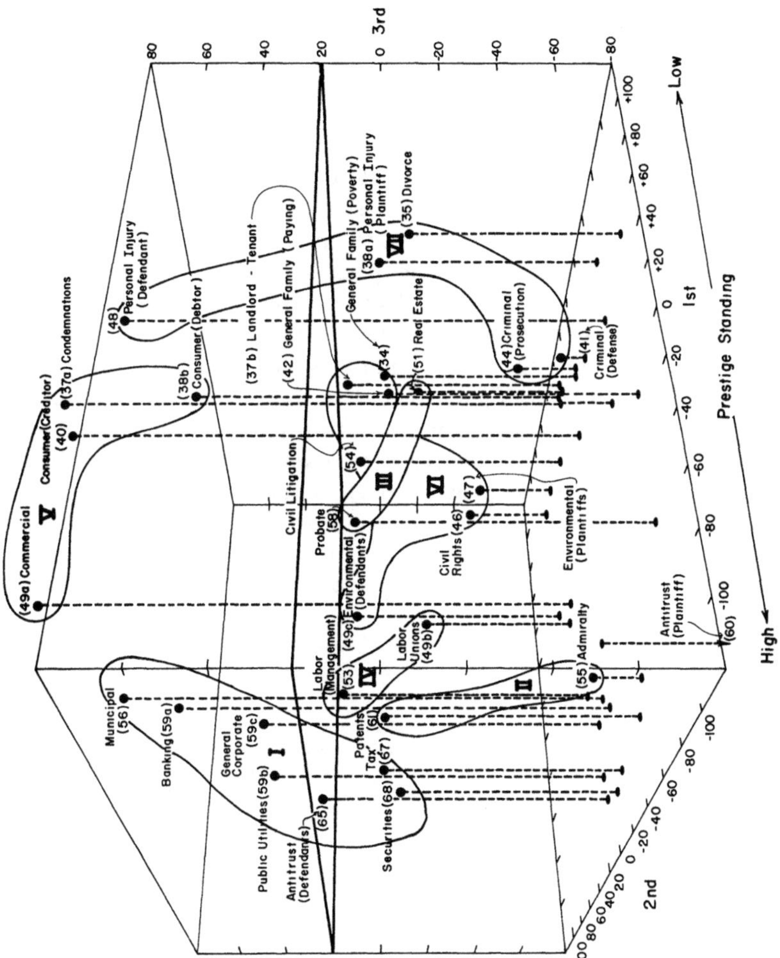

Figure 1. Three-Dimensional Smallest Space Solution for Prestige Judgments of Legal Specialties (Coefficient of Alienation = .129)

specialties from highest to lowest prestige, could not be found that did not distort the more complex order present in the original data beyond acceptable limits. Apparently the judges were responding to the specialties in a more complex fashion—*i.e.*, on the basis of a multifaceted conception of their similarities and differences with respect to prestige or deference entitlements.[57] It is true, however, that the locations of the specialties on the first axis of the three-dimensional solution are highly correlated (– .89) with the standardized prestige scores given in table 1, indicating that general prestige standing accounts for the lion's share of the ordering of the specialties on the first axis.[58]

Quite clearly, generalized prestige standing has a powerful influence on the location of specialties in the spatial solution. Also apparent, however, is the operation of other factors in determining perceived prestige similarities among the specialties that are not so easily organized according to a single dimension. One of the special attractions of smallest space analysis over other data-reduction techniques is the fact that one is not limited to using unidimensional ordering principles in interpreting the spatial configurations.[59] It is, for example, quite permissible to look for localized regions in the space in which the points are relatively homogeneous with respect to some nominal or qualitative characteristic distinguishing them from all other points in the space. In another context, we have called such regionalization "sector differentiation."[60] Another aspect of the configuration that may be interpretable is the relative distances of the points from the centroid of the solu-

57. *Cf.* Shils, *supra* note 10.

58. Of course, because the data used to construct the standard prestige scores are the same as those used to calculate the original matrix of correlation coefficients, there is a sense in which the two are not strictly independent, despite the very different manipulations of the data involved in the two procedures. Lacking any independent fine-grained estimates of the prestige order of the specialties, we must run the risk of some circularity in our reasoning on this point. In our defense, however, we should stress the high face validity of the prestige order and its congruence with orderings used by other researchers (*e.g.*, Carlin, *supra* note 29; Richard A. Watson & Rondal G. Downing, The Politics of the Bench and the Bar: Judicial Selection under the Missouri Nonpartisan Court Plan (New York: John Wiley & Sons, 1969); Erwin O. Smigel, The Wall Street Lawyer: Professional Organization Man? (New York: Free Press, 1964)) and also point out that the high correlation between the first axis and the standard scores—whether or not it is, in part, artifactual—is not crucial to our subsequent analysis.

59. The coordinates of the smallest space solution are themselves completely arbitrary and can be rotated to any other orientation without changing the order of the Euclidean interpoint distances—a feature that facilitates interpreting the generating principles organizing the space (*cf.* Laumann & Pappi, *supra* note 8, at 6-9). Being arbitrary, the coordinates are not always substantively interpretable (although, for the case in hand, the first axis of the solution happened to be substantively interpretable in terms of a general prestige rank order).

60. *Cf.* Edward O. Laumann & Franz Urban Pappi, New Directions in the Study of Community Elites, 38 Am. Soc. Rev. 212, 221-23 (1973).

tion[61]—that is, points in peripheral locations may differ in systematic ways from more centrally located points.[62]

To identify localized regions or clusters of points in the space disciplined by criteria more objective than visual impressions, we submitted the original matrix of correlation coefficients to a hierarchical clustering analysis using the maximum or diameter method.[63] Essentially, this method of analysis successively creates more and more inclusive clusters of specialties on the basis of their intercorrelations with one another until there is only one cluster containing all the points. A point (*i.e.*, a specialty, in our case) is added to a cluster at a given stage when it has at least a stipulated minimum correlation with all the other points in the cluster. The investigator can then examine the resulting nested hierarchy of clusters to determine the most meaningful set for his analytic purposes. Figure 2 presents a graphic representation (called a dendrogram) summarizing the results of this analysis. Reading the dendrogram from left to right, the reader can readily see how specialties were successively added to particular clusters as the correlation coefficients linking given specialties declined in value.

Inspection of the dendrogram suggests that a minimum value of .20 would provide a meaningful cutoff point for identifying the clusters; and, for ease of reference, these are listed in table 3 (and indicated in figure 1 by Roman numerals and encircling lines around the relevant points). Note, however, that most of the specialties in a given cluster are much more highly correlated with one another than this minimum correlation to add an outlier specialty to the cluster would imply. The average correlation of the pairs of specialties in the big business cluster (I), for example, is .40. Table 3 also indicates that these seven clusters can be grouped into two mutually exclusive clusters, *i.e.*, higher status specialties with predominantly corporate clientele versus lower status specialties with small business or individual clients, labeled clusters A and B, respectively. Indeed, this penultimate clustering is finally joined in the last step of the hierarchical clustering (in which all points are put

61. The centroid is the center of the smallest space solution. A physical analogy gives an intuitive sense of its meaning: if all points in a two-dimensional smallest space solution were a set of equal weights resting on a weightless plane, the centroid would be that point on which the plane would balance. For a technical discussion, see E. Roskam & J. C. Lingoes, A Mathematical and Empirical Study of Two Multidimensional Scaling Algorithms, 1 Mich. Mathematical Psych. Program 1 (1971).

62. *Cf.* Laumann & Pappi, *supra* note 60, at 221-23.

63. *Cf.* Stephen C. Johnson, Hierarchical Clustering Schemes, 32 Psychometrika 241 (1967); Kenneth D. Bailey, Cluster Analysis, *in* David R. Heise, ed., Sociological Methodology 1975, at 59 (San Francisco: Jossey-Bass, 1974); Ronald Burt, Positions in Networks, 55 Soc. Forces, in press.

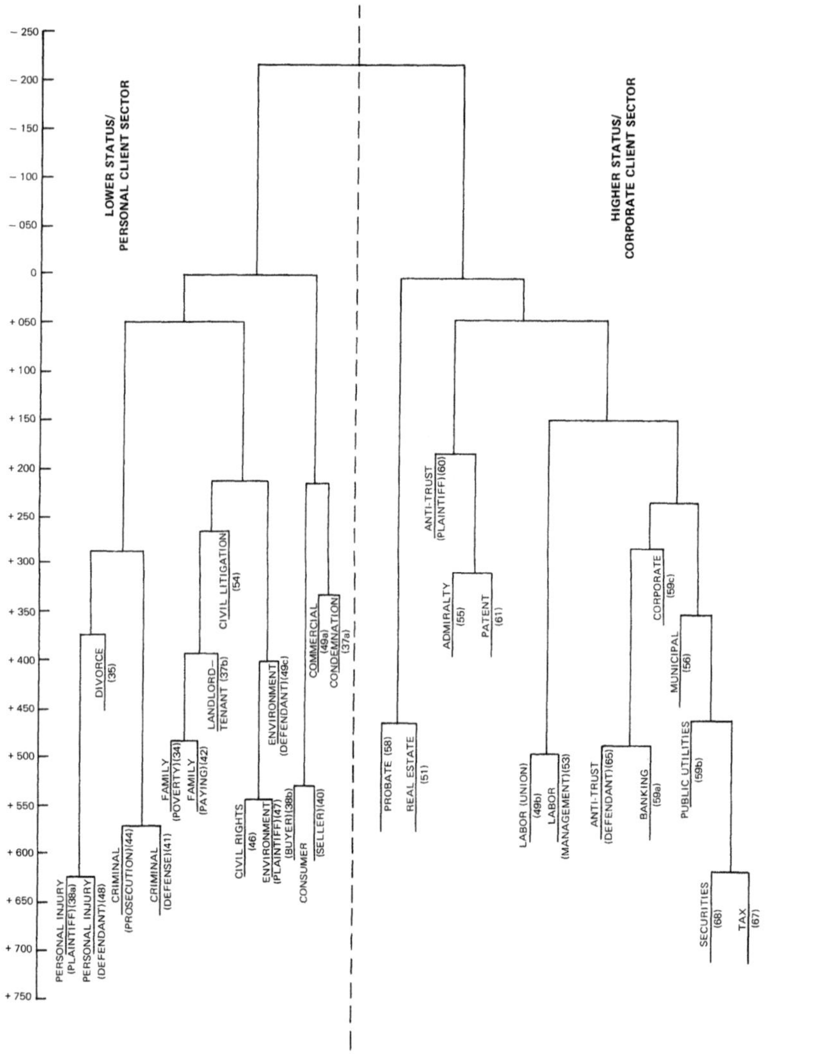

Figure 2. Hierarchical Clustering Solution for Correlations Among Prestige Ratings of Legal Specialties Made by a Subsample of Chicago Lawyers, Diameter Method

into one all-inclusive cluster) with a negative correlation of −.21, indicating that prestige evaluations of specialties in one cluster are negatively correlated with those of specialties in the other.

Within cluster A, one can discern an internal order among the component clusters that follows a gradient of specialties, from those serving "establishment," big business, and government clients to those serving relatively less esteemed clients in the corporate world—viz., the labor unions. Similarly, cluster B appears to be internally ordered from specialties serving "respectable" small business and personal clients to those having to do with more unsavory and disreputable clients.

TABLE 3
Clusters Identified by Hierarchical Clustering Analysis of Original Matrix of Correlation Coefficients, Diameter Method with +.20 Criterion

	Cluster No.	Cluster Label	Specialties in Cluster (with Standardized Prestige Score)[a]
(A) Higher status/ corporate clientele clusters	I	Big business	Securities (68), tax (67), antitrust (defendants) (65), banking (59a), general corporate (59), public utilities (59b), municipal (56)
	II	Classic specialties	Patents (61), admiralty (55)
	III	Property	Probate (58), real estate (51)
	IV	Labor	Labor (management) (53), labor (union) (49b)
(B) Lower status/ small business/ individual clientele clusters	V	Small business/ commercial	Commercial (49a), consumer (creditor) (40), consumer (debtor) (38b), condemnations (37a)
	VI	Public interest & litigation	Civil litigation (54), environmental (defendant) (49c), environmental (plaintiff) (47), civil rights (46), family (paying) (42), landlord-tenant (37b), family (poverty) (34)
	VII	Unsavory litigation	Personal injury (defendant) (48), criminal prosecution (44), criminal defense (41), personal injury (plaintiff) (38a), divorce (35)

[a]Antitrust (plaintiff) (60) was not assigned to any of the above clusters at the criterion specified.

Figure 1 tells essentially the same story that the dendrogram told us, but with the added advantage of showing how the clusters are related to one another. (Remember that the closer two points are in the space, the more highly correlated they are *and* the more similar their profiles of correlations with all the other points.) The seven clusters (plus the one nonclusterable specialty, antitrust plaintiffs' work) all roughly fall on the surface of a sphere. Using the first axis as an orientation for examining the spatial arrangement, we can divide the sphere into hemispheres with the left-hand hemisphere mapping cluster A and the right-hand hemisphere mapping cluster B. Roughly the upper half of the "globe" consists entirely of commercially oriented practice specialties, whether the clients are major corporations or small businesses (note how personal injury defendants' work in cluster VII is pulled into this region because its clients usually are corporations), while the lower half of the globe consists of specialties serving individual clients, whether reputable or unsavory. The reader may verify our characterization of the broad regions of the space by consulting the appropriate columns in tables 1 and 2 describing the differentiation of the specialties.

ACCOUNTING FOR THE DIFFERENTIAL ALLOCATION OF PRESTIGE

We are now in a position to examine more systematically how we might account for the differential allocation of prestige among the legal specialties. We remarked earlier on some of the conceptual and methodological difficulties in coming to terms with the concept "prestige," especially as it relates to the differing evaluations of an occupation's specialized activities. While we should not lose sight of the central proposition of the preceding section that the evaluation of the legal specialties is fundamentally multifaceted in nature, we want now to pull together the disparate analytic threads of our empirical analysis by focusing on explaining the rank order of the standardized prestige scores reported in column 1 of table 1.

In the course of noting the diverse ways in which the legal specialties are differentiated, we developed specific rationales for expecting each mode of differentiation to be related to varying prestige judgments. To be sure, of the many possible attributes of a social position that theorists and empirical researchers have suggested might be grounds for differing prestige evaluations, we have included in our analysis only one or two representatives of each of the major varieties of deference entitlements recognized in the literature. Given the limited theoretical closure in the field and the limitations on the data that we could realistically gather on the various specialties, we can certainly make no claim that our list of attributes is theoretically or empirically exhaustive, although we believe it to be as comprehensive as possible under the constraints of the study design. Attributes imputed by scholar judges, presented in table 1, for example, were specifically designed to tap what we thought were the most important, analytically independent aspects of the work tasks having probable implications for prestige judgments, irrespective of the other social characteristics of the persons who perform such tasks. (We recognize, of course, that our judges' evaluations might well have been "contaminated" by their also knowing the sorts of people involved in particular specialties.)

Four of these five attributes proved, in fact, to be significantly correlated with prestige, giving some support to our initial ideas. We can only appeal to face validity, however, to justify our claim that these five attributes are analytically independent of one another. In examining the intercorrelation matrix of the five imputed characteristics (given in table 4 in the Technical Appendix, *infra*), we found that five of the ten correlations were statistically significant, but these were usually of only modest strength. The correlational structure had no simple pattern, although the relative strength of specific correlations made good sense. For example, as one might have expected, intellectual challenge and rapidity of change of the law relevant to a specialty were correlated .69, and the *pro bono* and ethical conduct scores were correlated .62. Similarly, in table 2 we presented a number of measures relevant to assessing one or another of four broad categories of deference entitlements. Most proved to have statistically significant, zero-order associations with the allocation of prestige standing among the specialties (see the first column of table 5 in the Technical Appendix). But they too are correlated to varying degrees among themselves.

The crucial question thus becomes: given the extensive information we have about the characteristics of the specialties and their practitioners, many of which are known to co-vary with one another in highly predictable ways, can we devise a parsimonious account of the crucial features of the specialties that appear to explain the differential allocation of prestige among them? In attempting to answer this question, we decided to construct several alternative theoretical models of the prestige-allocation process in which we specified in advance a set of specialty characteristics (which are called the set of independent variables) that we believe determine differing prestige standings. We were then interested in determining the net effect on prestige standing of each specialty characteristic, holding constant the effects of all the other independent variables in the model. The statistical technique of multiple regression analysis has been designed to do just this sort of task.[64] Because of its highly technical nature, which requires some familiarity with advanced statistics, however, we are putting a detailed discussion of the results obtained by the technique in a Technical Appendix. (Incidentally, we have attempted to write this appendix in a way that should be comprehensible even to uninitiated laymen, although they might have to skip some of the technical details.) Here we shall simply summarize the main results to be drawn from this analysis.

64. For a good, brief introduction to this mode of statistical analysis, see Blalock, *supra* note 51, at 326-58.

The most parsimonious account that we can offer for the prestige ordering of the legal specialties would focus attention on the simultaneous operation of only five features of these specialties, each of which appears to make an independent "net" contribution to explaining the overall outcome of the evaluative process. These five features together account for 92 percent of the total variation in prestige scores (that is, only 8 percent of the variation in prestige scores remains unexplained by these five predictive factors). The reader should consult the Technical Appendix to learn some of the reasons why we must be cautious in accepting this particular account of the relative importance of the five independent variables. Particularly noteworthy here is the problem that there are some statistical sources of instability in our estimates that might result in some probably modest changes in our conclusions, were we to replicate our analysis on another sample of respondents.

Our results, based on the analysis of composite model III in the appendix, indicate that the most important feature of a legal specialty in accounting for its relative prestige standing is its *pro bono* score. The higher a specialty stands in its reputation for being motivated by altruistic (as opposed to profitable) considerations, the lower it is likely to be in the prestige order. Moreover, intellectual difficulty and reputation for ethical conduct make about equally weighted positive contributions to a specialty's standing in the prestige order. Of the many specialty characteristics of practitioners and their practices that we have considered, two stand out as being of particular importance. The higher the mean percentage of blue collar clients and the higher the percentage of Jewish practitioners in the specialty, the lower we find the specialty in the prestige order. Since we have only data gathered at one point in time and, therefore, are hardly in a position to demonstrate a cause-and-effect relationship between any of our independent variables and the dependent variable, how we are to interpret these results is very much an open question. Our concluding section, to which we now turn, attempts to place these and our other results in a broader interpretive context.

CONCLUSIONS

Sorting out the elements of the prestige of legal specialties is quite difficult because of the high degree of intercorrelation among several of the hypothesized independent variables. Some interpretations of the results, however, seem relatively clear. The general pattern of the prestige ranking, with specialties serving "big business" clients at the top and those serving individual clients (especially clients from lower socioeconomic groups) at the bottom, is unambiguous. Here again, however, we may run up against a confounding of effects. The degree of intellectual challenge of the specialties is highly correlated not only with their prestige (.65) but also with their percentages of blue collar clients (− .59). Thus, what may appear to be an effect of client type on the prestige rankings may, in fact, be in large part an effect of peer opinions of the intellectual demands of the different sorts of practice.

But one may question whether the lower intellectual challenge ratings assigned to the specialties that serve persons from lower socioeconomic groups might not reflect simply the social class or socioeconomic status bias of the group of scholars who rated intellectual challenge. We think this unlikely.[65] Their ratings probably reflect a quite accurate or objective perception of some of the realities of law practice. That is, work done for personal clients may well be, in fact, characteristically less intellectually challenging than are businesses' legal problems, and for that reason, *inter alia,* less prestigious. One divorce, title search, automobile accident, or repossession of a refrigerator is likely to be very much like another. What law there is to learn on these subjects may be mastered relatively quickly, after which the cases begin to become rather routine. At least, these may well seem to be the characteristics of work for individuals and small businesses when compared with, for example, a corporate acquisition or merger with complex tax and antitrust implications.

Rather than resorting to further techniques of multivariate analysis to attempt to unravel the confounding of effects of intellectual challenge and client type, a condition that may well exist in the real world, let us simply look at a few specialties where the degree of intellectual challenge is held constant. Our list of 30 specialties encompasses six fields of law where the adversary system creates clearly distinguishable specialties representing the two sides of the case—antitrust, labor, environmental, personal injury, criminal, and consumer law. The intellectual challenge ratings of the two sides of each of these specialties are, of course, substantially identical.[66] (Dealing with the legal substance of

65. The reason why we think this unlikely is presented in note 66 *infra.*

66. The differences between the intellectual challenge scores of each of these pairs are, in fact, very small, ranging from zero to three points. In the five comparisons in which there is a difference in the intellectual challenge scores of the two sides of the case (in environmental law, the scores are identical: 61), however, the difference is always in the same direction—the higher score is given to the "nonestablishment" side of the specialty. Thus, the direction of the differences suggests that the scholars who served as our judges of intellectual challenge did not share any possible status bias or proestablishment view of those who assessed prestige, but may instead have been somewhat biased in the other direction.

a case requires the lawyer, on whichever side of the case, to anticipate and respond to the law on the other side. Differences in the burden of proof or extralegal differences in resources available might conceivably make it easier to try one side of the case than the other, but the direction of these differences is certainly not consistent.) In each of the six fields of law listed above, the side that represents the more "establishment" client is consistently rated higher in prestige. That is, those who defend criminals are given less prestige than those who prosecute; labor union lawyers rank lower in prestige than do the labor lawyers who represent management; lawyers who represent plaintiffs with personal injury, environmental, or antitrust claims are assigned lower prestige scores than the lawyers who represent the insurance companies and other businesses that are the defendants in such actions; and the advocates for buyers of consumer goods have less prestige than do those who represent the sellers. The consistency of result in these comparisons seems to us to be rather persuasive support for the hypothesis that client type has an effect on prestige that is independent of the intellectual difficulty of the subject matter. And that effect is, quite clearly, to enhance the prestige of work done for corporate, establishment, or big business clients and to derogate that done for small businesses or for individuals, particularly those from the lower classes.

A similar tendency is observed in the strong negative correlation of prestige with the rating of the degree of altruistic motivation of practitioners in each of the specialties (the *pro bono* score), a variable that emerged in the regression analysis as one of the most important predictors of prestige. While we doubt that altruism is directly or consciously derogated, even in the practice of law, it seems clear that the profit motive and the values associated with it are given precedence in the allocation of prestige within the profession. Service to the sorts of clients that the lawyer profits by serving is more likely to enhance the prestige of a specialty—the American legal profession seems, in fact, to be preoccupied with economic enterprise. Llewellyn observed long ago that the "main work" of the metropolitan bar was "in essence the doing of business," and he drew some further conclusions.

> Now, any man's interests, any man's outlook, are shaped in greatest part by what he *does*. His perspective is in terms of what he knows. His sympathies and ethical judgments are determined essentially by the things and the people he works on and for and with. . . . Hence the practice of corporation law not only works for business men toward business ends, but develops within itself a business point of view—toward the work to be done, toward

> the value of the work to the community, indeed, toward the way in which to do the work.[67]

Thus, the legal profession is more concerned with the facilitation of business, with "getting things done," than with alleviating human suffering or with helping people. There is an important difference of degree, at least, between the legal and the medical professions in this respect. This is not to say that the legal profession does not perform useful social functions–it obviously does. The values it serves may be caricatured in catch phrases, such as, "The business of America is business," "What's good for General Motors is good for the country," or "Chicago–the city that works!" but the values served by the legal profession are the core economic values of our society.[68] The more a legal specialty serves these values, the higher its prestige within the profession.

Llewellyn's characterization of the twentieth century corporation lawyer may be contrasted with C. Wright Mills's evocation of the nineteenth century advocate:

> Before the ascendancy of the large corporation, skill and eloquence in advocacy selected nineteenth-century leaders of the bar; reputations and wealth were created and maintained in the courts, of which the lawyer was an officer. He was an agent of the law, handling the general interests of society, as fixed and allowed in the law; his day's tasks were as varied as human activity and experience itself. An opinion leader, a man whose recommendations to the community counted, who handled obligations and rights of intimate family and life problems, the liberty and property of all who had them, the lawyer personally pointed out the course of the law and counseled his client against the pitfalls of illegality. Deferred to by his client, he carefully displayed the dignity he claimed to embody. Rewarded for apparent honesty, carrying an ethical halo, held to be fit material for high statesmanship, the lawyer upheld public service and was professionally above business motives.[69]

Though Mills's picture may be somewhat exaggerated or idealized, it does seem likely that the prespecialized lawyer dealt with a greater range of human problems–all of the problems, save for those of health and of the soul, that were of greatest consequence to the individual. They dealt with, in Mills's felicitous phrase, "the liberty and property

67. Llewellyn, *supra* note 2, at 177.
68. *Cf.* Francis X. Sutton et al., The American Business Creed (Cambridge, Mass.: Harvard University Press, 1956).
69. C. Wright Mills, White Collar: The American Middle Classes 121 (New York: Oxford University Press, 1951).

of all who had them." The modern lawyer, by contrast, encounters a much smaller range of problems, and those are unlikely to be the intimate problems of an individual or his family. Relatively few lawyers now confront human suffering very directly in the course of their work, and those who do lose social standing as a result.

In the practice of law—as on the assembly line and in many other sorts of work—an almost inevitable consequence of the division of labor has been a routinization of tasks for most of the workers.[70] There are few sorts of specialized law practice where a high proportion of the problems call for truly unique solutions, and these sorts of practice are likely to be at the top of the prestige ladder, in the service of the most influential, most wealthy clients; unique problems and unique solutions are most likely to be generated when the stakes are high, and high for more than a few people. In this sense, also, the law is unlike medicine, since an exotic disease may be contracted by anyone, rich or poor (though it is, no doubt, more likely to be detected in the well-to-do). Thus, the value placed on "intellectual challenge" in the allocation of prestige within the legal profession is also an essentially elitist tendency. Service to the individual client is likely to be repetitious, and therefore dull. Though a divorce, a limb wasted by an automobile or by medical malpractice, a home mortgage foreclosure, the death of a loved one and the consequent estate problems, a sanity hearing, a criminal charge, the loss of a job, or an adoption or child custody proceeding may all involve great anxiety and suffering for the client, they are likely to be routine cases for the specialized lawyer. The intellectual challenge they present will usually not be great, and thus the profession does not assign much prestige to those sorts of work.

According to Mills, the nineteenth century lawyer was "an opinion leader, a man whose recommendations to the community counted" and was "held to be fit material for high statesmanship"—"the lawyer upheld public service and was professionally above business motives." While it is hard to believe that the profession can have been so pure in the nineteenth century (or, indeed, so "professional"), it is plausible that the modern specialized lawyer may be less involved with his community and its political affairs than was the old general practitioner. In part, this may simply be a concomitant of urbanization, a difference between the ethos of the big city and of the small town. But the same result might also follow from the process of specialization. It may be

70. *Cf.* Robert E. Blauner, Alienation and Freedom: The Factory Worker and His Industry (Chicago: University of Chicago Press, 1964).

that the highest prestige lawyers now tend to operate more as technicians or as anonymous advisers to the top management of major corporations. These are roles that, perhaps, are less likely to make the lawyer a public figure. Corporation lawyers advise, they negotiate business deals, and they draft complex and sophisticated documents, but they are less likely to make speeches or to become involved in major issues of public policy. But is this so? There has certainly been a conspicuous succession in high office in the modern era of such men as Henry Stimson, John J. McCloy, Dean Acheson, Cyrus Vance, Roswell Gilpatric, and George Ball. Since these are conspicuous cases, their willingness or ambition to assume public roles is, no doubt, atypical of their fellow corporation lawyers, but do they differ from their fellows in more fundamental, professional respects? The long tradition of dominance by lawyers of much of American government, particularly the legislatures, seems to continue.[71] But are these public offices—particularly, the elective ones—held mostly by lawyers who practice in the lower prestige specialties, lawyers whose practice brings them into contact with a wider segment of the populace? These are issues that we are not prepared to deal with fully at this time, but we believe that some of these questions should be placed high on the research agenda.

The more fundamental question is whether the prestige of legal specialties can be translated into more generalized influence, either within or outside the profession. Public office would, of course, provide one sort of opportunity for such influence. Another type of influence, however, is almost a necessary consequence of the role of adviser to big business. Lawyers who influence the expenditure of many millions of dollars, who determine whether corporate acquisitions or mergers will or will not take place, undeniably have an important sort of power. But there is also the question of who controls the pattern maintenance institutions of the profession, especially the bar associations. That is, who is given the authority to speak in the name of the profession as a whole? We have data on the positions of leadership in the Chicago Bar Association (CBA), the principal professional association in Chicago, that have been held by the lawyers in our sample. We find that the percentage of practitioners in a specialty who have held positions of leadership in the CBA correlates .56 with the prestige of the specialty. More than 20 percent of the securities, patent, and public utility lawyers in our

71. Alexis de Tocqueville, Democracy in American (Henry Reeve, trans. New York: Oxford University Press, 1947); James Bryce, The American Commonwealth (rev. ed. New York: Macmillan, 1911); Heinz Eulau & John D. Sprague, Lawyers in Politics: A Study in Professional Convergence (Indianapolis: Bobbs-Merrill, 1964).

sample had been CBA leaders, while 5 percent or fewer of the criminal defense and of the personal injury lawyers had held such positions. The direction of the causation (if any) seems quite clear; it is not very plausible that the proportion of CBA officers in a specialty would enhance its prestige appreciably. Rather, it seems much more likely that lawyers are chosen for CBA office, at least in important part, on the basis of their personal prestige, some of which is attributable to the prestige of the sorts of work they do. Thus, there is some substantial evidence that the prestige of the legal specialties may be convertible into influence, at least within the profession.

Another important consequence of the prestige structure may well be its effects on the recruitment of lawyers into the various specialties. Most of us value deference, and there will thus be an important incentive to enter the types of legal work that will earn one that deference. Thus, many of the lawyers who practice in the specialties that serve "persons of moderate means"[72] are probably not as highly qualified as are those who serve the large corporations, and many probably entered the lower prestige specialties more from necessity than from choice. As we have noted, the proportion of practitioners who attended the most prestigious law schools is much higher in the corporate practice than it is in the specialties serving individuals and small businesses (see table 2, column 6). The other side of this coin is that the percentage who attended law schools of only "local" repute ranges from a high of 70 to 80 percent in criminal defense, divorce, and personal injury plaintiffs' work to a low of 15 percent in securities, antitrust defense, and public utilities work.[73] Presumably, the resources available for legal education are substantially fewer in the local than in the elite schools,[74] and we may then expect the lawyers who serve individuals to be substantially less well trained than those who serve corporations. Since the income that a lawyer receives from his practice is not significantly associated with the prestige of his specialty, the monetary rewards available may induce some lawyers—even some well-qualified ones—to enter a lower prestige practice. A desire for "service" or a desire to appear (in his own eyes or those of others) to be motivated by altruism might also lead, of course, to that same result. But to the extent that lawyers making career choices are concerned with their prestige within the legal

---

72. Barlow F. Christensen, Lawyers for People of Moderate Means: Some Problems of Availability of Legal Services 92-97 (Chicago: American Bar Foundation, 1970).

73. *Cf.* Heinz et al., *supra* note 6. These "local" schools are DePaul, IIT-Chicago Kent, Loyola, and John Marshall, all located in Chicago.

74. Charles D. Kelso, Adding Up the Law Schools, Learning & L., Summer 1975, at 38.

profession—concerned, that is, with receiving deference or respect from their fellow professionals—they will tend to choose service to big business rather than to poor people.

The breadth of the issues considered in this paper defies easy summary or conclusion, and the unfolding empirical analysis has doubtless raised more questions than it has answered. Rather than rehearse what has gone before, then, we will conclude with a brief agenda for future work that is designed to answer more systematically the key issue raised in our introductory remarks: what are the consequences of prestige differentiation among the specialties for eliciting deferent behavior and, more specially, for channeling individual and interpersonal behavior of consequence to the stratification of the legal profession? As Shils[75] has suggested, deferent behavior may consist of relatively superficial courtesies, such as door holding or forms of address, but differential prestige may also have effects of much more far-reaching consequence on interactive behavior, friendship choice, and the like. As a matter of fact, we have in hand data that are relevant to just such issues. Each of the respondents in our cross-sectional survey, for example, was asked to identify several characteristics of their three closest professional associates. In addition to the standard demographic variables, these characteristics included various features of the associates' law practices. We also have information on the respondents' membership and participation in professional associations, social clubs, and civic or fraternal organizations and on their acquaintanceship with a list of selected notables in the legal profession in Chicago. Thus, we have a substantial body of data on the extent to which friendship choice and social intercourse within the profession may be patterned according to the principle of equal status contact.[76] In further papers resulting from this project, we propose to analyze the degree to which relations within the profession may be structured by the differential allocation of prestige and the degree to which this segregates segments of the bar from one another and thus diminishes the social integration of the profession.

75. Shils, *supra* note 10.
76. *Cf.* Laumann, *supra* note 17; Laumann, *supra* note 44; Collins, *supra* note 8.

TECHNICAL APPENDIX

Inspection of the intercorrelations among the many indicators of specialty characteristics we had in hand (see tables 4 and 5 for the complete intercorrelation matrices drawn from tables 1 and 2, respectively) reveals substantial redundancy among some subsets of the indicators. In identifying the set of characteristics we would finally include in the multiple regression analysis predicting the standardized prestige scores, we attempted to select only one indicator from each of the subsets manifesting substantial intercorrelations among themselves, subject to the constraint that we include at least one indicator from each of the theoretically identified categories of deference entitlements. In short, we wanted to steer a middle course between a raw empiricist approach, which would permit the computer to do our thinking for us by sorting through all the indicators to find, according to some statistical criterion, the optimal set to use in the regression equation, and an abstract, theoretical approach that would specify *a priori* what should or should not be considered in the regression analysis, free of any consideration of what the empirical world was telling us. The latter course is the preferable strategy, but is only reasonable when one is able to articulate a complete and unambiguous theory at the outset—an ability notably lacking in the relevant literature at the present time.

TABLE 4
Matrix of Correlation Coefficients Between Imputed Characteristics[a] and Prestige for the 30 Specialties Reported in Table 1

	Intellectual Challenge Score	Rapidity of Change Score	*Pro Bono* Score	Ethical Conduct Score	Freedom of Action Score
Rapidity of Change Score . . .	0.69*				
Pro Bono Score	0.05	0.44*			
Ethical Conduct Score	0.51*	0.11	0.20		
Freedom of Action Score . . .	−0.09	0.20	0.72*	−0.19	
Prestige	0.65*	0.08	−0.51*	0.53*	−0.54*

[a]See discussion of variables accompanying table 1.
*Statistically significant at the .05 level (two-tailed).

Table 6 presents three regression models that are intended more as concise summaries of the structure of the data in hand and as bases for further discussion than as demonstrations of the relative importance of different hypothetical constructs in a general theory of prestige generation. Model I considers all five of the characteristics imputed to the specialties by the scholar judges because we believed at the outset that they all would make analytically independent contributions to our understanding of prestige allocation. Model II considers six selected characteristics drawn from the much larger set of differentiating attributes of the practitioners and their practices in the various legal specialties. The proportions "Jewish

TABLE 5
Matrix of Correlations Between Selected Characteristics[a] and Prestige for the 23 Specialties Reported in Table 2

	Mean Age	% Metro-politan	% Jewish	% Repub-lican	% Elite School	% Solo	% Large Firm	Mean % Blue Collar Clients	Mean % Major Corporate Clients	% Stable Clients	% Profes-sional Expertise	% Negoti-ating & Advising	% Concen-tration	% Law Incomes $50,000 or More[b]
Percent Metropolitan	0.00													
Percent Jewish	0.26	0.18												
Percent Republican	0.25	−0.62*	−0.17											
Percent Elite School	−0.33	−0.42*	−0.33	0.38										
Percent Solo	0.58*	0.46*	0.42*	−0.14	−0.52*									
Percent Large Firm	−0.47*	−0.56*	−0.52*	0.38	0.67*	−0.45*								
Mean Percent Blue Collar Clients	0.40*	0.59*	0.41*	−0.54*	−0.52*	0.56*	−0.70*							
Mean Percent Major Corporate Clients .	−0.51*	−0.51*	−0.57*	0.19	0.41*	−0.72*	0.68*	−0.59*						
Percent Stable Clients	0.33	−0.34	0.03	0.48*	0.10	−0.35	−0.13	−0.11	0.22					
Percent Profes-sional Expertise . .	−0.30	−0.47*	−0.05	0.30	0.48*	−0.59*	0.30	−0.41*	0.38	0.26				
Percent Negotiating & Advising	0.38	0.02	0.37	−0.03	−0.23	0.52*	−0.16	0.41*	−0.19	−0.04	−0.42*			
Percent Concen-tration	−0.36	−0.29	−0.17	0.15	0.08	−0.55*	0.18	−0.37	0.53*	0.28	0.49*	−0.43*		
Percent Law Incomes $50,000 or More . .	−0.27	−0.22	−0.20	0.08	0.62*	−0.21	0.47*	−0.33	0.41*	0.05	0.08	−0.16	0.10	
Prestige	−0.23	−0.69*	−0.45*	0.67*	0.57*	−0.58*	0.63*	−0.86*	0.54*	0.33	0.49*	−0.42*	0.52*	0.40

[a]See discussion of variables accompanying table 2.

[b]Age adjusted.

*Statistically significant at the .05 level (two-tailed).

origin" and "elite law school attended" are intended to represent the social origins based on deference entitlement; proportions "working in law firms with 30 or more lawyers" and "professional training required for specialty practice" tap the complex of work context and work characteristics as bases of deference entitlement; "percent blue collar clients" taps client characteristics; while "proportion earning

TABLE 6
Multiple Regression of Selected Variables Predicting Prestige of Legal Specialties

	Unstandardized Coefficients	Standard Error	Partial *F*	Standardized Coefficients
Model I: Characteristics of Specialties Imputed by Legal Scholars				
1. *Pro Bono*	–.81	.27	9.18**	–.62
2. Intellectual Challenge .	.84	.32	6.80**	.62
3. Ethical Conduct	.55	.32	2.95*	.33
4. Freedom of Action . . .	.16	.22	0.51	.11
5. Rapidity of Change . . .	–.15	.31	0.25	–.11
Multiple R^2 = .88; F = 24.73, $p < .001$.				
Model II: Selected Characteristics of Practitioners in Specialties				
1. % Blue Collar	–4.63	1.03	20.07	–.73
2. % Professional Training	1.41	.99	2.01	.20
3. % Jewish Origin	–1.29	1.05	1.53	–.16
4. % Law Income $50,000 or More (Age Adjusted) .	1.48	1.43	1.08	.16
5. % Firm Larger than 30	–.45	.86	.27	–.10
6. % Elite Law School . . .	.02	1.33	.00	.00
Multiple R^2 = .80; F = 10.90, $p < .001$.				
Model III: Composite Model				
1. *Pro Bono*	–.56	.14	16.56**	–.43
2. Ethical Conduct	.54	.13	15.85**	.33
3. Intellectual Challenge .	.44	.14	9.51**	.33
4. % Blue Collar	–1.48	.85	3.04*	–.23
5. % Jewish Origin	–1.43	.61	5.54**	–.18
Multiple R^2 = .92; F = 41.77, $p < .001$.				

*Statistically significant at the .05 level.
**Statistically significant at the .01 level.

$50,000 or more" is intended to tap extrinsic rewards associated with particular task performances. Of course, all these indicators are resultants of very complex social processes and cannot, consequently, be expected to measure precisely only one hypothetical construct in our theoretical argument. The proportion working in large law firms, for example, is highly associated with the proportion reporting major corporations as clients, while the proportion in solo practice—which we have treated as a work context attribute—is strongly associated with the proportion Jewish origin—a putatively social origin attribute. Thus, since we expected some confounding and redundant effects among the various indicators, caution in interpreting the results is advisable. Model III is a composite model that considers simultaneously the five variables in Model I and the six in Model II to construct the best predictive model.

Table 6 lists the variables for each model in the order of their standardized coefficients (see last column). These standardized coefficients may be compared with one another in a given model in order to determine the relative impact each variable has on the dependent variable, the standardized prestige score. The partial *F*'s in the third column permit one to test whether the independent variable in question still contributes significantly to the explained sums of squares once the effects of the other variables in the model have been statistically removed. The unstandardized coefficients in the first column are the *b* coefficients or partial slopes for the multiple regression equation that can be used to predict the prestige scores; the second column gives the standard errors of these coefficients, providing a different way to evaluate the significance of a given unstandardized coefficient in the multiple regression equation as a whole.[77]

The reader can readily see that all three regression models are able to explain very high proportions of the total variance in prestige scores (the multiple R^2's range from .79, or 79 percent, for Model II to .92, or 92 percent of the total variance, for Model III). But in fact, in the case of Models I and II, only one to three variables are required to achieve these high R^2's. In Model I the first two variables, *pro bono* and intellectual difficulty, achieve a multiple R^2 of .80, which rises to .87 with the addition of ethical conduct. The remaining two variables, freedom of action and rapidity of change, make no significant contributions to the explanation of the prestige score, once the effects of the first three variables are taken into account. In Model II an even more dramatic result emerges. Only the first variable, percent blue collar clients, is significantly involved in explaining prestige scores among the specialties, achieving an R^2 of .74. The addition of all the other variables does not appreciably improve the prediction of the prestige scores. Especially noteworthy in this connection is the total absence of any impact of the differential monetary rewards of the specialties on prestige judgments—a negative finding of considerable theoretical import.

Model III confirms the results of the other two models by selecting only the top three variables from Model I and the top two from Model II (from the eleven it was originally given) to construct the optimal prediction of the prestige scores. It also informs us, however, that our fears about the problem of disentangling the confounding effects of the various indicators were justified. The percent blue collar clients, the single most powerful predictor in Model II, drops to relative insignificance when the imputed characteristics are taken into account. This result suggests that this variable is indeed acting as a complex proxy or compound indicator for several different aspects of legal specialties. Once it is placed in the context of

---

77. If an unstandardized coefficient is less than twice its standard error, one cannot assume that it departs significantly from zero (or no association between the independent and dependent variables, net of the effects of all the other variables in the model) with a probability less than .05. Such a test is ultimately equivalent, however, to the partial *F* test in the third column.

indicators more directly measuring these aspects, it loses its explanatory power. In an important sense the performance of the other variables at the expense of the percent blue collar clients helps us to specify more precisely what this complex variable may be measuring.[78] The sorts of cases blue collar clients bring to lawyers, while of great personal moment to the clients, are matters that require the applica-

---

78. The following detailed statistical analysis of aggregation and multicollinearity effects was prepared by our research assistant, Charles Cappell:

"The linear models in table 6 were inspected for redundancy among the independent variables. Eigenroots and eigenvectors were extracted from the intercorrelation matrices of the two sets of independent variables in Models I and II. The ratio of the first eigenroot to the sum of all the eigenroots was obtained for each solution. For Model I, this value was .3454; for Model II, .5212. This comparison indicates a greater degree of redundancy among the independent variables of Model II than among those in Model I. An inspection of the sixth eigenroot indicated that the matrices were of full rank.

"The effects of this redundancy can be observed in the size of the standard errors of the betas in the models. The effects are more pronounced, as they would have to be, for the standard errors in Model II. We can be reasonably certain (statistically) about the direction of effects only for the characteristics of percent blue collar clientele and percent Jewish.

"The original data used in Model I consisted of 19 observations on six attributes for the 23 specialties. The results of a two-way analysis of variance indicated the absence of an interaction effect; and a measure of the profile similarity of the judges, $R = 57$, indicated a moderate degree of similarity in the judges' reponses (see Ernest A Haggard, Intraclass Correlation and the Analysis of Variance, chs. 5, 7 (New York: Dryden Press, 1958)). In regression Model I, the mean observation across judges was used as the value for the attribute on a given specialty. This linear function relates a set of experts' mean judgments on six attributes for 23 specialties to the mean specialty prestige score obtained from a larger sample of lawyers. In this case, inferences regarding the size of the relationship can be extended to the individual level. Evidence suggests that the relationship for individuals would not be as large and that the inflation in the aggregate R^2 is substantial even when the intercorrelations among the independent variables is moderate (see Yehuda Grunfeld & Zvi Griliches, Is Aggregation Necessarily Bad? 42 Rev. Econ. & Statistics 1 (1960), especially sec. 1).

"In Model II a slightly more complicated problem arises. Here the measures on the independent variables were obtained by grouping and then finding the mean of the independent observations. (Individual lawyers were conceptualized as observations on specialties.) The grouping criterion was the amount of time the lawyer spent on the given specialty. Previous observations on the effects of redundancy and aggregation apply to this model also, but further complications arise if the grouping criterion is not random with respect to the independent variables. See Hubert M. Blalock, Jr., Causal Inferences in Non-experimental Research 97-125 (Chapel Hill: University of North Carolina Press, 1964); Grunfeld & Griliches, *supra*; Michael T. Hannan, Problems of Aggregation, *in* H. M. Blalock, Jr., ed., Causal Models in the Social Sciences 473 (Chicago: Aldine-Atherton, 1971). An extended multivariate analysis was not warranted; instead the extent of grouping effects was determined by inspecting the analysis of variance results obtained during the grouping operation. Intraclass correlation coefficients indicate the effect grouping had on the variance of the attribute for the grouped specialists compared with the variance of the attribute for the sample. In only a few instances did the intraclass correlation exceed .10. This indicates that, for the most part, the assumption of random grouping with respect to the independent variables seems reasonable. Extrapolating the findings to the individual level, one can infer that the relative strength of the betas would be maintained.

"However, a subtle substantive difference results from shifting levels of analysis in Model II. In this model at the grouped level, the mean of an attribute for a group of specialists, not judges, is related to the mean specialty prestige score. This implies, at the individual level, that an individual, in allocating prestige to a specialty, may be doing so on the basis of a vector of attribute means for each of the specialties. He must, therefore, be aware of the central tendency of each of the attributes for each of the specialties. Given the highly indirect nature of this allocation process (and the degree of redundancy among the attributes), the ability of Model II to fit the prestige scores is surprising."

tion of relatively routine procedures. These cases, in short, lack intellectual challenge—an attribute tapped more directly by the inclusion of the intellectual challenge variable in the composite model. Similarly, we have noted that certain types of cases, *e.g.*, personal injury, criminal defense, and divorce, are more likely to be handled by lawyers who employ sharp practices that are contrary to the prevailing ethical norms of the profession. These cases, too, tend more often to involve blue collar clients. Thus, as with intellectual challenge, our measure of ethical conduct more directly measures this aspect of legal work. Finally, blue collar clients, being persons of limited financial means, are more apt to be involved in the less profitable sorts of litigation and legal work—at times even requiring *pro bono* treatment, as in family practice with poverty clients. As Model III shows, *pro bono* work is disvalued in allocating prestige to legal specialties. Indeed, according to the standardized coefficients, it plays the strongest role in predicting the prestige scores. We tentatively conclude, then, that the percent blue collar clients is better treated as a compound indicator that is a complex function of legal work that varies in intellectual challenge, ethical conduct, and profitability (the obverse of *pro bono* work).

The negative impact of the percentage of practitioners of Jewish origin, a nonsignificant variable in Model II but now of some importance in Model III, is difficult to explain. Clearly, it is tapping an aspect of the prestige of legal specialties that is no longer masked by the effects of the other variables in the model. The negative impact on prestige standing of high concentrations of Jews in a specialty may simply reflect the historical and possibly continuing discrimination against the entry of Jews into the higher status specialties serving major corporate clients.[79] But given the nature of our data that measure the state of affairs at one point in time, we may only conjecture whether the relative concentration of Jews is causally implicated in raising or lowering prestige judgments of specialties, or whether it reflects an historical process that has run its course.

More generally, the regression models are best regarded as providing at this stage of research only some broad clues to understanding the empirical processes generating prestige judgments. The most serious limitation of our analysis rests on the widely varying measurement status of the several indicators considered. The relatively weaker roles that variables based on characteristics of practitioners in particular legal specialties played in the regression analysis, when compared with the imputed characteristics of the scholar judges, is probably due to their more confounded status as compound indicators of diverse social processes, sharing at least some common functional dependencies, in contrast to the analytically more homogeneous and empirically abstracted judgments of the legal scholars (see note 78 *supra*). It is well known that the variables subject to the least measurement error and contamination in a given regression analysis will tend to have the greatest explanatory power.[80] For this reason we should not take too seriously the results

79. *Cf.* Ladinsky, *supra* note 4.

80. *Cf.* Paul M. Siegel & Robert W. Hodge, A Causal Approach to the Study of Measurement Error, *in* Hubert M. Blalock, Jr., & Ann B. Blalock, eds., Methodology in Social Research 28 (New York: McGraw-Hill, 1968); Robert A. Gordon, Issues in Multiple Regression, 73 Am. J. Soc. 592 (1968).

regarding the relative impact of the different variables in explaining prestige differences. Only when research on an empirical phenomenon has accumulated to a point where good estimates of the reliability and validity of different measures can be made is one in a position to make realistic assessments of these troublesome issues. However tentative we must remain in assessing the relative importance of these variables, we should add on a more positive note that these several models do indicate that we have succeeded in identifying a relatively small set of theoretically interesting variables that are remarkably powerful in explaining the allocation of prestige.

Part V
Policing

[12]

THE POLICE ON SKID-ROW: A STUDY OF PEACE KEEPING *

EGON BITTNER

Langley Porter Neuropsychiatric Institute

Following the distinction proposed by Banton, police work consists of two relatively different activities: "law enforcement" and "keeping the peace." The latter is not determined by a clear legal mandate and does not stand under any system of external control. Instead, it developed as a craft in response to a variety of demand conditions. One such condition is created by the concentration of certain types of persons on skid-row. Patrolmen have a particular conception of the social order of skid-row life that determines the procedures of control they employ. The most conspicuous features of the peace keeping methods used are an aggressively personalized approach to residents, an attenuated regard for questions of culpability, and the use of coercion, mainly in the interest of managing situations rather than persons.

THE prototype of modern police organization, the Metropolitan Police of London, was created to replace an antiquated and corrupt system of law enforcement. The early planners were motivated by the mixture of hardheaded business rationality and humane sentiment that characterized liberal British thought of the first half of the nineteenth century.[1] Partly to meet the objections of a parliamentary committee, which was opposed to the establishment of the police in England, and partly because it was in line with their own thinking, the planners sought to produce an instrument that could not readily be used in the play of internal power politics but which would, instead, advance and protect conditions favorable to industry and commerce and to urban civil life in general. These intentions were not very specific and had to be reconciled with the existing structures of governing, administering justice, and keeping the peace. Consequently, the locus and mandate of the police in the modern polity were ill-defined at the outset. On the one hand, the new institution was to be a part of the executive branch of government, organized, funded, and staffed in accordance with standards that were typical for the entire system of the executive. On the other hand, the duties that were given to the police organization brought it under direct control of the judiciary in its day-to-day operation.

The dual patronage of the police by the executive and the judiciary is characteristic for all democratically governed countries. Moreover, it is generally the case, or at least it is deemed desirable, that judges *rather than* executive officials have control over police use and procedure.[2] This preference is based

* This research was supported in part by Grant 64-1-35 from the California Department of Mental Hygiene. I gratefully acknowledge the help I received from Fred Davis, Sheldon Messinger, Leonard Schatzman, and Anselm Strauss in the preparation of this paper.

[1] The bill for a Metropolitan Police was actually enacted under the sponsorship of Robert Peel, the Home Secretary in the Tory Government of the Duke of Wellington. There is, however, no doubt that it was one of the several reform tendencies that Peel assimilated into Tory politics in his long career. Cf. J. L. Lyman, "The Metropolitan Police Act of 1829," *Journal of Criminal Law, Criminology and Police Science,* 55 (1964), 141–154.

[2] Jerome Hall, "Police and Law in a Democratic Society," *Indiana Law Journal,* 28 (1953), 133–177. Though other authors are less emphatic on this point, judicial control is generally taken for granted. The point has been made, however, that in modern times judicial control over the police has been asserted mainly because of the default of any other general controlling authority, cf. E. L. Barrett, Jr.,

on two considerations. First, in the tenets of the democratic creed, the possibility of direct control of the police by a government in power is repugnant.[3] Even when the specter of the police state in its more ominous forms is not a concern, close ties between those who govern and those who police are viewed as a sign of political corruption.[4] Hence, mayors, governors, and cabinet officers—although the nominal superiors of the police—tend to maintain, or to pretend, a hands-off policy. Second, it is commonly understood that the main function of the police is the control of crime. Since the concept of crime belongs wholly to the law, and its treatment is exhaustively based on considerations of legality, police procedure automatically stands under the same system of review that controls the administration of justice in general.

By nature, judicial control encompasses only those aspects of police activity that are directly related to full-dress legal prosecution of offenders. The judiciary has neither the authority nor the means to direct, supervise, and review those activities of the police that do not result in prosecution. Yet such other activities are unavoidable, frequent, and largely within the realm of public expectations. It might be assumed that in this domain of practice the police are under executive control. This is not the case, however, except in a marginal sense.[5] Not only are police departments generally free to determine what need be done and how, but aside from informal pressures they are given scant direction in these matters. Thus, there appear to exist two relatively independent domains of police activity. In one, their methods are constrained by the prospect of the future disposition of a case in the courts; in the other, they operate under some other consideration and largely with no structured and continuous outside constraint. Following the terminology suggested by Michael Banton, they may be said to function in the first instance as "law officers" and in the second instance as "peace officers." [6] It must be emphasized that the designation "peace officer" is a residual term, with only some vaguely presumptive content. The role, as Banton speaks of it, is supposed to encompass all occupational routines not directly related to making arrests, without, however, specifying what determines the limits of competence and availability of the police in such actions.

Efforts to characterize a large domain of activities of an important public agency have so far yielded only negative definitions. We know that they do not involve arrests; we also know that they do not stand under judicial control, and that they are not, in any important sense, determined by specific executive or legislative mandates. In police textbooks and manuals, these activities receive only casual attention, and the role of the "peace officer" is typically stated in terms suggesting that his work is governed mainly by the individual officer's personal wisdom, integrity, and altruism.[7] Police departments generally keep no records of procedures that do not involve making arrests. Policemen, when asked, insist that they merely use common sense when acting as "peace officers," though they tend to emphasize the elements of experience and practice in discharging the role adequately. All this ambiguity is the more remarkable for the fact that peace keeping tasks, i.e., procedures not involving the formal legal remedy of arrest, were explicitly built into the program of the modern police from the outset.[8]

"Police Practice and the Law," *California Law Review*, 50 (1962), 11–55.

[3] A. C. German, F. D. Day and R. R. J. Gallati, *Introduction to Law Enforcement*, Springfield, Ill.: C. C Thomas, 1966; "One concept, in particular, should be kept in mind. A dictatorship can never exist unless the police system of the country is under the absolute control of the dictator. There is no other way to uphold a dictatorship except by terror, and the instrument of this total terror is the secret police, whatever its name. In every country where freedom has been lost, law enforcement has been a dominant instrument in destroying it" (p. 80).

[4] The point is frequently made; cf. Raymond B. Fosdick, *American Police Systems*, New York: Century Company, 1920; Bruce Smith, *Police Systems in the United States*, 2nd rev. ed., New York: Harper, 1960.

[5] The executive margin of control is set mainly in terms of budgetary determinations and the mapping of some formal aspects of the organization of departments.

[6] Michael Banton, *The Policeman in the Community*, New York: Basic Books, 1964, pp. 6–7 and 127 ff.

[7] R. Bruce Holmgren, *Primary Police Functions*, New York: William C. Copp, 1962.

[8] Cf. Lyman, *op. cit.*, p. 153; F. C. Mather, *Public Order in the Age of the Chartists*, Manchester: Manchester University Press, 1959, chap-

The early executives of the London police saw with great clarity that their organization had a dual function. While it was to be an arm of the administration of justice, in respect of which it developed certain techniques for bringing offenders to trial, it was also expected to function apart from, and at times in lieu of, the employment of full-dress legal procedure. Despite its early origin, despite a great deal of public knowledge about it, despite the fact that it is routinely done by policemen, no one can say with any clarity what it means to do a good job of keeping the peace. To be sure, there is vague consensus that when policemen direct, aid, inform, pacify, warn, discipline, roust, and do whatever else they do without making arrests, they do this with some reference to the circumstances of the occasion and, thus, somehow contribute to the maintenance of the peace and order. Peace keeping appears to be a solution to an unknown problem arrived at by unknown means.

The following is an attempt to clarify conceptually the mandate and the practice of keeping the peace. The effort will be directed not to the formulation of a comprehensive solution of the problem but to a detailed consideration of some aspects of it. Only in order to place the particular into the overall domain to which it belongs will the structural determinants of keeping the peace in general be discussed. By structural determinants are meant the typical situations that policemen perceive as *demand conditions* for action without arrest. This will be followed by a description of peace keeping in skid-row districts, with the object of identifying those aspects of it that constitute a *practical skill.*

Since the major object of this paper is to elucidate peace keeping practice as a skilled performance, it is necessary to make clear how the use of the term is intended.

Practical skill will be used to refer to those methods of doing certain things, and to the information that underlies the use of the methods, that *practitioners themselves* view as proper and efficient. Skill is, therefore, a stable orientation to work tasks that is relatively independent of the personal feelings and judgments of those who employ it. Whether the exercise of this skilled performance is desirable or not, and whether it is based on correct information or not, are specifically outside the scope of interest of this presentation. The following is deliberately confined to a description of what police patrolmen consider to be the reality of their work circumstances, what they do, and what they feel they must do to do a good job. That the practice is thought to be determined by normative standards of skill minimizes but does not eliminate the factors of personal interest or inclination. Moreover, the distribution of skill varies among practitioners in the very standards they set for themselves. For example, we will show that patrolmen view a measure of rough informality as good practice vis-a-vis skid-row inhabitants. By this standard, patrolmen who are "not rough enough," or who are "too rough," or whose roughness is determined by personal feelings rather than by situational exigencies, are judged to be poor craftsmen.

The description and analysis are based on twelve months of field work with the police departments of two large cities west of the Mississippi. Eleven weeks of this time were spent in skid-row and skid-row-like districts. The observations were augmented by approximately one hundred interviews with police officers of all ranks. The formulations that will be proposed were discussed in these interviews. They were recognized by the respondents as elements of standard practice. The respondents' recognition was often accompanied by remarks indicating that they had never thought about things in this way and that they were not aware how standardized police work was.

STRUCTURAL DEMAND CONDITIONS OF PEACE KEEPING

There exist at least five types of relatively distinct circumstances that produce police activities that do not involve invoking the law and that are only in a trivial sense determined by those considerations of legality that determine law enforcement. This does not mean that these activities are illegal but merely that there is no legal directive that informs the acting policeman whether what he does must be done or how it is to be done. In these circumstances, policemen act

ter IV. See also Robert H. Bremer, "Police, Penal and Parole Policies in Cleveland and Toledo," *American Journal of Economics and Sociology*, 14 (1955), 387–398, for similar recognition in the United States at about the turn of this century.

as all-purpose and terminal remedial agents, and the confronted problem is solved in the field. If these practices stand under any kind of review at all, and typically they do not, it is only through internal police department control.

1. Although the executive branch of government generally refrains from exercising a controlling influence over the direction of police interest, it manages to extract certain performances from it. Two important examples of this are the supervision of certain licensed services and premises and the regulation of traffic.[9] With respect to the first, the police tend to concentrate on what might be called the moral aspects of establishments rather than on questions relating to the technical adequacy of the service. This orientation is based on the assumption that certain types of businesses lend themselves to exploitation for undesirable and illegal purposes. Since this tendency cannot be fully controlled, it is only natural that the police will be inclined to favor licensees who are at least cooperative. This, however, transforms the task from the mere scrutiny of credentials and the passing of judgments, to the creation and maintenance of a network of connections that conveys influence, pressure, and information. The duty to inspect is the background of this network, but the resulting contacts acquire additional value for solving crimes and maintaining public order. Bartenders, shopkeepers, and hotel clerks become, for patrolmen, a resource that must be continuously serviced by visits and exchanges of favors. While it is apparent that this condition lends itself to corrupt exploitation by individual officers, even the most flawlessly honest policeman must participate in this network of exchanges if he is to function adequately. Thus, engaging in such exchanges becomes an occupational task that demands attention and time.

Regulation of traffic is considerably less complex. More than anything else, traffic control symbolizes the autonomous authority of policemen. Their commands generally are met with unquestioned compliance. Even when they issue citations, which seemingly refer the case to the courts, it is common practice for the accused to view the allegation as a finding against him and to pay the fine. Police officials emphasize that it is more important to be circumspect than legalistic in traffic control. Officers are often reminded that a large segment of the public has no other contacts with the police, and that the field lends itself to public relations work by the line personnel.[10]

2. Policemen often do not arrest persons who have committed minor offences in circumstances in which the arrest is technically possible. This practice has recently received considerable attention in legal and sociological literature. The studies were motivated by the realization that "police decisions not to invoke the criminal process determine the outer limits of law enforcement."[11] From these researches, it was learned that the police tend to impose more stringent criteria of law enforcement on certain segments of the community than on others.[12] It was also learned that, from the perspective of the administration of justice, the decisions not to make arrests often are based on compelling reasons.[13] It is less well appreciated that policemen often not only refrain from invoking the law formally but also employ alternative sanctions. For example, it is standard practice that violators are warned not to repeat the offense. This often leads to patrolmen's "keeping an eye" on certain persons. Less frequent, though not unusual, is the practice of direct disciplining of offenders, especially when they are juveniles, which occasionally involves inducing them to repair the damage occasioned by their misconduct.[14]

The power to arrest and the freedom not to arrest can be used in cases that do not involve patent offenses. An officer can say to a person whose behavior he wishes to control, "I'll let you go this time!" without

[9] Smith, *op. cit.*, pp. 15 ff.

[10] Orlando W. Wilson, "Police Authority in a Free Society," *Journal of Criminal Law, Criminology and Police Science*, 54 (1964), 175–177.

[11] Joseph Goldstein, "Police Discretion Not to Invoke the Criminal Process," *Yale Law Journal*, 69 (1960), 543.

[12] Jerome Skolnick, *Justice Without Trial*, New York: Wiley, 1966.

[13] Wayne LaFave, "The Police and Nonenforcement of the Law," *Wisconsin Law Review* (1962), 104–137 and 179–239.

[14] Nathan Goldman, *The Differential Selection of Juvenile Offenders for Court Appearance*, National Research and Information Center, National Council on Crime and Delinquency, 1963, pp. 114 ff.

indicating to him that he could not have been arrested in any case. Nor is this always deliberate misrepresentation, for in many cases the law is sufficiently ambiguous to allow alternative interpretations. In short, not to make an arrest is rarely, if ever, merely a decision not to act; it is most often a decision to act alternatively. In the case of minor offenses, to make an arrest often is merely one of several possible proper actions.

3. There exists a public demand for police intervention in matters that contain no criminal and often no legal aspects.[15] For example, it is commonly assumed that officers will be available to arbitrate quarrels, to pacify the unruly, and to help in keeping order. They are supposed also to aid people in trouble, and there is scarcely a human predicament imaginable for which police aid has not been solicited and obtained at one time or another. Most authors writing about the police consider such activities only marginally related to the police mandate. This view fails to reckon with the fact that the availability of these performances is taken for granted and the police assign a substantial amount of their resources to such work. Although this work cannot be subsumed under the concept of legal action, it does involve the exercise of a form of authority that most people associate with the police. In fact, no matter how trivial the occasion, the device of "calling the cops" transforms any problem. It implies that a situation is, or is getting, out of hand. Police responses to public demands are always oriented to this implication, and the risk of proliferation of troubles makes every call a potentially serious matter.[16]

4. Certain mass phenomena of either a regular or a spontaneous nature require direct monitoring. Most important is the controlling of crowds in incipient stages of disorder. The specter of mob violence frequently calls for measures that involve coercion, including the use of physical force. Legal theory allows, of course, that public officials are empowered to use coercion in situations of imminent danger.[17] Unfortunately, the doctrine is not sufficiently specific to be of much help as a rule of practice. It is based on the assumption of the adventitiousness of danger, and thus does not lend itself readily to elaborations that could direct the routines of early detection and prevention of untoward developments. It is interesting that the objective of preventing riots by informal means posed one of the central organizational problems for the police in England during the era of the Chartists.[18]

5. The police have certain special duties with respect to persons who are viewed as less than fully accountable for their actions. Examples of those eligible for special consideration are those who are under age [19] and those who are mentally ill.[20] Although it is virtually never acknowledged explicitly, those receiving special treatment include people who do not lead "normal" lives and who occupy a pariah status in society. This group includes residents of ethnic ghettos, certain types of bohemians and vagabonds, and persons of known criminal background. The special treatment of children and of sick persons is permissively sanctioned by the law, but the special treatment of others is, in principle, opposed by the leading theme of legality and the tenets of the democratic faith.[21] The important point is not that such persons are arrested more often than others, which is quite true, but that they are per-

---

[15] Elaine Cumming, Ian Cumming and Laura Edell, "Policeman as Philosopher, Guide and Friend," *Social Problems,* 12 (1965), 276–286.

[16] There is little doubt that many requests for service are turned down by the police, especially when they are made over the telephone or by mail, cf. LaFave, *op. cit.,* p. 212, n. 124. The uniformed patrolman, however, finds it virtually impossible to leave the scene without becoming involved in some way or another.

[17] Hans Kelsen, *General Theory of Law and State,* New York: Russell & Russell, 1961, pp. 278–279; H. L. A. Hart, *The Concept of Law,* Oxford: Clarendon Press, 1961, pp. 20–21.

[18] Mather, *op. cit.;* see also, Jenifer Hart, "Reform of the Borough Police, 1835–1856," *English History Review,* 70 (1955), 411–427.

[19] Francis A. Allen, *The Borderland of Criminal Justice,* Chicago: University of Chicago Press, 1964.

[20] Egon Bittner, "Police Discretion in Emergency Apprehension of Mentally Ill Persons," *Social Problems,* 14 (1967), 278–292.

[21] It bears mentioning, however, that differential treatment is not unique with the police, but is also in many ways representative for the administration of justice in general; cf. J. E. Carlin, Jan Howard and S. L. Messinger, "Civil Justice and the Poor," *Law and Society,* 1 (1966), 9–89; Jacobus tenBroek (ed.) *The Law of the Poor,* San Francisco: Chandler Publishing Co., 1966.

ceived by the police as producing a special problem that necessitates continuous attention and the use of special procedures.

The five types of demand conditions do not exclude the possibility of invoking the criminal process. Indeed, arrests do occur quite frequently in all these circumstances. But the concerns generated in these areas cause activities that usually do not terminate in an arrest. When arrests are made, there exist, at least in the ideal, certain criteria by reference to which the arrest can be judged as having been made more or less properly, and there are some persons who, in the natural course of events, actually judge the performance.[22] But for actions not resulting in arrest there are no such criteria and no such judges. How, then, can one speak of such actions as necessary and proper? Since there does not exist any official answer to this query, and since policemen act in the role of "peace officers" pretty much without external direction or constraint, the question comes down to asking how the policeman himself knows whether he has any business with a person he does not arrest, and if so, what that business might be. Furthermore, if there exists a domain of concerns and activities that is largely independent of the law enforcement mandate, it is reasonable to assume that it will exercise some degree of influence on how and to what ends the law is invoked in cases of arrests.

Skid-row presents one excellent opportunity to study these problems. The area contains a heavy concentration of persons who do not live "normal" lives in terms of prevailing standards of middle-class morality. Since the police respond to this situation by intensive patrolling, the structure of peace keeping should be readily observable. Needless to say, the findings and conclusions will not be necessarily generalizable to other types of demand conditions.

THE PROBLEM OF KEEPING THE PEACE IN SKID-ROW

Skid-row has always occupied a special place among the various forms of urban life. While other areas are perceived as being different in many ways, skid-row is seen as completely different. Though it is located in the heart of civilization, it is viewed as containing aspects of the primordial jungle, calling for missionary activities and offering opportunities for exotic adventure. While each inhabitant individually can be seen as tragically linked to the vicissitudes of "normal" life, allowing others to say "here but for the Grace of God go I," those who live there are believed to have repudiated the entire role-casting scheme of the majority and to live apart from normalcy. Accordingly, the traditional attitude of civic-mindedness toward skid-row has been dominated by the desire to contain it and to salvage souls from its clutches.[23] The specific task of containment has been left to the police. That this task pressed upon the police some rather special duties has never come under explicit consideration, either from the government that expects control or from the police departments that implement it. Instead, the prevailing method of carrying out the task is to assign patrolmen to the area on a fairly permanent basis and to allow them to work out their own ways of running things. External influence is confined largely to the supply of support and facilities, on the one hand, and to occasional expressions of criticism about the overall conditions, on the other. Within the limits of available resources and general expectations, patrolmen are supposed to know what to do and are free to do it.[24]

---

[22] This is, however, true only in the ideal. It is well known that a substantial number of persons who are arrested are subsequently released without ever being charged and tried, cf. Barret, *op. cit.*

[23] The literature on skid-row is voluminous. The classic in the field is Nels Anderson, *The Hobo,* Chicago: University of Chicago Press, 1923. Samuel E. Wallace, *Skid-Row as a Way of Life,* Totowa, New Jersey: The Bedminster Press, 1965, is a more recent descriptive account and contains a useful bibliography. Donald A. Bogue, *Skid-Row in American Cities,* Chicago: Community and Family Center, University of Chicago, 1963, contains an exhaustive quantitative survey of Chicago skid-row.

[24] One of the two cities described in this paper also employed the procedure of the "round-up" of drunks. In this, the police van toured the skid-row area twice daily, during the mid-afternoon and early evening hours, and the officers who manned it picked up drunks they sighted. A similar procedure is used in New York's Bowery and the officers who do it are called "condition men." Cf. *Bowery Project,* Bureau of Applied Social Research, Columbia University, Summary Report of a Study Undertaken under Contract Approved by the Board of Estimates, 1963, mimeo., p. 11.

Patrolmen who are more or less permanently assigned to skid-row districts tend to develop a conception of the nature of their "domain" that is surprisingly uniform. Individual officers differ in many aspects of practice, emphasize different concerns, and maintain different contacts, but they are in fundamental agreement about the structure of skid-row life. This relatively uniform conception includes an implicit formulation of the problem of keeping the peace in skid-row.

In the view of experienced patrolmen, life on skid-row is fundamentally different from life in other parts of society. To be sure, they say, around its geographic limits the area tends to blend into the surrounding environment, and its population always encompasses some persons who are only transitionally associated with it. Basically, however, skid-row is perceived as the natural habitat of people who lack the capacities and commitments to live "normal" lives on a sustained basis. The presence of these people defines the nature of social reality in the area. In general, and especially in casual encounters, the presumption of incompetence and of the disinclination to be "normal" is the leading theme for the interpretation of all actions and relations. Not only do people approach one another in this manner, but presumably they also expect to be approached in this way, and they conduct themselves accordingly.

In practice, the restriction of interactional possibilities that is based on the patrolman's stereotyped conception of skid-row residents is always subject to revision and modification toward particular individuals. Thus, it is entirely possible, and not unusual, for patrolmen to view certain skid-row inhabitants in terms that involve non-skid-row aspects of normality. Instances of such approaches and relationships invariably involve personal acquaintance and the knowledge of a good deal of individually qualifying information. Such instances are seen, despite their relative frequency, as exceptions to the rule. The awareness of the possibility of breakdown, frustration, and betrayal is ever-present, basic wariness is never wholly dissipated, and undaunted trust can never be fully reconciled with presence on skid-row.

What patrolmen view as normal on skid-row—and what they also think is taken for granted as "life as usual" by the inhabitants—is not easily summarized. It seems to focus on the idea that the dominant consideration governing all enterprise and association is directed to the occasion of the moment. Nothing is thought of as having a background that might have led up to the present in terms of some compelling moral or practical necessity. There are some exceptions to this rule, of course: the police themselves, and those who run certain establishments, are perceived as engaged in important and necessary activities. But in order to carry them out they, too, must be geared to the overall atmosphere of fortuitousness. In this atmosphere, the range of control that persons have over one another is exceedingly narrow. Good faith, even where it is valued, is seen merely as a personal matter. Its violations are the victim's own hard luck, rather than demonstrable violations of property. There is only a private sense of irony at having been victimized. The overall air is not so much one of active distrust as it is one of irrelevance of trust; as patrolmen often emphasize, the situation does not necessarily cause all relations to be predatory, but the possibility of exploitation is not checked by the expectation that it will not happen.

Just as the past is seen by the policeman as having only the most attenuated relevance to the present, so the future implications of present situations are said to be generally devoid of prospective coherence. No venture, especially no joint venture, can be said to have a strongly predictable future in line with its initial objectives. It is a matter of adventitious circumstance whether or not matters go as anticipated. That which is not within the grasp of momentary control is outside of practical social reality.

Though patrolmen see the temporal framework of the occasion of the moment mainly as a lack of trustworthiness, they also recognize that it involves more than merely the personal motives of individuals. In addition to the fact that everybody *feels* that things matter only at the moment, irresponsibility takes an *objectified* form on skid-row. The places the residents occupy, the social relations they entertain, and the activities that engage them are not meaningfully connected over time. Thus, for example, address, occupation, marital status, etc., matter much less on skid-row than in any other part of society. The fact that present whereabouts, activities, and affiliations imply neither continuity nor direction means that life on skid-row lacks a socially structured background of accountability. Of course, everybody's life contains some sequential incongruities, but in the life of a skid-row inhabitant every moment is an accident. That a man has no "address" in the future that could be in some way inferred from where he is and what he does makes him a person of ***radically reduced visibility***. If he disappears from sight and one wishes to locate him, it is virtually impossible to systematize the search. All one can know with relative certainty is that he will be somewhere on some skid-row and the only thing one can do is to trace the factual contiguities of his whereabouts.

It is commonly known that the police are expert in finding people and that they have developed an exquisite technology involving special facilities and procedures of sleuthing. It is less well appreciated that all this technology builds upon those socially structured features of everyday life that render persons findable in the first place.

Under ordinary conditions, the query as to where a person is can be addressed, from the outset, to a restricted realm of possibilities that can be further narrowed by looking into certain places and asking certain persons. The map of whereabouts that normally competent persons use whenever they wish to locate someone is constituted by the basic facts of membership in society. Insofar as membership consists of status incumbencies, each of which has an adumbrated future that substantially reduces unpredictability, it is itself a guarantee of the order within which it is quite difficult to get lost. Membership is thus visible not only now but also as its own projection into the future. It is in terms of this prospective availability that the skid-row inhabitant is a person of reduced visibility. His membership is viewed as extraordinary because its extension into the future is ***not*** reduced to a restricted realm of possibilities. Neither his subjective dispositions, nor his circumstances, indicate that he is oriented to any particular long-range interests. But, as he may claim every contingent opportunity, his claims are always seen as based on slight merit or right, at least to the extent that interfering with them does not constitute a substantial denial of his freedom.

This, then, constitutes the problem of keeping the peace on skid-row. Considerations of momentary expediency are seen as having unqualified priority as maxims of conduct; consequently, the controlling influences of the pursuit of sustained interests are presumed to be absent.

THE PRACTICES OF KEEPING THE PEACE IN SKID-ROW

From the perspective of society as a whole, skid-row inhabitants appear troublesome in a variety of ways. The uncommitted life attributed to them is perceived as inherently offensive; its very existence arouses indignation and contempt. More important, however, is the feeling that persons who have repudiated the entire role-status casting system of society, persons whose lives forever collapse into a succession of random moments, are seen as constituting a practical risk. As they have nothing to foresake, nothing is thought safe from them.[25]

The skid-row patrolman's concept of his mandate includes an awareness of this presumed risk. He is constantly attuned to the possibility of violence, and he is convinced that things to which the inhabitants have free access are as good as lost. But his concern is directed toward the continuous condition of peril *in the area* rather than *for society in general.* While he is obviously conscious of the presence of many persons who have committed crimes outside of skid-row and will arrest them when they come to his attention, this is a peripheral part of his routine activities. In general, the skid-row patrolman and his superiors take for granted that his main business is to keep the peace

[25] An illuminating parallel to the perception of skid-row can be found in the more traditional concept of vagabondage. Cf. Alexandre Vexliard, ***Introduction a la Sociologie du Vagabondage,*** Paris: Libraire Marcel Riviere, 1956, and "La Disparition du Vagabondage comme Fleau Social Universel," ***Revue de L'Instut de Sociologie*** (1963), 53–79. The classic account of English conditions up to the 19th century is C. J. Ribton-Turner, ***A History of Vagrants and Vagrancy and Beggars and Begging,*** London: Chapman and Hall, 1887.

and enforce the laws *on skid-row,* and that he is involved only incidentally in protecting society at large. Thus, his task is formulated basically as the protection of putative predators from one another. The maintenance of peace and safety is difficult because everyday life on skid-row is viewed as an open field for reciprocal exploitation. As the lives of the inhabitants lack the prospective coherence associated with status incumbency, the realization of self-interest does not produce order. Hence, mechanisms that control risk must work primarily from without.

External containment, to be effective, must be oriented to the realities of existence. Thus, the skid-row patrolman employs an approach that he views as appropriate to the *ad hoc* nature of skid-row life. The following are the three most prominent elements of this approach. First, the seasoned patrolman seeks to acquire a richly particularized knowledge of people and places in the area. Second, he gives the consideration of strict culpability a subordinate status among grounds for remedial sanction. Third, his use and choice of coercive interventions is determined mainly by exigencies of situations and with little regard for possible long range effects on individual persons.

The Particularization of Knowledge. The patrolman's orientation to people on skid-row is structured basically by the presupposition that if he does not know a man personally there is very little that he can assume about him. This rule determines his interaction with people who live on skid-row. Since the area also contains other types of persons, however, its applicability is not universal. To some such persons it does not apply at all, and it has a somewhat mitigated significance with certain others. For example, some persons encountered on skid-row can be recognized immediately as outsiders. Among them are workers who are employed in commercial and industrial enterprises that abut the area, persons who come for the purpose of adventurous "slumming," and some patrons of second-hand stores and pawn shops. Even with very little experience, it is relatively easy to identify these people by appearance, demeanor, and the time and place of their presence. The patrolman maintains an impersonal attitude toward them, and they are, under ordinary circumstances, not the objects of his attention.[26]

Clearly set off from these outsiders are the residents and the entire corps of personnel that services skid-row. It would be fair to say that one of the main routine activities of patrolmen is the establishment and maintenance of familiar relationships with individual members of these groups. Officers emphasize their interest in this, and they maintain that their grasp of and control over skid-row is precisely commensurate with the extent to which they "know the people." By this they do not mean having a quasi-theoretical understanding of human nature but rather the common practice of individualized and reciprocal recognition. As this group encompasses both those who render services on skid-row and those who are serviced, individualized interest is not always based on the desire to overcome uncertainty. Instead, relations with service personnel become absorbed into the network of particularized attention. Ties between patrolmen, on the one hand, and businessmen, managers, and workers, on the other hand, are often defined in terms of shared or similar interests. It bears mentioning that many persons live *and* work on skid-row. Thus, the distinction between those who service and those who are serviced is not a clearcut dichotomy but a spectrum of affiliations.

As a general rule, the skid-row patrolman possesses an immensely detailed factual knowledge of his beat. He knows, and knows a great deal about, a large number of residents. He is likely to know every person who manages or works in the local bars, hotels, shops, stores, and missions. Moreover, he probably knows every public and private place inside and out. Finally, he ordinarily remembers countless events of the past which he can recount by citing names, dates and places with remarkable precision. Though there are always some threads missing in the fabric of information, it is continuously woven and mended even as it is being used. New facts, however, are added to the texture,

[26] Several patrolmen complained about the influx of "tourists" into skid-row. Since such "tourists" are perceived as seeking illicit adventure, they receive little sympathy from patrolmen when they complain about being victimized.

not in terms of structured categories but in terms of adjoining known realities. In other words, the content and organization of the patrolman's knowledge is primarily ideographic and only vestigially, if at all, nomothetic.

Individual patrolmen vary in the extent to which they make themselves available or actively pursue personal acquaintances. But even the most aloof are continuously greeted and engaged in conversations that indicate a background of individualistic associations. While this scarcely has the appearance of work, because of its casual character, patrolmen do not view it as an optional activity. In the course of making their rounds, patrolmen seem to have access to every place, and their entry causes no surprise or consternation. Instead, the entry tends to lead to informal exchanges of small talk. At times the rounds include entering hotels and gaining access to rooms or dormitories, often for no other purpose than asking the occupants how things are going. In all this, patrolmen address innumerable persons by name and are in turn addressed by name. The conversational style that characterizes these exchanges is casual to an extent that by non-skid-row standards might suggest intimacy. Not only does the officer himself avoid all terms of deference and respect but he does not seem to expect or demand them. For example, a patrolman said to a man radiating an alcoholic glow on the street, "You've got enough of a heat on now; I'll give you ten minutes to get your ass off the street!" Without stopping, the man answered, "Oh, why don't you go and piss in your own pot!" The officer's only response was, "All right, in ten minutes you're either in bed or on your way to the can."

This kind of expressive freedom is an intricately limited privilege. Persons of acquaintance are entitled to it and appear to exercise it mainly in routinized encounters. But strangers, too, can use it with impunity. The safe way of gaining the privilege is to respond to the patrolman in ways that do not challenge his right to ask questions and issue commands. Once the concession is made that the officer is entitled to inquire into a man's background, business, and intentions, and that he is entitled to obedience, there opens a field of colloquial license. A patrolman seems to grant expressive freedom in recognition of a person's acceptance of his access to areas of life ordinarily defined as private and subject to coercive control only under special circumstances. While patrolmen accept and seemingly even cultivate the rough *quid pro quo* of informality, and while they do not expect sincerity, candor, or obedience in their dealings with the inhabitants, they do not allow the rejection of their approach.

The explicit refusal to answer questions of a personal nature and the demand to know why the questions are asked significantly enhances a person's chances of being arrested on some minor charge. While most patrolmen tend to be personally indignant about this kind of response and use the arrest to compose their own hurt feelings, this is merely a case of affect being in line with the method. There are other officers who proceed in the same manner without taking offense, or even with feelings of regret. Such patrolmen often maintain that their colleagues' affective involvement is a corruption of an essentially valid technique. The technique is oriented to the goal of maintaining operational control. The patrolman's conception of this goal places him hierarchically above whomever he approaches, and makes him the sole judge of the propriety of the occasion. As he alone is oriented to this goal, and as he seeks to attain it by means of individualized access to persons, those who frustrate him are seen as motivated at best by the desire to "give him a hard time" and at worst by some darkly devious purpose.

Officers are quite aware that the directness of their approach and the demands they make are difficult to reconcile with the doctrines of civil liberties, but they maintain that they are in accord with the general freedom of access that persons living on skid-row normally grant one another. That is, they believe that the imposition of personalized and far-reaching control is in tune with standard expectancies. In terms of these expectancies, people are not so much denied the right to privacy as they are seen as not having any privacy. Thus, officers seek to install themselves in the center of people's lives and let the consciousness of their presence play the part of conscience.

When talking about the practical necessity of an aggressively personal approach, officers do not refer merely to the need for maintaining control over lives that are open in the direction of the untoward. They also see it as the basis for the supply of certain valued services to inhabitants of skid-row. The coerced or conceded access to persons often imposes on the patrolman tasks that are, in the main, in line with these persons' expressed or implied interest. In asserting this connection, patrolmen note that they frequently help people to obtain meals, lodging, employment, that they direct them to welfare and health services, and that they aid them in various other ways. Though patrolmen tend to describe such services mainly as the product of their own altruism, they also say that their colleagues who avoid them are simply doing a poor job of patrolling. The acceptance of the need to help people is based on the realization that the hungry, the sick, and the troubled are a potential source of problems. Moreover, that patrolmen will help people is part of the background expectancies of life on skid-row. Hotel clerks normally call policemen when someone gets so sick as to need attention; merchants expect to be taxed, in a manner of speaking, to meet the pressing needs of certain persons; and the inhabitants do not hesitate to accept, solicit, and demand every kind of aid. The domain of the patrolman's service activity is virtually limitless, and it is no exaggeration to say that the solution of every conceivable problem has at one time or another been attempted by a police officer. In one observed instance, a patrolman unceremoniously entered the room of a man he had never seen before. The man, who gave no indication that he regarded the officer's entry and questions as anything but part of life as usual, related a story of having had his dentures stolen by his wife. In the course of the subsequent rounds, the patrolman sought to locate the woman and the dentures. This did not become the evening's project but was attended to while doing other things. In the densely matted activities of the patrolman, the questioning became one more strand, not so much to be pursued to its solution as a theme that organized the memory of one more man known individually. In all this, the officer followed the precept formulated by a somewhat more articulate patrolman: "If I want to be in control of my work and keep the street relatively peaceful, I have to know the people. To know them I must gain their trust, which means that I have to be involved in their lives. But I can't be soft like a social worker because unlike him I cannot call the cops when things go wrong. I am the cops!"[27]

The Restricted Relevance of Culpability. It is well known that policemen exercise discretionary freedom in invoking the law. It is also conceded that, in some measure, the practice is unavoidable. This being so, the outstanding problem is whether or not the decisions are in line with the intent of the law. On skid-row, patrolmen often make decisions based on reasons that the law probably does not recognize as valid. The problem can best be introduced by citing an example.

A man in a relatively mild state of intoxication (by skid-row standards) approached a patrolman to tell him that he had a room in a hotel, to which the officer responded by urging him to go to bed instead of getting drunk. As the man walked off, the officer related the following thoughts: Here is a completely lost soul. Though he probably is no more than thirty-five years old, he looks to be in his fifties. He never works and he hardly ever has a place to stay. He has been on the street for several years and is known as "Dakota." During the past few days, "Dakota" has been seen in the company of "Big Jim." The latter is an invalid living on some sort of pension with which he pays for a room in the hotel to which "Dakota" referred and for four weekly meal tickets in one of the restaurants on the street. Whatever is left he spends on wine and beer. Occasionally, "Big Jim" goes on drinking sprees in the company of someone like "Dakota." Leaving aside the consideration that there is probably a homosexual background to the association, and that it is not right that "Big Jim" should have to support the drinking habit of someone else, there is the more important risk that if "Dakota" moves in with "Big Jim" he will

[27] The same officer commented further, "If a man looks for something, I might help him. But I don't stay with him till he finds what he is looking for. If I did, I would never get to do anything else. In the last analysis, I really never solve any problems. The best I can hope for is to keep things from getting worse."

very likely walk off with whatever the latter keeps in his room. "Big Jim" would never dream of reporting the theft; he would just beat the hell out of "Dakota" after he sobered up. When asked what could be done to prevent the theft and the subsequent recriminations, the patrolman proposed that in this particular case he would throw "Big Jim" into jail if he found him tonight and then tell the hotel clerk to throw "Dakota" out of the room. When asked why he did not arrest "Dakota," who was, after all, drunk enough to warrant an arrest, the officer explained that this would not solve anything. While "Dakota" was in jail "Big Jim" would continue drinking and would either strike up another liaison or embrace his old buddy after he had been released. The only thing to do was to get "Big Jim" to sober up, and the only sure way of doing this was to arrest him.

As it turned out, "Big Jim" was not located that evening. But had he been located and arrested on a drunk charge, the fact that he was intoxicated would not have been the real reason for proceeding against him, but merely the pretext. The point of the example is not that it illustrates the tendency of skid-row patrolmen to arrest persons who would not be arrested under conditions of full respect for their legal rights. To be sure, this too happens. In the majority of minor arrest cases, however, the criteria the law specifies are met. But it is the rare exception that the law is invoked merely because the specifications of the law are met. That is, compliance with the law is merely the outward appearance of an intervention that is actually based on altogether different considerations. Thus, it could be said that patrolmen do not really enforce the law, even when they do invoke it, but merely use it as a resource to solve certain pressing practical problems in keeping the peace. This observation goes beyond the conclusion that many of the lesser norms of the criminal law are treated as defeasible in police work. It is patently not the case that skid-row patrolmen apply the legal norms while recognizing many exceptions to their applicability. Instead, the observation leads to the conclusion that in keeping the peace on skid-row, patrolmen encounter certain matters they attend to by means of coercive action, e.g., arrests. In doing this, they invoke legal norms that are available, and with some regard for substantive appropriateness. Hence, the problem patrolmen confront is not which drunks, beggars, or disturbers of the peace should be arrested and which can be let go as exceptions to the rule. Rather, the problem is whether, when someone "needs" to be arrested, he should be charged with drunkeness, begging, or disturbing the peace. Speculating further, one is almost compelled to infer that virtually any set of norms could be used in this manner, provided that they sanction relatively common forms of behavior.

The reduced relevance of culpability in peace keeping practice on skid-row is not readily visible. As mentioned, most arrested persons were actually found in the act, or in the state, alleged in the arrest record. It becomes partly visible when one views the treatment of persons who are not arrested even though all the legal grounds for an arrest are present. Whenever such persons are encountered and can be induced to leave, or taken to some shelter, or remanded to someone's care, then patrolmen feel, or at least maintain, that an arrest would serve no useful purpose. That is, whenever there exist means for controlling the troublesome aspects of some person's presence in some way alternative to an arrest, such means are preferentially employed, provided, of course, that the case at hand involves only a minor offense.[28]

The attenuation of the relevance of culpability is most visible when the presence of legal grounds for an arrest could be questioned, i.e., in cases that sometimes are euphemistically called "preventive arrests." In one observed instance, a man who attempted to trade a pocket knife came to the attention of a patrolman. The initial encounter was attended by a good deal of levity

[28] When evidence is present to indicate that a serious crime has been committed, considerations of culpability acquire a position of priority. Two such arrests were observed, both involving checkpassers. The first offender was caught *in flagrante delicto*. In the second instance, the suspect attracted the attention of the patrolman because of his sickly appearance. In the ensuing conversation the man made some remarks that led the officer to place a call with the Warrant Division of his department. According to the information that was obtained by checking records, the man was a wanted checkpasser and was immediately arrested.

and the man willingly responded to the officer's inquiries about his identity and business. The man laughingly acknowledged that he needed some money to get drunk. In the course of the exchange it came to light that he had just arrived in town, traveling in his automobile. When confronted with the demand to lead the officer to the car, the man's expression became serious and he pointedly stated that he would not comply because this was none of the officer's business. After a bit more prodding, which the patrolman initially kept in the light mood, the man was arrested on a charge involving begging. In subsequent conversation the patrolman acknowledged that the charge was only speciously appropriate and mainly a pretext. Having committed himself to demanding information he could not accept defeat. When this incident was discussed with another patrolman, the second officer found fault not with the fact that the arrest was made on a pretext but with the first officer's own contribution to the creation of conditions that made it unavoidable. "You see," he continued, "there is always the risk that the man is testing you and you must let him know what is what. The best among us can usually keep the upper hand in such situations without making arrests. But when it comes down to the wire, then you can't let them get away with it."

Finally, it must be mentioned that the reduction of the significance of culpability is built into the normal order of skid-row life, as patrolmen see it. Officers almost unfailingly say, pointing to some particular person, "I know that he knows that I know that some of the things he 'owns' are stolen, and that nothing can be done about it." In saying this, they often claim to have knowledge of such a degree of certainty as would normally be sufficient for virtually any kind of action except legal proceedings. Against this background, patrolmen adopt the view that the law is not merely imperfect and difficult to implement, but that on skid-row, at least, the association between delict and sanction is distinctly occasional. Thus, to implement the law naively, i.e., to arrest someone *merely* because he committed some minor offense, is perceived as containing elements of injustice.

Moreover, patrolmen often deal with situations in which questions of culpability are profoundly ambiguous. For example, an officer was called to help in settling a violent dispute in a hotel room. The object of the quarrel was a supposedly stolen pair of trousers. As the story unfolded in the conflicting versions of the participants, it was not possible to decide who was the complainant and who was alleged to be the thief, nor did it come to light who occupied the room in which the fracas took place, or whether the trousers were taken from the room or to the room. Though the officer did ask some questions, it seemed, and was confirmed in later conversation, that he was there not to solve the puzzle of the missing trousers but to keep the situation from getting out of hand. In the end, the exhausted participants dispersed, and this was the conclusion of the case. The patrolman maintained that no one could unravel mysteries of this sort because "these people take things from each other so often that no one could tell what 'belongs' to whom." In fact, he suggested, the terms owning, stealing, and swindling, in their strict sense, do not really belong on skid-row, and all efforts to distribute guilt and innocence according to some rational formula of justice are doomed to failure.

It could be said that the term "curb-stone justice" that is sometimes applied to the procedures of patrolmen in skid-rows contains a double irony. Not only is the procedure not legally authorized, which is the intended irony in the expression, but it does not even pretend to distribute deserts. The best among the patrolmen, according to their own standards, use the law to keep skid-row inhabitants from sinking deeper into the misery they already experience. The worst, in terms of these same standards, exploit the practice for personal aggrandizement or gain. Leaving motives aside, however, it is easy to see that if culpability is not the salient consideration leading to an arrest in cases where it is patently obvious, then the practical patrolman may not view it as being wholly out of line to make arrests lacking in formal legal justification. Conversely, he will come to view minor offense arrests made solely because legal standards are met as poor craftsmanship.

***The Background of* Ad Hoc *Decision Making*.** When skid-row patrolmen are pressed to explain their reasons for minor offense arrests, they most often mention that it is done for the protection of the arrested person. This, they maintain, is the case in virtually all drunk arrests, in the majority of arrests involving begging and other nuisance offenses, and in many cases involving acts of violence. When they are asked to explain further such arrests as the one cited earlier involving the man attempting to sell the pocket knife, who was certainly not arrested for his own protection, they cite the consideration that belligerent persons constitute a much greater menace on skid-row than any place else in the city. The reasons for this are twofold. First, many of the inhabitants are old, feeble, and not too smart, all of which makes them relatively defenseless. Second, many of the inhabitants are involved in illegal activities and are known as persons of bad character, which does not make them credible victims or witnesses. Potential predators realize that the resources society has mobilized to minimize the risk of criminal victimization do not protect the predator himself. Thus, reciprocal exploitation constitutes a preferred risk. The high vulnerability of everybody on skid-row is public knowledge and causes every seemingly aggressive act to be seen as a potentially grave risk.

When, in response to all this, patrolmen are confronted with the observation that many minor offense arrests they make do not seem to involve a careful evaluation of facts before acting, they give the following explanations: First, the two reasons of protection and prevention represent a global background, and in individual cases it may sometimes not be possible to produce adequate justification on these grounds. Nor is it thought to be a problem of great moment to estimate precisely whether someone is more likely to come to grief or to cause grief when the objective is to prevent the proliferation of troubles. Second, patrolmen maintain that some of the seemingly spur-of-the-moment decisions are actually made against a background of knowledge of facts that are not readily apparent in the situations. Since experience not only contains this information but also causes it to come to mind, patrolmen claim to have developed a special sensitivity for qualities of appearances that allow an intuitive grasp of probable tendencies. In this context, little things are said to have high informational value and lead to conclusions without the intervention of explicitly reasoned chains of inferences. Third, patrolmen readily admit that they do not adhere to high standards of adequacy of justification. They do not seek to defend the adequacy of their method against some abstract criteria of merit. Instead, when questioned, they assess their methods against the background of a whole system of *ad hoc* decision making, a system that encompasses the courts, correction facilities, the welfare establishment, and medical services. In fact, policemen generally maintain that their own procedures not only measure up to the workings of this system but exceed them in the attitude of carefulness.

In addition to these recognized reasons, there are two additional background factors that play a significant part in decisions to employ coercion. One has to do with the relevance of situational factors, and the other with the evaluation of coercion as relatively insignificant in the lives of the inhabitants.

There is no doubt that the nature of the circumstances often has decisive influence on what will be done. For example, the same patrolman who arrested the man trying to sell his pocket knife was observed dealing with a young couple. Though the officer was clearly angered by what he perceived as insolence and threatened the man with arrest, he merely ordered him and his companion to leave the street. He saw them walking away in a deliberately slow manner and when he noticed them a while later, still standing only a short distance away from the place of encounter, he did not respond to their presence. The difference between the two cases was that in the first there was a crowd of amused bystanders, while the latter case was not witnessed by anyone. In another instance, the patrolman was directed to a hotel and found a father and son fighting about money. The father occupied a room in the hotel and the son occasionally shared his quarters. There were two other men present, and they made it clear that their sympathies were with the older man. The son was whisked off to jail without much study of the relative merits of the conflicting claims. In yet another case, a middle-aged woman was forcefully evacuated from a bar even after the bartender explained that her loud behavior was merely a response to goading by some foul-mouth youth.

In all such circumstances, coercive control is exercised as a means of coming to grips with situational exigencies. Force is used against particular persons but is incidental to the task. An ideal of "economy of intervention" dictates in these and similar cases that the person whose presence is most likely to perpetuate the troublesome development be removed. Moreover, the decision as to who is to be removed is arrived at very quickly. Officers feel considerable pressure to act unhesitatingly, and many give accounts of situations that got out of hand because of desires to handle cases with careful consideration. However, even when there is no apparent risk of rapid proliferation of trouble, the tactic of removing one or two persons is used to control an undesirable situation. Thus, when a patrolman ran into a group of four men sharing a bottle of wine in an alley, he emptied the remaining contents of the bottle into the gutter, arrested one man—who was no more and no less drunk than the others—and let the others disperse in various directions.

The exigential nature of control is also evident in the handling of isolated drunks. Men are arrested because of where they happen to be encountered. In this, it matters not only whether a man is found in a conspicuous place or not, but also how far away he is from his domicile. The further away he is, the less likely it is that he will make it to his room, and the more likely the arrest. Sometimes drunk arrests are made mainly because the police van is available. In one case a patrolman summoned the van to pick up an arrested man. As the van was pulling away from the curb the officer stopped the driver because he sighted another drunk stumbling across the street. The second man protested saying that he "wasn't even half drunk yet." The patrolman's response was "OK, I'll owe you half a drunk." In sum, the basic routine of keeping the peace on skid-row involves a process of matching the resources of control with situational exigencies. The overall objective is to reduce the total amount of risk in the area. In this, practicality plays a considerably more important role than legal norms. Precisely because patrolmen see legal reasons for coercive action much more widely distributed on skid-row than could ever be matched by interventions, they intervene not in the interest of law enforcement but in the interest of producing relative tranquility and order on the street.

Taking the perspective of the victim of coercive measures, one could ask why he, in particular, has to bear the cost of keeping the aggregate of troubles down while others, who are equally or perhaps even more implicated, go scot-free. Patrolmen maintain that the *ad hoc* selection of persons for attention must be viewed in the light of the following consideration: Arresting a person on skid-row on some minor charge may save him and others a lot of trouble, but it does not work any real hardships on the arrested person. It is difficult to overestimate the skid-row patrolman's feeling of certainty that his coercive and disciplinary actions toward the inhabitants have but the most passing significance in their lives. Sending a man to jail on some charge that will hold him for a couple of days is seen as a matter of such slight importance to the affected person that it could hardly give rise to scruples. Thus, every indication that a coercive measure should be taken is accompanied by the realization "I might as well, for all it matters to him." Certain realities of life on skid-row furnish the context for this belief in the attenuated relevance of coercion in the lives of the inhabitants. Foremost among them is that the use of police authority is seen as totally unremarkable by everybody on skid-row. Persons who live or work there are continuously exposed to it and take its existence for granted. Shopkeepers, hotel clerks, and bartenders call patrolmen to rid themselves of unwanted and troublesome patrons. Residents expect patrolmen to arbitrate their quarrels authoritatively. Men who receive orders, whether they obey them or not, treat them as part of life as usual. Moreover, patrolmen find that disciplinary and coercive actions apparently do not affect their friendly relations with the persons against whom these actions are taken. Those who greet and chat with them are the very same men who have been disciplined, arrested, and ordered around in the past, and who expect to be thus treated again in the future. From all this, officers gather that though the people on skid-row seek to evade police authority, they do not really object to it. Indeed, it happens quite frequently that officers encounter men who welcome being arrested and even actively ask for it. Finally, officers point out that sending someone to jail from skid-row does not upset his relatives or his family life, does not cause him to miss work or lose a job, does not lead to his being reproached by friends and associates, does not lead to failure to meet commitments or protect investments, and does not conflict with any but the most passing intentions of the arrested person. Seasoned patrolmen are not oblivious to the irony of the fact that measures intended as mechanisms for distributing deserts can be used freely because these measures are relatively impotent in their effects.

SUMMARY AND CONCLUSIONS

It was the purpose of this paper to render an account of a domain of police practice that does not seem subject to any system of external control. Following the terminology suggested by Michael Banton, this practice was called keeping the peace. The procedures employed in keeping the peace are not determined by legal mandates but are, instead, responses to certain demand conditions. From among several demand conditions, we concentrated on the one produced by the concentration of certain types of persons in districts known as skid-row. Patrolmen maintain that the lives of the inhabitants of the area are lacking in prospective coherence. The consequent reduction in the temporal horizon of predictability constitutes the main problem of keeping the peace on skid-row.

Peace keeping procedure on skid-row consists of three elements. Patrolmen seek to acquire a rich body of concrete knowledge about people by cultivating personal acquaintance with as many residents as possible. They tend to proceed against persons mainly on the basis of perceived risk, rather than on the basis of culpability. And they are more interested in reducing the aggregate total of troubles in the area than in evaluating individual cases according to merit.

There may seem to be a discrepancy between the skid-row patrolman's objective of preventing disorder and his efforts to maintain personal acquaintance with as many persons as possible. But these efforts are principally a tactical device. By knowing someone individually the patrolman reduces ambiguity, extends trust and favors, but does not grant immunity. The informality of interaction on skid-row always contains some indications of the hierarchical superiority of the patrolman and the reality of his potential power lurks in the background of every encounter.

Though our interest was focused initially on those police procedures that did not involve invoking the law, we found that the two cannot be separated. The reason for the connection is not given in the circumstance that the roles of the "law officer" and of the "peace officer" are enacted by the same person and thus are contiguous. According to our observations, patrolmen do not act alternatively as one or the other, with certain actions being determined by the intended objective of keeping the peace and others being determined by the duty to enforce the law. Instead, we have found that *peace keeping occasionally acquires the external aspects of law enforcement.* This makes it specious to inquire whether or not police discretion in invoking the law conforms with the intention of some specific legal formula. The real reason behind an arrest is virtually always the actual state of particular social situations, or of the skid-row area in general.

We have concentrated on those procedures and considerations that skid-row patrolmen regard as necessary, proper, and efficient relative to the circumstances in which they are employed. In this way, we attempted to disclose the conception of the mandate to which the police feel summoned. It was entirely outside the scope of the presentation to review the merits of this conception and of the methods used to meet it. Only insofar as patrolmen themselves recognized instances and patterns of malpractice did we take note of them. Most of the criticism voiced by officers had to do with the use of undue harshness and with the indiscriminate use of arrest powers when these were based on personal feelings rather than the requirements of the situation. According to prevailing opinion, patrolmen guilty of such abuses make life unnecessarily difficult for themselves and for their co-workers. Despite disapproval of harshness, officers tend to be defensive about it. For example, one sergeant who was outspokenly critical of brutality, said that though in general brutal men create more problems than they solve, "they do a good job in some situations for which the better men have no stomach." Moreover, supevisory personnel exhibit a strong reluctance to direct their subordinates in the particulars of their work performance. According to our observations, control is exercised mainly through consultation with superiors, and directives take the form of requests rather than orders. In the background of all this is the belief that patrol work on skid-row requires a great deal of discretionary freedom. In the words of the same sergeant quoted above, "a good man has things worked out in his own ways on his beat and he doesn't need anybody to tell him what to do."

The virtual absence of disciplinary control and the demand for discretionary freedom are related to the idea that patrol work involves "playing by ear." For if it is true that peace keeping cannot be systematically generalized, then, of course, it cannot be organizationally constrained. What the seasoned patrolman means, however, in saying that he "plays by ear" is that he is making his decisions while being attuned to the realities of complex situations about which he has immensely detailed knowledge. This studied aspect of peace keeping generally is not made explicit, nor is the tyro or the outsider made aware of it. Quite to the contrary, the ability to discharge the duties associated with keeping the peace is viewed as a reflection of an innate talent of "getting along with people." Thus, the same demands are made of barely initiated officers as are made of experienced practitioners. Correspondingly, beginners tend to think that they can do as well as their more knowledgeable peers. As this leads to inevitable frustrations, they find themselves in a situation that is conducive to the development of a particular sense of "touchiness." Personal dispositions of individual officers are, of course, of great relevance. But the license of discretionary freedom and the expectation of success under conditions of autonomy, without any indication that the work of the successful craftsman is based on an acquired preparedness for the task, is ready-made for failure and malpractice. Moreover, it leads to slipshod practices of patrol that also infect the standards of the careful craftsman.

The uniformed patrol, and especially the foot patrol, has a low preferential value in the division of labor of police work. This is, in part, at least, due to the belief that "anyone could do it." In fact, this belief is thoroughly mistaken. At present, however, the recognition that the practice requires preparation, and the process of obtaining the preparation itself, is left entirely to the practitioner.

[13]

Police Deadly Force as Social Control: Jamaica, Argentina, and Brazil*

*Paul G. Chevigny***

INTRODUCTION

Until recently, interest in human rights has centered around problems that arise out of overtly partisan repression, as in the Soviet Union or in Argentina before the Malvinas (Falklands) war. There is increasing interest, however, in the human rights problems of ordinary street confrontations between police and petty criminals or poor people under governments that are not engaged in systematic political repression but, instead, present themselves to the world and to their own citizens as protecting civil rights and preserving order through routine police patrol.[1] Although there plainly

** Professor of Law, New York University School of Law, New York, New York, U.S.A.; B.A, Yale University 1957; LL.B., Harvard University 1960. My thanks are due to Bell Chevigny, Russell Karp, and Lois Whitman; to Americas Watch for sponsoring human rights investigations in Brazil and Jamaica; to the Centro de Estudios Legales y Sociales in Buenos Aires, Argentina; to Paulo Sergio Pinheiro and to the Nucleo de Estudos da Violência in São Paulo, Brazil; and to Frances Piven and Anne Buckborough for essential research assistance. Thanks to my colleagues from the Law and Society Colloquium at New York University and from the 1988 annual meeting of the Law and Society Association for helpful comments. I am grateful for the generous support of the Filomen D'Agostino and Max E. Greenberg Research Fund of New York University School of Law.

1 This subject was extensively explored at a 1988 conference I attended, "Mortes anunciadas: a (des)proteção da vida na America latina" [Deaths Foretold: The (Non)protection of Life in Latin America], Salvador, Bahia, Brazil, Dec. 4–7, 1988, sponsored by the Inter-American Institute for Human Rights and other organizations.

is a political aspect to this sort of police activity in developing nations, just as elsewhere, it is not outright political repression in the partisan sense. And while police violence is endemic to cities everywhere, it is of increasing concern in countries that are trying to make the transition out of a bureaucratic-authoritarian regime.

The targets of coercive police action are drawn mostly from the poor, and it is the fear of demands from this class that has often given rise to overtly political repression. Thus, "partisan" and "routine" police violence can be seen on a continuum. If nonpartisan police violence can be made legitimate—tolerable to the population as a whole—it can be carried out under governments that are formally democratic. That is, police violence can serve as an instrument of coercive social control[2] as long as it can be characterized as a justifiable response to violent crime.

This article examines the problem of police use of deadly force in three settings—the island of Jamaica (chiefly, the city of Kingston), the capital city of Buenos Aires, Argentina, and the urban states of Rio de Janeiro and São Paulo in Brazil. For each of these locations, data have recently become available through human rights investigations and other sources, showing striking similarities in the pattern of use of deadly force by the police. Although the three societies are culturally diverse, differing in population, in language, and in political tradition, they still have some notable characteristics in common. Perhaps most important, Jamaica, Argentina, and Brazil suffer continuing conditions of debt and underdevelopment, with their cities swollen by an influx of poor people from the hinterlands.[3]

These societies also share some political characteristics with the United States and Canada. All are (now) liberal-democratic polities, with popularly elected officials and a free press. In each, the police bear a roughly similar relation to the executive power; while the police constitute protomilitary bureaucracies, answerable formally to civilian law enforcement officials, they enjoy a large amount of customary discretion.

At the same time, Jamaica, Argentina, and Brazil present striking differences—both among themselves and from their northern neighbors—that in some ways aid comparison. The recent long-term bureaucratic-authoritarian repression in Argentina and Brazil might suggest, for example, that

[2] *See* Mayer, *Notes toward a Working Definition of Social Control in Historical Analysis*, in *Social Control and the State* ch. 1 (S. Cohen & A. Scull ed. 1983).

[3] *See generally* A. Portes & J. Walton, *Urban Latin America* (1976).

problems with police violence are merely a carryover from the military regimes that only lately ceased to exercise political control. The history of police use of deadly force in these countries, although rather sketchy, points, however, toward a conclusion that police abuses go back beyond the immediate political past. Moreover, the experience in Jamaica, which has never had this sort of repression, tends to confirm that the causes of police violence are likely to be independent of the authoritarian model. In fact, critics of police abuses in Brazil have argued that the causality runs chiefly the other way: A tradition of police violence makes the transition to political repression easier.[4]

To take another tack, if we look only at Jamaica and Brazil, we might conclude that the tradition of official violence is a legacy of slavery; however, the experience of Argentina, which was never a slave society in the same way, suggests that this explanation is simplistic. Again, if we were to look only at Brazil, we might attribute the source of police violence to racism since many of the victims are black. But the similarity of the problems in Jamaica and Argentina, which are not multiracial societies in the same way, suggests that the poverty of the victims, as much as their race, is a determining characteristic.

One way we can examine the phenomenon of police violence in the Caribbean and Latin America is to draw on the results of extensive investigations of this problem in North America. Research in United States cities[5] has documented a dramatic decrease (about 50 percent) in the number of civilians killed by police officers from 1971 to the mid-1980s. In New York City, for example, police killings of civilians dropped from a high of eighty-seven in 1971 to twelve in 1985.[6] By identifying the causes of this downward trend, we can begin to suggest ways to curb police abuses elsewhere.

The sharp decline in police killings in the United States appears to be largely the result of a policy decision by police officials over the past twenty years. It was notoriously the case that the urban rebellions of the sixties were frequently precipitated by police actions (not always by the use of deadly force, to be sure) and that they were exacerbated by the indiscriminate use

---

4 P. Pinheiro, *Escritos indignados* 58–60 (1984); Pinheiro, *Policia e a crise política*, in *Violência brasileira* 57 (M. Paoli ed. 1982).

5 L. Sherman & E. Cohn, *Citizens Killed by Big City Police* (1986).

6 *Id.* at 36; New York City Police Firearms Discharge Review Bd., *Report* (1985).

of gunfire.[7] Protesters were not cowed but, rather, provoked by the excessive use of force. Indeed, there is a rough correlation between violence by and against the police; that is, the two tend to rise and fall together.[8] Thus, to some extent, police violence begets a like response, although the causal relation is not always clear since violence directed at the police may cause them to react with fearful and intense repression. Recognition of this pattern apparently prompted a policy decision to restrict police violence. In addition, the downward trend in police violence in the United States may reflect the personal principles of individual officers and officials who think that there is insufficient reason to shoot a person who does not present a threat to the life of another. These factors have led not only to the abolition of the substantive rule justifying the shooting of any unarmed fleeing felon[9] but also to a radical reduction in the use of deadly force. There still are occasions when armed police shoot civilians, but policy clearly limits police use of deadly force to situations in which the civilian threatens the life of an officer or another person.

The experience in the United States tells us a great deal about the use of police deadly force in nonmilitary situations. When such force is broadly used, it indicates a policy of social control by violence. Moreover, this policy is, ultimately, a conscious one: Senior officials have sufficient command over their subordinates to change the way they use their weapons. Finally, the policy of social control through police violence fails when it systematically provokes a violent response; it ceases to be legitimate when it is perceived as begetting an endless round of violence. The increasing willingness of juries and judges in civil suits to award substantial damages to the victims of police abuse demonstrates that, at least in the United States, this policy has lost its legitimacy.[10]

The Data

Studies of police deadly force were conducted in Jamaica in 1986 and in São Paulo and Rio de Janeiro in 1987, by missions on which I served on behalf

---

7 Fogelson, *From Resentment to Confrontation*, 83 Pol. Sci. Q. 217 (1968); National Advisory Comm'n on Civil Disorders, *Report* 329 (1968).

8 L. Sherman & E. Cohn, *supra* note 5, at 8.

9 Tennessee v. Garner, 471 U.S. 1 (1985).

10 L. Sherman & E. Cohn, *supra* note 5, at 13–15.

of the human rights monitoring group Americas Watch,[11] and in Buenos Aires in 1987 and 1988, by the Centro de Estudios Legales y Sociales ("CELS").[12] The Americas Watch reports on Jamaica and Brazil relied on statistics and cases compiled from direct complaints, as well as from newspaper tallies made by local human rights groups. For this article, I have also included official figures collected subsequently by the Nucleo de Estudos da Violência at the University of São Paulo.[13] The CELS data include both official statistics and figures the center collected itself.

These investigations show that there are proportionately more police homicides in the island of Jamaica, in Buenos Aires, and in the states of São Paulo and Rio de Janeiro in Brazil than there are in the United States. The contrast with the United States raises the question whether the more frequent use of deadly force is minimally legitimate in those societies and, if so, how it is made legitimate. Moreover, insofar as the pattern of violence seems to be repeated from place to place, we need to ask whether it reflects common cultural and socioeconomic patterns.

Problems of Method

Blocking the way to any comparison either among the three countries or with the United States, however, is the customary official explanation for police use of deadly force. In liberal-democratic states such as these, it does

11 Americas Watch, *Police Abuse in Brazil: Summary Executions and Torture in São Paulo and Rio de Janeiro* (1987) [hereinafter Brazil Police Report]; Americas Watch, *Human Rights in Jamaica* (1986) [hereinafter Jamaica Report].

12 Centro de Estudios Legales y Sociales, *Muertos por violencia policial* (unpaginated mimeograph 1987 & rev. ed. 1988) [hereinafter 1987 CELS Report and 1988 CELS Report].

13 Nucleo de Estudos da Violência, Universidade de São Paulo, Violência do estado e militarização: mortes em conflitos policias em São Paulo nos anos 1980 (unpublished report 1989). A tabulation from newspaper accounts was initially made in Brazil and Jamaica because at the time of the Americas Watch reports, *supra* note 11, those governments declined to give Americas Watch official counts. Curiously, since the publication of the Americas Watch reports, both governments have started to release official figures. Tables 3 and 4 include unofficial, as well as official, figures.

Note that until recent years, municipal police departments in the United States also did not release official counts. *See* Sherman & Langworthy, *Measuring Homicide by Police Officers*, 70 J. Crim. L. & Criminology 546 (1979).

not appear to be politically acceptable for the police to admit that they kill a large number of people arbitrarily; they must appear to act under the rule of law. In all but a small fraction of cases, then, the government justifies shootings of civilians on the ground that the civilians were armed and, often, on the ground that the victim shot first.

Fortunately, studies conducted in the United States during the past fifteen years,[14] in the course of the effort by police officials to reduce the number of shootings, suggest some methods for seeing roughly what is going on behind the statistics and the justifications. Unfortunately, even if these methods help us show that the official account is untrue, we are still left wondering why police violence prevails in these societies, as well as why most people in both elite and victim groups in Jamaica, Argentina, and Brazil tolerate, or even support, the level of violence. To explore these questions, I have constructed a comparative index, admittedly very rough, of the perceived threat of unrest in South America and the Caribbean (Tables 1 and 2, respectively). In addition, I have looked at public attitudes expressed directly in opinion polls and indirectly in such indicators as the incidence of vigilantism.

People generally do not see the level of official violence in their own society, whether they approve of it or not, as relative to the level at another time or place. They are unaware whether there are more incidents in the present than there were in earlier years or than there currently are in some other city or nation. Consider, for example, Canada in relation to the United States. Because of the decentralization of law enforcement in the United States, it is impossible to get an accurate count of the number of homicides each year by police; estimates vary from about four hundred, at one extreme, to about seven hundred, at the other.[15] In contrast, one study of Canada reported 119 police killings in the years 1970–1981, about 10 per year,[16] a very low figure by United States standards (not to speak of the level in the other countries in the Americas discussed in this article). Nevertheless, because the investigators criticized police conduct in some individual cases,[17]

---

14 *See* sources cited *infra* notes 19–21, 23 & 25.

15 *See* K. Matulia, *A Balance of Forces* 9 (1982); Blumberg, *Issues and Controversies with Respect to the Use of Deadly Force*, in *Police Deviance* ch. 11 (T. Barker & D. Carter ed. 1986).

16 D. Chappell & L. Graham, *Police Use of Deadly Force: Canadian Perspectives* 10 (1985).

17 *Id.* at ix.

the Vancouver police union passed a resolution attacking the study. Apparently, it did not occur to the union to refrain from commenting even though the number of killings was very low in comparison to rates elsewhere. In other words, people become agitated about police shootings (or they don't), and the public relations officers of police departments react defensively regardless of how many incidents there are.

By implication, the studies in North America raise the question how to decide, without a detailed investigation of individual cases, that a given level of the use of deadly force is excessive. Although cities of comparable size may have very different levels of police violence, for example, this discrepancy taken by itself is at best a weak signal that the higher levels might be excessive. There may be a large number of shootings by the police, but every one of them may turn out to be justified in response to some life-threatening situation, as officials in Jamaica, Argentina, and Brazil often claim about the shootings in their countries.

Nevertheless, the studies in the United States[18] provide several ratios that can suggest persuasively when the police are using a relatively extreme level of deadly force: When the number of civilians killed exceeds the number wounded by the police, when the number of police killed by civilians constitutes only a small fraction of the number of civilians killed by police, and when the number of homicides by police represents a large fraction of all homicides, we can infer that deadly force is being abused. Taken by themselves, these ratios cannot reveal what happened in a particular case or even in a group of cases; read together with the details of exemplary cases, however, they give us a way of evaluating claims by police that all the homicides in many hundreds of instances are justified.[19]

1. *Relation between the number of shootings and the number of deaths attributable to the police.* Every police shooting is a potential killing. Therefore, the

---

[18] *See* sources cited *infra* notes 19–21, 23 & 25.

[19] There is a fourth possible statistical relation, suggested by Fyfe, *Blind Justice: Police Shootings in Memphis*, 73 J. Crim. L. & Criminology 707 (1982). Fyfe used figures for "shootings per officer," in relation to the total number of arrests for "violent felonies," to compare police killings in Memphis with those in New York City. This approach gives a very suggestive picture of the relationship between police use of deadly force and danger to police. I have not used this relationship because I do not have figures on shootings, as distinguished from homicides, and it is not clear that reliable figures on arrests for violent felonies could be assembled.

real indicator of how much deadly force is being used is not the number of deaths but, rather, the number of shootings (possibly even the number of occasions on which shots are fired). In the normal situation, many more persons are wounded than killed. For example, one study found that in Chicago in the five-year period 1974–1978, the police shot 523 persons, killing 130 of them; in a later five-year period (1981–1985), the New York City police shot 481 persons, killing 147 of them.[20] If the police kill more persons than they wound, or if the ratio of homicides to injuries suddenly starts to rise, we can infer that the use of deadly force may be excessive.

2. *Relation between the use of deadly force by and against the police.* If police are constantly in life-threatening situations, we expect them to use deadly force more frequently. Thus, the ratio between shootings *by* police and shootings *of* police is always significant. In Chicago, the ratio for 1974–1978 was 4.8:1, while in New York for 1981–1985 it was 5.2:2.[21] Such ratios are probably to be expected in United States cities. The relation between the number of civilians killed by police and the number of police killed in the line of duty is a much rougher estimate because some shootings will not be included, but it is still a useful comparison. In most developing nations, it is the only ratio that can even be approximated. In the period 1974–1978, the ratio of civilians to police killed in Chicago was 8.7:1; for New York in the period 1978–1985, the ratio was 7.8:1.[22] A ratio of roughly 7:1 is expected in the United States overall.[23] When up to fifteen times as many civilians as police are killed, as has happened in some of the cases discussed below,[24] this suggests that deadly force may be employed for purposes other than the protection of life.

3. *Relation between the number of homicides by police and the overall homicide rate.* Police use their weapons within a more or less violent society, and they

---

20 Figures for Chicago from Geller & Karales, *Shootings of and by Chicago Police* (pt. 1), 72 J. Crim. L. & Criminology 1813 (1981); figures for New York City from Press Relations Office, New York City Police Dep't, June 10, 1986.

21 Figures for Chicago from Geller & Karales, *Shootings of and by Chicago Police* (pt. 2), 73 J. Crim. L. & Criminology 331, 354 (1982); figures for New York City from Press Relations Office, New York City Police Dep't, June 10, 1986.

22 *See* sources cited *supra* note 21.

23 Personal communication from criminologist Mark Blumberg, Central Missouri State University, June 1986.

24 *See infra* Tables 3 & 4 and text accompanying notes 47, 71 & 88.

use them sometimes to protect other persons. There is, moreover, a positive correlation between violent crime and police use of deadly force. Nevertheless, we expect the number of homicides by police to constitute but a small fraction of the total homicide rate. According to one estimate, 3.6 percent of all homicides in the United States in the years 1971–1975 were by police officers.[25] I do not mean to suggest that the percentage in other countries need be that low; when the number of police killings becomes a very large percentage of the total homicide rate, however, we can infer that the police are not so much reacting to incidents within a violent society as using violence for purposes of social control.

Although these *disproportionate violence ratios*, as I call them, taken together with the details of particular cases, can help us to understand a pattern of violence, they can tell us little about what causes a police body, or the city or state of which it is a function, to persist in a policy that emphasizes deadly force. Some studies focusing on this issue in the United States have assumed that a high rate of the use of deadly force correlates with a rising rate of violent crime and specifically with a rising homicide rate.[26] For reasons given above in connection with the three disproportionate violence ratios, however, the equation of deadly force with violent crime is misleading. It implies that the use of deadly force is justifiable or even natural—that it rises in mere response to the threat of deadly violence. But the recent United States experience shows that the causation is not automatic; police commanders have the ability to control the use of deadly force even when the crime rate is perceived to be rising.

Some studies[27] have argued that police use of deadly force is correlated with the degree of economic inequality in the locale where it occurs, on the theory that the latter is an indicator of social conflict. This correlation may have some power when income inequality can be compared from city to city within a country.[28] However, all too often the underlying economic statistics are not available. Students of social mobilization have remarked on how dif-

---

25 Sherman & Langworthy, *supra* note 13, at 553; *see also* L. Sherman & E. Cohn, *supra* note 5, at 3, 10.

26 *See, e.g.*, K. Matulia, *supra* note 15, at 39.

27 *See, e.g.*, Jacobs & Britt, *Inequality and Police Use of Deadly Force*, 26 Soc. Probs. 403 (1979); Blumberg, *Research on Police Use of Deadly Force*, in *The Ambivalent Force* ch. 9 (A. Blumberg & E. Niederhoffer ed. 1985).

28 As Jacobs and Britt, *supra* note 27, have tried to do.

ficult it is to obtain reliable evidence of inequality.[29] As it happens, evidence of economic inequality in Brazil and Jamaica[30] is both dramatic and notorious, but comparative figures for cities and for other countries are hard to come by.

Moreover, the causal relation implied by the assumed correlation between official violence and economic inequality is ambiguous. At least two related scenarios are possible:

1. The relative poverty of the community results in a rise in the incidence of life-threatening crime, which in turn increases the incidence of police use of deadly force.

2. In societies marked by extreme economic inequality, elites and the polity as a whole may perceive a need for a show of violent force to discourage civil disturbances.

Although these two scenarios may, and often will, prevail at the same time, the second is more significant for us.[31] Among the things we are after, then, is an index of the perceived threat of social unrest among the poor. For this purpose, economic inequality, taken alone, has not been found to be determinative.[32] Continuing misery does not necessarily produce active protest; at a minimum, a sense of relative deprivation must be present.

Since at least the early sixties, students of social conflict have been trying to create indexes that correlate social conditions or changes in social conditions with social turmoil or rebellion.[33] One such index brought together factors of "social mobilization," including urbanization and means of mass communication, discounted by factors of "social welfare," including liter-

---

29 E. Duff & J. McCamant, *Violence and Repression in Latin America* 80 (1976); M. Ward, *Political Economy of Distribution* 165 (1978).

30 J. Lang, *Inside Development in Latin America* 151 (1988); T. Skidmore, *Politics of Military Rule in Brazil, 1964–85* at 286 (1988); S. Chernick, *Commonwealth Caribbean* 87–88 (1978).

31 The first scenario reiterates the "crime begets police violence" argument, rejected above. *See supra* text accompanying note 26.

32 E. Zimmermann, *Political Violence, Crises, and Revolutions* 46 (1983); Grofman & Muller, *The Strange Case of Relative Gratification and Potential for Political Violence*, 67 Am. Pol. Sci. Rev. 514 (1973).

33 E. Zimmermann, *supra* note 32, at 46.

acy, nutrition, medical care, and gross national product, on the hypothesis that the difference would be an indicator of social dissatisfaction and conflict.[34] While this approach did uncover a correlation between the welfare-mobilization differential and violence/repression in Latin America, the figures are out of date. I updated this index with recent statistics for South America and prepared a similar index for the Caribbean (see Tables 1 and 2, respectively). Each table includes a ranking of the countries in the order of the greatest differential between the social mobilization and the social welfare factors.[35]

Correlations of this sort, insofar as they are offered as indexes of rebellion or revolt against the established order, have come under increasing and successful attack in the past twenty years.[36] Critics have argued that social conflict is so pervasive in modern society that merely charting the reasons for conflict will not reveal the reasons for social upheaval; the real indicators are thought to be the conditions that mobilize the resources necessary to create a structure or organization for directing the underlying dissatisfaction.[37]

However, even assuming that such indexes cannot explain rebellion, they may still help to explain the underlying, unmobilized conflict. Indeed, the social mobilization-social welfare index has been correlated with civil violence.[38] With regard to the societies discussed in this article, the index is offered to show that there is at least some reason to expect or fear unrest as a result of dissatisfaction.[39] That is, the index points to a *risk* of social unrest

---

34 E. Duff & J. McCamant, *supra* note 29, ch. 3.

35 Rank is only suggestive and should be evaluated in terms of all the component factors. In the case of Brazil, for example, the large GNP has moved it down on the index, although it may be that the GNP does not much affect the lives of poorer people.

36 Jenkins, *Resource Mobilization Theory and the Study of Social Movements*, 9 Ann. Rev. Soc. 527 (1983); C. Tilly, *From Mobilization to Revolution* (1978); A. Oberschall, *Social Conflict and Social Movements* (1973).

37 *See generally* sources cited *supra* note 36.

38 E. Duff & J. McCamant, *supra* note 29, at 72, 92; E. Zimmermann, *supra* note 32, at 115; Zimmermann, *Macro-comparative Research on Political Protest*, in *Handbook of Political Conflict* 175 (T. Gurr ed. 1980).

39 Brazil is problematic for this scale, however, because the GNP distorts its placement. *See supra* note 35 and *infra* text accompanying note 94.

Table 1. Social Mobilization and Social Welfare in South America.*

	Social Mobilization					*Social Welfare*				
	Newsprint	*Radios*	*TVs*	*Urban*	*Total*	*Literacy*	*Calories*	*Doctors*	*GNP*	*Total*
Argentina	.04	.45	.38	.55	1.42	.18	.36	.12	.32	.98
Bolivia	−.21	−.15	−.10	−.50	−.96	−.25	−.21	.01	−.65	−1.10
Brazil	−.14	−.08	.12	−.30	.20	−.35	.06	.003	.43	.57
Chile	.10	−.07	.07	.55	.65	.15	.06	.04	.28	.53
Colombia	−.06	−.11	.01	.06	−.10	−.09	.02	.04	−.39	−.42
Ecuador	−.05	.01	−.10	−.36	−.50	−.09	−.26	.07	−.40	−.68
Guyana	−.16	.07	—	−.95	−1.04	.17	−.05	−.17	−.80	−.85
Paraguay	−.20	−.15	.25	−.65	−1.25	.09	.15	.02	−.05	.21
Peru	.25	−.10	−.15	.09	.09	−.04	−.07	.05	−.45	−.51
Suriname	−.03	.0	.11	−.24	−.16	.06	−.06	−.003	.60	.60
Uruguay	.21	.18	.11	.55	1.05	.17	.08	.10	.55	.90
Venezuela	.26	−.07	.11	.50	.80	−.02	.06	.08	.60	.72

Mobilization Ranking		*Welfare-Mobilization Differential*		*Welfare Ranking*	
Argentina	1.42	Peru	−.60	Argentina	.98
Uruguay	1.05	Argentina	−.44	Uruguay	.90
Venezuela	.80	Colombia	−.32	Venezuela	.72
Chile	.65	Ecuador	−.18	Suriname	.60
Brazil	.20	Uruguay	−.15	Brazil	.57
Peru	.09	Bolivia	−.14	Chile	.53
Colombia	−.10	Chile	−.12	Paraguay	.21
Suriname	−.16	Venezuela	−.08	Colombia	−.42
Ecuador	−.50	Guyana	.19	Peru	−.51
Bolivia	−.96	Brazil	.37	Ecuador	−.68
Guyana	−1.04	Suriname	.76	Guyana	− 85
Paraguay	−1.25	Paraguay	1.46	Bolivia	−1.10

Source note. The data were taken from the following sources:

Newsprint per capita: *Statistical Yearbook for Latin America and the Caribbean* (1987) [hereinafter SYLAC].

Radios per thousand persons: *World Bank Social Indicators* (1987) [hereinafter SI]; *United Nations Statistical Yearbook* (1983–84) [hereinafter UN].

Televisions per thousand persons: SYLAC; UN.

Urban population as a percentage of total population: *Economic and Social Progress in Latin America* (1987) [hereinafter ESPLA]; SI.

Literacy rate: SI; ESPLA.

Calories per diem: SI.

Doctors per capita: SI.

GNP per capita: SYLAC; *World Bank World Development Report* (1986).

*All scores are standardized. The factors in the social mobilization and social welfare indexes carry the following weights: in the social mobilization index, urban = 1/2 and the remaining factors = 1/6 each; for the social welfare index, GNP = 1/2 and the remaining factors = 1/6 each.

Table 2. Social Mobilization and Social Welfare in the Caribbean.*

	Social Mobilization					*Social Welfare*				
	Newsprint	*Radios*	*TVs*	*Urban*	*Total*	*Literacy*	*Calories*	*Doctors*	*GNP*	*Total*
Antigua/Barbuda	—	−.08	.06	−.62	−.64	—	−.26	0	—	−.51
Bahamas	—	.09	−.05	.41	.45	.07	.06	.09	.62	.84
Barbados	.26	.16	.06	−.26	.22	.13	.30	.10	.20	.73
Bermuda	—	.40	.55	—	.95	.13	—	—	.87	1.00
Cuba	.03	−.05	−.01	.47	.44	.12	.14	.17	−.22	.21
Dom. Repub.	−.06	−.19	−.10	.12	−.23	−.08	−.02	.05	−.41	−.46
Grenada	—	−.04	−.08	−.03	−.15	.12	−.09	−.02	−.43	−.42
Guadeloupe	—	−.15	−.07	.27	.05	—	—	.12	.11	.23
Haiti	−.26	−.20	−.18	−.74	−1.38	−.46	−.32	−.45	−.52	−1.75
Jamaica	−.07	−.04	−.10	.03	−.18	−.12	.003	−.04	−.38	−.54
Martinique	—	−.13	−.06	.30	.11	—	—	.13	.34	.47
Neth. Antilles	—	.68	−.01	.83	1.50	—	—	.05	.17	.22
St. Lucia	—	.18	−.18	—	0	−.03	−.08	−.03	−.38	−.52
St. Vincent	—	—	—	—	—	—	.07	−.29	−.43	−.65
Trinidad	.10	−.08	.11	−.88	−.75	.11	.16	.12	.70	1.09

Mobilization Ranking		*Welfare-Mobilization Differential*		*Welfare Ranking*	
Neth. Antilles	1.50	Neth. Antilles	−1.28	Trinida	1.09
Bermuda	.95	Haiti	−.37	Bermuda	1.00
Bahamas	.45	Jamaica	−.36	Bahamas	.84
Cuba	.44	Grenada	−.27	Barbados	.73
Barbados	.22	Cuba	−.23	Martinique	.47
Martinique	.11	Dom. Repub.	−.23	Guadeloupe	.23
Guadeloupe	.05	Bermuda	.05	Neth. Antille	.22
Grenada	−.15	Antigua/Barbuda	.13	Cuba	.21
Jamaica	−.18	Guadeloupe	.18	Grenada	−.42
Dom. Repub.	−.23	Martinique	.36	Dom. Repub.	−.46
Antigua/Barbuda	−.64	Bahamas	.39	Antigua/Barbuda	−.51
Trinidad	−.75	Barbados	.51	St. Lucia	−.52
Haiti	−1.38	Trinidad	1.84	Jamaica	−.54
				St. Vincent	−.65
				Haiti	−1.75

Source note. The data were taken from the following sources:

Newsprint per capita: *Statistical Yearbook for Latin America and the Caribbean* (1987) [hereinafter SYLAC].

Radios per thousand persons: *Caribbean Economic Handbook* (1985); *World Bank Social Indicators* (1987) [hereinafter SI]; *United Nations Statistical Yearbook* (1983–84) [hereinafter UN].

Televisions per thousand persons: SYLAC; UN.

Urban population as a percentage of total population: *Economic and Social Progress in Latin America* (1987) [hereinafter ESPLA]; SI.

Literacy rate: SI; ESPLA.

Calories per diem: SI.

Doctors per capita: SI.

GNP per capita: SYLAC; *World Bank World Development Report* (1986).

*See Table 1 statistical note. St. Lucia and St. Vincent are missing from the welfare-mobilization differential because of lack of data for the mobilization ranking.

from the point of view of the political elite; for that reason, I call this the *perceived threat of unrest scale.* The hypothesis is that awareness of the risk may make an increase in official violence more likely, at least where the climate of opinion would favor this response. On the other hand, official violence can provoke, as well as quell, social unrest.[40] When there is little protest against prevalent police violence, that passivity itself requires some explanation.

I propose, then, to examine the widespread use of deadly force in law enforcement in light of three factors:

1. Likelihood of social unrest. In this connection, Tables 1 and 2 are meant only to be suggestive. A strongly negative differential on the perceived threat of unrest scale points toward problems that might create enough apprehension to give rise to repressive police action.

2. Elite opinion concerning coercive social control and police use of deadly force.

3. Mass attitudes concerning coercive social control and police use of deadly force.

JAMAICA

Cases and statistics collected by the Jamaica Council for Human Rights, which were supplemented by official figures that became available later, demonstrate an extraordinary pattern in the use of deadly force by the Jamaica constabulary. It was at first impossible in Jamaica, just as it used to be in the United States,[41] to get an official count of homicides by police. We were forced to rely on newspaper accounts, which fortunately had been carefully tabulated for the period 1979–1985.[42] Although this method is likely, at best, to yield an undercount, the results turned out to be consistent with the official figures for succeeding years. After the release of the Americas Watch report, the government finally began to make official figures

[40] Feierabend, Feierabend & Nesvold, *Social Change and Political Violence*, in 2 *Violence in America* 497 (T. Gurr & H. Graham ed. 1969).

[41] *See supra* note 13.

[42] Jamaica Report, *supra* note 11, at 10.

available[43] (official and unofficial tallies set forth in Table 3). The average for the period 1979–1988 was 208 killings per year.

Whether underestimated or not, these figures are large and puzzling, in an island with less than three million people—about as many as, say, Brooklyn, New York—and a constabulary of roughly six thousand officers, assisted by about two thousand auxiliaries[44]—a force proportionately some-

Table 3. Homicide Statistics for Jamaica.

Homicides by Constabulary, 1979–1988

1979	1980	1981	1982	1983	1984	1985	1986	1987	1988	Average
199	206	319	101	196	288	210	178	205	181	208

Other Homicides, 1984-1987

1984	1985	1986	1987	1988	Average
484	434	449	442	414	445

Police Killed in the Line of Duty, 1980–1985

1979	1980	1981	1982	1983	1984	1985	
—	22	4	7	13	13	4	Regulars
		[31]*			7	5	Auxiliaries

Source note. Homicides by constabulary, 1979–1985, from the *Gleaner* (Kingston, Jamaica), collected in Jamaica Report, *supra* note 11, at 10. All other figures are official statistics from the Jamaican government.

*In the period 1979–1983, a total of 31 auxiliary police were killed in the line of duty, but no annual breakdown is available. Figures for regulars killed before 1980 also are not available.

[43] Letter from Lois Whitman, Americas Watch, to President Edward Seaga (Mar. 10, 1988); letter from Lois Whitman, Americas Watch, to President Michael Manley (Mar. 30, 1989). Ms. Whitman was reporting in each case information she had received from Jamaican law enforcement officials.

[44] Jamaica Report, *supra* note 11, at 9.

what smaller than that of New York City. But of course, despite the thousands of Jamaican immigrants living in Brooklyn, it is scarcely like Jamaica.

Jamaica has one large, poor city, Kingston, where many of the nation's social problems are concentrated, and is otherwise farm country and small towns, through which the police are thinly distributed. In but a handful of the numerous police homicides, the government admits that an error was made. The official explanation for the overwhelming majority of police killings is that Jamaica is an extraordinarily violent society and that in each case the police were responding to an "ambush" or a "shoot-out" in order to protect their lives.[45] If this claim were true, it might indicate a dire social situation, but at least the figures would be less puzzling.

The three disproportionate violence ratios afford a way to start evaluating the official explanation. Jamaica's statistics for homicides, apart from killings by police, in the five-year period 1984–1988, yield an average of 445 per year (see Table 3). The average for homicides by police in the same period is 212 (see Table 3), or not quite half the civilian homicide rate. In other words, the police account for nearly one-third of all homicides in the island. Official figures for the number of civilians killed and wounded are available only for 1988. During that year, 98 persons were wounded; 188 were killed.[46]

The relation between deadly force used by and against the police is also revealing (see Table 3). In the year 1985, for example, over twenty times as many civilians were killed by police as police were killed in the line of duty. For that year, furthermore, we received an extraordinary official statistic concerning the risk of injury run by officers in the shooting incidents. In 372 reported shooting incidents involving police in 1985, 22 police were injured, in addition to those killed.[47]

These figures suggests that something is wrong with the government's ambush/shoot-out scenario. The Jamaica Council for Human Rights has a dossier of a dozen officers who have been involved repeatedly in alleged abuses of deadly force. We identified police officers who were famous for having killed many people. Some of these officers not only had escaped any

[45] *Id.* at 12.

[46] Whitman letter (Mar. 30, 1989), *supra* note 43.

[47] Jamaica Report, *supra* note 11, at 15.

discipline but even had received promotions. The most notorious of them, who calls himself "Trinity," became part of former Prime Minister Edward Seaga's security staff.[48] We linked another of these officers, Alfred Laing, a detective corporal, to thirteen shootings in a three-year period; there may well have been more. One of Laing's cases can serve as the paradigm. In April 1985, Laing arrested a suspect and had him arraigned on a charge of gun possession, a rather serious charge in Jamaica. When Laing failed to produce certain documentation required by the court, the suspect was released on bail. At this point, Laing said to the suspect, "Tell your mother to get your burial suit ready." Three weeks later, Laing arrived at the suspect's house with a heavily armed squad and killed him. They then took the other young men who were present in the house into custody and beat them in an attempt to find out where the supposed gun was hidden.[49]

From the records of cases like this one, together with interviews of witnesses and lawyers in the island and the disproportionate violence ratios, we in the Americas Watch mission concluded that many of the police homicides are summary executions of suspects, usually in routine cases, whom the police simply kill in lieu of leaving the case to the courts. In connection with these killings, the police often use semiautomatic weapons, so that in crowded neighborhoods other individuals are shot either through indiscriminate firing or through mistaken identity.

Function of the System

Since its independence in 1962, Jamaica has been a Westminster style democracy with two dominant political parties, the Jamaica Labor Party, led by Edward Seaga, which is conservative, and the Peoples National Party, led by Michael Manley. The two parties replace one another at the polls regularly, although often in the midst of violence brought about by partisan gangs. The prevalence of police violence is not associated with one party or the other and the police do not, for the most part—with some exceptions in election years—appear to be attacking people for partisan reasons. Supporters of Manley, although they were very critical of Seaga, as well as of the police, did not pretend in conversations with us during the Americas Watch mission in 1986 that there were significantly more police killings in the

48 *Id.* at 25.

49 *Id.* at 21–25, 62.

Seaga than in the preceding Manley administrations. Although under the present administration, Manley has expressed concern about police violence,[50] the situation does not appear to be under control.

Social and economic relations prevailing in the island are menacing from the point of view of propertied Jamaicans. Unequal distribution of land and income, while traditional in Jamaica, has been increasing.[51] In turn, problems of land distribution, among other factors, have led to the increasing urbanization of the poor. On the perceived threat of unrest scale (discounting social mobilization by social welfare factors) for the Caribbean, Jamaica has one of the largest negative differentials (see Table 2), even though the island is not among the poorest in resources. It is interesting to note that in Trinidad, which has somewhat less than half the population of Jamaica and has one of the most favorable threat of unrest ratios (see Table 2), there have been about two hundred police homicides in the period 1970–1986.[52]

Under these socioeconomic conditions, we were afforded a window into the attitudes of elite opinion makers concerning police violence through their reactions to the Americas Watch report on human rights in Jamaica. The island's one newspaper, the *Gleaner* (Kingston) serialized the report in the fall of 1986, spawning an avalanche of commentary. Not surprisingly, government officials denied the conclusion concerning the prevalence of summary executions. For example, the minister of national security branded the report "a wholesale slander of the police."[53] The columnists for the

---

50 *Manley Concerned about Killings by Cops*, Weekly Gleaner (Kingston), Feb. 26, 1990 (int'l ed.).

51 C. Stone & A. Brown, *Essays on Power and Change in Jamaica* ch. 1 (1977).

52 H. Delroy Murray, then the legal officer of the Jamaica Council for Human Rights, attending a conference of the Bar Association of Trinidad and Tobago in 1986, commented wryly:

> So whereas [the Bar Association's] President was rightly alarmed at the fact that 200 or so persons had been killed by the police since 1970 in Trinidad, I had to chuckle—not because the situation he describes isn't serious, but because compared to the Jamaican statistics, you are still, comparatively speaking, living in, for want of a better term, a fairy tale world.

H.D. Murray, Police Excesses, the Courts, and Human Rights in Jamaica at 2 (paper presented at "Law and Civil Liberties in the Caribbean," a conference of the Bar Association of Trinidad and Tobago, 1986).

53 Gleaner (Kingston), Oct. 26, 1986; *see also* N.Y. Times, Oct. 24, 1986, at A13.

Gleaner, however, took a curious middle course: They did not so much deny the conclusion as seek to explain the practice.

The noted social scientist Carl Stone, a regular contributor, wrote at least four columns about the Americas Watch report.[54] In his column of October 15, 1986, Stone commented sharply:

> The average policeman in uniform cannot shoot straight enough to handle the tough criminals with M-16 rifles and to protect you and me against serious criminals.
>
> . . . .
>
> The much criticised Eradication Squad which wiped out many such criminals was designed for that purpose. Sharp-shooting CIB [Criminal Investigation Bureau] men at various Police stations have earned the support of citizens by demonstrating a capability to shake down criminals and send them in flight from sheer fear of their awesome reputations and their daring deeds of violence.
>
> . . . .
>
> . . . Even if this macho type Police strategy really does not work, it gives citizens a deep sense of confidence that there are tough cops who they think drive fear into the hearts of criminals.
>
> . . . .
>
> Some way has to be found to reduce the incidence of killing of innocent citizens and to prosecute policemen who kill outside of circumstances when their lives are threatened. But tough macho cops the country needs to maintain a "balance of terror" in the streets.
>
> The excesses must be curbed but there must be no removal of the frontline cops who strike fear in the hearts of the violent criminals and have the courage to confront them on the battlefield of violence.
>
> To do that is to ensure tha[t] many citizens would have to fill the vacuum and become frontline men fighting crime in highly organised vigilante squads along the South American pattern.[55]

Regular columnist Morris Cargill claimed that Jamaica is a "violent and anarchic society" with a crime rate "far in excess of [that of] any other coun-

---

54 Gleaner (Kingston), Oct. 1, 13, 15; Nov. 10, 1986.

55 *Id.*, Oct. 15, 1986.

try with even a vestigial claim to be civilised."[56] He expressed despair about the quality of prosecutors and court personnel in Jamaica, adding that the island is too poor to afford proper law enforcement:

> [W]e have not got the police capacity to track down and arrest our criminals in a nice, orderly, civilized manner.
>
> . . . .
>
> . . . The police do shoot down known murderers and armed gangsters when they catch them, sometimes in cold blood. This is not the best way of justice, but in our present circumstances my only complaint is that they don't shoot enough of them.[57]

For opinion makers in the island, then, police use of deadly force is an inescapable consequence of underdevelopment, crime, and poverty. Through a curious reversal of loyalties, they justify a system of repression by a supposed lack of access to a more "civilized" system, painting a picture of Jamaica as so anarchic, so filled with terrorists, as to have no alternative to police violence.[58] To lend support to these views, they rely on factors that are often correlated with police violence. Jamaica does have the highest homicide and robbery rate in the Caribbean.[59] More important, perhaps, the rate of crime has risen rapidly: There were more than ten times as many

---

56 *Id.*, Oct. 19, 1986.

57 *Id.*

58 While I do not want to clutter the text with data concerning relative crime rates, the argument that Jamaica has a crime rate that is so high as to put the island in a moral class by itself, a point made explicitly by Cargill, *supra* note 56, and less vigorously by Stone, *infra*, should not pass unchallenged.

The overall homicide rate in Jamaica per 100,000 is about the same as that in large American cities. According to Stone, Gleaner (Kingston), Oct. 13, 1986, the homicide rate in the Kingston area is 43.5 per 100,000. While this figure is indeed hair-raising, it should be noted that the homicide rate in Detroit, Michigan, is higher. *See* U.S. Dep't of Justice, *Uniform Crime Statistics* (1984). My objective is not to show that some places in the United States are "as bad as Jamaica," because the conditions are bound to be largely incomparable, but rather to suggest that people manage to live with high crime rates elsewhere.

59 Albuquerque, *A Comparative Analysis of Violent Crime in the Caribbean*, 33(3) U. West Indies Soc. & Econ. Stud. 93 (1984).

homicides in the island in 1983 as there were in 1953.[60] But these factors taken alone, as we have seen, do not serve to explain why police violence is acceptable to Jamaica's opinion makers; indeed, the threat of unrest may give them an extra reason to fear violence from the poor.

Not surprisingly, the views of the island's social commentators are reflected in the public's attitudes. On some occasions—for example, when the police make a mistake and kill the "wrong person," particularly if the person is popular—there is a public outcry and sometimes a prosecution. But, in general, the public attitude toward the police is ambivalent: Whereas one poll indicated that 66 percent of the public throughout Jamaica felt that the police do not respect citizens' rights,[61] another revealed that 68 percent of the respondents in the Kingston area rejected the idea that the police use excessive force.[62] Indeed, 41 percent thought that not enough force is used, and 10 percent said that "certain types . . . should not be brought in alive."[63] The public thus seems to share the opinion makers' sense that the police, like the criminal justice system as a whole, are not competent enough to deal with crime through legal methods and that extralegal measures, including homicide, are required.

Class relations in Jamaica also have tended to support a system of summary punishment. Commentators have remarked repeatedly that postcolonial social relations replicate those that existed before independence. Jamaicans who are "educated," who have "manners," often manifest a contempt for those who are not that is close to the contempt white colonial administrators exhibited toward black Jamaicans generally.[64] Under the unstable economic conditions prevailing in the island, moreover, many of those who are not in the underclass run the risk of being thrust into it. Their fear of social unrest and of the sort of persons associated with it is so strong that they deny a common social bond.

In addition, vigilante violence has been increasing for several years. The parliamentary ombudsman, condemning both official and nonofficial vio-

60 A. Lewin, *Social Control in Jamaica* 106 (1978).

61 Stone, *The Police and Our Rights*, Gleaner (Kingston), Oct. 13, 1986.

62 C. Stone, *Political Opinions of the Jamaican People* 68 (1982).

63 *Id.*

64 D. Austin, *Urban Life in Kingston, Jamaica* 156–59 (1984); G. Lewis, *Growth of the Modern West Indies* 188–92 (1968).

lence, counted thirty-five instances of vigilante killings in 1984;[65] similar incidents in which suspects are summarily killed seem to be at least as frequent today. A typical summary execution occurred in July 1986, for example, when vendors in a local market disarmed and beat a robber to death.[66] Lynch law and police violence are two aspects of the same problem; police use of deadly force can be seen, in many cases, as official vigilantism and it is notable that, so far as I can determine, arrests are never made for private vigilantism.

> Vigilante killings are popular and supported by a majority of Jamaicans because they feel that the Police are not able to control crime effectively due to inadequate manpower, guns and motor vehicles and because they fear that the courts system does not work for them. To protect themselves, they take the law in their own hands and seek to establish their own "balance of terror."[67]

As we shall see more vividly in Brazil, society presents a particularly terrifying prospect to those just above the underclass when government functionaries, supported by opinion makers, depict the state as too poor and the authorities as too incompetent to protect the underprivileged and promote self-help as the only recourse. This situation creates a grim world of vengefulness in which persons accused of crime are literally outlaws, subject to execution by anyone, official or private.[68]

---

65 Jamaica Report, *supra* note 11, at 34.

66 Gleaner (Kingston), July 3, 1986.

67 *Id.*, Oct. 15, 1986, at 8.

68 One example of lynch law, exercised by the police together with a citizen, is illustrative. The victim had hired a driver and a car to help him transport some work materials. As they were driving, the police drew alongside the car and fired shots. The car, it later turned out, had been stolen; the driver, who was probably aware of that fact, pulled over to the curb and ran away. The owner of the car, who was riding with the police, urged them to kill the victim. When he ran away, the police shot and wounded him, then shot him again as he was begging for his life, by putting a gun in his open mouth. The victim lived to collect damages from the government. He was able to corroborate the last, most grisly, aspect of the story by introducing medical evidence that there was an exit wound in the back of his neck but no entry wound. This case was reported by Richard Small, the lawyer who represented the claimant. Jamaica Report, *supra* note 11, at 34.

Apart from the public opinion polls cited earlier,[69] which sometimes do not distinguish with respect to class, the attitude of the poorest people, who are the chief victims both of police violence and of crime, is hard to determine. No doubt many ghetto dwellers share the view that criminals deserve no more consideration than a lynch mob would give them. They sometimes also accept the values of those who are a little better off than they are. Some rely on traditional patron-client relations, formed not only with politicians but with police officers as well. A Jamaican defense lawyer who did not wish to be quoted told us that many people in Laing's precinct do not consider him a bad fellow, despite the number of persons he has killed, because he has the reputation of not killing the innocent. Moreover, Laing has personally financed local dances, which are said to be well attended. People in the neighborhood also have been known to bring Laing gifts from their friends and relatives abroad, apparently to remain in his good graces.

In sum, there has been little protest, organized or otherwise, from any sector of Jamaican society. Neither major party stands to gain a substantial political advantage by making police abuse into an issue because it has not seemed to be a matter of central public concern. Although we learned that a handful of superior officers in the Jamaican police would like to curb the use of deadly force, they can find little political support for reform. Poor Jamaicans who might protest against abuse are surrounded by people who are ambivalent about it and, from their position of isolation, they are intimidated by the possibility of retaliation.[70] From a certain point of view, then, the policy of social control by the use of deadly force could be said to be working passably well.

ARGENTINA: BUENOS AIRES

For generations, the city of Buenos Aires, which by itself is as populous as the island of Jamaica, has been the center of trade and culture for Argentina and a magnet for immigrants. Since the collapse of the military dictatorship and the election of Raúl Alfonsín in 1983, the Centro de Estudios Legales y Sociales ("CELS"), a human rights organization in Buenos Aires, has been monitoring police violence in cases that do not involve overt political re-

---

69 *See* sources cited *supra* notes 61–62.

70 Personal communication from Florizelle O'Connor, Jamaica Council for Human Rights, Oct. 1986.

pression but are apparently "routine." Based on official figures and news reports, the CELS studies show a pattern in the city and the larger surrounding province of Buenos Aires similar to that of Jamaica. Police statistics for the period December 1983-July 1985 indicate that 304 civilians were killed by the police, while 26 police were killed (a ratio of not quite 12:1).[71] Most indicative of the deliberateness of the shootings are the figures on woundings for the same period: According to police figures, 172 "public servants" were injured and 199 "criminals" were injured.[72] In other words, only about one-eighth of shootings against police resulted in death, whereas three-fifths of all police shootings resulted in death. During the year 1984 alone, the police accounted for over a quarter of all homicides.[73]

Interestingly, CELS found that commanding officials seemed to have a considerable amount of control over the number of homicides by police. Both when an opposition deputy in the legislature demanded an explanation of the violence and again when a scandal broke out about a kidnapping masterminded by a police inspector, the killings dropped precipitately for a short period.[74] Like the history of the decline of police killings in the United States, this suggests that superiors can curb abuses if they choose to do so.

In a pattern evident also in Jamaica and Brazil, the victims generally are not powerful or socially important criminals but rather, in some cases, even the most petty of wrongdoers, if they can be described as criminals at all. In one case reported at length by CELS, the victim was chased by police and eventually shot because he was dead drunk, fell heavily over a car, and ran away.[75] Another victim was an addict accused of petty thievery.[76]

The history of Argentina does not at first make it seem a likely candidate for such police violence. The country has maintained a relatively high standard of living, has not suffered from overpopulation, and has attracted hundreds of thousands of European immigrants. Under the surface, however, the socioeconomic indicators point in a rather different direction.

---

71 1987 CELS Report, *supra* note 12.

72 *Id.*

73 *Id.* Many of the figures were taken from official statistics reported in Clarín (Buenos Aires), Aug. 17, 1985.

74 1987 CELS Report, *supra* note 12.

75 Testimony of Gerónimo Pastine, 1988 CELS Report, *supra* note 12.

76 Testimony of Rosario Alegre, *id.*

The negative spread between social mobilization and social welfare is one of the greatest in Latin America, not because welfare is low in relation to welfare in other nations but because the elements of mobilization are so much more developed (see Table 1). Moreover, the situation of the poor has worsened over the last generation, with increasing external debt and unemployment. Argentina is a nation of blasted hopes.

The ruling groups of Argentina have been haunted by the fear of rebellion among the poor for some sixty years. Indeed, the political arrangements from the Great Depression up to the collapse of the last military government in 1983 were established, at least in part, for the purpose of forestalling revolution. Juan Perón played upon that fear and justified his policies and later his power on the basis of the danger of revolution.[77]

Although there would seem to be objective reasons in Argentine social relations for the elite fears, in fact the mass of working people has never been mobilized around a revolutionary ideology or program. The dominance of authoritarian labor leaders during and after Perón made such mobilization even less likely. The oligarchy and its allies, however, have never had much trust in popular government, and until the Malvinas debacle they contrived usually to prevent it. During the 1970s, for example, elements of the landed bourgeoisie engaged in a policy of deindustrialization, in a successful effort to decrease the size of the working class, and hence its bargaining power, through increasing unemployment.[78]

Despite the success of the dominant class in containing the working class, there is a long tradition of elite fear of, and contempt for, the lower classes in Argentina. While outright political repression and military rule is one aspect of these attitudes, a tradition of repressive police action outside the arena of partisan politics may be seen as another. The police violence that CELS identified for the Alfonsín years is nothing new. The journalist Rodolfo Walsh, who "disappeared" in the seventies, complained about this problem twenty years ago.[79] Similarly, the father of a recent victim is quoted shouting at the police who informed him of his son's death, "I get it. I know this kind of shoot-out with the police all too well. My father was a police-

77 C. Waisman, *Reversal of Development in Argentina* ch. 6 (1987); J. Corradi, *Fitful Republic* ch. 4 (1985).

78 C. Waisman, *supra* note 77, at 280.

79 1988 CELS Report, *supra* note 12.

man and I have relatives in the police, so you'll see if I know! . . . First you shoot him and then you fire a gun for him. It's an old story."[80]

At the same time, there is some liberal agitation against police violence in Buenos Aires because, after all, the level of social mobilization is high. CELS itself has campaigned, together with opposition politicians, newspapers, and lawyers. There also have been demonstrations over particular incidents, but police killings did not become an issue against the Alfonsín regime. As Eugenio Raúl Zaffaroni, a noted criminologist and criminal appeals judge in Buenos Aires who is sharply critical of the police, has commented:

> The deaths are published in the daily papers and are taken by the population as a "natural" phenomenon. Death by violence on the part of the criminal justice system is "naturalized" with the phrase "he who acts bad, ends badly." It is not seen as a social phenomenon; from the point of view of newspaper reporting, the deaths are considered as a problem of the individual, as something produced by the victim himself. . . .
>
> . . . .
>
> It is a . . . sort of intimidation exerted on a whole social sector, carried out by persons drawn from that sector, which shows the clear purpose of exacerbating the contradictions in that sector. . . .
>
> These deaths have the object of generating or deepening the antagonism, the fragmentation, and of dissolving the bonds of solidarity within the poor sector.[81]

BRAZIL: SÃO PAULO AND RIO DE JANEIRO

With fourteen to fifteen million people, the city of São Paulo alone is roughly five times as populous as the entire island of Jamaica or the city of Buenos Aires and half again as populous as Buenos Aires province. The state of São Paulo is an industrial giant, producing half of Brazil's manufactured goods. Nevertheless, more than half the people live in substandard slums around the city. Rio de Janeiro is somewhat smaller (although it is larger

80 Testimony of Gerónimo Pastine, *id.*

81 Zaffaroni, *Reflexiones criminológicas sobre los datos de muerte de violencia policial*, 1988 CELS Report, *supra* note 12.

than New York City), with a lower percentage of its people living in slums.[82] Still, the Baixada Fluminense, a rural slum surrounding Rio, houses some three million people.

State governments in Brazil maintain two police forces: The civil police, who do mostly investigative work and run the police stations; and the military police (PM), who do most of the patrol.[83] It is the PM that is responsible for most of the use of deadly force.

In São Paulo and Rio, as in Buenos Aires, one can speculate that long years of military repression left a legacy of directing violence against the population in day-to-day encounters. Some middle-class liberal reformers, however, like some Argentines,[84] do not see the abuse of ordinary suspects as a result of the long-standing authoritarian repression. They say that the police have always violated the rights of suspects; indeed, interest in human rights burgeoned during the military dictatorship because in those years police abuses also involved members of the middle and upper classes. Now that the repression has passed, abusive police practices, having reverted to their usual victims among the poor, have become invisible again.[85] Nevertheless, there is some evidence that violence became more systematic against all sorts of suspects during the years of the dictatorship and that in part that system has been carried forward. For instance, the PM in São Paulo have continued to operate an elite extermination patrol, called the ROTA, numbering over seven hundred. During one nine-month period in 1981, just as the country was emerging from the military dictatorship, members of the ROTA shot 136 civilians, killing 129 of them, while suffering 1 officer dead and 18 injured.[86]

In 1982, the administrations of Andre Franco Montoro in São Paulo and Leonel Brizola in Rio de Janeiro swept in, dedicated to the reform of the police, as well as other service institutions. The Montoro administration

---

82 *Brazil: A Country Study* 130, 136, 339 (R. Nyrop ed. 1983).

83 The designation "military police" is somewhat misleading in the Brazilian context. This body is not, except in times of military repression, under the jurisdiction of the armed forces. Instead, the designation is meant to identify a body similar to the French *gendarmerie*, upon which the PM is based.

84 Zaffaroni, *supra* note 81.

85 Nucleo de Estudos da Violência, *supra* note 13, at 5; Brazil Police Report, *supra* note 11, at 3.

86 Pinheiro, *supra* note 4, at 89.

sought in particular to abolish the ROTA and to dismiss individual police officers who had been brutal. While the new administration did succeed in dismissing some fifteen hundred officers in four years, support for the ROTA, both inside and outside the police, has been so strong that this force has not been disbanded (although its officers have received some retraining).[87]

The disproportionate violence ratios for São Paulo are revealing. Table 4 reports civilian deaths at the hands of the police; these figures were drawn from newspaper or official counts and may well be too low. Moreover, they can be compared only roughly with deaths of PMs in service because the latter figures include accidental deaths. Despite the skew in the figures, the ratio of civilians to officers killed is very high. More indicative, perhaps, is the ratio of civilians killed to civilians wounded by police; at least twice as

Table 4. Deaths and Injuries among Military Police (PM) and Civilians (Civ.) in São Paulo State, 1982–1987.

Year	Civ. Killed by PM	Civ. Injured by PM	PM Killed in Service	PM Injured in Service*
1982	286	74	26	897
1983	328	109	45	819
1984	481	190	47	654
1985	585	291	34	605
1986	399	197	45	599
1987	305	147	40	559
Tot.	2394	1008	237	4133
Ave.	399	168	39	689

Source note. Nucleo de Estudos da Violência, *supra* note 13, at 20. These figures were compiled from official statistics supplied by the PM, supplemented, where data were lacking, by newspaper reports.

*The figures for PMs killed and injured in service include accidental injuries and deaths. At the same time, the table does not report the relatively small number of civilians killed by the civil police. In an incomplete count, the Nucleo de Estudos da Violência identified 42 such killings in the period 1983–1987. *Id.* at 54.

[87] Brazil Police Report, *supra* note 11, at 13.

many were killed as were wounded, and in some years the proportion was much higher.[88]

Some police homicides in Brazil, as in Jamaica, are summary executions of suspects, many of whom are black youths.[89] The PM tend to dispose of criminals this way not in major cases but in fairly routine ones involving drugs or theft, in which the victims are anonymous. Occasionally, the circumstances are revealed when the victim turns out not to be so anonymous, as in the case of Fernando Ramos da Silva, killed on August 25, 1987. Ramos da Silva was apparently a petty criminal, but eight years earlier he had starred in the film *Pixote*. Although the PM claimed that he had been killed in a shoot-out when he was being chased after an attempted robbery, it is fairly clear that Ramos da Silva was executed. He was shot eight times while crouching or lying down—and after a witness heard him say, "Don't kill me. I have a daughter to support."[90]

Cases like this of killings on duty are probably less common than they used to be: The reformers in São Paulo have worked very hard, and a large number of criminal charges are pending against PMs in the courts.[91] Nevertheless, public support for reform is spotty, and support for summary violence is very strong. A "security group" has been elected to the state legislature, including a ROTA captain cashiered after killing more than a hundred suspects by his own count; and Afanasio Jazadji, a staunch supporter of the ROTA, who hosts a call-in radio program famous for stories about violence. Afanasio, as he is universally called in Brazil, is fond of de-

---

88 It is possible to draw a ratio between the homicide rate as a whole and the police homicide rate. I have not done so because, as will be clarified in the text, the overall homicide rate includes some unknown number of killings by off-duty police.

89 Brazil Police Report, *supra* note 11, at 27. It is nearly impossible to obtain a precise count of police killings. According to the Nucleo de Estudos da Violência, *supra* note 13, at 45, of some 1,147 official reports of police killings in the period March 1983-March 1987 (during the Montoro administration), 63.6 percent occurred in "resistance, reaction, and return fire" (*revide*), 8 percent in "flight or pursuit," and 5.8 percent "in flagrante delicto." The category "shoot-out" (*tiroteio*) accounted for 13.3 percent. The categories are thus vague enough to encompass almost any police action.

90 Brazil Police Report, *supra* note 11, at 20, 52–54.

91 *Id.* at 26.

scribing a criminal class, ever stronger against a police force inadequately trained and equipped and weakened still further by the policies of the reformers.[92]

The social indicators that might imply a threat from the have-nots against the haves in Brazil are not simple. At first glance, the social mobilization-social welfare disparity seems rather favorable for Brazil (see Table 1). But the scale is distorted by the country's enormous GNP. If we look only at the other factors in the social welfare index (literacy, caloric intake, and the availability of doctors), it becomes apparent that the GNP masks an enormous disparity. Inequality in income is both extreme and increasing. In 1960, the richest 5 percent of the population received 28 percent of the income; in 1980, the same sector received almost 38 percent of the income; over the same period, the share of income absorbed by the bottom 50 percent of the population declined from 17.4 to 14.1 percent.[93]

The ruling class, as well as the bureaucratic elite, has reason, then, to fear unrest. These groups traditionally have mistrusted the political participation of the masses and have contrived to limit it through a hierarchical structure likened to Max Weber's patrimonial state.[94] Under President José Sarney, the federal government increased welfare expenditures without, however, making much difference in the lives of the poor.[95]

Officials, like the so-called security group in the São Paulo state legislature, have sometimes found it to their political advantage to take a very tough law enforcement line. In 1988, for example, when the new commander of the PM announced his intention to try to curb police violence, Afanasio delivered a typically vague diatribe:

> This campaign . . . is only a smokescreen to please the groups that defend human rights. They encourage violence and pay the PMs a starvation wage. This is the time for them to make their "mea culpa" and treat the police with a little more respect in order to get better control.[96]

---

92 *Id.* at 14.

93 J. Lang, *supra* note 30, at 151.

94 *See generally* R. Roett, *Brazil: Politics in a Patrimonial Society* (3d ed. 1984).

95 Riding, *Improving Brazilian Social Welfare Proves Far Easier Said Than Done*, N.Y. Times, Aug. 9, 1988, at A8.

96 Folha de S. [São] Paulo, Apr. 29, 1988, at A15.

Similarly, Waldemar Gomes de Castro, subsecretary of the civil police in Rio de Janeiro during part of 1987, liked to distribute to visitors a passage from a dialogue by Plato in which the speaker advocates killing, as one would a scorpion or other poisonous animal, men whose rational faculties degenerate. During the same period, civil police with reputations for violence, known as *pistoleiros*, held responsible positions on the force.[97]

There is also a large amount of vigilante violence, both in Rio and in São Paulo. Some of it takes the form of spontaneous lynchings of suspected thieves. Brazilian sociologists counted eighty-two such incidents reported in the press in the two states during the period September 1979-February 1982; thirty-eight resulted in death.[98] When Evaristo Cardinal Arns of São Paulo held a special mass for the victims of lynchings, Afanasio organized a demonstration in opposition. Arrests are occasionally made for lynchings, but not often; indeed, the police sometimes encourage such actions.[99] As Gomes de Castro remarked some years before becoming subsecretary in Rio, "Lynchings make the bandits see that they do not own the streets. It is not a matter of doing justice with hatred for criminals, but with love for their victims."[100]

An even more common form of vigilantism is the work of death squads or individual gunmen. The number of death squad killings each year can only be estimated; the figure often given of hundreds is surely not too high. The death squads, in turn, are often staffed and organized by off-duty police. "Cabo Bruno," a São Paulo PM who moonlighted as a gunman, claimed to have killed more than fifty people before being convicted of murder in 1983. In 1984, when the head of homicide investigations in the Montoro administration sought to solve the murders of more than eighty youths found shot death squad style in the slums of São Paulo, he found that several PMs were involved. Similarly, a commission in Rio de Janeiro determined that the police had been involved in a majority of nearly two hundred crimes—for the

---

97 Brazil Police Report, *supra* note 11, at 28.

98 Benevides & Fischer Ferreira, *Respostas populares e violência urbana: o caso de linchamento no Brasil (1979–82)*, in *Crime, violência e poder* 230 (P. Pinheiro ed. 1983).

99 In April 1986, when the PM captured three youths accused of kidnapping, they turned the suspects over to the victim. He killed two and wounded the third, who lived to be interviewed by the newspapers. Brazil Police Report, *supra* note 11, at 12.

100 *See* Benevides & Fischer Ferreira, *supra* note 98, at 237.

most part death squad style homicides—committed between 1983 and 1986 in the huge slum of Baixada Fluminense.[101] Much of the death squad activity thus involves police vigilantism. It is worth noting that this involvement makes the figures on the numbers of killings by police, of the sort set out in Table 4, still more suspect because they do not include vigilante killings by off-duty police.

Much of the obvious support of vigilantism and police violence is traceable to small business people, who employ death squads and individual gunmen to kill thieves. In 1986, when there was yet another shake-up in the ROTA after some scandalous killings, the São Paulo taxi drivers, who are often the victims of crime and constitute a law-and-order pressure group, protested by tying up traffic outside PM headquarters. Merchants demonstrated against the investigation into the Ramos da Silva (*Pixote*) killing, driving a truck decorated with a sign saying, "Society ought to thank the police."[102]

At the same time, support for the police is not combined with much confidence in them. According to one study, more than half of the persons in Rio and São Paulo who claim to have been victims of crime do not file complaints with the police.[103] Afanasio himself has commented on the relative ineffectiveness of the police.[104] The constant threat of violence, combined with the sense that the police not only will not (or cannot) control it but instead actually participate in it, and the burden on citizens to use self-help to solve their problems increase anxiety to a level that one of the reformers has called "a psychosis of fear."[105] It is a curious state of mind in which lack of confidence in the power of the government to keep order is combined with vocal support of police violence.

The attitude of the very poor, the victim class, toward deadly force is not easy to gauge. On the one hand, their reactions seem passive. Observers of Brazilian politics have commonly remarked that the urban poor remain immobilized; populist leaders, while calling on the people for support, have avoided organizing the have-nots.[106] Interviews conducted twenty years ago

---

[101] Brazil Police Report, *supra* note 11, at 12–13, 29–32.

[102] *Id.* at 26–27.

[103] Benevides & Fischer Ferreira, *supra* note 98, at 239.

[104] Brazil Police Report, *supra* note 11, at 14.

[105] *Id.*

[106] *See* R. Roett, *supra* note 94, at 42–44; P. McDonough, *Power and Ideology in*

among the poor in Rio indicated that these people thought they had "important rights," among them the "right to respect the authorities" and the "right to obey the laws."[107] Apparently, most poor people today still do not perceive that they have rights as against authority.[108]

The poor are just as frightened of crime as any other sector of the population; they strongly supported Afanasio in his election campaign in São Paulo. Many poor people seem to take it for granted that a person who commits a crime does not deserve anything better than a retaliatory death. The attitude expressed by the father of a boy who had been killed by the PM after some late-night pranks with other boys is perhaps typical: "If my son had been robbing, then he could have been killed. No one likes a thief. But he was not that. They [the boys] were having a party and threw some stones at a house."[109] In another case that is revealing although not typical, a mother called the police to deal with her violent son and expressed approval when the ROTA killed him.[110] The PM, who are recruited largely from the poor, seem to share this attitude and bring it to bear on other poor people.

A study of lynchings found that 44 percent of those interviewed in Rio in 1980 supported the practice, although chiefly because of the shortcomings of the police.[111] The investigators described an intricate relation between support for private and official violence:

> The stigmatization of the poor is incorporated by the population in general, creating a reaction of support for arbitrary actions, at the same time that the recognition of the ineffectiveness of police procedures to guarantee the security of the community provokes reactions of revolt, of which lynchings are dramatic examples.

Brazil at xxxiii (1981); Leeds & Leeds, *Accounting for Behavioral Differences: Three Political Systems and the Responses of Squatters in Brazil, Peru, and Chile*, in *The City in Comparative Perspective* 193 (J. Walton & L. Masotti ed. 1976).

107 J. Perlman, *The Myth of Marginality* 188 (1976).

108 Personal communication from journalist and political scientist Paulo Sergio Pinheiro, University of São Paulo, July 1987.

109 Brazil Police Report, *supra* note 11, at 51–52.

110 *Mãe chama a ROTA para matar o próprio filho*, Noticias populares (São Paulo), Mar. 2, 1983, at 1. The mother, who had nine other children, was quoted: "I did not want his life to end this way, but it was he who brought on this end. My son has tried many things in his life, and now he has suffered the consequences. It was better for him and better for us." *Id.* at 6.

111 Benevides & Fischer Ferreira, *supra* note 98, at 230.

> . . . [The] effect of this contradictory relation between the police and the people is an atomization that represses personal and collective expression and makes each citizen isolated and abandoned. The means the state employs for the control of social participation lead the citizens—chiefly, but not only, from the most needy economic strata—to consider its institutions like superior and distant tribunals, impervious to collective or individual action. This is probably the situation of greatest separation—either at the level of action or conception—between the individual and the state.[112]

Nevertheless, it is an oversimplification to view the reactions of the Brazilian poor as mere passivity. Certainly, the mass movement of squatters onto unoccupied urban land in the last two generations cannot easily be perceived as passive. While many of the poor do not seem to conceive of citizenship and rights in relation to the state as a chief arena for conflict, they have perhaps made a practical judgment to bargain with the elites for more immediate goals. In the Baixada Fluminense, local leaders told us they were much more concerned with getting the train to run more frequently into Rio so that residents could get to work than they were with police violence.

In recent years, moreover, the police have been taking action against poor neighborhoods as a whole, organizing sweeps through slum districts in search of suspects, breaking into and searching houses, and sometimes killing bystanders. This practice, among others, has led to mass protests in Rio that spurred the replacement of one particularly tough secretary of the civil police. Thus, police action that is perceived as running against the community as a whole, rather than solely against its criminal elements, may lead to solidarity among the poor.[113]

CONCLUSION

When we consider a variety of indicators concerning the disproportionate use of deadly force by police—the ratio of civilians killed to those wounded, the ratio of civilians killed to police killed, and the ratio of police killings to the total homicide rate—the statistics, both official and unofficial, for Jamaica, Buenos Aires, São Paulo, and Rio de Janeiro all point toward the

---

[112] *Id.* at 242.

[113] Brazil Police Report, *supra* note 11, at 28.

conclusion that the police are summarily executing suspects in routine, non-partisan cases. Directed almost exclusively against anonymous, poor people, this abuse of deadly force appears as an extreme form of coercive social control. When the threat of social unrest seems high—because of increased social mobilization together with increased economic misery—the police may summarily execute a large number of suspects, providing that both elite and lower-class opinion tolerates the executions as legitimate. In all these locations, while opinion is split, the police violence is minimally acceptable; indeed, the prevalence of private vigilantism signals its acceptability with the mass of people.

Nonetheless, because Jamaica, Argentina, and Brazil are liberal states, it is difficult to view police homicides as legitimate except under the rubric of crime control and under the rule of law. Accordingly, virtually all police killings are justified to the public as acts of self-defense, typically in the context of shoot-outs. This justification appears to be essential for organizing public opinion even though, for at least some people at all socioeconomic levels, summary executions, like vigilantism, are considered the proper punishment for alleged crimes. Experience in other countries suggests that it is possible for the authorities to limit and even prevent police violence. This effort will not be made in Jamaica, Argentina, or Brazil, however, so long as police use of deadly force constitutes a means of social control acceptable to both elite and mass opinion.

[14]

Irony of Effective Supervision and an *Enabling* Legal Environment

Setsuo Miyazawa

Most detective supervisors at the Eastern Police Station generally maintained remarkable procedural restraint in spite of their very heavy work loads. Police executives at the Hokkaido Police Headquarters made a shrewd decision when they chose the Eastern Police Station as my research site. Supervisors at the Eastern try hard to keep their control over every major action of police detectives even when detectives are away from the station. For instance, detectives are required to telephone the station to get approval for arrest even when they have a warrant in hand. In cases of violent crime, supervisors immediately rush to the scene and take command of the investigation. Moreover, at least two supervisors are usually involved in a single case. It is typical for the assistant station chief in charge of criminal investigation and head of one of the two Detective Departments to work together to direct an investigation.

This system of tight control makes the job of section heads a particularly difficult one. Section heads do not have independent authority as police supervisors to apply for warrants to the court and see themselves as lower-ranking detectives. They feel more in sympathy with detectives than with supervisors, yet they must direct their co-workers according to the demands of supervisors.

Previous studies of Japanese police suggest that this situation is more or less true of all police stations in Japan. We may conclude therefore that internal control of police detectives in Japan is more effective than is reported for police in the United States, Canada, and the United Kingdom. The visibility of detectives' actions to field supervisors is higher in Japan, and it is difficult to imagine that clearly illegal actions would go unrecognized by supervisors.

However, this effective internal control is double-edged. Supervisors can push detectives in either direction of procedural restraint or of aggressive investigation. Moreover, the internal reward system makes one edge sharper than the other. Aggressive detectives with higher productivity in the solution of crime are rewarded either morally or with tangible benefits, while there is no significant reward for procedural restraint.

It is also apparent in this research that detectives are not necessarily morally committed to aggressive criminal investigation. In chapter 11 I presented strong evidence that a substantial number of detectives question the legality and legitimacy of their own behavior and complain about many aspects of their working conditions. Even these detectives, however, do not hesitate to take questionable actions when they perceive strong internal pressure for higher productivity.

We have seen in chapter 13 how this combination of effective internal control and rewards for aggressive behavior works. Criticized by the Hokkaido Police Headquarters for poor performance in theft crime investigation, supervisors at the Eastern Police Station announced that they would rigorously evaluate individual performance of theft crime detectives and tie in that evaluation with personnel relocation. Detectives had an instant response to this policy. Police station detention cells immediately filled up. That can quite adequately explain their apparent devotion to hard work by the institutional arrangement of rewards and controls.

Case studies in chapter 4 and descriptions of investigative tactics in part 2 have clearly indicated that Japanese police detectives can be quite cynical in their relationships with suspects and will manipulate a detained suspect to their advantage. In this sense, detective work in Japan is fundamentally the same as that reported in other countries. The former image of a Japanese police detective as a benevolent caretaker of the suspect and his family is not accurate.

I should note, of course, that even the most aggressive and questionable forms of investigative behavior at the Eastern Police Station look benign compared to the situation often reported for North American police forces. For instance, I did not observe any physical abuse of a suspect, much less a shooting, not an uncommon event in the United States.

That is so because Japanese police officers need not behave as aggressively as their North American colleagues. As I have argued in chapter 2, police work loads are generally lighter, serious crimes are more rare, firearms are prohibited, and, most importantly, the legal environment is more enabling in Japan. Japanese detectives rarely need to apply physical force to a suspect because the legal system of criminal investigation is designed and implemented to give the detained suspect sufficiently strong psychological pressure to admit guilt.

In routine cases, the police do not need to worry about judicial scrutiny of their tactics. The court, when requested, routinely issues warrants and routinely approves detention at a police station detention cell. There is no need for the police to hurry an investigation. Detention is often lengthy enough to allow them to investigate separate offenses as well. Moreover, most suspects confess to a crime even without detention; they know what will happen if they refuse. Coupled with these very enabling legal resources, relatively benign tactics still can have a significant impact on a suspect.

Ease of getting a confession has long been the most important foundation of criminal investigation in Japan. Japanese detectives work on the assumption that the suspect will confess and that this confession will match the physical evidence. Therefore, they do little other than interrogate the suspect. Their enabling legal environment has precluded the development of other investigative skills. Indeed, the detectives' single-minded pursuit of the constantly changing confessions in Case 17, for instance, can be frustrating and puzzling to the uninitiated observer.

Japanese police detectives panic when they discover that a confession does not match the physical evidence. A clear example is Case 17. Detectives were caught in a vicious cycle of coercive interrogations and false confessions. When one confession did not fit the physical evidence, the detectives simply pressed the suspect to make another confession, which again failed to match physical evidence. It did not occur to the detectives that their original hypothesis was incorrect.

Fortunately, there was another crime for which to indict and detain the same suspect, so the detectives earned additional time to continue the investigation. Otherwise, they might have been tempted to use more coercive and manipulative tactics in interrogation in order to *make crime* which fits their hypothesis within the approved time limit.

Herein lies the seed of more serious cases of coerced false confessions and other procedural illegalities such as those capsulized in chapter 1. Serious cases are not qualitatively different from more routine ones. They simply magnify the problems inherent in criminal investigation in Japan.

Here we can see an essential irony of the enabling legal environment and effective internal control.

While the legal system allows detectives to spend more time in investigating each case, the internal control system allows supervisors to closely manage subordinates. Ericson (1981: 210) concluded in his study that both the structure of formal legal rules and the condition of low visibility sets the organizational framework for detective work in Canada, which allows the police to dominate the interactive process of *making crime*. The organizational framework of Japanese police detectives shares only one of these two elements, and one might expect that the higher visibility with tighter control more effectively restrains detectives.

However, the reality is that this organizational framework in Japan does not necessarily result in a higher degree of civility and restraint on the part of investigators. The legal system has caused detectives to rely heavily on interrogation of the suspect and the internal control system is administered in such a way as to demand higher productivity. If detectives fail to get an expected confession at an early stage of investigation in an important case, they are tempted to take more abusive or manipulative actions.

From a detective's perspective, emphasis on proving motivation at a trial is also a major reason for a preoccupation with confessions. In 1987, trial courts in Japan passed judgment on 76,483 defendants (Saiko Saibansho, 1988: 157). Among them, 69,851 completely admitted their guilt. Therefore in most cases, the real issue becomes sentencing, and mitigating and aggravating circumstances are central concerns for the court and, thus, also for the prosecution and defense. Motivation naturally plays a leading role in sentencing, and confession of the defendant becomes indispensable as evidence.

Reform proposals in Japan focus on the enabling legal environment, with the basic idea to make it less enabling by increasing direct intervention by the defense counsel during investigation, particularly in regard to questioning of the suspect in police custody. For instance, in chapter 1 I referred to a survey of falsely accused people which was administered by the three bar associations in Tokyo in order to find support for their proposal to abolish or limit the use of police station detention cells as substitute detention centers (Tokyo San Bengoshikai, 1984). It is no surprise that prosecutors oppose any such proposals.

A more serious problem is that influential judges are also against many of reform proposals, or at least reluctant to support them. A recent publication in which well-known judges, prosecutors, and attorneys wrote on the same subjects from different perspectives (Mitsui et al., 1988) provides some ideal material to see this pattern.

Attorney Kumamoto (1988) proposes, for instance, the following measures for crimes punishable by a prison term of three years or longer:

(1) Require the judge to provide the suspect with a state-appointed attorney when he authorizes the suspect's detention.

(2) Establish a clear rule which specifies minimum requirements on frequencies and length of meetings with the attorney during detention.

(3) Require the prosecutor to provide the defense attorney with a record of interrogations upon indictment.

(4) Give the defense attorney a right to read and xerox all the statements taken from the suspect upon indictment.

It is apparent that the Miranda decision in the United States in 1966 has influenced Kumamoto's proposals. However, Judge Sato (1988) compares Kumamoto's paper with another by a prosecutor (Harada, 1988) on the same subject and comments:

> In light of my practical experience of more than twenty years, I do not believe that the present system requires a radical reform, except some needs for improvement in its implementation. Of course, as Prosecutor Harada admits, secret interrogation always contain the danger of coercion, and the interrogator should always keep it in mind that he should not go beyond the limits allowed by the law. From this perspective, too, the proper attitude of mind [*kokorogamae* in Japanese] proposed by Prosecutor Harada for interrogators is truly important.

What Sato means by "the proper attitude of mind" is the following: an effort to understand the suspect's perspective; the patience to listen to the suspect and prudence to see the truth; and an understanding about the inevitable limits of human perception and memory (Harada, 1988: 184). No one would deny the wisdom of these recommendations. However, this influential judge still denies the need for reform of the system itself.

Akiyama (1988), another attorney, makes proposals similar to these of Kumamoto and offers additional recommendation. First, he wants to provide a state-appointed attorney for every arrested suspect. In 1985, excluding traffic offenses, there were 124,000 arrested suspects, about ten suspects per each attorney. He argues that this is not an impossible figure and that the bar has to make such a system possible. Second, he proposes the establishment of minimum standards for meetings of suspects with an attorney. Third, he argues that Article 34 of the Constitution, which says that "[n]o person shall be arrested or detained...without the immediate privilege of counsel," guaranteees a right to effective defense, so that the suspect should be able to secure the presence and advice of an attorney during interrogation. Fourth, he proposes to introduce various measures to make the suspect's right to remain silent more meaningful. He advocates, for instance, the suspect's right to refuse interrogation even after arrest or detention, and also recommends the tape-recording of interrogations. Fifth, he proposes to reduce the time allowed between arrest and the detention application from forty eight hours to twenty four hours, as well as to introduce bail before indictment. Finally, he argues for the need for exclusionary rules in regard to illegally obtained evidence.

Judge Horigome (1988) comments on Akiyama's paper, and is sympathetic to some of the proposals. He says that "[i]t seems worthwhile to explore the feasibility of state-appointed attorneys and bail before indictment." Horigome argues, however, that "while interrogation of the suspect should be a voluntary measure,...it is not true that voluntary investigation is permitted only when the suspect consents," and that "within the limits deemed reasonable under concrete circumstances, some investigations can be permitted as lawful voluntary investigations even when the suspect does not consent." He argues that investigators may continue to persuade the suspect to confess even after a refusal to be investigated, otherwise, large-scale cases of bribery or election law violation would never be indicted. He also points to the difficulty of investigating briberies and election law violations in order to justify his opposition to other proposals by Akiyama. Since these represent only a small portion of crimes in Japan, we can question the general validity of Horigome's argument. However, he strongly believes that confessions are indispensable in criminal justice as well as in criminal investigation. Judge Horigome says, therefore, that "we should also pay attention to the recent tendency in the United States to limit applicability of the Miranda rule and exclusionary rules," implying that the Japanese judiciary has stayed on the right track from the beginning in its rejection of such rules.

Similar patterns appear in other exchanges between defense attorneys and judges. For instance, Attorney Ishii (1988) argues that detention at a police station detention cell should be the exception, but Judge Nakayama (1988) counters that, in spite of the language of the Code of Prisons, "in practice, there is no relationship of principle and exception between detention centers and police station detention cells, and the judge uses his discretion and considers all the factors of each case." Attorney Muraoka (1988) argues that the suspect's right to retain counsel as provided in Article 34 of the Constitution implies the counsel's right of meeting and communicating with the client, and this right should enjoy priority over the right of investigation. Judge Nakayama (1988) argues, however, that while that right of counsel is recognized by the Code of Criminal Procedure on the basis of a principle established by the Constitution, it is not in itself a constitutional right, and thus does not have priority over the right of investigation.

Given these judicial opinions, reform proposals of these nature are not likely to find many supporters among judges. Some judges in the same publication went further. For instance, Judges Nitta and Yasui (1988) doubt even the necessity of a court procedure to disclose the cause of detention to the suspect.

Even if the judiciary becomes more supportive of reform proposals, legislative changes would not be made easily. Under the parliamentary cabinet system of Japan, major legislative proposals always come from relevant governmental agencies (Upham, 1987: 14). In the case of criminal procedure and policing, these would be the Justice Ministry and the National Police Agency. No one would expect the ministry and agency to propose legislations which reduce their power. Rather, the National Police Agency has made every effort to pass a bill called the Confinement Facility Act in order to legitimize confinement and detention in a police station detention cell. Prosecutors also want to increase their power. Prosecutor Masui (1988), for instance, argues that weekends, national holidays, and periods around New Year's Day should be excluded from the calculation of the detention period, even though convenience of interrogation is not recognized as a cause for detention in the Code of Criminal Procedure.

A remote possibility for change may lie in following the path toward improvement of procedural protection of the suspect introduced by the English Police and Criminal Evidence Act of 1984 (see, *The Criminal Law Review*, 1985; Dixon et al., 1990).

The Japanese bar could point to the English system of a ninety-six-hour limitation of police detention (Section 44), the availability of a duty solicitor at the police station (Section 59), and tape-recording of interrogations (Section 60) as comparative law evidence of the feasibility of some of its own proposals. However, "the thrust of the 1984 Act...has been to facilitate their [suspects] removal into police custody to a greater extent and for a longer period than previously" (Gibbons, 1985: 566). Procedural safeguards are strengthened in order to protect the suspect from the enabling apparatus which favors relatively unimpeded police work.

Likewise, the Japanese defense bar may consider legitimizing detention at a police station detention cell to a limited extent, in return for the introduction of state-appointed attorneys before indictment, counsel's prerogative to meet with the client, tape-recording of interrogations, and a shorter detention period. Judge Horigome (1988) mentions, for instance, that criminal immunity for collaborators and the use of police decoys could be alternatives to interrogation. The bar might consider such measures for white-collar crimes in return for improved procedural safeguards in other kinds of cases.

Unfortunately for reformers, however, there is no real impetus for prosecutors and the police to make such a deal with the bar. The present system is sufficiently enabling for them. Application for detention at a police station detention cell is granted routinely, and investigators can interrogate the suspect without interference of counsel for a long period of time. The prosecution and police do not have any need to make concessions to the bar.

Another possibility is a unilateral act on the part of the defense bar to establish a Japanese version of the duty solicitor scheme in England. With an annual budget of only 380 million yen in 1989 (approximately $3 million

U.S.), the Legal Aid Society in Japan is extremely small compared to the legal aid systems in other developed countries. Its official purpose is civil legal aid and the government contributed only 100 million yen limiting its use for that. With the contribution of 136 million yen, attorneys were the largest contributor, and, in fact, the activities of the prefectural offices of the Legal Aid Society are managed by officials selected from among local attorneys. In spite of this small budget, the society established in 1990 the Pretrial Criminal Defense Assistance System in six prefectures, including Tokyo and Osaka. This system provides a suspect with an attorney with a fund of up to 100 thousand yen (approximately $720 U.S.) on a loan basis. The number of the beneficiaries will be small, but this is nonetheless a good start.

However, not every attorney is willing to take a state-appointed case, even under the present system. According to a national survey of attorneys in 1980 (Nihon Bengoshi Rengokai, 1988: 102), 57 percent of the respondents were willing to take state-appointed cases. The major deterrent is the small compensation for such work. The overwhelming majority of such attorneys receive only 50 thousand yen or so (approximately $360 U.S.) per case. Then the question becomes, how many attorneys are willing to volunteer their time for pre-indictment suspects without meaningful compensation? If only one quarter of the attorneys are willing to participate in a Japanese version of duty solicitor scheme, each attorney will have to take four times the estimate by Akiyama, namely, forty cases a year. We cannot be too optimistic about the feasibility of such a blueprint.

There are no criminal defense specialists in Japan, much less organized specialists such as public defenders or legal aid attorneys in the United States. Celebrated cases such as those summarized in chapter 1 are often handled by activist lawyers with a strong commitment to civil rights. However, even these lawyers spend most of their time on civil cases. Most criminal work is carried out by an individual attorney who work on the case in his spare time. Most likely the attorney lacks expertise in criminal defense and cannot effectively challenge the police and the prosection. Therefore, the Japanese Federation of Bar Associations recently decided to establish so-called Criminal Defense Centers in major cities as depositories of information about successful defense actions, so that less experienced attorneys might learn from them. This is another good beginning; however, it is still very far from an organized defense bar with full-time specialist attorneys.

Finally, the public will very likely be opposed to any significant steps to make the legal environment for the police less enabling as the preceding section of this chapter demonstrated.

In 1977, researchers at Kyoto University asked a national sample of adults in Japan to name both a "violator" and a "protector" of "individual liberty and rights" (Kyoto Daigaku Hogakubu, 1978: Question 8). The largest category of responses to both questions was "none" (45.7 percent about "violator" and 29.6 percent about "protector"). A very interesting pattern appeared for other response categories. Mass media was the most frequently named "violator" (25.5 percent), followed by big business (21.9 percent) and then the government (9.3 percent). The police were named as a "violator" only by 2.8 percent of the respondents and were the most frequently named "protector" of individual liberty and rights (31.9 percent), followed by the family (30.4 percent) and the court (25.5 percent). Only 3 percent of the respondents regarded the mass media as a "protector." This finding tells us that most people in Japan do not view the police as part of the government, nor do they define liberty and rights as requiring protection from the governmental infringement. They rather think of more immediate interests such as safety of property, person, and privacy as examples of liberty and rights. Thus, other than the most intimate protectors (family members) of their interests, the police and court who apprehend and punish criminals are seen as the particularly important protectors of their liberty and rights.

The Japanese also do not perceive themselves as potential targets of police activity. This attitude appears in public opinion regarding *junkai renraku* or house visits by patrol officers. The official justification of house visits is the need for detailed information regarding each household for public service purposes, particularly for helping a visitor locate an address. Ames (1981: 39) has reported, however, that the real purposes of collecting such information include the potential use in criminal investigation and the surveillance of gangsters, ex-convicts, and leftist organizations. This has been understood for many years by police observers in Japan. Nevertheless, the Japanese public generally welcome house visits. For instance, in 1984, the Office of Prime Minister asked a national sample of adults about their impressions of contacts with police officers (Naikaku Sori Daijin Kanbo, 1985: survey number 8). Fifty-one percent of the respondents said they had no contact with the police in the preceding year; the most frequent contacts were house visits (21.1 percent). Fifty-five percent of the visited respondents reported a good impression, while only 0.2 percent said they harbored a bad impression. Similar opinions were found in a survey conducted by the National Research Institute of Police Science (Nishimura and Suzuki, 1986). In 1984, a sample of residents of seventeen urban police jurisdictions were asked about house visits. Sixty-four percent answered that "they understood well the purposes of house visits," compared to only 1.4 percent who said that they did not. Thirty-seven percent answered that "the officer was kind and courteous," while only 1.6 percent said that "the officer asked too much about details." Thirty-two percent wanted "more visits," compared to only 0.9 percent who denied the necessity of house visits. Only a small minority in Japan view house visits as an invasion of their privacy or appreciate the possibility that information collected during house visits might be used against them.

Of course, these surveys by governmental agencies were conducted to support the government's position that present police practices were acceptable to the public. It is also very likely that most people did not know the real purposes of house visits. Given the attitudes found by the Kyoto University survey, however, I doubt if people would criticize house visits even when they were told the real reasons. Since police are the most important public protectors of their private interests, the surveys suggest that they support more effective use of information about undesirable neighbors for more aggressive crime control.

Thus, I have to reach a somewhat pessimistic conclusion. It seems unlikely that effective measures will be introduced very soon to mitigate this combination of strong internal control over police detectives and the very enabling legal environment. The prevailing attitudes of the judiciary, the structure of the legislative process, the present situation of the bar, and dominant public opinion all contribute to maintain the present environment of criminal investigation in Japan.

In spite of some of their own doubts about the legitimacy of aspects of police practices and related working conditions, many detectives may continue to be forced to manipulate the suspect and to otherwise engage in questionable actions. If this hypothesis is correct, then for as long as this situation continues, morally involved detectives will appear in the ranks of the detectives exhibiting primarily calculative involvement.

Police behavior illustrates the principle of cognitive dissonance (Festinger, 1957). If the action cannot be avoided even where it is against the person's original will, cognitive dissonance may be reduced by placing a positive value on the behavior. If a reward is associated with the behavior, then to the extent that this reward is provided, the behavior will tend to become more pronounced.

In the Hokkaido police internal magazine, *Hokkai-keiyu* (Police Friends of Hokkaido), it is possible to locate some information suggestive of this process.

Initially, we find these statements by young officers:

- I am making the efforts I should to conform to the police organization.
- Because I entered this society as a police officer, and because in police society, those who persist in their own way will likely be banished from the organization, that is what I must do.
- It is a great thing to live with pride in one's work. We are drawn to such a man.

- For a man whose thoughts are on his paycheck, every day exhausts his body and his spirit, but for the man with passion and fight, rigor and stress awaken his enthusiasm, and become the vitality of the next day.

From such statements, it seems that there are many individuals who are making positive efforts to conform. However, there are others:

> I took the exam [to join the force] in an offhand way, and after I had joined up, I felt resistant. However, with the passage of time, in the course of my transformation as a member of the force, this resistance gradually began to fade.

Also, a junior member of the riot squad mustering out for guard duty against a demonstration wrote:

> When asked "Are you a human?" [by a demonstrator], I became agitated. But thinking, "I grow agitated because I have no confidence," I read the notes of a member headed for service in the Asamasanso case [in which a squad leader was shot to death by extreme leftists], seeking confidence and pride in myself. Now I carry my chest out further than anyone, and can declare in a full voice, "Yes! Send me, sir!" (on the Asamasanso case, see Bayley, 1976: 160-62).

And from another:

> I was distressed to be caught between youth and duty, but as I listened to the mustering-out song, "To make this world a flower" while setting out, I came to think, "What is the matter with you?" There is work to do to foster a peaceful society. What's with this stupid whining?

Of course, these statements were written and published with the full anticipation that supervisors and family members would read them. However, they still suggest that the perception of many recruits, who are initially plagued by resistance and doubt, is transformed gradually toward a feeling of satisfaction in the performance of their duty. If a similar process of cognitive modification were to exist in a detective department, the involvement of detectives in aggressive investigations may more readily change from calculative involvement to moral involvement. Geertz (1973: 126–27) argues that culture is a device through which people accept reality as morally right and cognitively natural. My data indicate that many police officers in Japan perceive aggressive actions and stressful work conditions in this light.

As recent experiments of police effectiveness in the United States have proven, styles and levels of police activities often are not causal factors in determining crime levels (for a summary of these studies, see Skolnick and Bayley, 1986: 1-6). Still "the police have been assigned, and have taken on, an impossible responsibility for controlling crimes as the key indicator of their success at reproducing order" (Ericson, 1982: 4). Only when the public ceases to demand the impossible of the police will there be any hope for a corresponding change in the direction of internal controls, and in the attitudes and behavior of lower-ranking police officers. With general public support of the status quo, increasing "professionalism" now means an emphasis on increased efficiency, rather than a deeper concern over legality (Skolnick, 1966: 238).

Recently, there has been a growing number of articles by police executives boasting of the competence of the Japanese police, often citing the great regard for the Japanese police system overseas. Indeed it is safe to say that in relative terms, the international standing of the Japanese police is very high. This does not deny, however, that they have their own problems. Given the lively international interest in Japanese police today, this book offers important new data on the day-to-day functioning of police departments, in order to present a more realistic picture of everyday criminal investigation and a deeper understanding of the perspective of lower-ranking police detectives.

Bibliography

Akiyama, Mikio. 1988. "Defense Activities of the Suspect and Counsel before Indictment" (in Japanese), in Mitsui, et al., 1988: 347–63.

Ames, Walter L. 1981. *Police and Community in Japan*. Berkeley: University of California Press.

Bayley, David H. 1976. *Forces of Order: Police Behavior in Japan and the United States*. Berkeley: University of California Press.

Dixon, David, et al. 1990. "Safeguarding the Rights of Suspects in Police Custody," *Policing and Society* 1: 115–40.

Ericson, Richard V. 1981. *Making Crime: A Study of Detective Work*. Toronto: Butterworth.

Ericson, Richard V. 1982. *Reproducing Order: A Study of Police Patrol Work*. Toronto: University of Totonto Press.

Festinger, Leon. 1957. *A Theory of Cognitive Dissonance*. Evanston: Row, Peterson.

Geertz, Clifford. 1973. *The Interpretation of Cultures*. New York: Basic Books.

Gibbons, Thomas. 1985. "The Conditions of Detention and Questioning by the Police," *The Criminal Law Review*, 1985: 558–68.

Harada, Akio. 1988. "Interrogation of the Suspect: From the Perspective of a Prosecutor" (in Japanese), in Mitsui et al., 1988: 177–86.

Horigome, Yukio. 1988. "Comment [to Akiyama, 1988]" (in Japanese), in Mitsui et al., 1988: 364–67.

Ishii, Yoshikazu. 1988. "Place of Confinement and Detention: From the Perspective of a Defense Attorney" (in Japanese), in Mitsui et al., 1988: 281–88.

Kumamoto, Norimichi. 1988. "Interrogation of the Suspect: From the Perspective of a Defense Attorney" (in Japanese), in Mitsui et al., 1988: 187–95.

Kyoto Daigaku Hogakubu (Kyoto University Faculty of Law) (ed.). 1978. *Ho Ishiki to Funso Shori* (Legal Consciousness and Dispute Processing). Unpublished research report.

Masui, Kiyohiko. 1988. "Comment [to Nitta and Yasui, 1988]" (in Japanese), in Mitsui et al., 1988: 266–69.

Mitsui, Makoto et al. (eds.). 1988. *Keiji Tetsuzuki* (Criminal Procedure), 1. Tokyo: Chikuma Shobo.

Muraoka, Keiichi. 1988. "Meeting and Communication of the Counsel and Client: From the Perspective of a Defense Attorney" (in Japanese), in Mitsui et al., 1988: 329–42.

Naikaku Sori Daijin Kanbo (Office of the Prime Minister) (ed.). 1985. *Seron Chosa Nenkan* (Almanac of Public Opinion Surveys), *1985*. Tokyo: Okurasho Insatsukyoku.

Nakayama, Yoshifusa. 1988. "Comment [to Ishii, 1988]" (in Japanese), in Mitsui, et al., 1988: 289–90.

Nihon Bengoshi Rengokai (Japanese Federation of Bar Associations) (ed.). 1988. *Nihon no Horitsu Jimusho* (Law Offices in Japan). Tokyo: Gyosei.

Nishimura, Haruo, and Suzuki, Shingo. 1986. "Citizen-Helping Role of the Police and the Attitudes of Residents in the Community (2)" (in Japanese), *Kagaku Keisatsu Kenkyujo Hokoku Bohan Shonen Hen* (Research Report of the Department of Crime Prevention and Juvenile Delinquency, the National Research Institute of Police Science) 27–1: 54–63.

Nitta, Mutsuo, and Yasui, Hisaharu. 1988. "Detention and Bail: From the Perspective of Judges" (in Japanese), in Mitsui, et al., 1988: 243–65.

Saiko Saibansho (Supreme Court) (ed.). 1988. *Shiho Tokei Nenpo Keiji Hen* (Annals of Judicial Statistics: Criminal Cases), *1988*.

Sanders, William B. 1977. *Detective Work*. New York: Free Press.

Sato, Fumiya. 1988. "Comment [to Harada, 1988, and Kumamoto, 1988]" (in Japanese), in Mitsui et al., 1988: 196–97.

Skolnick, Jerome H. 1966. *Justice Without Trial: Law Enforcement in Democratic Society*. New York: John Wiley and Sons.

Skolnick, Jerome H., and Bayley, David H. 1986. *The New Blue Line: Police Innovation in Six American Cities*. New York: Free Press.

Tanaka, Hideo (ed.). 1976. *The Japanese Legal System*. Tokyo: Tokyo University Press.

Tokyo San Bengoshikai (Three Bar Associations of Tokyo). 1984. *Nureginu* (Falsely Charged). Tokyo: Seihosha.

Upham, Frank K. 1987. *Law and Social Change in Postwar Japan*. Cambridge: Harvard University Press.

Part VI
Administrative Law and Regulation

[15]

The Contradictions of Immigration Lawmaking: The Immigration Reform and Control Act of 1986

KITTY CALAVITA

This paper argues that the Immigration Reform and Control Act of 1986 is a composite of contradictory measures. On one hand, employer sanctions are meant to curtail the employment of undocumented workers and preserve the U.S. labor market for legal residents and citizens; on the other hand, special foreign worker programs are designed to enhance the supply of immigrant workers. In an effort to make sense of these contradictions, the author places the legislation in historical context and proposes a dialectical model of immigration policymaking.

I. INTRODUCTION

On November 6, 1986, President Reagan signed the Immigration Reform and Control Act (IRCA, also known as the Simpson-Rodino Law), signalling the culmination of more than a decade of attempts by the U.S. Congress to "regain control of our borders" (U.S. Department of Justice, 1982). The new law is touted as the first comprehensive reform of U.S. immigration policy since the McCarran-Walter Act of 1952.

Scholars who have engaged in the debate surrounding immigration reform have tended to focus either on the question of the desirability of curtailing immigration, given the role of immigrant labor in the U.S. economy (Bustamante, 1987; Cornelius, 1987; Taylor, 1987), or on the difficulties of enforcing various provisions of the new law (Garcia y Griego, 1983; Portes, 1983). This paper draws from that debate, but recasts it by directing attention to the historical context of IRCA and the consequences of that context for the formulation of the law's major provisions. Specifically, it argues that the law's key reforms pull in opposite directions at once, and that this apparently contradictory nature of the law reflects a conflict between economic pressures and political forces of the type that have plagued U.S. immigration policy-makers since the 19th century. The nature of the law's contradictions, as well as its predictable impacts, are such that it cannot be accounted for simply as a pluralist compromise between conflicting special interest groups; rather, the law represents an attempted resolution to incompatible forces in the political economy itself.

The paper begins by providing the historical background for this latest immigration reform, focusing on the longstanding role of immigrant labor in the U.S. economy, side-by-side with recurring anti-immigrant nativism.

It then outlines specific provisions of the Simpson-Rodino Law and discusses their likely impacts. The final section addresses the contradictions implicit in the law and links these contradictions and the law's predictable impacts to the broader economic and political forces constraining immigration policy-makers.

Before beginning, a note of caution is in order. The purpose of this paper is not to document the effects of the new immigration law, an endeavor that would clearly be unfeasible at this early juncture. Rather, it addresses the formulation of specific provisions of the law and the likely impacts of those provisions in an effort to highlight and make sense of the contradictions that have permeated the law from the beginning. The details of the implementation of IRCA, employers' strategies in reacting to it, and actual long-run effects are issues that must be left to future research.

II. THE HISTORICAL CONTEXT

A. IMMIGRATION AS THE MOVEMENT OF A WORKFORCE

The dominant theory of international migration places economic imbalances at the center of analysis and posits that impersonal economic forces simultaneously propel immigrants from poor countries and attract them to opportunities in the industrialized world. Put this way, these push-pull factors seem to operate outside of the realm of human intervention. Indeed, the only deliberate ingredient in this depiction is the rational decision of the individual migrant.

In contrast to this view, the history of immigration to the United States suggests that U.S. policies have often provided the catalyst for the movement. In other words, the "pull" of the push-pull formula derives from deliberate policies of encouragement over time, and not simply from the magnetic force of the U.S. economy.

As early as 1791, Alexander Hamilton (1791:123) warned Congress that if the U.S. were develop into an industrial power, immigration must be encouraged so as to mitigate the "scarcity of hands" and the "dearness of labor". The following century witnessed recruitment efforts by the federal government and the states, as well as private employers who saturated Europe with promotional campaigns to stir up emigration to the United States. As Andrew Carnegie (1886: 34–35) explained it, "The value to the country of the annual foreign influx is very great indeed . . . These adults are surely worth $1500 each—for in former days an efficient slave sold for that sum." Later in the passage, Carnegie referred to immigration as "a golden stream which flows into the country each year." The *New York Journal of Commerce* (1892: 2) expressed it this way: "Men, like cows, are expensive to raise and a gift of either should be gladly received. And a man can be put to more valuable use than a cow".

Policy-makers throughout the 19th century extolled the economic benefits of abundant immigration and fashioned U.S. immigration policies to maximize the flow (Calavita, 1984). Until 1875, there were no restrictions of any kind. Indeed, the first comprehensive federal immigration law, passed in 1864, was *An Act to Encourage Immigration* (13 U.S. Statutes at Large). Among other things, this law established the first Immigration Bureau, whose primary function was to increase immigration to provide American industries with an adequate supply of workers to meet war production needs during the Civil War (U.S. Congress, Senate Report, 1864: 1–4).

The end of the 19th and early 20th centuries saw the enactment of a number of apparently restrictive measures, including the exclusion of anyone "likely to become a public charge," those with pre-arranged work contracts, the criminal, the diseased, and the politically undesirable. In practice, however, these measures excluded only about 1% of the total flow (Jenks, 1913), in large part because they were designed "along conservative lines [so as to] avoid measures so drastic as to cripple American industry" (*Congressional Record*, 1902: 5763–64). In addition, the implementation of these restrictions was carefully gauged so that the "golden stream" was uninterrupted. As one immigration inspector of the period explained it, "Better to run the risk of the occasional admission of an alien inadmissible under the law than to slow up the process." (quoted in Van Vleck, 1932: 28). Within the context of these formal and informal policies of encouragement, immigration to the United States averaged close to a million entrants a year during the early years of the 20th century.

Mexican migration gained momentum in the pre-World War I period, just as the U.S. government and even some employers were beginning to reconsider the costs and benefits of European migration. At this time, the European immigrant was getting the reputation as a kind of trouble-maker, increasingly forming the backbone of strikes and, more often than not, remaining to become a permanent member of society.

In 1911, the Dillingham Commission on immigration, in response to these concerns, noted the special advantages of Mexican migration:

> Because of their strong attachment to their native land . . . and the possibility of their residence here being discontinued, few become citizens of the United States. The Mexican immigrants are providing a fairly adequate supply of labor . . . While they are not easily assimilated, this is of no very great importance as long as most of them return to their native land. In the case of the Mexican, he is less desirable as a citizen than as a laborer (U.S. Congress, Senate Immigration Commission, 1911: 690–691).

Initially, the bulk of the Mexican migration was legal. In fact, the most significant restrictions of the early 20th century specifically exempted Mexicans from their orbit. In response to warnings from Southwest growers that the success of their harvests depended on a plentiful supply of Mexican labor, Mexicans were excluded from the literacy test requirement of 1917. When the Quota Restrictions of 1921 and 1924 reduced European immigration, Mexicans were again exempt, as this "back-door" was seen as a valuable substitute for European labor—a preferred one in fact, given the vicinity of Mexico and the ability to regulate the supply at a moment's notice. One scholar, summarizing the Congressional debate over possible restrictions on Mexican immigration in the 1920s, paraphrased Congress's anti-restrictionist sentiment:

> The Mexican, they pointed out, was a vulnerable alien living just a short distance from his homeland . . . He, unlike Puerto Ricans or Filipinos . . . could easily be deported. No safer or more economical unskilled labor force was imaginable (Reisler, 1976: 181; paraphrasing Hearings of the House of Representatives Committee on Immigration, 1929).

When European immigration was temporarily halted by World War I, U.S. industries as far north as Chicago drew labor from Mexico. Between 1915 and 1920, Mexican immigration went from 11,000 per year to 51,000, and during the 1920s, approximately 500,000 Mexicans migrated to the United States (Lopez, 1981: 660).

The shift from European to Mexican immigration as a source of labor did increase flexibility, as evidenced by the "repatriation" of thousands of Mexican workers and their families during the depression of the 1930s, and the increasingly rigorous interpretations of the public charge clause which reduced dramatically the number of legal entrants without resorting to statutory changes. As war production refueled the U.S. economy in the 1940s, Mexican contract laborers were imported through the Bracero Programs, a series of bilateral agreements which provided Mexican workers to southwest agriculture.

The Bracero Programs are interesting not only because they attempted to institutionalize the flexibility and temporary nature of the Mexican labor supply (which had always been recognized as its primary virtue), but also because formal and informal policies during this period contributed to the increase of illegal migration that characterizes the contemporary movement. For example, the Bracero agreement of 1949 provided that "illegal workers, when they are located in the United States, shall be given preference under outstanding U.S. Employment Service Certification" (quoted in Galarza, 1964: 63). Furthermore, illegals, or "wetbacks" as they were called, were often "dried out" by the Border Patrol who escorted them to the Mexican border, had them step to the Mexican side, and brought them back as legal Braceros. In some cases, the Border Patrol "paroled" illegal immigrants directly to employers (Garcia y Griego, 1981: 25). The President's Commission on Migratory Labor estimated in 1951 that from 1947 to 1949, more than 142,000 undocumented Mexican workers were legalized in this way, at a time when only 74,600 new Braceros were recruited from Mexico (cited in Samora, 1971: 47–48).

In addition to these more or less official policies of encouragement of illegal migration, Immigration and Naturalization Service (INS) district directors used their discretion to supply growers with seasonal undocumented labor. The chief inspector at Tucson, for example, reported that he "received orders from the District Director at El Paso each harvest to stop deporting illegal Mexican labor" (Kirstein, 1977: 90). The implicit message from Congress was consistent with this laissez-faire approach. As one observer put it, Congress was "splendidly indifferent" to the rising number of illegals during the Bracero period, reducing the Border Patrol budget just as the undocumented migration increased (Hadley, 1956: 334).

By the time the Bracero Programs ended in 1964, a relationship of symbiosis between Mexican migrants and U.S. employers had become well-entrenched, facilitated and nurtured by over fifty years of policy-making. Almost 5,000,000 Mexican workers had been brought to the U.S. as Braceros; approximately 5,000,000 illegal aliens were apprehended during the same period (Lopez, 1981: 671).

A key Congressional decision made employers immune to any risk involved in the employment of the undocumented. In 1952, the McCarran-Walter Act made it illegal to "harbor, transport, or conceal illegal entrants" (66 U.S. Statutes at Large 163). An amendment to the provision, referred to as the Texas Proviso after the Texas growers to whom it was a concession, excluded employment from the category of harboring. The amendment was interpreted by the INS as a virtual *carte blanche* for the employment of undocumented workers (for a discussion of this interpretation, see Greene, 1972: 453–55).

Having set the stage for high levels of documented and undocumented migration, U.S. policies in the post-Bracero period have perpetuated the pattern largely by default. Most important, budgetary decisions have had the consequence of effectively eliminating the counter-pressure to illegal migration. As the Congressional subcommittee that holds the pursestrings of the INS put it in 1981, the agency "has been chronically underfunded, undermanned and neglected" (quoted in Harwood, 1983: 108).

B. ANTI-IMMIGRANT BACKLASHES

Since the Irish migrations of the mid-1800s, the appreciation of the economic role of the immigrant has almost always been accompanied by anti-immigrant nativism and public pleas for restriction. Based on varying combinations of racism, visions of tax increases, cultural and political protectionism, and organized labor's concerns over bargaining power, these anti-immigrant backlashes have tended to intensify in periods of economic crisis and/or perceived threats to the national security (Higham, 1955; Cornelius, 1982).

Although similar in many respects, the backlash against Mexican immigrants in the mid-twentieth century has differed in specific ways from anti-immigrant reactions of the earlier period. Most important, given the vicinity of Mexico and the undocumented status of many Mexican immigrants, they, unlike their European counterparts, have been subject to abrupt policy changes at the administrative level in response to such backlashes.

Mass expulsions and round-ups of Mexicans during "Operation Wetback" in 1954, for example, were reminiscent of the depression policies of the 1930s. This periodic tightening of the border with Mexico, which has usually been accomplished without recourse to statutory changes, is eminently compatible with the longstanding perception of Mexican migration as a flexible and temporary supply of labor.

The last decade has witnessed a new round of nativism. As in the past, the new immigrants have been blamed for virtually every social ill of modern society. And, as in the past, it is in large part *because* immigrants supply a cheap labor force (i.e. precisely that which employers and policy-makers have appreciated) that they provide an easy target of backlash by wary taxpayers and domestic workers. The predominantly illegal nature of the contemporary flow enhances the reaction. As the fear spreads that the U.S. has "lost control of its borders", antagonism against those who personify this lack of control is intensified.

This new round of nativism is unique in at least one respect. It has often been pointed out that nativism and xenophobia have been correlated in the past with high unemployment rates (for an excellent discussion of this phenomenon, see Cornelius, 1982). Indeed, each serious recession since the mid-19th century has heightened anti-immigrant racism, as the new arrivals are scapegoated for the economic downturn (Calavita, 1984). The apparent irony of today's restrictionism is that while its roots can be traced to the "stagflation" of the 1970s, its heightened pitch in the 1980s occurs at a time of *declining* unemployment.

This is not to say that the new nativism is unrelated to economic factors. The increased restrictionism has been accompanied by major dislocations and transformations in the U.S. economy. As the heavy manufacturing sector has contracted and the service sector expands, an increased proportion of new jobs are located in the less desirable secondary labor market. A study prepared for the Congressional Joint Economic Committee estimates that close to 60% of the workers added to the labor force between 1979 and 1984 earned less than $7000 per year ("Minimum Wage Hike's Real Payoff", *Los Angeles Times*, May 12, 1987, Part IV: 3). Individual wage and salary income fell 10% from 1973 to 1985, and the proportion of households with incomes of less than $20,000 a year increased by 8% in the same period ("America's Dwindling Middle Class", *Los Angeles Times*, May 26, 1987, Part IV: 3).

In the past, the increased levels of unemployment that triggered immigrant scapegoating at the same time temporarily reduced the need for immigrant workers and hence tended to slow down the influx (as occurred during the 1930s, for example). In contrast, the economic processes underway since the early 1970s in the United States simultaneously increase the demand for immigrants as the proportion of minimum-wage, unskilled jobs proliferates, and enhance anti-immigrant backlashes. In other words, the structural changes in the economy which *fuel* undocumented migration are the same transformations that contribute to restrictionist sentiment.

C. SUMMARY

This brief historical overview suggests 1) that immigration to the U.S. can be characterized from the beginning as the movement of a workforce—a movement that is firmly rooted in economic realities; 2) that U.S. policies have both reflected those realities and acted as a catalyst for the movement; 3) that anti-immigrant nativism is often juxtaposed with this appreciation of the immigrant as a source of labor; and, 4) that a conflict has emerged between this anti-immigrant nativism and the economic forces which accelerate the undocumented flow. In the following sections, it will be argued that the Simpson-Rodino Law can best be understood within this context, as it attempts to respond both to the longstanding economic realities of immigration and to the new nativism that generates demands for restriction.

III. IRCA AND ITS POTENTIAL IMPACTS

IRCA consists of three fundamental components. First, the legalization provision allows undocumented immigrants who have been in the United States in an illegal status since before January 1, 1982, to apply for legal residence. Second, the employer sanctions provision makes it illegal for an employer to knowingly hire undocumented workers. Finally, the special agricultural workers program allows certain undocumented workers in the agricultural sector to apply for legalization, and provides for additional farm workers to be admitted, should a shortage of farm labor develop.

This paper focuses on employer sanctions and the provisions that pertain to agricultural labor, as these two components taken together provide unique insights into the political economy of this round of immigration policymaking. Before turning to a more detailed discussion of these two provisions and their predictable impact, the following section provides a brief legislative history of the reform and the key political actors involved in the reform process.

A. LEGISLATIVE HISTORY OF IRCA

IRCA's roots can be traced to 1971 when Rep. Rodino's Subcommittee on Immigration held a lengthy series of hearings on the topic of illegal aliens, a substantial portion of which dealt with the possibility of enacting a federal employer sanctions law.[1] Over the next few years, a number of employer sanctions bills were introduced in both houses. Consistently, only the House of Representatives took any action on these bills, which they passed by wide margins in the 92nd and 93rd Congresses. In spite of strong support from both the Nixon and Ford Administrations, these bills regularly died in the Senate without a vote, in large part due to the staunch opposition of Senator Eastland of Mississippi, then Chair of the Senate Judiciary Committee. Eastland, a cotton planter with strong ties to Southern agricultural interests, refused to hold hearings on the issue. It is reported that the Senate Subcommittee on Immigration, over which Eastland resided, did not even meet as a committee during these years (Schuck, 1975).

In 1975, the first amnesty provision was attached to the House bill. Public opinion polls have consistently shown the majority of Americans to be opposed to the concept of amnesty for the undocumented; however, the legalization provision was to be instrumental in garnering votes for the reform effort, both from liberal advocates of immigrants' rights and from those concerned with offsetting the effects of employer sanctions and stabilizing the supply of labor. The same year, President Ford established a Cabinet-level Domestic Council on Illegal Migration, chaired by the Attorney General. The recommendations of this council included both a federal employer sanctions law and a legalization plan.

The Carter Administration continued to push for reform, and in 1977 introduced a bill which included employer sanctions, legalization, and increased border enforcement. The Carter bill did not get far in either house. Instead, a prestigious 16-member Select Commission on Immigration and Refugee Policy was appointed. In 1981, the Commission published its report, and to noone's surprise, recommended employer sanctions, a legalization program, and increased resources for the Border Patrol. Consistent with the earlier Congressional proposals, the Commission's recommendations included no provision for special agricultural worker programs.

Just one year after the Commission published its recommendations, the first Simpson-Mazzoli Bill was reported out of the House and Senate Judiciary Committees. Both versions followed closely the Commission's proposals with only relatively minor differences between them. Once again, no mention was made of a special farm labor program, although the Senate bill would probably have expanded significantly the old H-2 program.[2] The Senate—where Senator Alan Simpson, Republican from Wyoming, had taken over as Chair of the Subcommittee on Immigration—passed its bill by 80 to 19 after only three days of floor debate. The bill foundered in the House, however, where civil rights advocates were concerned over the potential for abuse and discrimination against Hispanics, growers' groups lobbied for additional provisions for foreign labor, and the Chamber of Commerce persistently opposed sanctions against employers. So controversial was the bill in the House that over 300 amendments were introduced in a successful effort to forestall a vote.

A second Simpson-Mazzoli Bill finally passed both houses in 1984, squeaking by the House 216–211, only to come apart in the conference committee, ostensibly over the issue of cost. This year marked an important turning point for the reform effort. First, employer opposition to employer sanctions (most notably that of the Chamber of Commerce) began to subside, placated at least in part by the "affirmative defense" clause in the law which explicitly releases employers from any obligation to check the authenticity of documents presented to them. Second, agricultural employers shifted their focus from opposition to employer sanctions to a concerted campaign to secure alternative sources of foreign labor. As opposition to employer sanctions waned and growers' lobbying efforts for extensive temporary worker programs intensified, agricultural worker programs began to outrank the employer sanctions component as the most controversial element of the reform. What had begun as a restrictive effort based on employer sanctions, had now come full circle to be mired in a debate over how best to *expand* the supply of foreign labor.

The following year, Senator Simpson reintroduced the bill that Congressional opponents were now calling "The Monster from the Blue Lagoon" because of its eerie ability to rise from the dead. By September, this Senate version had already passed, after an impressive show of strength by the Western Growers' Association. Arguing that employer sanctions would cut off an invaluable source of agricultural labor, and seeing an opportunity for political horse-trading, Senator Wilson of California introduced an amendment on the floor of the Senate in the closing days of debate to create a temporary farm labor program outside of and in addition to the old H-2 program. The amendment was defeated 50 to 48, only to be passed four days later after intensive grower lobbying. The Wilson amendment provided for a short-term guestworker program for agriculture in which each year up to 350,000 foreign workers would be given visas for a limited period to harvest perishable crops.

A number of key democrats in the House vowed to kill any bill with such a "de facto slave labor program" attached to it, and it seemed at first that the controversy might unravel the limited consensus that had been achieved the previous year in the House. What ultimately provided the House bill with support from both sides of the farm labor issue and facilitated the final compromise with the Senate, was a Herculean effort engineered by Reps. Schumer of New York and Panetta and Berman of California. The original Schumer amendment would have provided legal status to undocumented aliens who could prove that they had worked in agriculture for at least 60 days in the year ending May 1986. By the end of the amendment process, House Republicans and Democrats had agreed to a complicated formula that provided temporary residence status and eventual eligibility for citizenship to those who had worked in agriculture for at least 90 days, and included a generous future replenishment clause, under the assumption that newly legalized workers might abandon farm labor. The compromise struck a delicate balance between civil rights advocates who argued against traditional guestworker programs on the grounds that they provided employers with a captive workforce and hence invited abuse, and growers' representatives who were assured a plentiful and continual supply of foreign labor through the replenishment clause. This precarious alliance was more than sufficient to outweigh the opposition of organized labor, particularly the AFL-CIO and the United Farm Workers, who continued to oppose the importation of additional workers.

On October 9, 1986—more than a year after its Senate passage—this rather unwieldy bill finally passed the House, and on October 14, House and Senate conferees endorsed a compromise. As the President signed IRCA less than a month later, he noted that the law was "the product of one of the longest and most difficult legislative undertakings of recent memory" (cited in Montwieler, 1987: 18). As we will see, the difficulties of this "legislative undertaking" were at least in part the product of the fundamental contradiction with which these legislators wrestled—a contradiction that was embodied *in toto* in two of the law's major provisions.

B. EMPLOYER SANCTIONS

Employer sanctions has been the centerpiece of immigration reform efforts since the early 1970s and has consistently been the political motor behind these efforts. Despite widespread political support for employer sanctions (see, for example, George Gallop, *The San Diego Union*, November 30, 1980, Part A, p. 22), the approach is fraught with difficulties. Specifically, it will be shown that: 1) employer sanctions are inherently difficult to enforce, and 2) voluntary compliance will not be sufficient to offset these difficulties.

A 1982 General Accounting Office (GAO) study, commissioned by Congress to report on the experience with employer sanctions in 19 foreign countries plus Hong Kong, documents some of the difficulties with this approach. The GAO study concluded that "Although each country had laws penalizing employers of illegal aliens, such laws were not an effective deterrent to stemming illegal employment . . ." (U.S. Government Accounting Office, 1982: 2).

In addition to problems related to inadequate enforcement resources and "lack of enforcement resolve" (Ibid., p. 2), the GAO report found that in countries such as Canada where there is no national identification system, "proving that the employer knowingly violated the law [i.e. was privy to their workers' undocumented status] can be difficult" (Ibid., Appendix 4). In countries with a secure system of worker identification, such as West Germany, the report concluded that "employers have been able to evade responsibility for hiring illegal workers altogether by subcontracting for work through firms that obtain illegal aliens on a temporary basis" (Ibid., Appendix: 14).

This GAO report received scant attention in Congress, perhaps because it reached conclusions antithetical to the goals of the employer sanctions sponsors who had commissioned it. In 1985, a second study was commissioned, with the GAO instructed this time to focus only on those nine countries plus Hong Kong where there was reason to believe there might have been some improvement since the earlier study. In this follow-up study, five of the eight countries that responded, plus Hong Kong, reported that employer sanctions were having some effect (U.S. Government Accounting Office, 1985). However, in three countries (including Canada) the deterrent effect was reported to be even weaker than in 1982. Furthermore, the number of undocumented aliens had decreased in only Austria and Hong Kong, and in the case of Austria, the decrease was reported to be the consequence of a reduction in labor demand, not employer sanctions. Curiously, France reported that employer sanctions was having a moderate deterrent effect, yet the same country reported an *increase* in the number of aliens working illegally.

Richard Norton, Associate Commissioner for Examinations of the INS, in his study of employer sanctions in France and West Germany (1985), comes to more optimistic conclusions on their deterrent effect, but the study is so seriously flawed that one wonders about the objectivity of the INS official/researcher. Norton concludes from his research that Germany "has had remarkable success with sanctions" (p. 49) and that France has been only somewhat less successful, with sanctions showing "fitful efficacy" (p. 16). However, these conclusions are based almost entirely on interviews with state officials, academics, and a handful of employers in these countries, the purpose of which is to document their *opinions* on sanctions' effectiveness. Nowhere in his study does he gather primary data, nor does he even mention migration rates or alien apprehension statistics, a curious omission when the task is to gauge the deterrent effect of sanctions. Furthermore, much in Norton's study seems to *confirm* the difficulty of enforcing sanctions effectively. For example, he documents the tendency of German employers to circumvent sanctions by subcontracting, French workers' increased use of false documents, and the greater concentration of immigrant workers in the underground economy in both countries. Norton —ever watchful for signs of sanctions efficacy—cites these trends as a reflection of employers' "voluntary compliance", i.e. these tactics are only necessary because of employers' compliance with the letter of the law. A more meaningful interpretation of these same data, however, leads one to the conclusion that a variety of employer and worker strategies can effectively nullify the deterrent potential of sanctions.

Miller and Papademetriou (1983) are somewhat less sanguine than Norton regarding the effectiveness of sanctions in Western Europe and the implication of that experience for the United States. While they do maintain that in many European countries sanctions have produced "some positive impact", they point out that "similar employer sanctions in the United States context would clearly not necessarily produce the same beneficial results" (p. 290). They conclude that "Employer sanctions in any advanced industrial democracy are more difficult to enforce than to legislate" (p. 292).

The United States probably represents the least amenable scenario for effective employer sanctions, given the absence of a national identification system, a 2000-mile border with Mexico, and a long history of employer dependence on immigrant labor. Indeed, since California passed its own version of an employer sanctions law in 1971, twelve other states have enacted similar laws, yet there have been only a handful of convictions and no reductions in either illegal alien employment or undocumented migration in these states (Schwarz, 1983).[3]

Immigration scholars at a symposium held to evaluate the potential impacts of what was then called the Simpson-Mazzoli Bill, were virtually unanimous in their prediction that employer sanctions would have little deterrent effect in the United States. Portes (1983: 27) reasoned that "passage of the proposed legislation will neither stop clandestine immigration nor deter its utilization". Instead, "Work settings will become more clandestine. . . . Production can be subcontracted. . . . Piece-rate homework will become still more common" (Ibid., p. 27). Keely (Ibid., p. 36), focusing on the absence of any national identification card in the United States, argued that "there can be scant confidence that an employer sanctions system can work . . . until we know what the secure worker-identification system is to be". Garcia y Griego (Ibid., p. 66), emphasizing the economic function of undocumented immigrants, concluded that "a serious effort to implement (employer sanctions) is likely to prove impractical".

In response to researchers' and others' skepticism of the employer sanctions approach, officials of the INS declare that employers' voluntary compliance will minimize enforcement difficulties and maximize the deterrence potential of sanctions (Alan Nelson, Commissioner of the Immigration and Naturalization Service, July 9, 1987). There are at least two problems with the expectation that voluntary compliance with employer sanctions will reduce illegal alien employment and stem undocumented migration.

First, depending on what is meant by "voluntary compliance", it may or may not make any difference. The employer sanctions provision of IRCA, as implemented by the INS, requires employers to ask all new employees for documentation indicating their identity and eligibility to work in the United States (a driver's license and social security card being a typical combination). It further requires employers to fill out an "I-9" form attesting to their having seen such documentation and to keep this form on file. Except in cases of blatantly fraudulent documents (an Attorney for the INS suggested, for example, that a birth certificate upon which "white-out" had been used should be considered suspect), the employer is not required to verify the validity of these documents. Furthermore, if the employer has completed this document check, and the document presented to the employer "reasonably appears on its face to be genuine", the employer has an affirmative defense against prosecution even if the worker is in fact illegal. In other words, voluntary compliance as defined by the law and its regulations, in practise means asking workers for documents and keeping completed I-9 forms on file. Given the ready availability and moderate cost of fraudulent documents, combined with the employer's lack of responsibility for verifying documents, this kind of "voluntary compliance" by itself is unlikely to alter either employment practises or the flow of illegal migration. As one employer put it, "If my employee brings me a fake document, I don't want to know about it. I'm here to comply with the law, not enforce it." (quoted in the *Wall Street Journal*, May 4, 1988: 15).

One study of 177 immigrant-dependent employers in California (Cornelius, 1987)[4], interviewed several years before IRCA was passed, lends support to the prediction that voluntary compliance will have little impact. More than half of these employers either thought there already was a law against hiring illegal aliens or were not sure whether there was such a law. Furthermore, more than half of the employers in the study requested some verification of their workers' eligibility to work in the U.S. Nonetheless, virtually all of these employers hired a significant number of illegal aliens. In other words, many of these employers were technically already in compliance with the terms of IRCA in so far as they requested documentation from their workers; yet this had little discernible impact on the kinds of workers they hired.

Preliminary findings from a follow-up of this study (Cornelius, 1988), in which 103 immigrant-dependent employers[5] and 500 of their workers have been interviewed since the passage of IRCA, confirm the effects of this disjunction between voluntary compliance and effectiveness. While the vast majority of these employers are requesting the specified documentation from their workers, and hence are complying with the letter of the law, these same employers report that the law has neither affected their hiring practices nor the types of people they hire; most of the employers admit that they "probably" have undocumented workers in their workforce; and, the overwhelming majority report that despite high compliance rates, they believe sanctions will have little or no deterrent effect.

If, on the other hand, voluntary compliance with employer sanctions means refusing to hire workers whom one suspects are illegal, this too is problematic. In the first place, such refusal potentially violates the anti-discrimination clause of IRCA (the Frank amendment) which makes it illegal to discriminate against workers on the basis of citizenship or alienage. Thus, unless an employer is somehow *certain* of a worker's undocumented status, there is a fine line between this kind of "voluntary compliance" and discrimination on the basis of foreign appearance.[6]

In addition, this kind of voluntary compliance in the absence of a serious threat of detection and conviction, is unlikely to be widespread in those industries where the undocumented predominate. This is the case both because such compliance would require a fundamental restructuring of the workforce in these industries and because many of these industries depend for their survival on this labor supply. While some large and highly profitable firms that only occasionally employ undocumented workers, may attempt to comply with employer sanctions by refusing to hire those suspected of illegal status, many firms where the undocumented predominate are less likely to have this luxury.[7] This forecast is lent tentative support by the sectoral distribution of fines in the first year of employer sanctions implementation. As of April 15, 1988, heavy industry had received only one fine for employer sanctions violations, while the service sector had received 56, or 77% of the total (unpublished INS report, "Employer Activity Report by Industry Through April 15, 1988"). While the distribution of fines inevitably reflects to some degree INS enforcement strategies, nonetheless the magnitude of the discrepancy is probably at least partially a reflection of employer behavior.

Since IRCA went into effect, some observers have maintained that there are signs that employer sanctions are working. INS officials (*Christian Science Monitor*, May 18, 1987; Nelson, 1988) cite an overall decline in apprehensions of undocumented border-crossers, as evidence of the law's deterrent effect. A closer look at the pattern of these apprehension statistics, however, suggests that this decline may be misleading (see Table 1). It is true that the first months after IRCA was signed saw an immediate downturn in border apprehensions, a decline that peaked in May, 1987.[8] However, apprehensions began to rise again in June, and by the winter of 1988, apprehensions were significantly higher than they had been the year before.

Table 1. Southern Border Apprehensions by U.S. Border Patrol for Fiscal Years 1986, 1987, 1988

	FY 1986	FY 1987	FY 1988
October	105,229	135,983	67,010
November	92,658	76,431	55,744
December	76,419	57,463	50,229
January	131,518	97,641	100,875
February	140,782	93,192	109,585
March	163,128	100,300	115,119
April	167,622	80,453	94,426
May	164,033	69,921	72,483
June	133,421	93,775	64,208
July	152,033	125,813	72,479
August	149,552	113,636	72,702
September	139,459	81,603	65,809
TOTAL	1,286,854	1,122,067	937,679

Source: U.S. Immigration and Naturalization Service

A number of factors help to explain these early reversals. Most important, the rumor mill in Mexico, fed by the Mexican news media, had disseminated the fear that IRCA would precipitate mass deportations in May 1987 (the month that the legalization program was to be launched).

The rumor was so widespread and the fear so prevalent that many who otherwise would have migrated remained at home in April and May (Bustamante, 1987). When no major deportations were carried out and when those who had travelled north in spite of the rumors continued to find employment, border apprehensions once again increased.[9] (That the initial declines were a result of rumors and misunderstandings rather than the direct effect of employer sanctions, is lent support by the fact that these early reductions *preceded* the implementation of employer sanctions [July 1, 1987] by several months.)

The spring and summer of 1988 saw a renewed decline in apprehensions, and once again sanctions advocates have pointed to the decreases as the product of the new law, and specifically the end of the employer "warning" period on June 1, 1988.[10] However, in light of independent studies (Bustamante, 1988; Cornelius, 1988) that conclude that the migratory flow has not been significantly altered, the magnitude of these decreases (for April through August of 1988, apprehensions were more than cut in half compared to the same period in 1986) is suspect. An alternative explanation for these dramatic apprehension reductions is straightforward and commonsensical: IRCA has *legalized* a substantial portion of the flow. In other words, it is not that migration has been reduced by employer sanctions; rather, the legalization and SAW provisions of IRCA have extended legal status to many of the same persons who in the past were apprehended by the Border Patrol. With hundreds of thousands of farm workers receiving temporary legal status in the last months, it was inevitable that apprehension statistics would be affected. And, it should not be surprising that the recent "reductions" have occurred in the spring and early summer, just as farm workers traditionally cross the border for the season.

Some sanctions proponents maintain that the full deterrence potential of employer sanctions will only be realized in the long-run, as employers become persuaded of the seriousness of the enforcement effort. However, preliminary evidence points to the opposite conclusion. The experience with sanctions in other countries suggests that the legal and practical difficulties of successfully convicting employers, and employers' use of circumvention strategies such as subcontracting, are among the most fundamental logjams to effective implementation. Yet, these are long-term stumbling blocks which are not necessarily revealed in the initial stages of implementation.

There is already evidence that the use of fraudulent documents has increased since the passage of IRCA. As Ernest Gustafson, INS District Director in Los Angeles, has observed, "What we're seeing is an increase in these documents. If we didn't have this new law [employer sanctions], we wouldn't see all these counterfeit documents" (quoted in the *San Diego Union*, October 22, 1987, Part A, p. 3).[11] In other words, not only are the problems inherent in employer sanctions likely to show up primarily in the longer run, but as fraudulent documents proliferate, the stage is being set now for the legal paralysis ahead.

This discussion of the deficiencies of employer sanctions suggests that whatever voluntary compliance occurs will have little impact on the volume of undocumented migration, and that inherent enforcement difficulties are likely to emasculate the measure. The limited potential of this restrictive component of IRCA contrasts sharply with the potential of the law's generous farm labor provisions, as outlined below.

C. THE AGRICULTURAL PROVISIONS OF IRCA

When Congress began discussing immigration reform in the 1970s, the focus was exclusively on employer sanctions, and special provisions for agricultural workers were not seriously considered. By 1984, however, the importation of foreign labor for agriculture had become one of the most central and controversial issues of immigration reform. Western growers, resigned to the eventual passage of an employer sanctions provision, had shifted their focus to securing alternative sources of immigrant labor. With the 1984 bills, growers achieved much that was on their wish-list. So generous was the Senate provision that it was likened by some to the old Bracero Program.

Indicative of the controversial nature of these programs, their perceived importance to agriculture, and the persuasive powers of agricultural pressure groups, when the 1984 bill died in conference, discussions were initiated as to the possibility of removing the issue from the legislative arena altogether and placing it in the less visible administrative arena. To this end, the INS issued informal proposals for a large new agricultural program to be put into effect solely on the basis of regulatory changes ("Proposed Revision of H-2 Agricultural Program by Regulation", INS unpublished document, January 1985; see also "U.S. Plans to Ease Alien Labor Rules", *New York Times*, January 27, 1985, p. 1). As Alan Nelson, Commissioner of the INS, put it, this shift "might facilitate [the] legislation" (quoted in the *New York Times*, January 27, 1985, p. 13).

This by no means would have been the first time that Congress had delegated to the INS the unenviable task of constructing—not just implementing—immigration policy, nor the first use of that delegation to advance agricultural interests. A vast literature speaks to the increased role of federal administrative agencies in public policymaking, and an accompanying decline in the role of Congress (Davis, 1969; Rourke, 1969; Heclo, 1977; Rosenbloom, 1983). Rosenbloom (1983) suggests that the increased legislative role of the administrative agency is at least in part the consequence of a deliberate delegation of authority on the part of Congress. He argues that Congress delegates authority in the interests of efficiency, since the administrative bureaucracy has more "fluid rule-making procedures", unencumbered as it is by electoral politics (1983: 23). What is more, "members of Congress have developed an inclination to delegate not just authority, but also controversial political issues to public administrators. By doing so, they . . . avoid making enemies of those who would oppose their policy stands" (p. 24). It should not be surprising, then, that in the controversial realm of immigration policymaking, the INS has historically been given wide latitude.[12]

Nor should it be surprising that the INS was prepared to use that latitude in 1985 to advance agricultural interests, for a special relationship has developed over time—a relationship that is predicated on structural and bureaucratic imperatives. Davis (1969), Davidson (1977), Lowi (1979), and others, argue that special interest groups are courted by administrative agencies as a base of power, and as a way to ward off hostile intervention in their programs. As Wildavsky (1971: 390) puts it, "For an agency that has a large and strategically placed clientele, the most effective strategy is service to those who are in a position to help them". Agribusiness has in the past provided the INS with this base of support, and has periodically protected the agency from aggressive Congressional oversight, particularly during the 1960s and early 1970s when Senator Eastland reigned over the Senate Judiciary Committee.

Agricultural interests and those of the immigration bureaucracy are curiously intertwined in another way as well, hinging on the border control function of the agency. Specifically, to the degree that growers and ranchers have access to legal foreign labor, they present less of an enforcement problem to the INS. This relationship and its consequences were most clearly apparently during the Bracero period, when the INS enforcement function ironically subordinated the agency to agricultural demands. As one ranchers' association president wrote to the INS commissioner in 1958, as he jockeyed for a liberal approach to the importation of braceros: "Unless a supply of legal labor is available, we will be faced with the wetback (sic) problem again. . . . *None of us want this to happen*". (letter from T. A. Kincaid, President, Texas Sheep and Goat Raisers' Association, to General Swing, Commissioner of the INS, July 2, 1958; emphasis added). One INS official responded to such threats by warning his colleagues, "We can cope with a threat from a solitary rancher to go back to wets within the next year; however, unless some means is found to avoid it, this situation will magnify a thousand-fold" (memo from E. De Witt Marshall, INS District Director, San Antonio, Texas, to L. W. Gilman, Associate Deputy Regional Commissioner, INS Western Region). These thinly veiled threats and INS reactions not only suggest a bureaucratic-structural basis for the INS alliance with agricultural employers, but also are indicative of the balance of power in that relationship.

Given this historical context of the Congressional delegation of power to the INS and the agency's alliance with growers over time, it makes sense that when the controversial issue of farm labor programs emerged in the 1980s, proposals were developed to shunt the issue into the administrative arena, should it continue to hamstring the legislative process. The political motor behind immigration reform was provided by *restrictive* demands, with which employer sanctions were eminently compatible and with which the importation of additional foreign workers was clearly incompatible. Caught between conflicting political and economic pressures, policymakers prepared to satisfy both with a carefully considered division of labor between the executive and legislative branches.

Ultimately, this proved unnecessary, as the reform measure that finally passed in 1986 incorporated the largest foreign labor program since the Bracero period. So generous were its provisions that a *Washington Post* editorial called it a "cave-in" to agricultural interests ("The Immigration 'Compromise'", July 16, 1986).

Three categories of Special Agricultural Workers (SAW's) are provided for in IRCA. The first group (SAW I) includes those who have performed 90 days of farm labor in the three consecutive years before May 1986 and who are otherwise admissible as immigrants. These workers can apply for temporary resident status and after one year, permanent residency. There is a limit of 350,000 in this category, on a first-come, first-served basis.

The second category (SAW II) includes those who applied in the first category, but after the ceiling of 350,000 had been reached, and also includes those who worked in agriculture for 90 days between May 1985 and May 1986. These workers would have to wait two years before becoming eligible for permanent residency. Neither SAW I's nor SAW II's would be tied to agriculture after being granted temporary resident status.

The third category is the "replenishment" group. Beginning in 1990 and lasting for three years, the Secretaries of Labor and Agriculture will annually evaluate the size of labor shortages in agriculture and allow for the importation of foreign workers to fill the gap.[13] These "Replenishment Agricultural Workers" (RAW's) will be given temporary resident status and after working in agriculture for at least 90 days each year for three consecutive years, may apply for permanent residency. After two more years doing such seasonal work, they could apply for citizenship, at which time their obligatory tie to agriculture would be terminated.

Clearly, the SAW program is as much a legalization plan as it is a foreign worker program. Once they have been legalized and are no longer tied to agriculture, some workers will move into other sectors; hence the perceived need for replenishment. Whether or not large numbers of these newly legalized workers do move out of agriculture[14], the fact that they will not constitute a captive workforce made the plan acceptable to those in Congress who opposed Wilson's Bracero-like program. At the same time, of course, it provides a potential supply of additional workers to non-agricultural industries.

Although the SAW program has received the most public attention, two other provisions of IRCA have immediate implications for the supply of agricultural labor. The new law creates a temporary worker program—the H-2A program—designed specifically for agriculture. A variation on the H-2 program, H-2A will minimize the time required to obtain imported farmworkers, reduce paperwork, and thereby presumably increase their numbers, particularly in the southwest where H-2 workers have historically been shunned in favor of readily available undocumented workers. In addition, growers won a major victory in IRCA with the establishment of a requirement that the INS must obtain a warrant before they search open fields for undocumented farm workers. According to some INS officials (cited in *The Christian Science Monitor*, February 23, 1986, p. 4), this new requirement was responsible for an immediate and dramatic reduction in Border Patrol activity in the agricultural sector.

The combined effect of these agricultural provisions of IRCA will undoubtedly be an increase in the supply of immigrant workers to agriculture. By August 30, 1988—still three months from the November 30 application deadline—almost 800,000 work permits had been extended under the first stage of the SAW program. As undocumented farm workers legalize, replenishment workers are imported, and fields are protected from unannounced INS searches, growers will benefit from a new potpourri of foreign labor comprised simultaneously of legal immigrants, temporary workers, and undocumented aliens.

Although it is difficult to predict with precision the long-term impacts of these agricultural provisions of IRCA, it is ironic that this law, precipitated by restrictionist demands and with employer sanctions as the primary political fuel, contains within it the potential to increase the supply of foreign labor. The irony is even more striking when this potential of IRCA is contrasted with the limited potential of employer sanctions to reduce the size of the undocumented worker population. The following section represents an attempt to untangle this apparent contradiction. Using the historical context of immigration policy as a building block, it argues that the conflicts between these two major components of IRCA reflect the contradictory economic and political demands to which the law responds.

IV. IRCA AND THE CONTRADICTIONS OF IMMIGRATION POLICYMAKING

An upper-level INS official has referred to IRCA as "Christmas-tree legislation". Asked what he meant, he replied, "It offers something for everyone, like ornaments hung on a Christmas tree." (Interview, September 1986). At one level, he was right. It is clear from the legislative overview presented above that employer sanctions is designed to satisfy restrictionists; legalization is intended to offset this punitive approach and placate advocates of immigrants' rights; and the agricultural provisions are a direct response to growers' demand for a continued supply of foreign workers.

But, this Christmas-tree analogy, essentially a pluralist rendition, is misleading in its oversimplification. First, not only is the new law a hodgepodge of *ad hoc* measures designed to please everyone, but some of these measures—most obviously employer sanctions and the foreign labor provisions—pull simultaneously in opposite directions. Second, in *practise*, some of the "ornaments" of the law will be far more meaningful than others. Ironically, employer sanctions, the *raison d'etre* of this reform and by far the most strongly and consistently endorsed in Congress as well as by the majority of Americans, is the least likely to realize its potential. In other words, not only does the law contain contradictory principles within it, but the law-in-action is likely to vitiate its original and overrriding political purpose of restriction. As the following sections demonstrate, the contradictory nature of the law's provisions and the limited potential of its restrictionist measures, can both be explained by reference to the clash between economic pragmatism and political demands.

A. EMPLOYER SANCTIONS AND THE POLITICAL DEMAND FOR RESTRICTION

It was suggested earlier that historically periods of economic downturn have been associated with increases in anti-immigrant sentiment. The early 1970s perpetuated this pattern, as illegal immigrants were blamed for many of the symptoms of the deepening recession. The *Wall Street Journal* (September 29, 1971, p. 1) declared in a headline that "Illegal Immigrants . . . Pose Economic Threat", and the *Los Angeles Times* (October 22, 1971, p. 1) warned "Illegal Alien: Growing Peril to U.S. Worker". California Assemblyman Ray Seeley was concerned that illegal Mexican workers might damage the U.S. economy "beyond repair" (Press Release, October 21, 1971). The message continued unabated throughout the 1970s. The *Sacramento Union* (May 4, 1976, p. 1) suggested that "illegal aliens prey on the economy". *U.S. News and World Report* (May 30, 1977, p. 30) editorialized that illegal aliens are "outlaws, figuring only as a frightening burden."

It was within this political and ideological context that a federal employer sanctions law was first debated in the 1970s. It represented a response to the collective perception of immigration as an "invasion" and the corresponding political pressure to "regain control of the border". As we have seen, it is a response that is likely to remain primarily symbolic, a monument to the political pressures and ideology that produced it, but with little objective impact.

To say that the employer sanctions provision is a symbolic measure does not necessarily imply that it is the deliberate construction of an empty law by cynical lawmakers. Murray Edelman, in *Political Language: Words that Succeed and Policies that Fail* (1977) suggests that political language is often "symbolic" in that it "evoke[s] strong political beliefs even when there is little warrant for the self-assurance". Furthermore, he points out that such "strong political beliefs" are often used to justify policies that advance the interests of the powerful. Edelman argues, however, that it can not be deduced from this outcome that such policies are the product of detached policymakers who are somehow immune to the collective myths of their society. Rather, "cognitions are complex because they are social in character, not confined inside the head of a single person" (page 11). Thus, the symbolic acts of policymakers both perpetuate *and* are derived from, the collective definition of the problem at hand. As Edelman (page 9) puts it, "public policies rest on the beliefs and perceptions of those who help make them, whether or not those cognitions are accurate."

It may occasionally be the case that symbolic law is the product of policymakers whose goal is to deceive and hence to placate those who demand some political response. For example, a close look at the Congressional debates surrounding the Anti-Alien Contract Labor Law of 1885 makes it clear that this response to organized labor's demands for restriction was, as one outspoken Congressional critic put it, a "sham and a pretense. . . . a sop to Cerberus" (*Congressional Record*, 1885: 1835). Both proponents and opponents expressed doubt that the law, which was introduced as the "salvation of American labor", would have any significant effect, since it would only bar a few skilled workers with pre-arranged work contracts. Ultimately, the law passed by overwhelming margins, with its advocates convincing potential naysayers with the argument that, "I do not understand the harm [it] can do if it has no effect" (Ibid., p. 1629).

More often, however, public policies are rendered symbolic as the ideological or political "cognitions" upon which they are based, and which are shared by the policymakers themselves, clash with countervailing realities in the amendment process, in the process of enforcement, or in their judicial interpretation. As outlined above, it is primarily enforcement difficulties that will emasculate the potential of employer sanctions. There is an important link between the cognitions and beliefs that underlie employer sanctions—and the strength of those beliefs—and its predictable enforcement difficulties. For, once illegal migration has been defined as an "invasion" and restriction in the form of employer sanctions the appropriate response, evidence documenting the predictable ineffectiveness of this approach, is discounted. Thus, the overwhelming evidence that employer sanctions had neither worked in other countries nor at the local state level, was ignored by employer sanctions proponents. In fact, the 1982 GAO study that concluded that sanctions were not a deterrent to illegal migration, was effectively buried, until it was leaked to the *New York Times* by a Congressional aide. As Edelman (Ibid., page 3) describes such loyalty to "myth" in spite of the evidence, "Large numbers of people continue for long periods of time to cling to myth, . . . and to reject falsifying information when prevailing myths justify their interests, roles, and past actions, or assuage their fears."

Employer sanctions is thus the product of a dialectical process, in which the collective definition of an invasion incites fears and demands political action based on those fears. In this sense, the law is "symbolic" in that it is a symbol, or concrete embodiment of, the collective definition. *Because* of these symbolic qualities and its effectiveness in assuaging fears, countervailing evidence as to its inoperability is ignored. Thus, while policymakers may not *begin* the political process with the intention of constructing a purely symbolic law, their adherence to myth in the face of reality, guarantees this result.

B. FOREIGN LABOR AND ECONOMIC PRAGMATISM

The last decade has witnessed an ongoing debate among immigration scholars over the net impact of undocumented workers on the national economy. Some of these scholars (Briggs, 1984; Bouvier and Gardner, 1986) echo the concerns voiced since the 19th century that immigrants (in this case, the undocumented) take more in social services than they contribute in revenues, have an adverse impact on wages, and contribute to unemployment by taking jobs away from U.S.-born workers. Others (McCarthy and Valdez, 1985; Muller and Espenshade, 1985) argue that, while some local entities may experience social service burdens, in general immigrants—both documented and undocumented—make a net contribution to the U.S. economy and tax coffers.

Among the most thoughtful participants in this debate are those who have done detailed case studies of specific sectors. Such an approach generally leads to the conclusion that while job displacement and adverse effects on wages may accompany large-scale undocumented employment in some sectors, in other sectors there is a positive ripple effect (Cornelius, 1987; Mines, 1987). According to this "ripple effect" argument, not only do the undocumented generally take jobs that the U.S.-born would eschew (in which case there is little direct displacement), but their very presence in certain sectors allows for the survival and expansion of those sectors and creates a series of related job opportunities for the documented and U.S.-born.[15]

Regardless of the pros and cons of these arguments, it is clear that certain industries—such as garment, agriculture, hotels and restaurants—have a long history of dependence on documented and undocumented immigrant labor, and that a number of new industries—electronics assembly being the prototype—depend on this labor supply for expansion. Whether or not the elimination of the undocumented workforce, and the economic restructuring that this would imply, would have a long-term ameliorative impact, is largely irrelevant here. What is important to note is that the foreign labor provisions of IRCA represent an official recognition of this ongoing reality of dependence on immigrant labor.

The fact that special provisions for foreign labor were focused on agriculture, is consistent with this interpretation. This singling out for special treatment not only reflects the lobbying power of growers' associations, but, more important for this analysis, it represents a concession to the longstanding relationship of symbiosis between growers and Mexican immigrant workers. In other words, it is not that legislators calculated that growers, compared to other employers, would be less likely to be able to mechanize and/or attract domestic workers with improved wage rates (After all, the profit margins in western agriculture are high compared to many other immigrant-dependent industries). Rather, the law is a reflection of the current reality that while only approximately 15% of undocumented Mexicans work in agriculture, in the western states anyway, agriculture is still the single largest employer of undocumented immigrant labor and depends on them for the bulk of the workforce (Mines and Martin, 1986).

It should also be noted that, although the H-2A and SAW-RAW legalization provisions are explicitly geared only toward agriculture, in practise IRCA will bring an additional contingent of immigrant workers into non-agricultural sectors as well. Not only will some newly legalized farmworkers seek employment opportunities in urban areas, but H-2 workers may be admitted in significant numbers for the first time to work in non-agricultural sectors. Ironically, although the employer sanctions provision is unlikely to have a major impact on levels of undocumented migration, it may operate as a persuasive political tool with which to convince policy-makers of employers' need for additional legal workers.

The question is begged at this point: If employer sanctions can be characterized as a symbolic law with little concrete potential, why then was it necessary to provide alternative avenues for labor importation? The answer relies on an understanding of the distinction between laws that are deliberately rendered symbolic in the legislative process and are passed because of their limited potential for impact (as was the case with the 1885 law prohibiting contract labor), and the more subtle process by which a law that symbolizes or embodies a collective myth wends its way through the legislative process not *because* of but in *spite* of its deficiencies. In the case of employer sanctions, it was the strength of the conviction that the law was sound that fueled its passage; at the same time, however, this conviction necessitated a corresponding concession to economic realities.[16]

A few members of Congress observed that IRCA—presumably a restrictive reform—would in practice have just the opposite effect. Rep. Roybal of California, on the day of the final vote in the House, complained: "I do not think that every member of this House knows what is in this bill. . . . They thought, for example, that they voted for immigration reform with sanctions, but they did not. What they voted for is a farm labor bill, a bill that is designed to provide cheap labor for the farmers and growers of this country" (*Congressional Record*, 1986: H 10589–90). Rep. Gonzalez of Texas said sardonically, "Let there be no mistake about it. This bill solves some problems; that is the problem of the exploiter who will be given a 20th century version of indentured servants to work with. . . . It guarantees that those who want to exploit cheap, foreign labor on farms and ranches can continue to do so with impunity" (*Congressional Record*, 1986: H 10588). But, "It does not address in any meaningful way the big pretext for this legislation, and that is the immigration problem that confronts the country" (Ibid., p. H 10588). Senator McClure of Rhode Island said simply that the bill was "a failure, a sham, and a fraud" (*Congressional Record*, 1986: S 16892).

An overview of U.S. immigration policies since the 19th century suggests that rather than a smooth evolution, the immigration policy landscape looks more like a patchwork of *ad hoc* policies. A closer look reveals that not infrequently this patchwork is fashioned out of mutually contradictory pieces. Furthermore, these contradictions are often the product of attempts by lawmakers to respond to conflicting pressures in the political economy. Particularly recurrent is the political demand for restrictions side-by-side with the economic reality of the need for immigrant labor.

Thus, for example, the Anti-Alien Contract Labor Law of 1885, purportedly enacted to protect U.S. workers from competition with European immigrants, was passed in the midst of an open-door era, in which the consensus of Congress was that, "We need the leaven of immigration" (*Congressional Record*, 1902: 5773–74). The 1950s present perhaps the best example of such apparent inconsistencies, as immigration policy veered from the *de facto* encouragement of illegal migration associated with the Bracero Programs and the immunity extended to employers through the Texas Proviso, to the mass deportations of "Operation Wetback".[17] What makes IRCA unique is that for perhaps the first time, such contradictions are incorporated into the same piece of legislation.

Thurman Arnold (1937: 207–13), in his analysis of the Sherman Anti-Trust Laws, noted that the ideal of free competition and an anti-trust ideology conflicted with economic pressures toward monopolization. As he put it, "Granted an insistent demand, which opposes a deeply felt ideal, and a conflict of this kind between two institutions (the economic and the ideological), the result is as inevitable as the reaction of a man sitting on a hot stove." He continues, "such a process is inevitable when an ideal meets in head-on collision with a practical need."

While Arnold was attempting to explain the lax *enforcement* of certain types of legislation, his analogy may apply equally well to contradictions within legislation itself. Remember that it was the ideology of restrictionism that precipitated employer sanctions, and it was the strength of this ideology (or "myth" as Edelman would put it), that explains its enactment in spite of its apparent deficiencies. But, at the same time that IRCA embodies this restrictionist ideology, its foreign labor provisions represent an official recognition and endorsement of the role of immigrants in the economy. This contradiction between restrictionist ideology and economic pragmatics can be conceptualized as the legislative embodiment of the "head-on collision" between the "ideal" and the "practical need".

V. CONCLUSION

This paper began by providing an historical overview from which to view the current round of immigration reform. It became clear from that discussion that U.S. immigration policy since the nineteenth century has been driven by economic realities, in particular the utility of immigration as a source of labor. Counterposed to the appreciation of immigrants as workers, anti-immigrant nativism has periodically racked the policy debate. Such nativism has occasionally triggered restrictionist policies against particular groups (for example, the Chinese in the 1880s and Southern Europeans in the 1920s) and mass deportations of others (Mexicans in particular). However, in most cases these anti-immigrant backlashes neither seriously limited the volume of migration nor reflected any change in policymakers' perception of immigrants as an important source of labor.

It was against this historical backdrop that the Immigration Reform and Control Act of 1986 was enacted. The law has been hailed both as landmark legislation that will "regain control of our borders", and as an ingenious creation painstakingly fashioned through the political art of compromise and concession—a showcase for pluralism. This simplified depiction of IRCA is wrong on both counts. First, while the mandate to regain control of the borders did provide the political motor of the reform effort, the sole restrictive provision of the law—employer sanctions—will remain a symbolic measure with little impact on immigration flows. At the same time, other provisions of IRCA, such as the special agricultural worker programs, will predictably add to the stock of immigrant workers. Thus, not only does IRCA pull both ways at once, but the long-term impact of this reform, which originated in and was fueled by restrictionist fervor, is likely to be a continued increase in immigration, both documented and undocumented.

Second, while it may be true that on one level IRCA is a carefully crafted balance of provisions designed to satisfy a myriad of interest groups, the pluralist paradigm proves inadequate to account for the apparent paradoxes in the bill's legislative history and in its potential outcome. Most important, it can not explain why restrictionists tenaciously held on to the concept of employer sanctions (indeed made it the centerpiece of the reform) in spite of consistent and extensive evidence calling into question its efficacy; it can not explain the "head-on collision" between two of the main provisions of the bill; and, finally, it can not account for the virtual transformation of this "restrictive" bill into a *de facto* labor stabilization/replenishment device.

The dialectical account of IRCA presented here treats the bill as the product of a conflict embedded in the political economy, between the ideology of immigration restrictionism and the economic pressure to provide employers with immigrant labor. The "resolution" to this conflict is comprised of, on one hand, a symbolic act of restrictionism—employer sanctions—that responds to the political demand to "regain control of the border", and, on the other hand, a series of measures designed to ensure an uninterrupted supply of labor.

Rather than a break with the past, IRCA represents a continuation of the historical pattern. In acceding to the demand for immigrant workers at the same time that it symbolically responds to restrictionist sentiment, it simultaneously accommodates the economic pragmatism and the anti-immigrant restrictionism that have alternately characterized U.S. immigration policy for more than a century. Nor are the contradictions that are generated by this accommodation unprecedented. As progeny of the same type of conflict that has confronted immigration policymakers for decades, they bear a striking resemblance to the policy contradictions of previous eras. What is perhaps unprecedented, and complicated considerably the legislative process, is that IRCA embodies the conflict *in toto*, and in so doing, brings into sharp relief the dialectical nature of immigration policymaking.

The focus of this paper has been on the shape of the new immigration law, on its apparent contradictions, and on the use of history as a way to make sense of these contradictions. It is hoped that future research will investigate the actual implementation and impacts of IRCA, and that the analysis presented here will be of use in this endeavor.

KITTY CALAVITA *is Assistant Professor in the Program in Social Ecology at the University of California, Irvine. She is currently doing research on administrative decision making and discretion in the U.S. Immigration and Naturalization Service, under a grant from the National Science Foundation. Her previous works include* U.S. Immigration Law and the Control of Labor: 1820–1924 *(Academic Press, 1984) and "California's 'Employer Sanctions' Legislation: Now You See It, Now You Don't"* (Politics and Society, *Volume 12 #2, 1983*).

NOTES

1. That same year, the first state employer sanctions law was passed in California.
2. The H-2 program allows for the seasonal importation of workers to areas where a labor shortage in specific sectors has been certified by the Department of Labor. Approximately 25,000 temporary workers—the largest single group being agricultural workers—are imported annually under this program, a number which has declined steadily since the 1970s (U.S. Government Accounting Office, 1984: 5). Growers in the southwest have never made extensive use of the H-2 program, probably because of the ease with which undocumented Mexican labor can be obtained as compared to the difficulties imposed by the bureaucratic regulations and requirements of the H-2 program.
3. For an analysis of the California case, see Calavita (1983).
4. The study was conducted from 1982 to 1984 in San Diego, Los Angeles and Orange Counties and in the San Francisco Bay area. The average proportion of Mexican immigrants in these firms was 65%; more than half of the total workforce included in the study was undocumented.
5. This follow-up study includes most of the original 177 employers with the exception of those in the San Francisco Bay area, which was excluded for budgetary reasons.
6. Employers who have participated in a pre-IRCA program organized by the INS, known as Operation Cooperation, in which employers pledge not to hire the undocumented in exchange for the freedom from disruptive factory raids, report that the approach has inevitably led to some discrimination against those who appear to be foreign (*Christian Science Monitor*, September 6, 1986, p. 6).

7. The effect may be an increased concentration of the undocumented in more economically marginal and less stable industries, rather than an overall reduction in the migratory flow. It follows that whatever discrimination results from such voluntary compliance, would be concentrated in those sectors offering the best working conditions and most stable employment.
8. Due to the seasonal nature of much migration, statistics for any given month must be compared to those of the same month in previous years.
9. Border apprehension statistics of course are not a precise indication of the number of undocumented border-crossings, since not all undocumented border-crossers are apprehended, some are apprehended more than once, and arrest statistics are sensitive to changes in enforcement efforts and resources. However, major increases and decreases may be useful for comparative purposes.
10. From June 1, 1987 to June 1, 1988, the INS generally issued warnings and citations to employers on their first offense.
11. Although many of these counterfeit documents are what the INS refers to with frustration as "50-footers", in apparent reference to the fact that they can be detected to be fraudulent from 50 feet away, INS officials do not, and can not under the law, require employers to verify their validity (Ibid., Part A, p. 3).
12. Perhaps the most noteworthy example of this delegation of power concerns the so-called "green-card commuter". These commuters are aliens who once obtained legal resident status in the United States, but who reside in contiguous foreign countries—primarily Mexico—and return to the U.S. daily or seasonally to work. There is no statutory basis for this category of commuters, and in 1965 Congress seems to have implicitly prohibited the practice by defining "residence" unequivocally as one's "principal, actual dwelling place in fact" (8 USC, Section 1101 [a] [33]), and restricting green-card entry to "returning resident immigrants" (8 USC, Section 1181 [b]). Greene (1972: 443) argues that "the INS continued the [commuter] status to provide a substitute for the terminated Bracero Program". Invented by the INS and tolerated by Congress and the courts, the green-card commuter practice continues today and stands as a powerful reminder of the role of the INS in immigration lawmaking.
13. The Department of Labor has had official responsibility for the H-2 program in the past and is perceived to be more difficult to convince of labor shortages than is the Department of Agriculture with its historically close ties to growers. IRCA, in making the Department of Agriculture an equal partner with the Labor Department in determining labor shortages, increases the likelihood that future replenishments will be generous.
14. It has been estimated that approximately 85% of undocumented workers are currently employed in non-agricultural sectors of the economy. It has furthermore been pointed out that pre-emigration factors such as place of origin, years of schooling and skill levels are more determinant of urban versus farm employment, than is immigration status (Mines and Massey, 1985). Such considerations suggest that the proportion of newly legalized farm workers who will leave agricultural employment, may in fact be quite low.
15. Mines (Ibid., p. 13) points out that "This usually occurs in sectors (like garments and shoes) where capital is highly mobile and footloose and where recent immigrants can help preserve or enlarge a sector. But, it can also occur in sectors like restaurants and irrigated agriculture where although capital is fixed, a low cost, flexible immigrant labor force . . . creates indirect employment for domestic workers."
16. The ideology of restrictionism in the 1970s and 1980s (as during virtually every such restrictionist period in the past) is influenced by, if not the product of, underlying economic factors, as discussed earlier. Thus, the discussion here is not meant to imply a rigid and arbitrary separation of the ideological and the

44 *Calavita IMMIGRATION LAWMAKING*

economic. In fact, it is precisely because immigrants have historically provided employers with cheap labor that the backlash against them—often in the form of racism and nativism—has achieved such momentum. But, to say that economic motives often feed the ideology of restrictionism is not to deny the ideological nature of the backlash that is unleashed.

17. Such contradictions are not confined of course to the conflict between restrictionism and economic pragmatism. Perhaps equally frequent are the tensions between the conflicting ideological functions of immigration policy. A particularly blatant case of such tension was evident in the House debate in 1921 on the issue of whether or not political refugees should be exempt from the forthcoming quota. On one hand, it was argued that refugees should be exempt since, "one of the great principles upon which this government is founded is that we should give asylum to those who are being prosecuted because of their religious or political beliefs" (*Congressional Record*, 1921: 586). On the other hand, it was pointed out that the prevailing policy of deporting or barring anarchists and communists precluded offering asylum to all refugees. As one befuddled Congressman asked, "What would be our attitude when a member of the communistic party . . . may be deported under our present law? We would be admitting an alien under this [proposed] law who would be deported after he got here (Ibid., p. 587).

BIBLIOGRAPHY

ARNOLD, T. (1937) *The Folklore of Capitalism*. New Haven: Yale University Press.

BOUVIER, L. and R. GARDNER (1986) "Immigration to the United States: The Unfinished Story," *Population Bulletin* 41: 1–51.

BRIGGS, V. M. (1984) *Immigration Policy and the American Labor Force*. Baltimore: The Johns Hopkins University Press.

BUSTAMANTE, J. (1987) Presentation to the Bilateral Commission on the Future of United States–Mexican Relations, Institute of the Americas, University of California, San Diego. August 28, 1987.

—— (1988) Presentation to the Annual Conference on Immigration Law, American Immigration Lawyers Association, San Diego, California. June 19, 1988.

CALAVITA, K. (1983) "California's 'Employer Sanctions' Legislation: Now You See It, Now You Don't," *Politics and Society* 12: 205–30.

—— (1984) *U.S. Immigration Law and the Control of Labor: 1820–1924*. London: Academic Press.

CARNEGIE, A. (1886) *Triumphant Democracy, or Fifty Years March of the Republic*. New York: Charles Scribners Sons.

CHRISTIAN SCIENCE MONITOR. February 23, 1986, p. 4. September 6, 1986, p. 6. May 18, 1987, p. 7.

CONGRESSIONAL RECORD. 48th Congress, 2nd Session (1885). 57th Congress, 1st Session (1902). 67th Congress, 1st Session (1921). 82nd Congress, 2nd Session (1952). 99th Congress, 2nd Session (1986).

CORNELIUS, W. A. (1982) "America in the Era of Limits: Nativist Reactions to the 'New' Immigration," Working Paper 3. La Jolla, California: Center for U.S.-Mexican Studies, University of California, San Diego.

—— (1987) "Potential Impacts of New Federal Immigration Legislation on Immigrant-Dependent Firms in California," Paper presented at the Annual Meeting of the Association of American Law Schools. Los Angeles, California. January 1987.

—— (1988) "The Persistence of Immigrant-Dominated Firms and Industries in the United States: The Case of California," Paper presented at the Conference on Comparative Migration Studies, Institute of Political Studies, Paris, France. June 20–23, 1988.

DAVIDSON, R. H. (1977) "Breaking Up Those 'Cozy Triangles': An Impossible Dream?" In S. Welch and J. G. Peters (eds) *Legislative Reform and Public Policy*. New York: Praeger Publishers.

DAVIS, K. C. (1969) *Discretionary Justice: A Preliminary Inquiry*. Baton Rouge: Louisiana State University Press.

EDELMAN, J. M. (1977) *Political Language: Words That Succeed and Policies That Fail*. New York: Academic Press.

GALARZA, E. (1964) *Merchants of Labor: The Mexican Bracero Story*. Santa Barbara: McNally and Loftin.

GARCIA Y GRIEGO, M. (1981) "The Importation of Mexican Contract Laborers to the United States, 1942–1964: Antecedents, Operation and Legacy," Working Papers in U.S.-Mexican Studies, 11. La Jolla, California: Center for U.S.-Mexican Studies, University of California, San Diego.

—— (1983) "Employer Sanctions: Political Appeal, Administrative Dilemmas," In W. A. Cornelius and R. A. Montoya (eds) *America's New Immigration Law: Origins, Rationales, and Potential Consequences*. La Jolla, Calif.: Center for U.S.-Mexican Studies, University of California, San Diego.

GREENE, S. L. (1972) "Public Agency Distortion of Congressional Will: Federal Policy Toward Non-Resident Alien Labor," *George Washington Law Review* 40: 440–63.

HADLEY, E. M. (1956) "A Critical Analysis of the Wetback Problem," *Law and Contemporary Problems* 21: 334–57.

HAMILTON, A. (1791) "Report on Manufacturing." *American State Papers, Finance*.

HARWOOD, E. (1983) "Can Immigration Laws Be Enforced?" *The Public Interest* 72: 107–23.

HECLO, H. (1977) *A Government of Strangers: Executive Politics in Washington*. Washington, DC: The Brookings Institute.

HIGHAM, J. (1955) *Strangers in the Land: Patterns of American Nativism, 1860–1925*. New Brunswick, New Jersey: Rutgers University Press.

IMMIGRATION AND NATURALIZATION SERVICE (1985) "Proposed Revision of H-2 Agricultural Program by Regulation," Unpublished Document, January, 1985.

—— (1988) "Employer Activity Report by Industry Through April 15, 1988," Unpublished report. INS Central Office, Washington, DC.

JENKS, J. W. (1913) *The Immigration Problem; A Study of American Immigration Conditions and Needs*. New York: Funk and Wagnalls.

KEELY, C. B. (1983) "The Failure of United States Immigration Policy". In W. A. Cornelius and R. A. Montoya (eds) *America's New Immigration Law: Origins, Rationales, and Potential Consequences*. La Jolla, Calif.: Center for U.S.-Mexican Studies, University of California, San Diego.

KINCAID, T. A. (1958) Letter to General Swing, Commissioner of the INS. July 2, 1958. INS Central Office Files, CO214K-P (Accession 67A233, Box 6).

KIRSTEIN, P. (1977) *Anglo Over Bracero: A History of the Mexican Worker in the United States from Roosevelt to Nixon*. San Francisco: R and E Research Associates.

Los Angeles Times. October 22, 1971, Part I: 1. May 12, 1987, Part IV: 3. May 26, 1987, Part IV: 3.

LOPEZ, G. P. (1981) "Undocumented Mexican Migrants: In Search of a Just Immigration Law and Policy," *UCLA Law Review* 28: 615–714.

LOWI, T. (1979) *The End of Liberalism: The Second Republic of the United States*. New York: W. W. Norton.

MARSHALL, E. D. (1960) Memo to L. W. Gilman, Associate Deputy Regional Commissioner, INS. June 9, 1960. INS Central Office Files. CO214K-P (Accession 67A233, Box 6).

MCCARTHY, K. and R. B. VALDEZ (1985) *Current and Future Effects of Mexican*

Immigration in California: Executive Summary. Santa Monica: The Rand Corporation.

MILLER, M. J. and D. G. PAPADEMETRIOU (1983) "Immigration Reform: The United States and Western Europe Compared," In M. J. Miller and D. Papademetriou (eds) *The Unavoidable Issue: U.S. Immigration Policy in the 1980s.* Philadelphia, Pennsylvania: Institute for the Study of Human Issues, Inc.

MINES, R. (1987) Presentation to the Workshop on The Changing Roles of Mexican Immigrants in the United States Economy: Sectoral Perspectives. Center for U.S.-Mexican Studies, University of California, San Diego, August 1987.

MINES, R. and P. MARTIN (1986) *A Profile of California Farmworkers.* Berkeley: Giannini Foundation Report 86-2.

MINES, R. and D. MASSEY (1985) "Patterns of Migration to the United States from Two Mexican Communities," *Latin American Research Review,* 20: 104–23.

MONTWIELER, N. H. (1987) *The Immigration Reform Law of 1986: Analysis, Text, Legislative History.* Washington DC: The Bureau of National Affairs.

MULLER, T. and T. ESPENSHADE (1985) *The Fourth Wave: California's Newest Immigrants.* Washington, DC: The Urban Institute Press.

NELSON, A. (1986) Statement to U.S. Congress. House of Representatives, December 17, 1986.

—— (1987) Presentation to the Seventh Annual Briefing Session for Professional Journalists. Center for U.S.-Mexican Studies, University of California, San Diego, July 9, 1987.

—— (1988) Presentation to the Eighth Annual Briefing Session for Professional Journalists. Center for U.S.-Mexican Studies, University of California, San Diego, June 17, 1988.

New York Journal of Commerce. December 13, 1892: 2.

New York Times. January 27, 1985: 1.

NORTON, R. E. (1985) "Employer Sanctions in France and West Germany." Unpublished Report, sponsored by the German Marshall Fund of the United States.

PORTES, A. (1983) "Of Borders and States: A Skeptical Note on the Legislative Control of Immigration," In W. A. Cornelius and R. A. Montoya (eds) *America's New Immigration Law: Origins, Rationales, and Potential Consequences.* La Jolla, Calif.: Center for U.S.-Mexican Studies, University of California, San Diego.

REISLER, M. (1976) *By the Sweat of their Brow: Mexican Immigrant Labor in the United States, 1900–1940.* Westport, Connecticut: Greenwood Press.

ROSENBLOOM, D. H. (1983) *Public Administration and the Law: Bench v. Bureau in the United States.* New York: Marcel Dekker, Inc.

ROURKE, F. E. (1969) *Bureaucracy, Politics, and Public Policy.* Boston: Little, Brown and Company.

Sacramento Union. May 4, 1976: 1.

SAMORA, J. (1971) *Los Mujados: The Wetback Story.* Notre Dame, Indiana: The University of Notre Dame.

The San Diego Union. November 30, 1980, Part A, p. 22. October 22, 1987, Part A, p. 3.

SCHUCK, P. H. (1975) *The Judiciary Committees: A Study of the House and Senate Judiciary Committees.* New York: Grossman Publishers.

SCHWARZ, C. E. (1983) "Employer Sanctions Laws, Worker Identification Systems and Undocumented Aliens: The State Experience and Federal Proposals," *Stanford Journal of International Law* 19: 371–405.

SEELEY, R. (1971) Press Release, October 21, 1971.

TAYLOR, J. E. (1987) "Illegal Immigrants in the California Farm Labor Market." Presentation to the Workshop on The Changing Roles of Mexican Immigrants in the U.S. Economy: Sectoral Perspectives. Center for U.S.-Mexican Studies, University of California, San Diego, August, 1987.

U.S. CONGRESS. HOUSE OF REPRESENTATIVES (1986) "Immigration Reform and Control Act of 1986." 99th Congress, 2nd Session. *House Report* 99-1000.

U.S. CONGRESS. SENATE IMMIGRATION COMMISSION (1911) *Immigration Commission Report*. 61st Congress, 3rd Session. Senate Document 747.

U.S. CONGRESS. SENATE (1864) 38th Congress, 1st Session. *Senate Report* 15.

U.S. DEPARTMENT OF JUSTICE (1982) "The Immigration Control and Reform Act of 1982." Unpublished Department of Justice Report.

U.S. GOVERNMENT ACCOUNTING OFFICE (1982) *Information on the Enforcement of Laws Regarding Employment of Aliens in Selected Countries*. GAO/GGD-82-86. August 31, 1982.

—— (1984) *Information on Aliens Admitted into the United States as Nonimmigrant Workers*. Report to the Chairman, Committee on the Judiciary, House of Representatives. GAO/GGD-85-27. December 26, 1984.

—— (1985) *Illegal Aliens: Information on Selected Countries' Employment Prohibition Laws*. Report to the Chairman, Subcommittee on Immigration, Refugees, and International Law, Committee on the Judiciary, House of Representatives. GAO/GGD-86-17BR, October, 1985.

U.S. News and World Report. May 30, 1977: 30.

VAN VLECK, W. C. (1932) *The Administrative Control of Aliens: A Study in Administrative Law and Procedure*. New York: The Commonwealth Fund.

The Wall Street Journal. September 29, 1971: 1. May 4, 1988: 15.

The Washington Post. July 16, 1986.

WILDAVSKY, A. (1971) "Budgetary Strategies of Administrative Agencies". In R. E. Wolfinger (ed) *Readings on Congress*. Englewood Cliffs, New Jersey: Prentice-Hall, Inc.

STATUTE CITED

8USC, Section 1101

—— Section 1181

13 U.S. Statutes at Large

66 U.S. Statutes at Large

[16]

BARGAIN AND BLUFF

Compliance Strategy and Deterrence in the Enforcement of Regulation

KEITH HAWKINS
Centre for Socio-Legal Studies
Wolfson College
Oxford

A strategy of compliance in which enforcement agents rely on negotiation is identified as a characteristic feature of water pollution control work. The strategy arises from the nature of the conduct and activities subject to regulation and from the need to maintain a continuing relationship with the regulated. In securing compliance regulatory agents shape their enforcement tactics by reference to assumptions held as to why polluters fail to comply. Bargaining is central to compliance strategy, but if a conciliatory approach fails, a more threatening posture will be taken in which a variety of mores, including bluffs about legal sanctions, may be employed. Law enforcement is treated as a matter of compliance as well as compulsion.

I

> We don't take people to court just like that. It's a history of problems. We've tried everything with them: negotiation, discussion, etc. When we take them to court it's like saying all the other methods have failed [Pollution control field officer].

It is a commonplace in the sociology of law to observe that a characteristic of industrialized societies is the use of the criminal

---

AUTHOR'S NOTE: *An earlier version of this article was delivered at the conference on Perspective on Regulation: Law, Discretion and Bureaucratic Behavior, sponsored by the Baldy Center for Law and Social Policy and the Oxford Centre for Socio-Legal Studies, SUNY Buffalo, May 1980. I am grateful to Richard Lempert for comments on an earlier draft.*

law to regulate economic life. Yet it is remarkable that so few analyses of the nature of the regulatory process are to be found in the literature,[1] especially given the fact that postwar Anglo-American sociology of law is largely a sociology of criminal justice. In this article, which is drawn from a forthcoming monograph about the control of water pollution,[2] I want to explore some of the distinctive features of the routine enforcement of regulation.

In order to throw the analysis into bolder relief I shall contrast two strategies or systems of enforcement, which I shall call compliance and sanctioning.[3] In focusing upon what are in effect broad characteristics, however, I do not wish to give a spurious impression that the world is such a neat place. The analytical contrast is employed simply as a way of organizing thinking about rule enforcement. A strategy of compliance appears to be the primary system of enforcement employed in regulatory control. Enforcement agents here are concerned with securing conformity to a rule or standard; rule-breaking tends to be conceived of as a problem. If repair is the primary objective in a compliance system, in a sanctioning system it is retribution. Central to this approach is a preoccupation with the application of punishment for harm done; conformity to the law may be the consequence of this, but that is not the main issue. While it is possible to pursue theoretical distinctions between these enforcement systems (see Hawkins, forthcoming), I propose to map out in this essay some of the characteristics of a compliance system.[4]

Existing studies of regulatory control from a sociological perspective have drawn attention to a marked reluctance to employ the formal machinery of law enforcement. Though enforcement agents may work in such widely contrasting fields as consumer protection, housing, industrial health and safety, or forestry, they all appear to display a clear preference for a strategy of enforcement by securing the compliance of rule-breakers.[5] Pollution control officers are no exception to this pervasive pattern of regulatory control, and from their point of view there is good reason for the strategy of compliance. They are confronted with a fundamental dilemma of regulatory work: How are rules to be enforced when much of the rule-breaking consists of morally problematic[6] states of affairs, when legal sanctions are widely regarded as derisory,[7] and when the regulated have good economic incentive not to observe the law?

Criminal law and its ceremonies are laden with moral overtones. Yet the nature of the conduct subject to control in systems of regulation invites moral ambivalence, an ambivalence reflected in the frail legal sanctions provided in the legislation for breach of regulation, and the extreme reluctance with which the formal law is invoked. In Britain, modest (some would say feeble) levels of sanction and unwillingness to prosecute are two of the major characteristics of regulatory law and practice. The ambivalence surrounding regulatory deviance is shared by polluters and enforcement agents alike and is presumably attributable in part to the recency with which new values have been invented and proscribed, and the recognition that economic activity, proscribed only when in excess, is responsible for the material well-being of the community. In general, though routine breaches of regulation are morally evaluated, it is not as common a response to draw unfavorable moral conclusions as it is upon the breaking of a rule in the traditional code.[8] Though the law recognizes no distinction, most people are unwilling to talk of crime when they discuss pollution. This sort of language is considered appropriate only where clearly blameworthy conduct exists: where there is a calculated breach of regulation or where the polluting substance is widely known to be dangerous and there was carelessness in handling it. Lawyers will recognize here a lay conception of mens rea, but the irony is that pollution control legislation in Britain (in keeping, so far as I know, with other forms of regulatory legislation) is framed in terms of rather strict liability, whereas the mental element is the hallmark of traditional crime.[9]

Whether it be murder, rape, robbery, arson, theft, or any of the other familiar forms of rule-breaking, an act in the traditional code is essentially a discrete event with an identifiable beginning and end. It is momentary, closed (Mileski, 1971). Enforcement is compressed in time to a once-and-for-all decision and discretionary outcomes tend to be binary—to arrest or not to arrest—rather than a choice among options. Such criminal acts are committed by specific (sometimes identifiable) offenders who create victims who themselves are specific and identifiable. The enforcement response is penal: to prepare for the administration of a deserved sanction.

In many forms of regulatory deviance, however, it is often difficult to conceive of or identify either a specific victim or an individual offender. Victims may be diffuse and remote, with harm accumulating over a period of time; while individual offenders (even if the source of the rule-breaking can be detected) may be lost in the organization, which is the commonest perpetrator of regulatory misconduct. This is particularly true of pollution. More importantly, rule-breaking behavior here tends to be open-ended and continuous, not "sealed in time by anything but a response" to it (Mileski, 1971: 11). It is a state of affairs—unfenced machinery, substandard housing, a badly smoking chimney, a dripping pipe—where that which gives offense is readily recognized as a problem. The response of regulatory officials is preventive or corrective: They seek to administer a needed remedy.

Remedy must be brought to problems that regulatory agents and others regard as not only economic but technological in character. So far as water pollution is concerned, effluent and waste control involves chemical, biological, and mechanical applications whose functioning is sometimes only imperfectly understood. The constituents of deviance and control in such a setting are readily regarded by enforcement agents as "technical" or "scientific" issues. The economic implications of compliance with pollution and other forms of regulation can, of course, be substantial. All pollution control staff are well aware that it costs money and takes time to stop breaking the rules. Those enforcing the traditional code need not be involved with such niceties. Cultural values and mens rea doctrine alike instruct them to be concerned with the deviant actor's opportunities to do otherwise, which, after all, is what the moral notion of blameworthiness is all about (McHugh, 1970). Besides, compliance consists of restraint, not action. This same conception of morality inculcates in the regulatory agent an acceptance of the fact that physical, technological, and economic impediments provide good, or at least plausible, grounds for noncompliance with the rules—and for continued noncompliance while efforts are made to overcome the impediments.

In order to accomplish remedy efficiently in a setting requiring money, time, and organizational will, regulatory agents direct their efforts toward the cultivation and maintenance of a network of amicable social relationships. Though they can do nothing about polluters' financial capacities to comply, they can use a variety of tactics to persuade them of the necessity of a measure of compliance for now and for the future. Regulatory enforcement in general takes place in the context of continuing relationships with that segment of the community defined by its economic activity as subject to the rules. Where law enforcement is practiced by the police in continuing relationships, it should be noted (with drunks or prostitutes, for example) that it too resembles a compliance strategy (Banton, 1964; Bittner, 1967; Wilson, 1968).

A compliance strategy is expressed in practical terms by the adoption of various negotiating and bargaining tactics organized over a period of time both to secure and maintain compliance with regulatory standards. In all of this, however, the formal legal process—prosecution—though thrust very much into the background, still plays a subtle but important role in this approach to enforcement.

II

Though I have stressed the state of affairs as a major characteristic of much regulatory deviance, by no means all pollutions are states of affairs. Field staff draw a practical distinction of considerable general importance for enforcement behavior between continuous and discrete rule-breaking—between "persistent failures to comply" and "one-off" pollutions. It is the persistent failure to comply that is the state of affairs: the continuing pollution that is frequently or consistently above consent limits,[10] either owing to inefficient treatment plant or inadequate attention to pollution control on the part of the discharger. The nature of this deviance is open-ended and persisting. It often comes to agency attention through proactive enforcement by routine monitoring and may have been in existence for a very long period and only recently discovered or recently defined as pollution.[11] Most such polluting activity is typically not regarded as serious.

The normal control response is the prescription of remedial measures made possible through the continuing relationship between enforcement agent and polluter. It is only where the polluter's behavior over a long period of time is considered "uncooperative" ("bolshie") that employing the law as the ultimate sanction for intransigence becomes a possibility. The use of the law here is both a penalty for misconduct, as in a sanctioning system of enforcement (for the uncooperativeness smacks of moral culpability), and it is also demanded to protect the credibility of the organization as an enforcement agency against this symbolic assault on its authority and legitimacy.

Though the responses of the persistent polluter are carefully monitored by field staff, most persistent failures to comply are treated as routine, uneventful:

> I think people see discharges as outside consent conditions, and have been for a long time, and people don't take that much notice.

The agency enforcement response is correspondingly modest; "We would," in the words of an area supervisor, "just tend to niggle away at the bloke." A persistent failure to comply will be treated more seriously only where the discharge is regarded as substantially beyond consent limits and where the pollution is noticeable.[12] The process of securing compliance, where the persistent failure to comply is concerned, is an organized sequence of requests and demands placed upon the polluter. It is a continuing, adaptive process, viewed by field staff in longitudinal perspective as a career, one that creates a context for the exercise of enforcement discretion. Compliance is therefore an elastic concept in practice that depends on the apparent progress made by polluters and other exigencies, such as their demeanor, which may affect their relationship with the field officer. The issue is not usually one of whether or not dischargers will take the action demanded of them by the field officer so much as whether they will take some remedial action as quickly as the officer wishes, and whether they will do—"for now"— as much as they are required. The stance adopted by the field officer during negotiations and the sorts of demands subsequently made of the polluters will be influenced as much by interpretations the officer places upon the polluters' response as by the nature of the problem to be remedied and the resources available for tackling it. That such interpretative work is possible is a reflection of the repetitive nature of the enforcement relationship. There is recurrent contact between the officer and the person designated in the factory or farm as responsible for pollution control (actually referred to as the "contact"). While inspection and sampling are infrequently done with small discharges, major sources of effluent may be monitored every few weeks or even days. The regulatory agency's enforcement domain is circumscribed by the activity to be policed, providing for the development of personalized relationships between regulator and regulated.

The technical implications of the behavior addressed by law require, in practice, this fluid conception of compliance. The nature of the problem has to be diagnosed, a remedy prescribed, installed, and made to work efficiently. This is the case even though the practical cure may be a relatively simple affair of digging a hole to serve as a settlement pit, for action has to be taken and the remedy maintained by the polluter. In some cases compliance may involve a complex plant installation requiring heavy expenditures of money and time, and constant vigilance by field officers as to performance and progress. Such plants frequently demand regular attention and maintenance to produce an acceptable effluent. Compliance here is subject to constant negotiation. Field officers do not work to a notion of instant compliance when dealing with persistent problems; compliance is instead measurable in months or years. Furthermore, to the extent that discharges are subject to continued monitoring and the standards to which the polluter is held are open to change, compliance has a quality of endlessness about it.

It often happens that economic or technical impediments also rule out instant compliance. What a field officer has to go on in these circumstances amounts to nothing more than the polluter's protestations of pious intention and good faith. Such pleadings normally serve as evidence of compliance.

The one-off pollution has its own significance in terms of compliance, for though the enforcement agent can achieve a more or less instant conformity (so far as the rule-breaking is concerned), preventive work may be necessary to foreclose the possibility that a similar event can happen in the future. In general, the one-off pollution is altogether a more important matter. Almost by definition it will be serious simply because it is unpredictable and less open to detection through routine monitoring, thus to ready control, than a continuing pollution. The one-off is a discrete event; it may be momentary or longer lasting, but it has a finite beginning and end. It normally comes to agency attention (in contrast with the persistent pollution) reactively, as a result of complaint from a third party, and sometimes it is difficult to link deviance with offender: a discharge can be turned off or an effluent diluted before a field officer arrives on the scene, only to find the slug of pollution has moved downstream or has begun to dissipate. And where the persistent pollution may be regarded by enforcement agents as either "inevitable," owing to technical or economic incapacity to comply on the part of the discharger, or "careless," through inadequate attention to pollution control, the one-off is given to different moral categorization. It is more likely to be regarded as an accident—a spillage, for example, a leakage, or a breakdown of treatment plant—or, more ominously, as deliberate—acid baths being emptied or settlement tanks being flushed out.

Since one-offs are more likely to be drastic instances of pollution, resort to the formal law, on those rare occasions when it is had, is not the ultimate sanction for nonconformity characteristic of a compliance strategy, but rather a punishment for wrong-doing, the more familiar response of a sanctioning style of enforcement. There is no problem as such to be remedied with a one-off (unless one of prevention); instead, enforcement activity is directed toward mitigating harm already done, preventing its recurrence, and deterring others. Because the one-off pollution by definition implies the existence of a discharge that is not normally made, or the presence of polluting matter in a normally clean discharge, compliance is relatively simple to secure where field officers discover the effluent actually discharging. They will demand that it cease. And the more serious the pollution appears to be, the sooner they will expect remedial action to be effective. Compliance here can be instant: taps can be turned off, an effluent pipe blocked off, polluting liquid diverted or disposed of in waste tankers.

III

Compliance strategy in pollution control work is founded on a number of assumptions made by enforcement officers. Two deserve particular attention. First, assumptions are made as to the cause of any pollution. Understanding cause—explaining the deviance, in other words—informs the officer as to the appropriate enforcement stategy and tactics to adopt.

Pollution control staff regard most dischargers as basically, if reluctantly, law-abiding. Thus polluters have to be talked into cleaning up their effluents or taking preventive steps since, as a senior officer put it, "Your priorities are not their priorities—that's the problem." What the water authority will regard as successful enforcement normally means expenditure—often heavy—for the polluter. The pollution control officer's art is to persuade polluters by a variety of tactics to bear costs in ways rarely justifiable commercially, hence their frequent description by field staff as "dead money."

In keeping with the image of water users as essentially law-abiding, field men claim considerable success in achieving compliance in the majority of cases; and, indeed, the physical evidence of compliance is clearly visible on any visit to factory or farm. Most dischargers are half-hearted in their resistance to the demands of the water authority; in fact most are described as responsible or public-spirited people: Those polluters who cause serious difficulties both in terms of their effluent and the trouble they make for field staff are in a small minority. This was not always so. The more experienced field staff all detect a change toward greater pollution consciousness among dischargers and public alike that took place in the 1950s and 1960s. This shift, it is thought, assists the task of control. This is not to suggest that dischargers are incapable of deviance, but field staff believe that serious pollution that is the result of negligence or deliberate misconduct does not now occur regularly or on a large scale.

Even so, field men maintain a dual image of dischargers, often explained by reference to the metaphor of the game. Securing compliance is a game to be played, in which the polluter's moves are directed toward resisting efforts at enforcement. Such resistance is portrayed as a ritual response even from a polluter who will be described as responsible or cooperative. For dischargers to "try it on" or "try to pull a fast one" is thought to be entirely normal behavior; they are expected to drag their heels or seek to avoid adopting in their full extent the measures required by the officer; "usually people are pretty slow to spend money," said an area man, "no matter which sector of the public they come from." Unless, however, the discharger is defined as belonging to an occupational or other group considered to be more likely to cause pollution, or has displayed an uncooperative attitude now or in the past, he will be expected ultimately to comply after some ritual reluctance or evasiveness. The motive for noncompliance is not questioned: it is taken for granted to be a desire to avoid trouble and costs that cannot be commercially justified and recouped:

> It's no skin off his nose if it carries on going down the stream. It's one less problem off his mind. He's got less slurry or less whatever to deal with. Or he hasn't got another soakaway to dig.

But relatively few dischargers, it is believed, resist enforcement efforts with any degree of seriousness.

In general, four working categories of dischargers are employed by pollution control staff. Most are regarded as *socially responsible*. Polluters here comply as a matter of principle: they are thse who, in Kadish's words, manifest a "personal disinclination to act in violation of the law's commands" (Kadish, 1963: 437). This categorization may address an individual or the corporate identity of a firm. Those dischargers most likely to be thought socially responsible—in sharp contrast with what appears to be the sentiment in some quarters in the United States—are usually the larger companies, including the nationalized concerns, which for the most part are viewed as helpful and responsive to the enforcement activities of the agency.[13] It is not that the socially responsible do not cause pollution, but rather when pollution occurs it does so as the result of an accident. It will almost certainly be an isolated instance of deviance—a one-off pollution. The socially responsible discharger in these circumstances will alert the agency and cooperate fully in clearing up and taking all necessary measures to prevent a recurrence.

Socially responsible dischargers, however, rarely possess unblemished virtue. It is taken for granted that part of the game of enforcement will be disclaimers, evasiveness, and delay in the application of remedial measures. "Everyone tries it on, at least to begin with. Even the big firms who will do what we want eventually," said a field man from a mixed catchment. "They will all say 'It wasn't us,' or 'It was an accident.'" When the officer, whose patch contained no towns or industries of any size, was asked how often dischargers tried to pull the wool over his eyes, he replied:

> Very regularly, very regularly. Nearly everyone to more or less a degree will try to kid you about something. Either the nature of the cause of the pollution, or how long it's been going on, or they weren't "aware that there was a pipe there," or "is it really? I've never been down and looked at that watercourse for the last 20 years, I didn't realize we were causing a problem." But nearly everyone tries some minor deception. . . . They will all have a go . . .

> even the biggest companies where you're going to get the perfect response, but they will still try to kid you that they "weren't aware that this was happening," or "it was while they were on leave" or, y'know, they "weren't doing it at all."

The three remaining categories describe compliance that is at best less than ideal, at worst nonexistent. One group might be described as *unfortunate*. These dischargers find it difficult to comply completely with the agency's demands owing either to technical inability or to physical or economic incapacity. Agencies recognize that effective treatment sometimes lies beyond the competence of the available experts. They also acknowledge that some dischargers do not possess the physical resources in the form of suitable land and appropriate topography to permit effective pollution control—quite apart from the economic costs in terms of capital outlay or potential unemployment that might sometimes be the consequence of overzealous enforcement. Economic incapacity is recognized by field officers as a genuine reason for noncompliance. For many of them it would be difficult to believe otherwise since they work in districts where their agencies' own sewage works are substandard in performance for that very reason. Field officers approach the task of enforcement in these circumstances with a feeling of resignation, if not impotence:

> I know before I get there the effluent's going to be bad, and all I'm doing is producing figures so that maybe we can present them at the end of the year. It does seem rather a waste of time in some cases.

Unfavorable inferences as to the willingness of the polluter to comply are not drawn here, in contrast with the two remaining categories.

The next group are often viewed as *careless*. These include the dischargers who are resistant to change. Many farmers, for example, find it difficult to adapt to new ways. And many old-established industries, which were in existence long before the water authorities or their predecessors, tend to behave as they have always behaved, only to find that the invention of new values recasts them as deviants. Then there are other dischargers who, through sloppy management, incompetence, inadequate internal sanctions, or a negligent labor force, regularly fail to maintain their effluents at an acceptable standard, or from time to time cause a one-off pollution (see Kogan and Scholz, forthcoming). For field staff, the worst form of carelessness amounts to outright negligence, and is particularly exemplified in the discharger whose failure to take the preventive measures recommended by field staff results in pollution.

Finally, the *malicious* are those who quite deliberately pollute watercourses either in a calculated desire to avoid the economic costs of treatment or disposal or through a symbolic rejection of the agency's authority. They are capable of both isolated and persistent instances of misconduct, but are not now regarded as numerous.

The second major assumption underlying compliance strategy is that dischargers are sensitive beings whose feelings may be easily bruised if urged—or forced—to do too much, too soon. To use the big stick or crack the whip too zealously may well be counterproductive. For a field officer to be too eager or abrasive is to risk encouraging in polluters an uncooperative attitude or even downright hostility. The assumption is translated into practice by field staff by recognition of two related imperatives aimed at preserving relationships: "be reasonable" and "be patient." These injunctions demand that field staff, rather than explicitly seeking to secure compliance at the outset by coercion, demonstrate an understanding of the polluter's problems by discussion and negotiation. Enforcement takes time.

The officer's understanding of the reasons why particular kinds of polluters comply and the kind of relationship he or she enjoys with each discharger mold the specific enforcement moves adopted. The broad approach, however, has a form of bargaining at its core. Some moves are organized around a noncoercive kind of bargaining because such bargaining carries with it the semblance of voluntariness essential in preserving a sense of reasonableness. If such bargaining is inappropriate or ineffective a more coercive bargaining stance relying on deterrence will be employed. Moves here are premised on a belief in the efficacy of individual and general deterrence for organizations concerned with their business prospects and public image. Since businesses and other organizations are regarded as rational institutions that act purposively, they are held to be ultimately amenable to law as a form of control. In practice, however, the working concept of deterrence, as I shall show, is rather broader than that contemplated by the law. The formal law is presumably founded on a belief that compliance occurs because those tempted to cause a pollution will be deterred by the threat of the legal sanction. During the research period the maximum penalty available to the courts for each charge was £100 on summary conviction in a magistrates' court and £200 on conviction on indictment in the Crown Court.[14] These sanctions were universally regarded by staff of all ranks as inconsequential as deterrents for all offenders except the most impecunious of farmers. Though this view was associated, not surprisingly, with a belief that individual or general deterrence would not be the result of a prosecution and fine, there was, however, no abandonment of deterrence as the principal rationale for enforcement. Deterrence, rather, resides in the serial and incremental nature of the bargaining tactics employed, particularly in the threats preceding use of the formal law or in the informal sanctions accompanying it, as more explicit reference to my empirical data in parts V and VI shows. In an agency mounting no more than a handful of prosecutions a year, threats and bluffs about legal powers become important tactics in everyday enforcement work.

IV

Negotiation is central to rule-enforcement in pollution control. It is conducted in various ways that reflect the officers' own style, their personal judgment as to the cause of the pollution, and features acquiring significance in the course of the enforcement relationship, such as the polluter's demeanor. There are clear patterns to the use of discretion.

Field staff have an array of measures that they employ serially and incrementally in the pursuit of compliance.[15] In a prototypical persistent failure to comply, the field officer may shift from a discussion of the polluter's problem and advice about the remedies which may be attempted, by way of requests and demands, warnings or threats, to the taking of a formal sample[16] of the polluting discharge. A formal sample may be followed by a Notice of Intention to Commence Proceedings and, finally, prosecution. Bargaining will continue throughout. The formal processes of the law are treated as the ultimate, logical consequence for the failure of a strategy of compliance and are portrayed by the field officer, if need be, as an awful culmination that, with a modicum of cooperation from the polluter, need never be reached. At any stage in this array of tactics field officers may support their position with letters to the discharger signed by their supervisor. Though the tactics form a natural gamut, becoming less and less conciliatory, officers will not necessarily follow the whole sequence, but will break into it or switch to a much less conciliatory move, bypassing others, depending upon their assessment of the problem to be solved, the progress being made, or the attitude of the discharger. In a one-off or a serious persistent failure to comply, enforcement can assume the character of a sanctioning strategy, with the array of tactics becoming extremely compressed, sometimes to the point that the officers begin matters by taking a formal sample.

Bargaining between field officers and polluters is central to all of this. Compliance strategy works because it is an exchange relationship (see Blau, 1963: 137ff). What polluters have to offer is a willingness to spend money, their cooperation, and their ultimate compliance. For their part, field staff possess two important commodities to offer the polluter in return. One is free advice and information about methods of treatment and costs of control. The other is forebearance.

Forebearance is the officer's major bargaining resource. It is valuable not only in the struggle for compliance, but in increasing the sensitivity of the agency's intelligence system. Forbearance helps generate a sense of trust that enhances the agency's ability to discover pollution and detect rule-breakers. Field staff are fond of pointing out that polluters who trust their field officers are willing to alert them on the first sign of trouble and will not seek to play problems down. Forbearance is all part of the officers' art of "being reasonable." For instance, reasonable officers will not ask for costly measures unless the problem is a major one or the polluter is undoubtedly wealthy. They will recognize the inherent constraints the polluter may be under, such as lack of space; and they will respect a previously good relationship. They will also offer time for the polluter to come into compliance. Most important of all, *they will not enforce the law in the manner in which they are theoretically entitled to enforce the law.* Bargaining, after all, is "based on the principle that success in pollution control is bought by giving up some of the demands that are fixed in the legal norms to be implemented" (Hücke, 1978: 18). Trust sustains bargaining.

Bargaining, however, can still be conducted when the fieldman is faced with intransigence and relationships are less amicable. It is sometimes laced with bluff. "You can always use a stat[17] you've taken as a bargaining weapon," said an officer from a difficult urban patch,

> in cases where you don't need to proceed, or the stat won't stand up. You can say "If you build this bund wall[18] or you take these steps we'll drop the stat." You can achieve a lot with this—*they* feel they've got you off their back, and *we've* got them to do something [his emphasis].

Field officers will do all of this in recognition of the belief that without forbearance, compliance is the more difficult to attain. What the officers will demand in return for forbearance on the polluter's part is some show of compliance with their requests. The bargaining implicit in the relationship between field officer and polluter emerges from the following conversation:

> *F.O.:* People are intrinsically very law-abiding, and if you tell them that they are in breach of a law you have very little difficulty in fact in practice in persuading them to spend the minimum amount of money required to avoid prosecution. It is a fact that they are very

ready to pay. Few people . . . I mean, I always explain to them . . . that they can do it in active cooperation with us, with us showing forbearance and we give them as much advice and help as possible, or they can be awkward and they can do it having been prosecuted . . . and with us watching them like a hawk forever afterwards. Which option would they choose? And when I sell it to them that way which way would anyone choose? They are obviously going to opt for the easier option. Now they might try back-sliding, but they can procrastinate once, but then we put dates on them. And legal samples are taken.

K.H.: When you say you put dates on them . . . ?

F.O.: Dates for them to meet the standards. If they say "Yes, we'll gladly spend the money required" and time goes by and they keep coming up with excuses and it clear that they are not in earnest, then in that case you put a date by which they are required to meet the consent. And if they do not then I feel no compulsion in taking a legal sample. After all, I have tried my best to get them to do it the easy way. And with good feelings all round.

In routine cases negotiations usually open with preparatory work by field officers designed to make the discharger receptive to their requests. A common ploy is to reason with their contacts and to appeal to their sense of social responsibility. Field officers will sometimes explain the various uses to which the water containing the effluent will be put downstream, a particularly appropriate tactic if the effluent is discharged into a potable supply river. Sometimes they will impose a moral burden upon the polluter by describing the treatment the water has already received upstream to render it suitable for their own use; this usually takes the familiar form, "How would you like it if you had this sort of discharge coming into your intake?" Sometimes, if the setting is right, rather than make apparently dispassionate appeals to what they hope is a sense of social responsibility, the officer will use overtly emotive language: "I tell people they're poisoning water," said one officer who worked on a major potable supply river. "I'll say anything like that to create the right atmosphere." Reasoning that is pursued too vigorously takes on the character of exhortation, a commoner response where implications of blameworthiness on the part of the polluter exist. It resembles the preaching of probation officers who picture "avoiding trouble . . . as a decision completely within the delinquent's grasp" (Emerson, 1969: 224).

If appeals to a sense of social responsibility seem to be having little impact, field officers can resort to a number of other moves. One is to portray compliance as ultimately inevitable and the enforcement process as inexorably moving to that end. This approach can be underpinned by an appeal to the financial sensibilities of most dischargers:

> Industry is only interested in pounds and pence. If you can base it on pounds and pence you're 75% home. . . . You do some simple arithmetic and you say, "Why the hell don't you do it now?" You go on to tell them what it will cost in a few years if they don't do it now.

Other field staff, especially those who claim no great negotiating skill, rely on achieving compliance less by what they say as by what they do. They adopt a tactic of enforcement by attrition. They rely on patience and persistence, by virtually making a nuisance of themselves to the discharger, a nuisance that can only be bought off by compliance:

> I wear 'em down. I go back again and again so they don't want to see me any more. . . . I get them into the position where they're saying to themselves, "Here's that so-and-so from the water authority again," and they put right what's wrong because they're fed up with me hanging around.

Another enforcement move involves a disguised threat based on the "give a dog one bite" principle.[19] When faced with a discharger unwilling to make expenditure on preventive measures, field officers seek to provide for themselves the grounds for serious action if a pollution should occur. By presenting their request as reasonable, enforcement agents establish the means by which inferences of negligence may be drawn if a mishap occurs in the future. For instance, pollution control officers possess, as yet, no legal powers to compel the bunding of oil tanks. Instead they request that bunding be carried out. This request is, rather, a threat masquerading as advice since it is so presented as to constitute a warning that if there is an escape of oil in future from an unbunded tank, grounds for prosecution are created, and prosecution is what the discharger should expect.

Sometimes field staff find it tactically useful to put polluters on the defensive by adopting a variant of the "wearing them down" move. For example, constant monitoring by field officers—regular sampling coupled with inspections conspicuously carried out—continually brings home to the polluters that their activities and their progress toward complaince are under close suveillance. With new pollutions a sample takes on special significance. It is visible evidence of the polluter's problem, which can be immediately displayed to them to preface discussions about corrective work. Confronting the dischargers on the spot with their poor effluent can have particular tactical value, the little piece of drama helping impart a sense of urgency that presentation of the actual sample results some weeks later may lack. A series of such samples can be employed to create an index of progress toward compliance. Even a couple of samples helps. A sample of the untreated pollution is taken, as one field man put it, "so I've got a record. I then have a sample at the start of the problem to show it was bad. And I can always take one later if nothing else has been done."

Yet another enforcement move relies for its force upon people's sensitivity to values connected with consistency of treatment. Field staff may exploit such sentiments, for example, by an alertness to the rivalry many companies enjoy with their competitors who, in many industries, are located close by. A field officer can subtly use a rival's performance to suggest that the polluter had no good economic grounds for not spending money, or claiming technical problems. Discreet enquiries in one firm about the prosperity currently being enjoyed by a particular industry also provides evidence by which field staff may judge the claims of poverty being made by another. Sometimes, however, there may be a confict of moral demands. For instance, the claims of even-handedness can put officers in the uneasy position of having to choose between what their sense of the reasonable tells them is unwarranted in an individual case, and their allegiance to a norm of consistency of treatment dictates. There seems to be a presumption in favor of the latter:

> We visited one of a cluster of sand and gravel works where the settlement pit was so small and the machinery and buildings so arranged that the pit could not be emptied by mechanical means. The manager claimed (presumably rhetorically) to have been up to his neck in slurry in the pit in the course of cleaning it out by hand. Redesign of the pit was impossible because there was simply not enough space. "I wouldn't like to have it on my conscience that that chap's up to here everyday," said Lawton, responding to the rhetoric and pointing to his neck, "to clean out his settlement pit when it's such a small discharge . . . it's not important. But we've done all the others, so we've got to do him."

Such close association, whether it be of industrial rivalry or physical proximity, can, however, be exploited in turn by polluters as a constraint upon a field officer's demands, because polluters too seem to give greater recognition to the value of consistency of treatment." I think it's a most difficult situation," said one junior official to whom the problem was familiar, "if you get someone saying 'you want me to do that, yet him down the road, he's not doing it.'" The "man down the road" can become a particularly powerful means of curbing the agencies' demands, founded as it is upon a moral desire for even-handedness of treatment that polluters and field staff recognize and share alike. "The man down the road" frequently raises a recurrent dilemma in those areas where the water authorities' sewage treatment works themselves produce a poor effluent. Officers find they must be careful in the standards they demand of discharges since their own agency is frequently unable to meet similar standards, and polluters know this. Exclusive stringency prompts noncompliance. One officer described the effluent from a dyeworks he was having trouble with as "black and purple," and it "often" resulted in "lots of complaints." But it was difficult for the officer to get his contact in the factory to cooperate "because he knows our sewage works is a far worse polluter than he is."

One distinctive feature prompted by the open-ended quality of compliance enforcement is the imposition of deadlines.[20] If a period of time is laid down by the field officer (or, better, agreed upon in consultation with the polluter) and articulated in the form of a calendar date, polluters are presented with an unambiguous target by which time they should have installed equipment, dug a hole, or replaced existing plant. A deadline is a good, seemingly nonproblematic index of compliance.[21] Deadlines also aid an enforcement officer's appreciation of the polluter's career as deviant. A deadline met offers an index of progress, of making headway, while a polluter who fails to meet a deadline can be mutually recognized as having failed, even as being uncooperative, since the expiration of a period of time is presentable as an unambiguous matter. In doing so field officer's inevitably put polluters on the defensive as they have to account for their failure to live up to their side of the bargain. What constitutes a plausible account so far as polluters are concerned usually involves the establishment of financial or technical impediments to compliance. Thus (to quote an example frequently treated as plausible by field staff) if polluters can claim the late delivery of equipment, this usually frees them from imputation of fault, and therefore gives them an excuse that demands forbearance from the officer. To have to account increases the polluters' sense of obligation to comply with the officers' demands in the future, especially if the officers can convincingly portray themselves as having been generous in the amount of time they have allowed. At the same time, however, failure to meet a date gives the field officer reasonable grounds for adopting a less forbearing attitude toward the polluter (if in the circumstances this is considered to be tactically desirable), in the face of their lack of cooperation. The use of dates in this way does not blur the issue as to whether the polluters have complied to the desired extent. To fail to meet a date without good excuse is to indicate unabiguously that polluters have breached the implied bargain between the field officer and themselves.

A series of unspoken understandings exist between field officrs and their contacts in those cases where relationships are well-established. The discharger learns, for example, that some indication of efforts made or money spent is the field officer's preoccupation, and that if these are interpreted as insufficient, more pressure will be exerted. Such understandings help endow relationships with a substantial measure of equilibrium that makes the business of securing compliance easier.[22]

But where the relationship is relatively new and there are uncertainties about the rules of the game, or where an uncooperative polluter forces the field officer's hand, the officer is faced with a problem of *enforcement credibility*. The polluter who does less than required poses a dilemma. On the one hand, the officer's need to demonstrate understanding of the polluter's problems may encourage a certain counterproductive inertia. "If you go too often," in the words of an experienced officer, "and talk in a friendly way about their problems they become complacent and don't do anything." On the other hand, officers who too readily veer toward the application of stiffer measures risk becoming locked inescapably into the array of more coercive tactics at their disposal, especially if they threaten that certain "action will be taken unless. . . . " If there is an unsatisfactory response from the polluter the officers may feel constrained to become less tolerant simply to preserve their credibility as enforcement agents. This invites further uncooperativeness on the polluter's part since it is generally accepted that more coercive measures risk further intransigence if the polluter regards such measures as unreasonable. This feature assumes considerable importance in an occupation in which there is a high measure of discretion as to how to do the job and how to secure compliance.

What the polluter actually does by way of compliance is probably no more important for the field officers than that some sign of compliance is made, a sign of respect for their ultimate authority symbolizing a willingness to comply. If a discharger is prepared to take action "fair enough. But if they don't do anything, then that's a different kettle of fish." The fact of action or response, in effect, is important in its own right, quite apart from what is actually done. To fail to respond to a request is to impugn the officer's authority, which calls for a show of strength, in which a more coercive tactic will be selected from the array: the involvement of a supervising officer (thereby underlining the gravity of the polluter's position), the imposition of strict time limits, the threat or actual taking of a formal sample, or talk of prosecution. More coercive measures are generally resorted to reluctantly, for they are regarded as potentially counterproductive to a relationship that must necessarily be a continuing and preferably amiable one (see Macaulay, 1963).

V

Much enforcement activity in pollution control work is premised on the assumption that dischargers are susceptible to extra-legal kinds of deterrence. Where a polluter is being less than cooperative and compliance has clear, easily quantifiable, and sometimes considerable economic costs attached to it, field staff bargain by generating contexts in which deterrence will take on significant meaning, by drawing attention, for example, to some of the difficulties which the dischargers will bring upon themselves if they are prosecuted. In particular, an individual's or an organization's public reputation is displayed as at risk if noncompliance continues. The aspect of the use of formal law believed to be most important for industrialists—"farmers are a different kettle of fish"—is the publicity associated with court appearance. Few officers suggest that there is a stigma with economic implications reflected in damage to sales and profitability attaching to a manufacturer found guilty of polluting a watercourse. Rather, the belief is that a company will seek to protect its reputation as a good in itself. Some field staff regard a company's motives to comply as also linked with a generalized desire to avoid the trouble stemming from public embarrassment. Publicity implies the construction of reputation, and a company does not want to be seen as a trouble maker, since the label will encourage others—especially public authorities that may have benefits to confer—to lay blame for all sorts of other problems at its door. Besides, other industrialists, it is thought, will not do business with those believed to engage in sharp practices. Thus where polluters are seen as potentially uncooperative, or their sluggishness suggests an unwillingness to comply, field staff may resort to the use of tactics based on such organizational susceptibilities to deterrence to attain compliance, exploiting links with other agencies with sanctions to impose or benefits to grant. The field officer's pragmatism, with its primary concern to get the job done as efficiently as possible, makes this fair game.

In some cases one way to get the job done is to work through another agency. The water authority is part of a network of relationships maintained by a variety of public bodies whose task is also to regulate other aspects of the behavior of farmers and industrialists. Deviance in which the water authority is interested is often the concern of another agency that might be in a better position to effect compliance:

> When it comes to things like oil jetties, they have to be surveyed regularly and given a licence by the local fire officer. And you do a joint survey and you often get the fire officer . . . you point out to him, you know. . . . You might also slightly touch on his fear if you've got a chance of a spillage, he might be interested as well from the fire safety aspect. So you've got the threat of stopping that licence—it's not your licence, but it's the Fire Brigade, but, y'know, you work together. . . . And then, of course, there's public health people. If you've got a problem of an area rather than just one industrial site, then you all get together, because you probably all got problems. . . . Obviously, it's an advantage to have a concerted front.

Sometimes field staff may be impeded in attaining their aim of controlling a discharge by the procedural requirements of the law. Working through another public agency is often a means of circumventing seemingly obstructive legal procedures. The following illustration of a case in which the officer was unable formally to connect the pollution to its source may be taken as typical:

> [There's a company in town where] they clean car components, rusty car components, by submersion in boiling caustic soda. . . .

The yard itself is concrete but there were obviously cracks in this concrete and this stuff, which is hosed down every day, had seeped through and accumulated beneath the site. Now this stuff contaminated a pool about a hundred yards away, but it was extremely difficult—well you couldn't see the stuff going in, although it was collecting in pools . . . there was no continuity between the pool of liquid and the pool of water. It subsequently was found that there were land drains between the company and the pool, but I, long before that . . . I simply phoned up [the] County Council and got the waste disposal inspector to come down, and we had a meeting with the company and he explained to them that the stuff that was in that pool which had come from their company was a toxic waste, and therefore it was deposited without—outside the law, and therefore they could be made to do something about it. But we had to sort of take the view that, alright, the pool would be polluted, but it was of lesser importance in this case. But by curing one you cured both.

The water authorities also have considerable scope for the application of authority over reluctant dischargers by virtue of the benefits they can confer or withold. It is in a company's interests to enjoy good relationships with the authority, as a supervising officer of wide experience pointed out. The conversation had turned to reasons why companies comply. Note the reference to the game:

S.O.: Because they want to have good relations with us, they see it as a great advantage.

K.H.: What's in it for them?

S.O.: Well for one thing, we can manoeuvre local authorities and things, etc., for them in terms of getting the dirty stuff into the sewers, in supporting them in developments—because we know they're going to do all the right things—and getting water supplies from the rivers. And also if they have got our support and things go wrong, you know, they know that we will look kindly upon them if we know the firm is playing the game. So it is to their advantage . . . for them to support us.

K.H.: And presumably [there's] sort of a negative of that: if they don't co-operate with you, you will . . . you are able to exert certain kinds of leverage?

S.O.: Yes. Oh yes.

There are, as the last question suggested, other kinds of tactics which are sometimes employed that constitute hints or warnings that unless the discharger does what is requested, the agency may withdraw or refuse benefits in its gift.[23] It will—discreetly—be made clear to an uncooperative discharger that the agencies derive considerable power from their position in the network of regulatory bodies and from the reach of their own authority into other areas of activity. "You may look on us as being something you've got to comply with," said a senior officer of many years' experience, "in order to carry on your legitimate business as an industrial person. And don't forget, without our goodwill it is almost impossible to develop or do anything." For example, legislation now requires that a county council consult the water authority if it is proposing to issue a license to dispose of waste: this was described by a senior official as an "obvious" opportunity for the water authority to secure the cooperation of a difficult discharger.

A more frequently cited instance involves planning permission. "The water authority's always consulted on planning matters," said a supervising officer, with a hint of ingenuousness, "and I assume that if there's a history of pollution the water authority would oppose consenting to planning applications." Applications for planning permission involving the use or discharge of water are sent to the pollution control sections of the authorities as a matter of routine. A field officer described how the process works:

> Certainly with planning applications . . . if you're fortunate enough to have an application in the pipeline at the time, or you're engaged in negotiations, then it's a very weighty stick to wave. We see all planning applications [involving use of water]. They go to the various sections for their reply: water supply, trade effluent, land drainage, also [pollution control. The field officer] will make comments, if necessary. So, if you weren't getting a good effluent from the factory, and they put in a planning application to extend the factory, then obviously you're in a very powerful position to say "I will object to that on the grounds of inadequate pollution equipment or control. We will object." And I often use that one.

The tactic can achieve striking results with recalcitrant dischargers. A senior officer gave an example of a company that is

> engaged in reclaiming metals. . . . Pollution has resulted—extremely heavy concentrations of metals have been found in the local surface water drainage system and this has been traced back to the factory. . . . Two or three months ago we had a planning application come through because they wanted to readjust the premises and alter them and so on. And we said "No, we will not give our"—I suppose you might say "approval. . . . We won't make any sort of favorable recommendations in this case because we don't know any details of what they're proposing." And within, I suppose, a week we had a telephone call from the company saying "Please come and discuss our proposal." Now that's the first time we'd got them to move in any way, shape or form, reasonably quickly. And we got more information out of that meeting as a result of delaying their planning application than we had done over eighteen months of somewhat patient and tedious negotiation.

VI

The field officer's perception of polluters as rational and responsive to deterrence by abating their pollution if sufficient threat is made, opens up a variety of other tactical opportunities to secure compliance. A significant part of the control exercised by field staff in general is derived from the polluters' lack of knowledge of legal provisions and procedures, the policies and practices of the authority (particularly the reluctance to use legal authority), and also their ignorance of field staff's status as enforcement agents possessing power to initiate prosecution. This lack of knowlege offers rich scope for the use of various forms of bluff.

"A helluva lot of bluff is used," said one urban field man. 'You use what tools you've got to exert what pressure you can. And if it's a bluff it's fine, so long as they don't call your bluff." Bluffing is a tactic employed in other forms of enforcement. Discussing the use of court proceedings in debt collection, for instance, it has been observed that:

> A creditor who refuses to employ these modes of enforcement may still try to exploit them. [He] will threaten the debtor with a sanction he has no intention of using [Rock, 1973: 66; see also Ross and Thomas, 1981].

In pollution control work, where uncooperative or potentially uncooperative polluters are concerned, field officers may threaten the use of procedures or sanctions they do not intend to employ, or, more interestingly, that are not theirs—legally—to use. That they can pull this off is a reflection of how little this branch of the law intrudes into the daily life of organizations and their members. Lawyers are not normally involved in negotiations with the water authority (in more than two years fieldwork I encountered only one case in which a lawyer attended a meeting with agency staff). Even in large companies that do employ lawyers, contact between enforcement agent and pollution control staff is normally at a point lower and relatively distant in the organizational hierarchy. Furthermore, enforcement staff trade on the disinclination of dischargers to explore the rules and procedures of the law. From the field officer's point of view, then, people know little about the law.[24] "They're not quite certain," said one, "what you can or cannot do to them." Recognizing that this gives scope for the use of bluff, he concluded: "I suppose it's in our interests not to let on to people what the law is; rather, you tell them about the law and its penalties when it suits you." A supervising officer, with due regard for delicacy, suggested that the result was that "we tend to have more impact than there is legislative backing for."

Bluffs tend to be concerned with legal sanctions or procedures, that is, with the penalties available or the risk of prosecution. In using the bluff, the field officer's general intention is to create the impression in the dischargers' eyes that they are in more trouble than they might actually be, or that they are dealing with a person of greater knowledge or power than is the case in fact. In trying to generate an impression of the awfulness of the criminal sanction, or the opprobrium following a court appearance, field officers do not necessarily believe that a criminal prosecution will produce such unhappy consequences for the polluter. It is enough that the criminal sanction is insufficiently used for there to be considerable unfamiliarity among company staff about the nature of the formal process and the implications of prosecution. This allows the possibility of a socially manufactured form of deterrence. In this way, the legislative sanction, and such deterrent force as it possesses, are socially mediated. Sometimes no more than a mention is called for to get the message across, but sometimes the tactic will be used quite blatantly where the context is right. Often a field officer only need hint about the unfortunate publicity that may follow a company's prosecution. In employing this tactic the officer is presenting a company's public reputation as at stake and is trading on the desire of most commercial organizations for an unsullied public image.

Sometimes field officers may find they are asked about legal penalties. To preserve the bluff where the penalties are low, many will evade giving a direct answer. This can be plausibly done: the penalty is determined by the court, and its decision can not be predicted; the penalty depends on the gravity or frequency of the violation; the court may ultimately impose a sentence of imprisonment, or the factory can be closed down. These latter two statements are pure bluffs because none of the field staff involved in the research could recall an instance in which such sanctions had actually been employed. But if the setting is appropriate, the bluff will be used:

> Returning to the scene of potentially serious oil pollution at a major car manufacturing plant the following morning, we were plied with tea in the company's pollution control office. Everyone seemed relieved that the problem had been solved. Griffith (the field officer) became a little impatient and began dropping hints that he needed to see for himself, just, as he explained later, to keep them on their toes. Back on the shop floor the cutting oil was being sucked out of the drains: "They've taken 160 gallons out of there so far," said Griffith. Lock, the company's own pollution control

officer, and Griffith both agreed that it would be useful to see the engineer responsible for that part of the shop floor in the hope of preventing a recurrence.

In an office nearby Lock told the engineer what had been happening, adding with great emphasis that it mustn't happen again. "This is red hot," he said, dramatically. The engineer looked at Griffith. "What's the fine? A thousand pounds?" Griffith did not give a direct answer but told the engineer instead that the company could be prosecuted and punished for every sample he took: "You can be prosecuted just as fast as I fill bottles." Lock, perhaps thinking that this might be insufficiently persuasive, then asked Griffith: "You can shut us down as well, Kevin, can't you?" "Yes, I can go to the court," said Griffith, "get an injunction, then they'll stick a bung in your discharge and I can shut you down with that."

Having left the factory Griffith explained his tactics. He agreed that he had deliberately given the engineer a misleading impression of the severity of the penalties, adding "I need to foster this belief"; he had done so because the formal penalties were so low. To let the polluter know what the fines were might encourage him to pollute with virtual impunity "I wouldn't go out of my way to disillusion anyone who thought the fines were higher," he said later, "because it is more of a deterrent. If a polluter *thinks* the fine is a thousand pounds, then you let him believe it." This was even truer, according to Griffith, when shop floor workers, as in this case, were paid piece-rate, since with their earnings at stake they would have no incentive to spend the time in taking preventive measures, or to clear up after a pollution [his emphasis].

Some field staff regard bluffing about penalty to be an integral part of enforcement practice in a regulatory agency whose legal sanction is considered to be totally inadequate to compel the respect of polluters. In a job where the practical concern for compliance is accorded such a central position, it is regarded as a natural response to circumvent the problem of an impotent law by portraying it, however subtly, as armed with a much more fearsome penalty. In fact in some cases where the penalties are not low, a direct answer about sanctions will be given. Here law is employed as a resource to support discretionary behavior. One field man who works on a large navigable river is, for example, prepared to tell dischargers suspected of having caused an oil pollution that the penalty on conviction is a fine of £ 50,000. What he does not say is that this fine must be imposed under the Oil in Navigable Waters Act, a piece of legislation which he and his colleagues do not enforce. If, on the other hand, oil is not involved, the officer will not specify the maximum (at the time of fieldwork £ 200, though under legislation not yet in force it had been raise to £ 400). "What do you think he'd say to me," the field man asked, "if I said [the maximum was] £ 400 where it's costing him eighty quid a load to tanker it away?" Because the penalty is perceived by the officer to be inadequate and his expectations of the polluter are that he, too, would find it very low, if asked directly what the maximum penalty is, it is imperative, as one put it, to "Hedge; at all costs."

Yet another form of bluff may address the individualized standards polluters must observe:

> A dyeworks was one of the more troublesome dischargers in Mullins' patch. There had been discussion in the past between the agency and the dyeworks about the introduction of a limit in the consent on the amount of coloring matter which the works could discharge. A color parameter had not, in fact, been added to the consent form. But the dyeworks staff were under the impression that a color standard which they were already required to observe had been incorporated in the consent. Mullins did not disabuse the staff of this—and had no intention of doing so—and generally behaved as if a color standard had actually been imposed.

In this case, the officer was able to represent the color problem as a difficulty that had to be dealt with. This tactic enhanced his control in general, first because more diligent attention to treatment has a broad beneficial impact on the effluent since attention to the improvement of one effluent parameter often results in the improvement of others as a natural consequence. Second, and more important, use of the tactic helped cast the dischargers into a defensive position: they were causing a problem, and were therefore obligated to the officer, in return for his forbearance, to do something about remedying it. With a nice regard for the distinction, the officer described his tactic as "I don't tell lies, but I do select the truth."

Bluffing tactics further support the field officers' view of the elaborate process of enforcing regulation by compliance strategy as a game to be played out with the polluter. "The whole thing's a series of bluffs," said one officer. "The problem arises," he continued, preoccupied with the question of enforcement credibility, "when you run out of bluffs." The impression of enforcement as a game to be played is derived also from officers' belief that polluters are often prepared to engage in bluffs of their own. This is in keeping with the prevailing view of dischargers, however compliant, as willing to try to pull a fast one. Field officers, inculcated as they and other enforcement agents are with a marked sense of suspiciousness, routinely expect polluters to seek to bluff them about their poverty, their willingness to comply, the efforts they have made to meet the field officer's demands, and so on. This raises the question (beyond the scope of this article) of enforcement agents' interpretative work: of how the officers "know" a bluff is being used, and how they treat some accounts as "plausible" or "reasonable" and others as disreputable of "trying to get away with it." It is upon such judgments that their future relationships with the polluter and their future enforcement activity will be premised.

VII

Enforcement in pollution control work is a social process, founded on reciprocity, which is serial in character: a patterned sequence of demands is placed upon the rule-breaker in return for forbearance. The strategy is normally incremental. Pressure is gradually exerted in the face of reluctance to comply, lack of cooperation, or outright intransigence with the threat or application of increasingly unpleasant consequences (see Rock, 1968, 1973). Field staff in effect work toward a sanctioning system.

Prosecution is the culmination of all this, a sanction occasionally threatened but actually employed only in extremis.[25] The structured career of enforcement may in one case be a compressed pattern, in another a protracted bout of negotiations spanning months or years. Law enforcement in a compliance system is adaptive: the continuing personal relationship between enforcement agent and the regulated offers a range of tactical options to be adjusted as circumstances demand. Control here is flexible and made possible by time and privacy. This is a far cry from the once-and-for-all decision of the policeman about the arrest of a person who has broken a rule in the sacred traditional code. So far as the regulatory rule-breaker is concerned a continuing relationship with an enforcement agent provides substantial opportunity to make efforts to comply: even scant display of attempts at remedy may be enough to win more time where states of affairs are concerned. Such a show is symbolically significant for the enforcement agent and tends morally to foreclose the possibility of sanctioning the deviants on the grounds of their noncompliance or uncooperativeness. In all of this, enforcement agents exploit for their own purposes the discrepancy between full enforcement and actual practice, the gap between legal word and legal deed.

A sanctioning strategy, on the other hand, is appropriate only when the officer is confronted by behavior possessing moral features aligning it with forms of traditional criminal conduct. Industrialists do sometimes empty their acid baths at three on a Sunday morning to avoid the cost of having the waste taken away in tankers for disposal; farmers do sometimes have escapes of oil from tanks which they have deliberately left unbunded, contrary to the urgings of the water authority; and some polluters do strike uncooperative or hostile postures when faced with requests from field staff to effect some remedial measure. But these are uncommon events. For the most part practical pollution control work is conciliatory control expressed in a display of tolerance and patience in a job whose supreme practical arts are common sense and being reasonable. After all, for the field officer the alternatives to bargaining about compliance have little appeal since they impose economic and human burdens that are morally intolerable.

In a well-known paper published nearly twenty years ago, Kadish argued that in the enforcement of economic regulation the criminal sanction "has not proved a major weapon for achieving compliance" (1963: 435). On the evidence of this research at least, this assertion cannot be supported. Indeed, the widespread reliance on bargaining, threatening, and bluffing to achieve compliance (itself a highly adaptable notion) produces results precisely because these techniques are practiced against a backdrop of the formal processes of the criminal sanction. The picture of the regulatory agency which can be pieced together from the scraps of data presented in this article is by no means one of an institution emasculated by an unused and impotent criminal sanction.

All of this suggests that it is possible to regard law enforcement in a wider sense than that in which it is usually understood: the simple recourse to the formal machinery of prosecution and the courts. In pollution control work (and, one suspects from reading between the lines of the available literature, in other areas of regulatory control as well), the reality of the law is negotiated. It is not presented or appreciated in clear, unambiguous, unproblematic terms (and indeed it is not in Britain even drafted that way). Instead the law is displayed as a vague, threatening entity of surpassing authority. In their various transformations the legal rules confer on field staff an authority that, for practical purposes, is in most cases ultimately persuasive. If enforcement is understood in this wider sense, as a matter of compliance as well as compulsion, we may wish to reexamine some of the familiar accusations about the failure or the ineffectiveness of regulation.

NOTES

1. There is, of course, a substantial political science literature dating back to prewar years, but this does not address the routine processes of regulatory control. Aspects of this

issue are dealt with to greater or lesser extent by Blau (1963), Carson (1970a, 1970b), Cranston (1979), Kagan (1978, 1980), Kelman (1981), Law Commission (1969), Mileski (1971), Ross and Thomas (1981), Schuck (1972), Silbey (1978), Stjernquist (1973), and the writers in Hawkins and Thomas (forthcoming).

2. Hawkins (forthcoming). This book should be consulted for information about the scope and methods of the research from which this article is derived and an account of the formal organization of pollution control. There will also be a companion volume from the pollution research project conducted at the Oxford Centre for Socio-Legal Studies that examines the control of trade effluent (Richardson et al., forthcoming).

3. Reiss and Biderman (1980), in a valuable study recently published, have conducted a similar analysis of compliance and penalty systems (see also Reiss, 1980). The first work to explore the distinction, so far as I know, was Mileski (1971). These contrasts are aligned with Black's concept of enforcement styles (Black 1976). One such style is conciliatory control, by which he means "remedial styles, methods of social repair and maintenance, assistance for people in trouble." Penal control, on the other hand, "prohibits certain conduct, and it enforces its prohibitions with punishment." Its stance is accusatory and enforcement here has a once-and-for-all character: "punishment or nothing" (Black, 1976: 4).

4. The data are drawn from the larger study (Hawkins, forthcoming) and were generated by extensive participant observation of the work of pollution control staff in areas of two English water authorities over a period of more than two years. These data were supplemented by lengthy interviews of both field and headquarters staff recorded on tape, and study of agency documents. The areas in which field work was conducted were deliberately selected to embrace as wide a range of control activities as possible. Some areas were predominantly rural, where the major pollution control problems tended to be connected with the preservation of existing high standards of cleanliness for potable supply or amenity value, and handling agricultural pollution (some forms of which can be extremely noxious). Other areas, in contrast, were heavily industrialized or extensively built-up. Here pollution control work was a matter of slowly trying to improve the quality of badly polluted watercourses. Many have been used for decades as dumping grounds for a variety of toxic wastes, or as carriers of poorly treated domestic or industrial effluents and urban run-off. Some urban rivers contain water that is of worse quality than the treated effluents from many sewage works on potable supply rivers.

5. See the references in note 1. Robert Kagan has, however, argued that in the United States there has been some shift away from a conciliatory approach (Kagan, 1980). This shift may prove to be short-lived with the advent of the Reagan administration (see Washington Post, 1981). The use of a strategy of compliance has provoked complaints that regulations are "poorly enforced" and legislation is "inadequate" (Gunningham, 1974: 56). Doubtless it is also responsible for the various criticisms by political scientists that regulatory agencies are fundamentally ineffective (e.g. Bernstein, 1955; Edelman, 1964).

6. Kadish (1963) uses the term "morally neutral"; in this context the term is inappropriate, however, since rule-breaking always appears to be evaluated morally.

7. The reference to the low level of legal sanction is made with the British position in mind. Many American regulatory agencies are armed with legal sanctions that are fearsome in comparison (see Clinard et al., 1979). However, the unwillingness to prosecute seems to be typical of regulatory systems in both the United Kingdom and the United States (but see Kagan, 1980). The circumstances in which prosecution is deemed necessary

is an interesting question, unfortunately beyond the scope of this article (see Hawkins, forthcoming).

8. By which I mean those crimes that "self-evidently warrant state intervention" (Matza, 1964: 161).

9. The law actually says that an offense is committed if a person "causes or knowingly permits to enter any stream any poisonous, noxious or polluting matter" (Rivers [Prevention of Pollution] Act, 1951: s. 2). While the phrase "knowingly permits" admits of a mental element, it is my impression that such prosecutions as are mounted under this section are for "causing" pollution, which, the House of Lords has held, is to be strictly interpreted (Alphacell v. Woodward, 1972).

10. The consent is the negotiable formal licensed to pollute up to certain specified limits on defined parameters granted by the water authority to any discharger to a watercourse. It is, in other words, an administratively fixed boundary marking out the formal limits of deviance and compliance (see further Hawkins, forthcoming).

11. I use the concepts of proactive and reactive enforcement in the tradition of Reiss and Black: Black (1973, 1980), Black and Reiss (1967), Reiss (1971), Reiss and Bordua (1967).

12. What constitutes a "substantial" breach or a "noticeable" pollution are, of course, problematic matters open to individual and organizational interpretation (Hawkins, forthcoming).

13. The epitome of the discharger with an ideal attitude toward pollution control was said to be one well-known company that gives its employees a course on pollution control and its significance, and a precise job to do if a spillage should occur in the factory.

14. Legislation subsequently raised the penalty to £400, and then £1000 on summary conviction.

15. The processes of incremental enforcement are analyzed in most detail in Rock (1973).

16. The formal sample is the solemn collection of incriminating evidence, a ritual that is treated as a prerequisite for the initiation of a prosecution.

17. A "stat" is agency argot for the formal (statutory) sample (variously referred to as the "legal," "tripartite," "prosecution," "sealed," or "official" sample). Taken according to strictly defined procedures that allow it to be admissible in court should the agency wish to mount a prosecution, the stat is particularly important for its use as a coercive tactic in its own right (hence the field officer's remark).

18. A bund wall is built around tanks containing polluting liquids to retain their contents should there be a leakage.

19. This is clearly akin to the "three strikes and you're out" rule in juvenile justice: see Emerson (1969).

20. A practice also observed in housing code enforcement (Mileski, 1971) and debt collection (Rock, 1973).

21. Such graduated enforcement may also help to soften the appearance of field officers' demands. Since compliance is often a lengthy and costly process, officers can spin out the time allowed for compliance, and present their demands in stages (see Kaufman, 1960: 225).

22. For an example of the consequence of disrupting this equilibrium, see Schuck (1972).

23. The use of hints or threats to withhold benefits, however, is a topic treated with some sensitivity by field staff: some denied using the tactic on the grounds that it is

improper, as a supervising officer put it, "to use one set of legislation to implement another." The unease some field staff feel in discussing such tactics for securing compliance is suggested in the justifications about bluffing ("everybody has to bluff"), which are sometimes put forward in quite elaborate form, as the following conversation suggests:

> *F.O.:* The truth is we couldn't in any way try and withhold planning permission for a responsible development on the basis of the fact that the effluent discharged by the firm was unsatisfactory. But that doesn't stop me hinting that it might be so [laughs quietly].
>
> *K.H.:* What you are saying is in fact you can't do it, but you can use the bluff again? You can give the impression that you—
>
> *F.O.:* Oh yeah. I am quite prepared to do that. . . . I work on the assumption that what I am doing is basically decent, and right, and to get it done quicker I am prepared to bluff a little bit. We all do that, every day. Everybody has to bluff, and I'm sure that they bluff with me as well when they come the, you know, the "you are going to close us down" bit. I am sure that most of them are bluffing—not that it is said to us too often—but there are bluffs on those kinds of lines.

24. This assumption is supported in a small study of dischargers undertaken by Brittan (forthcoming).

25. In one of the two water authorities studied, for example, there were 21 and 8 prosecutions in recent consecutive years. (This authority, incidentally, prides itself on its toughness.) The number of prosecutions amounted to less than 1% of the pollution incidents formally recorded as brought to agency attention. Officers handle many more cases in the field without reporting them and registering them as pollution incidents (see Hawkins, forthcoming: ch. 5).

REFERENCES

ALPHACELL v. WOODWARD (1972) A.C. 824

BANTON, M. (1964) The Policeman in the Community. London: Tavistock.

BERNSTEIN, M. H. (1955) Regulating Business by Independent Commission. Princeton, NJ: Princeton Univ. Press.

BITTNER, E. (1967) "The police on skid-row." Amer. Soc. Rev. 32: 699.

BLACK, D. J. (1980) The Manners and Customs of the Police. New York: Academic Press.

——— (1976) The Behavior of Law. New York: Academic Press.

——— (1973) "The mobilization of law." J. of Legal Studies 2: 125.

——— and A. J. REISS, Jr. (1967) "Patterns of behavior in police and citizen transactions," pp. 1-139 in Studies of Crime and Law Enforcement in Major Metropolitan Areas, Vol. II. U.S. President's Commission on Law Enforcement and Administration of Justice. Washington, DC: Government Printing Office.

BLAU, P. M. (1963) The Dynamics of Bureaucracy: A Study of Interpersonal Relationships in Two Government Agencies. Chicago: Univ. of Chicago Press.

BORDUA, D. J. [ed.] (1967) The Police: Six Sociological Essays. New York: John Wiley.

BRITTAN, Y. (forthcoming) The Impact of Water Pollution Control on Industry: A Case Study of Fifty Dischargers. Oxford: Centre for Socio-Legal Studies.

CARSON, W. G. (1970a) "Some sociological aspects of strict liability and the enforcement of factory legislation." Modern Law Rev. 33: 396.

——— (1970b) "White-collar crime and the enforcement of factory legislation." British J. of Criminology. 10: 383.

CLINARD, M., P. C. YEAGER, J. BRISSETTE, D. PETRASHEK, and E. HARRIES (1979) Illegal Corporate Behavior. Washington, DC: National Institute of Law Enforcement and Criminal Justice.

CRANSTON, R. (1979) Regulating Business: Law and Consumer Agencies. London: Macmillan.

DOUGLAS, J. D. [ed.] (1970) Deviance and Respectability. The Social Construction of Moral Meanings. New York: Basic Books.

EDELMAN, M. (1964) The Symbolic Uses of Politics. Urbana: Univ. of Illinois Press.

EMERSON, R. (1969) Judging Delinquents. Context and Process in Juvenile Court. Chicago: Aldine.

GUNNINGHAM, N. (1974) Pollution, Social Interest and the Law. London: Martin Robertson.

HAWKINS, K. (forthcoming) Environment and Enforcement: The Social Construction of Pollution. Oxford: Oxford Univ. Press.

——— and J. M. THOMAS [ed.] (forthcoming) Enforcing Regulation: Policy and Practice. Boston: Kluwer-Nijhoff.

HUCKE, J. (1978) "Bargaining in regulative policy implementation: the case of environmental policy in the Federal Republic of Germany." Prepared for Workship on Inter-Organizational Networks in Public Policy Implementation, European Consortium for Political Research, Grenoble, April.

KADISH, S. H. (1963) "Some observations on the use of criminal sanctions in enforcing economic regulations." Univ. of Chicago Law Rev. 30: 423.

KAGAN R. A. (1980) "The positive uses of discretion: the good inspector." Presented to the annual meeting of the U.S. Law and Society Association, Madison, Wisconsin, June.

——— (1978) Regulatory Justice: Implementing a Wage-Price Freeze. New York: Russell Sage.

——— and J. T. SCHOLZ (forthcoming) "The 'criminology of the corporation' and regulatory enforcement strategies," in K. Hawkins and J. M. Thomas (eds.) Enforcing Regulation: Policy and Practice. Boston: Kluwer-Nijhoff.

KAUFMAN, H. (1960) The Forest Ranger. A Study of Administrative Behavior. Baltimore, MD: Johns Hopkins Univ. Press.

KELMAN, S. (1981) Regulating America, Regulating Sweden: A Comparative Study of Occupational Safety and Health Policy. Cambridge, MA: MIT Press.

Law Commission (1969) Strict Liability and the Enforcement of the Factories Act 1961. Working Paper 30.

MACAULAY, S. (1963) "Non-contractual relations in business: a preliminary study." Amer. Soc. Rev. 28:55.

MATZA, D. (1964) Delinquency and Drift. New York: John Wiley.

McHUGH, P. (1970) "A common-sense conception of deviance," in J.D. Douglas (ed.) Deviance and Respectability: The Social Construction of Moral Meanings. New York: Basic Books.

MILESKI, M. (1971) "Policing slum landlords: an observation study of administrative control." Ph.D. dissertation. Yale University.

REISS, A. J., Jr. (1980) "The policing of organizational life." Presented for International Seminar on Management and Control of Police Organization, Nijenrode, Netherlands, December.

——— (1971) The Police and the Public. New Haven: Yale Univ. Press.

——— and D. BORDUA (1967) "Environment and organization: a perspective on the police" in D. J. Bordua (ed.) The Police: Six Sociological Essays. New York: John Wiley.

REISS, A. J., Jr. and A. D. BIDERMAN (1980) Data Sources on White-Collar Law-Breaking. Washington, DC: National Institute of Justice.

RICHARDSON, G., A. I. OGUS, and P. BURROWS (forthcoming) Policing Pollution: A Study of Regulation and Enforcement. Oxford: Oxford Univ. Press.

ROCK, P. (1973) Making People Pay. London: Routledge & Kegan Paul.

——— (1968) "Observations on debt collection." British J. of Sociology 19: 176.

ROSS, H. L. and J. M. THOMAS (1981) "Blue-collar bureaucrats and the law in action: housing code regulation in three cities." Presented for Association for Public Policy and Management, Washington, DC, October.

SCHUCK, P. (1972) "The curious case of the indicted meat inspectors." Harper's Magazine (September): 81.

SILBEY, S. (1978) "Consumer justice: the Massachusetts attorney general's office of consumer protection 1970-1974." Ph.D. dissertation, University of Chicago.

STJERNQUIST, P. (1973) Laws in the Forests: A Study of Public Direction of Swedish Private Forestry. Lund: C.W.K. Gleerup.

Washington Post (1981) "U.S. relaxing enforcement of regulations." November 15.

WILSON, J. Q. (1968) Varieties of Police Behavior: The Management of Law and Order in Eight Communities. Cambridge, MA: Harvard Univ. Press.

KEITH HAWKINS is a Senior Research Fellow at the SSRC Centre for Sociolegal Studies, Wolfson College, Oxford, England. He holds an LL.B. (Birmingham), Ph.D. (Oxford), and a diploma in Criminology (Cambridge). He has done extensive research and writing on penal law, criminology, the sociology of deviance, and the sociology of law.

[17]

JUDICIAL REVIEW OF ADMINISTRATIVE GUIDANCE: GOVERNMENTALLY ENCOURAGED CONSENSUAL DISPUTE RESOLUTION IN JAPAN

*Michael K. Young**

For centuries the shadow of the warrior turned bureaucrat has fallen long across Japan. With an awe bordering on reverence, American commentators have highlighted the role of these administrators in Japan's economic miracle.[1] Commentators have noted with equal frequency Japan's pervasive use of a regulatory technique known as administrative guidance (gyōsei shidō).[2] Stated simply, administrative guidance occurs when administrators take action of no coercive legal effect that encourages regulated parties to act in a specific way in order to realize some administrative aim.[3] This regulatory technique, with its apparent flexibility and attendant possibilities for unchecked administrative action, allegedly endows Japanese administrators with their unique ability to order and regulate economic and other aspects of Japanese life.

As this Article will show, however, a more careful examination of administrative guidance reveals a very different picture. Administrative guidance does have considerable attraction to administrators. It permits significant extension of their regulatory mandate and far ranging incursions into the affairs of regulated parties. But administrative guidance also suffers from the vices of its own virtues. The attributes that permit an agency to intervene in a variety of areas also strictly limit the form that intervention can take and circumscribe the degree to which the agency may actually intrude and attempt

---

* Associate Professor of Law, Director, Center for Japanese Legal Studies, School of Law, Columbia University. B.A. 1973, Brigham Young University; J.D. 1976, Harvard Law School. I am indebted to many American and Japanese colleagues for useful comments and helpful suggestions. Particularly generous with their time and thoughts were Bruce Ackerman, Peter Strauss, Cole Durham, Frank Upham, and Hiromi Naya.

1. See, e.g., C. Johnson, MITI and the Japanese Miracle 17-21 (1982); I. Magaziner & T. Hout, Japanese Industrial Policy 32 (1980); U.S. Int'l Trade Comm'n, Foreign Industrial Targeting and Its Effects on U.S. Industries—Phase I: Japan (1983). But cf. P. Trezise, Industrial Policy in Japan, *in* Industry Vitalization: Toward a National Industrial Policy 177 (1982) (government role in Japan similar to U.S.—little contribution to economic development); J. Wheeler, M. Janow & T. Pepper, Japanese Industrial Development Policies in the 1980's: Implications for U.S. Trade and Investment 1-13 (Oct., 1982) (Japanese industrial policies are not "undifferentiated, monolithic, or all-powerful device to enable Japan to pass or otherwise 'defeat' the U.S. and other advanced industrial countries.").

2. See, e.g., P. Davis, Administrative Guidance in Japan (Sophia U. Socio-Economic Inst. Bull. No. 41 1972); E. Kaplan, Japan: The Government-Business Relationship: A Guide for the American Businessman 30-32 (1972); Smith, Prices and Petroleum in Japan: 1973-1974—A Study of Administrative Guidance, 10 Law in Japan 81 (1977).

3. For a more complete definition and examples of administrative guidance, see infra notes 8-49 and accompanying text.

to order affairs. These limitations, moreover, give the parties a significant, indeed often dispositive, role in the regulatory process and make the frequent use of administrative guidance tolerable and often even welcome.

Judicial review of agency action taken through administrative guidance presents an equally complex picture. Because Japanese courts share the bureaucracy's sense of the need for flexibility in fulfilling important administrative tasks, they are understandably reluctant to scrutinize administrative guidance too carefully or to intrude too quickly to overturn administrative action. This impulse, however, does not motivate courts to abandon their historically mandated protective role. Indeed, careful review of the cases reveals a concerted effort to provide some oversight and protection against excessive administrative intrusion into private affairs. Again the matter is more subtle than casual descriptions suggest.

This Article examines both the fundamental nature of administrative guidance as a regulatory technique and the patterns of judicial review that have developed in response to its extensive use. Study of administrative guidance provides insight into the way Japanese administrative organs attempt to accomplish the variety of important tasks that fall to the bureaucracy in an industrialized, quasi-capitalist economy. Examining the judicial response to administrative guidance illuminates how Japanese courts provide protection against the bureaucracy without excessively limiting the scope of administrative activity. Of course the difficulty of striking a proper balance bedevils all legal systems committed to the rule of law. The particularly important historical role of Japan's bureaucracy and its apparent success, however, make examination of Japan's experience especially useful for all countries that are gradually moving into a postindustrial economy, with the attendant demands it places on government. As American dissatisfaction with our courts and traditional patterns of adjudication increases, moreover, some examination of how other cultures resolve major societal disputes is instructive.

Japan, with its clearly observable interplay between formal legal rules and institutions, on the one hand, and pre-existing social, political and economic structures, on the other, presents a good case study. Japan's modern court system, major codes, and even its first modern constitution, created and enacted late in the nineteenth century as part of the Meiji Restoration, all found their models in continental courts, codes and practice, particularly those of Germany, Switzerland and France.[4] The postwar occupation of Japan brought a number of changes, involving both the constitution and the codes. Yet again the model was foreign, this time American.[5] At the same

---

4. For a discussion of general developments see Young, The Japanese Legal System: History and Structure, *in* 2 Doing Business in Japan §§ 3.01[4]-3.02[2] (Z. Kitagawa ed. 1984); see also Y. Noda, Introduction to Japanese Law 41-63 (1976) (introduction of civil law system); Takayanagi, A Century of Innovation: The Development of Japanese Law, 1868-1961, *in* Law in Japan 5 (A. von Mehren ed. 1963) (same).

5. See J. Tanaka, Gyōsei Hō (Administrative Law) 21-28, 352-93 (1979); Tanakadate & Sonobe, Administrative Law in General, *in* 6 Doing Business in Japan, supra note 4, §§ 1.01, 1.02.

time, Japan possessed sophisticated indigenous legal institutions and traditions, as well as a historical, cultural and philosophical tradition that differed considerably from that of the countries in which the modeled legal institutions originated. This imposition or transplantation of foreign legal institutions and doctrines creates an interesting laboratory for examining the effects of law on society and, conversely, the effects of social norms, standards of behavior and traditions on the development and function of legal institutions.

The imposition of foreign institutions may, however, obscure indigenous legal attitudes and practices. Judges may become bound by a rigid conceptualism, slavishly attempting to recreate foreign legal developments with little attention to cultural, economic, social or even political differences between Japan and the country in which the law or legal institutions originated. Japanese administrative law has been strongly influenced by German law and, after the war, by American practices and procedures. The danger exists that when reviewing administrative action, Japanese judges may attempt simply to replicate the foreign result.

Yet challenges to administrative guidance find no easy analogue in modern German or American administrative law, given the nonbinding effect of this administrative technique. Moreover, whether accurate or not, the Japanese perceive administrative guidance as unique to Japan.[6] The lack of foreign models and the perception of administrative guidance as somehow capturing the Japanese attitude toward the proper role of government creates an environment in which judges can be more explicitly sensitive to the social, political, economic, cultural and legal context of the dispute at hand. These factors in turn allow Japanese judges to depart more easily from the rigid conceptualism that sometimes binds them and to give play to more indigenous attitudes towards adjudication, dispute resolution and the preferred role of the bureaucracy and judiciary in society. The cases in this area bear out the accuracy of this observation—judges struggling with the tensions and dilemmas created by a form of administrative action that is not easily accommodated within the traditional paradigms of administrative law, and fashioning innovative solutions that are sensitive to the needs of the individuals before the court and the society that the bureaucrats must serve.

---

6. Japanese commentators have stressed the distinctly Japanese nature of administrative guidance. See, e.g., Gyōsei Shidō Kenkyūkai, Gyōsei Shidō ni Kansuru Chōsa Hōkokusho (Report of a Study of Administrative Guidance), pt. 2, chs. 11-12 (1981); Narita, Gyōsei Shidō no Kinō to Kōzai (The Merits and Demerits of Administrative Guidance), 741 Jurisuto 36, 36-40, 42-44 (1981). While informal administrative action has not received the same attention in other countries, its practice is not unknown. Examples in the United States include informal wage and price controls that date back as far as President Kennedy's 1962 Economic Report. See G. Shultz & R. Aliber, Guidelines, Informal Controls, and the Market Place 2-4 (1966); see also Council on Wage and Price Stability Act, 12 U.S.C. § 1904 (1982) (creating the Council on Wage and Price Stability); White Paper: The President's Anti-Inflation Program, 14 Weekly Comp. Pres. Doc. 1845 (Oct. 24, 1978) (same). Indeed, though the amount of informal activity varies considerably from country to country, it makes up a large part of the administrative activity in all modern, industrialized countries. See R. Brickman, S. Jasanoff & T. Ilgen, Chemical Regulation and Cancer: A Cross National Study of Policy and Politics iv-vii, 84-89 (1982).

In examining the Japanese approach to the complex tasks that industrialized society imposes on the administrative state, this Article first describes the nature of administrative guidance, including liberation from legal restrictions, flexibility, recourse to collateral means of enforcement and input from regulated parties, as features that ensure bureaucrats' frequent recourse to, and parties' acceptance of this administrative device. Yet despite the appeal of administrative guidance to both administrators and regulated parties, disputes inevitably arise; Part II describes the form they generally take.

In a narrow class of cases, regulated parties seek judicial review of administrative guidance. Part III traces the judicial response to such challenges, from an initial refusal to entertain them through a series of cases that begin to elucidate a theory of judicial review. The Article concludes that the doctrine Japanese courts have developed adequately responds to the tension between safeguarding agency flexibility and protecting against overzealous administrative intrusion into private affairs, at least in the Japanese context. Finally, the Article suggests in Part IV that given the similarity of problems confronting modern industrialized societies, some understanding of Japan may illuminate some of the tensions and conflicts arising in the American regulatory context. In the best of all possible worlds, Japan may even contain a few modest lessons for its western teachers.[7]

I. The Principal Bureaucratic Behavior in Japan: Administrative Guidance

A. *Characteristics of Administrative Guidance*

Administrative guidance (gyōsei shidō) is a common Japanese regulatory technique that, although generally nonbinding, seeks to conform the behavior of regulated parties to broad administrative goals.[8] Two examples of administrative guidance clarify its scope. The first of these developed during late 1980 and early 1981, when the dispute between Japan and the United States over the

7. This Article contains occasional comparisons to other civil law jurisdictions and to the United States. Further comparisons undoubtedly will suggest themselves to the reader. The principal design of this Article, however, is not to limit readers' thinking by excessive comparative diversions. Instead, this Article seeks to present a considered framework for understanding the Japanese regulatory and judicial experience in context.

8. For introductory literature on administrative guidance in English, see, e.g., P. Davis, supra note 2; E. Kaplan, supra note 2; Narita, Administrative Guidance, 2 Law in Japan 44 (1968); Shiono, Administrative Guidance, *in* Tokyo Roundtable Organizing Comm., Int'l Inst. of Admin. Sciences, Public Administration in Japan 221 (1982); Smith, supra note 2; Yamanouchi, Administrative Guidance and the Rule of Law, 7 Law in Japan 22 (1974). Useful Japanese literature includes Hayashi, Iwayuru Gyōsei Shidō ni tsuite (On So-called Administrative Guidance), 4 Gyōsei to Kei'ei 17 (1962); Horie, Gyōsei Shidō (Administrative Guidance), 663 Shōji Hōmu 44 (1974); Narita, supra note 6; Suzuki, Gyōsei Shidō wo Meguru Hanrei no Dōkō (Trends of Decisions Dealing with Administrative Guidance), 741 Jurisuto 45 (1981); Tamura, Gyōsei Shidō no Igi to Yakuwari (The Meaning and Role of Administrative Guidance), 65 Toshi Mondai 15 (1974); Tanaka, Gyōsei Shidō to Hō no Shihai (Administrative Guidance and the Rule of Law), *in* 3 Gendai Shōhōgaku no Kadai: Suzuki Takeo Sensei Kōki Kinen Ronbunshū 1427 (K. Takeuchi

import of Japanese automobiles reached crisis proportions.[9] Threatened with the possibility of executive and legislative action restricting Japanese auto imports into the United States, the Japanese government agreed, in what is euphemistically known as an "Orderly Marketing Agreement," to restrict automobile imports "voluntarily" for a three-year period.[10] To implement this agreement, the principal ministry dealing with trade matters, the Ministry of International Trade and Industry (MITI), informed auto manufacturers that during each of the next three years they were to limit exports of passenger cars to the United States.[11] In its notification letter, the MITI found authority for this action in its enabling legislation[12] and in article 48 of the Foreign Exchange and Foreign Trade Control Law (FEFTCL).[13] To assure compliance, the MITI required each manufacturer to submit periodic reports on car exports. Falsification of such reports would be considered a violation of the reporting requirements under article 67 of the FEFTCL and would subject firms to liability for punishment under articles 72 and 73 of that same law.[14]

---

ed. 1975); Yamanouchi, Gyōsei Shidō to Hōchi Shugi (Administrative Guidance and Constitutionalism), 56 Jurisuto 14 (1974).

9. For a more complete treatment of this problem, see Auto Situation, 1980: Hearings Before the Subcomm. on Trade of the House Comm. on Ways and Means, 96th Cong., 2d Sess. (1980); id. at 99, 124–26 (statement of R.D. Hormats to the Subcommittee); Tate Special Report: Auto Industry Crisis, 38 Cong. Q. 1262–66 (1980); Ikema, Nichibei Jidōsha Masatsu (Japanese-American Automobile Trade Friction), Gendai Keizai, Summer 1980, at 35–49; Winham & Kabashima, The Politics of U.S.-Japanese Auto Trade, *in* Coping with U.S.-Japanese Economic Conflicts 73 (I. Destler & H. Sato eds. 1982).

10. See Winham & Kabashima, supra note 9, at 114–17.

11. See Letters from the MITI to Japanese auto manufacturers (May 7, 1981) (on file at the offices of the Columbia Law Review) [hereinafter cited as MITI letters]; see also Matsushita, Jidōsha Tsūshō Masatsu no Hōritsu Mondai (The Legal Problem of the Japanese-American Automobile Trade Friction), 914 Shōji Hōmu 171, 171–74 (1982) (discussion of content of Orderly Marketing Agreement and process of its implementation).

12. Tsūshō Sangyō Setchi Hō (Law Establishing [the Ministry of International] Trade and Industry), Law No. 275 of 1952, art. 3. The statute provides that the MITI shall be an administrative organ with the responsibility of effectuating in a unified manner the national administration of the following, including the adjustment and promotion of commerce and the administration of foreign exchange related to commerce, id. art. 3, ¶ 1, and the promotion of international cooperation in the trading economy, id. art. 3, ¶ 12.

13. MITI letters, supra note 11. The Foreign Exchange and Foreign Trade Control Law requires exporters to obtain MITI approval before exporting certain items when directed by a cabinet order to do so. Article 48 provides:

> A person who is to export goods of a certain type, or to a certain destination, or under a certain way of transaction or settlement might be obligated, as provided by Cabinet Order, to obtain approval from the Minister of International Trade and Industry.
>
> (2) No restrictions imposed by Cabinet Order under the provisions of the preceding paragraph shall exceed the limit necessary for the maintenance of equilibrium of balance of international payments, or for the sound development of international trade and national economy.

Gaikoku Kawase Oyobi Gaikoku Bōeki Kanri Hō (Foreign Exchange and Foreign Trade Control Law), Law No. 228 of 1949, art. 48 [hereinafter cited as FEFTCL], translated in Japan—Laws, Ordinances and Other Regulations Concerning Foreign Exchange and Foreign Trade (1984).

14. Article 72 reads in part:

> Any person who comes under any of the following items shall be liable to penal servitude

The MITI also indicated that if any company threatened to exceed its export allotment, the Government would amend the Export Trade Control Order[15] to subject car exports to the United States to export licensing, in accordance with article 48 of the FEFTCL. The MITI would then be able to seek sanctions against any noncomplying company under article 70 of the FEFTCL.[16]

Another interesting, important and, at least within Japan, well-known example of administrative guidance involves local governments' attempts at land use planning. During the postwar period, Japan experienced tremendous urban growth, much of it concentrated in the Tokyo metropolitan area, where almost one-quarter of Japan's population resides.[17] This rapid urban development seriously undermined the general living environment and placed tremendous strains on the ability of the government to provide adequate services.

While the national government undertook reasonably successful efforts to solve serious air pollution problems in Tokyo,[18] additional concerns surfaced in the late sixties that were not directly addressed at the national level. Two areas became the particular focus of residents' energies. First, concerned parents began to focus on the dislocations this rapid urban development caused in the schools. To a large degree, education is the key to an individual's future in Japan.[19] Even the slightest diminution in education opportunity

---

> not exceeding six (6) months, or a fine not exceeding two hundred thousand (200,000) yen: . . . (8) A person who submitted no report or a false report in contravention of an order provided by Article 67.

FEFTCL, supra note 13, art. 72, translated in Japan—Laws, Ordinances and Other Regulations Concerning Foreign Exchange and Foreign Trade (1984).

Article 73 reads in part:

> When a representative of a juridical person (including any organization defined by Article 26, Paragraph 1, Item (2) or (4) or Paragraph 5 thereof, which shall apply in this Paragraph), or an agent, employee, or other operator engaged by a juridical or natural person commits any offense mentioned in Article 70, Article 71, or the preceding Article in regard to the business or property of such a juridical or natural principal, the juridical or natural principal shall be liable for the fine specified in each Article, in addition to the punishment of the offender himself.

Id. art. 73.

15. Gaikoku Kawase Kanri Rei (Export Trade Control Order), Cabinet Order No. 379 of 1949.

16. Article 70 reads in pertinent part:

> Any person who comes under any of the following items shall be liable to penal servitude not exceeding three (3) years, or a fine not exceeding one million (1,000,000) yen or both. However, when three times the amount of the subject matter of contravention exceeds one million (1,000,000) yen, a fine up to three times that amount shall be applicable. . . .
> (29) A person who carries out any exportation of goods without obtaining approval as required by an Order provided by Article 48, Paragraph 1.

FEFTCL, supra note 13, art. 70, translated in Japan—Laws, Ordinances and Other Regulations Concerning Foreign Exchange and Foreign Trade (1984).

17. Japan's urban concentration is difficult to conceptualize. To find one-quarter of the population of the United States, one would have to visit the 10 largest cities; in the U.S.S.R., the 100 largest cities; and in China, over 1500 cities.

18. For a discussion of Japan's environmental successes and failures, see Environmental Law and Policy in the Pacific Basin Area (I. Kato, N. Kumamoto & W. Matthews eds. 1981); Environmental Policy in Japan (J. Gresser, A. Morishima & K. Fujikura eds. 1981).

19. See, e.g., H. Passin, Society and Education in Japan 117–48 (1982).

evokes great concern. The strain placed on the school systems during this period threatened the quality of educational opportunities and parents were quick to demand solutions.

Second, residents became increasingly concerned about the effect of highrise buildings on ventilation and sunlight.[20] This concern might strike Americans as odd, but Japan's climate, especially the high humidity of the Tokyo area, and the relatively late advent of air-conditioning and central heating, elevated sunlight and air above mere aesthetic interest. To enhance ventilation, walls are thin, windows and doors large, and many rooms are cross-ventilated. Few dwelling places are without a small patio used for ventilation, drying laundry, and growing plants. To the growing alarm of residents, the construction of apartment buildings, even if only three stories high, undermined ventilation and its significant benefits. Moreover, while Japanese courts have created a right to sunlight (Nisshōken), thereby affording some minimal protection against undue interference, effective injunctive relief is rarely available and damages are usually low.[21]

The national government addressed national standards for housing construction by adopting the Construction Standards Law.[22] The Law establishes a basic construction permit process, requiring builders to submit a complex set of plans and blueprints to the construction supervisor, an employee of the local municipal government.[23] The supervisor determines whether those plans conform to the requirements of the orders (meirei) and local ordinances (jōrei) based upon it.[24] Construction cannot lawfully proceed without a permit.[25]

---

20. For a general discussion of these and related concerns that gave rise to the administrative guidance discussed in this section, see K. Yamanouchi, Gyōsei Shidō (Administrative Guidance) 77-82 (1980); Goto, Musashino-shi Takuchi Kaihatsu Shidō Yōkō to Sono Ato no Seika (The Outline Guidance of the City of Musashino and its After-Effects), 529 Jurisuto 79 (1973); Ito, Yokohama-shi Nisshō tō Shidō Yōkō Seitei no Kei'i to Shushi (The Circumstances and Essence of the Establishment of 'Outline Guidance Regarding Sunlight, Etc., in the City of Yokohama'), 529 Jurisuto 82 (1973); Ito, Yokohama-shi no Nisshō Gyōsei—Yōkō Jisshi Igo (Sunlight Administration in the City of Yokohama—After Enforcement of the Outline), Tokushū Jurisuto—Nisshōken 155 (1974); Matsuda, Kanazawa-shi Nisshō Shidō Yōkō to Sono Genkyō (Sunlight Outline Guidance in the City of Kanazawa and Its Reality), Tokushū Jurisuto—Nisshōken 164 (1974); Matsuoka, Yōkō Gyōsei no Jittai—Kyoto-shi no Ba'ai (The Reality of Outline Administration—The Case of the City of Kyoto), Tokushū Jurisuto—Nisshōken 160 (1974); Tanabe, Tamachi-shi ni okeru 'Yōkō Shidō' no Jissai (The Reality of 'Outline Guidance' in the City of Tamachi), 529 Jurisuto 87 (1973).

21. See Ariizumi, Nisshōken wo Dono yō ni shite Mamoru Ka (How to Protect the Right to Sunlight), Tokushū Jurisuto—Nisshōken 14, 15-16 (1974); Matsuura, Nisshō Bōgai ni Motozuku Sashitome Seikyū (Requests for Injunctive Relief Based on Interference with Sunlight), Tokushū Jurisuto—Nisshōken 252 (1974); Shiomi, Nisshō Bōgai to Songai Baishō (Interference with Sunlight and Compensatory Damages), Tokushū Jurisuto—Nisshōken 237 (1974); Yamaguchi, Nisshōken ni Motozuku Kōji Sashitome (Injunctions Against Construction Based on the Right to Sunlight), Tokushū Jurisuto—Nisshōken 258 (1974).

22. Kenchiku Kijun Hō (Construction Standards Law), Law No. 201 of 1950.

23. Id. arts. 4-6.

24. Id. art. 6, §§ 2-4.

25. Id. art. 6, § 1.

Despite this regulatory mechanism, the law attempts only to guarantee health and safety and not to assure the availability of adequate educational facilities or of sunlight and ventilation. Nothing expressly authorizes the construction supervisor to deny a permit because a building might block sunlight from surrounding buildings or because the increase in population resulting from the occupancy of the new building would put a strain on schools.[26] Moreover, while the law allowed municipalities to establish additional building standards through local ordinances (jōrei),[27] no municipality enacted ordinances dealing with ventilation and local schools. Some commentators even doubted the legality of such ordinances,[28] as they would arguably exceed the scope of the law. Indeed, given the specificity of the law's provisions, these regulations might directly conflict with it, a preemption problem.[29] Moreover, while municipalities have a general mandate to enact local ordinances on matters within their jurisdictional ambit,[30] direct, legally binding solutions—such as the requirement that developers donate land and money for the construction

26. The Construction Standards Law was recently amended to explicitly give local authorities more extensive regulatory power over construction that impinges on the education, sunlight and ventilation concerns. See Chihō Kōfuzei Hō Tō no Ichibu wo Kaisei suru Hōritsu (Law Amending in part the Local Revenue Sharing Law, Etc.), Law No. 38 of 1978; Kenchiku Kijun Hō no Ichibu wo Kaisei Suru Hōritsu (Law Amending in part the Construction Standards Law), Law No. 83 of 1976.

27. See Kenchiku Kijun Hō (Construction Standards Law), Law No. 201 of 1950, arts. 3, 6–11; see also infra note 30 (discussing municipalities' authority to promulgate local ordinances).

28. See, e.g., K. Yamanouchi, supra note 20, at 74–76; Shiono, supra note 8, at 221–33.

29. For a decision discussing not only the problems of such preemption, but also the doctrinal and functional ramifications of this enhanced degree of judicial oversight in cases involving regulation of the use of one's property, see Yoshida v. Nakano Ward, 886 Hanrei Jihō 15 (Tokyo Dist. Ct. 1973). The case is discussed further infra text accompanying notes 141–51. For a discussion of the permissible scope of local regulation, especially in the face of comprehensive national treatment of the subject, see S. Kyomiya, 1 Kenpō (Constitution) 439–42 (1979); S. Tawara, Chihō Jichi Hō (Local Autonomy Law) 295–312 (1975).

30. This mandate resembles the notion of home rule possessed by some jurisdictions in the United States. See Vanlandingham, Municipal Home Rule in the United States, 10 Wm. & Mary L. Rev. 269 (1968). The Japanese Constitution expressly authorizes local public entities to issue "local ordinances (jōrei) concerning [their] organizations and operations," and "to manage" their affairs and administration. Kenpō (Constitution) art. 94; see also supra text accompanying notes 26–28. The Supreme Court has expressly validated this power, even in the case of local ordinances which purport to proscribe criminal conduct. In one case, for example, the defendant, charged with solicitation on the streets for purposes of prostitution under a local ordinance of the city of Osaka, contended, among other things, that imposition of a criminal penalty on the basis of a local ordinance (jōrei), as opposed to a national law (hōritsu), violated due process. The Supreme Court sustained the ordinance against this challenge, reasoning that a local ordinance, with its attendant degree of local discretion, was not an inappropriate method for dealing with the problem because the need for prostitution control varied between the large cities and rural areas. Matsumoto v. Japan, 16 Saikō Saibansho Keiji Hanrei Shū [Sai-han Keishū] 577 (S. Ct. Grand Bench 1962), translated in H. Itoh & L. Beer, The Constitutional Case Law of Japan 37 (1978).

of educational facilities—would probably conflict with the takings clause of the Japanese Constitution.[31]

Despite these disabilities, local constituencies placed considerable pressure on local governments to safeguard education and ventilation.[32] Local interest groups focused their energies on local solutions in part because they felt their needs and circumstances varied tremendously from area to area. The residential groups' resources would clearly be most effectively marshalled against the local—not national—government. Moreover, these groups refused to accept as an excuse for local-level nonaction the national government's failure to address their concerns adequately.

Municipalities initially responded to constituency pressure by urging national authorities either to undertake regulation of the incursions on sunlight and ventilation occasioned by housing construction, or to permit local regulation. The national authorities, however, were unresponsive and six concerned municipalities issued so-called "guidelines," known more formally as Outline Guidance (Yōkō Shidō).[33]

The Outline Guidance of the city of Musashino, a suburb in the Tokyo Metropolitan Area, typifies the response of the six original municipalities as well as that of the almost 800 municipalities that shortly followed suit.[34] Musashino issued "Outline Guidance Concerning Housing Development in the City of Musashino,"[35] which became effective on October 1, 1971. This Outline Guidance encouraged developers or builders of medium and large scale housing developments or apartment buildings to take two steps of particular significance.[36] First, in projects over a certain size, the developer was encouraged to provide free land for the construction of one elementary school for every 1000 units or fraction thereof and one junior high school for every 2000 units. Developers were also encouraged to bear the expense of constructing educational facilities on the land. Second, developers were to

---

31. At least one court explicitly stated that any attempt to impose formally such a requirement on the developers would have violated the Constitution. See Yamaki Kensetsu Kabushiki Kaisha v. The City of Musashino, 803 Hanrei Jihō 18, 22 (Tokyo Dist. Ct. 1975); see also infra text accompanying notes 176–80.

32. See Gyōsei Shidō Kenkyūkai, supra note 6, pt. 1, at 44–45.

33. See id. pt. 2, at 150–56.

34. See id.

35. Musashino-shi Takuchi Kaihatsu Tō ni Kansuru Shidō Yōkō (Outline Guidance Concerning Housing Development in the City of Musashino) (1971), reprinted in K. Yamanouchi, supra note 20, at 57–66. For a more complete explanation of this Outline Guidance, see K. Yamanouchi, supra note 20, at 57–66; Gyōsei Shidō Kenkyūkai, supra note 6, pt. 2, at 150–56.

36. Through this Outline Guidance the city encouraged developers to take other steps to reduce to a minimum the disruption to the local community caused by the development. These steps included the construction of roads to ensure adequate ingress and egress to the newly planned building, the development of surrounding parks and greenery areas, the protection of the television reception of the surrounding residents, and the installation of certain crime prevention aids or devices. None of these other steps, however, has been nearly as onerous or caused as much controversy as providing land for schools and reaching an agreement on sunlight and ventilation.

reach an agreement with the surrounding residents regarding the degree to which the planned building might permissibly interfere with the residents' sunlight and ventilation.

Although such Outline Guidance was not legally binding, the municipalities did not leave compliance entirely to the developers' good will. Musashino's Outline Guidance, for example, indicated that the city would not provide water or sewage services to uncooperative developers. Moreover, the city would not issue the construction permits required under the Construction Standards Law. Other municipalities outlined additional ways in which they would refuse to aid uncooperative developers. Some localities, for example, threatened to refuse uncooperative developers a waiver that would allow them to bring construction equipment to the construction site[37] under legislation entrusting to local officials' discretion the permissible size of vehicles allowed to pass over the roads.[38] These informal sanctions encouraged developers to heed residents' concerns over sunlight and ventilation.

These two examples of Japanese regulatory activity—municipalities' Outline Guidance and the MITI's Orderly Marketing Agreement—illustrate the broad scope of administrative guidance. They further demonstrate the major characteristics traditionally associated with administrative guidance.[39] These include an effect on behavior, a lack of legal effect and "voluntary" compliance.

1. *Modification of Behavior.* — Agencies adopting administrative guidance seek to encourage a regulated party to act or refrain from acting in order to advance a regulatory goal or objective. For example, both the MITI and the municipalities acted to accomplish a specific objective. The MITI wanted auto companies to limit their exports to the United States. The municipalities wanted developers to donate land, to bear the expense of constructing educational facilities and to reach some accommodation with the surrounding residents regarding the permissible degree of interference with sunlight and ventilation.

An agency's attempt to modify the behavior of regulated parties differs from an agency's merely explaining its interpretation of the law. Concededly, this latter interpretative activity may cause a regulated party to alter its

---

37. See, e.g., Nakano-ku Kōsō Kenchiku-butsu ni Kansuru Shidō Yōkō (Outline Guidance Concerning High-rise Construction in Nakano Ward) (1972); Suzuki, supra note 8, at 46. For a case examining the legality of this sanction, see Jūrakuen Yūgen Kaisha v. Nakano Ward, 931 Hanrei Jihō 79 (Tokyo Dist. Ct. 1978), aff'd, 36 Saikō Saibansho Minji Hanrei Shū [Sai-han Minshū] 737 (S. Ct. Petty Bench 1982), discussed infra note 150. For commentators' views of this sanction see Ito, supra note 20, at 79–80; Matsuda, supra note 20, at 164–65; Suzuki, supra note 8, at 46; Tanabe, supra note 20, at 87–88.

38. See Dōro Hō (Road Law), Law No. 180 of 1952, arts. 47, 47-2; Sharyō Seigen Rei (Vehicle Limitations Order), Cabinet Order No. 265 of 1961, art. 5, ¶ 2; see also infra note 151 (discussion of case that deals with legality of this sanction).

39. For a more particular examination of the basic characteristics of administrative guidance see authorities cited supra note 8.

conduct as, for example, when an agency predicts the tax consequences of a commercial transaction. Such administrative conduct fails, however, to qualify as administrative guidance because the agency did not intend to modify behavior in a specific way.

2. *Lack of Legal Effect.* — As Japanese commentators have pointed out, administrative guidance generally is an act of "factual" and not "legal" character.[40] Although exceptions exist,[41] administrative guidance does not alter the legal relationships of the regulated parties. For example, neither the MITI nor the municipalities took any steps, such as formally promulgating administrative orders, regulations or local ordinances, that would have enabled them to go into court or some other adjudicative forum and enforce with legal sanctions their demands against the regulated parties. The MITI directive admittedly gave the impression that the Ministry possessed legal authority to secure direct and immediate enforcement of the export limitations, but the actual request to limit exports was merely hortatory. The directive's reference to the FEFTCL and to the MITI's general mandate amounts to mere window dressing, intended to head off possible antitrust liability from disgruntled consumers in the United States.[42] Moreover, the

---

40. See, e.g., Narita, supra note 6, at 48.

41. In rare instances, certain laws do give legal effect to administrative guidance. For example, joint acts taken on the basis of certain types of administrative guidance are exempted from the antitrust laws. Shūzei no Hozen Oyobi Shuruigyō Kumiai Tō ni Kansuru Hōritsu (Law Concerning the Preservation of the Tax on Alcoholic Beverages and Alcoholic Beverages Industry Cooperatives, Etc.), Law No. 7 of 1953, art. 84, ¶¶ 2-3, art. 93. Other laws make the issuance of appropriate administrative guidance a prerequisite to compulsory enforcement of an agency's orders. See, e.g., Sōon Kisei Hō (Noise Regulation Law), Law No. 98 of 1968, art. 9, art. 12, ¶ 1, art. 15, ¶ 1; Shindō Kisei Hō (Vibration Regulation Law), Law No. 64 of 1976, art. 12, ¶ 1, art. 15, ¶ 1; Akushū Bōshi Hō (Offensive Order Prevention Law), Law No. 91 of 1971, art. 8, ¶ 1; Sekiyu Jukyū Tekiseika Hō (Petroleum Supply Rationalization Law), Law No. 122 of 1973, art. 10, ¶ 1. Finally, the law occasionally attaches legal effects to compliance with administrative guidance. For example, Shiteki Dokusen no Kinshi Oyobi Kōsei Torihiki no Kakuho ni Kansuru Hō (Law Concerning the Prohibition of Private Monopoly and the Maintenance of Fair Trade), Law No. 54 of 1947, art. 48, ¶ 1, provides that the Fair Trade Commission may terminate a case by issuing a decison similar in content to that of a previously issued warning (kankoku), if the regulated party has agreed to comply with that warning.

42. The relationship between administrative guidance and the antitrust laws has been the subject of a number of commentaries in both English and Japanese. For English language treatment of this problem, see, e.g., Matsushita, Problems and Analysis of the Oil Cartel Case Decisions, 15 Law in Japan 79 (1982); Pape, Gyōsei Shidō and the Antimonopoly Law, 15 Law in Japan 12 (1982). Useful Japanese works include Atsutani, Dokusen Kinshi Hō to Gyōsei Shidō (Antimonopoly Law and Administrative Guidance), 741 Jurisuto 53 (1981); Iyori & Shoda, Dokusen Kinshi Hō to Gyōsei Shidō to no Kankei (Antimonopoly Law and Administrative Guidance, Their Relationship), 366 Kōsei Torihiki 4 (1981); Kurusawa, Sekiyu Karuteru Hanketsu to Dokkin Seisaku (The Oil Cartel Judgment and Antimonopoly Policy), 729 Jurisuto 43 (1980). This relationship has also been the subject of major litigation. See, e.g., The Oil Cartel Cases, _______ Sai-han Keishū _______ (S. Ct. Petty Bench 1984); 32 Sai-han Keishū 515 (S. Ct., Petty Bench 1978); 985 Hanrei Jihō 3 (Tokyo Ct. App. 1980); 983 Hanrei Jihō 22 (Tokyo Ct. App. 1980) [hereinafter cited as The Oil Cartel Cases]; see also infra note 74.

MITI's only mention of sanctions involves penalties under article 67 for noncompliance with the reporting requirements—hardly an effective deterrent to exporting. Indeed, the MITI as much as admits its powerlessness by threatening to amend the Export Trade Control Order to permit direct legal enforcement of the export restrictions.[43] Thus, the MITI's request, like all administrative guidance, was only suppliant.

3. *"Voluntary" Compliance.* — This lack of binding legal effect highlights the third major characteristic of administrative guidance: all compliance with administrative guidance is "voluntary"—in a narrow, technical sense. Compliance is voluntary insofar as an agency cannot employ the judicial system or an administrative enforcement organ to compel a regulated party to obey the directive.[44] An agency's inability to enforce its mandate stems from administrative guidance's lack of effect on legal relationships between the parties.

Nevertheless, in most situations, agencies have available a broad array of devices to accomplish their goals. In the case of Outline Guidance, for example, the city explicitly threatened to withhold sewage and water services, in addition to necessary construction permits, from recalcitrant developers. Similarly, the MITI has at hand devices that would make noncompliance with its wishes ill-advised.[45] In other instances, administrative agencies encourage compliance not by punishing those who do not comply, but by rewarding those who do. For example, in the early 1960's, the Japanese government encouraged large-scale mergers in the shipping industry.[46] Those who followed this official encouragement received financing through the Japan Development Bank on particularly favorable terms. More recently, the government exerted similar pressure on the computer industry.[47] Imposition of these extralegal benefits and burdens raises considerable difficulties for regulated parties seeking to challenge administrative guidance.[48] Yet despite the array of devices available to agencies to secure compliance with their directives, direct legal enforcement is usually not an option.[49]

43. See MITI letters, supra note 11; supra notes 15-16 and accompanying text; see also Matsushita, supra note 11, at 171-74 (discussing the antitrust implications).

44. For example, even after the issuance of the MITI's directive, the MITI cannot go into a court (judicial, administrative or otherwise) and directly force a reluctant automobile company to restrict its exports to the United States. Neither can the city go into an adjudicatory institution and force a recalcitrant developer to donate land or reduce his building plan.

45. See infra note 103.

46. See D. Henderson, Foreign Enterprise in Japan: Laws and Policies 203-04 (1973).

47. Id.

48. See infra text accompanying notes 122-29.

49. In addition to the three elements I have discussed, some commentators also insist that administrative guidance includes only administrative action taken by an agency in a position of superiority to the regulated party—at least superiority with respect to those areas that fall within the agency's jurisdictional mandate—and that the party in the subordinate position be a private, not a governmental entity. Thus, attempts by an agency to control its own various departments or subagencies or to control or influence other agencies would not be considered administrative

B. *Prevalence of Administrative Guidance in Japan*

Japanese administrative agencies turn to administrative guidance as the preferred regulatory technique with notable frequency.[50] Administrative guidance enables agencies to avoid legal barriers such as constitutional prohibitions on action by statute and political difficulties such as local governments' inability to take action in certain areas. Administrative guidance further provides speed and flexibility. At the same time, administrative guidance is tolerable to regulated parties because they participate extensively in the formation of the regulation. The features of administrative guidance, essential to a strong administrative state, are consistent with Japan's historically activist approach to government.[51]

1. *Enhancement of Bureaucratic Power Despite Legal Restrictions.* — While Japanese bureaucrats no doubt genuinely fear appearing too "officious" and bureaucratic,[52] a more plausible explanation for their enthusiasm for administrative guidance lies in its ability to extend regulatory activity beyond strictly legal limits. Because an agency exercising administrative guidance anticipates no direct legal enforcement, it is less constrained to base its regulatory activity on a specific statutory authorization. In the usual regulatory situation, the enforcing agency must demonstrate a clear statutory mandate in order to persuade the enforcement organ to marshall its resources against the regulated party. When the agency does not intend to seek direct legal enforcement, however, it need not pay the statute the same deference in defining the permissible scope of agency action.

Thus, in Japan, agencies frequently attempt to accomplish through administrative guidance what by most admissions they cannot achieve under the governing legal regime. Until very recently, for example, laws regulating drugs

guidance. See, e.g., K. Yamanouchi, supra note 20, at 15-23. Of course, the MITI's actions with respect to the auto manufacturers and the city's with respect to the developers—both involving private individuals or organizations that fall within the agency's jurisdiction with respect to the activity under discussion—would satisfy this requirement.

Other commentators do not, however, confine their definition to guidance given only to private entities. See, e.g., Shiono, supra note 8, at 222. Indeed, the national government frequently issues to the local governments nonbinding, nonauthoritative directives that share the other characteristics of administrative guidance. Such was the case, for example, when the national government recently encouraged local governments to reduce what it considered "excessively high pay scales" for local officials. See id. Of course, legal differences exist between guidance given to a private rather than a governmental entity. Moreover, for some purposes, it is important to determine whether action given to a governmental entity falls within the boundaries of administrative guidance. Given the particular institutions and institutional relationships addressed in this Article, however, it is not necessary to resolve the definitional debate. This Article focuses only on the problems presented when an administrative organ attempts through administrative guidance to direct a private party.

50. Commentators estimate administrative guidance comprises over 80% of Japanese bureaucratic activity. See Narita, supra note 6, at 39-40; see also infra text accompanying note 120.

51. See infra note 84.

52. See K. Yamanouchi, supra note 20, at 111-13.

did not explicitly permit the government to force drug manufacturers to stop manufacturing and distributing drugs after permission was initially granted, even though subsequent data had proven them dangerous or capable of producing harmful side effects.[53] The government has nevertheless continually taken the position, both in testimony before the Japanese parliament, or Diet, and in actual practice, that permission to manufacture a certain drug can be withdrawn in appropriate cases through administrative guidance.[54] Evasion of possible legal limits also provided the motivation for instituting the Orderly Market Agreement regarding automobile exports[55] and the Outline Guidance dealing with sunlight and ventilation.[56]

Administrative guidance permits agencies to regulate not only beyond the limits of the law but also, on occasion, in direct contravention of the law. Such contravention is possible because any judicial inquiry into the propriety of the regulatory objectives will be limited. For example, during the oil crisis of 1973, the government strongly encouraged television stations to curtail late night broadcasts in an attempt to conserve energy.[57] The government no doubt had the power to issue regulations regarding conservation of electricity. It is commonly suggested, however, that the measures directed against television stations took the form of administrative guidance because the government wanted to minimize the possibility of a direct legal challenge.[58] Because these measures interfered with the editorial judgments of television stations, which enjoy some constitutional protection, their legal status was uncertain. Administrative guidance, by enabling the government to avoid a direct legal challenge to its action, may be understood as part of the inevitable and ever-present struggle between the governors and the governed to gain the upper hand—or at least coexist peacefully.

2. *Flexible Definition of Agency Mandate.* — Administrative guidance also provides agencies in Japan with a flexible means of handling tasks that the current legal regime fails to accommodate. Because the use of administrative guidance frees an agency from the specific moorings of the governing statutory language, it may not only expand the scope of its activity, but also redefine the very nature of its regulatory mandate. Many Japanese bureaucrats appear to view their enabling legislation not merely as establishing substantive areas over which they are to exercise regulatory control, but rather as descriptions of the various groups in society over which they have charge. The Ministry of Agriculture provides the best example of an agency redefining

53. See, e.g., Ogawa, Kikui, Shiono, Miyajima & Yamanouchi, Eigyō Seigen Rippō no Mondai (The Problem of Legislating Industrial Production Limitations), 592 Jurisuto 36, 41 (1975).

54. Id.; see also K. Yamanouchi, supra note 20, at 31–33, 53–54 (discussing the practice and attitude of government officials in this area).

55. See supra text accompanying notes 9–16.

56. See supra text accompanying notes 17–31.

57. Gyōsei Shidō Kenkyūkai, supra note 6, pt. 1, at 39–41.

58. Id.

its jurisdiction in this way. The Ministry's enabling legislation only vests it with responsibility for agricultural development. Yet the Ministry generally interprets this legislation as placing under its purview all farmers and their families for almost any conceivable purpose.[59] Thus, the Ministry has instituted programs that provide for medical examinations for farmers' wives, the maintenance of roads in farming areas, the construction of various public meeting facilities and recreational areas for farmers and their families, and the removal of sewage.[60] Many of these activities encroach upon the domain of other ministries, but jurisdictional disputes rarely arise because the other ministries acknowledge the Ministry of Agriculture's prime responsibility for the welfare of the farmers.[61]

The Ministry of Finance (MOF), though less explicit about its own inner workings, appears to take the same broad view of its jurisdictional mandate—to regulate banks and other financial institutions. Banking regulation thus extends as far as the establishment of energy conservation measures for banks, the encouragement of a five-day work week, and the provision of time off to permit bank employees to vote on election day.[62] Other ministries do not quarrel with these intrusions into areas that fall within their substantive jurisdictional mandate because the MOF limits its regulatory activity to financial institutions.[63]

---

59. Ministry officials themselves have given this view of their jurisdictional mandate. See id.

60. Id.

61. Id.

62. Id.

63. In this regard, it is interesting to note that for years the MOF and the MITI have had largely overlapping responsibility for the regulation of foreign investment and foreign trade in Japan. Yet, because each ministry defines its scope of activity more in terms of groups than transactions, they have rarely publicly clashed. Thus, prior to 1980, two largely overlapping (at least to Western eyes) laws regulating foreign trade were operative in Japan. Conceptual differences could be found between the two, with the Foreign Investment Law of 1950, Gaishi ni Kansuru Hōritsu (Foreign Investment Law), Law No. 163 of 1950, regulating foreign exchange activities for purposes of direct investment and the Foreign Exchange and Trade Control Law of 1949, Gaikoku Kawase Oyobi Gaikoku Bōeki Kanri Hō (Foreign Exchange and Trade Control Law), Law No. 228 of 1949, regulating trade transactions between residents and nonresidents. See D. Henderson, supra note 46, at 216–36. The specific content of the laws themselves, however, gave little indication that the Diet had been able to implement this neat theoretical distinction. In practice, moreover, the MOF and the MITI did not divide up their responsibilities in that way. Rather, the MOF focused on banks and other financial institutions and the MITI on manufacturing and distributing companies. The primary focus was not on the specific nature of the transaction, but on the institution engaged in that transaction, and one ministry seldom crossed the border into an area over which the other ministry claimed to reign.

Private, behind-the-scene disputes between these two ministries are not totally unknown, however. See C. Johnson, supra note 1, at 259. Such fights generally remain behind the scenes. More importantly, the real issue in such disagreements often is one ministry's attempt to exercise jurisdiction over the other's "group." Id.

At the same time, the MITI conflicts openly and regularly with the Japanese Fair Trade Commission (FTC). The FTC is one of the few major administrative agencies at the national level that has no limited and cohesive constituency defined by the substantive terms of its jurisdictional mandate. Its regulatory activity thus often encroaches not only on the substance, but also on the

When the Ministries of Agriculture and Finance redefine their regulatory mandate to embrace the regulated groups rather than merely to oversee certain types of activities, they gain considerable flexibility. The agencies can then use administrative guidance to implement a variety of substantive policies so long as they affect only the regulated groups' well-being.

3. *Collateral Enforcement.* — Use of administrative guidance enables agencies to gain additional flexibility by resorting to collateral methods of enforcement to effectuate quite unrelated regulatory objectives.[64] The MITI, for example, has been known to threaten restriction of the amount of coal a company could import if that company did not comply with the MITI's request to limit steel production.[65] The flexibility provided by such covert pressures, as well as by expanding regulatory activity to groups, enables administrative agencies to go into areas not otherwise subject to regulation.

4. *Party Input.* — At the same time, the flexibility that administrative guidance provides requires agencies to cooperate with the regulated parties.

---

groups that other agencies claim as their own. Id. at 259. One of the more recent and better known examples of that clash is found in The Oil Cartel Cases, supra note 42, where the FTC challenged certain allegedly collusive activities of oil companies. The companies defended on the grounds that the MITI had directed them (through the use of administrative guidance) to take the collusive steps. The FTC pressed its challenge even in the face of this defense, and persuaded the court to declare at least some portion of the MITI's guidance as violative of the antitrust laws. For a detailed discussion of these cases, see infra note 74. Though there are certainly a number of other occasions when one ministry has quite clearly encroached on the territorial limits of another, and perhaps even encouraged activity that would be illegal under a strict reading of laws and regulations administered by the second ministry, the *Oil Cartel Cases* are one of the few occasions when the conflict has become open and acknowledged, and required judicial resolution. Ministries, like the FTC, that fail to develop a group-oriented view of jurisdiction, are more likely to engage in open conflict with other ministries than those agencies that carve off a specific group upon which to focus their regulatory attention.

64. For example, in the drug recall case, discussed supra notes 53-54 and accompanying text, manufacturers feared that the relevant agenices would be appreciably less inclined to approve their new drugs if they were unwilling to withdraw drugs the government deemed hazardous. In actuality, not much evidence exists that bureaucrats in Japan operate so vindictively. There is even some evidence to the contrary. For example, tax officials often inform taxpayers of the availability of various appeals mechanisms. See Gellhorn, Settling Disagreements With Officials in Japan, 79 Harv. L. Rev. 685, 690 & n. 8 (1966). While this revelation is generally required by law, see Gyōsei Fufuku Shinsa Hō (Administrative Complaints Inquiry Law), Law No. 160 of 1962, arts. 41, 47, 56-58, it also suggests that perhaps appeals actually are not viewed so harshly. See Gellhorn, supra, at 690. Many tax attorneys in Japan, however, believe that filing an appeal against the rule of tax officials will indeed incur the wrath of those officials and lead to unfavorable dispositions in the future. Accordingly, the actual number of appeals is rather low. This very well may be one of those instances where the perception of reality, especially as it determines behavior, is more significant than the reality itself.

65. See infra text accompanying notes 100-03. Another good example of collateral enforcement arises in the Outline Guidance area. Municipalities often threaten to withhold vital services, including water and sewage removal, and various permits, including construction permits and permits for oversized vehicles to carry heavy equipment to construction sites, if developers do not comply with the municipalities' wishes as expressed through Outline Guidance. See supra text accompanying notes 17-38.

To assure voluntary compliance and substantial cooperation, agencies engage in practices designed to increase the informal, generally unreviewable input of parties into the regulatory process. Indeed, agencies that engage in administrative guidance undertake extensive consultations with regulated parties—who may include industry representatives[66]—about the need for regulation and the form it will take.

The Ministry of Labor, for example, engaged in comprehensive discussions with various industry associations and labor representatives before it suggested that companies gradually phase in a five-day work week.[67] Similarly, the Ministry of Construction encouraged construction firms and developers to form associations through which the Ministry then negotiated a series of reforms intended to strengthen and modernize the position and status of sub-contractors and other suppliers in the construction industry.[68] In the *Oil Cartel Cases*, the MITI committed to the Petroleum Federation, a major industry trade association, the task of allocating specific production shares among its members.[69] The price for which the oil subsequently sold was also determined in all but one instance by agreement with industry officials. In an equally extreme example, evidence exists that the Ministry of Transportation committed to an informal industry council the task of dividing up coveted railroad routes for private railroad companies.[70]

Consultation can take a variety of forms. All ministries have consultative and advisory committees comprised of industry representatives, academics, bureaucrats and representatives of other organizations, such as research institutes, the media and, on rare occasions, labor or consumer groups. Some of these councils, such as the MITI's Industrial Structure Council, are permanent.[71] Others are formed on an ad hoc basis to deal with a specific problem and disbanded after agreeing upon the substance and form of the guidance. Depending on the nature of the problem and the agency's desired objective, the consultation may be more informal and loosely structured. The agency

---

66. When bureaucrats consult with industry representatives, they sometimes focus on general business associations, such as Keidanren and the Keizai Dōyūkai, two powerful associations of leaders of major companies. Other times, they consult with specific trade associations, composed of representatives of all the companies in a particular industry. Interviews with government officials and representatives of industry and various industry associations in Japan (1981 & 1983).

67. Gyōsei Shidō Kenkyūkai, supra note 6, pt. 1, at 47-48.

68. Id.

69. See supra note 42 and infra note 74.

70. Gyōsei Shidō Kenkyūkai, supra note 6, pt. 1, at 49-53. This particular example also shows the pivotal role these implementing associations may play in the regulatory process, a role the bureaucrats are often reluctant to admit. The particular committee that divided up rail routes in a period of substantial economic expansion shifted gears during the more recent era of limited growth and prevented the government from rationalizing rail routes. This committee permitted private rail companies to hang on to unprofitable routes and claim redress from the government for the losses occasioned by running these routes long after the government itself was prepared to streamline private rail services. Id.; see also infra text accompanying notes 74-75.

71. C. Johnson, supra note 1, at 253.

may initially approach only selected representatives of a particular industry or trade, hoping their support will be sufficient to elicit cooperation from the other potential targets of regulation. While the manner and extent of consultation may vary markedly from case to case, consultation almost always takes place.[72]

Bureaucrats consult with involved parties before regulation both to build a consensus[73] and, on occasion, to elicit the cooperation of the regulated parties. Administrative guidance issued without such consultation may meet with disobedience and, in rare instances, litigation. Agencies avoid this result by committing much of the actual formation and implementation of guidance to the regulated parties themselves.[74] When the parties participate extensively in the design and execution of regulation, they can minimize the dislocations of particular regulatory burdens. They can also increase efficiency in accomplishing regulatory goals and introduce flexibility into the enforcement process, thereby ensuring that the regulations will not impose unnecessary, unfair or disproportionate burdens and compliance costs. They also may structure the compliance scheme to minimize the competitive disadvantages of regulation. If the parties are permitted genuine, regular, and unstructured input into the formation of administrative guidance, as it appears they necessarily are, it

72. Some consultation also undoubtedly occurs in Japan, as elsewhere, even when the agency plans to enforce its wishes directly. When the agency does not intend to invoke its enforcement powers, however, the need for such consultation increases because the success or failure of the regulatory venture will depend at least in part on the goodwill and cooperation of the regulated parties. Thus, while consultation may always play some part in any regulatory process, it has a particular place in, and a peculiar causal relationship to, that process when the ultimate mode of regulation is administrative guidance.

73. See K. Yamanouchi, supra note 20, at 111–13.

74. A particularly well-documented, though controversial, example of industry officials playing a major role in the development of a regulatory scheme occurred when the MITI attempted to relegate to the oil industry the creation and implementation of recession-type cartels. Long before the oil crisis of 1973, the MITI and petroleum industry officials agreed upon the need for production limitations and price stabilization measures. Price fixing became public knowledge in 1973, when the Japanese Fair Trade Commission (FTC) challenged these activities and the extent of industry participation in both the enforcement and establishment of production limitations. Indeed, company participation was so extensive that the FTC sought and secured consent decrees from the major oil companies to stop participating in these agreements, and in the next year it successfully sought criminal indictments against one major industry association and various petroleum companies and their officials for violations of the antitrust laws. See The Oil Cartel Cases, supra note 42. In these cases, one directed against the production limitations and the other against price-fixing, the accused defended on the ground that they were merely acting under the direction of the MITI and thus their activities were not illegal or at least not criminal. See id. For a translation of the first of these cases, see Ramseyer, The Oil Cartel Criminal Cases: Translations and Postscript, 15 Law in Japan 57 (1982). The courts acknowledged that the MITI had played some role in encouraging and facilitating these activities. Nevertheless, the courts rejected this defense because the activities were illegal and the MITI's guidance had not been sufficiently authoritative to eliminate that illegality. The defendants also claimed that even if the MITI's guidance did not have sufficient color of law to make these agreements legal, the MITI's encouragement and involvement had been pronounced enough to preclude a finding of criminal intent on the part of the defendants. Although the court thought the question close, it accepted

is no wonder they do not decry the frequency of its use. Indeed, in some instances, committing the formulation of policy to the parties results in regulation they consider not only less burdensome but also beneficial.[75]

Thus, whether Japanese bureaucrats perceive the consultative process as mere accommodation or as a necessary prerequisite to action, most guidance undergoes noticeable and significant changes before it becomes official policy.[76] The interactive consultation process that precedes the issuance of guidance is a significant and necessary step for the effective accomplishment of administrative goals and objectives.[77]

C. *Administrative Guidance: Enshrinement of Bargaining and Negotiation*

The flexibility that administrative guidance provides, together with the concomitant emphasis upon party input into the regulatory process, reveals a more fundamental feature of the Japanese administrative approach. Administrative organs in Japan often seek to enshrine bargaining and negotiation between parties as the principal device for allocating regulatory burdens.[78]

---

this defense in the production limitations case. With respect to price fixing, however, the court rejected even this defense, finding that the MITI's involvement had not been sufficient to make the parties think their activities might have been legal. The Oil Cartel Cases, supra note 42. For a discussion of various antitrust aspects of these cases, see, e.g., Atsuya, Keizai Hō Hanrei-Shinketsurei No Ugoki (Economic Law Decisions—The Movement of New Decisions), 743 Jurisuto 259 (1981); Sanekata, Gyōsei Shidō to Dokkin Hō Ihan no Tsumi—Sekiyu Karuteru Seisan Chōsei Jiken (Administrative Guidance and Violation of the Anti-trust Law—The Oil Cartel Production Adjustment Case), 743 Jurisuto 264 (1980); Ramseyer, Japanese Antitrust Enforcement After the Oil Embargo, 31 Am. J. Comp. L. 395 (1983).

In response to these cases, both the MITI and the FTC have issued separate statements regarding their quite different interpretation of the proper scope of governmental activities when such activities might involve anticompetitive behavior. See Japanese Fair Trade Comm'n, Dokusen Kinshi Hō to Gyōsei Shidō to no Kankei ni tsuite no Kangaekata (A Point of View About the Antitrust Law and Administrative Guidance and Their Relationship) (1981), reprinted in 741 Jurisuto 37 (1981); Ministry of Int'l Trade and Indus., Gyōsei Shidō ni tsuite no Kangaekata (A Point of View About Administrative Guidance) (1981), reprinted in 741 Jurisuto 37 (1981).

For a more general discussion of the relationship between administrative guidance and the antitrust laws, see, e.g., Iyori, Dokusen Kinshi Hō to Gyōsei Shidō (The Anti-Trust Law and Administrative Guidance), 342 Jurisuto 59 (1966); Kanazawa, Dokusen Kinshi Hō to Gyōsei Shidō (The Anti-Trust Law and Administrative Guidance), 65 NBL 8 (1974); Negishi, Sangyō Gyōsei to Gyōsei Shidō (Production Administration and Administrative Guidance), 628 Jurisuto 145 (1977).

75. See Gyōsei Shidō Kenkyūkai, supra note 6, pt. 1, at 46.

76. See, e.g., C. Johnson, supra note 1, at 258–61 (discussion of industrial structure measures law revisions).

77. See Gyōsei Shidō Kenkyūkai, supra note 6, pt. 1, at 46–47.

78. This pattern of forced bargaining or negotiation has identifiable historical ancestry in Japan. In his study of conciliation and Japanese law from Tokugawa (1603–1868) to modern Japan, Professor Henderson notes the tendency toward what he calls didactic conciliation. Such conciliation is "characterized by elements of background coercion, either because of the social context, the relative positions of the parties and the conciliator, or because there is in fact no practicable, alternative remedy in 'court.'" 1 D. Henderson, Conciliation and Japanese Law 5 (1965). Professor Henderson identifies among the major reasons for such a process an interest in

Such processes clearly occurred when industry officials conferred with their various regulating agencies in all the examples already discussed.[79] But nowhere is the Japanese emphasis on negotiation and private ordering more evident than in municipalities' Outline Guidance.

In promulgating Outline Guidance, the municipalities never attempted to establish the permissible degree of intrusion on the ventilation and sunlight of the surrounding residents. Rather, they simply indicated an unwillingness to cooperate with developers. The precise allocation of this regulatory burden thus depended almost entirely on negotiations directly between the developers and surrounding residents. These negotiations do not proceed through the medium of a government agency, and the government does not represent any particular interest in the dispute or even take sides—except when parties are acting unreasonably.[80] Indeed, except in an indirect way, the government does not even serve as the final arbiter of these disputes. Rather, the municipalities restructure the balance of power between the interested parties to ensure that each takes the other seriously and deals with the other in good faith. The municipalities then step out of the picture, reentering only when the parties have resolved the matter among themselves. Thus, in its ideal application, administrative guidance operates through bargaining and negotiation outside the realm of state enforcement mechanisms.[81]

In the United States, by way of contrast, the formal legal structure points in a different direction. When, for example, localities establish zoning guidelines, they can be varied by local administrative entities known as zoning boards.[82] Because the legal structure requires only that the board take some

protecting the dominant classes against the otherwise valid claims of the lower classes, id. at 8, and an interest in limiting the development of precedents that might be turned against the governors and diminish their scope of activity, id. at 9-10. Strains of this didactic conciliation exist in a variety of contexts even in modern Japan with its westernized system of law and government. Possibly, conciliation continues to be popular in part because it allows individualized solutions to complex problems of resource allocation.

79. See supra text accompanying notes 67-70.

80. See supra note 83; infra text accompanying notes 185-89, 190-94.

81. Of course, the very nature of the disputes that gave rise to the Outline Guidance in the first place may have influenced the municipalities to adopt this bargaining model. Residential patterns, needs and preferences regarding sunlight and ventilation vary tremendously, even among rather similar neighborhoods and residential districts. Even within a given neighborhood, moreover, individual situations vary greatly, in terms of environmental details and personal preferences. All this makes specific legislative and even administrative determinations of these matters difficult at best. Indeed, despite the relatively clear-cut legislative and administrative procedures governing zoning in most jurisdictions in the United States, many of the actual decisions regarding zoning, zoning variances, and enforcement of zoning rules appear to result more from compromises reached through negotiations among various interested and affected parties than from strict adherence to these formally mandated procedures. See R. Babcock, The Zoning Game 7-16, 130-35 (1966); R. Ellickson & D. Tarlock, Land Use Controls 234-80 (1981). That one should see a similar tendency in Japan is not surprising. The formalized structure is different in the United States, however, and these differences are suggestive as the discussion that follows in text indicates.

82. See D. Hagman, Urban Planning and Land Development Control Law §§ 106-15 (1975).

direct action on requests for variances, interested parties do not necessarily negotiate directly with each other. As in all civil disputes, of course, the parties may negotiate before committing their dispute to the government; they may even continue negotiating as the governmental organ examines the problem. The formal legal structure, however, requires that the parties eventually address their arguments to the zoning boards. The board stands as the ultimate arbiter, not of the reasonableness of the various disputants' positions, but rather of the ultimate legal and equitable merits of their arguments. The Japanese resistance to this sort of state institutional ordering of private affairs translates concretely into two specific features of the Japanese administrative approach—an emphasis on private ordering and a well-developed sense of individual rights.

1. *Emphasis on Private Ordering.* — Japanese administrators' reliance upon private arrangements to resolve complex disputes may very well stem from skepticism about the ability of agencies to identify and evaluate the competing interests that must inform governmental determinations. For example, the problems that Outline Guidance seeks to address involve an infinite number of geographical, environmental, and individual variables. Because Japanese expect their government to attempt solutions, governmental officials cannot evade difficult problems. The unrelenting, and ultimately irresistible, pressure on the over 800 municipalities that finally enacted Outline Guidance suggests the level and intensity of these expectations.

The pressure to resolve a problem that does not lend itself comfortably to a uniform solution encourages officials to search for a way of effecting an individualized solution that responds both to the variable circumstances in which the problem arises and to the competing societal and personal concerns inherent in the dispute. Rather than rely upon fallible agency determinations, Japanese administrators have turned to enforced bargaining and negotiation. Administrators reallocate bargaining power between the parties so as to assure serious negotiations,[83] but then distance themselves from the process, thereby allowing the parties themselves to make the difficult determinations. Such

83. For example, the municipalities in the Outline Guidance setting make no attempt to delineate any concrete rules or guidelines for solving specific problems. Instead, they simply nominate sunlight and ventilation as governmentally recognized concerns and encourage the parties to bargain out their own specific solution to the matter. Thus, administrative agencies acknowledge the generally indeterminate nature of interests and appropriate solutions, and do not attempt to impose a substantive solution on the parties. Rather, having denominated the broad category of interests to be protected, the general nature of the negotiating structure within which these interests are to be determined and protected, and the general category of people to be involved in the negotiations, the agencies distance themselves from the entire process, intruding only interstitially to insure the continuation of the bargaining and the ultimate resolution of the matter through that process.

Before stepping completely out of the matter, however, the municipalities, recognizing the disparity in bargaining power between the developer and surrounding residents, make some attempt to reallocate that power in such a way as to encourage serious, good faith bargaining. They accomplish this result by giving the residents an important bargaining chip—the ability to

modesty about the capabilities of a centralized government to assess citizens' needs—whether longstanding or newly discovered[84]—and to determine appropriate solutions runs counter to the commonly held American belief that the Japanese government is directorial and managerial in the extreme. Indeed,

---

forestall the issuance of a construction permit until they are satisfied. This bargaining chip is not quite as weighty in practice as it would seem in theory, even at the administrative level, because local officials confess they will issue construction permits even to developers who have not reached agreement with the surrounding residents if it appears the residents are not negotiating in good faith or are making totally unreasonable demands. Nevertheless, the basic shift in power effected by the municipalities encourages serious bargaining without the municipalities mandating specific solutions to the various problems.

84. Such awareness of the difficulty of this type of administrative determination may be a relatively new phenomenon in Japan. Regarding developments in the American legal system, for example, Professor Ackerman notes that the New Deal marked a radical departure from the view that "self-conscious state intervention in the market economy [was] a relatively extraordinary event . . . ." B. Ackerman, Reconstructing American Law 9 (1984). The perception of governmental intervention as nonexceptional placed new burdens on government to resolve difficult questions of resource allocation, distribution, and redistribution. Administrative determinations in these areas often affect important interests beyond those directly addressed by agency action. American administrative agencies have responded to these developments in a variety of ways, including expansion of the opportunity to be heard and to present evidence before the agency, and clearer articulation of the agency's responsibility to represent the "public interest" in various regulatory settings. See, e.g., Stewart, The Reformation of American Administrative Law, 88 Harv. L. Rev. 1667, 1723–48 (1975). Some commentators, recognizing the increased scope of interests affected by agency action in an era of large scale government and interrelated economic, political, and social interests, have suggested a marked expansion and facilitation of participation rights before agencies. Id. at 1748–81. Perhaps Japan too has entered an era in which it is no longer acceptable to view the state merely as a passive Lockean trustee of public order.

Evidence exists, however, to suggest that the Japanese view of the proper role of the state has long been at least moderately "activist." This view finds one of its clearest articulations in Prince Hirobumi Ito's commentaries of 1889 on the Meiji Constitution, enacted in 1889. In discussing Article 9, which authorized the Emperor to issue ordinances, Prince Ito notes that

> those also who maintain that the preservation of the public peace and order is the only object of administrative ordinances, are mistaken in defining the limits of the executive. In olden times, in every continental state of Europe, the maintenance of the public peace was regarded as the highest duty of a government, and simplicity as the sole principle of its internal administration. But when the turn of events had brought about a high degree of political development, owing to the advancement of civilization, it was found imperatively necessary to promote the welfare and prosperity of the people, both materially and intellectually, by economical and educational means. It thus came to be recognized that the object of the administrative ordinances is not confined to the negative measures of police, but that their object ought also to be to take the positive measures of promoting the material prosperity of the people by economical means and of cultivating the intellect of the people through education.

H. Ito, Commentaries on the Constitution of the Empire of Japan 9 (1889). Whatever the accuracy of Prince Ito's observations on European government, he was expressing views gained after long experience with general Japanese perceptions, both official and lay, about the proper role of government. In implementing this activist approach, the Japanese government may have long faced difficult and complex choices in positively promoting the public good and may have turned for solutions to forced negotiation and compromise. Certain evidence, though spotty and not entirely conclusive, supports this claim. See supra note 78.

American commentators sometimes depict the Japanese as a compliant populace merely marching in step to orders given by the central authorities, particularly the bureaucracy.[85] The tendency to forge individualized solutions to difficult problems of resource allocation and benefit and burden distribution is, however, marked in the case of Outline Guidance.

2. *Notion of Rights.* — The emphasis on private ordering notwithstanding, the Japanese also appear to retain a strong notion of rights or entitlements. When, pursuant to Outline Guidance, the local authorities compelled the parties to negotiate and bargain, they created in the surrounding residents something resembling a right or entitlement. In discussing the various ways in which a state may protect entitlements, Professors Calabresi and Melamed denote as property rules or property rights entitlements that, if removed from the holder, must be purchased in a "voluntary transaction in which the value of the entitlement is agreed upon by the seller."[86] Within certain limits, the administrative agencies overseeing municipal construction met this definition by attempting to provide the surrounding residents with an entitlement that could be taken away only with their consent and only at a price they specified. In particular, the Outline Guidance, as a practical matter, prevented developers from interfering with the surrounding residents' sunlight or ventilation without their consent.

Although the entitlement created by Outline Guidance differed in some superficial respects from a conventional right, it nevertheless bore the fundamental earmarks of a right. Local authorities did not follow the statutorily established procedures for creating binding ordinances (jōrei),[87] and they failed to use the language of entitlements. Moreover, the Outline Guidance did not speak directly to the surrounding residents, and it gave no suggestion as to the limits of this right or when encroachment would be permissible. The Outline Guidance did, however, clearly instruct developers not to interfere with the sunlight and ventilation—at least as those conditions existed in the dwellings when the Outline Guidance was issued.

One other divergence from the classical model of a property right does not lessen the entitlement created by Outline Guidance. Despite the Outline Guidance's broad language seeming to require the developer to reach agreement with the surrounding residents before securing the cooperation of local officials, as a practical matter those officials would issue the necessary building permits if they thought the developer had offered reasonable and sufficient compromises, and the surrounding residents' remaining demands were unreasonable.[88] Such a limit does not, however, undermine the value of the right. The surrounding residents were entitled not to all the sunshine and

85. See, e.g., C. Johnson, supra note 1, at 17–21; I. Magaziner & T. Hout, supra note 1, at 32; E. Vogel, Japan as Number One 66 (1979).

86. Calabresi & Melamed, Property Rules, Liability Rules, and Inalienability: One View of the Cathedral, 85 Harv. L. Rev. 1089, 1092 (1972).

87. See supra note 30 and accompanying text.

88. Interviews with local officials and developers, in Japan (1981 & 1983).

ventilation they desired, but rather only to a reasonable amount of those amenities. They could prevent not all, but rather only unreasonable encroachments on their sunshine. An entitlement to a "reasonable" amount of sunshine and ventilation has the basic characteristics of a property right, even though the "property" being protected and degree of protection itself are limited in scope. Indeed, few rights are unlimited in their description and even fewer in their enforcement. In Japan, moreover, legal doctrines exist that explicitly limit, to some extent, the ability to enforce virtually any legal right.[89] While the legal formulation of these doctrines takes a variety of forms, at base they resemble a standard of reasonableness.

Thus, within these limits of reasonableness, agencies confer on the residents a private right to bargain for the proper degree of sunlight and ventilation through their promulgation of Outline Guidance. As we have seen, the principal device for determining the allocation of burdens and benefits in this situation is the process of negotiation and bargaining over a paradigmatic private right. Resort to the courts and administrative agencies is infrequent in Japan perhaps not as a result of less developed notions of individual rights and duties, as is commonly asserted,[90] but rather because the use of the concept of rights and duties as a device for social order and control is frequently handled through private negotiating, albeit under agency supervision.

II. Process Breakdown and Dispute Resolution

Certain features of administrative guidance—the various informal consultative processes and the marked tendency to commit to the regulated parties the development and implementation of specific regulations—diminish significantly the number of disputes that arise after the issuance of administrative guidance. The parties may be genuinely pleased with the results, or simply happy to have escaped a heavier regulatory burden; in any event, they are generally unwilling to challenge the guidance in question. Yet disputes inevitably arise, usually caused by either the agency's failure to consult the parties or a perception of agency bias. The analysis that follows explores these causes of process failure, and the three responses open to regulated parties: noncompliance, resort to the political process or adjudication.

---

89. See infra text accompanying notes 173-75.

90. For the best known expositions of this view, see T. Kawashima, Nihonjin no Hō Ishiki (Japanese Legal Consciousness) (1978); Kawashima, Dispute Resolution in Contemporary Japan, *in* Law in Japan 41 (A. von Mehren ed. 1963); see also N. Kobayashi, Nihonjin no Kenpō Ishiki (Japanese Consciousness of the Constitution) (1968) (Japanese perceptions regarding the Constitution of Japan and its role in society); Gendai Nihonjin no Hō Ishiki (Modern Japanese Legal Consciousness) (Nihon Bunkakaigi ed. 1982) (survey of attitudes towards law); Nihonjin no Hō Ishiki (Japanese Legal Consciousness) (Nihon Bunkakaigi ed. 1973) (same)

A. *Process Failure*

1. *Inadequate Consultation.* — Inadequate consultation with the regulated parties is a leading cause of failure in regulation through administrative guidance. Exclusion from the consultative process may in some instances be directed at particular parties. For example, during the 1960's, the MITI attempted to rationalize the Japanese automobile parts industry by encouraging horizontal mergers and combinations. Despite the government's willingness to encourage mergers by making available to cooperative companies very low-cost financing, an incentive made particularly attractive by the high annual production growth rates, only a few mergers actually took place and the program was widely regarded as a failure.[91] The most commonly cited cause of the MITI's lack of success was its inability adequately to ascertain and consider the views of auto producers and primary parts manufacturers.[92]

In other instances, this failure to consult may be much more systematic, with certain groups and interests consistently excluded from participation in the regulatory process. For example, when the government primarily consults with an industry or trade association, nonmembers have little voice in the regulatory process.[93] At the national level, moreover, few vehicles exist for consistent consultation with representatives of consumer or other nonindustry interests or those of the general populace. Such systematic exclusion became most noticeable during the past two decades, as Japan struggled with severe pollution problems. Residents in areas particularly affected by pollution were excluded from regulatory consultation and resorted to the courts to bring to the government's attention the magnitude of the problem.[94] Once the government began the process of developing solutions, it again excluded or at least minimized local residents' participation in the regulatory process.[95]

---

91. See E. Kaplan, supra note 2, at 119–20.

92. Id. The MITI often drops plans when faced with strong or even moderate industry opposition. See, e.g., id. at 122 (in the 1960's, the MITI dropped plans to organize auto producers into groups based on cars' basic design type); id. at 123–24 (MITI failed in attempt to secure passage of law that would give it power to force mergers in auto industry in certain circumstances).

93. Gyōsei Shidō Kenkyūkai, supra note 6, pt. 1, at 46–48.

94. See Upham, Litigation and Moral Consciousness in Japan: An Interpretive Analysis of Four Japanese Pollution Suits, 10 Law & Soc'y Rev. 579, 583–88 (1976) (Many parties favored litigation over further negotiations in part because litigation was more likely to catch the public's and government's attention and force companies, and perhaps even the government, to acknowledge their respective roles in the tragedy.).

95. No doubt, as Japanese administrators often claim, the bureaucracy represented citizens' interests to some extent. Nevertheless, at least one commentator has persuasively argued that the apparently progressive solutions adopted by the Japanese government, such as the mediation system, were designed not with the intent of effecting a full solution to the problems confronting the average victim of pollution, but rather with the hope that a lesser solution would placate the victims and thus reduce the occasions on which they resorted to dispute resolution forums, especially courts, over which the government felt it did not have adequate control. See F. Upham, Law and Social Conflict in Contemporary Japan (1984) (unpublished manuscript). Moreover, major business interests did not find the government's chosen solutions particularly onerous, but instead enthusiastically, though quietly, supported them because they calculated their overall

This potential for systematic exclusion from participation in various critical stages of the regulatory process also may account for the differing perceptions between foreigners and Japanese about the nature of the Japanese administrative process. Foreigners tend to think that Japanese bureaucrats govern the country in a heavy-handed fashion, making all important decisions and implementing all significant policies in a directorial manner. According to this theory, Japan's economic success is a result of governmental interferences and carefully structured bureaucratic obstacles and hurdles. Japanese, on the other hand, tend to discount the influence of the bureaucracy. They praise the effectiveness and cooperative ethic of their bureaucracy, but rarely attribute their success to that segment of government. Moreover, Japanese do not perceive the bureaucracy as operating in an especially overbearing fashion. Rather, they view their bureaucracy as only one element, and perhaps not a very important element, in the decisionmaking and governance process.

This difference in perception may result in part from the systematic exclusion of foreigners from participation in the regulatory process, especially when the regulations at issue may affect foreigners' competitiveness in Japanese markets. Foreigners generally do not (and often cannot) belong, for example, to the associations assigned the task of developing specific product safety standards.[96] Not surprisingly, safety regulations often seem disproportionately burdensome to foreign companies. Foreign companies are equally excluded from the "old boy" network of former and current government officials. After an early retirement—often at age fifty or fifty-five—Japanese administrators generally accept positions in major Japanese corporations, usually the same ones they regulated during their tenure in government. This process, known as amakudari or descent from heaven, provides a substantial link between the companies and current bureaucrats[97] and assures a particularly good reception for the former bureaucrat's current employer. Foreign companies generally remain outside this important conduit into the administrative process.

Whether exclusion from the consultative process is systematic or particularized, it makes nonparticipants consistently feel more imposed upon by the Japanese administrative system than participants. Indeed, the participants are often insiders who can increase the likelihood that regulatory regimes will be as palatable as possible. It is no wonder outsiders feel more aggrieved at the onerous burdens they must bear and view the system with greater misgivings.

Of course, the debate about the appropriate degree of participation in the regulatory process is not confined to Japan. Much of the current literature about the American administrative process has focused on problems associ-

---

liability would be substantially lower under regulatory schemes in which they, more than any other groups, had the ear of the regulators.

96. See The Japan-United States Economic Relations Group, Report of the Japan-United States Economic Relations Group 59–60 (1981).

97. C. Johnson, supra note 1, at 11, 21, 63–73.

ated with inadequate participation by some groups[98] and many of the suggested reforms have been directed at restructuring that process to guarantee fair and adequate, but not excessive, participation.[99] Japanese literature on the administrative process has not devoted nearly as much attention to the institutionalization of participation, perhaps because groups systematically excluded do not feel sufficiently aggrieved to protest. Alternatively, the excluded groups may be so powerless or disenfranchised that they cannot generate debate about the possibility of reform. Whatever the reason for the lower degree of intensity with which this debate is pressed, however, the problem of exclusion is very real in the Japanese administrative system, and occasionally results in open conflict.

2. *Administrative Bias.* — A second major reason for dissatisfaction with decisions that emerge from the administrative process is a fear that the administrators are biased in favor of a particular party or interest. One of the better documented examples of such a perception occurred in 1965 when the MITI was helping the steel industry through rough times.[100] Through administrative guidance, the MITI encouraged some eighty producers to limit production and coordinate prices. All of the six major steel producers went along with the suggested price reductions and production limitations, but Sumitomo Metal Industries balked at the MITI's suggestion that these production limitations continue at least three months beyond the initial termination date. Sumitomo rested its objections on several grounds,[101] but it relied most heavily on a well-developed and long-harbored suspicion that the MITI determinations were consistently biased in favor of Yahata and Fuji Steel Companies—companies originally created and nurtured by the government.[102] The

---

98. See, e.g., Stewart, supra note 84, at 1723–48.

99. See id. at 1748–81.

100. For much of the postwar period, the MITI had kept a watchful eye over investment and price stability in the steel industry. The MITI, through its Industrial Rationalization Council, had helped the industry coordinate large-scale investment to minimize the possiblity of "excessive" price competition. It feared that such competition might jeopardize the industry's ability to repay loans taken for the huge investment in converters and blast furnaces. In 1960, the industry, through the Japanese Steel Federation and with the MITI's blessing, had taken over the task of coordinating investment and pricing. By 1965, however, conditions had so deteriorated that further remedial steps seemed essential. For a more complete discussion of this case, see, e.g., C. Johnson, supra note 1, at 268–72; Hibi ga Haita Tekkō no Seisan Chōsei (A Flaw Enters the Steel Production Adjustments), 338 Jurisuto 56–57 (1966); Narita, supra note 8, at 145–49.

101. Sumitomo considered itself one of the more effective export-oriented firms and believed the quotas penalized it for its success in foreign markets. It also thought that the MITI had not adequately allocated market shares in light of new production facilities. See C. Johnson, supra note 1, at 268–72.

102. The government originally founded the Yahata Company as the centerpiece of Japan Steel, a public corporation created in 1934 to strengthen Japan's steel production during a critical period of military expansion. Occupation authorities divided up Japan Steel into Yahata and Fuji (only to see it remerge into New Japan Steel in 1970), but the remaining major steel companies always suspected the government secretly favored the companies it had created and nurtured along. Thus, when the quotas seemed to Sumitomo to favor unduly Yahata and Fuji, it thought this was merely another example of the MITI's favoritism and felt particularly aggrieved. See id.

president of Sumitomo reacted to the perception of bias by publicizing the dispute, before finally settling with the MITI in 1966.[103]

Although the strong-willed personality of the particular bureaucrat and company president involved undoubtedly played a role in this dispute's becoming public, the underlying cause of Sumitomo's unhappiness was a sense of consistent MITI bias in favor of certain of their competitors. Parties regulated pursuant to the informal technique of administrative guidance expect occasionally to bear certain regulatory burdens, anticipating other regulatory concessions later on down the road. Yet if the regulated parties perceive that administrative decisions are consistently biased against them, they despair of the possibility of even-handed treatment—even over the long run. Under these circumstances, major disputes that the administrative system cannot resolve internally arise with greater frequency.

B. *Responses to Process Failure*

While the causes of open conflict are readily ascertained, the reasons a specific dispute takes a particular form are less certain. Nevertheless, some patterns do emerge. In particular, focusing on the power relationship between the agency and the regulated party reveals three important responses to conflict: noncompliance, resort to the political process and adjudication.

1. *Noncompliance.* — Noncompliance with administrative guidance that a regulated party finds unpalatable occurs most commonly when the agency is either unwilling or unable to resort to its collateral enforcement powers. In the 1960's, when the MITI encouraged mergers in the Japanese automobile parts industry, the targeted companies largely ignored the MITI.[104] In this case, the MITI failed to threaten to use any of its collateral powers, such as limiting the import of critical raw materials, to encourage compliance. Thus, the easiest and most straightforward response to this administrative guidance, which the regulated parties felt had not been adequately discussed and appropriately tailored to their circumstances, was simple disobedience. Such a response is

103. The MITI coerced this settlement by threatening to reduce Sumitomo's allotment of coal imports, an action likely to undermine completely Sumitomo's ability to produce. It is interesting to note that within a few months of this incident, the bureaucrat principally responsible for the MITI's determinations in this case retired, having "decided that he had exhausted his usefulness." Id. at 271. The failure to consult adequately and the inclination to operate in this heavy-handed fashion often undermines the effectiveness of bureaucrats and results in their exhausting their "usefulness."

Equally interesting was Sumitomo's subsequent decision to make a fundamental change in its policy and hire an ex-bureaucrat (amakudari). See supra note 97 and accompanying text. Up until that point Sumitomo had refused as a matter of principle to hire ex-bureaucrats. In 1969, however, it hired a retiring MITI vice-minister who became president of the company less than 10 years later. Even Sumitomo, as powerful as it was, ultimately recognized the importance of institutionalizing its input into the regulatory process.

104. See supra notes 91–92.

more common than non-Japanese commentators on Japanese administrative law suppose.[105]

2. *Resort to the Political Process.* — When an agency is willing to invoke collateral enforcement power to implement administrative guidance, a regulated party may resort to the courts or the political process. The aggrieved party is more likely to choose a politically oriented solution when it is subject to pervasive and comprehensive regulation by that particular agency. Under these circumstances, regulated parties may attempt to enlist public support for their cause in hopes of swaying bureaucratic decisionmaking, or more often, may attempt to enlist the support of industry associations and influential members of the business community in their fight.[106] Occasionally, a regulated party will even approach a competing ministry to persuade it that the regulating ministry has encroached upon its regulatory province.[107] Finally, regulated parties frequently approach politicians in an attempt to influence a ministry.[108] While Japanese politicians influence bureaucratic activities less than their counterparts in the United States, their control over budgetary decisions continues to assure some bureaucratic deference.

Regulated parties that expect an ongoing and comprehensive regulatory relationship with the agency in question clearly prefer the use of political pressure to adjudication. Indeed, of the approximately forty cases decided during the past decade that directly challenged the propriety of administrative guidance, virtually none involved a suit against a ministry with which the regulated party was likely to have future regulatory contact of any dimension.

Many commentators attribute this reluctance to litigate to vague, undefined, and empirically unverified cultural factors. Some, for example, stress an amorphous, but widely shared, national ethic that views litigation as disharmonious and thus inappropriate.[109] A related argument is that Japanese lack awareness or "consciousness" of the legal system and its ability to protect individual rights or advance societal objectives.[110] Other commentators point to the availability of alternate dispute resolution mechanisms.[111] Still others note the existence of a more cooperative ethic that has developed between government and business, perhaps as a result of the deeply rooted Confucian or Buddhist tradition or perhaps as a result of more recent structural factors.[112]

---

105. For a typical view of administrative guidance and the rarity of noncompliance or judicial challenge, see P. Davis, supra note 2, at 17-20.

106. This was Sumitomo's approach when the MITI attempted to impose production quotas in 1965. See C. Johnson, supra note 1, at 268-72.

107. Bankers, upset at the MITI's plans to include them in "discussion groups" (kondankai) that were designed to establish and carry out "promotion standards" for various industries under specially proposed legislation, took their case to the MOF and won. See id. at 258-60.

108. See id. at 260-61, 269-71.

109. See, e.g., Kawashima, supra note 90, at 43-45.

110. See T. Kawashima, supra note 90, at 15-36.

111. Henderson, Comments on Civil Disputes Resolution in the U.S. and Japan, 36 Bull. Int'l House Japan 35, 38 (1979).

112. See C. Johnson, supra note 1, at 311-16.

While some truth may be found in each of these observations, the long-term relationship between an agency and regulated party explains more fully the Japanese disinclination to sue. The first relevant institutional factor is a fear that administrative agencies will retaliate in other regulatory settings against parties who take that agency to court. The greater the agency's ability to intrude into the affairs of a party, moreover, the more that party may fear retaliation. Further, the availability of administrative guidance as a regulatory technique not only expands the number of areas into which the agency may intrude, but also tends to diminish any restrictions on the agency's ability to accomplish regulatory goals, regardless of the absence of any connection between a particular goal and a specific grant of regulatory power.[113] Thus, a regulated party who anticipates further dealings with an agency that views its mandate flexibly will think twice before bringing that agency into court, regardless of how onerous the burden of compliance may be in a particular case.[114]

Fear of retaliation is not, however, a wholly satisfactory explanation for the Japanese reluctance to challenge administrative action judicially. Such a theory fails to explain why adjudicatory confrontation threatens a ministry more than merely calling on business leaders or influential politicians, steps routinely taken even when the regulated party anticipates a future relationship with the agency. It may well be that administrators are more threatened by courts, either because they fear exposing to critical legal analysis the weak legal foundation of their regulation, or because they fear the rigidity that regular judicial review would impose upon regulation pursuant to administrative guidance. But whether or not Japanese administrators fear litigation more than political pressure—and therefore retaliate when judicially challenged—the regulated parties may also avoid adjudication out of a disinclination to legalize the regulatory relationship. The parties may perceive that the informal and unlegalized nature of the regulatory relationship generally works to their advantage. Even if they prevail in a particular case, consistent recourse to adjudication might rigidify the regulatory relationship in ways that would be to their long-run disadvantage. This appreciation of the benefits of administrative guidance, together with the fear of regulatory retaliation, explains the Japanese reluctance to adjudicate with greater precision than the cultural theses can.

3. *Adjudication.* — When the regulated party is threatened with collateral enforcement and does not anticipate extensive future regulatory contact with the agency, the way is open to pursue redress through the courts. The most frequent plaintiffs in the three dozen cases challenging the propriety of administrative guidance were developers seeking relief from municipalities' Outline Guidance. In these cases, the regulating authorities sought to bend the regulated parties—the developers—to their will through the imposition of

113. See supra text accompanying notes 52-58.

114. See supra note 64.

considerable collateral powers. The developers, however, planned to construct buildings and then either sell them outright or unit by unit to others. Thus, they did not anticipate a long-term, pervasive regulatory relationship with the municipalities.[115]

Other cases challenging administrative guidance also involve situations in which the likelihood of future involvement between the regulators and the regulated parties is minimal. A bankrupt company has sued the regulatory authorities it believed responsible for its demise,[116] political activists have challenged the Ministry of Foreign Affairs' refusal to allow them to travel to the Soviet Union,[117] and the retailing arm of a petroleum company has attacked the informal decision of local authorities to impose aesthetic restrictions on the building of a service station.[118] Of course, for every party that seeks redress, hundreds apparently choose to forgo judicial relief. Nevertheless, of the millions of Japanese regulatory decisions each year, only those made where the likelihood of future regulation is minimal have any possibility of ending up in court.

III. Judicial Review of Administrative Guidance

The narrow class of cases in which administrative guidance is challenged judicially imposes a significant burden on Japanese courts. They must develop doctrine that allows adequate scope for this important and necessary mode of regulatory power, since the demands placed upon administrative organs in the Japanese state require a broader scope of regulatory power than anticipated under the imported doctrines of judicial review. At the same time, the very mode of behavior that permits agencies to accomplish their tasks—administrative guidance—increases the danger of excessive or unfair intrusions into the affairs of regulated parties.

Judicial review of administrative guidance is particularly challenging due to the theoretically voluntary nature of compliance with administrative guidance.[119] In reality, however, noncompliance may significantly disadvantage regulated parties. Adhering too rigidly to a narrow concept of voluntariness would insulate from review much of the significant administrative activity in

115. It is interesting to note that a significant though somewhat overlapping percentage of the cases involving attacks on administrative guidance are judicial challenges directed towards local authorities and not national administrative officials. This perhaps suggests that the scope of administrative authority at the local level is more circumscribed, or that the number of areas of a regulated party's concerns into which local authorities can administratively intrude is more limited.

116. Shioda v. Ministry of Int'l Trade and Indus., 22 Gyōsei Jiken Saiban Reishū 1785 (Tokyo Dist. Ct. 1971); see infra text accompanying notes 130–33.

117. Okamura v. Japan, 8 Shōmu Geppō 1836 (Tokyo Ct. App. 1962); see infra text accompanying notes 122–26.

118. Sawarabi Kabushiki Kaisha v. City of Kyoto, 691 Hanrei Jihō 57 (Kyoto Dist. Ct. 1972); see infra text accompanying notes 134–37.

119. See supra text accompanying notes 40–49.

modern Japanese society. Yet once courts permit a direct challenge to administrative guidance, they must avoid the opposite extreme of placing severe limitations on the ability of agencies to use administrative guidance—which commentators estimate comprises over eighty percent of Japanese bureaucratic activity.[120] Such a result would be equally unfortunate and would hamper the achievement of a variety of legitimate regulatory goals and objectives in Japan. Japanese courts' response to this dilemma has evolved from a blanket rejection of challenges to administrative guidance to full scale review, but review of a most interesting kind.[121]

A. *Traditional Approach to Reviewing Administrative Guidance*

Japanese courts traditionally considered challenges to administrative guidance to be nonjusticiable. Thus the earliest cases dealing directly with administrative guidance accepted at face value the argument that compliance was voluntary and plaintiffs therefore had no claim for relief.

For example, in a 1963 decision, the Tokyo Court of Appeals rebuffed a challenge to administrative guidance issued by the Japanese Foreign Ministry.[122] The plaintiffs were part of an organization that traditionally participated in the Biannual Festival of World Peace and Friendship for Students and Youths. In 1957, the Festival was to be held in Moscow and its sponsors invited the Japanese organization to send 500 participants. Plaintiffs were encouraged to attend by the Japanese organization, which entered into negotiations with the Foreign Ministry regarding the size of the group that would be

120. Narita, supra note 6, at 39–40.

121. These cases challenging administrative guidance are useful not only because of the context in which they arise, discussed supra text accompanying notes 4–5, 83–90, 113–20, but also because they represent a relatively large percentage of the cases dealing directly with administrative guidance. See Suzuki, supra note 8, at 45–50.

The cases are also of interest due to the light they shed on informal bargaining situations—the most common means of dispute resolution in Japan and elsewhere. Cf. Eisenberg, Private Ordering Through Negotiation: Dispute-Settlement and Rulemaking, 89 Harv. L. Rev. 637 (1976) (exploring the operation of private negotiation as a method of dispute settlement); Mnookin & Kornhauser, Bargaining in the Shadow of the Law: The Case of Divorce, 88 Yale L.J. 950 (1979) (examining the impact of the legal system on bargaining outside the courtroom in the context of divorce). In all legal systems the judicial process and legal doctrines serve as a backdrop against which private negotiations occur, setting outer limits on the scope and content of those negotiations, and Japan is no exception. They provide, as commentators have noted, the "shadow" within which bargaining occurs. Mnookin & Kornhauser, supra, at 950. An examination of these administrative guidance cases makes clear not only the rules that govern these disputes, but also the role courts will play if called upon to intervene. These cases thus help us understand not only the doctrinal, but also the institutional, shadow of the law.

Case examination is also enlightening because the cases appear to have been test situations. Not only did they follow closely on the heels of the promulgation and implementation of Outline Guidance, but local officials in at least two different jurisdictions confirmed that a number of other local disputes of a similar nature were settled without litigation shortly after the court's decisions. Interviews with local officials and developers, in Japan (1981 & 1983).

122. Okamura v. Japan, 8 Shōmu Geppō 1836 (Tokyo Ct. App. 1962).

permitted to participate. The Foreign Ministry initially insisted that no more than fifty could attend, citing the Ministry of Finance's inability to supply foreign currency to any larger group and Japan's general political alignment with the Western bloc nations. As the issue assumed political dimensions, the Ministry eventually permitted 155 people to attend the conference, requesting that no more apply for passports. The remaining 345 brought suit against the government, claiming monetary relief for the injury allegedly resulting from the refusal to issue passports.[123] Plaintiffs argued, among other things, that the Ministry had acted in violation of both the Constitution[124] and the Passport Law[125] by determining in a broad, generalized way that attendance at the conference would undermine the national interest. Rather, the plaintiffs argued, such a determination should have been made on narrow grounds, only

---

123. Prior to World War II, aggrieved individuals could seek monetary relief for harms caused by the government only under general tort principles. Litigants based requests for relief primarily upon Mimpō (Civil Code), Law No. 89 of 1896, Law No. 94 of 1898, arts. 715, 717; see, e.g., S. Imamura & I. Ogawa, Kokka Hoshō Hō Gyōsei Soshō Hō (National Compensation Law and Administrative Litigation Law) 44–48 (1957), and special laws granting redress from harm caused by public employees acting in an official capacity, see, e.g., Yūbin Hō (Postal Law), arts. 68-75, 2 Genkō Hōrei Shūran, bk. 19, ch. 1, at 1 (1909); Yūbin Kawase Hō (Postal Exchange Law), art. 15, 2 Genkō Hōrei Shūran, bk. 19, ch. 2, at 168 (1909); Yūbin Chokin Hō (Postal Savings Law), art. 27, 1 Genkō Hōrei Shūran, bk. 13, ch. 3, at 45 (1909); Denshin Hō (Telegraphic Communications Law), art. 24, 2 Genkō Hōrei Shūran, bk. 19, ch. 3, at 235 (1909). The enactment of the present Constitution in 1946 greatly enhanced the possibility of monetary recovery against the state. Article 17 of the Constitution specifically provides that "[e]very person may sue for redress as provided by law from the State or a public entity, in case he has suffered damage through illegal act of any public official." Kenpō art. 17. The next year the Diet enacted the National Compensation Law, which provides in its first article that "when a public servant, in the course of his employment in an exercise of the public authority of the state or a local public body, illegally causes harm to another person either intentionally or negligently, then the state or public body has a responsibility for compensating the loss." Kokka Baishō Hō (National Compensation Law), Law No. 125 of 1947, art. 1. Although some debate continues about the exact relationship between this law and the tort provisions of the Civil Code, see, e.g., 19 Chūshaku Mimpō (Commentaries on the Civil Code) 271–72 (I. Kato ed. 1965), and the state remains liable in certain limited cases in tort under the Civil Code, see, e.g., 7 Mimpō: Jimu Kanri, Futō Ritoku, Fuhō Kōi (Civil Code: Management of Affairs Without Mandate, Unjust Enrichment and Illegal Acts) 203–05 (H. Endo, T. Kawai, S. Harashima, T. Hironaka, H. Mizumoto & S. Yamamoto eds. 1977), the principal thrust of the National Compensation Law is clear. It greatly expands the liability of the state for the tortious conduct of its employees. In particular, the state is now liable for harms negligently or intentionally committed by public employees even though those employees are engaged in an "exercise of the public authority"—a condition that previously permitted the state to avoid most liability in tort. Of course, there is still debate as to exactly what is an "exercise of the public authority." See, e.g., Sawarabi Kabushiki Kaisha v. City of Kyoto, 691 Hanrei Jihō 57 (Kyoto Dist. Ct. 1972), discussed infra text accompanying notes 134–37. Moreover, large areas of discretion and partial immunity still exist. Nevertheless, most demands for pecuniary relief against the state are made under the National Compensation Law.

124. Plaintiffs relied principally on the Constitution, Kenpō art. 22, ¶ 2, which reads: Freedom of all persons to move to a foreign country and to divest themselves of their nationality shall be inviolate.

125. Ryoken Hō (Passport Law), Law No. 267 of 1951.

after examining the merits of each individual applicant's situation. The court rejected this argument, however, on the ground that the 345 individuals did not apply for a passport and, as a result, the Foreign Ministry had not actually refused to grant passports. Thus, reasoned the court, the Ministry's failure to act on an individual basis could not be deemed illegal. The plaintiffs' voluntary compliance with the Ministry's instructions not to submit individual applications barred the success of plaintiffs' claim.[126]

A 1969 case, arising when the prefectural governor gave a fishing cooperative permission to reclaim certain public shore lands apparently for the purpose of enhancing the ability of the cooperative members to engage in their trade, provides another example of this view of the legal status of administrative guidance. After the reclamation project was well under way, the fishermen received permission to change the purpose of the reclamation project from development of land for fishing to construction of a housing project, which had been the fishing cooperative's objective all along. A company that built and operated tourist hotels sought to obtain the land because of its particularly favorable view of the Inland Sea, but applications for reclamation by private companies were rarely successful. The company had thus persuaded the fishing cooperative, in exchange for a large contribution, to make the application, begin reclamation and then request the modification of purpose. Plaintiffs, owners and operators of ryōkan or Japanese-style inns on the Inland Sea, sued the prefectural governor under the Administrative Case Litigation Law (ACLL)[127] for rescission of both the initial approval and the

126. Review of informal agency action also has not been easily granted in the United States. See, e.g., Helco Prods. Co. v. McNutt, 137 F.2d 681, 683 (D.C. Cir. 1943) ("[P]ronouncements, policies, and programs of a government administrative agency do not give rise to a justiciable controversy, save they have fruition in action of a definite and concrete character . . . .").

127. The Administrative Case Litigation Law specifies four different types of lawsuits. By far most common is a complaint lawsuit (kōkoku soshō). Gyōsei Jiken Soshō Hō (Administrative Case Litigation Law), Law No. 139 of 1962, art. 2 [hereinafter cited as ACLL]. Such a suit places at issue the definite rights and duties of a citizen, as well as the authority and responsibility of an administrative agency. In such a suit, an aggrieved party may challenge as illegal four different kinds of administrative acts. First, a regulated party can bring an action to revoke an administrative disposition (shobun no torikeshi no uttae) that he considers illegal. Id. art. 3, ¶ 2. Second, an aggrieved party can bring an action to revoke an administrative judgment (saiketsu no torikeshi no uttae) issued after a request for review or the filing of an objection pursuant to the Gyōsei Fufuku Shinsa Hō (Administrative Complaints Inquiry Law), Law No. 160 of 1962. ACLL, supra, art. 3, ¶ 3. Third, an aggrieved party can bring an action to challenge an administrative action he thinks not merely revocable, but void (mukō kakunin no uttae). ACLL, supra, art. 3, ¶ 4. If an administrative disposition is merely revocable, the regulated party must challenge the disposition and seek revocation within a specified period of time or he must follow that disposition. If the administrative action is void, however, the disposition has no legal effect and regulated parties need neither obey nor challenge the administrative disposition. As a practical matter, however, administrative agencies act on their dispositions until challenged through the action for confirmation of nullity. Fourth, a regulated party may seek a declaration that an agency's failure to take action is illegal (fusakui no ihō kakunin no uttae) and an order to act. ACLL, supra, art. 3, ¶ 5. If the plaintiff prevails, the court will direct the agency to act, although it will not dictate the substance of the action the agency should take. Challenges to agency

subsequent permission to change purposes. The ACLL's one-year statute of limitations had run on the challenge to the initial approval, however, so the success of their case turned on whether they could challenge the subsequent grant of permission for a change in purpose. The court found the subsequent permission for a change in purpose merely advisory.[128] Thus, the court reasoned, the grant of permission must have been achieved through administrative guidance, which was not a legal act or administrative disposition (shobun) that could be challenged by plaintiffs under the ACLL.

The courts' formalistic reasoning in both these cases ignores the real impact of the administrative determinations. In the first case, plaintiffs did not make a passport application because they were told in no uncertain terms their applications would be rejected. In the second case, only the subsequent grant of permission for a change in the purpose of the reclamation project revealed to plaintiffs the real danger the project posed to their livelihood. Indeed, everyone but the court agreed that a hotel could not have been built on the land except for the subsequent grant of permission. Nevertheless, the courts reasoned in both these cases, obedience to administrative guidance is voluntary and a regulated party that complies cannot come into court and challenge the governmental action that induced or encouraged compliance. Neither can an aggrieved party challenge administrative guidance given to others because ultimate compliance with that administrative advice is purely voluntary.

Courts' insistence that compliance was voluntary insulated from meaningful judicial review a significant amount of administrative activity with a pronounced impact on the affairs of the regulated parties. Indeed, in many instances, administrative guidance places regulated parties at the mercy of administrative agencies—in a practical, if not legal, sense.[129] As the dimension of this problem grew more apparent, courts became increasingly unwilling to use formalistic reasoning about the voluntary nature of compliance to preclude them from exercising even minimal oversight of administrative activity or from providing any protection for the rights and interests of regulated parties. The inadequacies of the strict conceptual approach to administrative determinations that fall under the rubric of administrative guidance led courts to search for ways to review this kind of administrative activity.

---

inaction are uncommon in the United States. See Note, Judicial Review of Administrative Inaction, 83 Colum. L. Rev. 627 (1983).

For a more thorough discussion of the Administrative Case Litigation Law, see J. Tanaka, supra note 5, at 352-440; R. Yanase, Gyōsei Hō Kōgi (Administrative Law Lectures) 227-65 (1973).

128. Kasai v. Governor of Kagawa Prefecture, 20 Gyōsei Jiken Saiban Reishū 452 (Takamatsu Dist. Ct. 1969). In large part, the court reasoned that the subsequent permission was only advisory because the initial approval did not expressly forbid the use of the reclaimed land for housing. Nevertheless, the explicit understanding, noted in both the application and the documents granting the initial approval, was that the reclaimed land would be used to enhance the fishing cooperative's operations.

129. See supra text accompanying notes 37-38, 45-59, 64-65.

B. *Recognition of the Need for Administrative Accountability*

Although unable to resolve fully the doctrinal difficulty inherent in judicial review of administrative guidance, Japanese courts began as early as 1971 to permit direct challenges to administrative guidance. In that year, the Tokyo District Court permitted a suit challenging a notice (tsūtatsu) issued by the MITI.[130] The plaintiff in this case manufactured and sold plastic rulers that measured in centimeters, inches, and even the traditional Japanese measurement standard. The MITI issued a notice that plaintiff's ruler was a measuring device under article 12 of the Weights and Measurements Law and thus must contain only the authorized units of measurement—centimeters. The notice also directed the local prefectural authorities to deal with the matter and report back to the MITI. Based on this notice, the prefectural authorities issued a warning (kankoku) to halt production of the ruler. The plaintiff lodged an objection (igimōshitate sho)[131] with the MITI, which was denied. Plaintiff then sued the MITI and the local prefectural authorities, seeking invalidation of both the notice and warning.[132]

The court held that plaintiff could challenge the notice but not the warning. The court reasoned, in the traditional manner, that the warning merely sought to gain plaintiff's voluntary cooperation and thus did not affect his rights and duties in a legal sense. The court also explicitly recognized that the notice was nothing more than an internal directive and did not change the concrete rights and duties of an individual. Moreover, the court acknowledged, a regulated party normally could bring an action against a specific administrative disposition based upon a notice, thereby adequately protecting his rights. Nevertheless, the court reasoned, in the reality of administrative affairs, notices play an important role and in practice can strongly affect the concrete rights and duties of individuals. Thus, in the rare case where an individual cannot obtain relief without directly disputing the validity of the notice, the court held a direct judicial challenge against the notice itself would be permissible. Although the court ruled against the plaintiff on the merits of his challenge, the significance of this opinion lies in its explicit acknowledgement that strict adherence to the notion that administrative guidance does not change legal relationships may insulate from meaningful judicial review significant administrative action.[133]

---

130. Shioda v. Ministry of Int'l Trade & Indus., 22 Gyōsei Jiken Saiban Reishū 1785 (Tokyo Dist. Ct. 1971).

131. Plaintiff actually mistakenly lodged a request for review (fufuku mōshitate sho), but the MITI regarded the filing as an objection (igi mōshitate sho) and dealt with it in its proper procedural posture.

132. Plaintiff sought revocation of the allegedly illegal administrative dispositions (shobun no torikeshi no uttae). See supra note 127.

133. Equally interesting is the court's realpolitik assessment that while the warning was the actual administrative step that adversely affected plaintiff (no retailers would buy his ruler because they thought it could not be legally resold), the true foundation of that administrative action was the notice issued by the MITI. Thus, instead of permitting plaintiff to challenge the

The following year, 1972, the Kyoto District Court also allowed a judicial challenge to administrative guidance.[134] The plaintiff, a company that owned and operated gasoline stations throughout Japan, had secured an option on land in a part of Kyoto that was designated a special area of scenic beauty (fūchi chiku). The city's Planning Bureau informed plaintiff that any gasoline station it built would have to conform to extremely restrictive aesthetic specifications, which the plaintiff determined would make the venture unprofitable. Plaintiff thus let the option on the land lapse, after which someone else purchased the land and built a gasoline station that did not conform to any of the requirements that had been presented to plaintiff. Plaintiff sued the city for damages under the National Compensation Law.[135] The court held that the city's actions, though administrative guidance, amounted to an "exercise of public authority" (kōkenryoku no kōshi) under article 1 of the National Compensation Law,[136] entitling plaintiff to damages if the action was illegal. Although the court found that defendant's actions were not illegal under the circumstances, the significance of its holding lies in the determination that even actions that do not directly change legal relationships and that involve at least theoretically voluntary compliance can be "exercises of public authority" and thus reviewed in court. The court was probably the first to construe "exercises of public authority" broadly enough to include many of those administrative activities that fall within the rubric of administrative guidance.[137]

In these two transition cases, the courts were clearly troubled by the prospect of dismissing a plaintiff's complaint when it was clear dismissal would leave a genuinely aggrieved party without legal recourse. Given the frequent resort to administrative guidance as a regulatory technique in Japan,[138] strict adherence to the narrow conception of an administrative disposition as the sole object of judicial review would leave entirely unreviewable the vast bulk of administrative determinations. The traditional doctrine regarding voluntary compliance simply could not provide the degree of flexibility necessary to assure some role for the judiciary in Japan's system of regulatory behavior. Thus, the courts were motivated to recognize the right of the aggrieved party to challenge the administrative directives and guidelines, despite the fact that these directives and guidelines had not yet crystallized into formal administrative determinations.

---

administrative action having the most direct adverse impact, the court permitted plaintiff to challenge the administrative determination upon which the warning was based. While this may seem odd, it reflects a realistic appraisal of where the power lies and the relationship between various decisional activities of related administrative agencies.

134. Sawarabi Kabushiki Kaisha v. City of Kyoto, 691 Hanrei Jihō 57 (Kyoto Dist. Ct. 1972).

135. Kokka Baishō Hō (National Compensation Law), Law No. 125 of 1947; see also supra note 123.

136. Kokka Baishō Hō (National Compensation Law), Law No. 125 of 1947, art. 1; see also supra note 123.

137. See 691 Hanrei Jihō 57, 57 (Kyoto Dist. Ct. 1972).

138. See supra note 120 and accompanying text.

C. *Judicial Review of Outline Guidance*

Having recognized a right to challenge administrative guidance, Japanese courts had to develop doctrine that would assure plaintiffs relief while affording administrators adequate flexibility. In resolving this dilemma, Japanese courts did not turn to the traditional civil law techniques of judicial review of administrative action, which ask whether the administrator conformed his acts to the legislative mandate and to constitutional imperatives.[139] Such sweeping review would eliminate a great deal of Japanese administrative flexibility, which commentators agree is essential to accomplish the difficult and complex tasks assigned the bureaucracy.[140] Instead, Japanese courts have, especially in cases reviewing municipalities' Outline Guidance, developed a unique approach to review of administrative action. These doctrinal steps are explored within the context in which they developed—cases challenging municipalities' Outline Guidance.

One of the earliest in a series of attacks by developers on Outline Guidance culminated in a 1973 decision of the Tokyo District Court, *Yoshida v. Nakano Ward*.[141] The plaintiff, who was planning to build an apartment complex within the Nakano Ward of Tokyo, applied to local authorities for a construction permit pursuant to the Construction Standards Law.[142] At the same time, pursuant to the local jurisdiction's Outline Guidance, he commenced negotiations with the surrounding residents in an attempt to reach agreement on the permissible degree of interference with sunlight and ventilation. Plaintiff continued these negotiations during the next four months, meeting with the surrounding residents six times and making at least one major modification in his plans. He also continued to press his case with the local authorities for approval of the construction permit. Despite these efforts, the surrounding residents refused to agree to his plan, even in its modified form. They held out in part because they hoped Tokyo would soon modify its zoning regulations, making plaintiff's project altogether unprofitable. Because the plaintiff had not reached an accord with the surrounding residents, the construction supervisor refused to pass on the permit, notwithstanding the legal requirement to do so within twenty-one days.[143]

---

139. Japanese law forbids both unauthorized administrative incursions on private activity and administrative action that conflicts with legislative pronouncements or constitutional strictures. For a detailed general discussion of these rules, see J. Tanaka, supra note 5, at 340–440.

140. Virtually all commentators mention this need when discussing administrative guidance. See, e.g., K. Yamanouchi, supra note 20, at 104–24; Shiono, supra note 8, at 225–27; Shiono, Gyōsei Shidō (Administrative Guidance), *in* Gyōsei Hō Kōza (Administrative Law Course) 13, 39–44 (J. Tanaka ed. 1965); Narita, supra note 6, at 39–42.

141. 886 Hanrei Jihō 15 (Tokyo Dist. Ct. 1973).

142. Kenchiku Kijun Hō (Construction Standards Law), Law No. 201 of 1950, art. 6; see also supra text accompanying notes 22–25, 35–38.

143. See Kenchiku Kijun Hō (Construction Standards Law), Law No. 201 of 1950, art. 6, ¶ 3; see also supra text accompanying notes 22–25; infra note 148.

Seeing little chance of persuading the surrounding residents, plaintiff sued the local authorities under the ACLL, seeking a declaration that their failure to pass on his application was illegal and that they should pass on that application as soon as possible.[144] While this case was pending, however, Tokyo rezoned, causing plaintiff to abandon the project and change his lawsuit to one against the local government for the harms occasioned by its delay in issuing his permit. In this amended suit, plaintiff sought damages under the National Compensation Law[145] for lost profits and expenses incurred in attempting to secure the financing necessary to complete the project.

The court agreed with the plaintiff that in determining whether to grant or refuse the permit, the construction supervisor could consider only whether the application conformed with the relevant laws, ordinances and regulations specified in the statute. The municipality had enacted no formal sunlight and ventilation ordinance.[146] Moreover, while the construction supervisor might have some statutorily granted discretion about whether the plans actually conformed to the law in certain cases,[147] once he determined the application did conform, he had no right to deny the permit. Finally, the court acknowledged the plaintiff's claim that, except in certain limited circumstances, the construction supervisor has twenty-one days to take action on an application.[148]

Despite this substantial agreement on legal theory, the court rejected plaintiff's claim. The court reasoned that reserving a decision on the application differed from taking adverse action. Moreover, the court noted, the Construction Standards Law permits the construction supervisor, when he has "proper reasons" (seitō na riyū), to notify the applicant that a decision cannot be reached within the twenty-one day period.[149] Thus, the twenty-one day limit is not absolute, but can be extended when proper reasons exist; propri-

144. This is the fourth kind of administrative challenge permitted under the ACLL. See supra note 127.

145. Kokka Baishō Hō (National Compensation Law), Law No. 125 of 1947; see supra note 123.

146. For example, both articles 29 and 33 of the Construction Standards Law permit the local authorities to determine that the plans generally conform to the requirements of the law and issue a permit, even when special circumstances make the plans not in total conformity with certain requirements. Thus, the authorities may waive compliance with article 29's requirement that dwellings above the first floor receive some sunlight, or article 33's requirements regarding lightning rods. Kenchiku Kijun Hō (Construction Standards Law), Law No. 201 of 1950, arts. 29, 33.

147. See supra notes 27–31 and accompanying text.

148. See Kenchiku Kijun Hō (Construction Standards Law), Law No. 201 of 1950, art. 6, ¶ 3. The rationale underlying the 21-day time limit is freedom to use one's property as one sees fit. Although regulations may restrict an owner's use (especially when it involves construction), the basic thrust of the law is to offset regulatory burdens upon ownership by assuring speedy regulatory decisions. Thus, the 21-day time limit must be regarded not merely as an internal directive to the agency, but rather as a mandatory provision. See Yoshida v. Nakano, 886 Hanrei Jihō 15 (Tokyo Dist. Ct. 1973).

149. Kenchiku Kijun Hō (Construction Standards Law), Law No. 201 of 1950, art. 6, ¶ 4.

ety, as the court somewhat elliptically explained, is appraised in the uncertain light of the "common sense of society."[150] Thus, reasoned the court, although the construction supervisor may not directly consider matters such as sunlight, ventilation and television reception when passing on applications, these factors—relevant to the "common sense of society"—may play an indirect role in the decision whether to withhold action on an application.

From a traditional civil or common law perspective, the court's approach thus far was predicated on the fundamental determination of whether the construction supervisor had advanced the law's "purposes." The court noted that the Construction Standards Law asserts as its general purpose the establishment of minimum standards concerning the site, structure, facilities, and use of construction to protect life, health and property, thereby contributing to the "public welfare." Yet in an impressive sleight of hand, the court at this point shifted its focus from the regulatory goals expressly mandated by the law to the more amorphous goal of resolving tensions and conflicts between competing interest groups in society. Out of whole cloth, the court asserted that the law's statement of general purpose, especially the invocation of "public welfare," supported a general duty of local authorities to attempt suitable resolutions of conflicts of interest that arise between various groups and individuals within the local authorities' jurisdiction.

By adopting this interpretation, the court read out of the statute any requirement that the agency base its decision solely or even primarily upon factors relating to the safety of the planned building. Instead, so long as an agency attempts to resolve conflicts among the various groups that fall within its jurisdictional mandate, it may delay a decision on a construction permit application based solely on the "common sense of society."[151] In defining what this standard required in a given situation, the court laid out criteria establishing the permissibility of agency action not in terms of substantive areas of regulatory control or the relationship of agency action to statutorily mandated administrative duties, but rather entirely in terms of dispute resolution technique.

More specifically, the court offered two standards for evaluating an agency's ability to resolve disputes. First, the administrative guidance must be performed in a manner recognized by society as proper or reasonable. In particular, the agency should take action that encourages the parties themselves to reach a settlement based on mutual consent. Second, the administra-

---

150. 886 Hanrei Jihō 15. In addition to general factors such as sunlight and ventilation, this standard would encompass technical reasons that may make action on an application inadvisable, such as when the documents are insufficient or the building project too complex to permit a reasoned judgment within the statutory time allotment.

151. See 886 Hanrei Jihō 15. Another example of this approach can be found in a 1978 Outline Guidance decision of the Tokyo District Court. In Jūrakuen Yūgen Kaisha v. Nakano Ward, 931 Hanrei Jihō 79 (Tokyo Dist. Ct. 1978), aff'd, 36 Sai-han Minshū 727 (S. Ct. Petty Bench 1982), plaintiff, the developer of a medium-size apartment building, sought to reach an agreement on light and ventilation with the surrounding residents as required by the local

tive guidance must be performed "sincerely" or "earnestly." In this regard, the court uses the word shinshi, a term of nonlegal vintage that suggests honest intent or genuine purpose. Fairly read, these two standards are vague exhortions to bargain in good faith and stay within the bounds of reason and societal sensibilities.

Perhaps realizing the difficulty of applying these two standards, the court also provided a more functional, real-world test for assessing the propriety of action taken on the basis of administrative guidance. The test asks whether during those periods when the agency was applying pressure, a reasonable expectation still existed that the dispute could be resolved by mutual agreement of the parties. When such an expectation disappears, further application of administrative guidance becomes impermissible. In the context of Outline Guidance, this test would permit the withholding of a construction permit so long as a reasonable possibility existed that the developer would reach agreement with the surrounding residents. Thus the court examined in great detail each of the various meetings between the developer and the surrounding residents, including the state of mind of all the participants at each stage of the negotiations. After examining with care all nuances of every communication, the court held that a reasonable possibility of compromise existed until Tokyo rezoned; therefore, the administrative authorities had not overstepped their bounds.[152]

---

jurisdiction's Outline Guidance. After long negotiations with the neighbors and unsuccessful importuning of the local authorities to issue a permit waiving the size and weight limitations under the Road Law, Dōro Hō (Road Law), Law No. 180 of 1952; see supra note 38 and accompanying text, to permit transport of the heavy construction machinery and materials, the developer finally reached an agreement with the neighbors. The local authorities then immediately issued the traffic permit.

Plaintiff sued the local authorities under the National Compensation Law, Kokka Baishō Hō (National Compensation Law), Law No. 125 of 1947; see supra note 123, for the financial injuries allegedly resulting from the long delay in construction occasioned by the local authorities' refusal to issue the necessary traffic permits. Plaintiff conceded that local authorities had some discretion in granting permission to use oversized vehicles, but argued that only the principle of safety could inform the exercise of this discretion. Because permission could not be withheld for any reason other than one relating to traffic safety, plaintiff argued, the local authorities' withholding of the permit was illegal.

The court agreed that viewed in the abstract, the purpose of the Road Law was safety and that it did not enable local authorities to withhold a permit for reasons unrelated to safety. Nevertheless, the court continued, local authorities perform many functions and may use one regulatory power to advance another, completely unrelated, regulatory interest. Because local authorities can use their powers under the Road Law to accomplish other, collateral regulatory goals, the propriety of their acts under the Road Law must be judged with an eye to their responsibilities in other areas. This exercise of power must be examined "in the totality of the circumstances"; under this standard, the court found their actions proper because they were encouraging various groups within their jurisdiction to settle disputes among themselves. For more details regarding this case, see Suzuki, supra note 8, at 46.

152. 886 Hanrei Jihō 15.

The 1979 decision of the Tokyo Court of Appeals in *Nakatani Honten Gōmei Kaisha v. Tokyo*[153] is even more striking in its articulation of this reasonable possibility of agreement standard. In that case, the court explicitly found continued inaction on a construction permit application illegal in the face of apparent impossibility of compromise or settlement. Plaintiff, planning to build an apartment complex, applied to the local construction supervisor for a construction permit under the Construction Standards Law. After an examination of the factors mandated in that law, the Supervisor reserved determination on the application because the plaintiff had failed to reach agreement with the surrounding residents on the permissible degree of interference with sunlight and ventilation. After continued unsuccessful negotiations, plaintiff's representatives appealed to the Tokyo Construction Inspection Committee, a legislatively created administrative organ, pursuant to article 94 of the Construction Standards Law. The plaintiff's representatives insisted that action be taken on the application or that the supervisor's inaction be construed as approval. Before the committee issued its decision, however, the plaintiff reached an agreement with the surrounding residents. After the permit was issued and construction began, the plaintiff sued the supervisor under the National Compensation Law for damages caused by the long and allegedly illegal delay.

The lower court dismissed the plaintiff's claim. It first held that the construction supervisor can withhold action on an application when circumstances exist that are "proper" and "logical" in light of the "common sense of society" and the "goals" of the law. It then determined that the construction supervisor's attempts to protect the local residents' sunlight and ventilation were proper goals within the law and thus constituted such circumstances. Therefore, the Supervisor's inaction could not be considered illegal.[154]

The Tokyo High Court disagreed. Relying on a reasoning process almost identical to that in *Yoshida v. Nakano Ward*, the court held that a construction supervisor's inaction becomes illegal when a reasonable possibility of compromise no longer exists. As in the *Yoshida* case, the court found that local authorities could delay action on an application for "proper reasons," again defined in terms of the common sense of society and the goals of the law. The court further found, as in *Yoshida*, that the purpose was acceptable. It defined the purpose not as the lower court had done, however, but rather focused mainly on the agency's mandate to resolve conflicts among various parties in an apparently consensual way. This permitted the court, like the *Yoshida* court, to focus its attention on the manner in which this guidance was given and to hold that it was proper so long as a reasonable possibility of compromise still existed. Unlike *Yoshida*, however, the court found, after a detailed analysis of the various meetings and the state of mind of plaintiff's representatives at each particular stage, that no reasonable possibility of

153. 955 Hanrei Jihō 73 (Tokyo Ct. App. 1979).
154. 928 Hanrei Jihō 79 (Tokyo Dist. Ct. 1978).

compromise existed after plaintiff applied to the Tokyo Construction Inspection Committee for review. Thus, the local authorities' refusal to act on the application after plaintiff filed its petition with the Committee was illegal. Accordingly, the plaintiff was entitled to increased costs caused by the delay.[155]

D. *Doctrinal Constructs of Judicial Review of Administrative Guidance*

These challenges to administrative guidance, and others like them,[156] significantly depart from traditional civil law notions of judicial review of administrative action. In seeking to strike the balance between administrative flexibility and protection against excessive bureaucratic intrusions, Japanese courts have developed a set of doctrinal constructs that enshrine bargaining and negotiation as the primary focus of judicial inquiry to evaluate the propriety of administrative action. First, the courts employ traditional and occasionally nontraditional judicial techniques to place limits on the agencies' power to force the regulated parties to reach an agreement. Second, the courts rearticulate the agency's regulatory mandate so as to focus on the voluntary nature of compliance. Finally, the courts refuse to determine the priority of competing claims of right. Each of these doctrinal developments will be examined in turn.

1. *Judicial Limits on the Bargaining Mode of Regulation.* — In striking the balance between judicial oversight and administrative flexibility, Japanese courts reviewing administrative guidance seek both to foster and to monitor the bargaining process. Yet courts employ several techniques designed to place

---

155. The court found, however, that most of the increased expenses were not compensable. The increased costs of subcontracting were not justified because, while costs were increasing rapidly in the construction industry, the period of time for which the local authorities were actually liable was not that long and costs could not have risen during that short period as much as plaintiff claimed. The amount equivalent to some predictable return that plaintiff would have received on his investment during that time had he been permitted to proceed (e.g., an amount of money essentially equivalent to the interest plaintiff would have earned had he otherwise invested the money during that period) could be measured, and was therefore compensable for the period of time between when plaintiff appealed to the Tokyo Construction Inspection Committee and when the permit finally issued.

The court's reasoning in this case also calls into question the validity of the subsequent agreement the developer reached with the local residents. If the agency was unduly pressuring the developer, the developer would have a strong argument that any agreement into which he subsequently entered was the product of duress or illegal government interference and thus voidable. The developer did not raise this argument, however, nor did he attempt to void the agreement. Thus, the court was not required to address this difficult question.

156. See, e.g., Taiyō Kensetsu Kabushiki Kaisha v. Nerima Ward, 952 Hanrei Jihō 18 (Tokyo Dist. Ct. 1979); Jūrakuen Yūgen Kaisha v. Nakano Ward, 931 Hanrei Jihō 79 (Tokyo Dist. Ct. 1978), aff'd, 36 Sai-han Minshū 727 (S. Ct. Petty Bench 1982); Fuji Enters. Kabushiki Kaisha v. Tokyo, 894 Hanrei Jihō 82 (Tokyo Dist. Ct. 1977); Yamaki Kensetsu Kabushiki Kaisha v. City of Musashino, 803 Hanrei Jihō 18 (Tokyo Dist. Ct. 1975). For a discussion of the *Jūrakuen Yūgen Kaisha* Case, see supra note 150, and for a discussion of *Yamaki Kensetsu Kabushiki Kaisha v. City of Musashino*, see infra notes 176–79 and accompanying text.

limits on the bargaining power of the parties involved and on the agencies' ability to structure the bargaining process. To constrain agencies from excessive and unwarranted intrusion into private affairs, courts permit them to encourage negotiation only where the goals of the bargaining conform with a broad, but informally determined social consensus. Courts further restrain excessive administrative zeal by conferring upon developers a limited right to halt all negotiations. These devices will be explored in turn.

The first major limit that courts impose on agencies is that they advance goals approved by societal consensus. Thus, in *Yoshida v. Nakano Ward*,[157] the court articulated a two-pronged test for evaluating the propriety of the interest advanced by the administrative agency: it must further the welfare of groups falling within the jurisdictional mandate,[158] and it must accord with the consensus of society.

While at first blush the *Yoshida* test may parallel traditional civil law purpose analysis, its emphasis on societal imprimatur signals a fundamental Japanese difference. The *Yoshida* court addresses the question of consensus despite the nonexistence of any authoritative legislative or even administrative enactment at either the local or national level on the question of sunlight and ventilation.[159] Of course the court was well supported in finding Outline Guidance socially accepted, given the over 800 jurisdictions that have enacted it in some form,[160] but the critical issue is the court's willingness to define consensus from informal rather than legal sources. Indeed, the court's view is that the basic inquiry for determining the validity of administrative action asks not whether those actions have been taken in accordance with legally established procedures that permit the government to take authoritative steps against the governed, but rather whether these actions have the more informal

---

157. 886 Hanrei Jihō 15 (Tokyo Dist. Ct. 1973).

158. The court's emphasis on groups accords with the group-oriented mandate of administrative guidance. See supra notes 59–64 and accompanying text.

159. Indeed, some speculate that this administrative action took the form of administrative guidance and not administrative regulations precisely because such regulations would be in conflict with the Construction Standards Law. See supra note 25–31 and accompanying text. This rationale suggests one of the more suspect uses of administrative guidance—action by the administrative agency taken in the form of nonbinding, nonauthoritative "suggestions" to insulate the administrative action from review. This misuse of administrative guidance attracted particular attention when the Ministry of Posts and Telecommunication attempted to regulate, without issuing any authoritative regulations or orders, the hours during which television stations could broadcast. See K. Yamanouchi, supra note 20, at 74–80; supra notes 57–58 and accompanying text.

160. See Gyōsei Shidō Kenkyūkai, supra note 6, pt. 2, at 152–54. Moreover, at the time of this decision, discussions of amendment to the Construction Standards Law were widespread. Indeed, in 1976, Kenchiku Kijun Hō no Ichibu wo Kaisei Suru Hōritsu (Law Amending in part the Construction Standards Law), Law No. 83 of 1976, and again in 1978, Chihō Kōfuzei Hō Tō no Ichibu wo Kaisei Suru Hōritsu (Law Amending in part the Local Revenue Sharing Law, Etc.), Law No. 38 of 1978, the law was amended to permit local authorities to regulate more extensively in the area of sunlight and ventilation.

sanction of society in general. Thus, the fact that agencies follow formally established rules is not highly significant in the judicial analysis.[161]

Japanese courts' emphasis on societal consensus rather than formal procedure in administrative guidance cases contrasts sharply with most civil law systems' respect, almost reverence, for the formalities of the legal process.[162] These cases suggest that the Japanese may not accord the forms and procedures of the legal process, at least at the legislative and administrative level, the same respect. In some sense, this lack of reverence for process leads to the generalization that the Japanese are less "legalistic" than Westerners. The Japanese may share or even exceed Westerners' concern that the substance of rights reflect majoritorian preferences or societal consensus, and that the average citizen actually enjoy the benefit of such rights. The Japanese may be less concerned, however, with the legislative and administrative processes that Westerners generally believe necessary to determine the substance of rights or so-called majoritarian preference.

---

161. Some legal commentators in Japan have embraced this view with enthusiasm. One commentator, for example, in addressing the legality of an individual's behavior that is in technical compliance with the law but in violation of Outline Guidance, argued that courts should permit the local authorities to take punitive retaliatory action if the Outline Guidance was developed through processes that allowed substantial, though admittedly informal, democratic participation by the residents, and if noncompliance were "illegal" in terms of "social reality." See Masago, Chihō Kōkyō Dantai ni okeru Gyōsei Shidō (Administrative Guidance in Local Public Entities), *in* Gendai Seiji to Chihō Jichi (Modern Politics and Local Automony) 247, 253 (T. Adachi, K. Kato, T. Fukushima, H. Fukui & Y. Muramatsu eds. 1975).

162. Like the Japanese attitude in administrative guidance cases, the common law commitment to the judiciary as a primary organ for developing law may reflect confidence that judges can determine which rules most benefit society. This initial confidence may have reflected some belief in a natural law that could be discovered by all men of learning and reason. More to the point, however, as Japanese judges are affirming (or perhaps renewing) their commitment to this judicial function, Americans are increasingly troubled by the exercise of judicial power. See, e.g., R. Berger, Congress v. The Supreme Court (1969); R. Berger, Government by Judiciary (1977); A. Bickel, The Least Dangerous Branch 1–19 (1962); Bork, The Impossibility of Finding Welfare Rights in the Constitution, 1979 Wash. U.L.Q. 695, 695–98. More generally, scholars are exerting even greater effort to determine, redefine, or defend the role of the courts in the development of law in the United States. See, e.g., G. Calabresi, A Common Law for the Age of Statutes (1982); J. Choper, Judicial Review and the National Political Process: A Functional Reconsideration of the Supreme Court (1980); J. Ely, Democracy and Distrust: A Theory of Judicial Review (1980); M. Perry, The Constitution, the Courts, and Human Rights (1982); Blasi, The Rootless Activism of the Burger Court, *in* The Burger Court 198 (V. Blasi ed. 1983). It is particularly interesting to observe Japanese judges, who come from the opposite legal tradition, moving in a quite different direction.

This different emphasis stems in part from cultural,[163] political,[164] and historical[165] differences. More concretely, however, courts' willingness to rely upon informal evidence of societal consensus derives from the nature of administrative guidance. All the literature addressing administrative guidance suggests general resignation that the tasks imposed on administrative organs in Japan may require them to act even without strict legal authorization.[166] Indeed, the courts in these opinions fear that bureaucratic organs will be unable to function properly if they must await specific legislative authorization in every case. To assure this flexibility while protecting individuals from arbitrary intrusion, courts rely on the notion of societal consensus. This test enables agencies to act without formal legal authorization but allows courts to assess whether administrative action falls within the perceived general public will. Keeping the barometer of societal consensus informal and vague allows agencies to continue to operate in a relatively free fashion. It nonetheless

---

163. Most Japanese view their society as extremely homogenous. Thus, they may well believe that determinations of societal "consensus" are easier to make and do not require strict compliance with all the technical formalities of the legal and political processes. This is not to say that the Japanese are necessarily any less concerned with respecting and following majoritarian views than other societies (indeed, at many levels they may be more concerned with the ascertainment of actual majoritarian preferences or the achievement of societal consensus through acceptable compromise or legislative and administrative determinations), but rather that they are more confident in the accuracy of less formal means that may be used to ascertain those views. Whether or not this confidence is misplaced, it remains true that the commitment to these forms and procedures appears to be less pronounced in Japan.

164. Politically, a gulf has long existed in Japan between formal legal and political institutions and the social and political reality within which they operated. Japan has long had a commitment to certain types of consensual decisionmaking processes that were democratic in their effect. Nevertheless, as a historical matter, the formal political and legal institutional arrangements were invariably quite authoritarian in coloring, if not in fact. This tension may inevitably have led to a reduced reliance on formal institutions, especially to the extent one actually possesses some basic inclination to respect majoritarian or consensual solutions to problems. Of course, the gulf between the formalities and realities of the legal and political systems is great in many, if not most, societies. One senses, however, that, at least historically, that gulf was perhaps wider in Japan.

165. The importation of political and legal institutions into Japan in the middle to end of the nineteenth century (and again at the end of World War II) and the imposition of these institutions atop a sophisticated preexisting legal and political order may also have distorted the normal operating modes of these institutions in ways relevant to this discussion. See supra text accompanying notes 4–5. It is commonplace that various legal institutions operate quite differently in different societies. Japan, however, may be an extreme example of that phenomenon. In light of the rapidity with which its legal institutions and legal order were imported and imposed, it would not be surprising if the various institutional formalities were occasionally considered less important than they might be elsewhere. These institutions, moreover, may not "fit" that society very well, or be responsive to the needs or concerns of that society. Perhaps the political and legal institutions adopted by Japan for the determination of various social policies do not mesh with the social and economic structure of the society upon which they were overlaid or perhaps the fit of that overlay is such that the technical procedures of these institutions are less significant in Japan than they might be elsewhere.

166. See supra note 140.

provides a minimal check on the substance of the regulations being advanced by the administrative organs. While cultural, social and historical factors may give Japanese courts confidence that their informal determinations of societal consensus will be accurate, the need for such informal determinations stems from the tasks imposed on the bureaucracy and the necessity of free form and unrestricted regulatory techniques to accomplish those tasks.

Courts place a second major limit on the excesses of the bureaucracy by vesting in developers the right to call a halt to further negotiation and insist upon the issuance of the permit. Use of this technique is particularly notable in the *Nakatani Honten*[167] case, where the court held the municipality liable for damages from the point in time when the developer firmly put his foot down and compromise became impossible. The rationale behind allowing developers to halt negotiations is the voluntary nature of compliance with administrative guidance. Because the basic jurisdictional mandate of the administrative agencies is to encourage negotiated settlement of disputes, when such a settlement is no longer possible, compliance is no longer voluntary and further pressure on the developer becomes improper.

It might be argued that the courts' attempt to prevent local authorities from exerting too much pressure on the developer acts merely as a roundabout way of validating the developer's claim of right. Permitting the developer to halt negotiations at any stage and insist upon the issuance of the construction permit places the surrounding residents at the mercy of the developer, just as they were before the local authorities attempted to create in them a substantive property right. Thus, this grant of power to the developers is merely an attempt to validate their rights through the back door, not an effort to place some limits on the ability of an agency to regulate.

Courts, however, attempt to contain any negative effect that judicial intervention would have on agency flexibility by limiting the developers' ability to terminate negotiations. The first major restriction that courts place on developers is an assumption that despite the developer's "right" to call a halt to the proceedings and insist on the issuance of a permit, the local authorities may assume at the outset the developer will not be inclined to cooperate. Indeed, the courts recognize not only that developers initially will be reluctant to concede their position, but that the very goal of this administrative pressure is to persuade recalcitrant, even obstinate, developers to be more cooperative. Thus, the courts permit the agency to presume—irrebutably—at the outset of the negotiations, regardless of the developer's actual state of mind or attitude at the time, that the developer in time might be persuaded. This presumption leaves no doubt that the local authorities can apply considerable pressure on the developer before developers finally invoke their "right" to call a halt to the negotiations. Moreover, allowing this amount of pressure—enough, but not too much, as it were—makes clear that

---

167. 955 Hanrei Jihō 73 (Tokyo Ct. App. 1979). See supra notes 136-40 and accompanying text.

the courts are not merely validating the developers' claim and rejecting the agency's attempts to create a right in the surrounding residents. To the contrary, the courts clearly refrain from deciding which right triumphs. Instead, they give the agencies some—although only some—leeway to restructure the bargaining situation and supervise the negotiations that occur within the confines of the newly created bargaining situation to make sure that real bargaining, with its attendant possibilities for meaningful compromise, actually occurs.

A second major limit courts place on developers' ability to terminate negotiations derives from a variant on the abuse of rights doctrine.[168] The abuse of rights doctrine, perhaps initially rooted in the roman legal concept *male enim nostro iure uti non debemus* ("we ought not to make a bad use of our lawful rights"),[169] first appeared in modern civil law jurisprudence in France.[170] In most civil law jurisdictions, the doctrine attempts to prevent individuals from using their rights with the sole intent of harming another, without any serious and legitimate interest or benefit to themselves.[171] In particular, the modern French concept continues to focus on the minimal benefit to the rightholder and his wrongful intent.[172]

In Japan, on the other hand, the abuse of rights doctrine has gradually evolved into an explicit tool for weighing the comparative harms and benefits attendant to the exercise of a particular right.[173] For example, in a 1972 decision on the proper use of the abuse of rights doctrine, the Japanese Supreme Court asserted that rights must be exercised only within "a scope judged reasonable in the light of the prevailing social conscience" and "the limit which is generally supposed to be borne in the social life . . . ."[174]

---

168. See Yamaki Kensetsu Kabushiki Kaisha v. City of Musashino, 803 Hanrei Jihō 18 (Tokyo Dist. Ct. 1975), discussed infra text accompanying notes 176-80.

169. 1 Inst. Gaius 36 (E. Poste trans. 1925).

170. Bolgar, Abuse of Rights in France, Germany and Switzerland: A Survey of a Recent Chapter in Legal Doctrine, 35 La. L. Rev. 1015, 1015-1023 (1975); Cueto-Rua, Abuse of Rights, 35 La. L. Rev. 965, 965-66 (1975) (quoting In re Doerr Colmar, May 2, 1855, D.P. 1856.2.9).

171. See Cueta-Rua, supra note 170, at 982.

172. See id. at 965 (quoting In re Doerr Colmar, May 2, 1855, D.P. 1856.2.9).

173. The doctrine was first transmitted to Japan through Germany around the turn of the century, see E. Makino, Kenri no Ranyō to Hōritsu ni okeru Shinka to Shimpo (Abuse of Rights and Evolution and Progress in the Law) 223, 223-237 (1924), where it early found expression in cases of the Great Court of Judicature, the forerunner of the Supreme Court, and enjoyed wide scholarly support. See H. Suekawa, Kenri Ranyō Gaisetsu (Outline of Abuse of Rights) 101 (1949) (tracing the development of the doctrine in Japan). Finally, in 1947, it became part of the Japanese Civil Code. See Mimpō (Civil Code), Law No. 222 of 1947, art. 1, ¶ 2.

174. Mitamura v. Suzuki, 26 Sai-han Minshū 1067, 1069 (S. Ct. Petty Bench 1972), quoted in Sono & Fujioka, The Role of the Abuse of Right Doctrine in Japan, 35 La. L. Rev. 1037 (1975). The quote reads in full:

> In all cases a right must be exercised in such a fashion that the result of the exercise remains within a scope judged reasonable in the light of the prevailing social conscience. When conduct by one who purports to have a right to do so fails to show social

Similarly, other cases suggest that Japanese courts balance the competing interests in assessing proper exercise of a right, weighing benefit against harm under the guise of the abuse of rights doctrine.[175]

In the context of Outline Guidance, however, at least one Japanese court has transformed the already unique Japanese version of abuse of rights into a potent device for reviewing administrative guidance and limiting the developers' ability to terminate negotiations. The 1975 decision of the Tokyo District Court, *Yamaki Kensetsu Kabushiki Kaisha v. City of Musashino*,[176] involved substantially the same facts as other Outline Guidance cases[177]—plaintiff-developer failed to reach an agreement with surrounding residents concerning sunlight and ventilation and the local authorities withheld the supply of water. The factual wrinkle in *Yamaki* was that the plaintiff borrowed water for construction purposes from nearby land and started construc-

---

reasonableness and when the consequential damages to others exceed the limit which is generally supposed to be borne in the social life, we must say that the exercise of the right is no longer within its permissible scope. Thus, the person who exercises his right in such a fashion shall be held liable because his conduct constitutes an abuse of right.

175. See, e.g., 22 Sai-han Minshū 817 (S. Ct. Petty Bench 1968); Denki Shōten Jiken, 16 Sai-han Minshū 639 (S. Ct. Petty Bench 1963). Little doubt exists that American courts not only would be reluctant to use some notion of abuse of rights as a device for weighing comparative benefits and burdens, but would be highly unlikely to use this doctrine to force a developer to negotiate with individuals who might be injured by construction. For example, the court in Fontainebleau Hotel Corp. v. Forty-Five Twenty-Five, Inc., 114 So. 2d 357, 359 (Fla. Dist. Ct. App. 1959) said

> There being, then, no legal right to the free flow of light and air from the adjoining land, it is universally held that where a structure serves a useful and beneficial purpose, it does not give rise to a cause of action, either for damages or for an injunction under the maxim *sic utere tuo ut alienum non laedas*, even though it causes injury to another by cutting off the light and air and interfering with the view that would otherwise be available over adjoining land in its natural state, regardless of the fact that the structure may have been erected partly for spite.

176. 803 Hanrei Jihō 18 (Tokyo Dist. Ct. 1975).

177. Plaintiff, a company engaged in the construction of housing developments, as well as buying, leasing, and managing real estate, planned to build a small housing development within the City of Musashino. In accordance with that city's Outline Guidance, plaintiff's representatives began discussing the problem of interference with sunlight and ventilation with the surrounding residents. However, even after extensive discussions and some modification of plaintiff's plans (from six to five floors and from 20 to 16 units) they were not able to reach an accord with the surrounding residents. The developer nevertheless submitted to the city officials its plan, both as originally conceived and as modified through subsequent discussions with surrounding residents. At the same time, it applied for a construction permit, as required by the Construction Standards Law. It is interesting to note that the city officials did not delay or obstruct the issuance of this construction permit, but rather issued the permit relatively quickly. The plaintiff then began construction while seeking informal assurances of local authorities' cooperation in the provision of water and sewage removal. The local authorities, relying on Outline Guidance, refused, however, because plaintiff had not attached to its building construction plans a document indicating agreement with the surrounding residents, nor had plaintiff indicated its intention to provide land or money for educational facilities as required by the Outline Guidance.

tion. When the city remained recalcitrant,[178] plaintiff sued the city under the Code of Civil Procedure, seeking a provisional disposition (kari shobun)—a judicial remedy quite similar to a preliminary injunction, but with more long-range effect—that would allow it to use the public water and sewer systems for servicing the tenants in the now completed building.

Although the court dismissed the complaint as to sewage removal services,[179] it held that the city's refusal to provide water could subject it to a provisional disposition under certain circumstances. The court evaluated the content of the city's administrative guidance in terms by now familiar.[180] In assessing the propriety of the local authorities' refusal to supply water in order to force plaintiff to reach an accord with the surrounding residents on sunlight and ventilation, the court focused on the bargaining situation rather than

178. When the project was almost complete, plaintiff again applied for water, this time on behalf of the soon-to-be occupants. Again the city refused. Plaintiff still had not reached agreement with the surrounding residents. Moreover, though it had made the required donation for educational facilities, it had not done so through the established procedures and thus the city, apparently wanting to make a point of some sort, had returned the money.

179. Under article 44 of the Administrative Case Litigation Law, ACLL, supra note 127, a provisional disposition (kari shobun) cannot be granted against an "administrative disposition" (gyōsei shobun) or other "exercise of public authority" (kōkenryoku no kōshi) of an administrative organ (gyōsei chō). The court held that the provision of sewage services was an exercise of public authority within the meaning of article 44, thereby immunizing the city's action from a provisional disposition. The court reasoned that provision of the services was an exercise of public authority because the law formally grants exclusive monopoly to the city to run these enterprises, makes provisions for legal mechanisms to enforce use of the public sewers and requires no approval or permission of the local authorities to use the sewer. Instead, the law makes it clear that all who live within the sewer district must use the sewage removal services.

The court treated the provision of water quite differently, however. First, the court held that the decision to provide water was not an administrative disposition or exercise of public authority under article 44. While the provision of water is indispensable to the well-being of the people and specially regulated, with local authorities actually monopolizing this service in most areas, the nature of the enterprise resembles a private law relationship more than sewage removal service. The party desiring water files an application, and the cost of the water is directly related to the amount used. Moreover, unlike the removal of sewage, where not only the individual but also those living in the same vicinity benefit, water service largely benefits the individual or individuals to whom it is provided. Thus, the court reasoned, the relationship between the provider and recipient of water services has more earmarks of private than public law and possesses few of the elements that normally characterize administrative dispositions or exercises of public authority falling within the purview of article 44. This part of the court's decision has generated substantial discussion in Japan and, at least from the perspective of Japanese commentators, is the most interesting part of the opinion. See, e.g., Nakanishi, Saishin Hanrei Hihyō (Analysis of New Decisions), 819 Hanrei Jihō 128 (1976).

180. The court first reasoned that the city's obligation to supply water was not absolute. The Water Supply Law permits the refusal of an application for a water supply contract for "proper reasons" (seitō na riyū). See Suidō Hō (Water Supply Law), Law No. 177 of 1957, art. 15, ¶ 1.

Thus, the fundamental question was whether noncompliance with the Outline Guidance was a "proper reason." The court then held that Outline Guidance was not a rule (kisoku) or an ordinance (jōrei)—which local authorities have the power to issue and which have binding legal effect in certain circumstances under the Local Autonomy Law, Chihō Jichi Hō (Local Autonomy Law), Law No. 67 of 1947; see supra text accompanying note 18. Nor did this guidance have any

upon whose right had priority. Because construction was ninety-five percent completed, the court reasoned, the advantages to be gained through negotiation were essentially lost. Accordingly, unless legal reasons existed to justify forcing the developer to remove the building—which would occur only in the most exceptional case—failure to reach an accord could not now constitute a "proper reason" for refusing to supply water.

At first blush, this holding might appear to take all the teeth out of administrative guidance—allowing the developer to borrow water elsewhere for construction and then forcing the city to supply water significantly reduces the developer's incentive to negotiate with the surrounding residents. The court avoided this result, however, by asserting that if the developer forges ahead with construction against the wishes of the city, his subsequent application for water, although technically within his rights, may be found an impermissible "abuse of right." Although the court did not find an abuse of right in the instant case, its use of the doctrine is a remarkable departure, even from the Japanese version of the doctrine.

Instead of regulating bad-intentioned exercises of rights as French courts do or even comparing the relative benefits and detriments attendant to the exercise of a particular substantive right as Japanese courts do, the *Yamaki* court sanctioned invocation of the abuse of rights doctrine to regulate the negotiating behavior of the developer. Although at some point the developer can call a halt to the negotiations and insist on the issuance of the permit, if his call is too quick, without at least the appearance of serious, good faith negotiations, he may be unable to secure the water necessary for his buildings. The court did not engage in any explicit, or even implicit, weighing of comparative benefits and detriments. Moreover, the court did not ask whether the harm to be borne by the surrounding residents is, as the Supreme Court suggested, beyond "the limit which is generally supposed to be borne in the social life." Nor did the court ask questions that would be asked under the traditional explications of the abuse of rights doctrine: whether the developer exercised his right with ill intent and without any legitimate benefit to himself. Instead, the court invoked the abuse of rights doctrine to place a limit on the ability of the developer to halt negotiations too quickly. The abuse of rights doctrine thus imposes a substantial limit on the power of the developer to refuse to bargain with the residents. In addition, by relying on the doctrine, the court defines the limits of judicial oversight of the administrative process, thereby striking the necessary balance between flexibility and protection by means of judicial review of administrative guidance.

---

legal basis for its promulgation. Thus, refusal based solely on noncompliance was not proper. See, e.g., Yoshida v. Nakano Ward, 886 Hanrei Jihō 15 (Tokyo Dist. Ct. 1973), discussed supra text accompanying notes 141-51. Nevertheless, administrative guidance could explicate proper justifications for refusing to enter into a water supply contract, reasons that found support in prior case law, for example. Such might be the case if the guidance indicated that a contract would be refused where there was not enough water to supply the increased demand that would be created by the new contract, where plans for adequate water removal had not been developed, or

2. *Rearticulation of Agency Mandates.* — Japanese courts are freed to use the legal devices just described for striking the balance between administrative flexibility and judicial protection because they rearticulate the administrative agencies' basic mandates. Japanese courts acknowledge the agencies' traditional mandate of executing and enforcing the law and the related task of determining the specific content of rules necessary to effectuate broadly worded legislative directives. But in administrative guidance cases, Japanese courts go further and view agencies as exercising a broader, less specifically executive, mandate to resolve conflicts among competing interest groups or at least to encourage settlement of those disputes.

This restructuring of the agencies' mandate is most clearly articulated in *Nakatani Honten Gōmei Kaisha v. Tokyo.*[181] There, the lower court, viewing the protection of access to sunlight as the main regulatory interest, held that the local authorities could delay action until the developer reached an accord that was substantively satisfactory—one that adequately protected access to sunlight. The appellate court agreed that the local authorities could delay action to advance regulatory interests. It disagreed, however, that protection of access to sunlight was the main regulatory interest. Instead, while the local authorities were legitimately enhancing the surrounding residents' access to sunlight, the principal regulatory interest was to encourage negotiated or apparently voluntary settlements of disputes between individuals and groups within the local authorities' jurisdiction. So long as some reasonable possibility of a compromise, or, in other words, some reasonable possibility of effectuating the primary regulatory concern, still existed, the local authorities could delay action on the developer's application. When that possibility disappeared, however, the local authorities' power to pressure the developer disappeared with it, precisely because the main regulatory concern was not the protection of a substantive right, but rather the negotiated settlement of a dispute. In this particular case, the higher court held that a reasonable possibility of agreement ceased to exist when plaintiff petitioned the Inspection Committee, making the local authorities' continued inaction on the application improper. Because the Court of Appeals perceived the agency's jurisdic-

---

where water could not be supplied for structural or technical reasons. Prior case law supports denial in these circumstances. See, e.g., Nakasone v. City of Osaka, 475 Hanrei Jihō 28 (Osaka Dist. Ct. 1967). See generally Nakanishi, supra note 179, at 130-32 (discussing this and other similar cases).

The court then turned to the content of the administrative guidance to determine whether the reasons for refusing the water supply contract were proper. The court rejected the local authorities' attempt to justify their refusal on the basis of plaintiff's disinclination to donate land or money for educational purposes. The Constitution provides that "[p]rivate property may be taken for public use upon just compensation therefor." Kenpō art. 29, ¶ 3. Donations of private property cannot be compelled, even though public use of the private property might be necessary to enhance the general living environment or for the public welfare. The court did indicate that an attempt to encourage such donations was another matter, but implicitly decided that the local authorities' attempts at persuasion had crossed the line from encouragement to compulsion.

181. 955 Hanrei Jihō 74 (Tokyo Ct. App. 1979), discussed supra notes 151-56 and accompanying text.

tional mandate as settling disputes, it reversed the lower court which had upheld the administrative inaction.

Judicial rearticulation of administrative mandate—from regulating sunlight to settling disputes—finds further support in the courts' handling of agencies' use of their collateral, or unrelated, powers of enforcement.[182] The courts permit the agencies to use certain of their unrelated regulatory powers—in particular, that of refusing to take any action on applications for construction permits—to accomplish the broad goals of administrative guidance.[183] The courts apparently recognize the inherent difficulties in permitting agencies to use one regulatory power to effectuate a very different regulatory concern, especially one that so differs in conception from tasks generally committed to adminstrative agencies. The courts' uneasiness finds expression in their unwillingness to permit agencies to exercise directly this collateral power to enforce administrative guidance. Nevertheless, viewing the promotion of amicable settlement of disputes as basic to the agencies' function, the courts permit the agencies to exercise their collateral powers indirectly. Indeed, in the various opinions,[184] the courts explicitly recognize that withholding action on an application is probably necessary to permit the agency to exert pressure on the developer for compromise and settlement; once the permit is issued, construction begins and the developers' incentive to settle substantially diminishes. By viewing such pressure to negotiate as permissible, Japanese courts have in effect transformed the agencies' mandate from effecting a specific regulatory goal—either protection of safety in construction or, even more far reaching, protection of sunlight and ventilation—to enhancing negotiated settlement of disputes.

3. *Refusal to Determine Priority of Competing Claims of Right.* — Courts' redefinition of agencies' regulatory mandate in administrative guidance cases allows them to avoid giving absolute priority to any of the competing claims of right. This doctrinal approach departs from the civil and common law traditions, which generally view courts as applying preexisting legal norms in dichotomous disputes to reach decisions that validate one party's claim of right over another's.[185] The basic binary structure of adjudication in most common and civil law systems facilitates this task by requiring the opposing parties to advance competing claims of right, to assert or deny claims of right, or to offer competing versions of the facts. Even when, as in the Outline Guidance cases, the facts are largely undisputed, most civil and common law jurisdictions expect courts faced with conflicting claims of right

182. See supra notes 64-65 and accompanying text.

183. See supra note 150 and accompanying text.

184. See, e.g., Nakatani Honten Gōmei Kaisha v. Tokyo, 955 Hanrei Jihō 73 (Tokyo Ct. App. 1979), discussed supra text accompanying notes 151-56; Yoshida v. Nakano Ward, 886 Hanrei Jihō 15 (Tokyo Dist. Ct. 1973), discussed supra text accompanying notes 141-51.

185. See, e.g., M. Shapiro, Courts: A Comparative and Political Analysis 1 (1981); Arnold, Trial by Combat and the New Deal, 47 Harv. L. Rev. 913, 920-21 (1934); Chayes, The Role of the Judge in Public Law Litigation, 89 Harv. L. Rev. 1281, 1283 (1976); Morgan, Judicial Notice, 57 Harv. L. Rev. 269, 269-72 (1944).

to determine which claim of right prevails, harmonize the conflicting claims or validate a claim of right against an assertion of the nonexistence of that right.[186]

The Outline Guidance cases present Japanese courts with the opportunity for a traditional determination of priority of competing claims. The developer claims a right under the Construction Standards Law to action within twenty-one days on his application for a construction permit.[187] The agencies make

186. Resolution of conflicting claims, advanced in complete good faith, poses a difficult task for courts. Systems of rules that speak in general terms and yet require application in highly specific and individualized situations create enormous doubt and uncertainty. The sheer number of organizations engaged in activities that create legal rules and other data whereby citizens can (and often must) order their public and private affairs leads inevitably to the emergence of conflicting rules. This welter of sometimes conflicting data results in a strongly felt need for mechanisms that can authoritatively determine the priority of the various rules. Which rules prevail in what type of situations? Which types of "rules" are most authoritative? Which "rule" governs when two or more rules are in conflict? Related to these questions are process and institutional concerns. What rules govern the determination of these priorities? To which government organs is committed the task of making those rules? Which organs apply those rules and thus actually decide specific questions of priority?

While the United States may have resolved many of these issues, cf. Marbury v. Madison, 5 U.S. (4 Cranch) 137 (1803) (Supreme Court final arbiter of whether administrative practice conflicts with the Constitution), questions invariably remain. Cf. Monaghan, *Marbury* and the Administrative State, 83 Colum. L. Rev. 1 (1983) (exploring what degree of deference reviewing courts should accord administrators). In Japan, the first volume of the major introductory treatise on the Japanese Civil Code devotes substantial attention to which legal rules prevail. See S. Wagatsuma, Mimpō Sōsoku (General Provisions of the Civil Code) 18, *in* 1 Mimpō Kōgi (Lectures on the Civil Code) (1974); see also S. Wagatsuma, Tampō Bukken 11–18 (Security Interest in Property), *in* 3 Mimpō Kōgi (Lectures on the Civil Code) (1976); S. Wagatsuma, Saiken Kakuron Jōhen 42–53 (First Part of the Specific Discussion of Obligations), *in* 5 Mimpō Kōgi (Lectures on the Civil Code) (1979). This treatment examines the abundant and detailed rules on the priority of a special law over a general law and customary law over some sorts of law, but not others. See, e.g., Fukoku (Rules for Conduct of Judicial Affairs), Decree No. 103 of 1875; Hōrei (Law Concerning the Application of Laws), Law No. 10 of 1898; Mimpō (Civil Code), Law No. 89 of 1896 and No. 94 of 1898, arts. 92, 236, 277, 294; Shōhō (Commercial Code), Law No. 48 of 1899, art. 1; see also S. Wagatsuma, Mimpō Sōsoku (General Provision of the Civil Code) 18, *in* 1 Mimpō Kōgi (Lectures on the Civil Code) (1974). The debate over the proper weight that should be accorded judicial precedent is equally intense. For early and extremely influential articles in this debate, see H. Suehiro, Hōgaku Nyūmon (Introduction to the Study of Law) 166–168 (1928); Hozumi, Kon'in Yoyaku Yūkō Hanketsu no Shin Igi (The True meaning of Judicial Decisions Validating Engagement Agreements), 9 Hōgaku Shinri 1, 19 (1917). Moreover, the Codes themselves devote space to questions of priority. The first article of the Japanese Commercial Code, for example, addresses this issue: "As to commercial matters, in cases where there are no applicable provisions in this Code, commercial customary law shall apply, and where there is no applicable commercial customary law, the Civil Code shall apply." Shōhō (Commercial Code), Law No. 48 of 1899, art. 1. Various articles in the Civil Code continue the process of establishing rules for the determination of priorities. See, e.g., Mimpō (Civil Code), Law No. 89 of 1896, Law No. 95 of 1898, arts. 92, 236, 277, 294. Special statutes, devoted entirely to the question of which laws apply in what situations, abound. See, e.g., Hōrei (Law Concerning the Application of Laws), Law No. 10 of 1898.

187. Plaintiffs also might be viewed as arguing that if their proposed construction project meets all the standards contained in the Construction Standards Law, they have a right not only to a decision on their application within 21 days, but also to a favorable disposition of that

two claims in response: either that the developers complied with the administrative guidance voluntarily by not formally submitting their applications for construction permits and thus have no grounds to complain, or that the developers were not entitled to a construction permit because the agencies may withhold action on the permit pending an agreement regarding sunlight and ventilation. Viewed in this light, these cases would seem to require that courts determine which of the claims prevail.[188]

Yet in sharp contrast to the traditional civil and common law approach, in the Outline Guidance cases Japanese courts refuse to determine which claims prevail. Instead, they implement legal standards that favor both plaintiff and defendant. They recognize that the developer has a right to some action on his application for a permit, which the agency may not deny based on considerations unrelated to the safety goals advanced by the law. At the same time, courts allow the agencies to withold action on the permit to advance unrelated goals of sunlight and ventilation. Still, agencies can withhold the permit only so long as a reasonable expectation exists that the dispute can be resolved by mutual agreement of the parties. The developers cannot, however, take advantage of this limitation on administrative action by refusing from the outset to consider the possibility of a negotiated settlement. Instead, the courts allow the agencies to presume irrebuttably that developers will negotiate; courts further impose limits on developers through the abuse of rights doctrine. By strengthening first one side and then the other, Japanese courts assure that neither side establishes the absolute priority of its claim of right. Such refusal to prioritize, though at odds with the civil and common law traditions, enables courts to protect individual rights without undermining the administrative flexibility that modern government requires.

In sum, Japanese courts' refusal to determine competing claims of right, together with their rearticulation of the administrative mandate and their invocation of certain legal doctrines to limit bargaining power on both sides, represents a solution to the dilemma posed by judicial review of administrative guidance. These doctrinal developments enable courts to police against abuses that may result from use of this informal regulatory technique without

---

application. This argument is not entirely necessary to these cases, however, because at this stage developers are only asking the court to declare the agency's inaction illegal. See supra note 116. Of course, to save time on the next go-round, they might prefer that the court also indicate the factors that the agency can legitimately consider in making its determination, but strictly speaking, such a disposition is not necessary to win. Indeed, the general consensus on this issue is that the courts may direct the agency to act when it has failed to act within the prescribed time limit, but cannot direct the agency to act in any particular manner. See J. Tanaka, supra note 5, at 380-82. For example, the courts could direct Construction Supervisors to act upon the applications, but could not direct them to act favorably. Plaintiffs could seek review of the substance of that decision at a later time.

188. Of course, these cases might be viewed from a slightly different perspective as cases involving one party (the developer) asserting a claim of right and the other party (the local authorities or, even more broadly conceived, the surrounding residents) denying the existence of

straight jacketing agency flexibility. Japanese courts' adept doctrinal accommodation to administrative guidance is an important departure from the traditional perception of the role of the bureaucracy under the civil law[189] and offers a most interesting mechanism for resolving future challenges to administrative action.

E. *Bargaining and Negotiation as the Principal Judical Inquiry*

The development of doctrines to handle judicial review of administrative guidance establishes bargaining and negotiation as the touchstone for evaluating the propriety of administrative action.[190] The various legal doctrines employed to limit or extend the bargaining power on each side, along with the redefinition of the agency's mandate and the steadfast refusal to determine the priority of competing claims of right, all serve this end.[191] Courts reviewing Outline Guidance allow the agencies to compel bargaining. At the same time, they evaluate the propriety of that compulsion by its faithfulness to the fundamental premise of bargaining, the ability to enter or avoid an agreement.

---

that right. This view, however, ignores the nature of the defense being advanced by the local authorities. The local authorities concede that developers generally have a right to a decision within 21 days on their construction permit applications. They counter, however, that special circumstances exist that make delay permissible. This argument brings directly into issue the validity of these special circumstances as reasons for delaying action on the applications. Thus, the nature of the defense brings into direct conflict the two claims discussed in the text. Moreover, even if one were to take the view that these cases involve only the validation or rejection of the developers' claims of right, the traditional view of the proper role of courts would require the court to decide whether the developers' claims of right are valid. Yet the courts depart from that traditional model.

189. Japanese courts' handling of administrative guidance illustrates their recognition that governmental intervention in the market economy and into heretofore private affairs no longer is a rare event of extraordinary dimension. See B. Ackerman, supra note 84, at 9. Moreover, when such intervention occurs, it no longer takes precisely predictable, well-established procedural forms. Finally, Japanese courts accept that the legitimizing principle underlying the administrative activity does not necessarily derive from a clear-cut statutory mandate or from formally promulgated rules or regulations.

190. Commentators in the United States and other traditional "western" societies have increasingly focused on alternatives to the typical adjudicatory pattern of dispute resolution. While much of their attention has been focused on certain sorts of consensually based resolution processes, such as bargaining, negotiation and mediation, the advantages they have identified generally vary from those that made such processes attractive to the Japanese courts in the case of Outline Guidance. See, e.g., Cappelletti & Garth, Access to Justice and the Welfare State: An Introduction, *in* Access to Justice and the Welfare State 14-20 (M. Cappelletti ed. 1982); Danzig, Toward the Creation of a Complementary, Decentralized System of Criminal Justice, 26 Stan. L. Rev. 1 (1973); Eisenberg, supra note 121; Felstiner, Influences of Social Organization on Dispute Processing, 9 Law & Soc'y Rev. 63 (1974); Fuller, Mediation—Its Form and Functions, 44 S. Cal. L. Rev. 305 (1971); Galanter, Justice in Many Rooms, *in* Access to Justice and the Welfare State 147 (M. Cappelletti ed. 1982); Susskind & Weinstein, Towards a Theory of Environmental Dispute Resolution, 9 B.C. Envt'l Aff. L. Rev 1, 311 (1980-1981).

191. Of course, even in common and civil law traditions, we are very conscious of the role that bargaining plays in the ultimate distribution of societal burdens and benefits. One of the central definitional tenets of a property right, for example, is that the holder cannot be divested of

Courts have embraced this notion of bargaining for reasons very different from those that make it appealing to the agencies, however. Agencies find this regulatory technique attractive because it permits considerable extension of their regulatory reach and helps them fashion individualized, particularized solutions to difficult social issues. For courts, the notion of good faith bargaining, with its necessary absence of legal compulsion to enter an agreement, provides a convenient and apparently effective device for checking administrative abuses while at the same time ensuring adequate administrative flexibility. It permits courts to strike a difficult balance between judicial protection and administrative freedom in a situation where traditional doctrines of judicial review are not satisfactory.[192]

---

it except through a voluntary transaction. See, e.g., Calabresi & Melamed, supra note 86, at 1092. Nor is there any doubt that judicial, legislative and even administrative determinations of the limits of a particular right significantly affect the parties in terms of their negotiations outside the courtroom. Even courts are conscious of the effects of their decisions on the comparative bargaining position of the litigants or those similarly situated. See, e.g., Eisenberg, supra note 121, at 665; Mnookin & Kornhauser, supra note 121, at 950. Generally, however, the principal concern is which of various competing claims of right should have primacy in a particular situation. The resulting analytical mode usually requires that courts focus upon the comparative weight, the specific language, the legislative history of various statutory enactments, the extent to which a decision will encourage or discourage a particular type of behavior, the extent to which a particular decision comports with fundamental principles underlying a certain type of relationship (e.g., "freedom of contract," "quiet possession," etc.), the consistency of a decision with previous decisions, and matters of "public policy." The courts may not be unmindful of the effects of their decisions on the relative bargaining strength of the disputants, but rarely will that be the principal focus.

In Japan, in the cases we have examined, the comparative bargaining strength of the disputants and the role of the agency as it affects that strength are the principal, indeed almost sole, focus of inquiry. The legal relationships and structures in their more strict and technical definitions receive passing attention, but only as devices to permit the restructuring of this bargaining situation. The propriety of the interests local authorities are advancing receives somewhat more attention, but the focus of that attention is not whether those interests have been legislatively sanctioned or are being advanced through legislatively authorized means, but rather whether the interests are matters about which some general, though rather informal, societal consensus has been achieved. Indeed, the courts spend most of their time examining the precise structure of the bargaining situation and supervising the bargaining that occurs. These are not tangential matters of only passing concern, but rather the principal thrust of the judicial inquiry.

192. Any doubt about whether the courts focus on the conduct of negotiations and whether they take this inquiry most seriously is dispelled by the amount of judicial attention devoted to determining exactly when the possibility of an agreement disappeared. The bulk of the opinions—well over half—deals directly with this question. See, e.g., Nakatani Honten Gōmei Kaisha v. Tokyo, 955 Hanrei Jihō 73, 76–77 (Tokyo Ct. App. 1979); Jūrakuen Yūgen Kaisha v. Nakano Ward, 931 Hanrei Jihō 79, 82–83, 86–89 (Tokyo Dist. Ct. 1978), aff'd, 36 Sai-han Minshū 737 (S. Ct. Petty Bench 1982); Taiyō Kensetsu Kabushiki Kaisha v. Nerima Ward, 952 Hanrei Jihō 18, 23–27 (Tokyo Dist. Ct. 1979); Fuji Enters. Kabushiki Kaisha v. Tokyo, 894 Hanrei Jihō 82, 84–87, 90–92 (Tokyo Dist. Ct. 1977); Yoshida v. Nakano Ward, 886 Hanrei Jihō 15, 16–21, 24–27 (Tokyo Dist. Ct. 1973). Moreover, in contrast to those parts that explore the legal status of the time limits in the Construction Standards Law and even those parts that deal with the propriety of the substantive interests the regulatory agency is advancing, this part of the opinions is extremely and laboriously fact-specific. The courts chronicle in painstaking detail, and explore plaintiffs' precise intentions before and after each meeting and at each other relevant point in time. They

In sum, Japanese courts have arrived at a solution to the problem posed by judicial review of administrative guidance. The approach they have adopted, as clarified in this Article, promises wide applicability. Certainly, this approach is a marked improvement over the early and transition cases that failed to protect adequately against agency intrusions into private affairs.[193]

IV. Ramifications of Japanese Emphasis on Private Ordering

A careful examination of these cases and the regulatory context in which they arise suggests that while the approach adopted by both agencies and courts in Japan may have been comfortable for cultural and historical reasons, the problems they addressed are not highly culturally or socially specific. Viewed in a broad context, administrative organs in Japan are often under considerable pressure to deal with a variety of problems confronting their constituents. Administrators are thus naturally drawn to use administrative techniques that provide them with flexibility and allow expansion of their regulatory mandate. Regulated parties have tolerated and often welcomed resort to administrative guidance because it necessarily gives them an expanded role in the governance process and it imposes inherent limitations on bureaucratic compulsion. This confluence of interests has led the bureaucracy to regulate by compelling bargaining and negotiation between the parties; an approach the parties have generally embraced with enthusiasm.

Viewed in the more narrow context of Outline Guidance, the bureaucracy has wrestled with a problem that defies, for legal and practical reasons, resolution through abstract, generalized rules. The bureaucracy is nevertheless under pressure to offer assistance in resolving disputes between developers and residents. It chose compelled bargaining as a useful regulatory technique that avoids difficult factual determinations and allows the parties to reach a solution among themselves in the first instance.

For different reasons, Japanese courts have endorsed the practice of compelled bargaining. The judiciary resists hampering unduly administrative activities, especially given the high level of demand placed on the bureaucracy to solve a broad variety of social, economic and political problems. The judiciary does not, however, wish to abrogate completely their responsibility

---

examine every nuance of every communication, leaving no doubt what courts consider important in these cases.

The fact-based inquiry that courts undertake also undermines the perception that Japanese judicial decisions are spare on their facts. These opinions suggest that at least some Japanese judicial decisions, while perhaps spare on the kind of facts we might expect in the opinions of a United States court, are extremely specific in their discussion of facts that are relevant to the inquiry in which the courts engage. The difference is not the degree of factual specificity, but rather the kinds of issues the courts consider dispositive and thus the kinds of facts they discuss extensively in the opinions. Japanese judicial decisions are as fact-specific as any in the United States, but the nature of the factual inquiry differs.

193. The only decisions to date embracing this bargaining model involve attacks on Outline Guidance. The success of this method, the speed with which it was adopted by the various courts, and the uniformity of its application, all suggest, however, the possibility of further judicial experiments when other appropriate cases arise.

to protect against excessive administrative intrusions. The more formal Japanese doctrines of judicial review of administrative action provide little help in striking this balance. At the very least, these doctrines strike the balance in formalistic and rigid ways, which judges find unacceptable in light of their perception of the proper role of the various governmental organs. Compelled bargaining, however, with its focus on the compulsion of good faith negotiating, rather than enforcement of an administratively determined substantive solution, provides a way to strike the proper balance. Moreover, because compelled bargaining leads to solutions that are individualized and command the parties' agreement, such solutions may well enlist a higher degree of voluntary compliance than normally found in more traditional adjudicated solutions. Thus, this approach commends itself, although its attraction for the courts is fundamentally different than for the bureaucracy.

The factors that make compelled bargaining attractive to Japanese courts and agencies may offer lessons for other legal systems. Foreign institutions and practices, of course, are not always easily transplanted. Situations arise, however, that might allow the United States to take advantage of this form of legally structured bargaining and negotiating, both as a regulatory technique and as a method for judicially supervising administrative activity.

Three elements emerge that tentatively would make the use of compelled bargaining both possible and attractive. First, the Japanese experience suggests that an ability to identify the interested parties is an important element in successful use of this technique. If an agency cannot reliably identify concerned parties, it cannot properly structure incentives to encourage good faith bargaining and negotiation. Uncertainty about the identity of the disputants also prevents the courts from meaningfully supervising either the propriety of the agency's incentive structure or the genuineness of the negotiations compelled by that administrative action. Second, the Japanese situations examined in this study generally have involved a relatively small number of competing interests. While bargaining may work in extremely diffuse and polycentric situations, the approach of restructuring the bargaining situation appears to have the greatest chance of success when the number of competing interests represented by the identifiable parties is low. These interests need not be entirely uniform, either within or among the various interested parties. Nevertheless, if the competing interests of the disputants are too great in number, restructuring the incentive patterns becomes very difficult and supervision of the process almost impossible. Finally, this regulatory and judicial approach works best when the elements relevant to an adequate resolution of the dispute are so inherently varied that the establishment of uniform rules creates uncomfortable or inadequate solutions. On occasion, of course, reasons of efficiency or fairness require a high degree of uniformity, even in problems otherwise suitable for individualized solutions. Absent such reasons, however, this regulatory technique may prove most useful in dealing with problems that lend themselves to a solution carefully tailored to the disputants' particular circumstances.

Two situations come to mind as possible candidates for application of this mode of dispute resolution. First, as in Japan, small-scale land use planning decisions have all the characteristics necessary to permit use of this approach. Both the parties and their competing interests are discrete in number and can be identified with certainty. The nature of the problems that arise in this context also lend themselves happily to individualized solutions. Indeed, by some accounts, individualized, particularized solutions to such problems are far preferable to generalized rules of dispute resolution.[194]

A second area where these principles may apply is in divorce settlements, particularly matters relating to child custody. Such disputes also share the characterisitics necessary for successful applicaton of this technique—the parties are easily identifiable, small in number, and their problems and circumstances vary tremendously. Moreover, negotiation is already the principal method for resolving these disputes.[195] Retailoring the administrative and judicial approach to emphasize negotiation more explicitly might allow more careful supervision and oversight of child custody negotiations and reduce enforcement problems.

It is not certain that this device will wear well in the United States even in the narrow contexts suggested. Nonetheless, some of the same motivations behind the Japanese adoption of this approach are present in the United States in these situations. Moreover, while this approach to regulation and judicial oversight is not without faults, its advantages militate in favor of at least a few small scale experiments. In any event, the Japanese experience with administrative guidance and the compelled bargaining that it creates suggests ways of rethinking both regulatory technique and judicial oversight in the administrative setting.

Conclusion

Administrative guidance, an administrative technique frequently used in Japan, is nonbinding administrative action that encourages regulated parties to act in a way that furthers an administrative aim. Although compliance with administrative guidance is technically voluntary, Japanese administrators rely

194. One commentator has recently called for a mediatory resolution process in the case of disputes arising out of small-scale land use planning decisions and issues, labeling such an alternate dispute-resolving model especially appropriate at the local or sublocal level. See Rose, Planning and Dealing: Piecemeal Land Controls as a Problem of Local Legitimacy, 71 Calif. L. Rev. 837, 887-93 (1983). For more typical treatment of these problems, especially in the context of disputes over sunlight, and a situation where the Japanese approach might have borne fruit, see Fontainebleau Hotel Corp. v. Forty-Five Twenty-Five, Inc., 114 So. 2d 357 (Fla. Dist. Ct. App. 1959), discussed supra note 175.

195. Some sort of mediated or negotiated solution to divorce and divorce-related disputes already has found some favor in the literature. See, e.g., J. Haynes, Divorce Mediation (1981); H. Irving, Divorce Mediation—A Rational Alternative to the Adversary System (1981); Mnookin & Kornhauser, supra note 121; Pearson, Child Custody: Why Not Let the Parents Decide?, 20 Judges J. 4 (1981); Winks, Divorce Mediation: A Nonadversary Procedure for the No-Fault Divorce, 19 J. Fam. Law 615 (1981).

The obvious limitation in this model in a pure bargaining form, however, is the relative inability of the child to represent and defend adequately his or her own interests in the negotiating

on informal pressure and other means of enforcement to persuade regulated parties to comply. This reliance on informal encouragement as opposed to legal coercion permits the bureaucracy to expand the areas into which it may intrude. It simultaneously limits the extent of those intrusions, however, and requires the bureaucracy to consult and negotiate extensively with the regulated parties. Indeed, administrators often leave largely to the parties the task of determining many of the details of the regulatory scheme and, on occasion, even the appropriate degree of regulation. Frequently, regulation amounts to little more than administrative organs' structuring of a bargaining situation in which the parties are compelled to negotiate with each other over the proper allocation of the benefits and burdens of regulation.

The absence of any legal compulsion in administrative guidance also initially deterred Japanese courts from reviewing such action, thereby insulating from judicial scrutiny a significant portion of Japanese regulatory conduct. More recently, however, courts have addressed the proper scope of review, particularly in cases involving municipalities' Oultine Guidance—regualtion designed to resolve informally disputes between building developers and residents over sunlight and ventilation.

From these more recent cases, this Article has distilled an approach to judicial review of administrative guidance. This approach directs courts to focus primarily on the agencies' attempt to restructure the bargaining situation. Courts accomplish this task by rearticulating the agencies' mandate and refusing to determine the priority of competing claims of right. Through use of traditional and sometimes not so traditional doctrines of judicial review the courts are then able to limit the extent to which agencies can compel negotiation. These doctrinal constructs, while perhaps appealing to traditional Japanese attitudes toward consensual dispute resolution, nevertheless offer important advantages that have little to do with culture or tradition; they enable the courts to strike a balance between protection of regulated parties and agency flexibility in a modern, industrialized state in which citizens place high demands on their bureaucracy. While not without potential pitfalls, the Japanese experience with administrative guidance offers Western legal systems a promising model for regulation and the resolution of certain kinds of disputes in a postindustrial era.

---

process. Various devices, such as judicial supervision or child representation, might be developed to deal with some of these concerns, however. See, e.g., Note, Lawyering for the Child: Principles of Representation in Custody and Visitation Disputes Arising from Divorce, 87 Yale L. J. 1126 (1978).

Name Index

For Product Safety Concerns and Information please contact our EU representative GPSR@taylorandfrancis.com Taylor & Francis Verlag GmbH, Kaufingerstraße 24, 80331 München, Germany

Batch number: 10726402

Printed by Printforce, the Netherlands